Emancipation's Diaspora

The John Hope Franklin
Series in African American History
and Culture
*Waldo E. Martin and
Patricia Sullivan, editors*

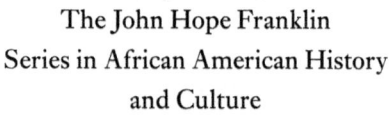

LESLIE A. SCHWALM

Emancipation's Diaspora

Race and Reconstruction
in the Upper Midwest

The University of North Carolina Press
Chapel Hill

© 2009 The University of North Carolina Press
All rights reserved

Designed by Jacquline Johnson
Set in Ehrhardt MT
by Keystone Typesetting, Inc.
Manufactured in the United States of America

The paper in this book meets the guidelines for permanence and durability of the Committee on Production Guidelines for Book Longevity of the Council on Library Resources.

The University of North Carolina Press has been a member of the Green Press Initiative since 2003.

Library of Congress Cataloging-in-Publication Data
Schwalm, Leslie A. (Leslie Ann), 1956–
Emancipation's diaspora : race and reconstruction in the upper Midwest / Leslie A. Schwalm. — 1st ed.
p. cm. — (John Hope Franklin series in African American history and culture)
Includes bibliographical references and index.
ISBN 978-0-8078-3291-2 (cloth: alk. paper)
ISBN 978-0-8078-5950-6 (pbk.: alk. paper)
1. African Americans—Iowa—History—19th century. 2. African Americans—Minnesota—History—19th century. 3. African Americans—Wisconsin—History—19th century. 4. Freedmen—Iowa—History—19th century. 5. Freedmen—Minnesota—History—19th century. 6. Freedmen—Wisconsin—History—19th century. 7. Iowa—Race relations—History—19th century. 8. Minnesota—Race relations—History—19th century. 9. Wisconsin—Race relations—History—19th century. 10. Reconstruction (U.S. history, 1865–1877) I. Title.
E185.93.I64S34 2009
305.896′07307709034—dc22
2009003098

Portions of this work have appeared previously, in somewhat different form, in " 'Overrun with Free Negroes': Emancipation and Wartime Migration in the Upper Midwest," *Civil War History* 50 (June 2004): 145–74; "Emancipation Day Celebrations: The Commemoration of Slavery and Freedom in Iowa," *Annals of Iowa*, 3rd ser., 62 (Summer 2003): 291–332; and " 'Agonizing Groans of Mothers' and 'Slave-Scarred Veterans': The Commemoration of Slavery and Emancipation," *American Nineteenth-Century History* 9 (September 2008): 289–304 and are reprinted with permission.

cloth 13 12 11 10 09 5 4 3 2 1
paper 13 12 11 10 09 5 4 3 2 1

Contents

Acknowledgments ix

Introduction 1

CHAPTER ONE
"A Full Realization of the Barbarities of Slavery" 9

CHAPTER TWO
"A Time of Scattering" 43

CHAPTER THREE
"Overrun with Free Negroes": The Politics of Wartime
Emancipation and Migration in the Upper Midwest 81

CHAPTER FOUR
"To Go and Help Be Free":
Migration and the Black Military Experience 107

CHAPTER FIVE
"The Building Up of Our Race":
Creating a Life in Freedom 135

CHAPTER SIX
"Freedom Was All They Had:"
Civil Rights and Northern Reconstruction 175

CHAPTER SEVEN
"Agonizing Groans of Mothers" and "Slave-Scarred Veterans":
History, Commemoration, and Memoir in the Aftermath of Slavery 219

Epilogue 265

Notes 267

Bibliography 339

Index 375

Table and Figures

TABLE

Black Enlistment in the Upper Midwest 108

FIGURES

Change in black population in the upper Midwest, 1860–1870 (map) 4

Place of birth of 1,400 antebellum arrivals in Iowa 13

Henry Harrison Triplett 20

Lydia Applewhite 28

Matilda Busey 44

The Mississippi valley (map) 48

Place of birth of 245 wartime arrivals in Iowa 50

"Negroes Driven South by the Rebel Officers," *Harper's Weekly* 63

An unnamed woman and two soldiers of the 22nd Wisconsin Regiment 70

"Fleeing from the Land of Bondage" (engraving) 75

"Contraban'" (image on Civil War envelopes) 87

"Southern Currency" (image on Civil War envelopes) 88

"I'm glad I'm not in Dixie" (image on Civil War envelopes) 89

Prince Hall Mason in regalia (ambrotype) 167

Albert Nuckols (ambrotype) 187

John Hays's life (cartoon) 220

"Dred Scott Sat in Iowa Shack" (article and cartoon) 221

Members of the Grand Army of the Republic, Biddle Circle #38, St. Paul 238

Samuel Hall 246

Acknowledgments

The historian's needs are many, and the opportunity to formally thank those who help are few. I am delighted to be able to acknowledge some of the assistance that came my way while working on this project.

The National Endowment for the Humanities, through its summer and major fellowship programs, provided critical support for this project. In addition, I have benefited greatly from the commitment of the University of Iowa to the members of its faculty and their research. The Offices of the Provost and the Vice President for Research Faculty Scholar Award and Arts and Humanities Initiative awards offered the two most important measures of support a historian could ask for: time and research funding. Both were crucial to this study. My deep appreciation to Darlene Clark Hine and Ira Berlin for their support and for enabling me to secure this important research help. The Department of History has also been an enduring supporter of this project, in part by supplying me with excellent research assistants from our graduate program. Richard Breaux, Brian Donovan, Kate Donovan, Shannon Fogg, Walter Gildersleeve, Jennifer Harbour, Wole Ife, Crystal Lewis, Kerima Lewis, Colleen Kelley, Claire O'Brien, Becky Pulju, Patricia Reid, Eric Roberson, Sharon Romeo, and Kate Stewart helped me comb archives, newspapers, and court cases, from Iowa City to Washington, D.C. Susan Stanfield assisted me in preparing the final manuscript for publication. I am indebted to all for their diligence and thoughtfulness. A few remarkable undergraduates also assisted with my research, including Noel Smythe, Stacy Bell, and Kellie Jackson. Several current and former graduate students at the University of Iowa have been engaged in their own important research, relevant in various ways to this project, and conversations about their work have also encouraged my own, including Kristen Anderson, Christy Clark, Heather Cooper, Jennifer Harbour, Colleen Kelley, Sharon Kennedy-Nolle, Crystal Lewis-Colman, John McKerley, Denise Pate, Yvonne Pitts, Patricia Reid, Sharon Romeo, Susan Stanfield, Charissa Threat, and Bridgett Williams-Searle. My colleague Colin Gordon helped me take baby steps into the world of maps, while Malcolm Rohrbough's lunchtime consultations were always a bright spot in my day.

The commitment, professionalism, and generosity of archivists made their mark on this book from its earliest stages. At the State Historical Society of

Iowa, Special Collections archivists Mary Bennett and Matt Schaefer (now at the Herbert Hoover Presidential Library Museum) steered me toward research collections, offered suggestions, and helped me track down lost people and lost places. Mary is a real hero to historians of the Midwest, with her unparalleled knowledge of the region's history and archives. Museum curator Jack Lufkin and Special Collections archivist Becki Plunkett were also generous in helping me with the Des Moines holdings. Jack Holzheuter, retired historian of the Wisconsin Historical Society, very generously shared his personal research files as well as his decades of interest and expertise in researching Wisconsin African American history. At the Minnesota Historical Society, Hampton Smith also shared his files and pointed me to the society's remarkable collections in African American history. At the University of Iowa's Main Library, Kären Mason, curator of the Iowa Women's Archives, and Bob McGowan, head of Special Collections (now retired), helped me navigate the marvelous holdings of both these important archives, and the staff in Interlibrary Loan kept the flow of research materials steady and uninterrupted. Bill Krueger, Librarian of the Iowa Masonic Library, was extraordinarily helpful and graciously fielded several inquiries about Masonry. As I explored the public libraries and county historical societies of the upper Midwest, I profited from the knowledge and interest of both library professionals and volunteers. Notable among them were Geraldine Lawson at the Keokuk Public Library, Susie Guest at the Burlington Public Library, and Lee Attenberg at the Lee County Historical Society. Many thanks as well to the staff at the National Archives, the Library of Congress, the Missouri Historical Society and Missouri State Archives, the University of Missouri Archives at St. Louis, the Western Historical Manuscripts Collection at St. Louis and Columbia, the library at the Iowa Wesleyan College, and the Nodaway Valley Historical Museum.

Several others shared their knowledge of regional African American history along the way, including Leola Bergman, author of the first serious study of black history in Iowa; Marv Bergman, Iowa historian and editor extraordinaire; Jan Nash, whose historical preservation efforts have benefited the community as well as my own research; Kim Painter, Johnson County (Iowa) Recorder, who scoured her archives for me; Professor Bridgett Williams-Searle (St. Rose College, New York), whose own work helped me think more clearly about midwestern slavery; and Professor Philip Webber, of Central College (Pella, Iowa), who shared his research notes on Clarinda's African American community. Professor Sharon Wood of the University of Nebraska made available her research in Davenport, as did Craig Klein, of Scott Community

College, whose devotion to uncovering and preserving the record of that city's African American history is matched by his generosity in sharing that work.

In the challenging process of turning a mountain of research into a book, I have had the privilege of working with a smart and generous writing group. Kathleen Diffley, Teresa Magnum, Kim Marra, and Laura Rigal brought their insight, intellect, wisdom, and good humor to bear on many a conference paper, article draft, and book chapter; they saved me from myself more times than I can remember. They could always envision the book that lay at the end of this project, and had faith that I would get there. Their presence around the dining room table nourished this study and me more than they probably realize.

Joanne Pope Melish and Louis Gerteis offered incredibly generous, insightful, and probative readings of the book manuscript. Chuck Grench warmly welcomed this project to the University of North Carolina Press, where Katy O'Brien, Ron Maner, and Stevie Champion brought their many fine talents to bear in transforming the manuscript into a book.

For the opportunity to present work in progress and receive helpful feedback from fellow panelists, commentators, and audience members, I wish to thank the Berkshire Conference on Women's History, the Organization of American Historians, the American Historical Association, the Southern Historical Association, the University of Minnesota Seminar on Race, Ethnicity, and Migration, the International Congress of Historical Sciences, the American Society for Legal History, the Atlantic Emancipations Conference at the MacNeil Center of the University of Pennsylvania, the University of East Anglia, the University of Northern Iowa, the Missouri Valley History Conference, the Hoover Presidential Library and Museum, the Missouri Graduate Conference at the University of Missouri-Columbia, the American Studies Program at the University of Iowa, the African American Historical Museum and Cultural Center (Cedar Rapids, Iowa), as well as the Lee County and Des Moines County Historical societies (Iowa).

Several people have sustained me and this project over the years. My fellow travelers from the first generations of the women's history graduate program at Madison—Juliana Barr, Kathleen Brown, Florence Deacon, Maureen Fitzgerald, Joyce Follet, Andrea Friedman, Jennifer Frost, Amy Hague, Nancy Isenberg, Maureen LaBerge, Nancy MacLean, Brenda Marston, Laura McEnaney, Leisa Meier, Leslie Reagan, Susan Smith, Landon Storrs, as well as Jeanne Boydston, Linda Gordon, Judy Leavitt, and Gerda Lerner—have been a treasured source of intellectual challenge, inspiration, hilarity, and renewed commitment to feminist scholarship.

Acknowledgments

The Schwalms—Bruce, Kim, Victor, Olivia, as well as Dad and Doris—have always rooted for me and celebrated my successes, but they also let me know that they expected me to get this book done.

Grace and Orin Stormoen provided a warm and welcome haven from the labor of book writing at their Arkdale home.

In Iowa City, Meredith Alexander and Kim Marra, Cheryl Hetherington and Lori Popp, kept me grounded, fed, inspired, and encouraged as only good friends (and great cooks) can. Otis, Beecher, and Tolliver, who get me out of bed in the morning and keep my computer warm, have helped this book along in their own special ways.

And then there is Doris Stormoen, for whom my sun rises. Every day spent researching and writing this book—and all the days between—were better for her presence in my life. Her insight, her wisdom, her kindness, her humor, and her patience with the long hours spent at my desk were exactly what I needed to complete this project, which would not have happened without her.

Introduction

For all its unintended consequences and unresolved implications, wartime emancipation was a singularly transformative event in American history. In its aftermath, four million people gained their freedom and a political economy based on chattel slavery was destroyed. Generations of scholarship have richly illuminated these consequences, particularly in the South.[1] But emancipation's immediate and postwar repercussions extended well beyond the South, forcing a renegotiation of the "place" of African Americans in the North—both geographically and in the imagined body politic. Northern whites, infamously unwilling to "tolerate negroes, except as slaves," according to *Harper's Weekly* in 1862, understood that southern emancipation not only unloosed the bonds of slavery from African Americans, but had also unloosed the meaning of race in American society.[2] By the time of the Civil War, northern whites had long since erased their region's own history of slavery and, in the process of stripping "free" blacks of their rights and opportunities, attributed the causes of racial disparities in the North to "race," rather than legally defined inequities.[3] Southern emancipation mattered, even in the North, because slavery had long anchored American ideas about race to how power, privilege, and citizenship were experienced and perceived. The persistence of southern slavery had allowed white Americans to project their conceptions of the "place" of people of African descent to the slave South.[4] Emancipation cut loose that anchor and, in so doing, changed the history of race throughout the nation. This book examines how one northern region contended with the repercussions of emancipation.

The phrase "emancipation's diaspora" refers to two key developments that forced the northern politics of race and emancipation into the open. One involved the wartime waves of migration by former slaves out of the South into northern and western communities, and the other concerned the public and private debates that wartime emancipation instigated in the North, as nonslaveholding Americans pondered their expectations and fears about the implications of slavery's destruction for the nation as a whole. The wartime diaspora of former slaves out of the South was one of several uprootings and dispersals that have characterized the experience of enslaved African and African-descended populations in North America, from the seventeenth century through the Great Migration that began during World War I. The first of these, the Atlantic slave trade, tore more than 12 million people from their African homes and transported them to the New World, 600,000 of them to North America. The second diaspora came with the American Revolution, when as much as a quarter of the enslaved African and African American population of the British colonies turned the chaos of war into an opportunity to flee their masters. Those who fled to British lines in anticipation of gaining their freedom were dispersed by evacuating British forces at the end of the war to slavery in the British West Indies, or as free people to Nova Scotia or London.[5] The third great diaspora occurred during the antebellum era with the internal slave trade, in which one million enslaved people became objects of speculation, were sold, separated from their families and their communities, and relocated onto the succession of American frontiers in the Southwest.[6] The fourth, and the last major dispersal during the period in which slavery was still legal in the United States, occurred during the Civil War. Hundreds of thousands of enslaved people, determined to gain their freedom, fled their masters and approached Union lines. Tens of thousands of those who struck out to gain their freedom during the war continued their journeys until they made their own way or were relocated by Union military or civilian authorities to northern homes and employers. Former slaves traveled to several northern and western destinations: up the Atlantic coast to Washington, D.C., and northward, up and across the Ohio River valley, west to Kansas, and up the Mississippi valley.[7] In each location, these migrants began new lives—in communities, towns, and cities already shaped by unique regional histories of black slavery and black freedom. Their arrival challenged both black and white communities to confront emancipation's aftereffects outside the South.

Emancipation's Diaspora considers those consequences in a seemingly unlikely location: at the northernmost reaches of the Mississippi valley, in the states of Iowa, Wisconsin, and Minnesota. Most Americans are not accustomed to thinking about this region of the country as a probable area for a significant or complex history of African Americans and their relationships with whites; after all, the population of African Americans in these three states has never been large. The 2,500 black residents of the upper Midwest in 1860 saw a net increase over the next ten years of about 6,100 people. Even after the wartime flow of formerly enslaved people into the region, the proportion of African Americans in the population remained small. While that proportion would rise and fall over the course of the twentieth century, it continued to be low. In 2005, it ranged from 2.3 percent in Iowa and 4.3 percent in Minnesota to 6 percent in Wisconsin.[8] But the force and extent of emancipation's impact on Americans and their ideas about race was not dictated by the relative size or proportion of African Americans in the population. *Emancipation's Diaspora* illuminates "race" as a historically contingent construction and a relationship created, contested, and experienced by and among white midwesterners as well as by African Americans. Moreover, this study shows that even in a region where black people were a very small proportion of the population, they self-consciously sustained and commemorated a history that merits further investigation and recognition.

To situate emancipation's impact on the wartime and postbellum Midwest, this study begins with the regional racial hierarchies that took shape prior to the war. African Americans whose antebellum journeys brought them into the upper Midwest carried with them personal and familial legacies of slavery, whether they arrived as free-born people, as recently freed from northern or southern slavery, as slaves, or as the children of slaves. They encountered a social landscape that had already been shaped by the early history and persistence of slavery, as well as by the institutional manifestations of white supremacy—in territorial and state constitutions, in codes of law, and in public policy. The practice of slavery in this region violated the Northwest Ordinance and the terms of the Louisiana Purchase, but African slavery had been tolerated in the "free" territories and states of the upper Midwest because it was consonant with the kind of society most of the area's white settlers preferred, one where their whiteness was understood to carry material, social, legal, and political privileges. Although by the antebellum era, slavery persisted only on a very small scale in the upper Midwest, it nonetheless reinforced these privileges by sustaining the associations between whiteness and mastery, and blackness and dependency. Black settlers in Wisconsin, Minnesota, and Iowa encountered this antebellum history of illegally sustained and extraconstitutional slavery as well as a western white frontier hostile to black freedom.[9]

The controversy of wartime African American migration from the South had a significant impact on residents of all three states. Although some white midwesterners were glad to have the opportunity to hire the new black refugees as farm laborers and servants, others saw black in-migration as an explicit threat to the white frontier. For the latter group of whites, the geographic mobility of former slaves became symptomatic of the equally undesirable social mobility of black people in the aftermath of emancipation. As a result, the upper Midwest's black and white residents became deeply and often antagonistically engaged in a process of redefining the meanings and implications of freedom and citizenship. Emancipation was not only about the destruction of

Change in black population in the upper Midwest, 1860–1870.

Introduction

the South's system of slavery, but also about the renegotiation of the place of African Americans throughout the nation and within the imagined body politic. An entire nation faced the meaning and consequences of emancipation.

This book is centrally concerned with the northern consequences of southern slavery's destruction. Most scholarship on emancipation's consequences during the era of Reconstruction has been southward-facing. Even those studies of Reconstruction that take northerners as their subject have typically focused on how those northern actors viewed and participated in the reconstruction of the South.[10] As a result, historians have underestimated southern emancipation's impact on the North. Moving the study of emancipation's uncertain Reconstruction-era resolution out of the South and into the upper Midwest, *Emancipation's Diaspora* finds that the transition to black citizenship involved the hotly contested politics of black enfranchisement, but also an extensive and persistent series of collisions over segregation, civil rights, and the more informal politics of race—including how slavery and emancipation would be remembered and commemorated. At the same time that African American residents in the upper Midwest pursued the formal rights and privileges they associated with citizenship, white midwesterners struggled to defend their own racial prerogatives—to send their children into all-white classrooms, to continue their exclusive right to serve in state legislatures, to travel in all-white cabins and cars, to take their meals in all-white dining rooms, to practice the rites of Masonry in all-white lodges. In party and nonpartisan conventions, in courtrooms, schoolhouses, lodge rooms, on steamboats and trains, in everyday interactions, black and white midwesterners, men and women, collided as they renegotiated the meaning attached to race—and its expression in social, political, and economic inequality—in northern postemancipation life.[11]

Even as African Americans challenged the public politics of segregation, they also turned their attention, as well as their social and material resources, to the work of creating the social, sacred, and institutional infrastructure that would sustain them as they set about the business of creating new lives in freedom. They contended with the politics of postemancipation life not only in conflicts with white men and women, but also in the black public sphere. Having claimed male citizenship on the basis of an idealized manhood, and a shared humanity by adhering to "civilized" gender conventions, many black midwesterners clearly recognized that gender was central to the public politics of race. But normative gender conventions were also subject to contestation and negotiation in postbellum black communities. African American women challenged the uses and abuses of male power and authority within their own

Introduction

communities; they refused to build and sustain sacred and secular community institutions only to yield absolute control over them to patriarchal authority. Even as the most economically disenfranchised of the Midwest's black residents, African American women claimed the prerogative both to endorse an idealized black manhood and to challenge the extent of male privilege in their communities.

As black men and women struggled to claim citizenship in the postemancipation North, they also sought authority over how their own and the nation's history of slavery and wartime emancipation would be remembered and represented. Emancipation Day celebrations were widespread in the decades following the Civil War, and they were a significant and widely enjoyed component of black expressive culture. But Emancipation Day celebrations were not simply holidays or festivals; they were richly and explicitly politicized events that commemorated collective memories of slavery and its destruction. Black midwesterners were publicly asserting a specific identity as an emancipated people, and therefore as former slaves, with the authority to interpret that past in the public sphere. More than just claiming their own history, black participants in Emancipation Day celebrations also insisted on emancipation as a central event in national history; they asserted that the postbellum legacy of slavery—particularly in the form of second-class citizenship for African Americans—demanded redress. In community festivities and in the many forms in which black memoir was publicly circulated, midwestern African Americans refused to abandon personal or collective memories of slavery to the misrepresentations that came out of white popular culture—whether in the literature of the "Lost Cause" or the increasingly romantic portrayals of the antebellum South. Emancipation Day celebrations, obituaries, and postbellum slave narratives kept public attention focused on the brutality of slavery, the violence white slaveowners had perpetrated on African American people, and the shameful fact of the nation's tolerance of that oppression for more than two hundred years. These forms of cultural expression challenged the caricatures that attempted to dehumanize the enslaved, as well as the portrayals of kind masters that attempted to exonerate slaveowners.[12]

Black midwesterners also reminisced about slavery, the war, emancipation, and its consequences in less formal circumstances. At family gatherings and in conversation with neighbors and fellow veterans, they continued to share their recollections about how they came to the Midwest, recounting the choices, dangers, and difficulties they faced as fugitives trying to make their way to freedom. Their recollections often included the perilous escape from slavery that began their journeys northward. While many white midwesterners attributed the destruction of slavery and the growing presence of African Americans in midwestern towns and villages to the humanitarian acts of courageous and sympathetic whites, reminiscing African Americans attributed their arrival in the Midwest to their own sacrifices, skill, bravery, determination, and desperation. By telling their stories to daughters, nieces, grandsons, and neighbors, black midwesterners challenged the notion that emancipation had been either a gift or a mistake. They claimed the battle for black freedom—in the past as well as in the present, in the Midwest as well as in the South—as their own and created a legacy of the Midwest's encounter with emancipation.

1 "A Full Realization of the Barbarities of Slavery"

Kate Thompson spent twenty-seven years in slavery. Born in Missouri, she was bought and sold five times and separated from her husband and the father of her children, until the chaos of war and the collapse of Missouri slavery created the opportunity for her to ensure that her children would never be taken from her. Kate took her four small children and fled to Iowa. There, for the remainder of the war, she supported herself and the youngsters by working as a farmhand. Like thousands of other enslaved people in the Mississippi valley, she gambled on the risks and uncertainty of flight to the unknown midwestern countryside, working and living amid strangers, rather than wait out the course of the war, risk the further devastation of her family, and hope for slavery's ultimate eradication.

Kate was not alone in her decision to seek freedom and safety in the North; tens of thousands joined her during the war. Some runaway slaves relied on protection and assistance from Union troops as they made their way north; others took matters into their own hands, like Jane Morgan, who boldly informed her owner, as she turned to leave, that "under Military rules then in Missouri she considered herself free." Still others, like Walter Bucklin, were sent out by unsuspecting masters to perform an errand and simply never returned. But all of these varied paths to freedom began with the decision to risk everything to escape the violence, compulsory labor, and brutal separation of families that marked the experience of slavery.[1]

The conditions of slavery helped fuel thousands of wartime decisions to take flight to the upper Midwest. Most of the enslaved people who became wartime migrants to this region also had shared experiences of involuntary migration and family separations prior to the war. Unlike slaves in the East, whose lives had been constantly overshadowed by the threat of separation by the slave trade, those from Kentucky westward had already been subjected to the involuntary relocations forced on them by the slave trade, estate dispersal, and the migrations of their owners. Their wartime migration often meant choosing to sever family and community ties, once again, as the only viable path to freedom. But this time, enslaved people took one of the most barbarous features of slavery—separation and involuntary relocation to a strange land—and turned it into an avenue to freedom.

Many black migrants were unaware of what awaited them at their midwestern destinations: the region's own history of slavery and circumscribed black freedom. The Midwest that they encountered was more accustomed to black slavery than white residents were willing to admit. In addition, black freedom was widely and openly impaired by legal restrictions that white citizens felt were appropriate and necessary, because they, like most white midwesterners, viewed African Americans as a "subject and subjugated people." Whether by holding them in slavery, or regarding them as innately disposed to enslavement, many white midwesterners saw people of African descent as slaves, slavelike, and a threat to white free labor and independence. "A full realization of the barbarities of slavery," as former slave Oscar McClellan referred to it, created a painful, common bridge of experience between wartime migrants seeking freedom and longtime black midwesterners.[2]

SLAVERY AND THE DIASPORIC COMMUNITY

Slavery meant many things to those whose lives were so deeply affected by it: brutality, sexual exploitation, unending labor, degradation, and treatment no different from other valuable livestock. As Samuel Hall (who at the close of the war made his way from Tennessee slavery to the small village of Washington, Iowa, and later published his postbellum slave narrative) would achingly describe it a half century after gaining his freedom, slaves were worked like horses and fed like pigs at a trough; their children were sold away like a calf from a cow. The threat of separation as well as promises to protect family ties were especially powerful tools in the hands of slaveowners seeking to "master" the people they regarded as property.[3]

Every enslaved person who made the journey north out of slavery to the upper Midwest, either before or during the Civil War, had already encountered "a full realization of the barbarities of slavery." Key among them was the loss of families to slavery. For Oscar McClellan, that "full realization" came in the unforgettable and unforgivable loss of his fourteen-year-old son to the slave trade; for Jefferson Holloway, it was being sold on "My own Birth Day," when he turned seven, "just like Horses or catle." For Titus and Ellen Shropshire, it was when their two children were sold away from them in 1860; for William Brown, it was the separation from his father and several siblings when he was only two years old, "parted, never to assemble together again in this world." Nathaniel Adams could only recall that he was "quite small" when he was "sold out of the Trader's Yard in Richmond and taken far away from his family to Tennessee." Fannie Jackson, born in Virginia, would be transported by her owner's son to Georgia at age four and to Alabama at age eight or nine. When "still a girl," she was removed again, this time to Louisiana; from there, she was sold at age sixteen to Putnam County, Missouri, and once again, while still a teenager, sold within Missouri. Clarissa Cox was moved five times; she was given as a gift to a child, traded for a plot of land, and delivered as a present to an illegitimate heir of her owner. Charles Thompson "did not know what trouble was" until sold away from his mother; in later life, he was hired out, repeatedly submitted to the cycle of severed kin and community ties. George Johnson recalled: "My mother said almost all the time 'round my grandmother's cabin there was weeping and wailing everyday or so when they'd come to buy some of 'em; 'Course as I say, I never saw it but I tell you it must a been awful." No matter their circumstances in the diversity of settings encompassed by American bondage, enslaved people lived at risk of being treated as chattel property repeatedly over the course of a lifetime: sold, passed on to heirs, seized for bad debt, hired out, traded for a plot of land.[4]

Every transaction in the slave South that reduced a person to chattel had an exponential effect—on those taken away, on the family members left behind, and on subsequent generations whose personal and family history was irrevocably marked by the loss of kinship ties.[5] Enslaved people carried not just their own grief but that of older generations as well. Samuel Hall learned as a child the story of his grandmother, whose anguish over her enslavement and forced removal from West Africa to Maryland without her beloved husband led first to a refusal to work, then to a refusal to learn English, and ultimately to a refusal to live. Hall not only carried this family history as part of his own identity, but also would himself be separated from three generations of his family by sale—from his wife and children, his mother, three half brothers, a half sister, and "other more distant relations." Merely witnessing such separations, let alone being subject to them, had a powerful impact. "I have seen slave mothers fall over in a dead faint when their children were sold away from them," Hall recalled. "The mothers would have to hand down their children and when they fell over in a dead faint men would pick the poor women up and carry them away just as if they were dogs. Those mothers loved their little children just the same as white mothers love their little babies and some of them were never happy again and some went insane as did my old mother when her children were sold away from her."[6] The physical journey of the Hall family—from Africa to Maryland and North Carolina, to Tennessee, and finally to Iowa—suggests the emotional and psychic travail that slavery caused for generations of family life.

The majority of black migrants to the upper Midwest (before and during the war) had spent much of their lives in and close to the Mississippi River valley; Missouri and Kentucky were their most common birthplaces. Among wartime migrants, Virginia and Tennessee were closely ranked third and fourth among their place of birth. But among those who had arrived before the war, many more claimed Virginia as their birthplace.[7] Few African Americans went directly from Virginia to the upper Midwest during the war; instead, the prevalence of birthplaces in that state points to its role as a starting place of the interstate slave trade, as well as the slave trade's dominance in the lives even of those who would become midwesterners.[8] In the 1850s, Virginia still exceeded all states in the number of exported enslaved African Americans. South Carolina, North Carolina, Maryland, and Georgia were less active than Virginia as exporters in the interstate slave trade; thus it is not surprising that, combined, they were the birthplace of only 8 percent of Iowa's civilian population. Virginia's frequent appearance as a birthplace among black midwesterners is testimony to the common experience of the slave trade's diaspora.

The life histories of the enslaved people who ultimately reached the upper Midwest had been shaped by the interstate slave trade but also by the westward movement of slavery over the course of the nineteenth century: the migration of slaveowners and potential slaveowners from Virginia to Kentucky and Tennessee, and later, to Missouri, made involuntary migration a central, commonly experienced aspect of life among the enslaved.[9] Even those born elsewhere could frequently trace their families back one or two generations to a Virginia birthplace. This westward movement of the nation's population and of the slave trade also meant that by the last decade of the antebellum era, Kentucky, Tennessee, and most of Missouri's eastern, Mississippi River–bordering counties had also become net exporters of slaves. This, too, would have an impact on the lives of those enslaved people who eventually became midwesterners. Slaves in the South's exporting states faced a greater vulnerability to family separation. In one of Missouri's most slave-intensive counties, 30 percent of a sample of slaves were children under age fifteen who had been sold without either parent.[10] As Michael Tadman, historian of the interstate slave trade, has shown, slaves in exporting states were three times more likely to face family separation than slaves in "importing" states.[11] After 1850, as some western states joined the ranks of those exporting slaves, birth in the Mississippi valley did not protect enslaved people from the most feared

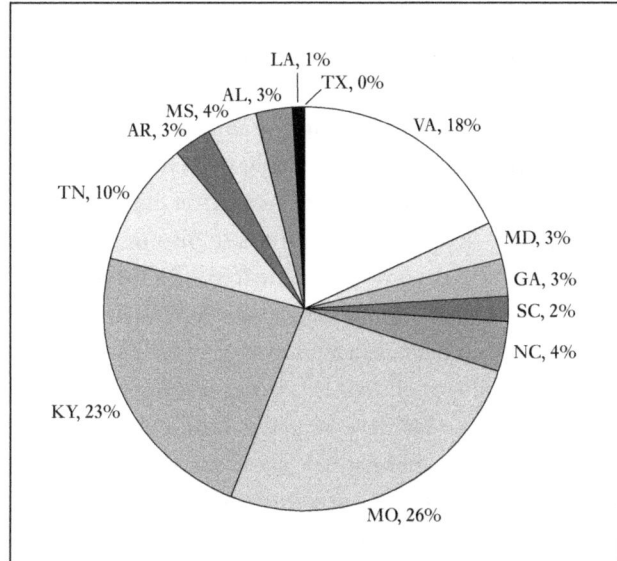

Place of birth of 1,400 antebellum arrivals in Iowa.

consequence of slavery: becoming lost to one's family and all that was familiar by means of the slave trade.

As common as involuntary separation was in the experience of enslaved people, not all separations and movements could be attributed to the interstate slave trade. A significant proportion of the involuntary relocation of the antebellum slave population—a low estimate suggests 30 to 40 percent—was a result of planter migration, the dispersal of slaves to heirs, and intrastate sales.[12] Furthermore, enslaved people often experienced the decimation of families and communities without being sold, and sometimes without even being sent out of state. Henry Vance's owner and his owner's daughter moved him four times around the state of Missouri before he fled slavery to enlist in the Union army. Indeed, Kate Thompson, whose experience of being sold five times opened this chapter, never traveled outside of Missouri before the war.[13]

Slave hiring contributed to the prevalence of involuntary slave movement in the South before the Civil War; as noted by the historian Jonathan D. Martin, slaveowners often offset the expense of their migration into the South's interior by hiring out their slaves.[14] In fact, Martin says, the risk of separation by the practice of hiring out was three to five times more likely than by sale. Iowan William Brown described the annual post-Christmas season of hiring out as yet another, grievous component of the "time of scattering" for slave families. The unpredictability of what the year might bring—"new and untried homes," exploitative and abusive employers—had to be accepted without comment; slaves "were not asked where they wanted to go. They had nothing to say about it. If they acted as if they were not pleased, they were very apt to take a lashing, and then go," Brown recalled. From age ten until gaining his freedom at age twenty, Brown was hired out to five different employers.[15] Ten-year-old Rachel Jackson, born in Missouri, was sold to Ned Thomas, who took her to his farm about six miles from Carrollton. After his death, his heirs "hired me out to work, out there in the country and also in this city. I worked out for different people until the slaves became free." As these experiences suggest, slave hiring was common in Missouri, as it was in most states where black midwesterners had been born. Hiring slaves gave nonslaveowning whites a welcome taste of the privileges of mastery; it was less expensive than hiring white labor and allowed these farmers to make more efficient use of their land or add to their holdings. At midcentury, slaveowners or their heirs earned a substantial (12 to 15 percent) rate of return on their investment. Good business and the pleasures of enhancing a man's household authority gave slave hiring a critical edge. From the perspective of enslaved people, hiring—and the annual exodus away from home and family that it usually entailed—was less permanent than the slave trade in the separations it caused but nonetheless heartbreaking for the children whom parents lost sight of and the parental nurturing the children knew only on rare occasions.[16]

The brutal violence of slavery was experienced not just in separation from family. As a child, Lucy Brown was tied and whipped for not bringing water as quickly as was expected of her. The Dandridge family—parents and children—hired out to a Mississippi cotton planter were beaten and watched other slaves being beaten to death.[17] When her biscuits were judged inferior, Rosy Robinson was thrown out of the house, down the porch, and kicked repeatedly by her owner. At age eleven, William H. Robinson was whipped so severely by his drunken master that "the blood had dried the shirt in the wounds on my back."[18] Samuel Hall knew as a child that in trying to learn to write, he risked having a finger cut off. He saw splits in the side of an older slave after his master had whipped him, was knifed as an adult by a master who sought to "break" him, and had his son taken and whipped by his master. He also recalled the horror of husbands being separated from their wives so patrollers could "use those same women for their pleasure."[19] The pain and horror of physical abuse, mutilation, and sexual exploitation echoed throughout families and communities when children, parents, spouses, and friends were forced to witness the violation of loved ones.

The enslaved people named here—men, women, and children—who would eventually make their way out of slavery during the Civil War and into the upper Midwest, knew slavery's barbarity. This was part of their inheritance, unwelcome, yet never to be forgotten, even in the later postwar decades when sectional reunion made forgetfulness a politically and culturally popular movement. It was also part of the immediate context that motivated and informed the wartime movement of former slaves from the slave South to the upper Midwest—a land of freedom, they must have imagined, where their families would finally be safe and where they might gain some distance from the chaos of war.

SLAVERY IN THE MIDWEST

Wartime migrants out of southern slavery may not have realized that their destination was marked by a legacy of bondage, that midwestern blacks had also very recently been held as slaves, subjected to sale, forced family separation, and the seizure of their children. Midwestern slavery—while often openly practiced—was rarely acknowledged at the time, and historians, too, have failed to come to terms with its extent or the experience of enslaved midwesterners.[20] Over the course of its development, midwestern slavery was a fluid institution, taking form in a variety of legal and extralegal practices, from open and legally sanctioned slaveownership, to term or lifetime indentured servitude, adoptions that were intended to mask child slavery, visiting or temporary bondage protected by law, and, of course, explicitly illegal slaveownership. All of these forms were found in the upper Midwest, and all of them were buttressed by black codes that, by circumscribing the rights of all black midwesterners, worked to perpetuate a regionwide presumption that white citizens were free, while residents of African descent most likely were not.[21]

Black servitude in Illinois played an important role in the spread of slavery north and west. Although not the sole source of midwestern bondage, the state's slaveholdings provided an accessible market to potential slaveowners regionwide, and Illinois owners themselves migrated with their slaves and servants to Wisconsin, Iowa, and Minnesota. The local and congressional interpretation that the Northwest Ordinance tolerated existing enslavement seems to have been infectious, promoting slavery and slaverylike practices well beyond the "Illinois Country" into the nineteenth century.

Slavery had been integral to eighteenth-century European and American exploration and colonization of the Midwest. Introduced around 1720 into the French settlements in the Illinois Country, African (and smaller numbers of Indian) slaves quickly became instrumental in that area's transition from mission centers and fur trading posts to an important grain-producing region.[22] Slave labor was also essential in colonial lead mines and saltworks. Slaves increased in number to 164 in 1732, when they were a quarter to a third of the area's population. Even after the French closed the slave trade to the Illinois Country in 1747, the black slave population increased; by 1752, 446 enslaved blacks resided in the region, and 41 percent of white heads of households owned slaves.[23]

In the colonial era, far fewer black slaves were found in the upper Midwest's fur trade, military outposts, and mining communities than in the more southerly Illinois Country; French authorities, believing that Africans would not survive harsh winters, joined with British and Canadians in relying largely on Indian slave labor. These enslaved people included war captives acquired from Pawnee tribes of the western plains, and, to a lesser extent, slaves obtained through imperial and intertribal conflict. However, as Americans took over the region, military conquest led to the removal of most Indian people to the West, and Indian slavery declined. African-descended slavery would take its place.[24]

As the legal historian Paul Finkelman has demonstrated, neither territorial officials nor the national government moved beyond the rhetoric of slavery's prohibition in Article IV of the Northwest Ordinance of 1787. Inhabitants of the original French Illinois settlements and the saline operators at Shawneetown had acquired explicit protection for their slave property, beginning with the 1783 cession of western lands by Virginia, the terms of which specified that slavery remain as previously practiced, and continuing with the interpretation offered by Congress, territorial officials, and local residents that the ordinance did not restrict the rights of resident slaveowners. Indeed, law and custom reinforced slavery in Illinois until it was finally excluded, without exception, by the 1848 state constitution. Until then, bondage not only continued, but also spread into the settlements of the upper Mississippi valley. From 1800 until 1848, neither territorial officials nor Congress moved to emancipate the region's slaves, and pro-slavery residents soon stopped petitioning for explicit legal protections when they realized that Article IV of the ordinance would not be enforced.[25]

As part of the Indiana Territory from 1800 to 1818, the former Illinois Country also profited from the territory's construction of an elaborate system of laws regulating and protecting slavery and black indentured servitude. By 1803, the territory had adopted a slave code drawing from those of Virginia and Kentucky. The territorial assemblies of 1805 and 1807 extended indentured servitude with a set of laws regulating the practice, a veritable form of slavery that would have a long history in the region.[26]

The Barbarities of Slavery

Although we know little about the texture of African American life under this system, the institution created by these laws confirms the proximity of indentured servitude to slavery. A statute set the terms of service at thirty-five years for males and thirty-two years for females. Moreover, since black servitude was heritable, their sons could look forward to thirty years of subjugation and their daughters, twenty-eight years. However, in both practice and indentures entered in the legal record, the terms of service frequently extended well beyond these limits; fifty- and ninety-nine-year terms meant that indentured servitude was, for many Illinois blacks, a lifetime of slavery. While the law of indentured servitude required the provision of sufficient food, clothing, and lodging, as well as freedom dues in the form of clothing and a blanket, it dictated the modes of control over the lives and mobility of black servants. Whipping—at forty lashes or less—was legal for a host of behaviors, from laziness to seditious speech and unlawful assembly. Idleness and unexcused absences could result in extended service. Indentures could be bought and sold and passed on to heirs, so servitude was heritable. Servants who wandered more than ten miles from their master's residence without a written pass were subject to seizure and corporal punishment. Through a series of Illinois Supreme Court rulings from 1825 to 1845, indentured servitude became more narrowly defined and servants were gradually emancipated, until the 1848 Illinois constitution finally ended the practices of servitude and slavery.[27]

However closely these laws may (or may not) reflect the lived experience of servants and slaves, particularly of those who were taken out of the Illinois Country and moved farther north, the law suggests the parameters of what was regarded as normative treatment of African Americans: legally sanctioned violence, restricted mobility, the continued centrality of reproduction to the perpetuation of servitude, and the entitlement of all whites to act punitively against blacks in the enforcement of these regulations. As servants and as slaves, African Americans were commodities. If some masters or mistresses were kind, if some servants performed compulsory labor that was less heinous than what was demanded in cotton fields of the South, if some attained their freedom at the age of majority, it is nonetheless clear that the power of the state, a culture of white supremacy, and generations of practice colluded to protect and expand black slavery in the Midwest.[28]

Well into the nineteenth century, enslaved African Americans were also conveyed to the upper Midwest by U.S. army officers assigned to upper Mississippi valley military outposts. These officers included slaveowners as well as those who took advantage of the army's special allowance to purchase, lease, or hire servants. At least through the 1840s, enslaved people were used to perform a wide range of service-related work (and to demonstrate the gentility of white officers' households) at Fort Snelling (St. Paul, Minnesota), Fort Crawford (Prairie du Chien, Wisconsin), and Fort Armstrong (Rock Island, Illinois). In addition, enslaved men and women were held by officers posted at Fort Winnebago (Columbia County, Wisconsin), Fort Des Moines (Montrose, Iowa), and the Sac and Fox Indian Agency (Wapello County, Iowa).[29] The largest slaveowners, including Major Lawrence Taliaferro at Fort Snelling, found fellow officers and their wives more than willing to purchase or hire the surplus African American laborers they brought to the forts.[30] The ownership and use of enslaved labor spread beyond the military families stationed at these forts; in 1842, interpreter Joseph Smart transported two enslaved black women from Missouri to Fort Des Moines to supplement the work performed by a Fox woman he also enslaved there.[31]

Some of the people held at these army posts had once been "Illinois" slaves; among them, Patsey was one of the few midwestern slaves whose lives—or at least genealogies—can be reconstructed. Patsey's history is especially useful in that it illustrates both the experience of midwestern slavery and how the institution spread through the region. Born into slavery in Kentucky in about 1800, the "nearly white quadroon" was initially owned by Thomas Posey.[32] As a young child, she was given to Posey's daughter, Emily. When Patsey's new mistress married fellow Kentuckian and slaveowner General Joseph M. Street, Patsey was taken away from her own family; at age twelve she was moved with the rest of the Street family belongings from Kentucky to Shawneetown in southern Illinois—an area where slavery was legal and still quite common; in fact, slaves served as the principal source of labor for the town's profitable saltworks. Six years later, knowing that their territory would not achieve statehood otherwise, delegates to the Illinois constitutional convention passed a law prohibiting slavery. Shawneetown slaveowners were granted an exception to the statute's enforcement until 1825, but Patsey's master acted as many southern Illinois slaveowners did in 1818—he secured his wealth in human property by having his five slaves sign indenture papers before the new constitution was enacted. Patsey, at age seventeen, and the man who was (or would soon be) her husband, London Triplett, at age sixteen, were persuaded or forced by General Street to indenture themselves to him—Patsey, for fifty years (which was thirty-six years more than permitted under territorial law); London, for sixty years (forty-one years longer than permitted under the law).[33] Their children would inherit and retain their indentured status until they reached the age of majority.[34] For London Triplett, who died sometime prior to 1850, his indenture would turn out to be a life sentence of slavery, despite his residence in three free midwestern states.

Patsey and London were forced to relocate in 1827, when Street was appointed Indian agent at Fort Crawford; the 1830 census records the presence of five slaves in his Wisconsin household, presumably including Patsey, London, and their infant son London. At the fort the Tripletts became part of a small slave community, consisting of 17 out of 313 residents in 1836.[35] While serving the Streets at Fort Crawford, Patsey would have at least three more children: Henry (1833), Lewis (1835), and Newton (1837). Despite their birth in a free territory, the children would be openly held as slaves in Wisconsin and then in Iowa until Street's death. As in the case of so many other enslaved mothers, Patsey's sons were "hers" only until her owner decided to exercise his prerogative. In 1835, when Joseph Street's daughter married George Wilson, a slaveholding officer at Fort Crawford, Street's wedding gift to his daughter was Henry Harrison Triplett, Patsey's two-year-old son. The gift came with the condition that Henry be granted his freedom in 1854, at age twenty-one. The latter provision, and the fact that the Wilsons remained at Fort Crawford for a time, may have lessened the Triplett family's grief, but their fears for his safety must have soon escalated, assuming they learned about George Wilson's subsequent actions as a slaveowner. Sometime between 1837 and 1840, Wilson, charging one of his female slaves with intolerable "unruliness," traded her for a pair of mules and she was never seen again. During this period, the Wilsons moved from Prairie du Chien, Wisconsin, to Dubuque, Iowa, separating Henry from his family. The word of Wilson's abrupt sale of an "unruly" slave must have made that separation a very anxious time for his parents. Henry was reunited with his family in 1839 or 1840, when the Wilsons rejoined the Street household in Wapello County, Iowa, on General Street's assignment as the new Indian agent there. Other slaves in the Street household included Charles Forrester and two women Street purchased in Missouri—and subsequently sold.[36]

On Street's death in 1840, Charles Forrester was freed by his will.[37] Henry remained a servant in the Wilson household; by 1850, still with the family, he was working as a blacksmith's apprentice in Fairfield, Jefferson County, Iowa. But we lose track of Patsey, her husband, and the rest of the Triplett family for the ten years following Street's death. During this decade, the elder London apparently died. Patsey and sons London, Lewis, and Newton seem to have gained their freedom (although Patsey still had eighteen years left on her "indenture"), suggested by their independent household as listed in the 1850

Henry Harrison Triplett, formerly enslaved son of Patsey and London Triplett. George Wilson, "George Wilson: First Territorial Adjutant of the Militia of Iowa," Annals of Iowa 4, January 1901.

census for Agency. Four years later, if Joseph Street's instructions were followed by his heirs, Henry Triplett, too, gained his freedom; by 1860, he was married and living in Keokuk, Iowa.[38] Patsey may not have known of her son's freedom and new family; she disappears from the record after 1850, probably to death.

As Patsey's life story reveals, the purchase, sale, and hiring of enslaved African Americans has been documented beyond Illinois to at least ten additional midwestern states, particularly during the territorial era, but in several instances up to 1860.[39] Well after they left Illinois for Wisconsin, then Iowa, the Tripletts were held as slaves by powerful public figures whose homes would have been open to frequent visitors. Whether those visitors were loathe to interfere in another man's household affairs, or were simply disinterested in the black laborers and servants they may have encountered, it would seem that at least some midwestern whites were tolerant of the ways in which their elite neighbors flaunted territorial, state, and federal laws at the expense of people of African descent.

In addition to the spread of slavery by military officers posted in the region, enslaved African Americans were taken to the upper Mississippi valley in the early decades of the nineteenth century by white settlers, including migrating slaveowners and whites willing to hire or lease enslaved and indentured African Americans. In the 1830s, a number of slaves were transported to Keokuk by fur traders and the commander of the local garrison.[40] In the 1840s and 1850s, enslaved men and women and their families were taken to Iowa, Minnesota, and Wisconsin by some of the region's most prominent figures. Judges, senators, governors, and other territorial officials, as well as ministers, were joined by more ordinary farmers, miners, and settlers in conveying their own slaves to the area. Enslaved people were bought and sold, separated from their families, and sometimes returned to the South with their owners after a brief sojourn in the "free" Midwest. A few of them are known to us by name— Samuel Cochran; "Uncle" Cassius; John Jackson and his children, Mary Jane and Andrew; the young boys "Bart" and Henry Hannah; siblings Charlotte and Paul Jones; Alexis Godar, his wife Rachel, and his brother Jule; eight-year-old Jerry Seers; America and her children; Proctor; "Black" Charlotte; and Moses Franklin.[41] But most illegally enslaved African Americans went unnamed in the historical record. They were referred to simply as, for example, the "mulatto woman" taken to Fort Des Moines in 1834 by garrison commander Stephen Kearney; the "large number" of slaves brought to Keokuk from Kentucky by Judge Frank Ballinger to construct his stone mansion in 1853; the twelve-year-old-girl and fourteen-year-old boy transported to Ringgold County, Iowa, by North Carolinian L. P. Allen in 1852; the two families conveyed to the Dubuque area by Augustus L. Gregoire; the woman taken to Potosi, Wisconsin, by a man named Woolfolk; the numerous slaves taken to Lancaster, Wisconsin, by several different settlers; the two slaves transported by the Reverend James Mitchell from Virginia to Wisconsin; and the "five or six slaves" located in Warren County, Iowa, by a Missouri slaveowner.[42]

Some enslaved midwesterners emerged from the obscurity of a disinterested historical record when they used the courts to challenge their continued bondage. Although Dred and Harriet Scott are the most well known of these plaintiffs, there were others who brought their cases to court, and, in contrast to the Scotts, several—though not all—succeeded in gaining their freedom. The extant records of these efforts fall into two general categories: freedom suits filed from Missouri, a slave state; and legal actions filed in midwestern courts, often in defense against recapture or in proceedings against fugitive slaves. In the first category, four extant freedom suits involved enslaved people taken from the South to the upper Midwest and returned to St. Louis, where they filed freedom suits based on their residence in free territory.[43] As Paul Finkelman has observed, in the 1820s and 1830s Missouri was one of a few southern states that frequently ruled in favor of the plantiffs when they could demonstrate residence in a free state; in at least eleven cases during this period, Missouri courts granted a petitioner's freedom.[44] One of these was brought by Rachel, a fellow slave undoubtedly familiar to Patsey and the rest of the Triplett family during their residence in the Fort Crawford slave community. Purchased at St. Louis on behalf of T. B. W. Stockton, Rachel had been delivered to Stockton at Fort Snelling in 1830 and brought by him in 1832 to Fort Crawford, where he kept her until the fall of 1834. During her last year at Fort Crawford, Rachel gave birth to a son, James Henry, and both were then taken to St. Louis and sold, at which point Rachel and her son sued for their freedom, based on her residence and his birth in what was then Michigan Territory. The case was remarkably similar to *Dred Scott*, but in this instance, after the Missouri court ruled against her, Rachel won on appeal; her son initially bested the slaveowner, but the outcome of Stockton's appeal is unknown. In 1835 Milly, a Kentucky-born slave, also sued for her freedom in the St. Louis courts in light of having been taken to Dubuque by her owner. Peter similarly sought his liberty on the basis of having been brought to Dubuque; there he had worked as a miner from 1833 to 1841, when, on being returned to St. Louis, he initiated his suit. The court ruled against Milly and Peter; both appealed the decision, but the outcome is unknown.[45]

In contrast to the mixed results encountered in the St. Louis circuit courts, midwestern courts more often ruled in favor of the plaintiffs. At age forty-five, Rachel Bundy had been sold at auction in New Orleans and conveyed by her new owner to Burlington, Iowa; four years later, in 1839, she fled and sought refuge in the household of Burlington's mayor. When her owner attempted to use the courts to regain custody, the mayor defended her and the territorial supreme court affirmed her freedom. When Ralph, a Missouri slave sent to labor in the Dubuque lead mines in 1834, faced the threat of seizure by his owner and a return to Missouri in 1839, he sued for—and won—his freedom. A similar case brought by Jim White in 1848 also met with success. In 1842, Paul Jones, described as an "Illinois" bondsman and one of some dozen slaves purchased and conveyed to Lancaster, Wisconsin, by General George W. Jones, successfully sued one of the region's most powerful and politically well-connected men for his wages and his freedom.[46] While the *Dred Scott* case was singular among midwestern freedom suits in its especially catastrophic outcome, territorial and state courts more typically presumed that slavery was and should be excluded from the region.

The cases of Rachel Bundy and Ralph reveal the overconfidence of attorneys and judges alike in the extent of midwestern freedom. Ralph's attorney, David Rohrer, argued that Ralph "became free as soon as, by consent of his master, he became an inhabitant of what is now the territory of Iowa."

The Barbarities of Slavery

Similarly, in Bundy's case—according to a local newspaper—Chief Justice Charles Mason of the Iowa Territorial Supreme Court ruled that "slavery cannot exist in Iowa." Yet neither assertion was fully correct; several states (Iowa included) had provisions permitting "sojourning" owners to bring their slave property into the state for temporary periods of time. For part of the antebellum era, slavery was, in fact, legal in every northern state as long as the owners were temporary visitors or travelers, or until the states acted to limit or remove these protections. Some states attached statutory limits to sojourning—nine months in New York, six months in Pennsylvania. Others (including Minnesota and Wisconsin) relied on interpretation of intent, distinguishing between those slaveowners seeking to establish a domicile in free territory and those who did not.[47]

Indeed, in the upper Midwest there were more court cases heard over the question of domicile than over the disposition of fugitive slaves. Evidence of intent to establish a permanent residence in free territory was the crucial factor yielding judgments for enslaved people in freedom suits brought to both midwestern and southern courts. As Chief Justice Mason said in his ruling for Ralph, if Ralph had been "sent upon an errand, or traveling in company with his master" he would have retained his status as a slave. "But this certainly cannot be the case where the journey was undertaken with the understanding of all parties that the slave was going to become a permanent resident of the free state or territory." Similarly, the crucial factor in Bundy's case was the indication of "an intention of making [free territory] her residence." Only some unavoidable occurrence—an impassable stream, a broken wagon, or illness—could allow a slaveholder to keep his or her slave in free territory "for a considerable length of time" and retain his (or her) right of ownership. Although Ralph and Bundy clearly benefited from it, this interpretation of the law was at odds with practice. The presence of sojourning owners in the upper Midwest—and longer-term residents who maintained the fiction of temporary residence—increased the presence of enslaved people, raised the threshold of risk for free blacks (who were all the more vulnerable to the presumption that they were slaves), and added another layer to the many forms that black servitude assumed in the region.[48]

BLACK FREEDOM IN THE MIDWEST

In this conflicting landscape, where courtroom pronouncements and day-to-day encounters told two very different stories about midwestern slavery, it is not surprising that the actual status of some black midwesterners cannot easily be sorted out. To what extent did former slaves experience freedom after migrating to the antebellum Midwest if they continued to reside with, and work for, their former owners? Why were whites reluctant to provide manumission papers to their "emancipated" slaves? Why would African Americans who migrated to Iowa continue to pay former owners for their liberty? These and other ambiguities suggest some of the ways in which consent, and perhaps freedom, eluded some former slaves who migrated to the upper Midwest before the Civil War.

Ellen Anderson, born into slavery in Frederick County, Maryland, in 1789, was manumitted by her owner, Major O. A. Warfield, probably in 1810. Her thirteen children—seven by her first husband, Edward Mathews, a free resident of Anne Arundel County, Maryland, and six by her second husband, Maryland-born Daniel Anderson—were apparently freed on reaching age twenty-five, although there is no record of the date or place of their birth or manumission. Presumably, some of them were still enslaved when she, husband Daniel, and one son, Benjamin, arrived in Muscatine, Iowa, no doubt in the company of the Warfield family, in 1837. There the Andersons were established in the household of David Warfield, Major Warfield's cousin. David Warfield owned and operated a sawmill, evidently relying on the labor of an unusually large number of African Americans in his household: in 1840, this included four black couples and their children—fifteen in total. Whether these individuals were all former Warfield slaves, whether they had all been manumitted, and the precise nature of the relationships between this former slave-owning family and these former slaves is provocatively undetectable from the historical record, which celebrates the Warfields as Iowa pioneers but elides the contributions, compulsory or not, of Ellen Anderson, her family, and the other black members of the Warfield household to Muscatine's settlement.[49]

In other instances, we are compelled to cast a critical eye on white accounts and memoirs explaining why and how former slaves came to accompany them west. Enslaved African Americans—assuming neither advanced age, illness, or disability prevented them from self-support—would have welcomed manumission, but many slave states required freed people to leave the state or severely constrained their mobility, occupational choices, and legal rights. Migration west may have been a choice of necessity. Members of the slave-owning Payne family, which migrated from Virginia in 1836 and later, recalled that their former slaves accompanied them to Iowa out of sympathetic loyalty "because the young masters knows nothin' about farmin'." But Virginia law since 1826 had required manumitted slaves to leave the state within a year of their manumission; after 1831, those who failed to leave were subject to reenslavement. During the same period, Virginia laws increasingly constrained free blacks.[50] The Paynes' manumitted slaves would have had few options and fewer resources if they had chosen to remain behind in Virginia.

Also suspect were the recollections of Jack and Catherine Gillihan, who migrated to Page County, Iowa, from Kentucky with the pair of slaves her family had given them as a wedding present: "Their slaves were set free, but had no idea how to make a living so they came along." But their migration may have been motivated by other factors. Since 1825, Kentucky allowed the children of free blacks to be involuntarily apprenticed if the parents were unable to provide for them; since 1834, state law required freed blacks to post a bond, on threat of reenslavement.[51] Other examples reveal much the same cloudy circumstances. Mary, a seventeen-year-old Kentucky slave, and "Uncle" Dick, "Aunt" Judy, and their children, who accompanied their owners to Des Moines, were apparently freed only on their arrival—in other words, their migration occurred while they were still enslaved; they trusted that the promise of manumission would be kept.[52] Betsey Henderson and her son Charles were conveyed to Davenport, Iowa, by their owner, George Williams, who did not file their freedom papers with the county recorder until February 1865.[53] With such fragmented documentation, none of it by former slaves themselves, it would be problematic to generalize or assign motive. What we can conclude is that these varied circumstances suggest a wide range between coercion and choice in the decision to migrate west with former owners.

Similarly, Catherine went to Iowa under conditions that make it difficult to ascertain her status and experience. Born in the early 1820s in western Virginia, a slave of Jacob Ankrom, Catherine—or "Cade," as she was called by her owners—was given as a wedding present (along with hogs, sheep, cows, and bedding) to Ankrom's daughter Rachel. Catherine would have been very young at the time, perhaps three years old, and she appears to have been one of three slaves held by Ankrom—the other two, adults, may have been her parents. When her new mistress married Patrick Cheadle, she moved to Morgan County, Ohio, and took the toddler Catherine with her, most likely severing Catherine's own family ties. In Ohio, Catherine's status is not evident from the historical record; the Ohio constitution outlawed slavery in 1803, but the state soon severely circumscribed African Americans with black laws, and as late as 1830 the federal census still recorded slaves (six in number) in the supposedly free state. The most suggestive piece of information we have about Catherine's status is a manumission record that was not legally signed until after Catherine and the Cheadles had left Ohio. Catherine accompanied the couple when they migrated to Iowa sometime before 1842, but it was not until 1851 that Patrick

Cheadle drafted Catherine's manumission papers, and it would be another six years before Rachel, his wife, would add her signature. By this time, Catherine had married, established her own household, and started a family in Muscatine; she had become politically active, joining with other African Americans in petitioning the state legislature to revoke Iowa's black codes. The record of Catherine's status is inconclusive, though she clearly sought documentation of her freedom—perhaps in the aftermath of her 1848 action to protect a fugitive slave from capture in Muscatine—and that documentation was given by her former mistress only reluctantly.[54]

Although we know even less about their lives, Ben and Kitty Gore provide another example of ambiguity in the status of former slaves who migrated to Iowa. Kentucky slaves who were allowed to buy their freedom (although not before seeing their only son sold south), the Gores were apparently relocated to Burlington in 1848 by their former owner. Despite their continued residence in a free state, they worked hard to complete their payments to their former owner until 1851, when the full price of their freedom had been paid.[55] What compelled the Gores to make those payments, when their permanent residence in Iowa should have conferred their freedom?

Indentures and adoptions also lent a veil of obscurity to the status of midwestern blacks. The prohibitions of the Northwest Ordinance against involuntary servitude and the general trend in courtrooms of the early republic to view indentured service as unfree labor had helped liberate white workers from coercive labor arrangements. But gradual emancipation laws in the East and flagrant violation of the antislavery directives of the Northwest Ordinance had only confirmed the overlap between slavery and indentured servitude for African Americans.[56] In February 1860, John L. Curtis claimed that the two young black girls—Mary, fourteen, and Vessy, ten—with whom he traveled from his Iowa City home toward Missouri were indentured servants, not slaves he intended to sell. A local constable suspected otherwise and forced Curtis to return with them to Iowa City to answer to a charge of kidnapping. Days later Curtis and his wife filed adoption papers for the girls, and in early March Curtis once again traveled south, taking Mary and Vessy with him, this time to Memphis where he netted $1,300 from their sale. No one in Iowa City—from the suspicious constable, to the judge who released the girls to his custody, to the mayor who signed the adoption papers, to neighbors—had presumed to intervene in Curtis's household arrangements to protect two African American girls from what many seemed to have understood was slavery.[57]

Mary and Vessy's story reveals the particular vulnerability of African American children to servitude in the West. General O. H. W. Stull, former territorial secretary and slaveowner, held a thirteen-year-old black girl at his Burlington home as a servant.[58] Lydia Applewhite, born into slavery in Missouri in 1845, lived to tell the story of how, as a child, she was placed on the auction block and sold to a family who "took her to Keokuk, separating her from the members of her own family"; only in womanhood did she gain her freedom.[59] The young boys "Bart" and Henry Hannah, siblings Charlotte and Paul Jones, Augustus Tindle, and Moses Franklin—among others whose names remain undocumented in the historical record—were held in slavery and indentured servitude, as commodities, each with their own, unrecoverable story of coercion and family separation.[60]

These examples of the constraint or violation of freedom, autonomy, and family integrity indicate how the concurrent practices of slavery and legal inequality could impact both black and white midwesterners. They reflect the "hardening ideology of race," a process that the historian Joanne Pope Melish observed of early nineteenth-century New England, when whites linked gradual emancipation with their efforts to excise not only slavery but also African Americans from the region's cultural, social, and political landscape.[61] Black laws, in hand with the practice of black slavery and indentured servitude, helped produce and sustain the belief held by many northern whites (whether in New England, New York, or the upper Midwest) that people of African descent were naturally dependent, appropriate targets of coercive and circumscribing behavior, and therefore deservedly outside the boundaries of respectability and citizenship. The upper Midwest underwent a process of racialization that occurred in local and historically specific circumstances, but the process and its outcome were familiar to other northern states and regions.[62] Because upper midwestern black laws were in place concurrent with the practice of slavery, these laws were not a replacement for slavery but rather expressions of the same ambition to exploit, coerce, and dehumanize people of African American descent in ways that produced and highlighted the status differences between black and white midwesterners.

Historians have long debated the origins of midwestern white supremacy; many identify the stream of white migration from the upper South as "importing" white racism from the slave South. But antagonism toward African Americans came to the region in the habits and culture of its earliest white settlers, whether those settlers were accustomed to the fact of southern slavery or the fiction of what Melish refers to as a "historically free, white New England."[63] Historians of the Midwest have been slow to recognize that northern

Early photo of Lydia Applewhite. "She recalls that when she was a young girl she was placed on the auction block and sold to a family from Keokuk, Ia. Her new owners took her to Keokuk, separating her from the members of her own family. . . . She grew to womanhood and obtained her freedom there." Newspaper clipping, n.d., Clippings File, Afro-Americans, State Historical Society of Iowa, Iowa City; photo courtesy of the late Mrs. Harold Clara Davis.

slavery and northern black laws were as important in shaping the settler communities of the upper Mississippi River as were the slaveholding experiences and expectations of settlers arriving from the South. Racism was not imposed on midwestern whites by outsiders; it was integral to the region's history and development. As one Iowa newspaper editor noted during discussions of the proposed revisions to the state constitution in 1857, Iowa's black laws had been written and passed by "wise and good men" who recognized blacks as a "subject and subjugated race." These legislators acted not "from prejudice against color," but (in the case of excluding blacks from juries) out of "a conviction of our inability of imposing upon them a sufficient sense of the obligations of oaths."[64]

The states of the upper Midwest varied in the extent to which they denied black residents the same rights enjoyed by whites. Wisconsin's laws were the least prohibitive, followed closely by Minnesota's; Iowa's laws were far more restrictive. Minnesota lawmakers considered but rejected bills to block black migration in 1854 and again in 1860, and one legislator suggested restricting black residency to St. Anthony and Minneapolis.[65] In all three states, the denial of suffrage resulted in further limitations, including exclusion from jury service. In Wisconsin, voters rejected referenda in both 1847 and 1857 to enfranchise black men. Iowa voters turned down a similar proposition in 1857, in an election in which "the old cries of Amalgamation, Negro Equality, &c., were raised with increased vehemence." Midwestern lawmakers returned regularly to debates over how they should restrict the black population and protect white civil and political prerogatives throughout the antebellum era.[66]

Even with strong pockets of abolitionist sentiment, protests by sympathetic legislators, and open resistance in several communities to the recapture of fugitive slaves, Iowa's territorial and state governments legislated white supremacy and a severely circumscribed form of black freedom with the overwhelming support of their constituencies, not only through disfranchisement, but also by prohibiting African Americans from testifying against whites in court, from serving in state militias or practicing law, and by segregating schools and prohibiting interracial marriage.[67] Black laws put the power of the state behind the enforcement of white supremacy and the constriction of black liberty. Both lawmaking and the power of enforcement lay in the hands of whites. As a resident of eastern Iowa wrote to the editor of the *Burlington Hawk-Eye*, "Have we no law to prevent the influx of free negro population into our State? . . . Almost every day this class of population seems to increase among us, and some of them of the most trifling character."[68] The letter implicitly communicated the writer's sense of the exclusive right whites exercised to claim the state as their own, as well as their prerogative—not simply rhetorical, but backed by the police power of the state—to define free African Americans as trifling and undesirable, whether as fellow citizens or fellow residents.

For Rose Ann McGregor and her husband, that power was exercised against them by their white neighbors on discovering that the McGregors were an interracial couple; they were appalled that an African American woman could claim to be the legal spouse of a white man. The neighbors called on the local constable to arrest her (not her husband) for violating the law against interracial marriage. When the McGregors obtained a change of venue to Quaker-influenced Oskaloosa and escaped prosecution, these neighbors persuaded county commissioners to direct the sheriff to arrest her for violating the laws governing black migration to Iowa. A posse went to their cabin and kicked in the door. Rose was bound. Her captors tried to take her into town, but she escaped. The next day she showed up in court to post the $500 bond for good behavior that marked her as an African American, someone who could be assumed to pose a threat to the peace and welfare of her community. Had she failed to provide the bond, she would have been sold into involuntary servitude for six months.[69] Iowa's territorial legislatures, constitutional conventions, and antebellum legislative assemblies made the status of African Americans a matter of white public interest; throughout the antebellum era they affirmed the premise that the state constitution reflected a social compact of rights and obligations to which blacks were not privy.

Rose McGregor had encountered the most severe aspect of Iowa's black laws: their intention to block free black in-migration to the state. Drawing on similar legislation from Michigan and Indiana, Iowa first limited (1839) and then barred (1851) black settlement.[70] The power of enforcement was wholly local; not only were local judges empowered to determine the racial identity of anyone against whom the law might be directed, but according to the 1851 law, local law enforcement officers were empowered to force new black immigrants out of the state:

> It shall be the duty of all township and county officers to notify all free negroes who may immigrate to this State, to leave the same within three days from the time of notice, and upon their failure to do so it shall be the duty of the constable of the proper township, sheriff of the county, marshal or other police officer of the town, to arrest such free negro and take him or her before a Justice of the peace or judge to fine such free negro the sum of two dollars for each day he may remain in the State after such notice, and

costs of prosecution; and to commit such free negro to the jail of the county, until such fine and costs are paid, or until he shall consent to leave the State, provided it shall be ascertained that he or she is unable to pay the fine and costs.[71]

Before and during the war, residents of both Minnesota and Wisconsin petitioned their legislatures to pass similar statutes.[72] Charles Forrester—one of the Street slaves finally manumitted in 1840—failed to post the required bond in Jefferson County, but citizens did not succeed in their attempt to compel county officials to enforce the law against him.[73] At least one municipality tried to pass similar (though redundant) legislation.[74] Although the laws limiting free black migration were unevenly enforced, some African Americans diligently registered their free papers as the law required and posted the $500 bond, hoping to secure a local reputation as a free person and the protection of local authorities against enslavement or reenslavement.[75] Given the exorbitant amount of the bond, some—and possibly most—would have been forced to turn to white patrons to cover the cost.[76]

As apprehensive as some upper midwestern blacks must have been about how or when their white neighbors might call on the state to act against them, they occasionally found allies among sympathetic white abolitionists who were willing to risk their own reputations and safety to aid them in their challenge to the illegal persistence of slavery. In a handful of small Iowa communities—most notably Salem, Denmark, Washington, Tabor, Whittenberg, and Amity—white opposition to bondage had been encouraged by antislavery Quakers, Congregationalists, Seceder Presbyterians, and a few Wesleyan Methodists. Like-minded communities developed in Wisconsin—in Burlington, Delavan, Racine, and Milwaukee. Beginning in the late 1830s in Wisconsin, and picking up in the early 1840s in Iowa, a regional antislavery movement emerged. Community debates, the organization of local antislavery societies and statewide conventions, the circulation of antislavery petitions, tours by the occasional antislavery lecturer, correspondence with the leading antislavery newspapers of the day and the start of both Wisconsin and Iowa Liberty Party newspapers, and the organization of the Liberty and Republican parties all offered evidence of pockets of abolitionist sentiment and activism among some of the upper Midwest's early white settlers.[77] Indeed, by the 1840s, a small but vocal minority of midwestern whites mobilized to protect fugitive slaves. A far smaller proportion and more radical segment of this minority also registered protests against their slaveholding and slave-trading neighbors, and they asked their legislators to repeal the "unjust and repressive" black codes.[78] These would have been the closest allies of African American midwesterners, whites who took what were widely regarded as extraordinarily radical moral and political positions to defend black freedom and racial equality.

In 1841, one of the few direct protests by white abolitionists against midwestern slavery occurred when a group of Salem Quakers visited Iowa governor John Chambers, one of Burlington's most prominent slaveowners, expressed their opposition to the fact that he had brought some of his slaves to Iowa, and left him with some antislavery literature. Chambers made no move to free his slaves, and the abolitionists made no effort to assist them directly.[79] In a second instance, North Carolinian L. P. Allen settled in Ringgold County with his family and two young slaves, who were siblings; pressure from local residents finally persuaded Allen to sell the two slaves to a Missouri buyer in 1853. In their desire to protect the "free soil" of Ringgold County from the practice of slavery, local whites seem to have acted without regard for the two children who were sold south to obtain this "Free Soil" victory.[80] Similarly, in 1858 Minnesota journalist Jane Swisshelm denounced the pastor of the Presbyterian church in St. Cloud for bringing a slave woman into Minnesota from Tennessee; the end result was the woman's return to Tennessee as a slave.[81] These instances reveal the shortcomings of white antislavery activism in the upper Midwest: most white residents shared with the larger population an antipathy toward African Americans; most believed that southern slavery was the central issue; most were not prepared to advocate for the equal treatment of African Americans before the law or in their social spheres. These attitudes also reflected the popularity of Free Soil politics in the Midwest.[82]

Among Iowa's attractions, according to boosters in the 1830s and 1840s, was the fact that the state was "forever free" not only of slavery, but also of blacks.[83] Authors of booster literature were fairly notorious for their prevarications, painting their subjects in the most attractive light, but they were also quite familiar with the expectations and desires of their audiences. Describing Iowa in this fashion tells us that white emigrants to the West were perceived as a population that preferred to cast their future apart from slaveowners but also apart from people of African descent.[84] The most organized expression of this desire came from the American Colonization Society, whose efforts to relocate African Americans to Africa were rejected both by white abolitionists and most African Americans.

Yet colonization drew enough white support for the organization in 1855 of the Colonization Society of the State of Iowa "to Colonize, with their own consent, the free people of color of the United States, in Africa or such other region as Congress shall deem expedient." The twenty-eight members who gathered at the 1857 annual meeting included current and former state legislators and secretaries of state, former Liberty Party men as well as Democrats and Republicans, antislavery men, ministers, lawyers, advocates of black laws, and activists who opposed Iowa's exclusionary law. The resolutions and speeches offered at the meeting were as diverse as the organization's membership. One speaker described the goals of the society in terms that condemned slavery and slaveowners: "The father is kid-napped, and carried in irons across the Atlantic, to promote the sordid gains of a so-called Christian people. The son is returned across the same ocean, not as the slave of his owner, but as a free man in Christ." Other speakers, however, pronounced African Americans "the most dangerous element that now threatens the peace of the nation," with a "natural mark that renders the Negro repulsive," making it impossible for whites and blacks to live together, let alone as equals. "Even with the lash of the master, and the force of absolutism, you cannot give it [referring to 'the Negro'] skill, you cannot instil into it, the force of enterprize, or the power of productiveness. As long as they remain, they must be outcasts and inferiors." Their degradation was so deep that in Africa "the mother would sell her child for a paltry gewgaw; and the father dispose of his family for a gawdy feather." The Iowa Colonization Society proposed that, as they were now "christianised and partially enlightened," African Americans should be returned to Africa, where they might serve as agents of civilization and Christianity.[85]

Black midwesterners also were questioning their future in the United States. The Fugitive Slave Law (1850), the Kansas-Nebraska Act (1854), and the *Dred Scott* decision (1857) all contributed to a growing radicalism as well as despair among African Americans, prompting some to consider emigration as an alternative to begging for citizenship in a nation determined to deny them not only political equality but also the most basic human rights. Black emigrationists were themselves a diverse group: some advocated emigration as a last-resort escape from slavery; others perceived the appeal of an independent black nation. On the other hand, many African Americans staunchly opposed emigration. When black Iowans gathered in convention at Muscatine in 1857, they proclaimed the United States as "our native land, which is as dear to us as the white man." A committee formed to consider emigration reported back to the convention that "our . . . interests and elevation had better be sought in this our native land, and especially while our enemies are conniving at every scheme to remove us from the soil of our nativity, it behooves us to stand fast and let our cry and our watchword be, by the help of God, we are here and we intend to live and die here." Other black midwesterners were willing to listen to the merits of emigration. Ambrose Dudley, a Milwaukee cook and waiter, had represented the upper Midwest at the 1854 Emigration Convention in Pittsburgh, and H. Ford Douglas, one of the nation's most prominent black advocates of emigration, toured the Midwest, lecturing at Rock Island and Moline, Illinois (drawing blacks from nearby Davenport, as well as Oskaloosa and Ottumwa).[86]

Another voice for emigration was that of Dr. J. Prescott, a white resident of Tama County, Iowa, who launched a public speaking tour in 1859 to gain support for his plan to settle eastern free blacks in northwestern Iowa. In his audience were members of Oskaloosa's tiny black Baptist congregation, from which there was enough enthusiasm to arrange a follow-up meeting and form a committee of correspondence with blacks in Cincinnati who were interested in his proposal. They also drafted a series of resolutions, noting that despite the "commendable progress" that African Americans had made, they tended to congregate in cities where jobs were scarce: "We have too long yielded to the unjust prejudices that have assigned us the more menial occupations; . . . even these employments are being taken away by foreign immigrants." Only the "wide and fertile prairies of the West," where land was yet unsettled and less expensive, would allow blacks to "arrive at the common rights of freedom and manhood."[87] According to newspaper reports, a significant attraction of Prescott's plan was the expectation that blacks would "occupy whole counties, to the exclusion of whites."[88] From whites in Oskaloosa, Tipton, Mason City, and Anamosa came a storm of protest that stopped the proposal dead in its tracks. "Iowa is now comparatively free from such a population—let it be our pride then to keep her so still, and not bring upon ourselves and upon our children this outrageous scourge." "We want to live among white people, and when we cannot we will leave the state."[89]

Despite white hostility toward black migration to the upper Mississippi valley, free black midwesterners did move into neighborhoods, settlements, and communities in the upper Midwest. During the Civil War, former slaves migrating out of the South would be drawn to them. (Few antebellum black migrants chose settlement on the edge of newly opened frontier lands; as Stephen Vincent has noted, those areas often presented greater dangers to free people of color than to whites.)[90] Of course, the black midwesterners that wartime migrants encountered were rarely more than one generation removed from slavery themselves. As late as 1850, half of Iowa's black population reported a slave state as their birthplace, and another 19 percent had been born in northern states where slavery persisted. That year Virginia and Kentucky predominated among the birthplaces of Minnesota's African Americans. Many—perhaps most—still had close family members in bondage, and

The Barbarities of Slavery

these separated families—like the Sheppards of Virginia and Wisconsin—yearned to reunite. "I have long hoped and wished to have been living in that happy land of freedom with you," Edward Sheppard wrote his brother in 1858.[91]

Even in light of a shared history of slavery with black midwesterners, the wartime migrants from the slave South faced a far more complicated landscape than the one imagined by Edward Sheppard. There were wide variations in the opportunities available, community histories, and relationships with whites. Those differences were important, but they were well below the magnitude of difference that existed between community life under southern slavery and community life in the upper Midwest. If southern migrants found that racism was more prevalent and more openly expressed than some might have anticipated, if occupations were more limited and laws more restrictive than hoped for, or if slavery's northward reach was longer and impacted more deeply than many expected, the upper Midwest offered, nonetheless, a sharp contrast to the slave South. The antebellum differences between two Iowa communities that drew large numbers of wartime migrants—Muscatine and Keokuk—illustrate the range of community life that the migrants would encounter.

MUSCATINE, A FLOUR and lumber-milling center with several factories and a stop for ferry and steamboat traffic on the Mississippi, was home to one of the antebellum upper Midwest's oldest and most politically active communities of free blacks, many of them former slaves. On the eve of the Civil War, the community had a higher percentage of black residents born in northern states (54 percent) than the statewide average (44 percent) and the largest percentage of residents who had been born in one of the eastern seaboard slave states (67 percent). African American men and women were among the town's earliest settlers before 1840, some arriving with former owners, and their numbers grew to at least 112 on the eve of the war.[92] Compared to Iowa's other communities, Muscatine's African American residents provided the human resources that made for a vibrant communal life that was simply not possible in more rural areas and counties where blacks resided in relative isolation. Day laborers and sawmill workers, farmers and farm laborers, teamsters and river men, barbers and blacksmiths, seamstresses and cooks, servants and washerwomen—this was the hard-working community that organized Iowa's first black African Methodist Episcopal (AME) congregation (in 1849) and one of the earliest schools for black children (in 1856), housed in the same church.[93]

Although small, Muscatine had exceptionally strong regional and national connections. Through the regional and general conferences of the AME Church, the national black convention movement, and Prince Hall Masonry, people like Alexander Clark (who attended the 1853 national black convention in Rochester, New York) helped sustain ties to black communities and activists in Ohio, Indiana, and Illinois, as well as in the East.[94] Itinerant ministers traveled the region, organizing and strengthening congregations, reporting on their experiences in nationally circulated papers such as the *Christian Recorder*, and attended regional and national denominational conferences. The black convention movement encouraged correspondence, coordination, and cooperation across the continent, and fraternal organizations rewarded local expansion with regional and even national recognition, prestige, and power. Muscatine's connections with these important networks of information, human resources, and political development belies both historical and contemporary notions of an isolated Midwest.

Beginning in 1842, Muscatine was home to Alexander Clark, a barber before the war, as well as Iowa's most prominent black leader and political activist. The son of emancipated slaves from western Pennsylvania, Clark was part of a migration stream composed of free blacks and freed northern slaves who hoped the West would open opportunities that industrialization in the East was foreclosing to African Americans.[95] After time spent in Cincinnati and on steamboats plying southern waters, Clark chose Muscatine, Iowa, as his new home. He married Catherine, a former slave from Virginia, in Iowa City. The Muscatine couple would protect a freed fugitive slave from illicit recapture in 1848. No one, however, was able to protect seven-year-old Milton Howard and his parents from being kidnapped from Muscatine and sold into slavery in Alabama in 1854.[96] Still, along with the Reverend Richard Harvey Cain (future bishop of the AME Church and a South Carolina state senator and U.S. congressman during Reconstruction), Clark joined with successful barber Thomas Motts, and many other men and women, in stepping into the region's political sphere in 1855, submitting to the state legislature the first petition from African Americans challenging the law that banned the migration of free blacks into Iowa.[97]

Muscatine's African American residents also organized and hosted Iowa's first statewide black convention in January 1857, asserting in its declaration of sentiments that "We, the colored people of the State of Iowa, in convention assembled, feel ourselves deeply aggrieved by reason of cruel prejudice we are compelled to suffer, in this our native land."[98] Committees on education, colonization, and emigration addressed the pressing issues of the day, including the injustice of taxing black Iowans for the support of public schools from which they were excluded. Later that year Muscatine's African Americans further staked out their claim on the public sphere with the first recorded Emancipation Day celebration in the region—a daylong, communitywide festival in commemoration of West Indian emancipation. Sponsored by members of the AME Church as a fund-raiser, the event included entertainment by a local African brass band, a supper prepared by church members, and speeches by Mt. Pleasant barber B. Bowser, Alexander Clark, and Reverend Cain on abolition and education. There was a procession through town and a ball later that evening. The day offered secular pleasures, serious political content, and the opportunity for African Americans to demonstrate their ongoing concern about slavery's impact on their nation, as well as its direct legacy in their lives.

Although the public record is relatively silent on how Muscatine's black residents negotiated their lives in a white-majority community, we do know that fugitive slaves and free blacks alike were vulnerable to kidnapping, that some African Americans seem to have occupied an ambiguous status in the households and employment of their former masters, that the black community chafed under its exclusion from public schools and the host of black laws that circumscribed their hopes for full citizenship. There is evidence that some were confronted with a range of indignities from whites who were confident in their right to exclude and belittle people of African descent—including the supposedly antislavery Congregational church that rejected a black woman's application for admission.[99]

ON THE EVE of the Civil War, Iowa's largest black community, with 245 residents in the city and surrounding county, was found in Keokuk, in southeastern Lee County, located on the Missouri border just two hundred miles north of St. Louis. Keokuk owed its development to the shallow Mississippi rapids, which required steamboats to unload their freight in order to get past the rapids; along with the work of establishing a settlement, the "lightering" business created an ongoing demand for river men and draymen that employed many African Americans. Keokuk was now a city of more than 15,000 residents, with more than 450 businesses ranging from mills and manufacturing to packinghouses and shops.

Keokuk's proximity to Missouri, its significant business ties to the South (particularly its inclusion within the orbit of St. Louis trade), and the steady stream of riverboats drew southerners to the city. Slaveowners were therefore welcome and prominent in its settling and development, but so were their slaves; in this regard, Keokuk perhaps ranked second only to Dubuque, where slave labor had been used in the area's lead mines. Yet Keokuk was also a "northern" city. Its proximity to Missouri and the rest of the slaveholding

South made it a stopping-off place for African Americans hoping to leave slavery behind—fugitives and those manumitted by their owners—who, in turn, helped establish the city's diverse black community. Keokuk's large percentage of southern-born black residents—at 68 percent, more than 20 percent higher than Muscatine's and 12 percent higher than the statewide average—confirms the impact of southern slavery on the city's black residents. Among the most well-known manumitted slaves to settle in and around Keokuk belonged to the Pyles clan. The extended Pyles family had been held in slavery in Washington County, Kentucky; Harry (1791–1870), the father of the clan, was said to have been the son of his owner and one of his slaves. Harry, his wife Charlotta (b. 1801), and sixteen children and grandchildren were manumitted in 1853 on the death of their owner, according to his wishes and his Wesleyan Methodist beliefs. After his sons sold one of the Pyles children south, ignoring their father's wishes, his daughter, Miss Ellen Gordon, with the remaining members of the Pyles family and a sympathetic Ohio preacher, fled Kentucky with Minnesota as their destination. Traveling by wagon through Louisville, Cincinnati, and St. Louis, the Pyles family and Gordon made it as far as Keokuk and decided they were far enough north for safety. Charlotta was now determined to raise the funds to buy the one remaining son who had been sold south and two sons-in-law. Arriving alone in New York, she appealed to local abolitionists and participants at a Morris Grove, New York, Emancipation Day celebration. Her daughter Julian went to Cincinnati for the same purpose. Donations to the family cause came from local elite whites and from as far away as Taunton, Massachusetts. With the required funds in hand, Charlotta proceeded to Kentucky to purchase and free her sons-in-law (her own son having been sold to parts unknown). Family tradition had it that the household in Keokuk aided other enslaved people—for example, sheltering fugitives—until the onset of the Civil War. Given the city's attraction as a gateway to the free Midwest, the Pyles family may have been busy, indeed, helping others complete the journey that they themselves had made.[100]

Between 1830 and 1850, Keokuk had developed from a frontier settlement where African Americans were openly held in slavery to a city where former and fugitive slaves gained some semblance of security. A few black residents achieved even more, for the city boasted some fairly prosperous black families and entrepreneurs. Butcher John Hiner and his wife owned real estate valued at $10,000 by 1860; even a drayman, like Flora Story, could accumulate over $3,000 in property and become financially secure. But if a few exceptional blacks could accumulate wealth in this river town, others found its race relations tense and threatening. Public acts of violence against African Americans, even when condemned by whites, suggested not only the privileges some white men assumed in their conduct toward black people, but also the legacy of slavery and slave ownership in midwestern cities and towns, and the tenuousness of safety that legacy created for African Americans. In 1842, when a recently arrived black man was accused of robbing a local merchant's warehouse, he was not arrested but rather tied to a tree and whipped. His Irish assailant, on the other hand, enjoyed the prerogative of treatment according to the rule of law.[101]

DESPITE THE UNDERLYING currents of tension and potential violence, by the 1850s African Americans in Keokuk had established themselves as efficient institution builders, beginning with the AME congregation, founded in 1857 (with forty members by 1859), and an "African School," established some time before the fall of 1859. Providing instruction to more than fifty students on the eve of the Civil War, theirs was the largest black school in the state, attracting well-trained instructors from around the region.[102] Although the facility was poorly furnished (in 1859 the school lacked desks), an inspection by the school superintendent in 1860 revealed the students' superior knowledge of geography and their achievement as "the best in reading," surpassing the city's white students.[103] If Keokuk lacked the regional and national connections nurtured by Muscatine's black residents, its African Americans were no less capable or devoted to creating a sustainable home in the gateway city.

But Keokuk's growth and economic success took a significant hit with the panic of 1857; wheat prices fell, crops failed, and the city suffered under a worsening debt as railroad construction proved far less profitable than anticipated. In the race for control over Mississippi River trade, Keokuk fell behind when its rival to the north, the city of Burlington, built a railroad connection in 1856 and secured its place within Chicago's economic orbit and solidified its ties to southern trade. According to one historian, these developments, together with the economic consequences of Keokuk's boom-and-bust cycle of the 1850s, shaped a uniquely "western version of free-labor ideology" among local Republicans, who cast the West as victimized by northern capitalists and eastern financiers in much the same way that the slaveholding elite had victimized white farmers of the South.[104]

As whites felt their economic future threatened, the year 1857 also became a turning point in the politics of race in Keokuk. In March, the U.S. Supreme Court issued the *Dred Scott* decision, one with particularly strong meaning for midwesterners. The judgment affirmed that African Americans held no rights that whites were bound to respect, while removing one of the key assertions that had allowed midwestern slaves to win their suits for freedom: residence in a free territory no longer could form the basis of a claim to liberty. In addition, the ruling increased the vulnerability of Keokuk's growing black population—many of them former slaves—who were competing with white laborers for jobs in the stressed economy of the late 1850s.[105] Further, as black workers found employment, sociability, and homes near the Keokuk levee, white residents blamed the growing black presence for turning the city's once prosperous (and white-dominated) place of pride into a landscape of bawdy houses and gambling dens.

Neighboring Fort Madison also saw increased racial tensions at this time. On a town dock, a conflict aboard the steamer *Saracen* between the white second mate and a black pantryman escalated when the pantryman made a saucy comment to the second mate. A fistfight ensued, and the pantryman jumped the boat and made his way to shore, only to be captured by pursuing white crew members. Back on the *Saracen*, he was stripped, tied to a stanchion, and beaten. When a black deckhand protested and residents in the area attempted to intervene, they were met with gunfire from the captain (who insisted on his prerogative to treat his property as he chose). He wounded fifteen residents of Fort Madison and killed a white bystander before steering the ship north, avoiding capture by officials at Burlington. After the coroner's inquest led to a charge of murder in the bystander's death, the city council posted a $300 reward for the return of the ship's captain and another officer. Locals insisted that no man—white or black—deserved to be stripped, tied up, and beaten. But the city council's reward was about meting justice to the murderer of the white bystander, not to the abusers of an enslaved African American.[106]

Only days later, racial tension in and around Keokuk erupted again. An exchange between two partisan, rival newspapers revealed that the city marshal was attempting to enforce Iowa's 1851 exclusion law; notices had been printed and apparently served on local African American men, threatening imminent enforcement of the law. The marshal insisted he was merely ridding the levee of criminal activity, though in doing so he ignored white criminals. In the midst of Keokuk's worst economic downturn to date, however, eliminating black workers from the levee would decrease the competition white workers faced. Yet the move may well have had other motivations; from January through March 1857, the constitutional convention had turned not only to pressing banking, railroad, and land grant issues, but also to the existing black codes and the white prerogatives they had inscribed into law. Race had become the most readily exploited issue of the day, and the marshal's brief attempt to enforce Iowa's exclusion law exemplified how partisan politics had merged with the city's strained race relations to create a more public, virulent, and threateningly racist public sphere.

In the politics of 1857, the state's new Republican Party, as well as southern sympathizers in the Democratic Party, made race the center of debates over revisions to the state constitution, including the issue of black enfranchisement. Democrats charged that Republican influence threatened to undermine white prerogatives and elevate black equality. Yet Republicans refused to advocate for black suffrage, insisting that the proposed constitution was a bipartisan product and that Iowa's voters had the final say. In the face of Republican backpedaling on suffrage reform, the Democrats—and their newspapers—deluged Iowans with a campaign that associated black enfranchisement with the removal of white privilege from every sphere of life. "Do you wish to see your children sit side by side with little darkies in our common schools? . . . Do you wish to pay taxes to support a mongrel pauper population? . . . Do you wish to amalgamate with negro bucks and wenches?" Democrats warned that hundreds of new black emigrants could be expected to swarm the state if the suffrage provision were approved.[107]

Keokuk's black population was less overtly political than Muscatine's throughout the antebellum era. Even in the context of physical assault, threatened enforcement of Iowa's exclusion law, and the politics of race in 1857, African Americans appear to have kept their thoughts and feelings to themselves. Perhaps they believed they could not afford an organized response; perhaps the economic downturn had forced them to concentrate on survival—just keeping their families fed and clothed. Perhaps their response is best measured by the success of their efforts to build a congregation of their own and to organize and staff the state's largest and best black school, institutions that, as the historians James and Lois Horton remind us, were both the foundation and the expression of black freedom.[108] Or perhaps their response was, by design, unreadable by the white observers who created the historical record; perhaps, like Charlotta and Harry Pyles, African Americans in Keokuk were acting outside the boundaries of the law, harboring and aiding fugitive slaves in search of freedom in the upper Midwest.

ON THE EVE of the Civil War, with sectional politics sharply escalating the local and national debate on the future of slavery and the place of African Americans in the nation, southern slaves continued to flee north to the cities and river towns where black midwesterners were creating community life. If the region and its inhabitants still bore the consequences of a hidden history of slavery and an attenuated black freedom, to enslaved people in the South the upper Mississippi valley nonetheless offered the promise of liberty; their flight northward points to the contrast they anticipated between southern slavery and "the happy land of freedom." The upper Mississippi valley provided enough distance from southern slavery and former owners to attract a small stream of fugitives who were already risking everything to make their way to the budding communities blacks had established in Minnesota, Wisconsin, and Iowa. When civil war finally erupted, the Mississippi River would open that small stream into an unprecedented flow of African Americans to the upper Midwest.

2   "A Time of Scattering"

From the tobacco plantation in the far southwestern corner of Kentucky where they and nine of their ten children were held in slavery, Matilda and James Busey watched the Civil War unfold. The Buseys may not have known of Kentucky's crucial role as a border slave state that did not secede, but by early 1862 they were aware that both Confederate and Union forces had invaded the state. They must have rejoiced when nearby Fort Heiman, just across the Tennessee River from Fort Henry, fell to the Union during General Ulysses S. Grant's successful attack in February 1862. Like thousands of other Kentucky slaves, the Buseys decided that the proximity of the U.S. Army created the opportunity they had been waiting for.

With remarkable stealth and at great risk, they managed to hitch up their master's wagon and team of oxen, and with nine children set out on the ten-mile journey to the fort. Along the way, James and one of his sons tried to approach the plantation where Tom, the Buseys' tenth child, was held, but bloodhounds made his rescue impossible. Arriving at Fort Heiman, the two adults and nine children were fortunate to be admitted, as official Federal policy required that fugitive slaves be expelled from Union lines. Their hope that the U.S. soldiers would protect them was sorely tested the next morning, when their irate owner arrived to reclaim them. At the time, Abraham Lincoln desperately hoped to keep Kentucky in the Union and had ordered his military commanders to leave its slavery intact. The Union army, the president insisted, could not afford to alienate white Kentuckians by acting as an army of liberation. But that policy proved hard to enforce; runaway slaves like the Buseys were overwhelming Union camps, and U.S. troops did not always agree that slavery should survive the war. The soldiers at Fort Heiman honored the slaveowner's claim to the wagon and oxen, but not to the Busey family.

Fearful, perhaps, that they might yet be returned to their master, or forced to leave the camp, the Buseys began to head northwest. For a time they were

Matilda Busey, ca. 1890. Born in North Carolina, Busey was in Kentucky at the start of the war and, with her husband and nine of her ten children, fled their owner and made their way to a Union army camp. Transported to another Union camp in Columbus, Kentucky, where her husband was "pressed into the service of the Union army" for several days, the family finally made their way to Davenport, Iowa, with two dollars to their name. Putnam Museum of History and Natural Sciences, Davenport, Iowa.

sheltered at the large but crowded contraband camp established by the U.S. Army at Columbus, Kentucky, nearly eighty miles away. There they may have received food and clothing, but they were also vulnerable to the labor demands of the army. At one point, James was conscripted to help throw up embankments, day and night, in the rain. Eventually, the family resumed its journey north, probably on a Union steamer heading toward the contraband camp at Cairo, Illinois. From there, like several hundred other African Americans who crowded into the Cairo and St. Louis contraband camps during the war, the family traveled up the Mississippi to Iowa. The Buseys arrived at Davenport, a Mississippi River town, in 1864, with two dollars to their name. There they would stay and make their new lives as free people; miraculously, they would be joined by their tenth son, Tom, who found them in 1869.[1]

The decision to flee slavery, to find a way out of the chaos of war and the threat of reenslavement, was made tens of thousands of times during the course of the Civil War. More than six thousand former slaves followed the path chosen by the Busey family, seizing the opportunities presented by wartime conditions to leave the South for the upper Midwest. It is impossible to determine exactly how many people were involved in this diaspora. In 1865, Wisconsin, Minnesota, and Iowa all conducted a state census—the most likely tool for measuring the demographic consequences of wartime migration to the region. However, only fragments of the Wisconsin census survive, and in

Minnesota and Iowa, enumerators completed their work before black soldiers were mustered out and returned to their new upper midwestern homes.[2] Still, for Minnesota and Iowa, the rate of increase in the black population between 1860 and 1865 was significant: 158 percent in Minnesota (from 259 to 411), and 337 percent in Iowa (from 1,069 to 3,608).[3] Between 1860 and 1870, the Federal census reported an overall net increase of 6,135 African Americans for all three states; from 1,171 to 2,113 in Wisconsin, 259 to 759 in Minnesota, and 1,069 to 5,762 in Iowa—an increase of 80 percent, 193 percent, and 439 percent, respectively. Another way to measure the impact of wartime migration is to consider more local consequences. In 1860, slightly less than half (45) of Iowa's 99 counties had no black residents (46 percent). By 1870, only 15 of those counties (16 percent) had no blacks, while 64 Iowa townships gained black residents.[4] Davenport, the Buseys' destination, was fairly typical: the black population there grew eightfold, from 25 black residents on the eve of the war to 210 by 1870.

In Wisconsin, African Americans often arrived en masse when local religious leaders answered the call to provide northern homes and employers for black refugees. Between the fall of 1862 and the spring of 1863, 40 or 50 blacks were led at one time to Beaver Dam, 75 to Fond du Lac, and 25 to Trenton. Racine, a larger city, received 150 black migrants at one time.[5] In Minnesota, Mississippi River steamboats in government service carried the largest numbers of former slaves, including about 30 on the *War Eagle* in the fall of 1862, then 125 on the *Northerner* and 233 on the *Davenport*, both in May 1863. Most of these refugees settled in the St. Paul, Minneapolis, and St. Anthony areas, as well as in southeastern counties bordering the Mississippi and Minnesota rivers.[6] Whether we look to the Midwest's rural counties or its cities, the numbers of African Americans newly arrived from southern slavery increased —sometimes overnight. Clearly, this wartime diaspora had a major influence on the region.

Census returns offer an incomplete portrait of this "time of scattering," but, in conjunction with other sources of demographic data, they do provide an important clue. Wartime migration had a dramatic impact on the composition of black communities in the upper Midwest. Among those black Iowans arriving before the war whose place of birth can be identified, 36 percent had been born in northern states. But of those who came during the war, 96 percent were southern-born; of those arriving after the war up to 1870, 95 percent were southern-born. Wartime black migration thus firmly tied the upper Midwest and its new inhabitants to slavery, to the slave South, and to the experience of wartime emancipation.[7]

A Time of Scattering

The movement of recently enslaved people into the upper Midwest was mirrored by similar migrations west into Kansas, north into the Ohio valley, and along the eastern Atlantic corridor. Carol Faulkner, who has studied wartime and postwar black migration to Washington, D.C., and northward, estimates that 17,000 freedpeople traveled north from Virginia during the war. Michael Johnson, who has researched the collective experience of black migration in the Midwest, approximates Civil War–era black relocation from the South to the greater Midwest at about 80,000.[8] Together, these figures suggest that close to 100,000 enslaved people made their way west and north during the war, a little less than a third of all slaves who are estimated to have fled their masters during the chaos of war.

Wartime migration transformed the meaning of movement in the lives of enslaved people. As the previous chapter emphasizes, the movement of black slaves prior to the war was involuntary, severing families, uprooting communities, decimating those left behind, and throwing those forced to leave into new circumstances where both master and fellow slaves might prove treacherous.[9] The social and economic chaos that civil war inflicted on the southern home front introduced yet new catalysts for the involuntary movement of slaves, adding fresh layers of uncertainty and unpredictability to this dispersal by slaveowners seeking to protect their property and their mastery. But the war also opened breaches in the institution of slavery that enslaved people used to transform movement from an inescapable aspect of oppression to an avenue for liberation. Those who made their way into the upper Midwest and the whites they settled among would contribute to the developing national debates about the meaning of emancipation during and after the Civil War.

"THE 'NEGRO QUESTION' IS A VEXATIOUS ONE"

Enslaved people throughout the South and in the slaveholding states of the Union anticipated that the Civil War would determine the fate of slavery and bring God's wrath—or at least the wrath of Union guns—down upon southern slaveholders. If, as Martilla Newbern recalled in later years, the war's turn of events "scared me nearly to death," she, like thousands of other slaves, negotiated and indeed accelerated the war's circuitous path toward emancipation.[10] For many, the path to freedom led northward, but only after they had contended with the hardships and risks posed by civil war, and only after enslaved African Americans forced Confederate and Union strategy and policy— directed by some of the most powerful men of their era—in directions that were not intended or anticipated. For enslaved people, the combined consequences of Union penetration into the Mississippi valley on one hand, and the innumerable local, departmentwide, and regional policies regarding slaveholders and the enslaved on the other, made northward flight a viable, preferable, and sometimes unavoidable choice.

In the western theater (the departure point for the Busey family and most African Americans who fled to the upper Midwest), Union policies on slavery were shaped as much by politics as by the military campaign. Initially, Lincoln hoped to support Missouri's decision not to secede and strengthen the fragile control Unionists held over the state, to preserve Kentucky's neutrality, and to encourage existing pockets of Unionist sentiment in the Confederate states. Especially during the first year and a half of war, Lincoln was unwilling to precipitate further secession by threatening border-state slavery or the property rights of slaveowning Unionists. He hoped that the demonstration of Federal neutrality toward slavery would convince the nonseceding slave states to remain in the Union and persuade reluctant southern Unionists to help defeat the Confederacy.[11] At this early point in the conflict, enslaved people who anticipated that Union soldiers would act as agents of their liberation were often sorely disappointed.[12] As one Union commander commented from his post in Missouri, "I am not a Nigger man [and] have had no fugitives in my Battery nor have none now and don't intend to have."[13] The Busey family had been lucky; they might have just as easily been returned to their master when he demanded his property from Union forces at Fort Heiman. Caution in Union policy prevailed, with significant consequences for enslaved people and for the Lincoln administration's policies on slavery.

But Lincoln's political and military strategy in the West changed over time, in part because of the actions of slaves who believed that the war should and would end bondage. African Americans thus acted to secure their freedom regardless of official policies devised to define their status and control their movements. Significant changes in Federal policy on slavery in the western theater occurred in three chronological phases. The first phase was marked by Lincoln's initial caution and "hands-off" stance regarding slavery in 1861. The second phase emerged in the first half of 1862, a consequence of what James M. McPherson has referred to as the "river war" in the Mississippi valley. Although Confederate forces held onto Vicksburg and controlled the Mississippi River, Union troops drove deeply, successfully, and disruptively into the plantation landscape of the Mississippi River valley. Tens of thousands of enslaved people used the chaos to flee their masters, approach Union lines, and challenge the fiction that war could be fought on southern soil with slavery left

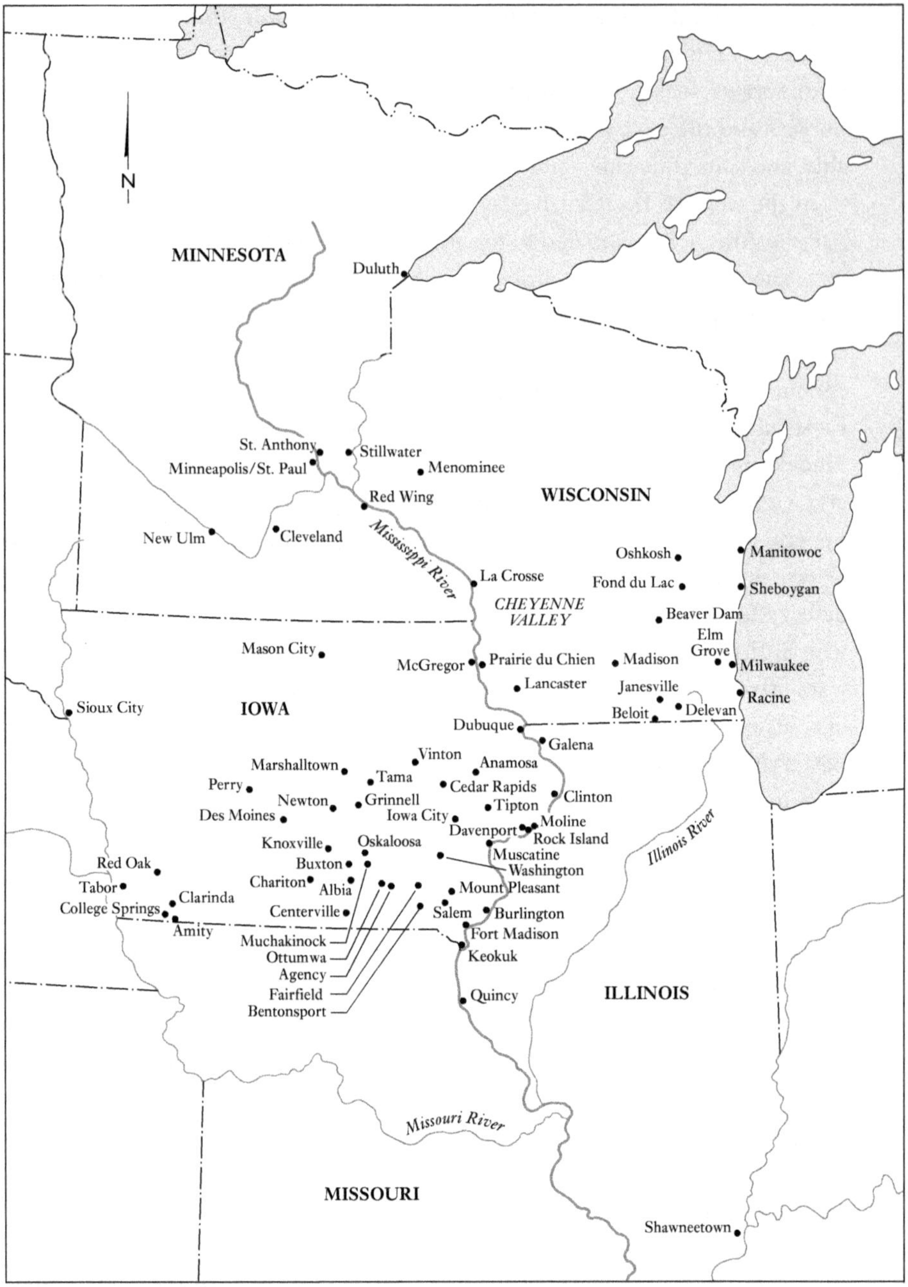

The Mississippi valley.

A Time of Scattering

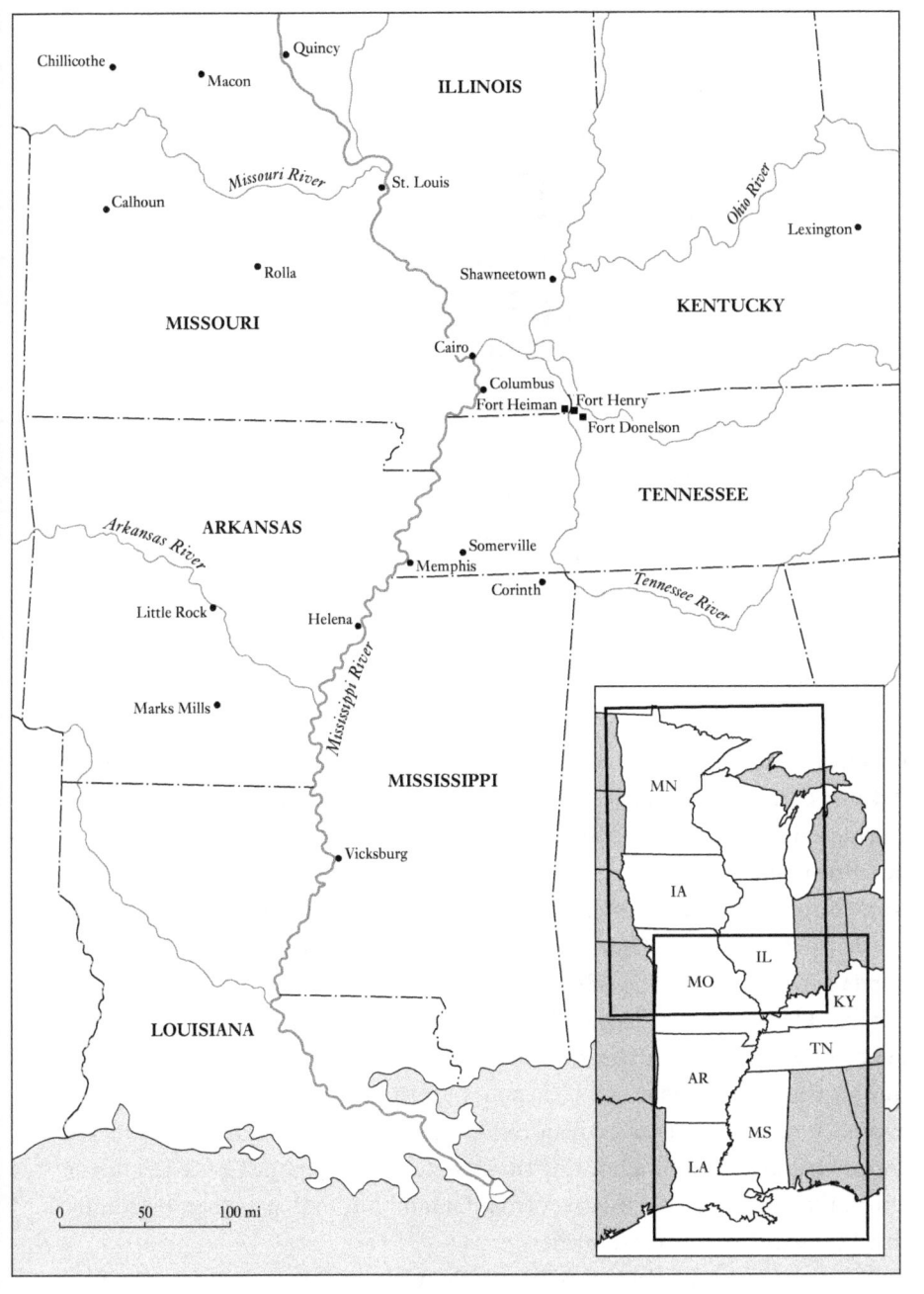

A Time of Scattering

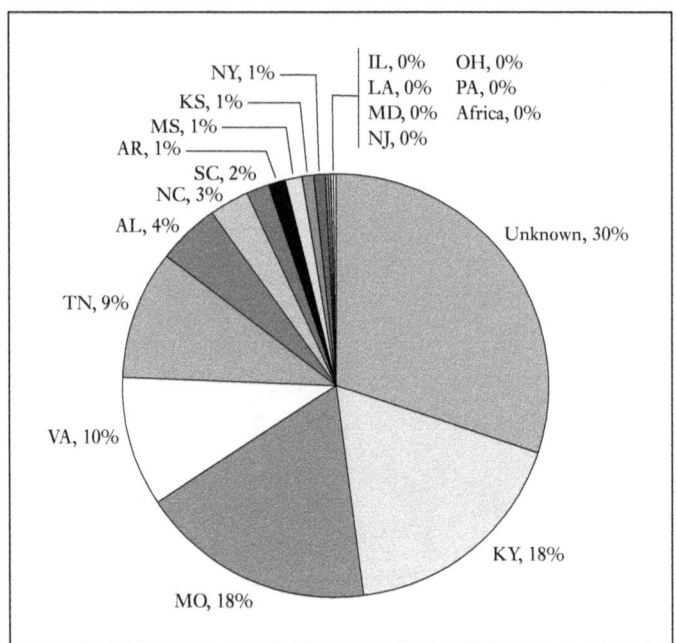

Place of birth of 245 wartime arrivals in Iowa.

intact. Among them was a couple held on adjoining plantations near Helena, Arkansas. Before the Emancipation Proclamation, William Brickley and Celia Curran ran to Union forces at Helena, not simply to gain their own freedom, but also to ensure that their children would not be born into slavery. Both worked for the army—Celia as a cook, William as a servant—before heading north to Iowa City.[14] They were among the thousands of people held in bondage near Helena who offered their labor to the Union army during this period. The July 1862 Second Confiscation Act, which replaced the earlier policy of excluding fugitives from Federal lines, was the most definitive feature of this second phase of U.S. policy in the West. Overwhelmed by the approach of thousands of civilian refugees, Union commanders and officers coped variously: first by admitting the slaves employed in the Confederate war effort, then by excluding fugitives from Union lines, and after that, by admitting the chattel of rebel slaveowners.

The third phase of Federal policy in the western theater was launched by the Emancipation Proclamation and the decision to enlist African American men in the military. Thus, by 1863, the war had indeed become a war to destroy Confederate slavery. But as the Union put the twin strategies of emancipation and black enlistment into action, there were unintended consequences: a weakening ability to protect loyal slave states from the war's emancipatory effects, confusion about policy regarding slaves and slavery on the local level, and the creation of a wartime diaspora among the western theater's enslaved population. For many people held in slavery, this third phase of war was dangerous and liberating at the same time.

As Union policy on slavery moved through these three phases, it also varied by location. The western theater, the starting point of most migrants to the upper Midwest, consisted of subregions and several shifting military departments. In making sense of the effect of war and evolving Federal policy on the enslaved people who ultimately fled to the upper Midwest, it is useful to think of a middle and a lower Mississippi valley. The middle valley included southern Illinois (whose port city of Cairo, at the confluence of the Ohio and Mississippi rivers, made it a critical location strategically) and the nonseceding states of Missouri and Kentucky. At least a third of a small sample of wartime migrants to the upper Midwest left from this region (although the point of origin for another third cannot be traced). The lower valley, including Arkansas, Tennessee, Mississippi, Alabama, and Louisiana, accounted for about 15 percent of the sampled migrants.[15] The differences in the process and experience of slavery's destruction in these subregions had significant consequences for the forced and voluntary movement of African Americans out of the South to the upper Midwest.

The Middle Mississippi Valley

Fugitives traveling through the middle Mississippi valley (Missouri and Kentucky) on their way to the upper Midwest found the border south treacherous to negotiate. In Missouri, during the first year of the war, the struggle between a Confederate state government in exile and both a pro-Union and a proslavery state government in residence helped turn Missouri into a theater of guerrilla warfare. Union general John C. Frémont, abolitionist commander of the Western Department since July 1861, tried to dampen Confederate operations and punish the guerrillas' Confederate slaveholding supporters. Since the outset of war, secessionists had threatened the important Federal arsenal at St. Louis, establishing a camp on the outskirts of the city and engaging in several skirmishes with Union supporters. In August 1861, Frémont proclaimed martial law in Missouri; he also declared that slavery was inconsistent with martial law in an attempt to emancipate Missouri's slaves. If Frémont's brash action provided a bright moment for African Americans and antislavery Unionists, slaveowners were outraged. Frémont's proclamation posed a direct threat to efforts by Lincoln and his ally, Missouri governor Hamilton R. Gamble, to appease loyal slaveowners and keep the state from seceding. Lincoln not only forced Frémont to rescind the order, he also replaced him in November with the more conservative and far more cautious General Henry W. Halleck as the new commander of the Department of the Missouri. Halleck would immediately try to impose order on a department still marked by great inconsistency and conflict over the army's relationship to slavery. For every Union soldier who insisted that fugitive slaves were unwelcome in his unit's camp, there were others who protected fugitive slaves, even those whose masters were loyal to the Union.[16]

The politics of border-state slavery continued to shape Federal and military policy for Missouri in the fall. To assuage concerns about the stability of slavery under a Unionist state government, Halleck issued General Orders No. 3, in November 1861, excluding all "unauthorized persons" from army camps within the Department of the Missouri—ostensibly to prevent fugitive slaves from feeding critical information about U.S. forces to the enemy, but more obviously an answer to the repeated demands by loyal slaveowners for the return of their slaves from Union army camps.[17]

Subordinate officers in the department flooded Halleck's aides with requests for clarification on how to distinguish between "authorized" and "unauthorized" camp dwellers. Major George Waring, commanding forces near Rolla, Missouri, ordered interviews with every African American in his camp to determine who should be excluded. Apparently fully apprised of the implications of the exercise, fugitives used all their persuasive powers to prevent their return to slavery. Waring reported:

> They all stoutly asserted they were free. . . . Some of them I have no question are so. Others I have as little doubt have been slaves,—but no one is here to prove it, and I hesitate to take so serious a responsibility. . . . If I turn them away, I inflict great hardship upon them, as they would be homeless and helpless. Furthermore, such a course would occasion much personal inconvenience and sincere regret, to other officers no less than myself. These people are mainly our servants and we can get no others. They have been employed in this capacity for some time—long enough for us to like them as servants, to find them useful and trustworthy, and to feel an interest in their welfare. . . . The negroes in my camp are employed, in accordance with the Army Regulations, as officers servants, teamsters, and hospital attendants, and, with the except[ion] of one little child, are such as we are authorized to have in the camp.[18]

Although Halleck offered no response to Waring's concerns, repeated inquiries from others about the order's inconsistencies with the First Confiscation Act pushed him to explain, by the end of the year, that his intention was not to exclude legitimately employed servants of officers or other blacks authorized to work in the camps. General Grant, commanding the District of Cairo (which included some of Missouri's southeastern counties), also made it clear that slaves "used to support the master, who supports the rebellion," were "not to be restored to the master by military authority."[19] By the end of 1861, Lincoln and his departmental commander had done much to reassure Union owners in Missouri that their slave property would be protected, but slave flight continued to escalate. The issue of border-state slavery remained far from settled, and emancipation remained for many enslaved Missourians a subject for prayer but not immediate hope.[20]

The greatest obstacles encountered by Missouri slaves who hoped to receive Federal protection or escape into urban anonymity were the aggressive measures by St. Louis police and state militia to enforce laws regulating the city's slave population. Lincoln's concession, at the time of the Frémont imbroglio, had been to expand the policing powers of city authorities and the state militia. This may have been politically astute, but in practice it created turmoil and posed a serious threat to local and migrating African Americans. Missouri state law required that captured runaway slaves be held in city jails for three months; after that, if no owner stepped forward, they were subject to sale. The St. Louis city jail was used throughout the war to house captured fugitive slaves. One of the many conflicts to arise over the state law occurred in December 1861, when department commander Halleck ordered his provost marshal general to prevent local authorities from selling sixteen African Americans. Halleck insisted that the First Confiscation Act (which since 6 August 1861 allowed Union forces to "confiscate" slaves being used directly in the Confederate war effort) superseded the state law. He also created a loophole to ensure their removal from city control to Federal protection: Since the slaves had been issued clothing by the U.S. Quartermaster's Department, they must be turned over to that department to pay off, through their labor, the cost of the clothing. Here Halleck revealed his nimble efforts to accommodate conflicting law and policy with the claims of fugitive slaves to freedom in a city that, after all, was under Union control. But neither Halleck nor his successors ever managed to establish order out of the colliding policies that claimed authority over Missouri bondage. Fugitive slaves continued to face capture and imprisonment in city jails for the duration of the war, if for no other reason than to "teach them to behave" by threatening them with sale into the Deep South.[21]

Judging from the large number of newspaper reports, the capture, jailing, and auctioning off of runaway slaves was a frequent occurrence during the war. Some of the fugitives who reached St. Louis had traveled from considerable distances. Thompson Rowland escaped from his owner in Platte City, Missouri, in June 1862; he was tracked down and brought before a judge, then confined in the city jail pending return to his master. Local police authorities were aggressive about returning fugitives to their owners or selling them to new ones. Three enslaved women who had been held in the city jail for the requisite three months were swiftly sold at public auction by the St. Louis County sheriff in June 1862. Jane, aged forty-five, was sold for $300; her daughter Sue, aged nineteen, for $485; and a six-year-old, probably Sue's child, for $175—all to different buyers. Ten days later a mother, her two children, and another slave woman who had escaped from their mistress were captured and returned by the city police, despite their reports of severe mistreatment. Slaveowners from across the state regularly notified the St. Louis chief of police when their slaves took flight, as was the case with some thirty or forty slaves from counties in and near the state's plantation belt of Little Dixie. During the first two years of war, Missouri slaveowners suspected that St. Louis was a favorite destination of runaway slaves; they expected the police and sheriff to protect their property rights.[22]

In addition to its use as temporary quarters for slaves on the run, the St. Louis city jail was also a preferred place of confinement for slaves regarded by their owners as "unruly." At least eighteen slaves were held there during a three-week period in March 1863, including a young mother with her infant, a mother with her toddler, and at least four more children.[23] F. B. Kennett's overseer proposed confining Kennett's slaves (from southeastern Washington County) in the St. Louis jail "until they agreed to behave," but apparently he waited too long to act, as several escaped and made their own way to the city, living and working as fugitives.[24]

Efforts to control the city's slave population, including fugitives, were further complicated by the proximity of Benton Barracks, a major rendezvous for white and then black enlistment. A fifty-acre enclosure outside of the city, the barracks maintained hospitals in addition to encampments where newly enlisted soldiers were organized, trained, and prepared for assignments in the South.[25] Missouri and St. Louis slaves lost no time in seeking protection at the barracks and, in 1863, the opportunity to enlist. Some accompanied white troops returning from farther afield in the state. A seven-year-old boy who fled slavery early in January 1862 was brought to the barracks by Union soldiers, only to be seized, taken to the city jail, and ultimately returned to his owner in

Lexington.[26] A group of thirty men, women, and children who escaped slavery in Chillicothe arrived at the barracks with white soldiers in November 1862.[27] This placed the barrack commanders in the unwelcome position of having to determine the legitimacy of the fugitives' claims to freedom. Soldiers at the barracks, who held varying political and personal beliefs, were also involved—not simply by virtue of having witnessed the arrival and departure of African Americans, but also by encouraging or discouraging their efforts to gain protection and freedom.[28]

Through the summer and fall of 1862, even as increasing numbers of Missouri slaves claimed their freedom under the Second Confiscation Act, department commander Halleck struggled to prevent the threatened collapse of Missouri slavery and the anti-Unionist sentiment he feared would result.[29] He and his successor, General John M. Schofield, were unable to contain the emancipatory effects of war or the threat to Missouri's western border by fugitive blacks in Kansas (who sought to retaliate against former owners and to rescue family members left behind). This prompted Lincoln to name yet another department commander, Major General Samuel Ryan Curtis, in September 1862. Curtis's appointment effected what Louis Gerteis describes as an important shift in the balance of power toward emancipationists in the state.[30]

Curtis moved quickly to ensure the widest possible application of the First and Second Confiscation acts. On Christmas Eve, 1862, he issued General Orders No. 35 instructing provost marshals to issue certificates of freedom to all fugitive slaves entitled to their liberty under the confiscation acts.[31] Lincoln, hoping for Missouri's continued loyalty, sent Curtis a note stating that he understood "there is considerable trouble with the slaves in Missouri" and urged him to "please do your best to keep peace on the question."[32] Curtis nonetheless continued to issue certificates of freedom; many recipients joined the northward migration of former slaves. But perhaps the greatest force for freedom in the state were the slaves themselves.

Enslaved people in and traveling through Missouri demonstrated both an astute awareness of wartime politics and a persistent determination to win their freedom. They soon learned the grounds under which the confiscation acts might help them and made persuasive claims for the enforcement of those acts. They also discovered which Union soldiers were most sympathetic, hoping to join those soldiers on their return north once they were discharged.[33] Such fugitives ignored the advice of Union officials who claimed to know what was best for them (like staying with their masters until they could "better their condition"). The legacy of family separation and involuntary relocation was transformed in the midst of war. Men and women struggled to keep families together, or at least prepare for a future where they might be reunited. Many slave men headed out on their own, some seeking new homes and returning for their families later. Former slave James Montgomery noted that his father "left perhaps a year before [his mother] left. . . . He went off, not with any intention of deserting her, but to be free." Archer Alexander, who fled in February 1863, left behind Louisa, his wife of thirty years, and their ten children, but hoped that they could be reunited in freedom.[34] Some male fugitives banded together, armed themselves, and demanded that owners release family members still held as slaves. Others simply walked away. Patty served her master's dinner one last time and quietly took her five children to a nearby Union camp and then to St. Louis, where she reunited with her father and other male kin. These everyday acts of claiming freedom sometimes came at a terrible cost when the state militia, guerrillas, Confederate troops, or angry slaveowners took matters into their own hands as they tried to shore up the institution of slavery. Louisa Alexander's master declared that she "would never get free[,] only at the point of a bayonet."[35] Entire families were subjected to brutal violence, and the military department was too understaffed to prevent it. Missouri slaves learned to create their own opportunities and rely on their own judgment about when, how, and where to obtain their freedom. They understood, far better than did Unionist or rebel Missourians, that their liberty would not be a gift from Union soldiers, but rather had to be seized.[36]

The Missouri state convention finally passed a gradual emancipation law in July 1863; under its provisions, most slaves would be emancipated by 1876, although some would have to wait until 1881 and beyond.[37] However, black enlistment, beginning in May 1863, sped the collapse of slavery in the state. Slaves and recruiters alike ignored efforts to limit enlistment to the disloyal southwestern corner of Missouri; recruiters were frequently approached by entire families, since enlisted men were realistically fearful of the repercussions for women and children left behind to face angry slaveowners.[38] During this period, the return of paroled Confederate soldiers captured at Vicksburg increased rebel guerrilla activity that frequently targeted slaves, especially those fleeing masters in search of an opportunity to enlist.[39] Thousands of men, women, and children fled at great risk, but with the understanding that gradual emancipation remained a distant promise while nearby Union forces offered the possibility of a more immediate release from bondage. As the historian Louis Gerteis has pointed out, it was nearly impossible for the Union commander at St. Louis to balance the demands of loyal slaveholders and a

War Department hungry for new recruits.[40] Enlistment produced "a perfect stampede" among slaves, altering relationships between slaveowners and slaves; according to one former master, in some instances "those who are left are so independent that to get them to work we have to pay them wages."[41] A second wave of black enlistments during the harvest season of 1863 was so disruptive to slavery in northern Missouri that Union officials suspended recruitment activities between September and November under new guidelines permitting loyal slaveowners to receive compensation when they lost their slaves to army recruiters. When, in January 1864, Congress decided to enlist even the slaves of loyal owners, slavery's collapse in Missouri was nearly guaranteed.

THE INSTITUTION OF slavery proved more resilient in Kentucky—another point of origin in the middle Mississippi valley for slaves making their way to the upper Midwest. Kentucky had not only declared its neutrality in the Civil War; it had also announced that invasion by either army would drive the state to the opposition. To ensure Kentucky's continued neutrality, Lincoln instructed his commanders to insulate the state's Unionist slaveowners from any military policies that might be interpreted as emancipatory. After all, Kentucky was a valuable military target; the Ohio River not only served as the slave South's northern boundary; it also offered navigable tributaries (the Cumberland and Tennessee rivers) that could permit a speedy Union advance into central Tennessee and northern Alabama. James McPherson has concluded that "Lincoln's forbearance toward Kentucky paid off," since statewide elections in 1861 bolstered the strength of Unionists in the legislature. A failed Confederate attempt to seize the railroad terminals at Columbus cemented Kentucky's loyalty to the Union; under General Grant, Union forces soon occupied all but its southwestern corner by the end of 1861. The Union's apparent political and military successes in Kentucky came at great cost to enslaved people, however, as Lincoln's instructions not to alienate the state's powerful slaveowning elites led to a precarious effort to distinguish between fugitive slaves who had been ejected from army camps and returned to their Kentucky owners and fugitives en route from the lower Mississippi valley. The latter were regarded as contrabands, presumed to be free and often employed or impressed by Union forces. With the exception of one contraband camp, the army refused to shelter or enlist Kentucky's fugitive slaves until 1864, when restrictions on border-state enlistments were lifted, and slaves and contrabands—men and women—rushed to Union lines to offer their services in exchange for their freedom. Kentucky slavery would then gradually collapse, but the surest path to freedom was continued migration out of the state.[42]

The Lower Mississippi Valley

The Union army's "hands off" policy toward slaves and slavery had helped to keep the border states in the Union as of the close of 1861. The nature of the war changed, however, in 1862, as the Federals drove deep into the plantation region of the lower Mississippi valley. The struggle between the chaos of war and the perpetuity of slavery moved south with the advance of Union forces, increasing the possibilities of slave flight and migration northward to the upper Midwest. That February, as the "river war" began, Federal troops won control of western and central Tennessee, part of Arkansas, northern Alabama, and northern Mississippi. Here, as in Missouri and Kentucky, Union commanders reassured loyal slaveowners that their slave property was not at risk. Federal policy was to avoid all entanglements that a desperate population of fugitive slaves—and an angry population of loyal slaveowners—might create. But it was a policy that contradicted developments in the East, where General Benjamin Butler—with Lincoln's approval—had decided to admit runaway slaves to Fortress Monroe (Virginia) so they might be used in support of, rather than against, the Union war effort.

As in the case of Missouri and Kentucky, not all commanders or soldiers in the more southern reaches of the western theater agreed with or even followed official policy on slaves. In Baton Rouge, Colonel Halbert E. Paine of the 4th Wisconsin was arrested for protecting two male fugitives who had brought him valuable information. Paine had returned the slaves to their owner, as required by his commander, but they soon reappeared at the camp with their backs gashed open and wearing "the horrid three-pronged iron collar" as punishment for their flight. This time Paine refused to return the men to their master, and during his subsequent arrest he was cheered by his regiment.[43] Captain William Moore, of a company of Wisconsin soldiers, noted in June 1862 that an order requiring "all officers having Negroes in their employ, as servants to turn them out of camp," was met by considerable resistance among his fellow officers. Similarly, officers of an Illinois regiment encamped nearby resigned rather than enforce the order.[44]

General Curtis (commanding the Army of the Southwest, and Halleck's successor as commander of the Department of the Missouri in September 1862) made one of the most dramatic departures from Halleck's (and Lincoln's) policies when he advanced through Tennessee and Arkansas, from Pea Ridge to Little Rock and on to Helena, by mid-July 1862. Repeatedly encountering obstructions built by slaves who had been taken from neighboring plantations by Confederate soldiers, Curtis targeted Arkansas's rebel slaveholders by applying General Butler's policy, for the first time, in the Mississippi valley. Curtis issued "freedom certificates" to fugitive slaves used in the Confederate war effort, declaring them emancipated and authorizing their removal from Arkansas to the North.

Rather than exclude slaves from his camps or become entangled in debates with slaveowners over their political loyalties, Curtis gave African Americans protection, leading to a "general stampede" of enslaved people to his encampment at Helena. By the summer of 1863, several thousand people had arrived or been gathered there, many of whom would eventually find their way to the upper Midwest.[45] These included Rachel Weeden, who fled her owner, made her way to Helena, and worked for the soldiers as a laundress. Martilla Newbern left for Helena after her master's plantation was raided by Union soldiers. Enos Luckadoo was "taken" from his owner in Summerville, Tennessee, by Union forces and brought to Helena. Nathaniel Adams fled ten miles from his owner's plantation to Helena, where he worked as a cook for five months. All of these fugitives would ultimately settle in the upper Midwest.[46]

This change in Union policy had been promoted by the Second Confiscation Act, coupled with the Federal advance against Vicksburg in 1862 and 1863. The Vicksburg assault drew Union soldiers deeper and deeper into the Mississippi valley's plantation landscape and confirmed the shortsightedness of the exclusion policy, given the labor needs of the U.S. Army as well as the humanitarian needs of refugee slaves. Although an article of war passed by Congress in March 1862 had allowed Union soldiers to refuse an order to return fugitive slaves to their owners, the Second Confiscation Act went beyond that article by *forbidding* Federal soldiers from returning fugitive slaves. The act confirmed what was already practice in some locations of the lower Mississippi valley where for some time fugitive slaves had been accepted into camps as laborers.[47] Individual soldiers as well as their commanding officers held varying opinions on the subject. In letters to his family, Iowan David James Palmer bragged: "I have a contraband to take care of my horse & black boots[,] brush pants[,] sweep out the tent[,] keep my sword bright &c. &c. . . . So you may be shure I aint going to heat myself in this southern Confederacy, while I can have it done by 'de colored Population.'" Soldiers in the 13th Wisconsin Regiment, stationed at Fort Henry, Tennessee, in late November 1862, benefited from the labor of nearly one hundred black men, "employed at the expense of the government as cooks, pioneers, mule-whackers, &c."[48] Robert Moyle's comrades in Louisiana were more ambivalent about black workers; traveling down the Mississippi, they refused pleas from fugitive slaves on the riverbanks to allow them on board. The soldiers were "considerably divided in reference to the niger[;] some of them threatened to shoot them[,] but the nigers are to be pitied[;] they are in a most deplorable condition[,] they are barefooted & ragged & look miserable[;] a good many of the soldiers have them to cook & wash for them."[49]

Fugitive slave women also made themselves valuable to the military effort by cooking, sewing, washing, caring for horses, and nursing the sick and wounded. Liz Fairfax joined up with the 26th Iowa Infantry early in its service and worked for the unit until it mustered out. Union soldier Thomas Montgomery wrote his parents back in Minnesota: "As it is we are quite comfortable. We have 2 boys and a woman to wait on us, and wash & sew for us, so we have no trouble but attend to our duties." In a later letter he noted that his laundress also "does some good cooking." Iowan A. F. Sperry, stationed at Little Rock, recalled a family of four moving into his unit's camp during the winter of 1863–64; the husband picked up what work he could, while the wife and two daughters "officiated as washer-women for the regiment." Slave women worked with white midwestern women in hospitals and Sanitary Commission field offices in the South; commission nurse Rhonda Amanda Shelton was glad to have the help of "Auntie," who scrubbed Shelton's lodgings, prepared her breakfast, and even screened her unwelcome male visitors.[50]

Federal policy toward slaves in the lower Mississippi valley entered a third phase once Federal officials conceded, in the aftermath of the Second Confiscation Act, that the military could not stem the flow of fugitives to Union camps. U.S. officials now acknowledged that a plan was needed to cope with this civilian population. Able-bodied black men like Samuel Hall were useful to the military as laborers, but the same army whose troops described the valuable camp labor provided by fugitive slave women and children now deemed them an encumbrance. "The problem," complained one Minnesota soldier, was that "every Sambo has his Dinah and maybe a litter of little 'pickaninnies' that we have no sort of use for, and don't know what to do with."[51] In November 1862 Grant appointed a chaplain of an Ohio regiment, John Eaton Jr., to organize these fugitive slave women and children and move them to the abandoned plantations along the Mississippi, there to work under white lessees and, by supporting themselves, begin their apprenticeship as free laborers. Eaton would be overwhelmed by the task, particularly as the numbers of freed slaves increased exponentially with the Emancipation Proclamation of January 1.[52]

Yet even as Union commanders became increasingly committed to the destruction of southern slavery and the protection of African American liberty, newly freed slaves were still vulnerable when Confederate forces overran Union lines. The Federal retreat from northern Alabama and middle Tennessee in the fall of 1862 left scores of slaves abandoned to rebel soldiers and former owners. Some of these fugitives escaped by following Union troops into Kentucky, but state law permitted local officials to jail them as runaways and sell them into the slave trade.

Former slaves who sought refuge in Union-occupied southern cities were also at risk. Those from surrounding cotton plantations who gathered in Memphis were seized by police and confined in the city jail, either to be sold or returned to their owners. Only the U.S. Army's need for labor to construct the city's fortifications ended this local challenge to a Federal policy progressing (however unevenly) toward emancipation.

Grant's 1863 assault against Vicksburg also drew thousands of slaves from Mississippi, Louisiana, and Arkansas to Union lines. For most enslaved African Americans, the arrival of Union troops and the defeat of Confederate forces at Vicksburg in mid-1863 offered a compelling opportunity for freedom that they pursued at their peril. That spring, Adjutant General Lorenzo Thomas had begun mobilizing Mississippi valley blacks on behalf of the Union war effort. This included enlisting able-bodied black men (more than seventy thousand blacks from the Mississippi valley freed themselves by signing up), lining the crucial riverways of the valley with a loyal population by putting freedpeople (predominantly female) to work on the plantations abandoned by Confederate owners and leased by northern entrepreneurs; and establishing temporary quarters for thousands more contrabands (mostly women, children, and the elderly) in camps. The fall of Vicksburg opened the Mississippi valley to the war's devastating impact on the institution of slavery, multiplied as Union troops marched into the interior of Arkansas, Louisiana, and Mississippi, and reoccupied northern Alabama.[53]

But even this two-pronged policy of emancipation and enlistment could prove dangerously incomplete for African Americans in search of freedom. The Reverend Uriah Eberhart, chaplain of the 20th Iowa Infantry, observed the workings of the new policy on the ground; "After the surrender of Vicksburg the so-called 'Contrabands' came in from the surrounding country by thousands, hoping to get something to eat, and something to do to make a living." Eberhart noted that thirty to forty thousand freedpeople streamed into the city, but there was nothing to eat and disease spread rapidly among them:

> So General Grant issued an order that they must immediately be removed, dead or alive, to the Louisiana side of the river. . . . Many were sick with small-pox, yellow fever and other contagious diseases, and a good many were already dead, and some of them had been dead for days, and all had to be removed. . . . In all my army life I witnessed nothing like this. It beggars description. I will give only one of the many cases. A woman had been dead several days, and her child was still nursing the dead mother. . . . For weeks they had neither hut nor tent to shelter them. But this was not the worst feature in their condition. They had nothing to eat save a little "hard-tack," given to some of them by the soldiers, and what they had picked up along by the way. On the day I entered on this work, Gen. Grant told me he would send over a boat-load of provisions the next day. So I made out a "requisition" and took it to the Quarter-master, who, to my great disappointment, would not honor it, saying: "We have no army regulations to feed niggers, especially when our soldiers and prisoners are on short rations."

Eberhart returned to Grant and obtained a special order for the provisions as well as a requisition for their transport across the river. "But all this time the poor contrabands were starving to death." He estimated twenty to thirty deaths a day: "In this wretched, starving condition, these poor creatures became very despondent, desperate, and even rebellious, . . . and came to the conclusion that the 'Yankees,' instead of being their friends, intended to starve them to death—as some of the masters had told them."[54]

Indeed, the war and U.S. policy created circumstances that threatened the very survival of former slaves, as peacetime slavery never had. Former slaves in flight were vulnerable to kidnapping: more than one thousand blacks were illegally sent from Missouri to Kentucky slave marts within a two-month period in the fall of 1863.[55] Confederate officers forced some slaves into service with them, which led to indeterminate—and sometimes permanent—separation from their families.[56] Other slaveowners, anticipating the Confederacy's defeat, were quick to "cash out" their investment in human chattel.[57] Still others drove their slaves south (referred to as "refugeeing" in the parlance of the times), away from Union forces, in an effort to protect their investment. Dr. Monroe Felkerson of Columbia was one of many Missouri slaveholders who sent their slaves south during the first year of the war; then he decided to move them to Texas, "where the Yankees could not find them." Felkerson had declared that "before he would let his niggers be free he would shoot

"Negroes Driven South by the Rebel Officers," Harper's Weekly, *8 November 1862. After the war, many formerly enslaved people reported being forced south away from Union forces and the possibility of escape. Special Collections, State Historical Society of Iowa, Iowa City.*

them down." Among his slaves, Saphronia Carter, her mother, her uncle, and an older woman were spared the forced march south—in Saphronia's case, because she was about to give birth to her second child. The others may have been too old or too ill to survive the journey.[58]

Not only recapture, but also vengeance, threatened fugitives trying to reach Union forces. Lieutenant Benjamin F. Pearson of the 36th Iowa Infantry was in a supply train overtaken by Confederate troops at Marks Mills, Arkansas, in April 1864; while Pearson was merely taken prisoner, half of the contrabands who accompanied the Union soldiers were gunned down or clubbed to death. "There was not an armed negro with us & they shot down our Colored servants & temsters & others that were following to get from bondage, as they would shoot sheep dogs." Their victims were men, women, and children. Another observer of the massacre added: "No orders, threats or commands would restrain the men from vengeance on the negroes, and they were piled in great heaps about the wagons, in tangled brushwood, and upon the muddied and trampled road."[59]

For many African Americans, bondage became much worse until the circumstances and chaos of war enabled them to escape northward. While Union policies were developed, debated, imposed, revoked, and refined at the nation's capital and military headquarters, those policies were only as effective as

A Time of Scattering

the individual officers and soldiers who ultimately enforced or ignored them, face-to-face with slaveowners and the enslaved.

"GLORY TO GOD AND THE YANKEES FOREVER. . . . MY TEN CHILEN ALL FREE HALILUYAH"

The emergence of a large population of female refugees contributed to the process of slavery's destruction, for it transformed antebellum patterns of slave flight that once favored single men over women (especially women with children). Out of a population of about four million, roughly 320,000 enslaved people—more than half of them women—became displaced during the war.[60] Slave flight, initiated well before the Union army abandoned its noninterventionist stance on bondage, compounded the war's threat to the plantation economy, undermined the stability of southern mastery, and gave the lie to the fiction of consent and the rituals of subordination that had marked social relations between slaves and their masters.[61] For enslaved women, the decision to flee also dramatically changed the meaning of reproduction in their lives. As they led their children out of bondage, these mothers rejected slavery's claims on their kin and absolved themselves of the terrible burden that enslaved motherhood had forced upon them: adding to the wealth of slaveholders and bringing a child into the world of slavery.

Not all displaced southerners were slaves; one of the outcomes of the war was its creation of a large number of white female refugees in the South.[62] But the causes leading to refugee status and the consequences for southern whites and southern slaves were as different as one might imagine. Among southern white women, those who were slaveowners often became refugees as a last-ditch effort to protect their chattel property, whereas nonslaveowners were more often displaced by the impending arrival of enemy forces. As one historian has noted, white women's refugee experience was marked by "danger, illness and catastrophic loss"—the loss of household belongings, social stability, and the social bargain of white female dependence in exchange for white male protection. Displacement brought calamity and chaos to white women, although those with more resources usually encountered far fewer risks.[63]

Among enslaved women, displacement was generally the result of a decision to flee slavery—to reject "home" and the fiction of "protection" offered by slaveowners for the freedom and relative safety slave women hoped eventually to gain behind enemy lines.[64] While chaos, illness, and catastrophe marked their experience no less than that of white female refugees, displaced slave women chose to become refugees as a strategy in the war against slavery. Their choice not only yielded a qualitative difference in their experience of displacement, but also reflected their decision—and ability—to challenge the pervasive threat of family separation and involuntary movement that slavery and war held over their lives. Enslaved families were now moving by choice, and many (though certainly not all) found a way to move together. Iowa soldier John Shepherd described how Alabama slaves greeted the arrival of Union troops: "Some of the Negros came out to meet us, and I Shall never forget one old Woman. I heard her shouting ¼ of a mile away. When we came up to where she was She was jumping up and down and Shouting Glory to God and the Yankees forever. She said my ten Chilen all free haliluyah." Other soldiers took a more active role in the liberation of slaves; Thomas Montgomery described "capturing" a "colored gal" from her master and bringing her into camp with his unit; there "she gave some of the boys their supper (as it was dark) and quizzed them some about escaping, and they encouraged her, & we did not object. Accordingly, she dressed in the pants, coat & cap of one of the boys, and took his gun and passed into the boat. She . . . was glad to get free."[65]

Unfortunately for these women, their decision to flee slavery sometimes worked against them. Because they *chose* to become war refugees, slave women were less likely to be regarded as innocent victims of war than were white Unionists in the South. One Missouri provost marshal advised slave women who were "humanely treated to stay with their masters until there in a prospect for them to better their condition by leaving," as though gaining their freedom did not fall under the category of "better[ing] their condition."[66] With "victim" status reserved for women who surrendered to the gendered expectations for noncombatants in times of war, the very term "refugee" referred to displaced whites; contemporary observers found themselves lacking even the terminology to describe fugitive slave women. The label that came into wide usage—"contraband of war," or "contrabands"—grouped refugee slave women (and men) with the wagons, horses, and miscellaneous enemy property seized by the U.S. Army. The technical military term bore little resemblance to the courage and desperation that prompted enslaved women and men to risk flight to Union lines.[67]

But terminology was the least of their difficulties. Given the Union's initial presumption that the war could be fought and won leaving slavery intact, the army was ill-prepared for the onrush of refugee slaves, particularly the large proportion of women and children. Very early in the conflict, U.S. military authorities relaxed the "hands-off" policy regarding slavery to allow the use of fugitive slave men as laborers and much later as soldiers. On the other hand, from the beginning to the end of the war, women and children were often viewed not only as an encumbrance to the army, but also as a diseased, demoralizing, and dependent population that drained valuable military resources. A few white soldiers conceded that their comrades were brutal in their treatment of black women in the South. In letters to his wife, William Ault, a private in a Wisconsin regiment, observed that, as a result of the racism and violence of his fellow Union soldiers, "A negro woman is not safe to travel if she is a decent woman."[68]

Although women and children comprised a larger proportion of the fugitive slaves approaching Federal lines, they were excluded from both the southern and northern view of war as a man's world of work and struggle, an attitude that prevailed throughout the conflict.[69] Yet the historian Jane Schultz has recently documented that black women's rate of participation in the war effort— 10 percent of over 21,000 paid hospital attendants—paralleled, and perhaps exceeded, the rate of participation of black men in the Union army (of course, the category of hospital attendant accounts for only some of the women who participated).[70] Unknown numbers of African American women—fugitive slaves and free northerners—accompanied black regiments to the South or traveled South to nurse sick or wounded husbands.[71] Despite their contributions to the Union cause, displaced women from the slave South were frequently seen as a "problem" by the northern military and became the target of a range of policies intended to remove the burden they were believed to represent.

"THEY FLOCKED INTO MY CAMP IN GREAT CROWDS"

"Migration" is a generic term that can obscure significant differences in wartime black mobility, differences in the experience of migration as well as in the responses to it. African Americans who fled slavery in the Mississippi valley traveled one of three distinct paths to the upper Midwest. All three paths involved careful decisions and volition on the part of enslaved people. The first path can be characterized as self-liberation by flight, in which the migration process was directed by enslaved people themselves. The second path involved arrangements made with white soldiers and officers from midwestern states to transport fugitive slaves north to the homes of family and friends. The third path entailed the organized relocation of large numbers of fugitive slaves to northern employers, initially under the auspices of military authorities, but later with the assistance of freedmen's aid societies, philanthropic civilians, and potential employers.

The first path to freedom—self-liberation by flight—had a long antebellum history, but its use increased dramatically with the proximity of Union forces and the disruptions of war. Lucius Hubbard, while serving in a Minnesota regiment stationed just east of Corinth to guard the crucial Memphis-Charleston Railroad in the fall of 1862, described the determination of slaves to gain their freedom: "The entire negro population of the valley, which at one time constituted nineteen twentieths of its inhabitants, seems to regard our mission here to be simply their deliverance, hence I am constantly besieged by men, women and children, who apply for 'protection,' and facilities for leaving the country."[72] Within the Mississippi valley, opportunities for flight continued to increase through the three phases of Federal policy on slavery and as U.S. troops advanced farther into the interior of the region. Pairing their control of the Mississippi valley with emancipation, the enlistment of slave men, and the employment of other former slaves on abandoned plantations, Union forces helped bring de facto freedom to thousands of slaves.[73]

Among the slaves who escaped to the upper Midwest were George Johnson and his family. They were safely led to Mt. Pleasant, Iowa, by Johnson's father, who drove them across the Missouri state border hidden in a grain-loaded wagon, as though he were making his usual trip to the closest gristmill.[74] In 1862 six slave families slipped out of Boone County, Missouri, made their way to St. Louis, and boarded a Union steamship that took them up the Mississippi to St. Paul.[75] Thomas Gordon Jones fled his master in Georgia, attached himself to a Union regiment, and eventually made his own way to Iowa.[76] Milton Howard and a "crowd of us" escaped from slavery in Alabama to the Midwest.[77] After bolting from Missouri plantations at night, John Miller, Aleck Nichols, and Andy and Henderson Hays all evaded slave hunters, bloodhounds, and Iowa Copperheads before arriving safely in Newton, Iowa.[78] William Jones and Reuben Washington left their owners in Chariton County, Missouri, and went to Des Moines; John Anderson and six other men fled Warrenton, Missouri, and found a route to Keokuk, Iowa.[79] In 1863 fugitive slave Thomas Green walked from Missouri to Prairie du Chien, Wisconsin.[80] Several of the former slaves who joined Iowa's black regiment, the 60th U.S. Colored Infantry (USCI), and the 29th USCI (which included many men who had enlisted in Wisconsin), had made their own way out of slavery to the Midwest in order to enlist.

In Missouri, perhaps the most important gateway to the upper Midwest for fugitive slaves, a unique set of circumstances shaped wartime black migration. By 1863, Lincoln still held out hope that the state would emancipate its slaves voluntarily—a realistic expectation, as the state legislature passed a gradual emancipation bill in July 1863, albeit one that would not free all Missouri slaves until 1881.[81] The decision to enlist blacks opened up new opportunities for freedom for Missouri's male slaves in the fall of 1863, but slave women and children accompanying men to recruiting stations were turned away or, worse, returned to the custody of loyal slaveowners, who responded violently to the erosion of their mastery. Thousands of these slave women and children, in fear for their lives and in pursuit of freedom, headed west to Kansas, east across the Mississippi to Illinois, or north to St. Louis, Iowa, or beyond. As one Canton County, Missouri, newspaper reported in June 1864, "Several families of African citizens stampeded . . . supposed to have gone up to Keokuk—that negro paradise. The institution has been on the wing for the last two years, and this last stampede, with the successful recruiting the following day, has about cleaned out the colored element of this place."[82] They fled on foot, on stolen horses or wagons, by steamboat and train, individually, in family groups, and, as slavery neared the brink of collapse, by the hundreds.[83]

Wartime flight was dangerous for slaves anywhere in the Mississippi valley. Missouri closely enforced state laws barring common carriers from transporting slaves without their owners' permission, and it was fairly common for slaveowners to pursue fugitives well into Iowa or Illinois.[84] Missouri rebels were not above "arresting all the contrabands in the County who had free papers" or threatening the lives of Federal authorities who tried to take them north.[85] These dangers reflect the tremendous hardships caused by military policies that left enslaved women and children to fend for themselves.

A second migratory path to freedom opened up when midwestern soldiers and officers decided to bring black servants home with them, or arranged to relocate individual fugitives or small families to neighboring farms and households in need of additional labor.[86] Because military policy excluded fugitive slaves from army camps (especially in Missouri) and protected the property rights of loyal slaveowners, it was not unusual for fugitives to be refused safe harbor in army encampments.[87] But enforcement of that policy had weakened as soldiers became increasingly unwilling to participate directly in the return to bondage of men and women whose labor had eased the harshness of camp life.[88] Lucius Hubbard, stationed east of Corinth, took advantage of his unit's distance from its command to act as he saw best: "I am doing quite a business in the confiscation of slave property. I have already sent about eighty human chattels away by railroad headed north, and have about fifty more in camp whom I shall send as soon as I can get transportation." Midwestern soldiers uncomfortable with official policy and opposed to returning fugitives to their owners were also more likely to send fugitive slaves north. An unnamed young woman, sold during the war for use in a "house of ill fame," escaped from her owner near Lexington, Kentucky, and approached the camp of a Wisconsin regiment; there sympathetic soldiers arranged for her transportation to Wisconsin. These men viewed their own actions as heroic and memorialized them in a group photograph made before she left for the North.[89]

For some soldiers, the wartime labor shortage and their concern for farms and property back home prompted their decision to send former slaves north. Edward Redington, stationed for a time in Helena, Arkansas, was one of several Wisconsin officers who viewed former slaves as transportable labor. A friend in the service escorted at least seven people to Wisconsin, one to Redington's Whitewater home and several more to LaCrosse.[90] Captain Charles Nelson, of the 15th Wisconsin Infantry, employed Peter Thomas as his servant until Nelson was injured, when Thomas helped him return to his home in Beloit and worked for a time on his farm while Nelson recovered from his injury.[91] Children were often considered likely candidates for relocation north. Thomas A. Ball, of Iowa's 32nd Infantry, wounded in the leg, was concerned about how he and his wife would make do on their farm when he returned. He wrote her: "Now Serrilda I want you to give me your opinion about haveing about three or four darkies brought to your house when I come home to work for us." They could take in "three boys about twelve years old, one to help you about the house and garden and cook for the other two that plows and so on as I never expect to be able to follow the plow on account of my leg." We do not have his wife's response, but his subsequent letters never raise the possibility again.[92] Men, women, children, and sometimes entire families accompanied the soldiers of the upper Midwest to their homes, seeking freedom, self-support, and a life outside the war zone.[93]

When soldiers sent former slaves to their families, they exercised their authority as heads of household, as well as to ensure that their farms and household economies would continue in their absence. But there is considerable evidence that their decisions were not always approved by their wives. White wives often found themselves in charge of a black laborer—sometimes, male, sometimes female—in places where African American residents were few in number. In this circumstance, wives might express doubt about the contributions these black strangers would actually make. Less explicit but clearly important were wives' concerns about how they and their households would be perceived in their white-majority and frequently white-supremacist communities. To her husband's announcement that he might bring home a fugitive slave boy, Mary Ann Graham Rogers of Tama, Iowa, responded: "I wondered what I would do with another boy and he a black one. There was not a colored person in our town or ever had been that I knew of."[94] Edward

An eighteen-year-old "mulatto" sold in Lexington, Ky., to a purchaser intending to put her in a house of "ill fame," flanked by two members of the 22nd Wisconsin Volunteers. "To this the poor girl refused to consent, every feeling of her nature recoiling at it. She had, though a slave, the instincts of a woman, and felt that death would be preferable to such a destiny. The day following, she came into the camp of one of our Wisconsin regiments. She was not repulsed, but found herself amongst a thousand true-hearted men, who assured her of all the protection of their power." They arranged her secret removal to Wisconsin; en route, "she with her escorts visited the daguerrean rooms and had their likenesses taken, she sitting in the center with a soldier on either side, with their revolvers drawn, showing their readiness thus to protect her, even at the cost of their own lives."
Rev. J. B. Rogers, War Pictures: Experiences and Observations of a Chaplain in the U.S. Army, in the War of the Southern Rebellion *(Chicago: Church and Goodman, 1863), 126–29; Photo G98S-CWP 145.54 (1862), U.S. Army Military Institute, Carlisle, Pa.*

Redington was more convinced than his wife Mary that a former slave could help her. Their dispute on the subject in January 1863 led Edward to joke about it in March, when he scolded Mary for the amount of heavy physical labor she was undertaking; he threatened to "send you another nigger" if she failed to hire someone locally to take up the slack.[95]

The perspectives of black migrants on the opportunities presented by relocation to the North are harder to document. Although they would be removed from the threat of reenslavement, many African Americans who agreed to make the trip north left spouses, family, and friends behind; were dependent on the trustworthiness of their benefactor and the soundness of his or her plans; and faced long, complicated, and dangerous journeys to unknown locations to live with white strangers for an indefinite length of time. Elizabeth Estell, a fugitive from Missouri, was sent by steamboat, train, and stagecoach to Cleveland, Minnesota, by the white officer commanding her husband's company. Restless throughout her stay in rural Minnesota, Estell especially missed her husband and two children, who were left behind. Perhaps the cooking, sewing, laundry, cleaning, and farm chores she was expected to perform for a family of four were harder or more tedious than she had expected, or the isolation more stark, or the lack of a firm arrangement concerning her wages too disappointing for her to appreciate the lessons in reading and writing and the occasional sleigh ride she received in exchange for her labor. Certainly her experience was not unique among the hundreds, perhaps thousands, of African American adults and children who migrated to the rural Midwest under similar circumstances.[96]

THERE IS GOOD reason to be skeptical about the quality of life and the extent of freedom encountered by isolated refugees like Estell. Some newly arrived blacks discovered a presumption among local whites (and potential employers) that their northern benefactor held a claim to their labor, as was the case for Emmanuel Craig, a young former slave from Tennessee, brought to Des Moines by Governor Samuel J. Kirkwood. Craig wanted to leave his situation with Kirkwood but found local businessmen unwilling to come between him and his powerful employer.[97] Some ex-slaves found themselves stranded without any arrangement concerning their wages or living quarters, as reported in Fairfield, Iowa, where, in June 1862, a soldier was charged with illegally bringing a slave boy, James Robinson, home and using him as a slave. Refugees who became sick and unable to work were sometimes abandoned to public charity. In October 1862, an unnamed man was taken to Keokuk by Colonel John W. Rankin and left at the Lee County poorhouse when he became ill.[98]

Other former slaves were threatened with return to the South should their work or behavior not meet expectations. Not the least of their worries was the threat posed by Iowa's law against the migration of free blacks into the state, as well as the sentiment supporting such laws expressed by a vocal minority in Minnesota and Wisconsin.[99]

Thomas Montgomery, who served in the 7th Minnesota Volunteers before becoming an officer in the 67th USCI, not only sent the wife of one of his black soldiers to his family farm, but also contemplated arranging for a number of men in his regiment to establish a black settlement in Minnesota's St. Peter land district. Montgomery made a detailed inquiry about the terms and prospects of the proposal; his soldiers were apparently wary:

> I have no doubt but I could form a good colony but the men as well as myself want to know on what conditions &c. we are to base our action. Will you [his father] please collect the required information and send it to me, as speedily as possible. . . . Will a receipt be furnished, or other papers sent, showing what was done with the money? So as to make myself safe, & give the men something to show that they have a claim on the land? Will the land be safely held for the men till after the war, free from taxes &c and for their heirs, in case they should die or be killed in the U.S. Service. . . . All my men are without homes and are desirous of procuring them and they could each bring their friends along. Some are tradesmen. All of them I have no doubt would make good industrious citizens. . . . I think they will be quite willing to go to Minnesota.[100]

With no further reference to the proposed settlement in his correspondence, the plan probably did not materialize.

The third path of wartime black migration—the organized relocation of former slaves from the Mississippi valley to the upper Midwest—began in earnest during the summer and fall of 1862. At that time large numbers of enslaved people fled to Union lines as the Union army advanced into west and central Tennessee, northern Alabama, northern Mississippi, and Arkansas.[101] As one observer described it:

> I have heard various accounts of what they thought and what they did when they heard '*dem big guns roar*'—how the men and women in the fields would prick up their ears and listen. . . . The overseers and the white folks generally had been telling them that the Yankees were their enemies, and they pretended to believe them until now. The overseers would tell them, 'Now, when you see the Yankees coming you must break for the woods or

Cainbreaks.' They would say, 'No, we think the best way would be to run to the Yankees and throw ourselves on their mercies, and they will be less liable to hurt us.[102]

Indeed, Union troops were less liable to hurt them, but so many slaves entered their lines at one time that many commanders and soldiers regarded them as "a burden and an encumbrance to the army and the cause." Military authorities were forced to improvise camps to accommodate the unanticipated influx.[103] For example, the camp at Helena was established in mid-July 1862, when General Curtis and his troops advanced into Arkansas down the White River.[104] Within ten days of their arrival at Helena, the quartermaster reported "a perfect 'Cloud' of negroes being thrown upon me for Sustenance & Support"; some—including a considerable number of women and children—had traveled long distances. Of the fifty contrabands the quartermaster had to feed, only twelve were men who could be "reasonably" worked. "What am I to do with them," he asked. "If this taking them in & feeding them is to be the order of the day[,] would it not be well to have some competent man employed to look after them & Keep their time, draw their Rations & look after their Sanitary Condition?"[105] As the camps grew increasingly overcrowded, they posed a significant humanitarian problem, drained the Union war effort of resources and material, and put post commanders in a vulnerable position of improvising on official policy.[106] The 50 contrabands who seemed so overwhelming to the quartermaster in July had increased to 900 by September and, after the Emancipation Proclamation on 1 January, to 4,000 that month.[107]

Although joyful to escape slaveowners and overseers, African Americans encountered stressful conditions at Helena. Their housing consisted of "old, dilapidated houses in town, or tents and cabins in Ethiopia encampment, not averaging [a] room to a family." Those who received rations were required to move within the lines of the encampment, leaving about three hundred people outside it to fend for themselves.[108] Helena was subject to severe flooding, drinking water was contaminated, and soldiers and contrabands alike were vulnerable to Confederate attack. Hundreds of contraband men were put to work on the post fortifications and to transfer government stores from ships, but they were paid irregularly—some not at all.[109] Women had far fewer opportunities to support themselves and their children, and they often lacked the most basic necessities.[110]

Federal forces were not simply unprepared for the large numbers of African Americans arriving at the camps in Helena; some troops treated them badly. Conditions at the hospital for black refugees, inspected by army chaplains in late December 1862, were appalling. The chaplains "found everything dirty, uncomfortable and cheerless" and much worse; suffering patients spoke of "cruelties and barbarities perpetrated on male and female," including many who were "brutally beaten." A "notorious number" of deaths had occurred at the hospital.[111] Union troops also mistreated the healthy. They took over their cabins, sexually assaulted the women, and attacked, even murdered, their defenders among the fugitives.[112]

Overwhelmed by southern blacks seeking freedom and protection, field and departmental commanders at Helena, in northern Alabama, and in Tennessee began sending them up the river or by train to the Union camp at Cairo, Illinois.[113] Finding the means to transport large numbers of contrabands was often challenging. White crews on steamships sometimes resented the civilian cargo, and railroad companies in the South found themselves targets of dozens of lawsuits when Union officers commandeered boxcars to send contrabands north, since most states prohibited the transportation of slaves on trains without the express permission of their masters.[114]

Many African Americans who were relocated to the upper Midwest thus spent time in Cairo.[115] The town occupied a critical location for Union forces, as it sat at the terminus of the Illinois Central Railroad and the junction of the Ohio and Mississippi rivers. Contrabands began arriving in the fall of 1862 from Union camps farther south in the Mississippi valley.[116] By mid-September, Grant was forwarding "large lots of negro women and children" from Tennessee to the Union barracks at Cairo.[117] A reporter for *Frederick Douglass' Paper* observed in September that "Cairo now begins to look as though the jubilee, sure enough has come, in this country. Besides what are here already, filling the old barracks, from one end to the other, still they come. Every evening, when I go down to the 'Ohio Levee,' I find it literally dotted over with new arrivals of contrabands. Old men and young men, old women and young women, and children are here."[118] By October, the *New York Times* reported that the 800 to 1,000 people at the camp were "in a most miserable condition" and suffered from the lack of clothing and bedding; "nearly all" were women and children, and many of them were sick.[119] By early November, when the refugee population reached 2,500, John B. Rogers, a Wisconsin chaplain who had been assisting with the contrabands at Corinth, was appointed to supervise the camp.[120] Although "a large number" of those at Cairo were relocated to abandoned plantations on Island No. 10 (in the Mississippi River near Tiptonville, Tennessee) by February 1863, that April 5,000 people were reported to be still in the camp, and over 2,000 former slaves remained there at the end of the war.[121]

"*Fleeing from the Land of Bondage*": a sympathetic portrayal of African American wartime migration by prolific American illustrator Felix Octavius Carr Darley (1822–88), engraved by J. J. Cade and published in 1887. Picture Collection, The Branch Libraries, The New York Public Library, Astor, Lenox and Tilden Foundations.

Like Helena, Cairo occupied a very unpleasant location. The town was on a low peninsula surrounded by a levee, subject to flooding, often muddy, and always rat-infested.[122] Old army barracks were used as shelters; most contrabands entered the camp with "very poor" clothing, "many of them hardly enough to cover their nakedness." Unlike the fugitives who occasionally arrived at southern camps with horses, oxen, wagons, and cotton, most contrabands went to Cairo with empty hands and empty pockets. Food rations were somewhat better than those provided in other camps—at Cairo, they were of the same kind and quantity as soldiers' rations. Three hospitals were established, and Quakers took up the work of organizing and teaching a school there. The former slaves found employment with the Quartermaster's Department, the navy, and in the hospitals.[123] But in Cairo they were not safe from depredations either by soldiers or citizens, some of whom would be described at the close of the war as "bitter negro haters" guilty of committing "petty abuses and outrages" against the former slaves in camp.[124] One observer in November 1862 reported that the prejudices of local whites were "raging intensely and fiercely here against those unfortunate and innocent people. I believe the Irish would murder every man and woman of them if they thought they dare do it. Indeed, were it not for military authorities here, you might not be surprised to hear of a mob here any day." The attacks against women and their daughters "would shock the moral sensibilities of any well-regulated mind or community."[125]

By mid-September 1862, Cairo had become a temporary stop for former slaves who then would be sent farther north. Their relocation to the upper Midwest was first attempted that month, when seven hundred runaway slaves, mostly women and children, who had recently arrived at Cairo, were directed (under the authority of the secretary of war, at government expense, and with the assistance of secular and denominational charities) to potential employers in Chicago, Iowa, Wisconsin, and Minnesota.[126] Their numbers included "large lots" of women and children sent to Cairo from Tennessee by General Grant, many of them the families of black men employed by the army.[127] Among them may have been the six women and two "likely" boys directed to Muscatine, Iowa, on Sept. 30, 1862, in response to a request made by a committee of Muscatine residents to the commander at Cairo. The eight, who were apparently the former slaves of Confederate general Gideon J. Pillow in Mississippi, drew a crowd of "curiosity seekers" on their arrival.[128] About 120 women and children—at least 40 of them under age twelve—traveled in four boxcars from Jackson, Tennessee, to Cairo, then northward.[129] Officers in the field welcomed the opportunity to relieve their camps of fugitive slaves. From northern Alabama in September 1862, Minnesotan Lucius Hubbard wrote: "I am constantly besieged by men, women and children, who apply for 'protection,' and facilities for leaving the country. . . . I was sorely puzzled to know what to do with them." Within a month, he described sending five hundred former slaves north: "They flocked into my camp in great crowds, and I shipped them as fast as I could get transportation. They are in a free state by this time."[130]

While military authorities were relieved and many midwestern farmers and employers were eager to hire the black refugees, government-sponsored relocation of former slaves to the North provoked considerable white opposition. Fearing that such a move might undermine support for Republican candidates in the upcoming election, the secretary of war brought organized relocation to an abrupt but temporary halt in October 1862. After the election, it was quickly resurrected and former slaves were once more transported north from Cairo.[131] Although in 1863 the military (under pressure from the Lincoln administration) looked to black enlistment and employment on abandoned plantations to curb the flow of fugitives into Union lines, organized relocation continued, as did the demand for black laborers.[132] Many of the army chaplains running contraband camps used their association with denominational and freedmen's aid societies to assist in conveying large numbers of former slaves to northern employers. These included Chaplain Rogers, superintendent of the Cairo camp, who helped to relocate seventy-five contrabands to his hometown of Fond du Lac, Wisconsin, and several more to Vinton, Iowa.[133]

Cairo was not the only gateway for organized relocation. Early in March 1863, former slaves were also sent from Helena to St. Louis. Brigadier General B. M. Prentiss, then in charge at Helena, arranged for five hundred contrabands—again, mostly women and children—to be transferred by steamboat to St. Louis.[134] There, Samuel Curtis—then commanding the Department of the Missouri—was reported to have met the steamer with exasperation: "I have more of these, unfortunately, than I know what to do with. The State of Missouri must not be made the depot for the paupers of Arkansas . . . the subject is troublesome and perplexing, but I respectfully suggest that you only transfer it by sending the negroes to my command. . . . I will have to send [them] back if you repeat the shipments," he warned Prentiss.[135] However, Samuel Sawyer, an Indiana chaplain escorting the boat and soon to be the superintendent of contraband at St. Louis, encouraged Prentiss to send up as many fugitives from Helena as he wished.[136] Prentiss would continue shipments at least through June 1863.[137] Among those relocated might have been Rachel Morton, who had escaped from her owner in 1862 and cooked for an Iowa cavalry regiment at Helena until she was taken by boat to Keokuk. Nathaniel Adams also fled his owner's plantation and made for Helena; there he cooked for soldiers for five months before he, too, was sent to Keokuk.[138]

Despite Curtis's initial response and his fear that contrabands would not be safe in a state where bondage remained legal, St. Louis quickly became a major gathering place for African Americans who hoped to leave slavery behind them. On the arrival of the first shipload of fugitives from Helena, Curtis designated the abandoned Missouri Hotel for their use, and Sawyer spent the next week organizing a plan for distributing them to employers. In little more than a week, 300 had been "disposed" of, and requests had already come from Wisconsin, Illinois, Iowa, Kansas, and Missourians to hire the remainder. With over 2,300 applications for workers and 250 more people arriving from Helena soon after the first shipload, Sawyer expected the Missouri Hotel to become "the leading contraband intelligence office for the great Northwest."[139] Sawyer himself contributed to the influx of former slaves, traveling into western Missouri to find and transfer black men who were needed as teamsters by the quartermaster's department.[140] By April 18, he had processed free papers for more than 1,100 people; 18 percent stayed in St. Louis (Curtis forbade their hiring outside the city) and the remainder were sent north. Applications continued to come in for thousands of additional workers, including one requisition for two hundred teamsters by the Union army.[141] As Missouri senator Benjamin Gratz Brown commented in June 1864: "There is scarcely a steamboat that comes from the lower Mississippi and lands in my own city that does not bring up hundreds of these freedmen. They are congregated there, and there is a demand for them, not only in my own State and in my own city and county, but in my neighboring States along the Mississippi river. I think that that dispersion should be encouraged."[142]

Civilian relief activities also helped make St. Louis a gateway to the North for former slaves. When the first steamer arrived from Helena, Curtis and Sawyer had a very efficient organization to turn to: the city's female Contraband Relief Society. The society had formed in late January 1863, splitting off from the St. Louis Ladies Union Aid Society when members of the Union Aid Society insisted it was not "proper to use funds contributed for sick and wounded soldiers for any other purpose."[143] Although established to collect donations for contrabands at Helena, Cairo, Memphis, and other locations, the Contraband Relief Society appealed to Curtis to "make some provision for freedmen daily arriving in the city." From March through July 1863, when the largest numbers of fugitives arrived from southern Missouri and farther south, the society worked with a small staff—including a guard from an Iowa regiment—to provide for the constant flow of inmates to the Missouri Hotel, offering meals, clothing, and a hospital for sick and dying freedpeople, staffed and supported by Contraband Relief. The society also helped establish two "very prosperous" schools, aided by two teachers—one each from New York and Iowa—provided by the American Missionary Association. Finally, the society took on the work of organizing the relocation of freedpeople, "sent up the river at the urgent request of patriots of all parties, who need their labor." Society members screened applicants and covered the costs of transportation for most of the estimated 2,500–3,500 freedpeople who were housed at the hotel.[144] They worked closely with the provost marshal's office to ensure that written contracts were drawn up, that all former slaves obtained a certificate of their freedom, and that they were better outfitted for the northern climate.[145] The Union soldiers assigned to the Missouri Hotel also helped with the relocation project; Major Lyman Allen of the 37th Iowa offered to send "a large number" of refugees to his hometown of Iowa City, "if they were wanted, as there are many brought up the river at this time." He also planned to send a man and a woman to his own family.[146]

Of the three major camps—at Helena, Cairo, and St. Louis—through which the former slaves of the Mississippi valley were likely to pass in their difficult, complicated, and sometimes desperate journeys north, the conditions in the "camp" at St. Louis were by all accounts the safest. There is a certain irony in this, because city slaves, fugitive slaves, and even those relocated with certificates of freedom provided by Curtis were all vulnerable to kidnapping and sale south. Slaveowners and slave traders alike supported an active business with "professional man-hunters" in recapturing runaways (or men and woman the traders claimed were runaways) and transporting them out of state where they could be sold.[147] These included people relocated from Helena but living outside the Missouri Hotel, such as fourteen-year-old Alice Jones, whose "free papers" from the Helena superintendent of contrabands did not prevent a local slave trader from having her confined in jail while he tried to come up with witnesses willing to testify that she was Adelade, a twenty-year-old runaway belonging to Joseph Conway.[148] Women, men, and children were tracked down and dragged from their city residences, beaten senseless, and hurried away before anyone could intervene.[149]

At that time, a city grand jury inspected the jail and found the conditions "dilapidated and unfit even for felons"; it recommended that the jailer of St. Louis County end the practice of holding slaves at the request of their owners for safekeeping or punishment. Although the city was instructed to so limit its traditional role in regulating and controlling the urban slave population, this change had the unintended consequences of obscuring the underground slave trade. Traders who could no longer avail themselves of the jail now confined their victims in hotel rooms and private dwellings prior to sending them out of state.[150]

African Americans in St. Louis were at the center of the open, ongoing contest between slave traders, city police, provost marshals, and Union soldiers over the status of slaves, suspected runaways, and contrabands in the city. An extension of the internecine struggle in Missouri between radical and conservative Unionists and pro-slavery Confederate sympathizers, the tug-of-war between anti- and pro-slavery forces continued to have dire consequences for African Americans in the city. Fugitive slaves, like Lucy Ann Davis, were threatened with arrest and confinement in the city jail, only to be rescued by Union soldiers and then threatened again with arrest by soldiers from a different unit.[151] Other slaves relied on compromises with slaveowners and, when necessary, physical force and open resistance to challenge the illegal smuggling operations in St. Louis.[152] With a blossoming underground market in slaves, and civilian and military officials at loggerheads over whose authority took precedence, the safety and freedom of blacks outside the Missouri Hotel were at considerable risk. Throughout the war, the *Missouri Democrat* documented the constant threat these various forces posed to African Americans.

In May 1863, President Lincoln responded to persistent political factionalism in Missouri by replacing Curtis with his predecessor, General Schofield, hoping to reduce the fighting and conflict caused by Curtis's very public antislavery position and practices.[153] Schofield soon implemented changes in the disposition of contrabands. He applied new restrictions on the issuance of certificates of freedom under the provisions of the Second Confiscation Act and limited the distribution of aid to fugitive slaves.[154] By early September 1863, Schofield ordered the Missouri Hotel closed, and refugees were instead gathered at Benton Barracks. Members of the Contraband Relief Society continued their work, now focusing on the families of black enlisted men. On 1 December, they provided clothing for forty contrabands who were needed in Iowa, noting that "they were all destitute—wanting shoes and stockings and dresses and all kinds of garments, to fit them out to go to Iowa. These were women and children," as most of the men had served in the army since the late summer.[155] Among them may have been Mary Crutchfield, an Arkansas slave who later said: "We were all captured by the Union army and taken to Helena & kept us for a time & then took us to St. Louis Missouri & from there to Keokuk Iowa where we were left."[156] The transfer to Benton Barracks grouped fugitives with black soldiers and family members who accompanied them. Between the fall of 1863 and early 1864, more than 900 additional people entered Benton Barracks.[157] By the end of 1863, more than 1,500 black Missourians had enlisted in the Union army.[158] As black enlistment accelerated in 1864, thousands more African Americans went to St. Louis; women and children, as well as the men ineligible for military service, were frequently relocated north.

AS SOUTHERN SLAVES pursued their freedom, the wartime collapse of bondage added yet another layer of voluntary and involuntary movement and migration to the experiences of thousands of Mississippi valley slaves. Enslaved men and women fled the new threats posed by war: forced labor on Confederate fortifications, separation from their families, removal to distant locations far from the protection of Union forces. Although it is the story of black enlistment and black soldiering that dominates most accounts of black agency during the Civil War, the flight of noncombatant women and children to Union lines also played a significant role in accelerating slavery's downfall, in creating a northward diaspora, and in making emancipation a national event.

A Time of Scattering

3 "Overrun with Free Negroes" The Politics of Wartime Emancipation and Migration in the Upper Midwest

Major Lyman Allen wrote to his hometown newspaper in March 1863, inquiring: "Are there any contrabands wanted in Iowa City, or its vicinity for help this spring? If so, please let me hear from you. I could send a large number to Iowa, if they were wanted, as there are many brought up the river at this time." Writing from St. Louis, he noted that many former slaves gathered there "prefer going to Iowa than any other place." But at home, some of Allen's Iowa neighbors had other plans. They organized a public meeting to oppose "all schemes . . . to fill our schools and domestic circle with the African race." They believed that recently emancipated African Americans, "unaccustomed to our climate, unskilled in our mode of agriculture, undisciplined in habits, and unfit for society," would "destroy the dignity of white labor" in Johnson County.[1] That white Iowans were not all of one mind about the arrival of emancipated slaves was also suggested in the tone of press coverage when former slaves appeared at a nearby Mississippi River town. Rife with sarcasm, the local paper reported that potential employers for the new arrivals were not difficult to find: "When the negroes arrived, there was a great fluttering . . . for the best 'take.' Philanthropy ran very high indeed—provided the services of a good stout negro could be obtained for his victuals and clothes. Visions of retired gentlemen and gentlewomen, with black servants to attend their every want and wish, overcame some . . . [who] felt as though 'it were the happiest day of their lives.' "[2] White midwesterners were divided on the implications of their recent arrival in the region, but whether they welcomed the newly freed African Americans as a new source of labor or feared workplace competition, whether they participated in philanthropic work on behalf of former slaves or distrusted the motives of those who did, white midwesterners agreed on one thing: that the consequences of emancipation extended well beyond the slaveholding South. As they imagined and responded to the consequences of emancipation, midwesterners helped create a regional as well as a national public politics of race.

By the eve of the Civil War, public debate and conflict over the social place of African Americans in the nation already had a long history, often expressed as concerns about their physical location. These apprehensions occasionally erupted into violence against northern blacks, but among some blacks and most whites, their anxieties coalesced more peacefully in the colonization and emigration movements, whose advocates asserted that white supremacy left no opening for black political and civic equality in the United States.[3] These disputes about "place" and location—and their consequences for African Americans—gained urgency when northerners contemplated the possibility of slavery's wartime destruction. As Harriet Beecher Stowe observed early in the conflict: "Many well-meaning people can form no idea of immediate emancipation but one full of dangers and horrors. They imagine the blacks free from every restraint of law, roaming abroad a terror and nuisance to the land."[4] From the Connecticut soldier fed up with emancipation celebrations in Beaufort, S.C., who threatened to kill any former slave who tried to "get in on" him, to the Iowan who complained of freed men and women "crowding" whites on local sidewalks, many northern whites shared the fear that removing the bonds of slavery would bring unwelcome change to the "place" of African Americans—and, by implication, the place of whites—in a postemancipation nation.[5]

In 1862, *Harper's Weekly* condemned those attitudes as petty and unchristian but joined Stowe in acknowledging their strength and persistence. The nation could not "tolerate negroes, except as slaves. We can't bear them. We don't want them in our houses. We won't meet them in public assemblages, or concede to them any rights whatever, except the bare right of living and working for us, sometimes for wages, generally without." The *Liberator*, William Lloyd Garrison's radical abolitionist newspaper out of Boston, confirmed the "existence of a very extensive hostility of feeling against the negro among the people of the free States," most notably "on the part of some of the North-Western States, to expel, or other-wise oppress, the unhappy blacks who are now seeking refuge among them."[6]

As readers and writers, legislators and city council members, farmers and dockhands, workers and employers, northern women and men debated the possible outcomes of emancipation. Among them, most northern blacks rejected the prospect of colonization and instead embraced the hope that southern liberation would lead to full political and civic equality. That hope was not without foundation; besides the real and symbolic importance of emancipation and black enlistment, during the war there was some erosion of discriminatory laws in Iowa, Illinois, California, and Ohio, as well as successful challenges to streetcar segregation in New York and Washington, D.C. Still, advocates for racial equality knew that more would be needed to end, as one black journalist described it, the "mockery of freedom" that northern blacks endured, with the "pain, the penalties, the soul-cutting degradations" of their circumscribed citizenship.[7] State laws, public support, and generations of practice fortified legal and customary discrimination against any easy incursion, yet the war seemed poised to threaten this status quo. From Washington, D.C., to Canada West, whites anxiously predicted that liberation would be followed by an unwelcome northward migration of African Americans. Many whites feared the consequences if Republican efforts to expand black freedom in the South enlarged the expectations of former slaves as they made their way north. By framing emancipation as a southern problem that southern blacks might bring into the North, northern whites participated in a powerful national amnesia about the extent, duration, and consequences of northern slavery.[8]

As whites increasingly apprehended that African Americans fleeing slavery might choose to leave the South, they began to link emancipation and migration as possible outcomes of the war. National debates over "place," the social position of African Americans in a racially stratified society, became yoked to white anxieties about "location," as slavery's wartime collapse accelerated the migration and relocation of former slaves out of the South. The war's emancipationist direction brought with it the unanswered question: What would be the social, political, and geographic destiny of African Americans in the aftermath of slavery's destruction? Opposition to black migration and the defense of white privilege were expressed not only in fiery rhetoric, or in caricatures circulated in the popular press, but also in action: in efforts to use the power of the state to sustain white privilege and black exclusion from the region; in assemblies that ranged from local protest meetings to larger mass gatherings and ritualized mob actions; in threatened and actual physical violence. Sharply aware of the extent of opposition to black migration among northern and border-state whites, Congress and the president brought colonization proposals forward with nearly every discussion of emancipation.[9] The arrival of former slaves in the upper Midwest fueled this debate.

Among many midwesterners, emancipating and aiding former slaves who intended to stay in the South were viewed as a humanitarian issue. But when former slaves—by their own volition or with the help of others—made their way north, emancipation became an increasingly critical and vigorously debated matter of public policy. Revealing a deep-seated belief in the benefits and necessity of a racially stratified society, many whites assumed that any black gains in the region would diminish their own status and citizenship. For those midwesterners whose understanding of white supremacy had been premised on their right and ability to exclude first Native Americans and then African Americans from the region, the physical mobility of former slaves suggested an undesirable change in racial boundaries and practices in a post-slavery nation.

On midwestern farms, in the churches and shops of small towns, and on the streets and levees of midwestern cities, the entry of newly emancipated slaves into the region inspired partisan debate, infiltrated political rhetoric, and informed political behavior. Their arrival became a lightning rod for regional debate over the causes and consequences of war, the proper reach and function of the Federal government, and the meaning of masculinity in households seemingly turned upside down by the war, as well as over the definition and implications of black freedom and citizenship. From the threat of a "black tide heading up the Mississippi" to the portrayal of African Americans "coming in vast herds to the fair prairies of the North West," the caricatures of black migration appearing in the regional Democratic press and a larger popular culture drew their exaggerated imagery out of the midwestern landscape, dehumanizing black migrants by likening them to the cattle and hogs driven to Mississippi valley market towns. Even more exaggerated were the portrayals of migration's consequences, threatening that jobs left vacant by Union soldiers would be "filled by lazy, shiftless negroes," and that the dependents of white workingmen would be driven to the same economic and social level as blacks, "until the white man conscious of the outrage inflicted upon him, would rise up and throw off the incubus."[10] These inflated images of the scale and consequences of black migration have largely been treated by scholars as partisan tools to derail Radical Republican agendas and rally Democratic votes, as expressions of "negrophobia," a descriptive term that does little to locate racialized rhetoric in time or place. This collection of images, caricatures, and language was part of the overt expression of a complex and multidimensional politics of race, and its exaggerations and escalated racial anxieties attest to the war's challenges to racial thought and practice in the upper Midwest. Most importantly, this rhetoric was never limited to political campaigns or party schemes; it quickly found wide expression in the political behavior of everyday life—in mass meetings, in associational life, in households and private correspondence, as well as on farms and levees. It also found expression in mob violence, attacks on recently relocated blacks and their white employers, and efforts to enforce state laws excluding the in-migration of free blacks. Its power and pervasiveness persuaded the Lincoln administration and the president's commanders in the field to develop alternatives to the relocation of contrabands outside the South.[11] For former slaves migrating to the upper Midwest, the wartime politics over the place and location of black people made their homes, their livelihood, their very freedom a site of conflict.

This conflict began in earnest during the early spring of 1862. Of the unknown number of southern slaves who migrated to the upper Mississippi valley during the first year of civil war, only a few appear to have relocated with the assistance of northerners—aid provided under a veil of secrecy, apparently in fear that the Fugitive Slave Law might be enforced.[12] By the winter and spring of 1862, U.S. troops began arranging for the transportation north of individual former slaves who had made their way into Union camps. These were some of the same soldiers and officers who had experienced high-level, home-front support for their defense of fugitive slaves from forcible return to rebel masters. In the national press and to President Lincoln, Iowa's Senator James W. Grimes and Governor Samuel Kirkwood defended officers in their state who refused to enforce more fully Henry Halleck's November 1861 exclusion order.[13] But when midwestern soldiers and officers not only protected southern slaves in the South but also began helping some of them in relocating north, official and public support evaporated. Relocated former slaves were then viewed not as recipients of philanthropy but a source of conflict and unwanted change.[14] Thus, while relocation temporarily eased the pressures on Union officers and military resources in the South, it aroused the fears of white midwesterners that Federal authorities would unleash a flood of black migrants in their region.

Newspapers were instrumental in popularizing and framing the increasingly inflammatory prospect of large-scale black migration northward. The wartime press, Mark McNeely reminds us, with its "snarling and confrontational tone," was an integral component of party politics, existing to promote political interests rather than to render calm, disinterested reporting of the news. The financial survival of newspapers depended on direct funding from political parties, on government printing contracts offered by the party in office, and on subscriptions from party members.[15] The racist and anti-abolition campaigning that had marked Democratic partisanship politics on the eve of war now turned to the political mileage to be gained from slavery's wartime erosion. Beginning in May 1862, and intensifying with the confluence of the Preliminary Emancipation Proclamation, the 1862 election campaigns, and the first arrival of large groups of former slaves relocated to the upper Midwest under the auspices of the Union army, newspapers of all political persuasions became engaged in a virulent war of words about the potential consequences of slavery's demise and the implications for race relations in the Midwest. While black migrants from the South were the primary targets of this discourse, whites were also targeted—particularly those considered to be advocates or agents of black migration.

As they questioned and castigated the motives and actions of white advocates of black migration, Democratic newspapers asserted that such individuals were neither charitable nor philanthropic. Rather, they were cynical employers in search of cheap labor, "cold-hearted," "selfish partisans," exploiting vulnerable freed slaves who would accept dismally low wages. Whites employed former slaves because they wanted to "play the lord" and "imitate the patriarchs of old," having black servants meet their every imagined need, while brutally mistreating them. These were not merely inflammatory characterizations; they also served to politicize, in explicitly racialized ways, the already contested terrain of Civil War relief work—a terrain where men and women, as well as local and national organizations, competed to position themselves as the appropriate arbiters of charity and of the recipients of charity work.[16] Politicizing aid to southern freedpeople in this manner may have influenced a wider public opinion. Consider that in 1861 and 1862, not even those white midwesterners most sympathetic to abolition felt compelled to act.[17] It was late 1863 before Iowa Quakers began systematically organizing relief at the local level. Wisconsin Methodists were tentative in 1862; not until late 1863 did they adopt a sympathetic posture toward emancipation and assistance to former slaves at their annual conference.[18] For most northern whites, white soldiers and needy white families presented a far more compelling and legitimate call on their energies and financial resources. Indeed, the women who joined in the first attempts to help former slaves were ridiculed. A Minnesota paper offered a harsh assessment of the female teachers and missionaries "gadding about Beaufort pretending to instruct lazy negroes," in contrast to the "industry and soothing care of the pious, blessed Sisters of Mercy among the thousands of sick soldiers at Louisville."[19]

In their evasive responses to Democratic charges, Republican newspapers confirmed—and, in their own way, contributed to—the persuasive appeals to northern racism. Their strategy was not to defend black relocation, but instead to deflect Democratic accusations of Republican involvement in relocation. They denied "any great love" for African Americans and refused to engage in substantive discussions about racial equality. To the contrary, they suggested that Democratic threats of black competition with white laborers revealed a presumption that blacks were somehow superior to whites—which Republicans were quick to reject. Iowa's oldest Republican newspaper con-

Civil War Envelope, 1861. Several versions of this image appeared on commercially printed Civil War envelopes. The image and the caption refer to General Benjamin Butler's 1861 decision to employ the labor of fugitives from Confederate slaveowners at Fort Monroe, Virginia, declaring them "contraband of war"—enemy property subject to confiscation. M. W. Davis Scrapbook, Ss 5, Special Collections, State Historical Society of Iowa, Iowa City.

tended that African Americans were of such inferior ability and intelligence that they could never compete with white workers.[20] Black migration northward, the paper insisted, was not the result of an invitation extended by abolitionists or Republicans. Rather, it was the consequence of Democratic resistance to emancipation in the South. Republican newspapers also appealed to a crude scientific racism by asserting that African Americans were "better suited" to the southern climate and would not want to relocate northward. So great was that "southward pull" that a reverse migration southward of northern blacks would occur if only the Union army would pursue a more consistent emancipation policy. Democratic exaggerations of the numbers of former slaves moving northward were dismissed as a "dirty trick," part of a baseless partisan effort to exploit "the prejudices against the 'nager.'" It was Democratic partisanship that instigated the many cruel race riots that occurred in the summer and fall of 1862. Lastly, Republicans charged midwestern Democrats with duplicitous complicity: Democrats were eagerly employing the newly arriving contrabands themselves. (Later in the war, Republicans said, Democrats eagerly hired blacks as substitutes for the draft.)

Not all of the heated debates about the arrival of former slaves in the North were partisan, of course. Commercial envelopes bearing illustrations and messages were quite popular during the war (at least 277 northern companies sold these "patriotic covers"), and dozens of the more than 2,500 designs since discovered by collectors and researchers focused on the flight of former slaves from their masters to Union lines and to the North. These caricatures of "contrabands" did not simply illustrate black flight; they also conveyed the

Civil War Envelope, 1861. Following the popularity of commercially printed "contraband" envelopes that commented on the flight of enslaved people to Union lines, some manufacturers began to produce new images that emphasized the northward migration of black fugitives. These images drew on antebellum antislavery popular culture, with images of the North Star and references to enslaved people as chattel property. American Broadsides and Ephemera, ser. 1, no. 24740, American Antiquarian Society and Newsbank, Inc.

North's ambivalence toward it by sometimes portraying contrabands as cartoonish buffoons. The historian Alice Fahs has argued that these images provided "a circumscribed vision of how freedmen and freedwomen would become part of a new national family."[21]

But it was the Democratic Party—in newspapers, campaigns, and several dimensions of political behavior during the war—that kept the issue of labor competition before the public eye and proved most effective in framing the racial politics of war, slavery's demise, and the consequences for working

Civil War Envelope, 1861. A significant subgroup of commercially printed Civil War envelopes commented, through image and caption, on the arrival of so-called contrabands in the North. Most of the covers used caricatured speech, clothing, and facial features to ridicule and denigrate black migrants, and contributed a widely circulated vicious satire to northern white debates about the "place" of African Americans in the North. M. W. Davis Scrapbook, Ss 5, Special Collections, State Historical Society of Iowa, Iowa City.

people in the North.[22] Local newspaper reporting and editorializing provided an important interpretation of the much larger national print culture of the war, which scholars such as Fahs and Kathleen Diffley have identified as wide ranging and abundant, from newspapers and periodicals to photographs, stationary and envelopes, song sheets, engravings, and a variety of popular literature. In the Midwest, photographs of soldiers in camp attended by contrabands, commercially printed envelopes caricaturing slaves in flight from the South, and illustrations of the uneven and violent wartime collapse of slavery in *Harper's Weekly* would have been filtered through the interpretive lens of local, partisan newspapers.[23] The outcome of the 1862 elections offered a tremendous boost to midwestern Democrats, and while the vote against Lincoln's handling of the battlefield and the home front drew on a number of issues, the racist campaign against black relocation had reverberated loudly throughout the region.[24]

MIDWESTERN UNDERSTANDINGS OF emancipation were compounded by regional perceptions of national developments. The Democratic Party's success in focusing resistance to relocation tapped not only into the region's racism, but also into growing apprehensions about the changing role of the Federal gov-

Wartime Emancipation and Migration

ernment. The Preliminary Emancipation Proclamation was but one of a series of developments that led midwesterners, like many other northern whites, to associate the Republican Party with an increasingly centralized, powerful Federal government whose policies were affecting daily life in unprecedented and unwelcome ways.[25] Steady inflation had already brought home the cost of war, and some midwesterners felt that Federal aid to fugitive slaves was depriving more worthy citizens of support. Civilians and soldiers alike ruminated on the expense of helping the contrabands. On the cost of assisting contrabands during five months at Fortress Monroe in Virginia, one Minnesota newspaper reported: "$62,000 of your money taken . . . to keep in idleness a lot of vagrant negroes." In Wisconsin, the *Manitowoc Pilot* complained that the expense of relocation was shouldered by the public treasury, while the cost of supporting blacks once they had arrived would be assumed by local white residents. "Meanwhile," the paper continued, "the white laborer . . . through out the north, has to pay about double for everything . . . everything must go 'up,' 'up,' if we white men must be compelled thus to feed, clothe, nurse, and take care of the millions of lazy contrabands, which the abolitionists threaten to loose upon us."[26]

It was not only the cost of Federal aid that excited midwestern criticism, but also the symbolic meaning of the unprecedented expenditure of human and financial resources seemingly on behalf of African Americans. Although their votes helped elect Abraham Lincoln president, few whites in the region disagreed with Stephen Douglas's insistence that the nation was "founded on the white basis." Most expected both the state and the Federal government to protect their privileges as white citizens.[27] The editor of one Wisconsin newspaper, reporting on Lincoln's December 1862 address to Congress, complained that "the President is troubled with 'nigger on the brain.' The message commences with 'nigger,' and ends with 'nigger,'—not a word for the benefit of the white people of the country."[28] Public and private discussions of black migration and employment also revealed a growing resentment that the increasingly powerful Federal government was failing to safeguard what current scholarship would call the political and psychological wages of whiteness. That failure was viewed as part of the erosion of the racially determined economic and political privileges that many white midwesterners believed lay at the core of the republic.[29] In the Midwest, it was particularly because of the juxtaposition of the Federal government's conduct regarding the Dakota Sioux, white citizens, and former slaves that some came to believe Washington was failing to act in the best interests of white citizens, even demonstrating preferential treatment of nonwhites.

Wartime Emancipation and Migration

Regional antagonism toward the national government was significantly shaped by the events surrounding the Dakota uprising of 1862. Perhaps nothing was more critical to the racial self-consciousness of midwestern whites than their claim to have "civilized" the region by conquering, containing, and displacing Native Americans, a process enabled and mediated by Federal, territorial, and state authorities. The failure of U.S. Indian policy during the Civil War compounded the criticism of the government's wartime priorities and policies. In August 1862, in an uprising fueled by the malfeasance of Federal Indian agents and white settlers' disregard of Native American treaty rights, Dakota warriors in southern Minnesota killed about five hundred white settlers and militiamen; thousands of white midwesterners fled their homes. Alarm spread quickly to midwestern communities far from the fighting, including central and eastern Wisconsin, where rumors of imminent attack heightened anti-Indian racism and prompted hysteria and panicked flight.[30] From the perspective of many white midwesterners, the Federal response to the Minnesota uprising was characterized by inadequate relief for white victims, slow and ineffective military retaliation, and the ultimate insult of Lincoln's offer of clemency to all but 38 of the 307 Dakota and métis who were convicted by a military commission. The largest mass execution in American history did little to allay the anger of midwestern whites. In a region where the very presence of white settlers was sanctioned by the state-supported effort to dominate and expel Native Americans, the Federal government's failure to divert manpower and resources to a more immediate and brutal military response was viewed by whites as a deep betrayal.[31] That sense of betrayal was sharpened by the belief among white settlers that even while their needs were ignored, large sums of public funds were being spent to support fugitive slaves in the South. As one editor noted:

> The just demands and unquestioned rights of Minnesota have no chance in this Congress. Suffering from the horrors of an unparalleled Indian massacre, the fault or not of the very powers from whom she seeks redress, she comes to Congress with her country devastated, her women ravished—murdered a thousand times over—her suckling children hanging crucified to her door posts, her men lying on the plains and in the ditches, the victims of infernal fiends, and implores assistance—redress. The answer is, Wait. "Four millions of Southern slaves must have their freedom." . . . Little is expected of this Congress but the eternal discussion of the nigger question.[32]

Further aggravating Minnesotans' view of the misplaced priorities of the Republican administration was the army's transport of more than one hundred contrabands to St. Paul, ostensibly to support the military expedition against the Dakotas. More than half of those conveyed were women and children, whom local whites regarded as a burden, not a help, during this time of crisis. "Women and pickaninnies will not render material assistance in driving mule teams over the plains," grumbled the editor of the *St. Paul Pioneer*. On the levees, city policemen and Irish gangs physically resisted the arrival of the former slaves.[33] As citizens denounced the administration's response to the Dakota uprising and its aftermath, they affirmed a uniquely midwestern white perspective on Republicanism and free labor ideology. Easterners had repeatedly failed the West. From the panic of 1857 and its deadening impact on midwestern enterprises (blamed by many on eastern bankers and financiers), to wartime tariffs and inflated freight costs on eastern-owned railroads, to Washington's inadequately punitive response to the Dakota uprising, a midwestern identity was being forged that strongly reinforced white privilege and authority.[34]

In addition to the impact of national and regional developments on midwestern responses to emancipation and relocation, the most disparate of wartime incidents also evoked anxieties about the erosion of their status and prerogatives. Ignoring the efforts among African Americans to gain the right to enlist, some whites charged that, until late 1863, white families shouldered the burdens of military service while black families did not. Some argued that pension board authorities subjected the widows of black veterans to less rigorous rules than white widows. White soldiers "feel hurt; insulted" that Congress was putting "the African on equal footing." A Wisconsin officer declared that he had not gone to eastern battlefields "from the grand west . . . to wrangle over Virginia niggers and South Carolina niggers and other niggers." White soldiers "are placed under guard if they dare to say 'Nigger' to a darkey," asserted Iowa's *Oskaloosa Times*. When Senator Charles Sumner described a Union soldier's act of kindness toward a slave girl as "the most touching" act of the war, he was furiously criticized in the Midwest for making a symbol of a black child rather than highlighting the wartime sacrifices of white women. Others contended that the loss of family farms to mortgage companies drew little sympathy because only white families were affected; had those farmers been black, they suggested, a host of philanthropists would be offering aid. St. Louis shoemakers posed the question many midwesterners asked among themselves: "Have we no eye for the relief of anybody but negroes? Are we not just as much entitled to freedom as the negro?"[35] Early in 1862, Iowa legislators were presented with a resolution demanding "that at least one-half of the time be given to legislating for white men."[36]

As military service took a greater and greater toll on white families (midwestern troops experienced particularly high mortality rates in the western theater of war, and working-class households were hard hit by the absence of wage earners and farmhands), resentment increased; some believed that white soldiers were frequently slighted to the advantage of fugitive slaves and free blacks. As one Minnesota soldier said, "I am as much in favor of abolishing slavery as anybody . . . but since I have been in the Army and seen them better treated than White Men . . . I lost all my love for the colored Gentlemen."[37] A Wisconsin newspaper asserted that white soldiers—their families in want and themselves without food or clothing—"must stand aside" while the government attended to former slaves. "In some countries," the paper concluded, "it is an advantage to be a nigger."[38] According to a Minnesota paper, contrabands received better rations (fresh bread) than white soldiers ("hard, mouldy, wormy crackers").[39] Rumors spread that white soldiers were arrested for using commonplace derogatory language to former slaves, whereas blacks were free to insult white soldiers. White men in uniform were reported to have been barred from public events that admitted African Americans. Rumors flew on the home front about "the pernicious workings of the 'Freedom Policy,'" in which "hundreds on hundreds of the hated negroes . . . flock to the stations on rail roads running north, claiming protection and transportation to the exclusion of sick soldiers, and army stores." Shocked that their accustomed racial privileges seemed under assault by a government in which African Americans could not even claim to be citizens, white soldiers, their families, and their larger communities were loud and clear in their protests. "What next will the colored people get from our long heeled despots superior to that which they dole out to white people?" asked one Iowa editor.[40]

The ideas white midwesterners held about race and place in their society became explicit in the public dialogue that accompanied wartime black migration. Male or female, former slaves were often derided as impertinent and disrespectful to whites, eager to challenge the public rituals of racial domination and subordination, and anxious to claim privileges associated with whiteness. Men and women alike were portrayed as "impudent and fresh" in their bearing toward whites. Whites claimed to suffer "many and gross outrages at the hands of these fugitives from the South," who refused to yield on city sidewalks, refused to doff their hats when spoken to, refused to remain silent when treated in a disrespectful or demeaning manner.[41] Midwestern whites involved in freedmen's aid work in the South were "troubled" to see former slave women preferring the long dresses that white women regularly wore rather than the shorter dresses that seemed better "suited to their form, color, condition."[42] Newly arrived former slave women were caricatured as styling themselves too good for menial household labor, falsely imbued with the notion that better things awaited them in their new homes.[43] If these accounts are suspect for their one-sidedness, they nonetheless confirm what many midwestern whites had feared about the uncontainable consequences of emancipation and relocation: former slaves rejected the notion that the destruction of slavery constituted the extent of black freedom, and, in so doing, challenged the very foundations of white privilege in the region.

Fear of how emancipation and the movement of former slaves northward would alter midwestern life often focused on the workplace. The war "multiplied and politicized laborers' grievances against the Republican Party," notes the historian Iver Bernstein.[44] Besides their efforts to improve conditions on the job and work hours, as well as to organize locally and nationally, white laborers fought against the ominous rate of wartime inflation. Though wages for most workers increased by 50 to 60 percent, those increases failed to keep pace with an inflation rate of almost 100 percent.[45]

Not all workers' grievances were material. As Jacqueline Jones observes in her study of race and American labor, "Jobs are never just jobs; they are social markers of great real and symbolic value."[46] How fragile were the ideas and practices that protected white privilege in the midwestern workplace, that kept most black workers out of all but the most menial work, and that perpetuated the notion that independence and dependence were racialized? It seemed that white employers could not be counted on to maintain the exclusive white workplace. Both before and after the Federal government relocated contrabands to the North, some employers experimented with using former slaves to replace enlisted workers or as substitutes for striking workers.[47] "White" jobs were disappearing. The editor of one southeastern Iowa paper insisted that "a white drayman can scarcely live; neither can a blacksmith, plasterer, nor many other tradesmen, to say nothing of common laborers," because of the competition from black workers.[48] In July 1864, the *Constitution* decried the practice of "would be loyal merchants" who fired white men and hired "female shades to do their work at such reduced prices, that, considering the present rates for the commodities it would be impossible for any man of a family to keep his head above water."[49] "Why not?" asked one Iowa editor. "While the bones of your sons are bleaching on the southern plains, allow the accursed source of all our trouble to come here and enjoy the business your sons are deprived of, and compete with the poor laborers of your State?"[50] Again, the sense of government betrayal exacerbated white concerns: "White men and women in want of employment, are advised to black themselves with burnt cork, rubbed with lard, and make immediate application to the Government.... Ebony is all the go now, and who would not prefer a black skin to an empty stomach?"[51] Lincoln's assurances in December 1862 that emancipation would "enhance" the wages of white workers fell on disbelieving ears.[52]

Worries about losing jobs and, by extension, economic and political independence went far beyond the exchange of partisan editorials: black workers and their white employers were the targets of mass meetings, protests, threats, and occasional violence. Men gathered in Iowa's Wapello and Johnson counties to "resist the introduction of free negroes into Iowa; first by lawful means, and when that fails, we will drive them, together with such whites as may be engaged in bringing them in, out of the State or afford them 'hospitable graves.'" Many protests and physical attacks targeted farmers—the largest source of jobs in the Midwest. In Iowa, Page County farmers who had employed "some colored girls ... in their houses ... were soon notified, by a man in their neighborhood ... that they must send those 'niggers' back, or they would be burnt out." Similar threats were made against an Appanoose County farmer who had hired former slaves. A farmer in Muscatine County employing a contraband boy was visited by twenty local residents who hoped, "by threats of personal violence," to "convince him of his error."[53] Even the chaplains who assisted in the relocation process were not exempt. The Reverend James B. Rogers, superintendent of contrabands at Corinth, Mississippi, and then at Cairo, Illinois, escorted seventy-five people to his hometown of Fond du Lac, Wisconsin, so local farmers might hire them. Rogers's own home was set upon by late-night vandals. "Don't I know," recalled one of those contrabands, a small child who was sleeping there that night, "how they threw a rock through the window of his house?"[54] The African Americans in Fond du Lac were subjected to persistent harassment, according to Van Spence, who recalled of his arrival: "We couldn't walk down the street without having some one jeering at us" and calling out insults.[55]

While the intensity and occasional violence of these protests reflected a deep investment in a segregated economy and fears about the erosion of the social context of white labor, it is difficult to reconcile the fear of replacement by black workers with the widely acknowledged labor shortage affecting the region. The war not only increased demand for midwestern agricultural products, but also, through enlistments, had significantly reduced the agricultural workforce.[56] In 1864, in light of the farm labor shortage, Iowa's Governor William Stone issued a proclamation limiting out-migration from the state to those who obtained a pass signed by the provost marshal.[57] "No whites can be gotten," insisted labor-hungry farmers; blacks were the "last resort" of employers desperate for workers. When shiploads of contrabands disembarked at Mississippi River towns in the upper Midwest, they were often outnumbered by the employers who anxiously awaited them.[58] Furthermore, hundreds—if not thousands—of these African Americans were relocated to farms and households throughout the region not by the Federal government but by midwestern soldiers and officers to help their own struggling families.[59]

Competing claims among native-born, immigrant, and ethnic Americans to other prerogatives of whiteness were an underlying dynamic in shaping the response to emancipation and black migration. Wartime developments unrelated to black migration had already nurtured midwestern nativism. In Davenport, Iowa, for example, foreign-born men who obtained exemptions from the draft were singled out to have their names published in the newspaper, and the city council resolved not to offer public employment to any of them.[60] The *Milwaukee See-Bote*, the leading paper of Wisconsin's German Catholics and strongly critical of the Lincoln administration and the war, was banished from circulation in U.S. army camps in southeastern Missouri; its editor, Peter Deuster, was threatened with arrest by Federal marshals. The only antidraft riot in the upper Midwest centered in the German immigrant communities of Ozaukee County, Wisconsin (besides Indiana, Wisconsin was the only midwestern state that had to resort to the draft in 1862).[61] Native-born employers, who responded to strikes or labor shortages by hiring black workers, were willing to deny Irish and other working-class immigrants the privilege of an all-white workplace.[62] The tenuous hold of unskilled Irish workers, in particular, on white entitlements was also revealed in reports that blamed Irish workers for the most vigorous opposition to black relocation.[63] From St. Paul came comparisons of the "low Irish" and newly arrived African Americans: "The contrast between the two classes as they came in contact was decidedly in favor of the contrabands, and the Irish appreciated it by expressing fear of competition." Local newspapers announced that the Irish had good reason to fear competition from the more pliable contraband laborers, who were excluded from unions and unlikely to make the kinds of demands expressed by Irish workers.[64]

Some of the recent black migrants also encountered hostility from African Americans who had lived in the Midwest for some time. One former slave who left Missouri for St. Paul during the war would recall the clear "line of demarcation" between antebellum black residents of the city, then referred to as "colored people," and the wartime arrivals from the South, referred to as "contraband." He described the former as more settled, holding more skilled occupations, and as setting themselves apart from the latter.[65] In Iowa, one of the most explicit observations of similar tensions came from Moses Mosely, also a wartime migrant (along with his family) out of Missouri slavery. In his account of arriving in Mt. Pleasant, Mosely described a small portion of longer-term black residents who "kicked a little on the freedom of the colored man." Some had been free blacks in the South who insisted that "we are none of your low, contraband niggers; we came by our freedom honorably." According to Mosely, these black residents "seemed to think that their freedom would be impeded by such an influx of contrabands":

> When the time came for the general emancipation of the slaves, this fractional class, above named, was only lukewarm on the subject; there was some danger of losing their position at the head of the colored columns to be succeeded by some raw slaves from the lower grades of the human family, and this of course was not at all desirable on their part. . . . They . . . complained of the contrabands swarming into towns and other public places, taking the work from the free people and often making unbecoming remarks.[66]

Although firsthand observations of the reception provided by more settled blacks are rare, they reveal a credible source of conflict that would have sharpened the challenges faced by new arrivals. They also remind us that black communities in the Midwest were not unified in their response to wartime migration.

WITH ALL THE outrage over the erosion of white workingmen's rights in the face of emancipation and relocation, as well as the criticism of those whites who employed black workers, it would be easy to overlook the fact that the majority of relocated and migrating contrabands were women and children, and that their employers were very often white women.[67] Many midwestern women were eager to employ former slave women as household and farm workers, despite white men's intentions to defend the domestic circle from "the African race." Indeed, some women took an active role in encouraging and arranging for the transportation of former slaves north. White women who were sympathetic toward the plight of slaves, or were simply desperate for domestic and farm help, responded enthusiastically when authorities invited northerners to apply for contraband laborers. Several women made inquiries through Annie Wittenmyer, the Midwest's preeminent wartime relief organizer, hoping that her extensive contacts in the South could help them obtain black workers. Their detailed lists of specific preferences suggest the perception of former slaves as commodities: "If a good servant could be had I would take her even with a child—rather than not get one," wrote a woman from Bentonsport, Iowa. Another sought a "woman from 18 to 40—capable of general housework. Should she have a boy—or brother from 12 to 16—and even a young child—we will take them all." She noted that "there are quite a number here that would be glad to get them [women]—for servants"; she needed help "—oh so much—and what we get here is so poor." A number of families in and near Vinton, Iowa, were looking for contrabands to work as field hands as well as house servants. Many others made arrangements with missionaries and ministers working in contraband camps, as well as their enlisted male kin stationed in the Mississippi valley. Orrin Densmore wrote his son, a Minnesota soldier: "You know just what we want—a servant that is *neat honest* & *active*. I earnestly hope you will find a 'darkey woman' suited to your mind and ship her forthwith for Red Wing." With so many midwestern women struggling to keep households and farms afloat, the opportunity to hire contraband women was a welcomed development. In fact, as such efforts produced favorable outcomes, friends and neighbors soon followed suit. His own family's success, another Densmore commented, "had given house wives all around the wench fever."[68]

Former slave women were also widely employed as farmhands in the Midwest, and contrasting perceptions of black and white women's field work reveals the racializing consequences of wartime developments. Initially, northern whites complained about the predominance of women among the migrants; in November 1862, the *New York Times* thought it "unfortunate" that so many of the fugitive slaves entering Union lines were women, "when farm laborers would find a welcome in almost any part of the country."[69] Two days later, though, the paper conceded that former slave women were eagerly hired by midwestern employers.[70] Although white women could be found in the fields in the absence of male laborers, they were regarded as making a temporary, albeit important, contribution to the war effort. Black female farmhands, on the other hand, were seen as "able-bodied," "rough," "athletic" women; they were employed in physically demanding labor not because of temporary exigencies but because their womanhood was regarded as different from—and inferior to—that of their white counterparts.[71] The white perception was that whereas white women were heroines of the farm, whose patriotic sacrifices complemented their idealized womanhood rather than jeopardizing it, black women were well-suited for the physical demands of farmwork.

Some thought black women lacked the refinement to be domestic servants. Quakers involved in missionary and philanthropic work among the Cairo contrabands described former slave women there as more suitable for farm labor than household work. A potential employer seeking a woman for a house servant was warned that she took the former slave woman "at your own risk."[72] When military officials and civilian philanthropists involved in the organized relocation of former slave women described them as being "provided with good situations at fair wages," they meant that those "situations" were "good" for black women; no white woman would have been asked to take up such a position except out of temporary necessity.[73] Some observers went so far as to suggest that black women were not merely suited to farmwork, but in fact could die without it. According to one St. Paul newspaper in 1863, women who had been forced, as slaves, to perform "all manner of hard farm labor" were now dying "by the score" in contraband camps, in part because of the "want of exercise."[74] The different meanings attached to black and white women's farmwork—brute strength versus womanly sacrifice—point to the war's racializing impact on ideas about gender and about womanhood in particular.

Although the debate over emancipation's impact on white privilege in the workplace often focused on male workers and occupations dominated by men, the dynamic meanings of race and free labor were also played out in midwestern households. The employment of newly arrived black women as domestics and farmworkers introduced complicated dynamics into the relationship between servants and the women who hired them. In St. Paul, white servants became viewed by some potential employers as less desirable than blacks, leading to an increased demand for newly arrived black workers.[75] For their part, whether native born or immigrant, white female servants rejected the prospect of working alongside black women. Louisa Johnson, a Swedish employee in a Minnesota household, was described by her employer as having "a fear that she and a darkey would be identified as help or that she would be set aside for the ebony article."[76] Yet families seeking household and farm help turned to former slaves in part because white workers took advantage of the wartime labor shortage to pursue more advantageous positions, especially at harvesttime, when they could demand higher wages.

Native-born whites harbored resentment at their abandonment by white immigrant workers seeking better opportunities, and it seems that the turn to black workers was part of the larger struggle over the meaning of race in the Midwest.[77] It is also important to consider whether the "wench fever" that swept midwestern communities reflected a perceived change in the status of white women who hired black, rather than white, household workers. Up to the Civil War, the employment of black servants had been limited to an elite group of whites—southerners vacationing along southern Minnesota's lakes who brought their slaves with them, former southerners who took their slaves when migrating to the Midwest, and army officers stationed in the Midwest who hired or purchased slaves as household servants. The ability to employ African American women as laborers imparted a new aura of status and respectability to midwestern white women, who not only needed the help to run their households and farms, but might also have relished their racial authority over black workers.[78]

Whether the employment of blacks offered a remedy for wartime labor shortages or unreliable immigrant workers, or provided an opportunity to boost their status, white women seeking to hire newly arrived African Americans often faced their strongest opposition from white men. In meetings, rallies, and the ongoing editorial dialogue over the threat posed by black migration, white men repeatedly asserted their right and intention to defend the racial purity of the white household and the family it sheltered. "While our brothers, sons and neighbors are doing battle in our country's cause, and enduring the hardships of the battle-field, we will keep their homes unspotted by the black race," asserted men in Johnson County, Iowa, and echoed by others in northern Powesheik County. "On account of the respect and affection we have for our wives, sisters, and daughters, we will resist all schemes . . . to fill our schools and domestic circle with the African race."[79] It is unclear whether these men, so ready to defend hearth and home against the "threat" posed by black women, were directing their protests to other white men or to the women who were so anxious to find household workers. But there is little doubt that the war had already eroded masculine authority in the domestic sphere; more than half of Iowa's white men of military age enlisted or were drafted during the war, leaving many farms and households absent of husbands, fathers, and elder sons who now found themselves in positions of receiving orders rather than giving them.[80]

The wartime economy may have benefited some, but many men found their ability to support their families seriously impaired by inflation, the loss of southern markets for their produce, and the absence of labor at critical moments. Added to these developments, in both private and public settings many white women were taking on unprecedented responsibilities, assuming increasingly public roles, and making themselves arbiters of loyalty and patriotism as they defined and monitored the obligations of their congregations and communities on behalf of the soldier and the Union cause.[81] While many men publicly endorsed the patriotism of their women, they may not have welcomed all of the changes (however short-term) that war brought to gender relations within their own households. Men's strident insistence on defending hearth and home was at least in part an effort to shore up their own political authority by reclaiming both the ability and the right to dictate the goings-on in their own families. After all, men who insisted on defending their families against the new migrants were also implying their ability to do so. That a defense of their authority could be framed in racialized terms—protecting the racial purity of their households—suggests how intimately male authority was linked with racial prerogative.

Jean Baker, in her study of political behavior during antebellum America, has noted in reference to the politics of race: "In the public mind, the Negro had been a preeminent issue in the North for some time, and the transfer between popular culture and racial policy was complete when the blacks' changed circumstances emerged as a partisan symbol of public disorder and civic pollution." Midwestern efforts to reinforce white racial prerogative during the wartime controversy over black migration demonstrated not just the symbolic nature of public political behavior, but its instrumental consequences as well.[82] In the effort to protect white privilege and restrict black geographic and social mobility, white midwesterners used an array of political weapons: they deployed the power of the state and formal political structures; they organized in gatherings that ranged from local protest meetings to larger mass gatherings, to ritualized mob actions; they threatened and applied physical violence. Midwestern Democrats successfully used the threat and imagery of black migration to gain white working-class support for their party, for their candidates, and for their criticism of the unraveling of black bondage under the Republican wartime administration. In 1862, the Iowa Democratic Convention resolved that "this is the Government of white men, and was established exclusively for the white race; that the negroes are not entitled to, and ought not to be admitted to political or social equality with the white race"; they are an "inferior and dependent race."[83]

The link between emancipation and black migration became a point of considerable political debate, not just in the Midwest, but across the North, in the West, and in the halls of Congress. During the summer of 1862, white hostility toward blacks had already erupted into riots in Toledo, Cincinnati, Chicago, and Peoria. By mid-October, fearing that relocating former slaves into the upper Midwest would provoke further civil unrest—and undermine support for Republican candidates in the upcoming election—the secretary of war brought organized relocation to an abrupt halt. After the election, the program was quickly resurrected and former slaves were once more transported north with the aid of military authorities and civilian groups.[84] Not only did the politics of black migration shape the 1862 election; those politics also fashioned debate later in the war about the nation's responsibilities toward freed slaves.[85] By the summer of 1863, the Lincoln administration looked to black enlistment and employment on abandoned plantations to solve the problems posed by the flow of fugitive slaves into Union lines and northern anxiety about migration. Nevertheless, organized relocation continued—and so did opposition efforts. Throughout the war, petition drives to obtain stringent antiblack migration laws were a popular means of protesting the possibility of labor competition with African Americans; they also became an instrument for mobilizing voters to the Democratic Party.[86]

Midwestern whites turned to the power of the state early in the war, drawing on the momentum of the antebellum colonization movement (very active in the upper Midwest in the 1850s) to support Lincoln's proposals for colonization explicitly as an answer to regional anxieties about the consequences of emancipation.[87] The premise behind this support, of course, was that an integrated society was not only undesirable but perhaps impossible, a premise of such leading figures as Iowa's Governor Kirkwood, Senator James Harlan, and former territorial supreme court justice Charles Mason, as well as Wisconsin's Senator James R. Doolittle. Harlan introduced a bill that authorized Lincoln to acquire a territory to which freed slaves could be sent; Doolittle argued for the voluntary emigration of slaves freed in the District of Columbia and urged that a liberal budget be designated to support it. Kirkwood and Mason had publicly supported colonization prior to as well as during the war.[88]

Political action was not only in the hands of political leaders. When the Iowa Democratic Party urged Iowans to petition the state to prevent an influx of African Americans, whites responded favorably and in 1862 submitted petitions from at least four counties. The Emancipation Proclamation of 1 January 1863 inspired a new round of petitioning for exclusion laws in Minnesota and Wisconsin.[89] As citizens, voters, and leading elected and appointed officials, midwestern white men were not hesitant to use the privilege from which African Americans were excluded—the power of formally recognized political voice and action—to assert their right to a white republic.

UNLIKE WISCONSIN AND Minnesota, Iowa had, since 1851, prohibited black migration. Although that law had been spottily invoked since its passage, and some questioned its legality, the antiblack migration sentiment of white Iowans coalesced in a singular and ultimately failed effort to enforce the law in early 1863. On 8 January 1863, just days after local whites had gathered to celebrate the Emancipation Proclamation, migrant and former slave Archie Webb received notice from a local justice of the peace that he was subject to arrest under the 1851 law prohibiting the migration of free blacks to Iowa. Webb had been in the state perhaps a month or two, having made the same journey north that thousands of other slaves would make during the war. Early in the conflict, Webb had been held on a plantation in the interior of Arkansas. When Union troops arrived in Helena, Webb took advantage of his master's absence to run away. At Helena, he found work in a camp of Iowa soldiers from Dubuque. Later he accompanied one of those soldiers, Melville Wright, to his home in northeastern Iowa. There, Webb was hired by Wright's father, James C. Wright, the newly elected secretary of state. When James moved to Des Moines to take up his position, he arranged work for Webb as a farmhand for Stephen Brooks, a substantial farmer and active Republican in Des Moines. Webb was not the only former slave employed by farmers in that township; most local farmers, a neighbor noted, preferred white labor, but there was none to be had, and some had found it necessary to hire former slaves to help with the work. This had raised the ire of several white neighbors, who organized a meeting on 8 January in which they resolved "that no more 'darkies' shall be permitted to dwell in the State of Iowa!"[90]

Two days later, a group of local white men, emboldened by the meeting, served Webb with a notice (signed by a township trustee and prepared by a Des Moines law firm) that he had three days to leave the state or face imprisonment and a fine. According to the law, if Webb was unable to pay the fine ($12.00) and court costs ($2.90), he would be hired out by the county to earn the penalties and then sent out of the state. Webb refused to comply, having been advised by white friends that the notice was groundless. Indeed, some Iowans felt that the law had never been published and so could not be enforced; state legislators opposed to black migration had failed in an effort to introduce a new version of the law in September 1862.[91] Nevertheless, a day or two later the sheriff, accompanied by James Wright, who wanted to ensure that the proceedings were conducted fairly, arrested Webb and confined him in the Des Moines jail.

The ongoing dispute about the real and threatened arrival of former slaves from the South was intensified by news of Webb's incarceration. Under headlines like "Lawless Arrest," "Nigger on the Brain," and "Nigger in the Woodpile," Iowa papers in the winter of 1863 debated the legality and propriety of Webb's seizure and the implications of his case. Opponents to black migration organized meetings to declare their intention to resist further black arrivals.[92] Webb's supporters characterized his arrest as an effort to "embarrass the execution of the President's Emancipation Proclamation in the Mississippi Valley."[93]

Wartime Emancipation and Migration

As the debates raged, a writ of habeas corpus was filed on Webb's behalf. At the hearing, he was advised by the judge to claim he was a slave, since slaves were exempt from the exclusion law. But Webb refused. After insisting that he was a free man and entitled to his liberty, he was released from jail until his suit for freedom could be heard by Judge John Henry Gray. Gray's decision, rendered on 2 February before a filled courthouse, declared the 1851 law unconstitutional in its attempt to deprive African Americans of their citizenship. Webb, he pronounced, was free to go. In response to the ruling, the defendants said they would appeal the case to the state supreme court. The following winter, before the case had been heard, the Des Moines sheriff's office and law officers elsewhere in the state resumed enforcing the statute. With several African American men again held in the Des Moines jail for violating the exclusion law, James Wright—the same secretary of state whose son had brought Webb to Iowa—persuaded a state representative to introduce a bill repealing the exclusion law. In April 1864 the bill passed, ending the question of the legality of black migration. But the debates over the implications and consequences of black migration continued.[94] Within days of the Webb ruling, Minnesota and Wisconsin voters submitted petitions to their state assemblies calling for the passage of exclusionary laws.[95]

While mass meetings, political partisanship, and pressure on state legislatures to enforce the privileges of whiteness created a difficult and challenging climate for African Americans in the Midwest, violence constantly escalated the meaning of those threats to blacks, both long-term residents and those newly arriving from the South. The language of violence permeated debates over the consequences of emancipation and black migration. When newspapers referred to a "war of extermination" against newly arriving blacks, when at public meetings white opponents threatened to "drive" them and their employers into "hospitable graves," and when the same white employers were visited by mobs forewarning bodily violence and destruction of property, the targets of such extreme rhetoric would have fearfully anticipated the unpredictable moment when words might be transformed into deeds.[96] In 1862 and 1863, those debates were joined by threats and violence—in attacks on black workers in Chicago, Cincinnati, and Boston, and on African American communities in Massachusetts, Connecticut, New York, and New Jersey; in the particularly heinous race riots in New York City and Detroit; and in the numerous direct attacks on newly arriving black migrants in midwestern river towns, from New Albany, Indiana, to St. Paul, Minnesota.[97] Whether the attacks came from white soldiers, angry Irishmen, or other, "unknown" assailants, black victims of racially motivated violence knew that angry talk could quickly escalate into violence.⁹⁸

THE WARTIME CONFLICT over black mobility revealed how closely white midwesterners linked the stability of their own racial hierarchies with southern slavery. Until the war, the exclusion from the Midwest of all but a small population of African Americans—one of the region's characteristic features— had been accomplished by legislation and, indirectly, by antebellum slavery's containment of almost 90 percent of the nation's black population within the South.⁹⁹ When slavery's wartime collapse led to the northward migration of African Americans, midwestern whites encountered an unprecedented challenge to the practices and ideas that sustained white supremacy in their region. As they struggled to defend what they felt were the entitlements accorded them by race—to jobs and farm ownership and the political and economic independence they afforded, to a segregated workplace, to control over public spaces, to idealized gender roles, and to citizenship—they revealed how deeply white privilege saturated daily life even in a region with a small black population. At the same time, the response to black migration suggests how contingent midwestern white supremacy was on white mutuality, demonstrated when white men mobilized in political meetings, in informal gatherings, and in threatening visitations to wayward neighbors, to enforce errant men's obligations to white neighbors, to absent white soldiers, to white workers. Such collective action sought to repair the social fabric of white supremacy as well as to reinforce the public authority of white men, an authority challenged not only by black mobility but also by the war's intrusion on households and male authority over them.

Finally, the debate over race and place revealed that out of the circumstances of the Civil War came new claims that competed with antebellum practices in influencing midwestern beliefs and behavior. During the war, the need to unburden the army of its civilian encumbrance, the imperative to bring in harvests when labor was scarce, and the ability to protect independence and perhaps profit through the exploitation of vulnerable workers, competed with the region's history of black exclusion, ultimately demanding from white residents more elastic responses to the relocation and employment of former slaves. The men and women who helped former slaves move and settle in the North, and those who employed these black people in their homes, on their farms, and in their businesses, had not necessarily abandoned their own race-based prerogatives; instead, they tried to reconcile the unprecedented events of the war with an ideology that now required more flexible behavior. Farmwives and merchants who welcomed the opportunity to employ African Americans could accommodate their presumptions of white racial superiority by treating their new black employees as servile workers.

Ultimately, the proximity of African Americans proved less of a threat to racial hierarchies than many midwesterners might have expected. As a result, emancipation and black migration set the stage for a much longer battle over "place" and citizenship, a battle that would last well into the twentieth century. Nonetheless, the wartime struggle over the implications of emancipation represented a pivotal moment in the history of midwestern black political and social life. Wartime events not only increased the size of black communities, but, perhaps more importantly, mobilized black midwesterners to provide a collective and public defense of their race and a claim to citizenship that gained momentum through the enlistment of black men in the Union army, the mobilization of black women to support black soldiers, and the postwar demand for citizenship and challenges to discriminatory laws. For black midwesterners, the wartime conflicts over emancipation's consequences launched an unprecedented era of regional activism and organizing. Former slaves like Moses Mosely, who migrated to Iowa during the war, were glad to take their new freedom "in the rough," but they were also determined to "make the best of it we can." After the war, they pressed for a more expanded meaning of citizenship by means of the franchise and the law and by challenging the public and private politics of race that continued to be encountered in midwestern households, farms, and streets through the end of the nineteenth century.[100]

4   "To Go and Help Be Free" Migration and the Black Military Experience

Wartime African American migration in the Mississippi valley was not only directed northward. A number of the men and women, who had already risked so much to escape slavery and begin new lives in the Midwest, chose to set aside their new opportunities on the home front and return south. Answering the call to take up arms against bondage, many former slaves who had made their way to St. Paul, Keokuk, Davenport, Des Moines, Burlington, Mt. Pleasant, Newton, and a number of smaller communities decided to return south, "to go and help be free."[1] Most of them were soldiers, but some were the wives and children of soldiers.

Soldiering was a gendered and gendering experience. African American men held their own expectations of manly behavior, but they also had to contend with how their white officers and the War Department envisioned the utility and limitations of black military service.[2] Then, too, there were the material realities of war, ranging from the physical challenges and dangers to the varied social worlds of camp life created among men, men and women, and families and soldiers alike. From their own testimony and the observations of others, it is clear that black men and women experienced their participation in the military conflict in ways that included the subjectively symbolic, material, relational, and physical meanings of gender.

Black midwesterners served in a number of regiments, but the 60th U.S. Colored Infantry (USCI) directly tied the migratory flow of African Americans in the Mississippi valley to black enlistment.[3] With Keokuk as the regiment's rendezvous point, more than 267 black men—some joined by their wives and children—elected to leave the recently gained (and relative) safety of the North and return to the slave South, there to face their former masters on the field of battle and advance the cause of freedom.[4]

Enlistment was a political act and one of great personal courage on the part of former slaves. From the perspective of many military officials, black service was a welcome solution to the army's growing need for soldiers, as well as to

BLACK ENLISTMENT IN THE UPPER MIDWEST

	Iowa	Minnesota	Wisconsin	Total
Black population, 1860/1865	1,069/3,608	259/411	1,171/NA	2,499/incomplete
USCI enlistments: total/percentage of 1860 population	440/41	104/40	272/23	816/33
60th USCI enlistments/percentage of 1860 population	384/36	47/18	0	431/17
60th as percentage of USCI enlistments	87	45	0	79 (excluding Wis.)

Sources: Population figures are from University of Virginia, Geospatial and Statistical Data Center, U.S. Historical Census Data Browser, <http://fisher.lib.virginia.edu/collections/stats/histcensus/index.html>; [David Blakeley], *Annual Report of the Secretary of State to the Legislature of Minnesota* (St. Paul: N.p., 1866); and John T. Hull, *1836–1880: Census of Iowa for 1880* (Des Moines: F. M. Mills, 1883). A small percentage of the total population were men of military age; in Wisconsin, for example, only 25 percent of the total population in 1860 was eligible for service. Furthermore, there is no wartime census that allows us to estimate wartime populations of the upper Midwest in the course of black migration northward. USCI enlistment numbers come from Ira Berlin, Leslie S. Rowland, and Joseph P. Reidy, eds., *The Black Military Experience*, ser. 2 of *Freedom: A Documentary History of Emancipation, 1861–1867* (New York: Cambridge University Press, 1982), 12.

the "contraband problem" in the Mississippi valley. Nationally, black soldiers and sailors helped turn the tide of war and proved instrumental in the success of the Union's final strategy for defeating Lee's army. Soldiering would also turn the tide of racially proscribed citizenship, as African American men would use their demonstrated willingness and ability to shoulder the burdens of military sacrifice to make a strong claim for citizenship's prerogatives and rights. Recent arrivals in the upper Midwest therefore linked their geographic migration to their social migration—from slaves to contraband property, from contrabands to soldiers, from soldiers to citizens.

"A CHANCE TO EARN THEIR FREEDOM": THE RACIAL POLITICS OF ENLISTMENT

It is not surprising that there was considerable opposition among midwestern whites to black enlistment. Most local opponents feared that military service would put African American men "on equal footing with the brave [white] soldiers who are fighting the battles of the Union."⁵ Just as the physical migration of African Americans to the upper Midwest had threatened white presumptions about the "place" of blacks in society, so the prospect of black soldiering threatened white men's exclusive claim on the idealized masculinity of military service. Many white soldiers, on encountering former slaves in the South, regarded them as entertaining versions of the caricatures they had seen on the stage or in popular print culture. "They exhibit the plantation 'break downs' and 'shin-digs' to perfection," noted one white Iowa soldier. Similarly, a Minnesota soldier wrote home: "We have some great times here evenings.... We get some of them in a ring and get them to patting and dancing until nine or ten o'clock. It would make you laugh to see them. It is better than any nigger show you or I ever saw."⁶ Whites found it difficult to imagine African Americans as fellow men in arms, despite their service in the Revolutionary War and the War of 1812.⁷ In fact, in most venues of the white popular press, black men were rarely regarded as adults. As the historian Louise Newman has observed, white Americans believed that sex (and gender) differences were a product of civilization; black men and women were lower on the scale of civilization than whites and unable to claim the idealized characteristics of masculinity or femininity.⁸ The very notion of black enlistment required white Americans to recast their view of African American men into normatively gendered subjects.

Although historians widely attribute the accomplishment of this transformation in white public opinion to black service in the Civil War, it was by no means clear during the conflict if or when this change would occur. Even the earliest white advocates of black enlistment took care to subordinate black manhood to white manhood. One white Iowan officer of a black regiment, while explaining why he felt black men would make better soldiers than whites, nevertheless demeaned their manhood: black men were imitative, they were willing to subordinate themselves to their superiors, they were well-trained by slavery to obey orders. They had none of the independent spirit of white manhood, a spirit that often made white men unwilling to subordinate themselves to the demands of the service.⁹

In the fall elections of 1862 (by which time the Militia Act had authorized the employment, though not the enlistment, of blacks by the Union army), midwestern Democrats campaigned on a claim that they alone defended the interests of white soldiers. Only Democrats could be counted on to protect white privilege on the home front and to oppose the relocation of former slaves in the North—a Republican program that endangered the racial purity of the absent soldier's domestic circle and community.¹⁰ Midwestern white soldiers were also increasingly resentful (as they wrote to their families and hometown newspapers) that slaves and contrabands seemed better treated than white soldiers.

The tentative, experimental enlistment of black soldiers in South Carolina (1862), Louisiana (1862), and Kansas and Massachusetts (early 1863) first raised the possibility of black soldiering. The editor of the *Iowa Daily Statesman* spoke for many white midwesterners when he doubted that African American men had the mettle for soldiering: "They are better at almost anything else than fighting or working. A majority of them would rather run than fight, or steal than work."[11] To some midwesterners, however, enlisting black soldiers made sense as a way to save white lives. Iowan Jeff Hoge said he "would rather see them killed off than so many of the white soldiers. Wouldn't you?" he asked his wife. Indeed, a white woman from Iowa City wrote military officials to request that her fiancé's regiment be spared by allowing black regiments to take its place.[12] Many agreed with Wisconsin lieutenant Edwin Brown, who maintained that "more lives will be lost in the next big battle, more treasure expended than the necks of the whole negro race are worth."[13]

Some white soldiers endorsed black enlistment, but only if the threat of social equality or black migration could be strictly contained. One white Iowan advised the governor: "The army is willing to fight for the Union, and a majority of them would throw the negroes in any place to get peace, if they don't go North and want to be white folks. . . . I think two-thirds of the soldiers would fight against that. You can set me down as one who will never go for negro equality." Even state officials who were somewhat sympathetic to black enlistment insisted on a segregated army; black soldiers "would not be tolerated in one of our [white] regiments. However wrong this may be we cannot ignore the fact."[14] It is true that many midwestern white soldiers expressed bitter opposition to any implication of equality between black and white troops. Iowan Edward Davis, writing home from Missouri, offered his opinion: "Here it is D——n them. . . . I say let the nigger shovel and dig, and I will fight, but do not make him an equal with me. I can't stand that." Davis even questioned the humanity of African Americans; "(*Do you think a nigger is wholly human*[?]) I cannot exactly swallow it."[15] In the violent context of war, white soldiers easily turned to violent imagery in their defense of white supremacy: "I would shoot one ["nigger"] as quick as I would a dog if he did not keep his place."[16]

Yet some white midwesterners supported the arming of black men. Hiram Price, a successful Republican candidate for Congress in 1862, had noted on the Iowa campaign trail that "if necessity require it, muskets should be placed in the hands of negroes, and, as in the war of '76, they should be told to fight for their liberty and ours."[17] An Iowa soldier agreed: "We are in favor of using them any way we can. . . . Let them have a chance to earn their freedom."[18] Still other whites urged military service as a way of forcing blacks to pay the full cost of their freedom. From eastern Iowa came a newspaper editorial asserting:

> The negroes must be taught that their freedom has but resulted as an incident of the war, and that it is not their privilege to skulk off to comfortable corners in the North, where they can curl up in the chimneys and lazy away a life of useless indolence. The people of the North are beginning to feel a powerful desire to swap off the useless black refugees among them for their husbands, fathers, brothers and sons now languishing under poisonous miasmas which a negro may breathe with impunity.[19]

African American men did pursue enlistment, even when the War Department still prohibited it. Responding to inquiries by local black residents as early as 1862, Governor Edward Salomon of Wisconsin sought permission from the secretary of war to enlist them.[20] By then, at least a handful of midwestern blacks were already serving in the army or had attempted to enlist. In January 1862, a free-born, light-skinned African American by the name of Thomas Jeffries enlisted in the 15th Iowa at Knoxville. Jeffries was described as a "mulatto" by a white member of the regiment; the white soldier noted that Jeffries "was without doubt half negro" and that considerable prejudice was directed against him when he first joined the company. Yet a majority of his white comrades decided to allow him to remain. He reportedly proved to be a good soldier "in spite of his negro blood"; his service at the battle of Shiloh was especially notable. Jeffries died of typhoid fever within six months of enlisting.[21]

The army's color line was also crossed by residents of Wisconsin's Cheyenne Valley (near Forest in Vernon County), an unusually multiracial settlement of African Americans, Native Americans, and whites. Thomas Greene, although black, was apparently drafted into the 13th Wisconsin Regiment, Heavy Artillery, in October 1864.[22] Three sons of Cherokee-descended settlers Micajah and Mourning Jacobs Revels served in white regiments; two, John and William Revels, served together in the 6th Wisconsin Infantry. Although whites presumed them to be African American, these dark-complected soldiers were nonetheless remembered with respect by white fellow soldiers.[23] A fourth Cheyenne Valley resident, Leonard Barton, also served. Barton was the son of Illinois free blacks who carefully guarded their freedom, even after his family moved to the Cheyenne Valley sometime before 1851. Barton was openly drafted into the 32nd Wisconsin Infantry as an African American on 21 September 1864, at a time when service in a black regiment was the only officially sanctioned option. Less than a month later, his younger brother, Felix, was enrolled for enlistment in a black regiment.[24]

Two young men from a rural township in eastern Iowa found white midwesterners unwilling to serve with men whom they suspected might be of African descent. Described in the local newspaper as "of dark complexion, rather Indian than mulatto in color, but had light blue eyes and the general Caucasian features, though with rather woolly looking hair," the two brothers were anxious to serve and insisted they knew of no African-descended ancestors. But they were turned away by the officers of the company in 1862. Two years later, George Butler, a black resident and successful barber of Waterloo, Iowa, was recruited by an officer desperate to meet his county's quota and mistakenly assured Butler that he could choose his regiment. When Butler reported at the camp of the 4th Iowa Cavalry, he was informed that his only option was to serve with the state's black regiment.[25]

The War Department's decision to authorize the wide-scale enlistment of African American men in segregated regiments, commanded by white officers, was initiated in eastern states. Early in 1863, Secretary of War Edwin M. Stanton finally permitted the governors of Rhode Island, Massachusetts, and Connecticut to organize black regiments. Midwestern blacks eagerly signed on with the recruiting agents who traveled west in search of enlistments.[26] But midwestern governors and Mississippi valley officers were not permitted to enlist black men until several months later. The flight of southern slaves to army camps, the 1862 public and military controversies over black migration and relocation, and a decline in white recruits all promoted authorization for enlistment in the Mississippi valley. On 25 March 1863, Adjutant General Lorenzo Thomas was ordered to the Mississippi valley to recruit black soldiers and organize them into regiments. As the historian Michael T. Meier has noted, Thomas was encouraged by Stanton to use enlistment as part of a larger, more uniform effort to deal with combatants as well as noncombatants flooding Union lines—thereby extending Thomas's authority to resolve the "problem" created by the wives, sisters, parents, and children of enlisted men.[27] Thus, in addition to his recruiting efforts, from Cairo, Illinois, to Milliken's Bend, Louisiana, Thomas inspected contraband camps and supported the leasing of abandoned plantations and farms where soldiers' families could be employed and self-supporting. At every opportunity, he explained to white troops the new policy of enlisting black men in order to garner their support. As one of those soldiers—Iowan E. W. Gray—informed his hometown newspaper, Thomas "gave us assurance that it was not the intention of the government to send the negro North, to encounter the prejudices and struggle with the legal disabilities of the black man in the free States, but to leave him upon the soil and in a climate to which he has become accustomed, and to employ him upon precisely such work as he best understands."²⁸ Northern whites approved of the new policy in part because it promised to stem the flow of former slaves into the North. African Americans in the South responded eagerly when Thomas linked the privileges and responsibilities of freedom and citizenship, as well as when he spoke to the potential impact of black military heroism on white prejudice. Within ten months (during which time the Union victory at Vicksburg opened the Mississippi to Union control), at least fifty-eight black regiments were organized as part of Thomas's campaign.²⁹

Across the country, African Americans viewed military service as an avenue to respect, upward mobility, citizenship rights, and uncontested manhood for black men. Many of them saw enlistment as the black man's "main chance," offering the steady employment and opportunities for promotion that were rare in the racially segregated marketplace but key to a husband and father's idealized role as the support for his family.³⁰ In a letter to his son, Mathew Griffin, a black soldier from the midwestern 29th USCI, put it this way: in the army "I am looked upon as a man and not as a muel and a dog."³¹

White support for black enlistment increased markedly with the enactment of the draft in March 1863. Sharing the potentially fatal burdens of military service with newly arrived African American men became more immediate and persuasive to white midwesterners than their fears that black soldiers might one day demand the privileges of citizenship. As one Iowa newspaper asserted in July 1863: "Every negro soldier enlisted and sent to the field diminishes by one the number of white men to be drafted. Any squeamish fellow who objects to having his fighting done by a 'nigger' should at once report himself to the nearest recruiting officer and volunteer."³² Later, the same newspaper urged white employers of black migrants to release their employees for military service: "Let it be borne in mind that each negro enlisted saves a white man from the draft, and that the man in easy circumstances who keeps an able-bodied negro about him virtually condemns a white man to a servitude for which the negro is constitutionally better fitted. Rout 'em out."³³ In his correspondence with General Henry Halleck, Iowa governor Samuel Kirkwood also endorsed black enlistment: "I have but one remark to add and that in regard to the negroes fighting—it is this—When this war is over & we have summed up the entire loss of life it has imposed on the country[,] I shall not have any regrets if it is found that a part of the dead are *niggers* and that *all* are not white men."³⁴ Black soldiering thus became more palatable to whites when they could envision black soldiers serving white interests. A number of black men were also hired as substitutes by whites seeking to avoid the draft.³⁵

In the Midwest, many African Americans were anxious to assume the burdens of war. As General Thomas initiated his work at Cairo and farther south, midwestern civilians as well as state authorities inquired about black enlistment. Within two months, at least one hundred "colored citizens" of Henry County, Iowa (most of whom would have been recent migrants out of slavery), offered their services to the county recruiting officer. In June and July 1863, as the draft was initiated, officials in Wisconsin and Minnesota began asking about the possibility of enlisting African Americans and using them to fill state quotas. In 1862 Cornelius Butler, a black resident of Kenosha, Wisconsin, had offered to raise a company of Wisconsin blacks, and Alexander Clark, to raise black companies in Iowa.³⁶ In October 1863 John W. Birney, a prosperous black barber in LaCrosse, Wisconsin, sought a commission to raise a "colored company" in his state. A local bank president highly recommended that Governor Salomon approve the request. Birney was "well-behaved, intelligent, sober and gentlemanly . . . of very favorable appearance" (light-skinned), and someone who would "give as good satisfaction for a position as any man that may be found among his class of people. . . . And I have no doubt, but he can enlist nearly all the steamboat colored men in this section, whose number may amount to 30 or 40, besides others residing in this City and neighborhood."³⁷

Yet black midwesterners were not entirely unified on the matter of black military service. One Mt. Pleasant resident—Jerry Green—was arrested by federal agents for discouraging enlistment "among his people."³⁸ While the local Republican newspaper decried Green as a "black Copperhead," Green's reasons for his opposition went unreported. Green certainly would not have been alone among African American men in objecting to the terms under which they were permitted to serve, objections voiced by prominent black leaders such as Frederick Douglass and by black newspapers like the *Christian Recorder* and the *Anglo-African*. Not everyone believed that black enlistment was an open door to racial equality.³⁹

It was in this context of shifting public opinion toward black soldiering that Governor Kirkwood received permission from the War Department to organize a black regiment. When Keokuk, in southeastern Iowa, became the rendezvous point for the 1st Iowa Regiment, African Descent (later designated the 60th USCI) in August 1863, it was less a result of local initiatives than a consequence of the constraints placed on black recruitment in Missouri.[40] In June, Colonel William Pile, of the 33rd Regiment, Missouri Infantry, had been authorized to recruit African Americans in Missouri, but Governor Hamilton Gamble required him to abide by the state's black laws—that is, to limit enlistment to free blacks and the slave men of disloyal owners (thus protecting the "property" of loyal slaveowners), as well as to credit the black recruits to a state other than Missouri.[41]

Just across the border, a number of Keokuk businessmen and Republican political leaders, aware of the limitations imposed by the Missouri statutes, proposed to Governor Kirkwood that Keokuk be established as the rendezvous point for enlisting blacks regionwide. Their rationale was threefold: (1) a Keokuk rendezvous would be convenient to both southern and northern blacks, (2) an Iowa rendezvous would circumvent Missouri's black laws preventing the arming of African Americans, and (3) the soldiers recruited could be useful in the effort to maintain peace along the Iowa-Missouri border. They also asserted that this plan would be well received by loyal citizens; perhaps they believed that black enlistment could overshadow some of the negative associations of black migration with Republican policy. Among the vigorous advocates for the Keokuk rendezvous were Milton Collins, who would be commissioned as a lieutenant colonel in the regiment, and George W. Pittman, a wealthy Keokuk merchant who would become regimental sutler.[42] On 1 August recruiters began scouring northern Missouri, Iowa, Illinois, and Minnesota for eligible African Americans who would be conveyed to Camp Lincoln in Keokuk.[43] August and September saw a flurry of enlistments. The same midwestern communities that had become the destinations of former slaves now began targeting their new black residents to meet local quotas under the enrollment law.

By 12 September 1863, 300 men were gathered at Keokuk; in two weeks, that number had grown to more than 500. By the end of October, their numbers stood at 650. Of those who joined the regiment, 80 percent were enlisted in either Missouri (47 percent) or Iowa (34 percent). The great majority of men in Iowa were former slaves who had migrated or been relocated north during the first two years of the war. Others, also former slaves, were recruited in Missouri and transported to Keokuk.

The men who had been free before the war left few clues to explain their apparently weaker enthusiasm for enlistment. Few recruits had resided in the upper Midwest prior to the conflict.[44] Unlike recently arrived migrants, longer-term black residents had established a foothold—a home, a job, a business, a community—that may have seemed too vulnerable or too valuable to sacrifice. In contrast, recently arrived migrants had not been in the region long enough to settle their families and homes on a firm footing; moreover, enlistment bounties may have provided a strong incentive to impoverished recent arrivals. Too, many of the newer migrants reported being urged by enlisting officers to head south "to go and help be free."[45]

Despite the assumptions of many northern whites that African American men were incapable of performing a soldier's duties, a number of men joined the 60th USCI with previous military experience—not as soldiers, but as employees of the army, as unpaid workers in the war effort, or as servants who accompanied individual white officers onto the battlefield. Among the former military workers were George Hall, who had been "conscripted" out of slavery to drive a team for the 3rd Iowa Cavalry for thirteen months prior to going to Iowa and "joining on my own accord," and Ephraim Piles Ford, who had "worked digging trenches and rifle pits" at Fort Pillow and mounting heavy artillery at Helena, Arkansas.[46] Several men had been employed as army teamsters, including James Bradford, who was present at the assault on Vicksburg that summer.[47] Many who worked as cooks and servants had faced the dangers of battle. For example, before enlisting, Peter Thomas, as a servant for the captain of a company in a Wisconsin regiment, had accompanied him into battle at Chickamauga and Mission Ridge.[48]

Among those with prior military experience were several members of a company of recruits who enlisted in the 60th USCI from Minneapolis. Forty-eight men were signed up at St. Paul's Fort Snelling in September 1863, by Alexander Clark, a successful black businessman from Muscatine, Iowa, and the most prominent black rights activist in the region. The recruits, all former slaves, had gone to Fort Snelling that spring. In April 1863, General Henry H. Sibley (commanding the Department of the Northwest, formed in response to the 1862 Dakota uprising) had requested that a large number of contrabands be assembled from Missouri and Cairo, Illinois, and sent to him by steamboat. The men were needed as teamsters and cooks in Sibley's expedition against the Dakota Sioux following the Dakota uprising. There was considerable difficulty in finding the number of men requested. Sibley's request for black laborers competed with those of other officers; furthermore, Missouri railroad executives resisted the use of their lines to transport former slaves, fearing lawsuits by slaveowners. Contemporary reports offer conflicting accounts of the numbers sent to Minnesota, but at least three steamboats arrived at Minneapolis in April and May 1863, one carrying between 125 and 260 former slaves; a second, 233; and a third, 200 or more.[49] As Antoine Crawford, a former St. Louis slave, explained, "I . . . went with about 200 colored men in a barge from here to St. Paul, and went with General Sibley in an expedition against the Indians."[50]

The men who arrived at Fort Snelling at Sibley's request were accompanied by their families, eliciting considerable negative reaction among local whites. When the first group of contrabands arrived and half of them consisted of women and children, area papers wanted to know, "What will be done with them?" St. Paul police attempted to prevent them from going ashore, fearing they might become a public charge; local Irish river workers also tried to block their disembarkation, complaining angrily about job competition. After a time, the former slaves were allowed off the boat. The fort's quartermaster immediately began advertising in local papers for potential employers of the women and children now crowded into the garrison. The men who had joined Sibley's expedition in June returned on 12 September, having driven two hundred wagons that carried food and ammunition, as well as tending stock and cooking for the 2,300 soldiers involved in the punitive attack on the Dakota Sioux.[51] Within two weeks of their return to the fort, Alexander Clark recruited at least forty-eight of the men for Iowa's black regiment. As an inducement, Clark passed on to them the two-dollar fee he received as enlisting agent for each of the men he brought into the regiment.[52] Now they would finally get their uniforms and serve as soldiers—although at lower pay than they had earned as teamsters on the plains.[53]

In contrast, for most of the other men who enlisted in the 60th USCI, the transition from enslavement to freedom and from civilian life to the military was immediate and sometimes very brief. Some did not know of the Emancipation Proclamation until sought out by Union soldiers intent on signing them up.[54] Many men walked or made their way out of the South with stolen horses or wagons in order to enlist at Keokuk. Some spent only a few short months in the upper Midwest before deciding to enlist; others were targeted by white recruiting agents as soon as they arrived. William Early and Henry Cooper both took flight in Grundy County, Missouri, proceeded to Albia, Iowa, and enlisted only a month later; Jason Green joined up within two months of escaping to Iowa.[55]

Many of the 60th's members had become close comrades before entering the service; several had escaped slavery together. "A crowd of us ran off and came North," recalled veteran Milton Howard.[56] William Logan and George C. Young were plowing neighboring fields when they were approached by recruiting agents; the two men left their plows and oxen in the field and walked to Keokuk.[57] Friends Arge Washington and Robert Wilson fled on foot from Shelby County, Missouri, to Quincy, Illinois, then took a steamboat to

Keokuk. Both men knew several other fugitives from Missouri who enlisted at Keokuk; twenty-eight of thirty men in Washington's company were from the same area in Missouri.[58] Similarly, George Combs fled to Iowa with three other slaves.[59] Of the men who fled to Iowa to enlist, 220 chose to return to the state when the war was over; at least 5 went back to Minnesota.[60]

Some of the men who signed up with the 60th had already begun to forge a sense of community in their new midwestern homes before deciding to enlist. Recruiting agents took advantage of those community ties. Most of the men who enlisted from Mt. Pleasant, Iowa, served in Company H; most from Newton, Iowa, in Company F; and most from Minnesota, in Company F. Captain William A. Stuart, who would command Company D, recruited several recent arrivals to Des Moines, and, continuing his efforts, a Captain Brownell brought more than fifty men from Des Moines. For the members of Company D, their shared experiences of slavery, self-emancipation, migration, and war created lasting bonds.[61] Captain Stuart emphasized that the "boys from Des Moines can go in with their acquaintances."[62] Those close ties helped the men fight "like demons" against Confederate troops in July 1864 at Big Creek, Arkansas, where Company D, along with black and white soldiers from other units, were "attacked by overwhelming forces," surrounded on three sides, yet battled through enemy lines back to Helena.[63] The white officers proudly proclaimed that their company consisted of "good fighting men."

"THE BOYS ARE PROUD OF THE NAME SOLDIER"

As Union soldiers, former slaves found that their experience of manhood was tied to their appearance, their strength, their bodily integrity or its loss, to their sexual, familial, social, and military relationships; and to their ability to cope with and survive the demands and regulations of military life. Their experience was therefore distinct from what might be generalized as the universally masculine reality of soldiering. There may have been considerable distance between the gendered ideals and prerogatives that they laid claim to and the day-to-day realities of military life. Nevertheless, black men and women described their participation in the war in gendered language and imagery, and after the conflict they sought to elevate their claims to rights and to citizenship on the basis of those experiences.

One of the first tests faced by men who wished to become soldiers was the physical exam. Every potential soldier was ostensibly required to pass a physical examination before he could be mustered in.[64] Yet those exams were so superficial that more than four hundred women managed to pass and join the

Union army over the course of the war. But the men who enlisted in the 60th USCI described being subjected to very thorough inspections; perhaps African Americans were more closely examined. Abram Myers noted that "we were stripped naked, sounded . . . and bent . . . around in all shapes."[65] Arge Washington also recalled that they were "closely examined, stripped, made to jump up."[66] George Kebo said that the surgeon "had us to strip naked as we came into the world. He sounded our lungs, felt our arms and legs."[67] According to William Early, "The Drs. Made us take off all our clothes."[68] White recruits subjected to a similar exam may have felt embarrassment about the exposure or manipulation of their bodies, but for former slave men, that experience would be profoundly reminiscent of the objectification and commodification of their bodies by slaveowners and prospective buyers in slave markets. Black recruits found themselves once again subordinate to white men who could freely inspect, manipulate, assess, and comment on their physical soundness; perhaps worse, in this new setting former slave men probably could not exert the kind of influence or manipulation that many used in the slave market.[69] Despite the familiarity of being objectified, the exam was likely the first time that white men judged them worthy of something other than being a commodity; a successful exam meant access to a new, higher status. These African Americans were described as "sound," "stout," and "robust"— assessments that they had undoubtedly heard in southern slave markets. Not everyone passed the exam; indeed, Alexander Clark, who had devoted so much effort to the regiment and expected to be appointed one of its sergeants, was turned away when the surgeon discovered an old ankle injury that made Clark ineligible for service.[70]

While medical exams were intended to ensure that the regiment's soldiers were physically sound, the unusual thoroughness of the examinations conducted by the 60th suggests that the exams may also have served other purposes. George Kebo reported that the surgeon "even examined our privates— he tried to make us believe that we had to have the whole thing cut off—he said we could not be soldiers unless it was done." In his recollection of the event, Kebo acknowledged that "I was green like the rest of them[.] I told him I didn't want to be a soldier."[71] Although it is impossible to discern the motivations behind the examination itself, the medical officer's suggestion that castration was necessary for military service seems laden with meaning, even beyond the teasing of "green" recruits. Considering the importance of self-discipline in idealized nineteenth-century white manhood, the surgeon's taunt suggests that the disciplining of black men depended on depriving them of the most symbolic physical manifestation of their manhood.[72] At the very least, this particular white medical officer found amusement in the vulnerability of the nude black men assembled before him and in belittling them with the threat of castration.

Just as George Kebo refused to abandon his virility for the right to serve his counry, he and his comrades would find a host of ways to assert their own manhood as new recruits and as soldiers. Sometimes those affirmations rankled midwestern whites. In late August 1863, new black recruits in Des Moines allegedly felt "licensed to do pretty much as they please, and swagger about the streets with an air of insolence and a degree of impudence perfectly disgusting."[73] In a conflict with a white soldier at Camp Lincoln, one black soldier drew a pistol, shook the weapon in the white man's face, and "blackguarded him to his hearts content." The Democratic paper reporting the incident concluded that this example of black aggression was the outcome of abolitionist teachings. However, it would seem that the uniform and weaponry of soldiering, too, had altered the balance of power between black and white men.[74]

An especially personal accoutrement became instrumental in the assertion of a new identity among the former slaves of the 60th. When enlisting officers entered their names in the regimental rolls, many of the men chose to change their surnames. Some were encouraged to do so by enlisting officers; others had their own reasons. Henry Brown knew he had to change his name or run the risk of being recognized by rebel soldiers when the unit headed down to Missouri. William Harrison changed his to prevent his owner from attempting to locate and recapture him. Many men of the 60th rejected their "slave names," or the surnames of their former owners, and took the surnames of their fathers. For these former slaves, asserting their manhood was less about an invented, self-reliant identity (one that would have been more familiar to northern whites) than about claiming their rightful place in a male line and in their own families. For the rest of the war, when these men followed orders, those orders identified them as the sons of their fathers, not as slaves.[75]

When black recruits performed the part of soldiers, they were pleased when the general public took an interest. On 29 September 1863, for example, thirty-two men of the 60th USCI marched in formation through the streets of St. Paul on their way to the dock to board the steamboat that would ferry them down to Keokuk to rendezvous with their regiment. At their head was Alexander Clark, the recruiting agent responsible for their enlistment. The men looked sharp; according to the *St. Paul Daily Press*, they "made a very good appearance." Of course, white soldiers also sought to make a favorable impression when they marched.[76] But these soldiers-to-be must have been especially conscious of their public representation of an idealized black manhood in a city that had not wanted them to leave the boats that had brought them there. Too, local whites had doubted their ability to contribute to Sibley's violent reprisals against the Sioux. Having played a key supportive role in the punitive expeditions and perhaps accruing some social capital for allying themselves with the white victors over the defeated Sioux, the men now prepared to enter the military as uniformed soldiers rather than as civilian employees. In light of Clark's frequent references to military service as a supreme measure of manhood, his recruiting activities among the African Americans probably emphasized an idealized black masculinity. These were men who had already accepted the risks attending their escape from slavery, had agreed to be sent far from their homes to aid the Union army, and now were agreeing to return south to face slaveowners on the field of battle. Were they motivated to serve by what they had already accomplished, or by some measure of manhood against which they might still be found lacking?

The recruits demonstrated their "manly appearance" and "soldierly bearing" during a dress parade before "friends of the enterprise" in Keokuk as they boarded boats for St. Louis; when they marched through that city's streets to Benton Barracks, where they paraded for visiting dignitaries; and during their drills and inspections in Helena, where the unit spent the majority of its wartime service.[77] At St. Louis, their orderly marching earned them praise from white officers and soldiers alike; a white soldier from Minnesota thought they "looked well under arms" and might fight as well as white troops. Yet along with such praise came the scorn of their detractors. The latter included a group of white women who were watching the black men march; these onlookers did not hesitate to publicly express their poor opinion of black men in uniform and to unreservedly dispute the soldiers' claims to respectability and disciplined manhood.[78]

In their impressive, orderly appearance, these African American men evocatively challenged the public culture of racist ridicule in the North, a culture that regularly mocked, satirized, and dehumanized them. From minstrel shows to illustrated sheet music and political cartoons, white Americans had long amused themselves with a visual and textual caricature of black men as lazy, undisciplined, and unrestrained. Black soldiers drew on their own traditions, including the antebellum rituals of formal parades associated with fraternal activities, Emancipation Day, and other celebrations to present a new and powerful image of black manhood. It was impressive enough for one elderly former slave in Helena, having observed the inspection of the 60th USCI by a visiting dignitary, to exclaim, "Gentlemen, it's no use talking. You can whip the whole world."[79]

That image of black manhood was deliberately reflected back to the men of the 60th by some of their wives, sisters, and mothers. While the regiment was still in St. Louis, two of Iowa's most prominent (and likely wealthiest) African Americans received permission from Lieutenant Colonel Milton Collins to present the 60th with a silk flag, sewn by the African American ladies of Muscatine and Keokuk, in a formal gathering. At Benton Barracks in St. Louis on 20 November 1863, the regiment's companies were "drawn up in line" in a "fine" display and addressed by Alexander Clark; John Hiner, Keokuk's successful black butcher; and Lieutenant Colonel Collins. Clark's speech framed the event as one that demonstrated the ability of African American men and women to fulfill the highest ideals of manhood and womanhood. The wives, mothers, and sisters who offered the beautiful flag to the regiment had shown themselves to be worthy "ladies" through the patriotic sacrifice of their loved ones to the cause. In making a gift of the national emblem, these women publicly recognized their loved ones as true men—soldiers who would bravely defend their flag and their country against the rebel foe. For their part, the uniformed husbands, sons, and brothers would fight for their nation and their flag as they would fight for their wives, daughters, and sisters. Their loyalty and valor were cemented by the affectionate ties embodied in the flag. In response, Collins asserted that they would "defend their invaluable gift to the death"; the next day, Collins observed in his diary that "the boys are proud of the name soldier."[80]

While still stationed at Benton Barracks, the black soldiers also asserted their manhood when it came time for their first paychecks. On 28 November—payday, as Collins observed—black soldiers responded angrily "when it was announced [to] the men that they would not receive more than 7.00 per month[;] some of the men refused to sign the rolls." This was an insult to their dignity and a flagrant indication that the Federal government valued black manhood less than white manhood. In addition, many soldiers were deeply concerned about their ability to support their families on such paltry pay. (Protests, demonstrations, and threatened mutiny would accompany black soldiers' fight for equal pay across the nation.) For these impoverished former slaves, refusing to accept a wage that demonstrated racial prejudice and denied their equal manhood would have serious consequences for their dependents. By mid-June 1864, Congress would act to equalize their pay retroactively to January 1864, but for those first months of service, payday carried a painful reminder to African Americans that their lives were valued less than those of white soldiers.[81]

"A DIRTY, NASTY TOWN"

After a six-day journey down the Mississippi, the 60th USCI arrived at Helena on 20 December 1863. An important Arkansas port and commercial center prior to the war, Helena was occupied by Union forces in the spring of 1862 in support of the western theater's river war. There, the 60th USCI became part of a larger strategy to defend Federal control over the Mississippi River by garrisoning its banks with a loyal population. Black troops would not just defend the civilian population, but, as an army of occupation, free up white troops for combat.[82] The occupation in 1862 was closely followed by the Second Confiscation Act (extending freedom and protection from recapture to "contraband," and encouraging their employment by the military), drawing fugitive slaves to the Union outpost ("thick as blackberries," one white Wisconsin soldier noted in 1862) and leading to the extensive employment of contraband laborers.[83] Because Helena was one of the first Union outposts in the western theater to draw large numbers of fugitive slaves, it also contributed heavily to the flow of black migrants in the Mississippi valley. More than one thousand former slaves are estimated to have been relocated north from Helena; many chose Iowa, Wisconsin, or Minnesota as their destination.[84] With the arrival of the 60th USCI, many of those former contrabands—now soldiers—returned in the service of the Union. The regiment would remain in Helena for the next sixteen months, conducting expeditions against the enemy and seeing major action at Big Creek in July 1864 and Little Rock that fall, scouting rebel activities in the area, defending nearby leased plantations against Confederate attack, and performing an exhausting range of military assignments as well as garrison duty for this important Mississippi River outpost and nearby encampments of contraband workers.[85]

As they struggled to survive the fatigue duty that black troops were typically assigned in the Mississippi valley, these African Americans now fully experienced their transition from slave to free men, from civilians to soldiers, and from a private manhood they could only surreptitiously claim under slavery to a public manhood. There must have been an astonishing gap between the initial celebration of their manly appearance as uniformed, well-disciplined soldiers and the actual experience of soldiering. As former slaves, they may have been accustomed to the exploitation of their labor and to hard taskmasters on farms and plantations in the South, but the demands of heavy, unending labor led to disabling afflictions. Whether in loading and unloading cargo or moving the heavy timbers needed to repair fortifications or build shelters and bridges, soldier after soldier suffered injuries that would impair them for the rest of their lives.[86] Stout, strong men who had been "good and healthy as a rock" before the war would return as "frightful looking skeletons."[87]

Low-lying, muddy, surrounded by swamps, and susceptible to flooding in the spring and snow in the winter, Helena earned the sobriquet of "Hell-in-Arkansas" from another Iowa regiment.[88] The 60th USCI would have found Helena, as one observer noted, a "town like all other overflowed towns," dingy from the residue of past floods, or, as another described it, "a sickly, detestable village," a "dirty nasty town."[89] Surrounding the town were four batteries, as well as Fort Curtis, a major defense structure housing heavy artillery; a black "shanty-town," with neatly kept houses, composed of free blacks and former slaves inside the picket lines; and a contraband camp two miles outside of town, where black refugees from slavery found shelter, protection, and occasional jobs for the military. Black soldiers and contrabands alike were treated for illness and injury at a "colored hospital."[90] Beyond the town were the abandoned cotton plantations now leased by the Treasury Department to Unionist planters who employed former slaves.

Only five months before the 60th's arrival, Union forces had repelled a major Confederate assault on Helena's defenses. Since then, rebel guerrillas often kept the soldiers confined to picket lines, away from town and from the plentiful game that might have added considerably to their meager diets.[91] Yet if Helena seemed relatively safe from a major enemy attack, the men of the 60th and the family members who joined them would quickly encounter the less dramatic but deadlier consequences of the town's physical and disease environment, of overwork, and of inadequate shelter. Lieutenant Colonel Collins recorded with great pride the honors accruing to his regiment: the first black unit entrusted with picket duty at Helena, the conclusion of inspectors that his was the "finest disciplined Regiment in the field. . . . equal in drill and the Manual of arm to any other," his own selection to serve as officer of the day. Each development promised to "ever elevate the [race]."[92] But while Collins concerned himself with the appearance and reputation of the unit, his men—and their families—contended with the daily threats to their health and safety that garrison and fatigue duties often involved. Perhaps, too, they were aware that the arduous tasks they performed were regarded by white soldiers as beneath them. More than one white soldier wrote home complaining of being ordered to take on the fatigue duty that they usually derided as emasculating "slave work."[93]

From their experience in camp at Keokuk to their trip down the Mississippi to Helena, one of the challenges of soldiering for the 60th USCI was to withstand the winter cold. Keokuk papers wrote sarcastically about the men huddling around campfires—further evidence, they seemed to imply, that black men did not belong in the North. But the winter weather followed them south. In St. Louis, the soldiers encountered "awful cold." A few weeks later, as they boarded crowded ships bound for Helena, they were forced to remain on the exposed decks; the cold was so severe that "a good many men got their feet frozen," and a few lost toes. On arrival at Helena, their thin cotton tents provided little protection from the cold and unexpected snowstorms; they scrambled to gather lumber to build shelters, stables, and outhouses. "We suffered as much with the cold at Helena . . . as we did in Suthern Iowa," wrote Collins. "It was a cold bad winter," recalled George Kebo.[94]

Although the regiment was glad to leave St. Louis for Helena (according to Collins, the men "all appear anxious for the field and active service"), they soon discovered that "active service" meant garrison, picket, and fatigue duties. Although another black soldier (stationed in the East) insisted that "a man dies none the less gloriously, standing at his post on picket, or digging in the trench," he wrote from the battlefield, not from a post where hard physical labor was the order of the day.[95] The 60th's troops would have occasional, deadly opportunities to exchange fire with the enemy and were allotted their share of drilling and training for combat, but the great majority of their time was spent building and repairing roads, bridges, batteries, shelters, and encampments in the area, and loading and unloading the ships that delivered supplies and took off wood, cotton, soldiers, and civilians. No memoirs or reminiscences suggest that these soldiers felt they needed a chance to prove their manhood through battlefield valor, but nearly all of their accounts document the unheralded demands, dangers, and risks that permeated garrison and fatigue duties.

Disease was the biggest threat, and it struck as soon as they assembled at Keokuk (where 14 men died), when they trained in St. Louis (where 23 died), and during their entire service in Arkansas (where 225 died).[96] (For the army experience more generally, the historian Gerald F. Linderman has noted that the spread of infectious childhood diseases constituted the "first wave" of sickness encountered by new recruits in both Union and Confederate armies.)[97] Within the 60th, measles and mumps seemed to circulate very shortly after the unit's arrival at Keokuk.[98] At Benton Barracks, in St. Louis, disease spread even more rapidly; Company D, for example, was almost immediately reduced by more than a quarter by severe sickness.[99] But Helena proved more dangerous than anyone could have imagined. There, a "second wave" of disease and illness swept through the regiment; diarrhea, dysentery, pneumonia, malaria, scurvy, and even sunstroke took a tremendous toll.[100] Five men died from disease on the sixth day after their arrival; 65 percent of the regiment's total deaths occurred in Arkansas.[101] A white officer would recall that there was more sickness at Helena than he saw at any other place: "It was seldom that we had more than half a co. [at] a time that was fit for duty."[102]

The soldiers had their own explanations for such extensive illness. Lacking access to clean water, they were "compelled to drink stagnant and foul water from the pools and sloughs."[103] Sanitary conditions at Helena were poor, a fact worsened significantly by flooding. In January 1865, the men had to wade through waist-deep water to go on and off duty; they ultimately left their quarters for shelter in abandoned buildings. Soldier after soldier would remember sleeping in cold mud, with little more than a thin tent to protect them from the snowstorms that hit during their first winter at Helena.[104] When combined with overwork, the physical and disease environment posed the biggest threat to survival. As a captain recalled of one of the veterans (who had "made a good soldier" but suffered from disease, sunstroke, and a battle wound), "he never was the man after that he was before."[105] "We were nearly all sick," said Henry Cooper, "and many died—and we thought it was due to our exposure at Helena."[106]

Smallpox took a particularly severe toll on black soldiers in the Mississippi valley, including the men of the 60th USCI. Black troops were not only far more likely than whites to contract the disease while in the service (roughly 37 cases per 1,000 black men and 6 cases per 1,000 white men), but also they were more likely to die from it (35 percent mortality rates for black soldiers, compared to 23 percent for white).[107] The Union army required vaccination of its troops, including black regiments, but the vaccine matter used—sometimes taken from men who were sick with other diseases—often led to severe complications.[108] This was especially true when the scabs used as vaccine matter were taken from men infected with syphilis. Prisons and hospitals on both sides of the conflict reported the harmful, occasionally fatal consequences of impure vaccinations, from the spread of disease to the appearance of large, gangrenous ulcers at the point of vaccination—which could lead to amputation. Several hundred cases of these "spurious vaccinations" were reported during the war.[109]

Tragically, the army's own preventative treatment for smallpox—vaccinating uninfected soldiers—led to a second dangerous epidemic, this time of syphilis. In the spring of 1864, when smallpox broke out among the soldiers of the 60th USCI, their commander received orders to see that all of the uninfected men were vaccinated. The vaccine matter provided by the medical department was impure and infected many men with syphilis and other diseases. One company commander recalled that at least one hundred men were given the impure vaccine, and one soldier thought "it killed several of the boys."[110] The regimental surgeon acknowledged that "many of the men were severely poisoned with it, some of them carrying their arms in slings for three & four months." Twenty years later, George Kebo, one of the infected men, reported that he had "not got over it yet."[111] Kebo lived longer than some. London Triplett died in 1875 of the syphilis he contracted from the vaccine; according to his doctor, his final illness was both severe and painful.[112]

Although the army ultimately ordered a medical investigation of the vaccinations, it took time for the infected men to understand what had made them ill. Some blamed local miasmas (commonly associated with disease at the time), and those who were sick were teased and stigmatized—teased for having contracted a venereal disease from their wives or the women they socialized with in Helena; stigmatized because their sores were "loathsome" and the other men feared contracting the disease from them. Regarding one of the sicker men, a comrade would later say that "none of the boys wanted to sleep with him and we would not let him put his hands on anything we had about the table; the boys told him he had the pock, and I have heard them curse about it more than a little."[113]

Despite the official investigation and the fact that the regiment's surgeons acknowledged the army's mistake, many white military and pension officials during and after the war blamed the illness on the men themselves. Syphilis, they argued, was spread by the large number of black men who had contracted the disease before entering the service, when they had been infected by engaging in sexual relations with black women who were presumed to be both syphilitic and promiscuous.[114] Facts could not sway some whites from their presumption that African Americans were morally undeveloped and transgressively unrestrained in their sexual behavior and therefore frequent carriers of venereal disease.[115] In contrast, when white civilians contracted syphilis from contaminated vaccine matter (as several families did in Appanoose County, Iowa, in 1864), there were no rumors or assumptions that illicit sexual activity had caused the outbreak; all agreed that the vaccine was the culprit.[116]

The terrible toll of disease was not unique to the 60th USCI. In fact, illness decimated the white troops stationed at Helena prior to the regiment's arrival, immobilizing the Army of the Southwest in 1862.[117] But, as one white Iowan would later note, as miserable as his time in Helena was, for white troops "this state of things was not to last forever"; they would move on to play a role in the battles of the western theater.[118] Not so for black troops; assigned garrison and fatigue duties, black troops remained in the most unhealthy locations of the western theater and died there by the scores. Had they been used in combat instead, they no doubt would have had far higher survival rates. Black troops were ten times as likely to die from disease as from battle, compared to white troops, who were only twice as likely to die from disease as from battle. Put differently, one in twelve white soldiers died of disease, whereas the ratio for black soldiers was one in five.[119] When the disease environment of Helena collided with the racist policies of the U.S. military (requiring that black troops be assigned heavy physical labor and guard duties), the consequences were deadly. Furthermore, as white soldiers and officers readily observed, a soldier's death from disease was not always recognized as a heroic death.[120]

While conditions in the Mississippi valley were particularly severe, black soldiers in the eastern theater were equally outraged by the impact of racism on their ability to serve, survive, and be honored for their sacrifices. As a black soldier stationed in North Carolina wrote to the secretary of war, "We have come out Like men & we Expected to be Treeated as men but we have been Treeated more Like Dogs than men."[121] In both the eastern and western theaters of war, black soldiers and some sympathetic white officers—like General Lorenzo Thomas—protested the policies, the inadequate hospitals, and the racist white medical officers that made disease, illness, and injury a far worse threat to black troops than to white ones.[122]

IF THE STRAIN of unremitting hard labor and ill health compromised the exploration and expression of masculinity among black soldiers, camp life and after-duty hours offered many opportunities for sustenance and amusement. While the 60th was still in Iowa, local African Americans visited the troops at Camp Lincoln to socialize, donate reading material, fruits, and vegetables, while others—like the well-off butcher William Kay—gave speeches. Kay spoke about a long history of black warriors, including Hannibal and Othello, although his speech was mocked in local Democratic papers as an example of black buffoonery.[123]

St. Louis, with thousands of soldiers at Benton Barracks, just four miles outside the city, and thousands of contrabands entering the city, offered increased dangers as well as amusements. Exposure to infectious diseases such as mumps and measles increased exponentially, and the regiment's sick list grew quickly. With slave catchers surveilling the city's black population, black soldiers were not immune from being kidnapped and sold back into slavery. And confrontations with hostile white soldiers occasionally spilled over into violence.[124] But men of the regiment pursued a range of off-duty activities, from the sacred to the very secular. Some soldiers held prayer meetings, conducted by the preachers among their ranks, and the regiment's white chaplain organized a Sunday school. There was also a good deal of card playing and other games of chance, as well as the drinking that occurred in most army camps.[125] Some members of the 60th appear to have raided gardens and poultry pens outside the encampment, although their commanding officer suspected that some of the complaints from city residents were "greatly exaggerated," motivated by "prejudice to colored troops."[126]

Although Helena had less to offer off-duty soldiers than Benton Barracks or St. Louis, the men of the 60th were nonetheless drawn into town. The increasing popularity of drinking establishments, improvised horse racing, and gambling led to curfews, the regulation of troop movements in and out of town, and an order forcing officers to quarter with their troops to keep an eye on them.[127] The black soldiers were eager to socialize with the African Americans in town, and competed for the affections of the women they met.[128] At band parties in Helena, the regiment's musicians entertained black civilians and soldiers alike.[129] Some of the men dedicated their off-hours to self-improvement; they learned to read and write at the school established at Helena by the Western Sanitary Commission, and they led or participated in Sunday services, prayer meetings, and other religious activities.[130]

However, the longer the unit remained at Helena (and with the return of better weather), the more likely they were to venture outside their picket lines, "raiding and pillaging the private property of citizens." Besides helping themselves to the orchards and gardens of white residents in the countryside (even their commanding officers complained that the government rations were "not sufficient for their actual wants"), they appear to have targeted some white men in the area for repeated harassment. One commanding officer charged that black soldiers were going outside the lines primarily to insult white residents.[131] While there are few records of the discipline and punishments administered to wayward troops, at least one soldier was repeatedly tied to the ground, spread-eagled, for repeatedly leaving camp without permission.[132]

"MARY WENT TO WAR WITH HIM"

"When the soldiers left [Keokuk], and went to Helena I went along," recalled Mary White Brown, a former slave who made the journey to Iowa in order to join her husband when his regiment headed south. Brown said that she was with her husband, Jerry White, "all the time he was in the army." She shared his tent and split her time between working for the regiment as a cook and laundress, and nursing White through diarrhea ("I mean he had it *bad*"), consumption, and three gunshot wounds received during the battle at Big Creek.[133] Brown was not alone, since a number of wives, other family members, and sweethearts accompanied the 60th USCI. Among them was Celia Brickley, a North Carolina–born slave in her early thirties, who remained with her husband of three years, William Brickley, while his regiment was in Arkansas. According to his obituary, "He and his wife joined the northern army, he as a soldier in Co. A, Sixtieth Iowa Infantry, and his wife as a cook."[134] Other women—who had already made their way north—came down from the upper Midwest when they heard their husbands were sick or injured, as was fairly customary during the war. Although they, like Mary White Brown, played an important role in the life and functioning of the regiment, their experiences and contributions remain largely unstudied and unacknowledged by historians. Their presence in the regiment reminds us that military service was not exclusively a male undertaking. For many soldiers, wives and families were integrated into their experience of the war.[135]

Location was a key reason. From December 1863 to April 1865, the 60th's location at Helena meant that the regiment was both accessible by river traffic and garrisoned near a town where civilians could work to support themselves. This allowed frequent and long-term contact for some soldiers' families. The ostensibly masculine world of soldiering and camp life was in fact often interwoven with heterosocial and familial relationships, a fact that surely shaped the wartime meanings of masculinity for the men of the 60th.

When families left slavery together—whether through organized relocation or self-directed flight and migration—they often approached the regiment's rendezvous together and shared space in the Keokuk barracks. When the troops departed for St. Louis and then Helena, some were accompanied by their families, while others were joined later by wives and children. Thus it was not only black men who risked recapture when they entered the U.S. army; wives and children often assumed the same risk. Perhaps they accompanied the regiment because they were reluctant to sever family ties that had just been liberated from bondage, perhaps because of a sense of shared duty, or perhaps because they believed that Iowa, Minnesota, or Wisconsin were no safer or more secure than the regimental encampment. Perhaps, as recently escaped slaves, they simply had no other place to go.

Robert Hutchinson's wife Harriet and their two toddlers lived with him at the Keokuk barracks for six weeks after their successful flight from slavery; they were together until the regiment left for St. Louis.[136] James and Nancy

Richards resided in the barracks at St. Louis until the regiment departed for Helena; Nancy later traveled down to Helena to care for James when he became sick with camp fever, nursing him until his death.[137] Jackson and Malinda Henry, Violet Moulton and husband Sherrod Henry, Mary Cox, and Henry Dais all fled slavery in Mississippi and Arkansas for Keokuk in the spring of 1863; the men enlisted in the fall, and both Malinda and Violet lived with their husbands in the Keokuk barracks.[138] Elizabeth Stuart, who had married William Stuart before the war, traveled from Keokuk to Helena and stayed with her husband's regiment for more than a year. Like Mary White Brown, she worked as a cook for the 60th USCI.[139] These and other families maneuvered to remain together even after enlistment, or they reunited when illness or injury threatened, suggesting that African Americans felt that neither military service nor wartime masculinity demanded removal of noncombatants from the regiment. To the contrary, intimate and familial relationships and responsibilities were consonant with, and central to, black manhood.

Some of the soldiers' wives made the trek from Iowa to Helena with the regimental sutler, a wealthy white Keokuk merchant by the name of George Pittman. Among them was Mary Triplett, who was notified in the spring of 1864 that her husband London was very ill. Mary and London, a son of Patsey Street and London Triplett, were both free blacks. London's parents had been Illinois slaves who lived for a time at Fort Crawford, where the younger London was probably born; he had won his freedom sometime before the war.[140] Mary, born in Washington, D.C., was brought by her employer to Missouri before the war, when her path crossed with London's. In 1859, they were married at Keokuk's AME church. They had twins (and another unsuccessful pregnancy) before London enlisted in the 60th and headed down to Helena.[141]

Accompanied to Helena by the regimental sutler, Mary Triplett found London sick from "some loathsome disease."[142] Amazingly, she had brought with her their five-year-old twin girls. One of London's company commanders authorized an addition to London's tent so that Mary and the girls could stay with him. She remained in Helena for five months, nursing her husband and caring for their daughters, until he had improved enough to be assigned light duties.

At first, neither Mary nor London knew what disease had infected him. London, who thought it was something from the local miasma, felt well enough within the next weeks to resume sexual intimacy with his wife. She later stated that "we continued to have sexual connection right along as we pleased so long as I remained there."[143] But when Mary returned to Keokuk, she experienced genital swelling, which she attributed to London's problem with the vaccine. Both London and Mary soon became the target of bawdy teasing and accusations, he in Helena and she in Keokuk; it was rumored among the men of the regiment and their families that Mary had infected London with syphilis.[144] "They said he had the clap," recalled Elizabeth Stuart, another soldier's wife then working for the regiment. "It was talked all over the Company," one soldier recalled. "The boys said the Keokuk ladies were nothing and said what she had done," though several of their friends—male and female—knew that neither were known to pursue sexual partners outside of their marriage.[145] It was not long before Mary realized she had contracted syphilis. Unsure of how it had happened, she thought she might have been infected in her work as a laundress—washing sheets. News of the couple's illness and the alleged reason for it spread quickly and continued after the war. At one point, the elders of Mary's AME congregation in Keokuk consulted on the matter. "It raised quite a stir in town," recalled Elizabeth Stuart.[146]

This remarkable story of tragic illness, marital devotion, wartime risks and courage, honor and reputation reveals several elements of the gendered experiences of war. It illustrates, for instance, that there were "hidden" victims of the military's vaccination crisis; wives, sweethearts, and their offspring were surely infected by the vaccines, with terrible consequences for their families. The death rate for infants with congenital syphilis was very high, and those who survived faced disabling sickness.[147] We are able to catch a glimpse of the standards of sexual morality to which husbands and wives were held by their friends, comrades, and church members. Contrary to popular white assumptions that African Americans universally engaged in unrestrained sexual behavior, the suggestion of extramarital sexuality in this instance subjected the Tripletts to the moral judgment of their communities. Some of London's comrades condemned Mary (and, by extension, all black women in Keokuk) for her alleged promiscuity. But it was not only Mary who was judged; London, too, felt the scorn of his peers for his syphilitic infection and its implications of sexual misconduct. But his treatment, unlike Mary's, often veered off into good-natured teasing; as one soldier recalled, "The boys would get to deviling him about it." Mary faced a different battle, including defending her good name when the issue was raised by her church elders.[148]

While a proud public saw the men of the 60th off to war and cheered their courage in returning south to face their former masters on the battlefield, the women of the regiment—sometimes accompanied by their children—were never publicly acknowledged or honored for taking some of the same risks

Migration and the Black Military Experience

when they headed south to care for sick and injured soldiers and to work in support of the unit. Their names do not appear among those of twenty African American women whose wartime hospital work at Helena entitled them to apply for pensions.[149] Nonetheless, whether free born or recently enslaved, they risked capture and resale into slavery, as well as injury and illness, by taking an active role in the life of the regiment. Although some white officers made efforts to aid the wives of soldiers, by the spring of 1865 Colonel John G. Hudson intervened to stop any further travel to the post by wives and to block marriages between the black soldiers and the "common place women of the town." Any soldier seeking to marry had to obtain the written permission of his company commander as well as the colonel himself. Soldiers would also be discouraged from staying out of their quarters at night with wives if they had not received the colonel's permission to marry. The order led several couples to marry, but it also forced several couples who had long regarded themselves as married to remarry if they had taken their vows as slaves.[150]

When the 60th prepared to return to Iowa to be mustered out, Hudson restricted the transportation that would be made available to women to two officially employed cooks, servants, or laundresses per company.[151] Despite their risks and their investments in the health and smooth functioning of the regiment, African American women appeared to be nothing more than a potential problem to be regulated.

HISTORIANS HAVE GENERALLY agreed that it was the black soldier's valor in battle that forced whites to respect him, rather than the daily determination to outlive the threats of disease, sunstroke, and injury.[152] The same midwesterners who had cheered the uniformed African Americans who marched smartly in parade could not understand the challenges of survival at Helena, challenges that far outweighed the risks of dying at the hand of the Confederate army. Although many of the men in Iowa's black regiment saw active combat and performed well under fire, most of the 60th's service had been devoted to the military labor that white commanders felt black troops were best suited for. Black veterans would face an uphill battle in their efforts to claim the respect and honor they had earned while serving their country in uniform. African American women would never receive their due for their service to the regiment and to freedom.

5 "The Building Up of Our Race"
Creating a Life in Freedom

Twenty years after his family's wartime escape from Missouri to Mt. Pleasant, Iowa, Moses Mosely reflected on the experience and promise of slavery's destruction. He recalled that the enslaved

> had nothing, knew nothing, and desired nothing but his freedom; he regarded it as a pearl of great price. Although nothing but freedom, it was marvelous to the imagination of the slave; the transition from slavery to freedom was beyond description. It filled the soul at least for a while; there was but little room for anything else until some of the excitement had a chance to work off. . . . We were all glad enough to get our liberty in the way it came. We were willing to take it in the rough and make the best of it we can by improvement.

"We shall . . . go forward," Mosely asserted, "in the building up of our race and repairing as quickly as possible the breach which has been made in it by slavery."[1]

Midwestern African Americans could not make "the best" of their liberty without confronting the legacy of slavery and racial inequality in law and conduct. Their struggle in this endeavor reminds us that the consequences of emancipation were never contained within the geographic limits of the former slave South. In the upper Midwest, where the majority of the black population at the close of the war were recent and second-generation migrants out of bondage, slavery was both more significant and more formative in the postwar era there than it was in other parts of the North.[2] As one writer offered in the pages of the nationally read African Methodist Episcopal (AME) denominational newspaper, the *Christian Recorder*, "In the East where slavery has never been known by this generation there is not felt the effect to so great an extent, as in the South and Northwest, where the masses of the people are just out of bondage."[3] For these midwestern African Americans, the postwar civil rights movement was concurrent with their efforts to restore and reunite families separated by slavery, the chaos of war, and northward migration.[4]

Leaving their struggle for the more formal rights of citizenship in voting booths and courts of law for a later chapter, here we turn to the communities and public culture created by black midwesterners in the aftermath of slavery, migration, emancipation, and war. The region's new black residents turned to building a new, free life in unfamiliar communities, without any of the material resources that migrants typically brought with them—clothes, tools, household or personal belongings. Education was an immediate priority for children as well as for adults, who deeply resented their enforced ignorance under slavery. They created communities, institutions, and social networks that brought together the diverse population of recently arrived migrants and second-generation, longer-term black settlers. They risked and challenged the ridicule of white midwesterners as they moved into and through white-dominated public spaces, while they also created a black public sphere, where they discussed and contested everything from the politics of sexuality and gender relations to partisan loyalties.[5] The result was a vigorous and expansive black civic life.[6]

As they discovered commonalities and differences in their experiences and expectations of life after slavery, black midwesterners also considered how gender roles and relations shaped the social, cultural, and political landscape. Women's and men's experience of "freedom in the rough" and their hopes for a more fully realized citizenship were deeply and differently influenced by gendered ideals, expectations, and behavioral conventions. Gender shaped their opportunities, their working lives, and the political strategies they used to challenge the many constraints and obstacles they encountered. Sexuality, too, played a complex role in black public life in the postemancipation era. In their efforts to rebuke white caricatures of black people as barbaric and permanently outside the "pale" of civilization, black leaders—especially religious leaders—portrayed wayward members of their congregations and communities as victims of a legacy of rapacious and immoral white slaveowners. However, they also urged African Americans to abide by a strict code of behavior with double standards and consequences for men and women. As a result, African Americans used the black public sphere to debate and contest conflicting ideas and expectations about gender and sexuality in their communities, as well as in their fight for respectability and citizenship.

The struggle for a fully realized freedom and citizenship was undertaken in workplaces, churches, and fraternal lodges, as well as in statehouses, polling places, and courtrooms. Although civil rights claims were rarely contained by the boundaries of any one venue, each setting presented distinct challenges, offered a particular context and cast of characters, and frequently drew on uniquely discernible chronologies of events and developments. While the more informal arenas of civil rights activism are treated separately from the more formal venues in this and the following chapter, the informal and the formal also overlapped in their influence on the region's emergent black culture. Through both, African Americans created a counterdiscourse to the ideas and practices of white supremacy that shaped formal politics as well as everyday life in the upper Mississippi valley.

"WE ALL WORKED OUT BY DAYS WORK"

In the immediate postwar era, some black residents touted the Midwest's economic opportunities for individual prosperity as well as for advancement of the race. They offered encouragement to recent migrants not only from the South, but also from the East. One enthusiast in Keokuk, Iowa, called on eastern readers of the *Christian Recorder* to realize that while "the right of suffrage and of testifying before the Courts" were "indispensable" rights,

> another indispensable necessity, equally vital to our prosperity, is, that we engage, without delay, in agriculture and mechanics. The wide prairies of the west hold out many inducements to those who have a desire to engage in agricultural pursuits. . . . On these distant prairies . . . the emigrant settler from the East is not required, with axe in hand, to fell a forest, in order to prepare the way for the next generation to cultivate the soil. The Almighty has laid out these broad plains with not a stone or stump to stop the progress of the husbandman's plow. A slight preparation of the soil, is all that is necessary to raise abundant crops. . . . Now, sir, we want mechanics and agriculturists; and we must have them, or we cannot, as a people, compete with our white neighbors, who will ever consider themselves our superiors, in consequence. We want machine shops carried on by competent colored men, and agricultural societies formed to look after the interests of the colored farmers. Let your Eastern cities try the experiment with the youth, and, in my opinion, it will prove successful, and become a source of incalculable blessing to the rising generation.[7]

Perhaps this writer's optimism was based on personal success; but for many, the promise of economic opportunity too often delivered obstacles and traps.

Recent migrants out of the South discovered that their opportunities were not unbounded. Indeed, a group portrait of the world of black labor in the two decades following the end of the war reveals that the color line continued to demarcate the midwestern workplace, limiting the jobs available to African Americans and perpetuating their economic vulnerability. While the obstacles to black workers were rarely attended by the kind of violence and systemic enforcement of white supremacy encountered on southern plantations, the midwestern labor market was far more limited than suggested by the optimistic writer from Keokuk. Employers still openly advertised for workers with the caveat that "no niggers need apply," and the social meanings of work were still deeply racialized.[8] It was not only the struggle for economic survival (let alone mobility) in a segregated labor market that shaped midwestern race relations; it was also the way in which work became a scaffolding for the structures and ideologies that sustained white supremacy. White employment of black servants continued to carry freighted meaning into the postwar period, reinforcing white perceptions of black subservience and white dominance, as well as preserving the color line in hiring patterns. More than a decade after the war, in an article intended as a humorous piece, a Keokuk newspaper described two local white young ladies "who wanted to drive in style, but who lacked a 'nigger' to drive, put their heads together and captured a younger sister, a little girl, and blackening her face," dressed her in boy's clothes and drove through town.[9] The lessons of the racialized meanings of work (and their implications for gender conventions) were still being taught and learned in the postwar, postemancipation Midwest.

Drawing on the life experiences of more than 2,200 African Americans who resided in Iowa between 1865 and 1880, one can make a number of observations.[10] In the twenty years following the close of the war, their daily labor distinguished midwestern African Americans as a group from white native-born and immigrant midwesterners. Similarities among black workers were found in the extremes. Black men and women were concentrated at the bottom of the occupational ladder, and only a very small proportion practiced a profession. Black men and women were also barred, for the most part, from industrial employment.

There were important distinctions between men's and women's work. For example, women were far less likely than men to report an occupation to census takers, yet they performed labor that was vital to household economies. From the beginning of the wartime diaspora, black women worked as farm laborers; after the war, their unpaid farm labor at home often allowed husbands and fathers to hire out as wage workers to neighboring white farmers. Matilda Dandridge may have been typical. Her family members were tenant farmers, and, although she listed no occupation in the 1870 census, she would "take the children and go into the fields and hoe and pull weeds from around the plants" while her husband hired out as a day laborer at white farms. She and the children sustained the home farm while making it possible for her husband to bring in wages as a day laborer.[11] Many African American women also took in boarders (without reporting this as an "occupation"); 21 percent of all women in this author's database and 42 percent of women reporting an occupation brought income into their households this way. From the poorest households to those of ministers and teachers, taking in boarders was practiced by African American women of all classes. In contrast, taking in boarders was not as widely practiced by white women; rather, it was largely the endeavor of wives whose husbands worked in "high non-manual" occupations.[12]

Half of African American women described themselves as either domestic servants (34 percent) or laundresses (17 percent); both were distinctly female jobs. No men reported laundry work, and only 4 percent of men reported employment as servants (mostly in hotels). These were physically demanding occupations. Mary Triplett's son Alfred appreciated the hard work his mother had to do to support five children; she "raised us children by washing and ironing."[13] Many working women moved between laundry, service, and other day jobs, like Nellie Hutchinson, who "washes and does housework, and all kinds of work in order to support herself, and is a respectable hard working woman."[14] In the same way, Nancy Richards "was always willing to turn her hand to whatever kind of work offered—from laundress to ladies waiting maid."[15] Far fewer white women were similarly employed—in 1860, only 9 percent of the white women in one Iowa river town worked as servants.[16] Yet it is also true that black midwestern women enjoyed better job opportunities than black urban women in the South; in 1880, 98 percent of working black women in Atlanta were domestic servants.[17]

In the Midwest, black women were concentrated in low-wage occupations, but they were also far more likely than men to live in households with other servants (households that were economically vulnerable, given servants' low wages).[18] Former slave Rebecca Rakes, a resident of Des Moines, was fairly typical. Describing her living arrangements during and after the Civil War with several other former slaves, she noted simply that "we all kept house together" and "we all worked out by days work." Rakes, who was seventeen years old when she arrived in Iowa in 1862, found it took her own wages plus those of four young men, as well as contributions from an adult male, to meet the monthly rent of four dollars.[19]

Midwestern black families were also distinguished from whites by higher rates of child employment. More than one-fifth of the African Americans

Creating a Life in Freedom

identified as working in white households were age sixteen or younger.[20] Low-wage families relied on children's outwork as a way to shelter and feed them, but also as a strategy for generating income for the core family. Like their white counterparts, older black children were expected to contribute to family support; however, the marked vulnerability of African Americans to poverty placed a greater burden on all family members, including children.[21]

The small numbers of midwestern black women employed in skilled occupations were found in dressmaking, hairdressing, sewing, and midwifery (5.6 percent). Teaching in and administering black schools provided the only professional occupations available to black women; nine women reported working as teachers, and two of these eventually became principals of segregated schools.

Hard work was also the lot of most employed black men; 60 percent were day laborers in and around towns or on farms.[22] Black men were twice as likely as white men to work in unskilled day labor that was physically demanding, poorly paid, and inconsistent.[23] This included men like former slave Isaac Cox, who performed any work he could get—as a hod carrier, woodchopper, or simply breaking rocks. Edwin Swanson, a former slave and Civil War veteran, "worked around" as a farmhand in south-central Iowa for seven or eight years, then moved to Fort Madison, where he "huckstered," performed day labor, and rafted logs on the Mississippi for a chair company.[24] George Johnson, another former slave and veteran, dug wells, cleaned privies, was a farmhand, and worked as a fiddler.[25]

About 18 percent of black day laborers were farmhands, the vast majority employed by white farmers. Most black farmhands patched together their support with a range of seasonal jobs.[26] Kansas Wilson combined seasonal work as a farmhand with cutting and delivering ice during the winter.[27] Agricultural wage labor encompassed a diverse range of tasks, which former slave men were well acquainted with. As a plowman on a white farm, Henry Vance cultivated corn, wheat, and oats.[28] Jerry White had two jobs: working in a grain elevator and "grubbing wood" on a half acre for a different employer.[29] Veteran Frederick Douglass (a self-chosen name) reported that his job as a plowman paid about eighteen dollars a month, which was similar to what other farmhands could earn.[30]

After the war, some black veterans returned to the midwestern communities where they had found employment during the war; however, sickness and war injuries had reduced some men's capacity for self-support.[31] Others were more fortunate; they came back healthy and used their wartime wages and bounty money to rent farms. A few moved out of day labor into farm tenancy or sharecropping.³² Rufus Dandridge worked days on the farms of white neighbors in Lee County, then went home and plowed his own crops by candlelight. The obstacles to land ownership were many. While the evidence is fragmentary, it appears that for Iowa's black farmers, tenancy or sharecropping was not the step toward farm ownership that at least some historians have found it to be for whites.³³ Samuel Red worked on O. S. Conklin's farm for eight months, then moved with Conklin to Keokuk. But Conklin never paid him "anything more than to buy him tobacco and one pair of boots," leaving him no further ahead than he had been after slavery.³⁴ One former slave who went to Iowa soon after his discharge from the service used his back pay and his wages from day labor after mustering out to purchase land in Mills County. But he had been swindled, and the land was "no good at all for farming." Left penniless, he tried again in Nebraska, hoping to homestead land there, but once again he lost everything.³⁵

A step above unskilled day labor could be found in transportation—as carriage and omnibus drivers, draymen, porters, hostlers, teamsters, and related occupations in liveries (8 percent of the black male workers I studied). A surprisingly small proportion of men reported working on the river as engineers, firemen, deckhands, or simple boatmen, or chopping and hauling wood for the packets running the river (3 percent). This might easily reflect an undercount; their mobility made river workers especially difficult to track. Steamboating meant frequent and extended absences from home, as well as a certain unpredictability in employment. The families of these men were often left to support themselves and their wives left to raise the children.³⁶

African American men appear to have been largely shut out of manufacturing, a pattern that continued through the nineteenth century.³⁷ The rapid postwar expansion of midwestern rail lines, however, created new employment opportunities on track crews and in coal mining. Both occupations were governed by a color line that initially excluded most African Americans. In 1866, a group of black men from Mt. Pleasant (where a large population of former slaves had settled during the war) arranged with a subcontractor to lay track on the Ottumwa-to-Des Moines line. On their arrival, however, they were turned away by the job foreman, who employed mostly Irishmen who were "opposed to working alongside of colored men."³⁸ Blacks were more successful challenging the color line in Iowa's coal mines, but initially only as strikebreakers during labor actions by white miners. One company hired black replacement workers from coal-mining districts in Missouri (in February 1880, to work mines near Albia, Monroe County), West Virginia (in 1880, to work in Lucas County), and Virginia (in 1880–81, to work at Muchakinock).

By the end of 1881, more than 850 black workers had been brought to Muchakinock, where despite the initial hostility and violence encountered from white strikers and the dangerous working conditions, they developed a thriving black community.[39] As one white employer boasted, Muchakinock soon included "happy homes, a colored school, a Methodist church, Masonic and Odd Fellows lodges, a fine brass band, and in fact all the accessories of comfort."[40]

Midwestern black men fared better than black easterners in obtaining skilled work. Only 25 percent of antebellum blacks in northern cities east of Cincinnati were employed in skilled labor, and in 1870 just over 12 percent of the blacks in Washington, D.C., were similarly employed, while nearly a third of midwestern black men found jobs as skilled laborers.[41] Whether skilled or unskilled, black men felt the impact of midwestern racism in terms of limited intergenerational social mobility; even their better-educated sons could not hope for better opportunities. As one man observed in 1886: "Your sons graduate from your high school to have offered them as incentives to development—what? Positions as clerks, messengers, salesmen, agents? No, no, no! A position in the rear of the premises to rub horses at $3 per week. Here they may quote Cicero and Virgil to the horses, apply chemistry and physics to the coal scuttles, figure out geometry and trigonometry in the carriage wheels."[42] Such a limited patrimony would have surely been experienced as a denial of black manhood.

A strikingly small percentage of African American men (4 percent) found professional employment, a stark contrast to the 28 percent of white men in Dubuque in 1870 so employed, but higher than the 1 to 2 percent found among northern urban blacks before the war.[43] Ministers were the most numerous professionals, though many ministers could not rely entirely on their congregations for support. William Stuart reported that "I preach the gospel some," but he also worked as a plasterer.[44] Other professionals included a handful of teachers, school principals, and lawyers.

A few African Americans worked in hotels (3 percent), often as waiters. George Caldwell, one of Keokuk's most respected black men, was a hotel "runner," recruiting business from newly arrived steamboats on Keokuk's busy wharfs.[45] Ten percent of African American men reported working in the semiprofessional occupation of barbering in hotels, their own shops, and as employees of (usually African American) barbershop owners.[46] There were few entrepreneurs other than shop-owning barbers. John Hiner, who owned a butcher shop and packinghouse, was one; Alexander Clark, who had a lumber supply business and delved into real estate, was another. One of very few female entrepreneurs was Nancy Yancey, a former slave born in West Virginia who gained her freedom and studied at Oberlin College before emigrating to Iowa prior to the Civil War. Her family's sole support after the death of her husband in 1870, and apparently denied a teaching position at Fairfield, Yancey established a successful laundry business in the community that supported her family and provided jobs for several other African Americans as well.[47] Eliza Warren, a Tennessee-born former slave, also opened a laundry business, in Oskaloosa, which employed several additional black workers.[48] That the only examples of female entrepreneurship to emerge from the historical record involved laundry work suggests, on one hand, how opportunity could be carved out of the few prospects available to African American women but, on the other hand, how even the most entrepreneurial black women could be so limited in the possibilities they might pursue. Certainly Nancy Yancey may have preferred a teaching career, but her prosperous laundry business supported her family as well as others in her community, provided her children with an education, and even became a source of income in her old age.

After the war, most black midwesterners struggled to provide for their families. The barriers of poverty, illiteracy, white control over industrial and skilled work sites, as well as racism's broad impact on employer preferences, meant that African Americans were largely relegated to the unpredictable and poorly paid arena of day labor and domestic service. The promise of opportunity in the West, touted in black newspapers as the answer to the rigid segregation of eastern and urban labor markets, would prove to be overly optimistic. For black midwesterners, their struggle was a different and undoubtedly easier one than that experienced farther south, particularly among those who contended with former masters and mistresses as their employers. Yet despite their concentration in the lowest-paying occupations of the Midwest, African Americans used their meager resources not only to eke out an existence for themselves and their families but also to support the first institutions that black communities built: their churches.

"GREAT PRAISE IS DUE THE . . . SISTERS"

The Reverend John W. Malone, born a slave in North Carolina but freed by his family's self-purchase before the war, went to Iowa in 1862, when he first began his itinerancy for the AME Church. Later, looking back on a quarter century of missionary work, he recalled

> having unfurled the banner and planted the standard in Indiana, Illinois, Wisconsin, Minnesota, Dakota, etc. I have suffered much from cold and

hunger; sometimes twenty to thirty hours without a meal of victuals. I have walked from ten to twenty-five and thirty miles regularly, from appointment to appointment; at times plunging through the snow waist deep. Have been out all day and nearly all night when it was from twenty to forty degrees below zero; have been at railroad crossings and stations, where there was no building, waiting in the cold and snow for a train and had to jump and stir around to keep from freezing, etc. I have been away many months at a time before returning to my family in order to succeed in organizing Wisconsin, Minnesota, Iowa, and Dakota, etc. . . . During all these trials and hardships my family never suffered for food and raiment, etc. Thank the good Lord I am still in the field doing service.[49]

Malone may have romanticized the ability of itinerant ministers to overcome the difficulties they faced in the mid-nineteenth-century Midwest, but he was quick to acknowledge the important work of women in advancing the denomination. "Great praise" was due the sisters, he noted repeatedly in the pages of the *Christian Recorder*, as he listed the sums they had gathered to support the church and the food they had provided to ministers' families.[50] Malone's experience was multiplied many times over by the itinerant churchmen who—with their wives and families—began building congregations and churches throughout the upper Midwest. With antebellum black migration, the AME Church, from its origins in Pennsylvania, was transported west across the Alleghenies to Indiana, Ohio, and Illinois—where the Midwest's largest church, Quinn Chapel, became a symbol of denominational expansion. Beginning in 1848, many of the most prominent AME leaders played a role in bringing the church to the Midwest, including Bishops Paul Quinn, Alexander Walker Wayman, and Richard Harvey Cain. (Cain's first charge was Muscatine's AME church in 1856–57; he would serve as a South Carolina state senator and U.S. congressman during Reconstruction.)[51]

The spread of black congregations throughout the upper Midwest began with two of the earliest black communities in Iowa: Muscatine (1848) and Keokuk (1857). When the wartime diaspora out of the South created a demand for more churches, the upper Midwest became a fruitful vineyard for the major black denominations, particularly as the AME Church grew into a truly national organization.[52] During the Civil War, four new AME congregations were organized in Iowa (at Burlington, Washington, Cedar Rapids, and Mt. Pleasant). By 1885, eighteen additional churches had been created in Iowa, Minnesota, and Wisconsin. Black Baptists also extended their reach north and westward. The upper Midwest's first black Baptists worshiped in white congregations before and during the Civil War, at Burlington and Keokuk, Iowa. By 1864, midwestern black Baptists were organizing and building their own churches, with memberships that often exceeded those of black Methodist churches; by 1882, black Baptists had formed ten more congregations in the region.

Despite their similar pace of growth, there were some important differences in the efforts and successes of the two denominations. The AME system of quarterly meetings and an annual General Conference sustained a significant connection among churches and between regions. This network was further reinforced by the practice of itinerancy; by the national circulation of the denominational newspaper, the *Christian Recorder*; and by the frequent visitations of bishops throughout the conference. Baptist congregations, however, largely relied on the skills and enthusiasm of individual ministers, and black Baptists sometimes joined white congregations before black churches could be organized. Advocates for the cultural and spiritual authority of African Americans, like Reverend Malone, found it disgraceful that, as late as 1870, St. Paul's black Baptists were still "partially organized under the government of the whites and worship in a small room.... [where] a white man is boss over them."[53] Malone often was critical of the treatment of black congregations under white pastors or white-led denominations; he was not hesitant to publicize that fact when he encountered black congregations in Iowa that were "tired of being under the white folks."[54] After being governed by white State Conventions for a number of years, Iowa's black Baptists organized a separate black association in 1878 (later than in the South, where eight states had formed black associations by 1870).[55] But even after 1878, the new association had to ask the white convention for financial assistance to keep up with debt on church buildings and ministerial salaries. Annual reports from the 1880s reveal the frequency with which Baptist ministers were "compelled to resign, on account of the churches being unable to support them, and obliged to seek other employment."[56]

Although former slaves were widely distributed among upper midwestern denominations, the relative economic vulnerability and instability of Baptist congregations probably reflects in part the poverty of the recently arrived former slaves, who lacked the resources to sustain a church. Into the 1880s, the Iowa Baptist Association recognized the "commendable efforts to keep a house of God under the most difficult circumstances," referring to one church that "consists of a little band of sisters, who all alone hold up their banner in that town, and are worthy of all praise for their labor of love, and should be encouraged in every possible way by this body."[57] Despite their connection to the white Baptist State Convention (making reports and attending the annual meeting), within less than ten years the black Baptists became financially independent, and by the 1890s they ceased reporting to the white State Convention. Throughout the 1890s, white Baptists would call for renewed ties with the black association, assuming that it needed "patient watchful care and judicious aid" and "the moulding influence of those qualified to counsel and direct." Black Baptists offered no explicit rebuff to these expressions of white paternalism but appear to have simply gone about their business of self-support and self-governance.[58] In 1895, black Baptists developed a permanent national convention.[59]

Black congregations emerged and church buildings were built in the upper Midwest through not only the pioneering activities of ministers, but also the contributions and hard work of their wives and female congregants. Although denominational histories of the nineteenth century emphasize the toil of pioneering ministers (often eulogized as "battle-scarred and blood-washed warriors")—in what religious scholar Julius H. Bailey describes as "narratives of masculine achievement"—a careful reading of contemporary sources indicates the importance of women's work to church building in the Midwest.[60] In fact, the heroicized itinerancy of ministers like John W. Malone relied heavily on women's exertions, both visible and invisible: their income-generating and income-saving activities, their contributions to ministers' salaries and the cost of building and maintaining church structures and their organizational skills in unifying newly forming congregations.

When the Reverend Abraham T. Hall was appointed to the Keokuk Station during the Civil War and found his circumstances "rather close"—not only fifty dollars in debt but behind in his taxes and several months without a salary—we can surmise that his wife Johanna did everything in her power to keep their household afloat; that she found a way to feed and clothe their children, while maintaining the respectable appearance of a preacher's family. She may have been helped, as another pastor's family was, by donations of "many articles of comfort and utility" from the women of the church.[61] Indeed, shortly after the Halls arrived, several women in the congregation formed a sewing circle, and it was this society—with its many fairs and festivals—that provided the chief sustenance for ministers and their families during the difficult years of the Civil War.[62] By 1863, they had raised enough money to pay for seats and a pulpit in their new church.[63] So important were the group's contributions that the itinerant preachers who variously served the congregation later battled over who could claim to have helped organize the sewing circle.[64]

Creating a Life in Freedom

The support of churchwomen was vital to congregations throughout the upper Midwest. In Oskaloosa, Iowa, AME women raised $177 to pay for the furnishings of their new church at the close of 1865.[65] In 1866, the AME sewing circle in Davenport raised $64 toward the cost of their church building and lot; by hosting festivals and fairs, they maintained a steady flow of funding for the church in the 1870s.[66] In 1867, the women of the AME congregation in Des Moines offered a benefit Emancipation Day supper and, in 1873, a festival to raise funds for their church.[67] What is also notable about their pivotal role in building and sustaining congregations was the economic vulnerability of most midwestern black women. Although—despite their hard work—they were among the most impoverished people in the region, these women nonetheless found a way to ensure the viability of their churches.

In addition to their crucial material and financial support, African American women were among the charter or organizing members of many new congregations. In Keokuk, Muscatine (where female charter members of the AME congregation outnumbered their male counterparts), Burlington, and St. Paul, women were numerous among church founders.[68] Women sustained the region's black congregations with their hard-earned money, with fundraisers, with food for ministers and their families, but also with their religious devotion.

For long-term midwestern residents and those recently arrived from the South, the black church offered much more than a place to worship; it was the center of the black public sphere.[69] When men and women dedicated themselves to their churches, they were building and sustaining community centers as well as houses of worship. The black-controlled space of the church was a critical community resource in a region still dominated by practices of segregation and white supremacy. With public primary schools segregated into the 1870s (and African Americans excluded from public high schools), most black schools were housed in (and partially supported by) black churches. They provided education for school-age children, as well as Sunday schools and Bible classes (which included literacy education) for adults. One such class was organized explicitly for the "old sisters" of Muscatine's AME church.[70] In addition to serving as classrooms for their communities, black churches also became a major venue for political meetings, ceremonial occasions, and celebrations. Most Emancipation Day gatherings began or ended at black churches.[71]

Given their well-documented, publicly lauded efforts to sustain ministers' families and church edifices, it is not surprising that black women of the AME Church claimed an active citizenship in their congregations and in denominational proceedings. They made these claims despite, and perhaps in response to, church insistence on a male-dominated ministry and hierarchy during the antebellum era. At least three times before and once during the war, the AME Church considered and rejected petitions asking that female preachers be recognized.[72] Female exhorters and evangelists had a strong tradition in the denomination (consider the example of Mrs. Elizabeth Duffin of Galena, Illinois, who was well known among midwestern itinerants: "Hundreds of persons were awakened and saved by the fervor of her faith and prayers"; she was a "Shaft of fire" in the house of God, according to her obituary). But as Julius Bailey has pointed out, the AME General Conference moved to separate the roles of exhorter and preacher in the 1830s, as the denomination's male leaders sought to protect their own position and limit the role of women.[73] The historian James Campbell has observed that the AME Church became more concerned with limiting the position of women in the church as it sought to defend and assert black manhood in the late antebellum and Civil War eras: "Black women's struggle for equality," he asserts, "would be sacrificed on the altar of racial manhood."[74] Persuaded that the reciprocal nature of gender relations required women to follow if men were to lead, most ministers throughout the nineteenth century endorsed women's exclusion from the ministry. In 1884, the delegates to the General Conference finally allowed women to hold exhorter licenses (twenty years after these licenses were first proposed at the General Conference). But, once again, they agreed that "women had no right to go into the pulpit to preach"; "God had circumscribed her sphere, and whenever she goes out of it injury is done to society." Another delegate stated: "I vote in favor of their staying home and taking care of the babies." Several well-known, respected female evangelists were present during the discussion of this question, but they would continue their work in the Iowa Conference.[75]

Beyond the battle over the pulpit, AME women persistently defended what they viewed as their integral role in the denomination. For example, New Orleans pastor (and former Iowan) William A. Dove persuaded delegates of the Missouri Conference to hold their 1865 meeting in New Orleans, stating that his congregants would cover the travel expenses of all those who wished to attend. By July 1865, however, Dove wrote to the *Christian Recorder* that since "times were hard" in New Orleans and his congregation could not offer as much financial support as it had hoped, Dove now urged "my brethren" to "bring as little encumbrance as possible; in fact, ministers will be better off here without their families, as board is very high."[76] In the next several issues of the paper, members of the conference from Kentucky to Kansas leveled pointed criticism at Dove for failing to keep his promises and for characterizing ministers' families as an encumbrance. One of the sharpest critiques came from Mary A. Turner, who resented being portrayed as "combrous"; she pointed out that the annual conference was a time for the wives of ministers and bishops to meet and tend to denominational business. Dove's public dismissal of AME wives as inconsequential to denominational matters thus had prompted an immediate and a loud response.

By 1868, given the large proportion of women among its members and their instrumental role in fund-raising, AME Church leaders saw fit to create a new (if still limited) role for women as "Stewardesses" to shepherd members: that is, to care for the poor and needy, help maintain church discipline, and, of course, continue their fund-raising efforts. Over the next two decades, the General Conference repeatedly enlarged women's responsibilities and privileges, including creating a new role for them at the General Conference meetings. Nevertheless, there was enough resistance to delay action until the end of the century.[77] By that time, midwestern AME women had found alternate routes to influence, authority, and service in their congregations by assuming leading roles in Sunday school associations. Within the black Baptist denomination, women assumed new roles as church clerks and missionary society leaders.[78]

In men's exclusion of women from the pulpit, resistance to an expanded role for stewardesses and licensing of female exhorters, and unwillingness to accept new roles for women outside of Sunday schools and missionary societies, both denominations offered evidence of what Julius Bailey has called the "masculinization of the pulpit," an intensified claim by black men on the ministry as an exclusively masculine domain. The postbellum focus on the manhood of the ministry was also seen in the emphasis on an educated ministry and in the critique of an older, more emotive style of worship that was often associated with female religiosity.[79] The valorization of the earliest generation of itinerants to bring Methodism to the Midwest echoed this masculinist emphasis. In the *Christian Recorder*, the term "veteran" referred to these pioneering itinerants, not to the soldiers who had fought in the Civil War.[80] At this time, black men were denied the patriarchal role of family breadwinner by the continued economic necessity of female wage earning; by occupational barriers that restricted social mobility and the respectability denoted by social class; and by Jim Crow laws, north and south, all of which restricted black men's ability to protect wives and female kin from insulting public behaviors.[81] The black denominational ministry remained a refuge for male authority and prerogative. In this setting, some African American men laid claim to the idealized gender roles of the society against which they were constantly measured and found wanting.

Yet gender roles and relationships continued to be contested. As the historian Martha S. Jones has shown, beginning in 1872 and through 1880, the AME General Conference considered and passed (with little debate) several proposals to extend denominational voting rights to churchwomen.[82] It also debated the politics of gender and sexuality when it considered church discipline regarding marriage. In 1872, the General Conference entertained a proposal by the Reverend Thomas H. Jackson to strike the word "obey" from the matrimonial service. Although seconded, the motion was tabled without further discussion. Although we cannot know Jackson's reasons for proposing this change (nor why it failed to pass), his recommendation suggests an effort to reenvision the marriage relationship. It also indicates an astute awareness that "obedience" might be associated with enslavement by a generation so recently emancipated.[83]

In the postwar era, marriage was a reoccurring topic of discussion as church leaders attempted to enforce the denomination's expectations concerning marriage and divorce (the latter grounds for expulsion) among a following that included many former slaves. Many had been separated from their mates involuntarily, and their postemancipation marriages and intimate relationships sometimes departed from denominational doctrine that prohibited separation or remarriage except after the death of a spouse. "'Grass widows' [abandoned mistresses of married men] must take a back seat; nor must men with two wives come to the front," insisted a reader of the *Christian Recorder*.[84] During the war, debate about marital behavior had escalated as AME leaders disagreed about how the church should view relationships formed during slavery. Still others pressed successfully for a revision of doctrine, to distinguish between guilty and innocent parties in cases of adultery—allowing the innocent party to remarry.

By the 1880s, evidence of the denomination's turn to more conservative doctrine and policy surfaced when leaders called for a more rigid church law in the area of sexual and conjugal relations. This did not necessarily translate into wholesale support for male dominance, however. In 1883 the *Christian Recorder*'s editor critiqued domestic abuse and battery as regrettable carryovers from slavery, especially among men "brought up, if not in slavery, under its influence," who "believe that just as 'old massa' used to rule the plantation, even so they should rule their houses."[85]

The AME Church became increasingly conservative on matters of sexuality as whites increasingly turned to mob violence to control black men, whom they regarded as harboring a savage and criminal sexuality that threatened white civilization and white womanhood. Many black denominations were on the defensive, insisting on higher standards of "respectability" in their effort to distance themselves from whites' caricatures and their often violent consequences. In the upper Midwest, African American men charged with rape or attempted rape against white victims were likely to be met by violent white mobs or sometimes killed. Between 1864 and 1895, eight of ten black men accused of rape or attempted rape against white women were threatened by lynch mobs, and two were murdered.[86] Even the *Woman's Journal*, published by the American Woman Suffrage Association, called for an extralegal "manly outburst" by white men to answer an alleged assault on a white Iowa woman by an African American man.[87] In contrast, in none of the nine incidents where white men were accused of the rape, or attempted rape, of black women were the individuals charged threatened with or subjected to extralegal violence.[88] White caricatures of black men as aggressive sexual brutes and black women as promiscuous and indiscriminate were powerful cultural weapons that black communities were forced to contend with.

DESPITE THE INCREASED valorization of male authority in black denominations, female congregants in the upper Midwest made public claims in the arena of church and denominational governance and in surveillance over the actions and behavior of their clergy. In a number of conflicts and disciplinary proceedings occurring during and after the war, women demanded public accountability from male church leaders as well as male congregants—particularly when a female's reputation was at stake.[89]

The AME Church was a powerful advocate for black manhood and a patriarchal, Victorian-modeled black family in the decades following the war. From the inception of the denomination, family life, sexual mores and conduct, and gender relations were all subjects of concern, teaching, contestation, and surveillance, particularly as the church sought to reconcile male-dominant modes of organization and respectability with the essential work of women. In the Civil War era, men and women found their behavior scrutinized, and they appealed to the church to adjudicate conflicts relating to gender relations and sexuality. African American women also saw the church as a unique venue where they could call black men to justice without risking the consequences for entire communities when whites presumed to judge and punish them. In fact, the church served as an important site of recourse and deliberation when churchmen as well as laypeople were charged with misconduct. Few venues in black community life revealed more about their conflicts, behaviors, and values—actual and rumored—than did the AME Church.

Early in 1863, the Reverend William Dove left his post in Chicago and returned to his wife and family in Keokuk under a cloud of suspicion heightened by sensationalist reporting in Chicago newspapers, as well as by more cautious but pointed reports carried in the *Christian Recorder*. Dove, who had served widely in Indiana, Illinois, and Iowa before the war, was well known in the Midwest and highly regarded by many. But early in December 1862, while serving his Chicago congregation, his parsonage was "inked" (daubed with paint, graffiti-style, as a mark of public criticism). By the next day, a rumor had surfaced that Dove was responsible for the pregnancy of four young girls. The "rumor continued to increase until it was in the mouth of about all the colored people in the city."[90]

According to Dove, several months earlier one of these young unmarried women had confided in him that she was pregnant by a "big fish"—a notable member of the congregation—and that she planned to leave the city. Dove had counseled her to tell her mother, but she refused "because . . . her mother would destroy the child as she did her sister's." (Her mention of abortion was apparently unremarkable, as later testimony did not refer back to it.) According to the young woman's subsequent testimony, Dove had also suggested she identify the father as a young man in the congregation. When rumors of her pregnancy surfaced in December 1862, Dove conferred with her stepfather, who then took his daughter to confront the young man he presumed to be the father of her child. At this point the daughter, angry that Dove had revealed her pregnancy to her stepfather, insisted that Dove was the father.[91]

In the meantime, Dove interviewed each of the other girls in the presence of their mothers, and each denied any sexual contact with him. By the end of the week, the church stewards had investigated the matter and assembled the members of Quinn Chapel—about one hundred people—to hear their report exonerating him. However, as Dove later contended, the members, some of whom Dove referred to as his "avowed enemies," were not satisfied with the stewards' investigation and demanded that three of the girls be cross-examined before the entire congregation. Under "close questioning," the young women again denied Dove's involvement, and the congregation exonerated him. Still, his "enemies" sent for the fourth young woman to be interviewed. According to Dove, "She arose and made her statement, which was so much out of reason and such a lie, that the d——l himself would have blushed to have told it." Although her testimony was unsettling, Dove was absolved of all wrongdoing.[92]

But the denomination was not through investigating. A week later, the official Church Board (including stewards, class leaders, trustees, local preachers, exhorters, and a visiting minister) met to formally review the rumors, the stewards' investigation, and the congregation's vote. That board also voted to clear Dove of censure. The case then went to Bishop Quinn, who traveled to Chicago to investigate for himself. The fourth young woman's mother, in a meeting with the bishop, accused Dove of fornication or adultery, detailing dates and times of the alleged acts. The bishop initiated another inquiry. Meanwhile, the rumors surrounding Dove so disrupted the Chicago congregation that it interfered with the planned festivities to commemorate the Emancipation Proclamation on New Year's Day. When Dove attempted to lead the congregation in prayer during the celebration, he was hissed at by some of the congregants.[93]

Before the bishop concluded his investigation, the *Chicago Tribune* got wind of what it called a "Scandal in Colored Religious Circles." The circumstances gave the paper an irresistible opportunity to smear an African American man who claimed the moral authority and respectability of the ministry. Naming Dove as the suspect, the *Tribune* reported that he had been charged "with the ruin of a number of colored girls belonging to his flock," carrying on a "system of vile debauchery" for the past year. Moreover, "Dove [had] been once before suspended from all ministerial functions, for similar conduct in Indiana." Referring to Dove as a "sable lothario," the paper reported that he had "gone missing."[94]

The outcome of Bishop Quinn's final investigation was less clear than the *Tribune* suggested. Dove resigned his pastoral charge in Chicago and departed immediately for Iowa, "incensed at the malice of the people," but also to escape renewed efforts to "make the girl swear before the court her child upon me." He was "advised by friends to leave, and if possible save the colored people" from further public embarrassment.[95] Dove would later claim that he was acquitted by the bishop and arrived in Iowa "with my credentials in hand."[96] But A. McIntosh, one of the ministers aiding Quinn's inquiry, reported a different conclusion: the bishop's committee "did make enough out of it to silence Brother Dove from all official standing until the next ensuing Annual conference." And if "Bro. Dove did not know it, it was because he did not stay to hear the committee's report."[97]

By mid-February 1863 in Keokuk, where Dove had joined his wife and her mother, the AME congregation had become "very much divided, one against the other," over the charges.[98] That August, when the Indiana Conference met at Chicago, Dove's alleged behavior once again became a topic of community, denominational, and regional interest, especially when the conference decided to try Dove once more, "as though the case never had been." The conference then cleared Dove of all charges, asserting that "there was no testimony against him."⁹⁹ The *Chicago Times*, a Democratic newspaper, explained the outcome differently. Dove's acquittal, argued the *Times*, demonstrated that black "preachers and leaders" saw no impropriety in adultery or sexual immorality. "The race is sensual, brutish, incapable of those finer feelings which have developed the civilization of the white man, and unable to perceive sin in that which to our eyes is the worst kind of moral turpitude." The article, printed while the Indiana Conference was still in session, triggered an emphatic response by the delegates. The *Times* report, they declared, was not only a "slanderous attack" on the denomination and an ignorant insult to the gathered ministers, but also an attempt to degrade the entire African American race.¹⁰⁰

For denominational officials, the matter was now settled. Dove was transferred to a New Orleans congregation. He would not serve again in Illinois, Indiana, or Iowa, although apparently his family continued to live in Keokuk, and his wife became a leader in that city's postbellum civil rights struggle. Although neither denominational nor secular newspapers mentioned the sexual charges again, only two years later Dove became the target of denominational dissension over his reference to the wives of churchmen as costly "encumbrances" who drained the local finances needed to support annual regional conferences. Yet despite the Chicago charges and the resentment that arose around his demeaning reference to women's presence at the annual conference, Dove would be remembered in later years as one of the "western warriors" of the AME Church, an elder who filled several important posts "with uniform success," as some recalled.¹⁰¹

Dove was not the only midwestern AME minister to be the subject of church investigations demanded by female congregants. In December 1874, Milwaukee's congregation leveled serious charges of alleged immoral conduct against their pastor, the Reverend J. H. D. Payne.¹⁰² Bishop Alexander Walker Wayman assigned a committee to investigate, but Payne fled the state ("to escape the wrath of his people") and word soon leaked to the press. In typical sensationalist style, the *Chicago Tribune* reported a "Clerical Scandal" in the black community. With salacious details that read like popular fiction, the *Tribune* described a visit that Reverend Payne had paid to a Mrs. Shear, a "grass widow" and former member of his congregation. Their conversation reportedly "turned upon the plenty they enjoyed in the Sunny South, and the lady lamented her lack of coffee, sugar, and other pleasing adjuncts of a well-supplied larder" (implying unlikely fond reminiscences of a better life under slavery). Payne offered Mrs. Shear some provisions, which she later sent her daughter, described in the *Tribune* as "a buxom lass of 14," to Payne's house to collect. On her return, the daughter reported that she had been sexually assaulted by Payne "under threat of death." The following day, Mrs. Shear and her daughter "gathered their aprons full of stones and proceeded to church with the avowed intention of stoning the rascal out of the pulpit," hoping to "right the wrong." In response, local church leaders confronted Payne, who denied the charge and demanded an investigation. But by the next day, he had packed up his belongings and left Milwaukee for his home in Ohio. Mrs. Shear subsequently "swore out a warrant charging the Rev. J. H. D. Payne with rape" (although there is no evidence that the case moved forward).[103] According to later reports in the *Christian Recorder*, the bishop assigned a committee to hear the charges against Payne, and it found him guilty. Within two weeks, the minister had submitted his resignation, although he would attempt to vindicate himself at the next meeting of the General Conference.

We cannot know all the facts of these two cases or the truth behind the charges. What we do know for certain is that women, as vocal and active congregants, made claims they brought directly to church officials, testified before church representatives, and challenged the leadership, veracity, and moral authority of male church leaders. Nor were these isolated instances of churchwomen's influence. Women congregants in Fond du Lac, Wisconsin (one of the communities to receive a significant number of contrabands during the war), were also notably assertive. In 1879, several female members of the city's African Methodist Episcopal Zion (AMEZ) congregation objected so strenuously to having their names appear on a list of the membership's "backsliders" that they were arrested and fined for disturbing the peace. The following year, Liz Williams not only disrupted the proceedings of a special meeting called to investigate financial difficulties at the same church, but she also resisted the efforts of the pastor and male elders to force her to leave. The local newspaper reported that "Liz defied them," and the police were called to intervene.[104]

Another church trial, this one occurring in Des Moines in 1867, portrayed female congregants as assertive, even physically demonstrative, in claiming not only church membership but also church citizenship. Early in January 1867 (barely six months after the organization of Burns AME Chapel, the city's first black church), Samuel J. and Hannah Harris were tried before the membership for "keeping a house of ill fame." The church may have had a particular interest in trying Samuel because of his position as a church exhorter, but perhaps also because he had emerged as a public figure following his address at the city's 1866 Emancipation Day celebration.[105] After a regular Friday evening service, the congregation's pastor, the Reverend S. T. Wells (a very public and politically active figure), asked all the female congregants to leave, as well as any men who were not members. Hannah Harris, along with one other woman, refused to go. One of the male congregants, a class leader, made a statement about the case, and, according to later reports, Hannah not only accused him of lying but also threatened him physically. Unable to preserve order, Reverend Wells finally "called out to the men to 'put that woman out' (some say he used more violent language)." Hannah resisted when one of the church's "leading members" tried to carry her out. Wells then came forward with a stick in hand and forced her out of the building, though not before she had taken a good bite out of his ear. In response, at least three lawsuits were filed; in one, Hannah Harris sued Wells for assault and battery. Her case, heard before a packed courtroom of spectators, lasted a full day.[106]

The jury responded in this and the other cases with "not guilty" verdicts, endorsing and sustaining Reverend Wells's prerogative to exercise authority over his congregation. As in the cases involving Dove and Payne, the white press was derogatory in its portrayal of the trial participants ("amusing and ludicrous"), pandering to racist caricatures and inventing details that reinforced racist stereotypes.[107] But there is another, important sub rosa narrative revealed by these contentious developments. The churches involved were clearly regarded by congregants as constituting a public sphere, where grievances could be voiced, reputations defended, and disputes aired and settled. Yet if the church provided a space for open discussion and hearings of conflicts, it also inadvertently disclosed them to the wider (and whiter) public eye. Charges and countercharges quickly led to reports in the white press attacking the propriety and morality of church leaders as well as laity. Yet this reporting appears not to have dampened congregants' determination to express their differences within their church communities.

As these stories of female congregants reveal, the history of black church building and denominational expansion in the upper Midwest was far more than an account of heroic male itinerants contending with the natural landscape of the midwestern frontier. White efforts to diminish black men's authority were as persistent a feature of this landscape as harsh winter weather, and both features made the work of churchmen more difficult. But men were not alone in their work. Female congregants, along with ministers' wives, were central to the organization and maintenance of their church communities; furthermore, they provided a considerable portion of the money that paid for church buildings and ministers' salaries. They also laid the groundwork for the expansion of African American women's public activism in the next generation, widely referred to by historians as "The Woman's Era," which was

Creating a Life in Freedom

marked by the emergence of women's national secular and sacred associational life.[108] Although excluded from the pulpit, black women claimed citizenship in their churches and denominational structures. They challenged perceived abuses of authority and violations of church discipline on the part of male clergy, and they were quick to defend their role—however limited—in church operations. Neither poverty, nor economically vulnerable households, nor the workplace barriers that kept most black women in domestic service prevented them from playing an instrumental part in the process of community building. The patriarchal model of the black churches and their denominational governance could not restrain women's claims of citizenship in the institutions they had sacrificed so much to develop and sustain.

"TO BE CONSIDERED AS MEN AMONGST MEN"

In the postemancipation era, secular venues overlapped with sacred ones as central sites for community development and the articulation of shared values. Fraternal (and later, sororal) associations would grow along with black settlement in the upper Midwest. Associational life was especially important to the formulation of civic identities and as a training ground for civic activism. Black fraternal societies were "genuinely 'civic'": as the scholars Theda Skocpol and Jennifer Lynn Osler have noted, they enabled African Americans to participate "in parades and other public occasions, support education and community service, maintain halls that are also used by other groups, and from time to time get involved in legislative or policy campaigns."[109] In the upper Midwest, fraternal associations—especially black and white Masonry—became principal sites for the articulation of evolving racial ideologies, race organizing, and masculine identity. Importantly, Masonry's historic legacy of segregation was openly debated and confronted as black and white members considered the implications of the changing status of African Americans in the aftermath of emancipation. The debates that ensued reveal a great deal about contemporary perceptions of the relationship between manhood and race.

In the Midwest, as across the nation, Masonry was a major vehicle for building and sustaining regional homosocial networks. It provided an opportunity for individual men to develop and groom their leadership potential; it became a venue for the accrual, display, and contest over individual and group power; and it was one of the locations from which African American men challenged discriminatory practices as well as the ideologies of racialism and white supremacy. Membership gave both free and former slave men a chance to demonstrate their ability to learn, achieve, and behave like men, and, perhaps most crucially, to be recognized as men—despite the inequities perpetrated by a white-dominated marketplace and a larger public sphere that demeaned black manhood and black men's abilities.

The gendered significance of black fraternalism was also shaped by women's involvement in auxiliary associations (including the Order of the Eastern Star and the Heroines of Jericho), and in ceremonies and rituals that were open to the female family members and escorts of Prince Hall Masons.[110] For example, just after the close of the Civil War, the wives of Chicago's leading black Masons honored the members of the North Star Lodge by presenting them with "a beautiful silk flag of national colors, with Masonic emblems, costing over one hundred dollars." This event drew on familiar wartime rituals in which black women presented flags to black regiments as they headed off to battle. The Chicago ceremony was conducted entirely by women, who used the occasion to idealize black men as the protectors of women and the nation, especially by linking the military achievements of black soldiers to the black men, "dressed in full regalia," who marched around Metropolitan Hall "bearing the flag."[111]

The Heroines of Jericho (HOJ) was the earliest Masonic association of midwestern African American women, first appearing in nearby Missouri during the Civil War. Iowa courts were organized by 1870, and the Missouri Grand Court (presiding over the entire upper Mississippi valley) was formed at St. Louis in 1874, with the assistance of prominent black Masonic leaders Moses Dickson (who wrote the manual standardizing the organization's ritual) and Iowan Jacob Pritchard.[112] In her autobiography, Mrs. Amanda Smith, a well-known black evangelist, recalled her experience with the order:

> There was a new society started called the "Heroines of Jericho." None but Master Masons' wives and daughters could join it, and this society was very high-toned, and as my husband was a Master Mason, he was anxious for me to join. He came home one night and told me all about it. Nothing would do but I must join this. . . . Well, after some weeks I did, and we had flashy times, all the tinsel regalia and turn out and money and show; it took all I could gather to keep up with it, and I had no chance to draw anything, for I had good health and was never sick; but still I must go on paying my dues regularly, as I had begun; and so I did until 1868.

Her experience of sanctification, however, persuaded Smith that "these secret societies are the mothers of selfishness, pride and worldliness." Friends urged her to continue her membership. "They said, 'You were just come to where you would be in office, and you have paid so much money in, and you should not leave now.' "[113] Smith described the attractions of membership, including sociability and peer approval, the opportunity for social mobility, the provision of benefits should she become sick, the lure of officeholding, and her husband's belief that her participation would enhance his own status as a Mason. While Smith's religiosity ultimately led her to leave the order, other African American women viewed their membership in a much more positive light. St. Louis resident Lucy Delany, also an active member of the AME Church, saw her participation in the HOJ as an investment in her community "to benefit those for whom I live. And what better can we do than to live for others?"[114]

The Order of the Eastern Star (OES) was organized as a partner group with Prince Hall Masons in 1874 and, like the HOJ, offered membership to the female relatives of Masons. The earliest chapter of the OES in the upper Midwest was organized by 1881 in Keokuk, Iowa, a community with a strong history of Prince Hall Masonry.[115] While both the HOJ and the OES were structurally subordinate to Prince Hall Masons and endorsed the masculinist endeavor of Masonry, they offered opportunities for female leadership, activism, and organization of civic and social welfare activities.[116]

African American women in the upper Midwest were also very active in the Independent Order of the Good Templars (IOGT), one of several associations focused on temperance. According to the historian David Fahey, the order was unusual in that it welcomed women as well as men, African Americans as well as whites. In November 1863 the white Templars of St. Paul, Minnesota, generously opened their lodge to recently arrived black migrants so they could conduct their own Baptist church services.[117] Black members of IOGT lodges in the upper Midwest can be dated from 1865 in Janesville, Wisconsin, 1866 in Des Moines and Iowa City, and 1872 in St. Paul; but the Iowa and Minnesota lodges were segregated. In black, white, and integrated lodges, women joined with men not only as members but also as officers.[118]

Its open membership practices caused a deep schism within the IOGT by the 1870s, when white southerners began insisting on excluding African Americans from membership. That controversy permeated the 1872 national meeting, held in Madison, Wisconsin. Southern delegates rushed to relieve the psychic trauma of a white female delegate from Georgia when a male African American member of the Madison Templar Lodge joined the reception to welcome visiting delegates. The "noble sister shed tears at the humiliation" of being at a social event that a black man attended as her equal.[119]

Also popular among black midwesterners was the International Order of Twelve Knights and Daughters of Tabor. "The proudest and most distinctive of all African American orders," as it was pronounced by one group of scholars, was the brainchild of Moses Dickson, the author of its constitution and rituals. Dickson was described as "a master in the art of organization" because of his untiring activism throughout the Mississippi valley on behalf of slaves, freedpeople, black education, Prince Hall Masonry, the AME Church, and Republican politics.[120] After three years of preparation, Dickson organized the first Temple and Tabernacle in 1871. The order was established to support "homebuilding and the acquiring of wealth," education, and Christianity, as well as the promulgation of "true manhood and womanhood." Men and women were eligible for membership and enjoyed the same benefits and privileges. At its 1872 national meeting in Chicago, the order claimed 1,500 members from Missouri, Kansas, Illinois, Iowa, and Kentucky. Ten years later, in 1882, it had over 7,000 members in twelve states, but was most popular in the Midwest. By the end of the century, its membership topped 60,000.[121]

PRINCE HALL MASONRY became a particularly significant venue for community, state, regional, and national organizing among African Americans. It was an important part of the social network that midwestern African American men built and drew upon as they created new, postemancipation civic identities.[122] Too, the temples' furnishings, the members' apparel and paraphernalia, and the ritualized observances and behaviors that marked Masonic gatherings all provided ample opportunities for the development of a specifically male visual and performative, expressive culture. Increasingly popular in midwestern black communities, Masonry also became the source of substantial controversy and conflict, as members competed for recognition and leadership, as affiliations became politicized, and as communities vied for regional position and power within the organization.

Since the beginning of American Masonry, whites had insisted on excluding blacks from membership. White members interpreted the requirement that Masons be "free-born" as necessarily excluding the enslaved and the former slave. But they also understood that since Masons must be "of good report," "well-recommended," and possessing a "trade, estate, office, occupation, or visible way of acquiring a livelihood," all African Americans—even the free born—could, and must, be excluded.[123] In this way, whites turned their Masonic practices and their lodges into venues for asserting a racialized male identity. Whiteness alone was never considered a sufficient qualification for membership, but by aligning the Mason's idealized character exclusively with white manhood, every component of Masonic learning, fellowship, and ritual became an opportunity for whites to enact the meaning of race in their lives and as part of their individual and corporate identity as men.

Creating a Life in Freedom

African American Masonry, known as "Prince Hall Masonry" after its West Indian immigrant founder, traced its U.S. origins to Hall's apprenticeship and advancement within a British lodge in Boston on the eve of the American Revolution. Having been rejected for membership by the white Massachusetts Grand Lodge, Hall and his black fraternal associates were finally granted a charter by the (white) Grand Lodge of England in 1787. When they severed their connection to the British in 1847, they established their own Grand Lodge in the United States. Their growth was phenomenal. As Theda Skocpol and Jennifer Osler have documented, when the Civil War ended there were "more than 2,700 Prince Hall Masons meeting under the jurisdiction of 23 grand lodges in 22 states plus Canada and the District of Columbia."[124] Lodges enabled men to learn and practice the association's rituals; socialize new members; organize and furnish meeting rooms; acquire leadership skills; distribute charitable relief to ill members, widows, orphans, and others in need; and engage in public ceremonies—most prominently, laying cornerstones for black churches.[125] Annual meetings gathered the lodges under a Grand Lodge, where the membership discussed, debated, organized, and solidified regional social and political networks.

African Americans emigrating west prior to the Civil War took Prince Hall Masonry with them to Ohio, the border South, and the upper Midwest. Among those emigrants were Pennsylvania-born Alexander Clark and Jacob Pritchard, both of whom were instrumental in Masonry's westward expansion. Along with Moses Dickson, they helped organize lodges from Ohio westward. Pritchard, born around 1815, had migrated to Quincy, Illinois, by 1846, when he was the local agent for Martin Delaney's black newspaper, *The Mystery*. By 1848 he had moved to Muscatine, Iowa, and assisted in forming Muscatine's AME Church in the late 1840s. In 1857, Pritchard played an active role in that city's black convention and, with Alexander Clark, joined the St. Louis black Masonic lodge in 1851.[126]

Black Masonry had spread to Missouri under the jurisdiction of the Ohio Grand Lodge, but the growth of the westernmost lodge prompted Clark, Pritchard, Dickson, and others in 1866 to separate from Ohio and form the independent Missouri Grand Lodge, which included the upper Midwest in its territory. By that time the three men had also helped organize lodges in Iowa, Minnesota, Missouri, Arkansas, Kansas, and Mississippi; Grand Lodge membership consisted of 232 Masons. Six years later, in 1872, the Missouri Grand Lodge counted 1,000 members in six states.[127] Although Masons represented a small proportion of the region's adult male black population, they fought significant battles over racism and inequality during and after Reconstruction.

After the war, black Masons initiated a persistent, sharp critique of the racism that permeated white Masonic tradition. An Iowan made the first challenge to the region's white lodges. With the unorthodox recommendation of two sympathetic white Masons, the unnamed man sought initiation into a Decatur County (Iowa) lodge. His request forced both the local lodge and, later that year, the (white) Iowa Grand Lodge, to openly admit their racial policies, including their belief in the "general positive deficiency of natural endowments" in African Americans as well as the impossibility of sustaining Masonry's highly valued tenets of "good will" and "brotherly love" across the color line. Reasserting the tradition that had governed white Masonry since its organization in North America, Iowa's white members insisted that emancipation had not and would not alter their practices or beliefs.[128]

This reassertion of white supremacy revealed not only the continuity of racist Masonic tradition, but also the limited impact of emancipation on white midwestern racial ideologies and behaviors. It also exposed some of the contradictions embedded in the racist ideology that had shaped white Masonry. The association had long justified its exclusionary policy based on slavery's degrading effect on blacks. But with emancipation eliminating the stigma of ignorance, economic dependency, and dishonesty imposed by bondage, it followed that men of African descent could now be judged on the same grounds as other free men. Nonetheless, white Masons refused to reconsider their preemancipation position. That would introduce "the impossibility or at least the difficulty, of ascertaining once we commence, their free birth, and where the lines of intelligence and social elevation commences and ends, or divides portions of the race."[129] Emancipation had revealed that it was race, not just enslaved status, that mattered in the white Masonic worldview. White Masons could not imagine a world where race did not organize society hierarchically. Simply pondering the possibility that emancipation had created a breach in their rationale was overwhelming, and the feared costs to white privilege were enough to dissuade most whites from delving any deeper into the subject.

In 1867, white Masons were again forced into open and explicit dialogue about race when African Americans in Pilot Grove (Lee County) and Des Moines (Polk County) requested permission from Iowa's white Grand Lodge to organize affiliated black lodges. (Minnesota's two black lodges would use the same strategy in 1876.)[130] Grand Master Campbell Peck addressed the issue in his annual address to Iowa's white Masons. Emancipation and Reconstruction, he said, had brought to Masons "a new problem. . . . In consideration of the new position in which they [African Americans] have been placed, and the recognition of the constitutional declaration now being forced upon us as a nation, that 'all men are created free and equal,' does it not become us as Masons to weigh well our relation and duty towards them as members of the same order?"[131]

According to Peck, then, freedom had been "given" to slaves and racial equality was being "forced" on America. He went on to observe that African Americans were being elevated "from their illiterate and debased condition," which weakened the long-standing presumption that the slave's ignorance justified his exclusion from membership. Peck acknowledged that reconsidering the racial prerogatives of white Masonry meant not only tackling "a difficult and unpopular" issue, but also risking the disapprobation of other whites. "The time is within the recollection of all of us, when it was suicide, both professional and social, for a man to openly condemn slavery." Reevaluating white Masonic ideology and practice might "subject us as Masons to derision and abuse; but shall we, on this account, hesitate to grapple with it?" Peck warned against hasty action, but he raised several issues for further study, including the admission of Native Americans by some white lodges. In an implicit reference to the Minnesota uprising and the Plains wars, he asked: Did "recent developments indicate that [Native Americans] are so much more elevated in morals, habits, and Christianity, than the negro race, as to entitle them to their preference?"

The committee appointed to examine these issues characterized Peck's views as evidence of his liberal, "large masonic heart," but concluded that even questioning current practice would disturb white Masonry's requisite harmony and unity. Regardless of emancipation, their "Ancient Constitutions" required Masons to be free born (ignoring, of course, the population of African Americans who had been born free); any other action would "subject ourselves (and that justly) to the most severe . . . criticism from our sister Grand Lodges." Thus, two years after the Civil War ended, midwestern white Masons rejected the efforts of African Americans and a few fellow whites to expand the meaning and implications of black freedom and reconsider white racial beliefs and practices.

Prince Hall Masonry in the upper Midwest continued to challenge the discriminatory practices of its white brethren and the racist ideology that rationalized them. Energized by black Masonry's rapid growth, but also by the passage of the Civil Rights Act in 1866 and Republican success in the elections that year, the Missouri (Prince Hall) Grand Lodge proclaimed at its 1866 annual meeting that African America "has risen like the Phoenix from the ashes, and we are now considered a Race amongst nations, treated as equals by those formerly acknowledged as our superiors; and we are now admitted to all associations on an equality with all. . . . How glorious! How beautiful to know that our children will have the advantages of education; and when they arrive at maturity to be considered as *men* amongst *men*."[132]

Even as they heralded the triumph of slavery's destruction and the expanding protections for equality offered by the Freedmen's Bureau Act, the Civil Rights Act, and the proposed Fourteenth Amendment to the Constitution, African American men continued to press white Masons for recognition, proclaimed the legitimacy of their own order, and within it asserted an uncompromising masculine identity. As they positioned themselves in relation to white men, other black men, and the women and children in their families and communities, midwestern black Masons created themselves as male citizens. The historian Martin Summers has written brilliantly about the meaning of Masonic membership for African American men at the turn of the century, when greater resources and more stratified class relations among black Americans profoundly shaped the order's gendered meanings to its membership.[133] In the two decades following the war, however, midwestern black Masons faced what they regarded as an immediate requirement to extend and defend their newly won citizenship rights, challenging white Masonic tradition (and the philosophy behind it) to accommodate the altered status of formerly enslaved men, assist communities in need, and participate in the construction and dedication of community institutions. Through these activities, black Masons articulated and performed a new black manhood that was increasingly predicated on citizenship and equality among men.

Midwestern black Masons engaged in an extensive but focused campaign against white Masonic racism, the key elements of which were the efforts of individual black Masons to gain admission to white lodges and permission to organize black lodges under the jurisdiction of the white Grand Lodges. In addition, they initiated a wide correspondence with American and European white lodges in their attempts to gain recognition as a legally constituted order. American white Masonry had long rejected Prince Hall Freemasonry as "clandestine," that is, organized without appropriate and legitimate authority. While illegitimacy had a technical meaning in the Masonic world, the stigma of illegitimacy meant something very specific among African Americans, especially former slaves, whose familial relationships had been denied the recognition and protections of the law. In defending the legitimate genealogy of Prince Hall Masonry, black Masons were also challenging the wider use of that stigma as a prop for white supremacy while insisting on public recognition of a legitimate black manhood.[134]

In 1869, Iowan Alexander Clark, now Grand Master of the (Prince Hall)

Grand Lodge of Missouri, easily reconciled the apparent conflict between slavery and Masonry. In his annual communication to fellow Masons, he asserted that the former slave could be made a Mason because "Freedom is man's natural birthright—the gift of God."[135] Black midwesterners also extended the Reconstruction era's struggle for equal citizenship rights and legal protections into Masonic life when they attacked what they called the "black laws" of white lodges, the same laws that Iowa's white Grand Master Campbell Peck had recommended that his state's white lodges reconsider.

In 1871, Moses Dickson (then chair of the committee on foreign correspondence) informed his fellow Prince Hall Masons that white Grand Lodges in Georgia and Illinois had responded to his letters of inquiry by conceding that no Masonic law could be found that explicitly prohibited the admission of African Americans. That acknowledgment was seen as an important step in changing "public sentiment" toward black Masons.[136] By 1872, Grand Master Clark declared that the "criminal prejudice of caste is fast passing away before the beauties of masonry."[137]

As black midwesterners struggled to achieve equality in Masonry and to open its doors to the formerly enslaved, they were also articulating the responsibilities of manhood in an organization that maintained a close watch over the behavior of its members. Masons explored the meaning of manhood in their relationship not only to the "profane" world of noninitiates, but also to other Masons. Masonry conferred reciprocal obligations upon its members ("What consolation a stranger in a strange land must feel, when in poverty and sickness to have an affectionate loving Brother administer to his every want, furnish a home, food, clothing and medical attendance, with an unselfish spirit which alone characterizes our Noble Institution"), extending, perhaps, the corporate male camaraderie fostered in the armed services and in religious organizations.[138] An important part of the construction of Masonic manhood for the Prince Hall association lay in the obligation they assumed to care for the dependents of their deceased members. Many black Masons came to the order with experience in assuming this obligation in a denominational context; the AME Church had long offered partial support to ministers' widows, and in the upper Midwest, there was considerable overlap between Masons and men who were either active members or preachers in the AME or Baptist tradition. But in accepting the responsibility to furnish "ample provision" for "our widows and orphans," black Masons were also articulating a secular, masculine identity as providers, a role that slavery had denied to so many men and that occupational segregation and menial employment continued to undermine. By supporting a sinking fund, Prince Hall Masons assumed further pecuniary obligations to ensure that Masons and their families received an appropriate, dignified burial.[139]

As African Americans in the postemancipation, postwar Midwest entered an intensive era of institution building, black Masons played a notable role in dedication and cornerstone ceremonies. Through these ceremonies black Masons extended their rich, symbolic ritual into the public sphere and the life of the community, in full regalia and dress (although during this period, it is unclear how many Masons could afford the entire ensemble of "dark suits, white leather or lambskin aprons, medallions, white gloves, and, for the most worshipful master, a black top hat," as described by Martin Summers).[140] Cornerstone ceremonies could be quite elaborate.[141] With a wave of school and church building in the aftermath of wartime black migration to the upper Midwest, the opportunities for public performances of Masonic ritual would have positioned Prince Hall Masons increasingly in the wider life of communities while also contributing to the order's growth.[142]

The western spread of the order and its continued challenges to the ideas and practices of white Masonry led to two key developments in the 1870s and 1880s. One was a significant change in how white midwestern Masons rationalized black exclusion—a movement that Prince Hall Masons chose to laud as a partial victory in their struggle for equality and white recognition. The second development was seen in the emergence of conflicts among black Masons over governance and affiliation.

During the 1870s, Prince Hall challenges to white Masonry came to a head first in Ohio and then in Iowa. In 1865, Ohio's Prince Hall Grand Lodge (at that time, the second largest Prince Hall–affiliated Grand Lodge in the country) had petitioned the (white) Grand Lodge of Ohio to either admit the members of black lodges currently under Ohio Prince Hall jurisdiction or recognize the lodges as legitimate. In response, the white Grand Lodge proposed, in 1869, to abolish the "black laws" by which the Grand Lodge directed all lodges to exclude African Americans and make membership decisions based on the "ballots" of individual lodge members. Ohio's white Masons accepted this change in 1870. In the same year, when a similar proposal was made to the (white) Iowa Grand Lodge, Grand Master John Scott observed that the centrality of race to white Masonry would not quickly disappear: "It is difficult for any of us to divest ourselves of those prejudices which have grown with our growth and strengthened with our strength, and these prejudices will, doubtless, prevent our affiliating with those by this law declared rejected, during the natural lives of any now here; but, it is my firm belief that they can only be rejected by the ballot, and not by law."[143] Nonetheless, Iowa's

Prince Hall Mason in regalia, ambrotype, ca. 1860. National Heritage Museum.

white Masons joined with those of Ohio in ending their formal bar against black initiation.[144] As Scott suggested, individual Masons—rather than Masonic law—would now be responsible for the admission or rejection of black initiates.

Prince Hall Masons welcomed Ohio's decision. For other reasons, however, they still found their victory incomplete. The new membership regulations would treat Prince Hall Masons as applicants for admission, rather than recognizing their current standing as regular—in fact, equal—members of the order. "We are Masons," Ohio's Grand Master emphasized. "Our petition did not pray for the rights of profanes [people outside of Masonry], but the rights

Creating a Life in Freedom

of brother Masons." Frustrated by this treatment, Ohio's Prince Hall Masons began a period of intense correspondence with white lodges outside the United States, gaining recognition of their "legitimacy" from white Masons in Peru, Germany, the Dominican Republic, France, Italy, and Hungary. And so, in 1875, Ohio's white Grand Lodge again raised the issue of the color bar: "Shall it be because his skin is not colored like our own we shall spurn the colored Masons with contempt? . . . I am aware of the prejudice against the African race. I am not entirely free of it myself. . . . But . . . if he is a Mason and can prove himself such, he should be welcomed as a man and a brother into our Lodges and entitled to equal rights in our great brotherhood."[145] The white Masons then proposed to recognize Prince Hall Masonry "as a legitimate and Independent Grand Lodge"—if it changed its name to "The African Grand Lodge of Free and Accepted Masons of the State of Ohio." (The designation of "African" was a reference to the first black lodge in North America, which became standard usage until 1848, when black Masons chose instead to designate themselves as "Prince Hall Lodges.") Further discussion of the proposal was deferred for two years, and then it was not considered again for another century.

The proposed name change, with its implication that they were not "Americans," insulted black Masons and undoubtedly reminded them of the *Dred Scott* decision, which had stripped African Americans of their citizenship. One member asserted: "Our lodges are not made up of Africans. I cannot now recall in mind one brother in all these lodges of whom, it can, with certainty, be said, 'He is an African.'"[146] Despite their disappointment that white Masons had faltered at the moment when they seemed poised to abolish race-based privileges and exclusions, Ohio's Prince Hall Grand Lodge had accomplished in the temples of Masonry what Americans struggled with throughout the North and South: establishing the legal basis for freedom and equality. The outcome within Masonry would be similar to what developed in the outside world: laws establishing or protecting institutional discrimination were prohibited, but individual behavior would remain beyond legal challenge.

Masons across the country circulated reports of the developments in Iowa and Ohio, and Minnesota soon joined the debate. Minnesota's two Prince Hall Lodges (still under the jurisdiction of the Missouri Prince Hall Grand Lodge) petitioned Minnesota's white Grand Lodge for recognition, and Lewis Hayden, a prominent public figure, well-known black abolitionist, and Masonic leader, followed suit on behalf of the Massachusetts Prince Hall Grand Lodge. Minnesota's white Grand Master, Charles Griswold, an earlier advocate of black suffrage in the state legislature, offered a lengthy, thoughtful address on

Masonry and white racism during the 1876 annual meeting. He argued that if black Masons were illegitimate, white lodges shared the burden for that fact: "Again and again have they knocked at the doors of Grand Lodges, and as often they have been turned away; and to-day they exist as independent Masonic bodies, simply because they have to do so, or else give up their Masonic life. . . . Until we change our attitude towards them, it is with a very poor grace indeed that we hurl epithets and sneers and denounce them as clandestine."[147] Griswold recommended that a committee study the issue and report back to the membership at the next annual meeting.

His committee members were not persuaded. In 1877, one member argued that ending the black laws would be an imposition on white Masons:

> What right have we to *force* an unwelcome guest upon our brother, even though he be the best qualified Caucasian in the land? No white man can become a Mason, or enter a Lodge, if objection be made. *Shall the Ethiopian* be more highly favored? Shall the *color* of *his* skin exempt him from the ordeal to which the white man is subjected? And this, too, while we profess to ignore the question of color? In the name of masonry, *these things cannot be*.

He advised that there be no recognition of Prince Hall lodges and no change in the bar against black initiates.[148] The committee chair maintained that African Americans were seeking special privileges rather than equality:

> A large proportion of the members of these organizations were not free-born, to say nothing of other disabilities which, if they existed among white men, would prevent this Grand Lodge from accepting them. . . . We would extend to the negro every right, benefit and privilege which his manhood entitles him to, but are not in favor of extending to him, *because* he is a negro, privileges that we could not grant to the white man.[149]

Minnesota's white Masons voted as Ohio's had: to remove the Grand Lodge bar to black membership, but to withhold recognition of the legitimacy of Prince Hall Masons and their lodges. Other white Grand Lodges approved: "Minnesota has buried the matter so deep that it will be beyond the powers of resurrection to ever reach it again."[150] Thus, by 1877—the denouement of Reconstruction in the South—midwestern white Masons made their last concession for the next century. They agreed to remove the "legal bars" to an integrated Masonry—but were confident that individual lodges would sustain segregation. That confidence would prove well founded.

White refusal to recognize Prince Hall Masonry did not impede its growth.

Under the Missouri Grand Lodge, Minnesota and Iowa Prince Hall Masonry expanded in the 1870s and 1880s. Out of this growth, internal disputes over recognition and leadership arose and began to threaten the unity that had characterized the early years of black fraternalism. The first sign of conflict occurred in 1867, when Moses Dickson—so crucial to the order's early history in Missouri—challenged his fellow Masons for rejecting his nomination to the penultimate position of Most Worshipful Grand Master because of his failure to meet certain eligibility requirements. The current Grand Master, H. McGee Alexander, was reelected, but only after Dickson and his supporters threatened to disrupt and abandon the proceedings. Dickson clearly felt that his service should have earned him the respect and prestige afforded by the Grand Lodge's highest post, and he resented the reminder that he did not meet the formal requirements for that position.[151] In an organization where hierarchy, submission to established order, and appropriate conduct were among its most treasured values, Dickson's protest could have earned him, and possibly his followers, suspension. That no punishment was dispensed suggests Dickson's widely recognized importance to the order but also perhaps some sympathy with him. Alexander, who died in office, was succeeded in 1868 by Alexander Clark. Dickson served as Clark's Deputy Grand Master until elected Grand Master in 1869 (and again in 1878).[152]

The turmoil that had threatened the 1867 meeting foreshadowed more serious conflicts when the power and prestige associated with Masonic office became a source of competition and contention. The Missouri Prince Hall Grand Lodge grew steadily, with thirty-four lodges and 1,000 members in over six states by 1872. In 1879, the membership reached 3,000; when the Grand Lodge convened in Macon, Missouri, activities included a public procession of over 1,500 Masons in full dress and regalia. By 1881, Iowa alone had eleven lodges and a membership of 250.[153]

This was not only a time of growth but also of increased internal surveillance of members' behavior, resulting in a significant rise in complaints and disciplinary actions. It was a time of dissent and discontent that mirrored, in some ways, the political instabilities of the era and the growing stratification within black communities. One observer charged: "The leaders or representative members have resorted to all the practices of political tricksters to further their aims and have carried the issues from the Lodge to the Church, to the social circle and to the community at large."[154] With their political voice beleaguered by the white leadership of the Republican Party and their participation in party politics constantly under scrutiny, Prince Hall Masonry became all the more important as a site of self-government, where Masons laid claim to a long-standing cultural tradition in which black men conferred and enjoyed status, authority, respectability, and power.

By 1878, momentum began to build among Iowans for the organization of an independent Grand Lodge. That year, Grand Master Moses Dickson toured the Iowa lodges and declared that he saw a new Grand Lodge as a way to strengthen Masonry "among colored men in the West." Although Dickson's endorsement encouraged some members, it fueled the growth of an opposition movement—led by past Grand Master Alexander Clark. The ensuing debate and conflict launched an era in which midwestern black Masonry was less focused on challenging white Masonry and more centered around internally competing visions of the function and future of the order. Among the charges and countercharges were allegations of frustrated office seeking, conflict over the efficacy of leadership, perceived slights over the distribution of elected positions, charges of misuse of power and subjective reporting of the causes and consequences of the conflict, and unseemly competition of the two Grand Lodges over the membership and furnishings of existing subordinate lodges.

Inevitably, with one group pushing for a new organization and another defending older practices, the dispute became framed as one between established power and new claims on that power. Because Prince Hall Masonry was one of the principal sites from which black men articulated idealized gender identities, the conflict and dissension had an impact throughout the region's black communities.

In assessing this era of conflict, it is instructive to note what was not at stake. Both sides included men of means, some of them free born, as well as former slaves. Both sides included the most vulnerable black workers in the region— day laborers, farmhands, and servants—as well as well-to-do professionals and artisans.[155] Both sides included men from the same denominational affiliations; both sides included veterans. And both sides included recent arrivals as well as long-term residents of the upper Midwest. In the context of their struggle with white Masons in the immediate postwar era, it is interesting that those supporting Iowa independence identified themselves with an "African" Grand Lodge, a move that emphasized perceived differences in race and even nationality from white Masons. But Iowa Masons undoubtedly chose the "African" designation as a strategy by which they identified themselves with the long tradition of black Freemasonry in the United States.

Alexander Clark played a central role both in opposing the independent lodge and, nearly a decade later, in negotiating a solution to the conflict. Clark was not only one of the most politically experienced African American men in the region, but he also drew on powerful connections to regional and national networks—including denominational networks, the national black convention movement, and, of course, his widely recognized activism within the Republican Party. Undoubtedly he would have been viewed as a power broker, and perhaps a power broker who had let down his fellow black midwesterners, given the Republican Party's failure to nominate or appoint African American men to positions of significance. In fact, Clark's reputation may have suffered from growing black alienation from the party of Lincoln. Rightly or wrongly, some of Iowa's black Masons came to view Clark's powerful role in regional and national black politics with dissatisfaction and suspicion.[156]

Clark had immediately opposed the creation of an independent Grand Lodge for Iowa. He characterized the movement as the effort of "ambitious, disappointed office-seeking Masons of St. Louis, aided and abetted by a few ambitious, unthinking Masons of Iowa." Independence would be costly to Iowa's black Masons; their dues and taxes would increase significantly. Supporting a Grand Lodge was not an inexpensive endeavor. Better, Clark argued, to save that money, "and by economy accumulate means to furnish our lodge rooms, and a fund to care for our sick and disabled Masons, their wives, widows and orphans, and be able to bury them when dead."[157] Clark's inferences were twofold: that black Masons should focus on their gendered obligations as providers, and that Iowa Masons could not afford an independent lodge. The Iowans may have resented Clark's heavy-handed advice to save their money, considering he was, at the time, a wealthy man. They may also have perceived insult in the suggestion that they could not adequately meet their obligations as men to provide for wives and children. Keokuk's York Lodge informed the Missouri Grand Lodge of its intention to switch affiliation to the new African Grand Lodge of Iowa.

This act precipitated further conflict, as the members of the subordinate lodge wavered in their allegiances, as ownership over the lodge and its furnishings became hotly debated, and as York Lodge was placed under censure. A Grand Master who visited York Lodge reported being subjected to indignities and insults; he described its condition as "deplorable. . . . Discord and anarchy reigned." The Missouri lodge organized a new, loyal, competing lodge in Keokuk and ultimately recommended the expulsion of several officers of York Lodge.[158]

Between December 1879 and August 1881, there were several unsuccessful attempts to organize the new Grand Lodge in Iowa "independent of Missouri dictatation and control." Alexander Clark and Moses Dickson, who had reversed his position, subverted those efforts. It was a small but determined group that finally brought the effort to fruition in August 1881, attended by lodges from five Iowa communities.[159] By 1884 the African Grand Lodge had expanded to include lodges in six additional communities, including St. Paul, Minnesota.[160] The growth of new black communities, especially in southern Iowa's coal-mining belt, and the gradual movement of Iowa's black population away from the older Mississippi river towns to larger cities in the interior of the state, offered new territory from which black Masons could be drawn, including newcomers to the region who would not have held allegiances to an older generation of black leadership. Keokuk, however, would continue to anchor Masonic developments during this period.

In April 1884, the remaining Iowa members of the Missouri Grand Lodge, with Grand Lodge approval, began to organize their own Hiram Grand Lodge in Iowa. Alexander Clark helped bring this new Grand Lodge into being that summer at a meeting in Des Moines attended by lodges from eight Iowa cities and towns.[161] Members of the African Grand Lodge regarded this action as a hostile "invasion" of their territory, the "beginning of a new trouble."[162] They condemned Clark, in particular, for his role. In 1885, Austin Bland, Grand Master of the African Grand Lodge, reported with considerable disdain: "Now the worst element of our opposition [referring here to Clark] has left Missouri and come into Iowa. He has caused the few subordinate lodges that chose to stay on the *old farm* with the old folks, to leave and follow him out West where we have set up a prosperous Grand Lodge, and has here organized a second Grand Lodge." Bland's dig at Clark and his followers, as tied to the "old farm," cast them as plantation loyalists who were still bound to the place and practices of the Old South. Not only was this intended to slander Clark as an "Uncle Tom," but it also served to portray the African Grand Lodge as the more progressive of the two Masonic organizations.[163] There was considerable competition to see which Grand Lodge would be recognized by other states. Although the established and powerful Missouri Grand Lodge supported the new Hiram Grand Lodge, the African Grand Lodge garnered greater recognition.[164] The conflict led to open hostilities among black Iowans, including "slander and backbiting, disobedience of lawful authority, contumacy to the authority of the Grand Master and Grand Lodge; malfeasance in office, violation of ancient charges, departure from the original plan of masonry and ancient landmarks, disobedience to the Constitution and Laws," as observers would later recall.[165]

By June 1885, the two lodges began to exchange correspondence with hopes of finding a way to reunite. A joint meeting in 1887 helped pave the way, and within a month they had finally united as the United Grand Lodge of Iowa,

Ancient Free and Accepted Masons (A.F. & A.M.). Ironically, while the union brought an end to the "bitter and widespread" discord among Masonic men in the region, the order's female affiliate, the Heroines of Jericho, found union more difficult, and two years later had not yet reconciled.[166] Minnesota Masons would remain part of the United Grand Lodge—and a Minnesotan would serve as Grand Master—before Minnesota established its own Grand Lodge in 1894.[167]

IN THE AFTERMATH of emancipation, war, and military service, black midwesterners set out to establish new lives and communities in three important venues: work, worship, and associational life. Although the color line restricted nearly all African Americans to the most economically disadvantaged and vulnerable occupations, black women were most profoundly affected, as individual workers but also in terms of their households. Yet despite the barriers they encountered to steady subsistence and social mobility, midwestern African Americans invested in houses of worship that also served as venues for the creation of a black public sphere—where gender relations and sexuality became matters of community and denominational concern as well as part of the landscape of black social relations. So, too, black midwesterners invested in associational life. Within Prince Hall Masonry, in particular, African Americans not only reinforced black male authority and masculine identity, but also maintained a steady critique of the racist practices and ideologies sustained by white fraternal associations. Emancipation's diaspora—the flow of former slaves into the upper Midwest—had fueled an era of black institution building, an era in which the politics of gender and race were confronted within the community and in relationship to white Americans who were not easily persuaded that African Americans deserved unfettered freedom and full citizenship.

6   "Freedom Was All They Had" Civil Rights and Northern Reconstruction

In the aftermath of emancipation and the Confederacy's defeat, African Americans of the upper Midwest quickly became involved in the legal challenges and political conflicts raised by the Reconstruction process. Like many northern whites, midwesterners were southward-facing when they endorsed the necessity of Reconstruction, particularly given the array of issues at play in the political reconstitution of the former Confederate states. But whites in the Midwest always turned their gaze homeward when they contemplated Reconstruction's ramifications. This was especially true when African Americans forced their white neighbors to consider the meaning of black freedom and its relationship to citizenship, one of the most contentious issues the nation would confront after the war.

As the country entered the postwar era, northerners understood that they would soon have to reexamine the enduring impact of white supremacy on their own region's law, culture, and society. Despite emancipation and the passage of the Thirteenth Amendment, slavery was still very much alive in the memory and experience of northern blacks, including those who had arrived during the war, as well as those whose immediate and distant kin had gained their freedom as a result of the conflict.[1] In 1865, the upper Midwest gave former slaves a measure of freedom but did not yet offer them citizenship. Their story—how African American men and women in the upper Midwest shaped and contributed to Reconstruction—constitutes part of the poorly chronicled *northern* account of how black freedom and citizenship were understood, defined, and defended in the postemancipation, postwar United States.[2]

Both familiar and unexpected findings about the African American struggle for civil and political rights are revealed from a northward focus on the Reconstruction era. Black veterans' claim for the franchise, based on their manhood proved on the battlefield, will not be surprising. But, in the story of emancipation's aftermath, historians seldom consider *northern* battles for the franchise, for access to public schools and public accommodations, and for the dignity of citizenship. Even more unrecognized are the significant contributions of African American women to northern civil rights movements, most notably in the public venues and courtrooms where they challenged segregation. Furthermore, it would be women's activism that served as the barometer of change in black politics in the closing decades of the nineteenth century. Building on Steven Hahn's observation that postwar southern blacks "made and remade their politics and political history in complex relation to shifting events," this chapter turns to the more formal venues in which African Americans in the upper Midwest sought, extended, and defended the formal rights they associated with citizenship. This story culminates in the successes and failures that led these women and men into regional and national activism after the 1880s.[3]

African Americans in the upper Midwest pursued the more formal rights of citizenship in the complex legislative and constitutional context of Reconstruction, a highly politicized era of American governance that was uneven in its impact on northern states. Even so, the North encountered more local and far-reaching consequences of Reconstruction than some accounts have acknowledged. Although the Thirteenth Amendment placed the abolition of slavery firmly in the U.S. Constitution, it did not confer citizenship rights on African Americans, North or South.[4] The Civil Rights Act (passed on 9 April 1866 over President Andrew Johnson's veto) pronounced African Americans to be citizens, reversing the *Dred Scott* decision of 1857, but without conferring specific rights and privileges, or obligations, of citizenship. And while the First Reconstruction Act (passed on 2 March 1867) imposed black male suffrage on the former Confederate states, by plan and intent this statute did not strike down existing restrictions on black suffrage in the northern states. Sixteen months later, on 28 July 1868, the Fourteenth Amendment superseded the Civil Rights Act in providing protections for African Americans against discriminatory actions by states.

But by 1868 black men still could not vote in eleven of twenty-one northern states or in any of the five border states.[5] In fact, until the ratification of the Fifteenth Amendment on 3 February 1870, the North made very slow progress toward black male enfranchisement while northern Democrats advanced what the historian William Gillette has described as cohesive and vigorous opposition to the proposed amendment.[6] After it was ratified, northern whites still employed a range of tactics to limit black voting, from threats of violence (Ohio, 1870), to blocking the payment of taxes that was a prerequisite for voting (Delaware, 1873), to arresting black federal marshals to prevent their interference with fraud at the polls (New York, 1870).[7] In the period between the passage of a new Civil Rights Act in 1875 and the U.S. Supreme Court's reversal of that act in 1883, African Americans in the North sought federal protection of their civil rights from the discriminatory actions of states as well as individual citizens. The exercise of their political and civil rights often required a forceful defense.

The extension of the franchise to black men provoked heated debate in the North. By the end of the war, Radical Republicans had come to view black enfranchisement as a necessary check on the political power of former Confederates, for the political stability of the reconstructed states of the South, and for continued Republican dominance over Congress. But Radicals were a minority in their party, and their repeated efforts to persuade moderate Republicans and northern Democrats of that necessity ran aground on two key factors: states established voter qualifications, and most white northerners believed the franchise to be a privilege of white manhood and legitimately denied to black men. As a result, at the end of the war, unrestricted black suffrage was permitted in only five northern states (Maine, Massachusetts, New Hampshire, Vermont, and Rhode Island, with less than 7 percent of the North's black population); New York State limited suffrage to black property owners. White northerners reaffirmed their exclusive claim on citizenship after the war. During 1865–66, voters in three northern states (Connecticut, Minnesota, and Wisconsin) rejected referenda that would have given the vote to black men, and Republican leaders in six additional northern states (Ohio, Pennsylvania, New York, New Jersey, Indiana, and Michigan) prevented the issue from coming to the popular vote. In 1867, black suffrage was denied in Ohio, Minnesota, and Kansas; and in 1868, in Michigan and New York State.[8]

Northern voters and Republican congressmen were far more supportive of black enfranchisement in the South. Under military Reconstruction, the percentage of adult black men eligible to vote would increase from 0.5 percent to 80.5 percent, but all of the increase occurred in the former Confederacy. As Richard Valelly has noted, there was no Union League in the North and no northern version of the South's "registration summer" in 1867, when Republican-sponsored organizers and army-appointed registrars brought 200,000 to 300,000 black men into southern Union Leagues.[9]

Instead, as the historian Xi Wang has so carefully documented, northern Republicans preferred to postpone the debate over black suffrage in northern states, a debate they viewed as "hazardous" to the northern party.[10] The party thus continued to advocate a congressional mandate for black suffrage in the South but state control over franchise qualifications in the North. Republicans kept the issue of the black franchise alive because of their interest in protecting black voting rights in the South, rather than expanding them in the North.

The story of how the majority of white northern voters came to approve extending the franchise to northern black men, and then how these new voters participated in electoral politics, is incompletely understood. Yet as important as these events were to the North's "reconstruction," they were by no means the only components of northern Reconstruction. To African Americans seeking a full measure of liberty in the postbellum upper Midwest, the franchise was a crucial element in their definition of citizenship.[11] And while black men in Iowa, Minnesota, and Wisconsin were among those few northern African Americans to gain the vote prior to the ratification of the Fifteenth Amendment, this achievement was clearly neither the sole focus nor the culmination of their pursuit of citizenship. Midwestern blacks also vigorously pursued the rights accompanying the franchise (such as jury service), equal treatment in public accommodations and state-supported institutions, and what might best be described as a less formal array of claims that included self-determination, as well as the respect and dignity accorded free and equal members of the human race.

Midwestern African Americans, like blacks across the North, pursued the rights of citizenship in the streets, in schoolhouses, on trains and steamboats, in cemeteries, as well as in the arenas of formal politics, including party conventions and voting booths.[12] Black men, in particular, organized petition drives, conventions, and appeals to state legislatures and white midwestern voters "to recognize our claim to manhood." They relied heavily (and successfully) on their military service to strengthen their claims for manhood franchise. The gendered construction of those claims cannot be explained simply as a utilitarian political strategy. The vigor with which black veterans demanded the public prerogatives of manhood was consistent with their demands in other settings (such as fraternal associations) and reflected an explicitly gendered vision of the rights and responsibilities of the franchise, even if these men and their communities believed that male voters represented communal, rather than individual and gendered, interests.[13]

But black midwesterners entertained more than one vision of formal citizenship rights. During this period, women—and girls—played a central role in the fight for equal access to public education and public accommodations. Their consciousness of this activism as part of a significant national struggle for rights was suggested by the response of a group of black women in Washington, D.C., to the passage of the 1866 Civil Rights Act (guaranteeing African Americans "the full and equal benefit of all laws") over President Johnson's veto.[14] These women flooded the Senate chamber with beautiful bouquets of flowers for the senators who had supported the bill. "We exercise our civil right to express our gratitude," noted the attached cards, which were signed, "Colored Citizens."[15] Both men and women, then, were self-consciously engaged in a range of actions to claim a new realm of freedom.

Although African American women would not gain the full spectrum of political rights in the near future, they were nonetheless central to the evolving definitions of citizenship and its pursuit by black communities in the course of northern Reconstruction. As noted in the previous chapter's consideration of black churches and fraternal associations, African American women claimed citizenship within the black public sphere, simultaneously but selectively endorsing the efforts of black men to secure a full manhood—confronting male church leaders on some issues, supporting them (as well as black fraternal leaders) on others. Men and women worked separately and together to challenge the raced entitlements that midwestern whites had long laid claim to under the guise of civilization, of morality, and of racially exclusive gender ideals.

Notable gender differences emerged as black midwesterners sought full citizenship. Prior to the 1880s, African American women were less likely than men to use their single-sex secular societies or associations in the pursuit of civil rights. Rather, they confronted the denial of their civil rights on a more direct, personal level, often in concert with adult and youthful family members. The greater likelihood that women would challenge the law and practice of discrimination from a personal and familial standpoint reminds us that slavery's destruction entailed a transformation in the meaning of reproduction and reproductive labor for African American women. Slavery had deprived both men and women of the familial roles and protections that white Americans enjoyed, but for women, the burdens had been uniquely harsh, as motherhood had been agonizingly entangled with the reproduction of slavery. Freedom transformed the meanings and experience of motherhood among black women. In the postwar era, some black mothers became especially active in the struggle for civil rights.

A careful consideration of Reconstruction-era activism also reveals important changes over time in how black communities viewed themselves and how they chose to pursue their citizenship. After the war, black communities seeking white support for their enfranchisement drew together, in juxtaposition to white men, as a race and as a unified people. But once black men gained the franchise, black communities became both liberated and doomed to explore their heterogeneity, to pursue different and sometimes contesting strategies for full freedom and liberty. Too, after enfranchisement, black midwesterners discovered both how much and how little their votes mattered; they therefore took their claim to citizenship in new directions that laid the groundwork for the civil rights movements of the twentieth century. The well-studied era of fin de siècle political empowerment—in organizations like the Afro-American Council, the National Association of Colored Women's Clubs (NACW), and ultimately the National Association for the Advancement of Colored People (NAACP)—built on traditions and struggles rooted in the antebellum era as well as two full generations of postemancipation northern black political activism.

"TO SUPPORT OUR GOVERNMENT LIKE MEN"

The postemancipation call for citizenship in the upper Midwest was first led by the Civil War's black veterans, who believed that having shouldered citizenship's most dangerous responsibilities, they should be granted its privileges and prerogatives. This was certainly the case with the men (and their families) of the 60th U.S. Colored Infantry (USCI), which returned to Davenport, Iowa, to muster out on Saturday, 28 October 1865. Although plans had been made to greet the soldiers with ringing church bells, a brass band, a welcoming speech, and a crowd of civilians, the regiment arrived unexpectedly and to no welcoming fanfare. Instead, accompanied by the regiment's own brass band, they marched in cold sleet through the muddy streets to Camp McClellan, exhausted from their long journey from Arkansas by rail and steamer. The men soon recuperated, and two days before they were to be disbanded, the regiment's seven hundred soldiers held a convention to "prepare the way for our approach to the ballot box." They elected Alexander Clark as the convention's president and several noncommissioned officers as vice presidents and secretary, then listened to speeches by local community leaders and their own officers. Afterward, they formed committees and drafted resolutions, an address to the people of Iowa, and a petition to the state legislature. Their claims were singular: Without the rights of citizenship, "our well-earned freedom is but a shadow." They had been trusted with the musket and now asked to be trusted with the ballot. They spoke on their own behalf, both as veterans and as former slaves. Asserting that their natural, manhood rights were heralded in the Declaration of Independence, they spoke on behalf of a people who sought not only life and liberty but also equal rights and justice. They asked all black Iowans to join with them in presenting petitions for those rights to the legislature. At the same time, they urged their fellow black Iowans to prove to the larger society that they deserved the vote by demonstrating their respectability through "education, industry and thrift" and by abstaining from "intoxicating drink."[16]

Like similar conventions held across the nation and in the upper Midwest as black troops were mustered out of the service, this one might appear to confirm a familiar occurrence in the history of nineteenth-century northern black activism: male veterans claimed citizenship's benefits on the basis of having fulfilled citizenship's obligations. Some historians have argued that white voters eagerly satisfied this claim, their antebellum racism eroded by having shared the battlefield with black soldiers. Iowa's convention, however, points to a different, more complicated story of northern Reconstruction, of the transition from slavery to freedom and citizenship among African Americans whose battles lay largely with northern racism and the northern politics of Reconstruction. This was unlike southern Reconstruction, where freedpeople struggled against the resilience and violence of southern slavery, against former masters and mistresses, and against a well-established race-based system of labor exploitation in order to gain a measure of freedom. In the postbellum upper Midwest, racism more subtly saturated the public sphere. But midwestern racism also encouraged a legal framework that protected white supremacy and created a marketplace where race opened or closed doors to employment and social mobility.

Despite the important differences between southern and northern Reconstruction, most of the men who gathered that late October day in Davenport were southern-born and, like the rest of the upper Midwest's black population by 1865, they and their families had recently (or within the last generation) experienced slavery with its attending violence, exploitation, separations, and losses. Connected, despite emancipation's diaspora, to black southerners in the postwar nation, African Americans in the upper Midwest faced a different struggle than did their kin in the South; what they wanted, the context in which they asked for it, and who they asked to satisfy those demands would necessarily differ.

Wisconsin, Minnesota, and Iowa were among the few northern states to enfranchise African American men prior to the passage of the Fifteenth Amendment.[17] The path to black empowerment followed different trajectories in each of these three states bordering the upper Mississippi River. In Wisconsin, it came through a state supreme court decision in 1866; two years later (after two failed attempts), Minnesota voters authorized their legislature to alter qualifications for suffrage to include African American men; and in Iowa, the long process of amending the state constitution was completed, also in 1868, with a public referendum approving the state constitutional amendment that had been endorsed by two previous consecutive general assemblies. Despite these different mechanisms, similar dynamics shaped the political context in all three states. With some important exceptions, most Republicans in the upper Midwest were reluctant to advocate universal black suffrage or to associate their party with such an unpopular cause.[18] Those white Republicans who supported black enfranchisement framed their advocacy in terms of the political struggle between loyal former slaves and former masters in the South.[19] Few were as radical and outspoken as Iowan Warrington Howe, who argued in November 1865 that "to-day . . . is the August opportunity" for letting black men know they were "men among men—*pari passu* in all that makes the well-being of a common manhood."[20]

Democrats in all three states campaigned in opposition, heavily exploiting the threat that black enfranchisement posed to white supremacy and predicting massive black migration to any state that granted equal political rights to African American men. White "Soldiers' Conventions" were organized by Democrats in an effort to claim exclusively for whites the manly performance of wartime sacrifices.[21] Midwestern Republicans were far from unified on black enfranchisement. U.S. senator James Doolittle of Wisconsin argued that black suffrage would cost the party its power in six northern states and would result in the defeat of the Thirteenth Amendment.[22] In contrast, most Republican supporters focused on the importance of black voters in the South.[23] Opponents ultimately relinquished the fight, conceding that the small number of blacks to be enfranchised could have little impact on election outcomes.

Wisconsin was one of the first northern states to enfranchise African American men after the war. Black settlers and radical white abolitionists had repeatedly brought the issue to the territorial legislature in the 1840s. But the few legislators to support it met with overwhelming opposition, particularly from the southwestern part of the territory, where Democratic slaveholders (and African Americans) were most prominent, and from the communities most populated by foreign-born voters. In 1849, a referendum approved a bill enfranchising black men, but such a small proportion of men participating in that year's general election bothered to vote on the issue that the state decreed that the referendum had failed to meet the constitutional standard of majority approval. A similar bill was defeated in 1857. Thus black men remained disfranchised. In the spring of 1865, as the war drew to a close, African Americans continued petitioning the state legislature for their right to the franchise. That October, a "mass meeting" convened at Milwaukee, drawing black men from the river town of LaCrosse as well as Milwaukee, to call for black suffrage. Preceding the Iowa soldiers' convention by less than two weeks, Wisconsin's mass meeting offered many of the same arguments that the Iowans would make: Having assumed the obligations and duties of citizenship by fighting alongside white men, they had earned the rights and privileges of citizenship. Not only had African Americans proved themselves true to the Union in battle; in the South, they alone had been "faithful among the faithless, prompt to warn our armies of approaching danger, vigorous to discover the designs of the enemy, brave and always ready to aid and succor our prisoners in their flight."[24]

Advocates of black suffrage directed their claims to Wisconsin's white voters, but their strategies were not limited to persuasive rhetoric. During the fall elections of 1865, two African American men—an unidentified resident of Lancaster (populated by slaveowners and former slaves in the 1840s, then by black migrants during the war) and Ezekial Gillespie (a Tennessee-born former slave who had resided in Milwaukee with his family since 1854 and had participated in the October mass meeting)—attempted to vote. Expecting to be rejected, both men hoped to force the issue into the courts and win a reconsideration of the 1849 referendum. Gillespie's suit, argued by a white abolitionist lawyer who had earlier served on the state supreme court, persuaded the Wisconsin Supreme Court that the 1849 approval of the franchise referendum mandated black men's right to vote.[25]

In both Minnesota and Iowa, African American men obtained the franchise through approval of referenda submitted to the white voters of each state in 1868. Earlier bills to extend the vote to black men in Minnesota (brought to the territorial legislature in 1849, a state constitutional convention in 1857, and the state legislature in 1860) had all failed. In contrast, efforts to restrict the rights of black settlers had succeeded; the territorial legislature gradually extended the ban on black suffrage to cover all local elections and to prevent black officeholding as well as jury service (in Wisconsin, blacks could serve on juries prior to gaining the franchise).[26] Minnesota's black settlers delivered their first petitions for voting rights to the state legislature in January 1865. The men supported their claim based on the Declaration of Independence, their integrity and moral worth, and their demonstrated willingness to offer "our black bosoms as a rampart to shield the nation." They also accused Minnesota's white citizens of having "imposed a stigma upon us, that dampens our ardor in pursuing everything that is eminently best for the exemplary citizen to follow." Most of the forty-one men signing the petition, from St. Paul and vicinity, did not appear on any territorial or state census before 1865, suggesting that they were wartime migrants to the state.[27] Aware that they had few allies in the legislature, African American men from St. Paul formed a small committee to honor lawmaker Charles Griswold in March 1865 for introducing a bill endorsing black suffrage.[28] Brought to the state's white voters as a referendum that fall, the bill failed—as did another attempt in 1867. In 1868, the referendum was finally approved, although historians have argued that the physical form of the ballot was intentionally confusing; many voters were probably unaware that they had authorized black enfranchisement. Nonetheless, Minnesota's black men had gained the franchise, although the white voters in St. Paul (home to most of the state's black residents) registered overwhelming opposition.[29]

In Iowa, the debate over black enfranchisement was first raised in 1844 in a supportive petition from white abolitionists to the territorial constitutional convention. African American residents of Muscatine subsequently petitioned the 1857 state constitutional convention for the franchise, which was followed by a failed public referendum. In 1865, the question of extending the vote to black men was raised by white delegates at the Republican state convention: Would the state party take a stand on this divisive and contentious issue? Because the state legislators elected in 1865 would inevitably confront black suffrage, it became a central issue in the fall campaign, with Iowa Republicans resolving that "we are in favor of striking out the word 'white' " from suffrage qualifications listed in the state constitution.[30] The most radical white advocates argued that without political and civil rights, black men were left in a "swoon between life and death" that "may be grandly called *Emancipation*, but is not *Freedom*."[31] U.S. Secretary of the Interior and Iowa Republican James Harlan was far more moderate and pragmatic: Southerners would demand those rights of the North, and "here in Iowa, where there would not be enough colored votes to alter the result in any county, township or city election, there can surely be no injury in granting that right, even if he is not qualified to vote."[32] Opponents contended that black Iowans had not yet sufficiently recovered from the degrading experience of slavery to exercise the ballot wisely. Conservative Republicans insisted that freedom was more than adequate recompense for the military sacrifices made by black men. Better to delay and prepare both black and white midwesterners for such a revolutionary change, they cautioned. Others maintained that it was unfair to single out black men. Republicans should not invite African Americans to vote and shape public policy unless they offered the same opportunity to all other disenfranchised groups that had worked equally hard during the war—an allusion to white female suffrage.[33]

Over the resistance of men opposed to black male enfranchisement and those who feared a conservative white backlash at the polls, Iowa Republicans fell in line with the national party's endorsement of the proposed measure, and their candidates did well in the fall elections, including gubernatorial nominee

William Stone, a strong supporter. Southeastern Lee County, overwhelmingly Democratic but also the location of Iowa's largest black population, resisted the measure, but the general assembly endorsed black suffrage in both 1866 and 1867 sessions. Meanwhile, black Iowans continued to pressure the legislature; in January 1866, Alexander Clark presented petitions bearing more than one thousand signatures.[34] Despite the withdrawal of some conservatives into a new, third party (the Conservative Republican Party) in 1866, popular disapproval of the actions of former Confederate states and northern disdain for President Johnson's leniency toward former Confederates were the key issues that drew Iowa voters to the polls to support the Republican ticket.

Eliminating the racial restrictions on suffrage required final approval in a public referendum. In 1868, anxious that the issue be submitted to voters in the fall elections and looking for an opportunity to make their case with the public, African American delegates from around the state convened at Des Moines on Abraham Lincoln's birthday—seizing the moral weight of his martyrdom to back their claims for full citizenship. If their meeting was overly devoted to the minutiae of credentials, rules, and procedures for participation, the delegates were determined to demonstrate their capacity for fair and well-ordered self-government. The key speakers—Alexander Clark and the Reverend J. W. Malone—claimed the right to vote given "our full share of the hardships incidental to the war," "our natural rights," and the moral imperative of extending to black northerners the "equal rights and equal justice . . . asserted and enforced" in the South. Citizenship, they argued, must be a boon of freedom. "The colored people of Iowa," asserted Reverend Malone, sought "the power to protect themselves in their lives, liberty and property." The notion that white Iowans would safeguard the rights of African Americans "is the old argument in favor of slavery, when it was urged that the good and kind master would take care of the slaves, and do better for them than they would do for themselves." But they did not rely just on egalitarian political philosophy, for they highlighted a more pragmatic point as well. "The extension of the elective franchise to a few loyal colored men" would hardly unsettle the government. Clark reminded white Iowans that black voters would hold little collective political power.[35]

In the 1868 fall elections, white voters in Minnesota and Iowa approved the extension of the franchise to black men. African Americans celebrated their victory over the "insane appeals" that the Democratic press had aimed at the "rabble" to stir up racist outrage. In St. Paul, the enfranchised black voters immediately began to plan a state convention, to be held "in commemoration of their release from the odious political disabilities long imposed upon them, and to testify to their appreciation of this tardy act of justice." On 1 January 1869, the convention and victory celebration were combined with Emancipation Day activities attended by both men and women.[36]

The men who organized the Iowa convention and filled its various offices included former slaves who had moved to the state during the war as well as free blacks who had migrated to the territory in the 1850s, suggesting that suffrage may have provided a common goal for the two groups, which were described by a contemporary observer as having a "line of demarcation" between them.[37] Speeches were delivered by several of Minnesota's leading white Republicans and officeholders, as well as a Mr. Washington, a "colored orator" from Wisconsin. Charles Griswold stated that, with the franchise, African Americans were recognized as "men among men," with a "future bright with the promise of better things," whereas St. Paul's mayor was far more guarded in his assessment of enfranchisement's consequences. There would be whites who would "shut [blacks] out" from the schools, but who would raise a "hue and cry" if a black voter could not read his ballot; whites would provide little in the way of "openings and opportunities for work" but would be quick to insist on the "sin of colored idleness." Anticipating these responses, and perhaps to better ensure the success of their struggle for full citizenship, the black men in attendance organized the "Sons of Freedom." Its members (men only) would gather information on the progress of African Americans, publicize employment and training opportunities, and meet annually.[38]

In Iowa, black communities in Keokuk and Des Moines took to the streets to celebrate enfranchisement. Keokuk's torchlight procession included more than one hundred participants.[39] In Des Moines, beginning in the early afternoon of election day, a crowd of black families turned out for a "jubilee" that "was one of jollification" rather than a somber march. Their costumes, masks, and decorated wagons suggested that some (hopeful) planning had occurred before the election. The parade was styled as a shivaree, aiming a number of "laughable hits at the expense of the late Democratic party of Iowa," including costumed men caricaturing Confederate leaders. A wagon carried a coffin that was proclaimed to contain the Democratic platform. A brass artillery piece was pulled along in line, with armed veterans bringing up the rear. There were flags and banners everywhere as the crowd paraded down major streets and cheered the Republican city paper, the party's successful candidates, and the Iowa voters who had approved black suffrage. Later in the evening (for this was a celebration of several hours' duration), the celebrants were treated to a more formal torchlight procession and several speeches, one by the popular

Albert Nuckols, ambrotype, ca. 1868–70. Shortly after Iowa extended the franchise to African American men, Nuckols proclaimed: "I'm a man; have enjoyed citizenship two days out of forty years, and from the fullness of a grateful heart I beg leave to thank the loyal voters in our young state for the substantial test they have given of our sympathy for freedom by extending to the colored man the right of suffrage." Isaac A. Wetherby Collection, State Historical Society of Iowa, Iowa City.

Reverend S. T. Wells, a former slave who pronounced the election results a personal victory over his former master. "All we want is full liberty," he said. "We want to know more, we want to learn better how to discharge our duty here and to support our government like men." Arkansas-born Albert Nuckols, who had migrated to Davenport before the war, told the *Davenport Gazette* what enfranchisement meant to him: "I'm a *man*; have enjoyed citizenship two days out of forty years, and from the fullness of a grateful heart I beg leave to thank the loyal voters in our young state for the substantial test they have given of their sympathy for freedom by extending to the colored man the right of suffrage."[40] Nicholas Jones derided those northern states that still excluded or restricted black suffrage, asserting: "We have received the ballot and have been placed in possession of our rights and knowing them dare maintain them."[41]

Extant newspaper coverage offers little insight into how black voters in Wisconsin and Minnesota prepared to exercise their citizenship rights at the polls. There are no reports of black midwesterners gathering, as southern freedmen did under the auspices of the Union League, for the purpose of political education. Historian Gary Libman found evidence that John Richardson, living in Wabashaw County since his escape from Tennessee slavery during the war, was the first black Minnesotan to vote; he cast his ballot in a bond referendum in February 1869.[42] In Iowa, local newspapers reported that black men participated in a number of municipal elections in 1869, starting in Burlington, where, according to the *Iowa City Republican*, fifty or sixty African Americans "voted the Republican ticket, going to the polls quietly, and behaving themselves like the good citizens they are."[43] In early March, thirty-three blacks helped elect two white Republican aldermen in Muscatine.[44]

Although there is no evidence that black men encountered resistance at the ballot box, their free exercise of other rights of citizenship were still encumbered. White midwesterners were reluctant to accept black jurors, resisting their social proximity in the jury box, but also the idea of African American men sitting in judgment of whites and empowered to interpret the law.[45] Some court officials openly rejected black jurors; others seated black jurors only when cases involved African Americans. In most instances, the seating of a black juror was deemed notable by local, state, and sometimes regional newspapers for a number of years.[46]

In June 1869, Iowa and Chicago papers announced the seating of an all-black jury in Iowa City to hear a civil action involving two African Americans.[47] The first notice of an integrated jury in the region appeared in September 1869, when an Iowa newspaper noted that it was successfully "coming off."[48] Wisconsin's first reported instance of black jurors was in 1870, when an all-black jury was summoned to hear assault and battery charges against an African American man in Madison.[49] Minnesota and Iowa newspapers provided accounts of Minnesota's first occurrence of black jury service in 1873; "St. Paul," an Iowa report indicated, "has been greatly exercised over her first colored jurors," perhaps because local newspapers derisively caricatured potential black jurors as ignorant.[50] African Americans quickly learned that gaining rights was not the same as exercising them.

With their enfranchisement, black men anticipated playing an active role in Republican Party conventions. African American Iowans attended the state Republican convention for the first time in 1869, when five counties sent black delegates. Among them was Alexander Clark, whose address was "greeted with rapturous applause"; in recognition of his service to the party, he was elected vice president of the convention.[51] When Clark stumped for Republicans that fall, one eastern Iowa newspaper recommended that the party should expand his electioneering. "There are hundreds of white men . . . who ought to hear" him, the paper proclaimed.[52] Clark was joined by Keokuk's well-known black businessman, John Hiner, in addressing a large number of the city's African Americans in November 1869, a month before the elections. They outlined the Republican Party's work on behalf of blacks, referred to the "strong and persistent manner in which the Democratic party has always opposed and oppressed them," and reminded "both white and colored, of the duty" they shared on election day.[53]

Despite the symbolic importance of their enfranchisement, black voters in the upper Midwest would exercise little influence—let alone power—over regional politics. In contrast to the states of the former Confederacy, where concentrated black populations could and did elect black officials during Reconstruction, midwestern black voters and candidates were unable to garner support from the white electorate.[54] Over the next two decades, only two African American men in the upper Midwest were elected to local office. In 1869, William Jones, a well-off, Virginia-born black farmer in Tama County, Iowa, may have been the state's first black elected official, as constable for Perry Township, where he and his wife were the only black residents. It would be thirty more years before the municipal election of Frank Blagburn as Des Moines market master. In Wisconsin, Peter Thomas was elected to a two-year term as Racine County coroner in 1887. A Tennessee-born former slave who had relocated to southern Wisconsin with a white soldier wounded during the Civil War, Thomas enlisted in a black regiment and returned to the state in 1883.[55] James Kidd Hilyard, a Pennsylvania-born free black who went to St. Paul after the war, was, in 1891, the first black Minnesotan nominated for an elective position.[56]

Most of the political gains associated with citizenship rights were narrowly confined until the turn of the century, with the election of Minnesota's first black state legislator, John Wheaton, in 1898, and Wisconsin's first African American legislator, Lucien Palmer, in 1906.[57] White Iowans proved even more resistant to naming African Americans to government posts; in fact, until 1880, the state constitution prohibited black men from holding elective office.[58] Although black Republicans nominated first John Priestly (in 1885), then George H. Woodson (in 1899 and 1912), and Manson L. James (in 1944) to serve in the Iowa General Assembly, it would be 1964 before black and white voters saw fit to send an African American to the state legislature. In the meantime, black men were more likely to be selected as doorkeepers for the state house and senate, as they were in 1874 and 1883.[59]

The rewards were slim, but black voters in the upper Midwest were loyal to the party of Lincoln. Though rarely elected as delegates to state party conventions, they joined black "Cobblers and Tanners Clubs" (workingmen's Republican clubs) during Grant's 1868 and 1872 presidential campaigns. Black Republicans also enforced party discipline—challenging and publicly humiliating black men (like Henry Webb of Page County, Iowa) who dared to vote for Democratic candidates. But only a handful of black men won party recognition. Alexander Clark, among them, was asked to campaign for Republicans in Mississippi during the 1869 elections; in 1872 and again in 1876 he was elected an Iowa delegate to the Republican National Convention.[60] Few men, white or black, worked as hard as Clark did to support the party, with a long schedule of speeches nearly every election year. Like other black politicians, he used the podium not only for his party, but also in behalf of racial justice. Clark alerted midwestern audiences to the ongoing violence against black voters in the South, and he urged support of the Civil Rights Bill in 1874, when it was bogged down in congressional debate.[61]

The unshakable alliance that midwestern black voters built with the Republican Party would not survive the nineteenth century, however. A split in the party culminated during the 1872 campaign with the formation of the Liberal Republican Party, which attracted some black voters. As early as September 1871, at a Great Plains regional meeting in St. Louis, black Iowans joined delegates from Illinois, Nebraska, Indiana, Arkansas, and Missouri in departing from mainstream Republican positions, urging the removal of political disabilities from "repentant rebels of the South" and the extension of suffrage to women.[62] By 1872, even Liberal opponent Frederick Douglass acknowledged the substance of complaints "against the Republican party and the present administration": "They have overlooked and disregarded the claims of the colored voter in the bestowment of offices and honors; . . . they have assumed that colored men should be satisfied with the rights to vote for white men . . . ; and . . . they have done so in deference to the well-known prejudice against the colored race. We admit this, and if possible, much more against the Republican party."[63]

Encouraged, perhaps, by prominent black rights advocate George T. Downing's sympathy for the Liberal Party, by Radical Republican Charles Sumner's refusal to back Grant's reelection, or by their frustration with party corruption and the failure of the North's powerful Republican machine to deal fairly with black voters, a Colored National Liberal Republican Convention formed and met in Louisville; two Iowa delegates attended.[64] Some semblance of black support for the Liberal Party continued into the 1870s, enough to draw the venom of Alexander Clark in his keynote address at the 1876 Iowa black state convention, where he attacked Klan-like White Leagues, Grangers, and "recreant Republicans called Liberals" for their attempts to overthrow the Republican Party.[65]

The vast majority of black Republicans, alienated from what William Gillette characterized as "a coalition of racist reactionaries, reformist moderates, and disenchanted Republicans," continued to support the party of Lincoln.[66] But black voters made their choices carefully. In 1874, the year that saw the greatest upset in Republican power since the party's formation, they probably played a role in the defeat of Keokuk's Republican mayoral candidate, who had been an opponent of black suffrage.[67] Republican success in northern states and localities waned as northern white supporters, preoccupied with the impact of the national depression and flagging in their commitment to racial justice in the South, began withdrawing their support for federal intervention in the former Confederacy and began to lose their hold on state politics in the upper Midwest. By 1875, Republicans had also lost control of state governments in eight of the former Confederate states, although blacks continued to serve in southern local offices at least through the 1877 withdrawal of federal troops (marking the end of Reconstruction) and, in some locations, into the 1890s.[68]

By the 1880s, in the aftermath of "redemption," the Supreme Court reversal of the Civil Rights Act in 1883, and increasing violence aimed at disfranchising black southern voters, African Americans in the upper Midwest and black voters across the North more openly challenged their second-class status in the Republican Party, as well as criticizing the party's apparent abandonment of civil rights and southern black voters.[69] In 1883, when black Minnesotans gathered at a statewide convention in St. Paul, they did something that would have been unthinkable a decade earlier: they tabled a proposed resolution endorsing the statewide Republican ticket in that year's campaign.[70] Five years later, the Reverend William Hilary Coston, minister of the AME church in Mt. Pleasant, Iowa, complained that "we suffer in consequence of Republican perfidy on one hand and Democratic ku-kluxism on the other." Party loyalty held no benefits for blacks, according to Coston. "We have nothing to gain from either party. One has betrayed us, the other murders us with impunity." He told fellow black midwesterners: "We should place a political boycott on all who refuse us free access to the industrial mart."[71]

By 1884, midwestern black Republicans were tired of being "obliged to put up with the tail end of everything." Meeting in Des Moines, they formed the "Aspiring Club" to pursue an increase in the number of black candidates Republicans endorsed in state races as well as black delegates to the Republican National Convention. The county Republican organization responded by recommending to send at least one black delegate to that year's state convention.[72] Black party members in Mt. Pleasant similarly complained of exclusion from party gatherings as well as state elections; they also criticized the infighting among black Republicans that led to competition for political influence and positioning. These state-level concerns were mirrored at the 1884 Republican National Convention in Chicago. Although this assembly saw the first appointment of an African American (John R. Lynch, a former Mississippi congressman) as temporary chair, black delegates challenged the party to do more. John Green, a black Ohio legislator, rebuked white Republicans who believed "that the colored man should stick to the party to pay a debt of gratitude."[73] They wanted more.

The growth of Iowa's coal mining industry, in conjunction with the recruitment of black miners from Virginia and the corresponding growth of black communities in the southeastern tier of counties, encouraged the state's black voters to believe they had finally attained the political muscle they needed to shape local politics and more directly influence the state Republican Party.[74] By 1885, black voters in the mining community in and around Oskaloosa and Muchakinock convened, applauded speeches that were occasionally "revolutionary towards the Republican party," and nominated an African American—John Priestly—for the state assembly. At this meeting they announced that if the Republican Party failed to endorse Priestly's candidacy, they would choose their own nominees for county offices as well. Because black voters outnumbered the Republican majority in the county, they had reason to hope their demand for representation on the Republican ticket would be taken seriously.[75] But Iowa Republicans did not nominate Priestly. Perhaps black voters were wooed back to the party's standard by the appearance of the nation's best-known black politician, Mississippian Blanche K. Bruce, the first black U.S. senator, as the keynote speaker at a southern Iowa Emancipation Day celebration on 22 September 1885.[76]

The 1890s continued to see black midwestern men make demands on the Republican Party. At a campaign meeting in Illinois attended by black residents of several Iowa river towns, a speaker from Keokuk insisted that "the Republican party must change its policy toward the colored people or it would lose their votes. . . . The party has been using the colored man as a tool, getting the benefit of his political services and giving no political reward."[77] At Minnesota's Republican convention, African Americans confronted white party members: "Does the republican party of the State of Minnesota owe anything to its Afro-American constituency?" The answer to that question, they said, was yes: Their demonstrated loyalty had put the party in their debt, a debt that should be repaid at the upcoming national convention in Minneapolis. But the white Republicans rejected their demand that an African American delegate be seated at the convention. The 1892 Republican National Convention, which failed to address the issues of lynching and black voting rights, was a disappointment not only for black Minnesotans, but also for the country's black party faithful as whole.[78]

Some black midwestern Republicans thought they needed to take more initiative at the local, rather than the state or national, level. One anonymous writer in an Iowa newspaper, under the heading of "Colored Citizen," suggested that black voters make it their business to educate themselves about candidates, attend convention meetings, prepare position papers, and present their interests to party convention delegates. Another model for successful grassroots activism, this particular observer noted, could be found among black women. "We are in possession of the ballot, they are not, yet they are far in advance of us in the expression of their grievances and accomplishing the ends desired."[79] Indeed, African American women in the upper Midwest were making their own challenge to northern white supremacy.

"LET US LEARN VALUABLE LESSONS FROM THE HEROISM OF WOMEN"

The postbellum struggle for black citizenship and civil rights was both tenacious and gendered. While African American men sought the franchise and a representative role in party politics, women were more likely to be found in courtrooms pursuing civil rights. A number of black women in the Midwest joined with their peers across the country to confront public officials, transportation workers and the companies they worked for, the white public, and the courts in their struggle to defend their freedom and their citizenship. One of the most substantial archives of women's Reconstruction-era activism is found in the records of civil rights litigation, which show African American women—North and South—numerously engaged in courtroom challenges to the custom and law of segregation. One historian's survey of racial discrimination cases involving public transit between 1865 and 1920 found black female litigants initiating twenty-eight of the thirty-four cases with published legal opinions.[80]

In addition to these public transport cases (many of which occurred in the South), there are a number of published opinions on challenges to the denial of public education in Iowa, Ohio, California, New York, Pennsylvania, and

Kansas—cases that involved adult female litigants (mothers) or a female child seeking access to a public school.[81] Unreported cases were more numerous. For example, of an additional twenty cases from northern states that had unpublished opinions but were noted in the *New York Times*, the AME's *Christian Recorder*, or the African American *Cleveland Gazette*, ten involved plaintiffs who were mothers of students or girls who sought admission to segregated schools.[82] Many of these published and unrecorded cases occurred in the immediate postwar decade, what the legal scholar Davison Douglas has called "the most intense period of northern antisegregation activity of the entire nineteenth century," which began with hundreds of petitions, protests, and letters to boards of education.[83] Historians have been slow to recognize women's prominence in civil rights activism and legal cases in particular, and slow to appreciate the number of civil rights cases that challenged northern discriminatory practices.

Of course, not all civil rights activism by northern women culminated in legal action. Still, this record of civil rights litigation is important, not only because it documents civil rights injustices and women's responses to them, but also because these cases demonstrate women's participation in the movement to expand citizenship in postwar America. This litigation produced the earliest interpretations of the Fourteenth Amendment, contributed to a body of common law that judges frequently referred to in deciding appeals, and documented the actual usage of Reconstruction-era statutes designed to overcome racial inequality in the law.[84] It also provides a record of how and why African American women and their daughters came to stand at the front line of northern black efforts to challenge the state to fulfill the promise of freedom —at great risk to their dignity and personal safety. Moreover, these cases illuminate how African American women battled what one black midwesterner referred to as "that wily oppressor[,] public sentiment."[85]

The earliest recorded protest to Iowa authorities by a black woman against state-sanctioned discriminatory practices occurred before the Civil War in relation to school segregation. In 1855, Martha Reno, of Iowa City, a forty-year-old widow, refused to pay a newly instituted school tax assessed for the construction of new schools, a matter that the sheriff dutifully reported to the city council. Reno, he said, declined to pay the tax on the grounds that local schools would not admit her daughter.[86] Significantly, Reno dared to take this stand only because she and her husband had been very cautious since their arrival in Iowa in 1841. At that time, Iowa's territorial law required all free blacks entering the territory to post a $500 bond; Martha and her husband did so with the help of one of Iowa City's white entrepreneurs—most likely the couple's employer. Had they failed to post the bond, Reno's civil disobedience would have permitted the commissioners of Johnson County to reduce her to involuntary servitude for a six-month period before ejecting her, as well as her two children, from the state.[87] The city council made no effort to prosecute or penalize her, perhaps because a check of state law would have revealed that, since 1849, the property of black residents had been explicitly excluded from taxation that supported white-only schools.

For a few months in 1858, an Iowa statute allowed black children to attend public schools if white parents did not object, a measure that was quickly found to be unconstitutional. Subsequent laws concerning Iowa schools—between 1860 and 1866—made no mention of race or color, nor did they exempt African Americans from taxes assessed to support public schools, as earlier laws had.[88] The end result was that black children were far less likely than white children to have access to a common (public) school education. In 1860, just under a third of the state's 378 school-age black children attended school, in contrast to 67 percent of their white peers. Because there is no record that separate schools were built for black students, it is likely that some schools must have admitted black children, although Martha Reno's community was not among them.[89]

Without an explicit law to guide them in the mechanics of segregation, Iowa communities responded variously to the demands black residents made on local schools. In the fall of 1850, the entry of black children into the school in Tabor prompted one or more persons to burn the building to the ground. In Grinnell, between 1858 and 1860, a sixteen-year-old fugitive slave girl, employed in a local white household, entered the public school without apparent incident. But when she was joined by four young male fugitives, white opposition erupted into mob violence. The facility was forced to close until the school board announced that it would screen all black applicants, understood locally as a process by which the board would deny blacks admission.[90]

During and immediately after the war, Iowa's newest black residents made similar claims for their own and their children's education, claims they pursued under difficult circumstances. Local school boards offered an increasingly explicit pattern of segregation, some organizing or building separate schools. In other communities, unnamed private citizens provided financial backing for separate black schools; in still others, the new "black" schools were supported entirely through student subscriptions. In Ottumwa, the local AME congregation raised money to buy the land on which the school board built a new school "expressly for the benefit of the colored children."[91]

But just as local school boards and the white communities they represented found various means to arrive at segregation, so Iowa's recent black migrants drew from a range of strategies as they sought to secure their rights to education. Their decisions about how to proceed could not be made lightly. To whom would they entrust their children's schooling? What choice was the right one for their families and their communities? It was no secret among black Iowans that white adults often regarded them as ignorant, degraded, and shiftless. When black parents in smaller communities attempted to send their children to public schools, white parents and school boards made it clear that close association and mutual learning, when interracial, were unacceptable. School boards in Taylor and Mitchell counties expelled black youths who dared to enter their public schools; white parents in Perry petitioned for the expulsion of the single black child who went to the school. In Bonaparte, by what one observer described as the "will of the people," the school board banned the town's one black student from the public school classroom, then hired a teacher who instructed him in a room set off from the rest of the school. As a result, many black parents chose not to try to place their children in "white" public schools.[92] Black parents in Des Moines—most of them wartime migrants from the South—organized a school of their own. Although impoverished and aware that they had a legal right to attend the city's tax-supported schools, "most prefer not to excite the prejudices that might be awakened if they should attempt to avail themselves of their legal rights," explained a local paper.[93] The rare experiments with integrated schools could draw school boards into micromanagement in order to to accommodate the racist sensibilities of white parents; in Washington, Iowa, the school board rearranged classroom seating when a white father, claiming that a black student had an odor that made his son sick, insisted that his son's seat be moved away from the black student's.[94]

The Civil Rights Act of 1866 and the ratification of the Fourteenth Amendment in 1868 provided a new framework and venue for responses to discriminatory acts; both encouraged African Americans to consider the courtroom as a site of redress.[95] In this context, African Americans in the upper Midwest (and across the nation) accelerated their struggle against state-sanctioned segregation and imbued their pursuit of civil rights with unprecedented political significance. Black midwesterners included equal access to public institutions and accommodations, and equal treatment within them, as components of their newly confirmed citizenship. As one white lawyer asserted on behalf of a black female litigant: "The colored population being now all free, and being by constitutional amendments endowed with the right of the elective franchise, are a part of the public, a part of the body politic."[96]

This newly charged pursuit of citizenship was not only about what happened in the courtroom. It depended on the willingness of individual parents and children to confront teachers, principals, school superintendents, boards of education, and other local authorities, most if not all of whom were white. This was an African American movement; with the exception of the white lawyers who represented black plaintiffs, few whites expressed support—and then largely from a safe distance.[97] Importantly, African American women and female children were frequently central figures in litigation over school segregation in the North.[98] In the legal records of these confrontations, husbands and fathers often appear as plaintiffs, since common law subsumed minors and married women under the legal identity of fathers and husbands, but below the surface lay the central role of mothers and children.[99]

This was particularly true in Iowa, where adult women were directly involved in several important face-to-face confrontations that launched legal challenges to segregation. (In contrast, the extant record is silent on black women's involvement in organizing or staffing black schools or challenging de facto school segregation in Wisconsin or its legal complement in Minnesota.)[100] When St. Paul's population of school-age black children reached sixty in 1857, the local board of education organized a separate black school taught by a black male instructor. Limited attendance soon led to the school's closure, although it reopened in 1865 (under a white female teacher) in the wake of wartime black migration. The school building's dismal physical condition and lack of supplies prompted local African American men (veterans as well as members of a black men's literary club) to protest. By March 1869, the Minnesota legislature finally initiated an integrated system of education, although white protests against the admission of black pupils would continue for years to come.[101]

The decision of whether to challenge or to cooperate with school segregation could not have been an easy one for black families. But in Iowa, their challenges met with success in three lawsuits that survived appeals to the state supreme court. The first of these cases began in the fall of 1867, when twelve-year-old Susan Clark was turned away from a white grammar school in Muscatine. Eleven years earlier, black families in her community had organized their own, separate school, housed in the AME church. In the immediate aftermath of the Civil War, however, the black community determined to make an indirect challenge to segregation: the AME congregation informed the school board that it would no longer house (and financially support) the school. Soon afterward black families brought their children to the city's tax-supported white schools. In response, whites charged that African Americans were trying to "crowd white children out of our schools." While their children bore the initial brunt of racist reactions, local black parents achieved both a material and a symbolic victory when they succeeded in transferring responsibility for funding their school to the public treasury. Faced with the choice between integrating schools or financing a black school, Muscatine's white school board suddenly found the resources to support a school for black youth.[102]

In this context, twelve-year-old Susan Clark confronted public school segregation head on. When her request for admission to her neighborhood white school was denied, Susan's father sued the school board on her behalf. The lower court found in her favor, and the ruling survived an April 1868 appeal; the higher court determined that Iowa law did not grant local school boards the authority to segregate schools. By December 1868, Muscatine's schools were integrated.[103] But the victory of the Clark suit went beyond Susan's admission to her neighborhood school. Claiming the right to benefit fully from the taxes they paid, her parents had successfully challenged the practice of state-supported segregation and discredited white assumptions that segregation served the interests of black and white communities equally. More importantly, the court had decreed that, in Iowa, "all youths are equal before the law."[104] Yet, across the state, school boards ignored the ruling. Many black parents chose not to seek its enforcement, apparently preferring to entrust their children to separate schools under black teachers and black principals.

One of the places where school segregation continued unabated was Keokuk, located in southeastern Iowa on the Missouri border, just two hundred miles north of St. Louis. Keokuk was Iowa's largest city and home to its largest black community. The war had brought change to Keokuk, increasing its black population more than 400 percent—from about 220 to more than 1,000 residents. As the rendezvous point for the state's black regiment, the city drew black recruits and their families from as far south as Alabama and as far north as Minneapolis, contributing to the growing black population. The African Americans in Keokuk were efficient institution builders, beginning with the founding of an AME congregation in 1857 and an "African School" some time prior to the fall of 1859. Providing instruction to more than fifty students on the eve of the war, this was the largest black school in the state, boasting well-trained instructors and an expanding enrollment.[105]

By the end of the war, the school had three graded classes and three female teachers to handle the demands of its continued growth; by 1869, enrollment exceeded three hundred students. Susan Caldwell, the school's first teacher, was later joined by Martha Anderson and Mary Mann. Formerly of Cleveland, Anderson was an experienced teacher and active in the Ohio Colored Teachers

Association before moving to Keokuk.[106] By 1867, she was the school's principal but continued to hold classes, even after a male teacher was hired. Mann, born in Zanesville, Ohio, went to Iowa by way of Chicago, where as a student she had successfully challenged segregation in the city's high school. In fact, she may have been the first African American to graduate from a public high school in Illinois. Ironically, having championed desegregation in Chicago's high school, Mann's first teaching job was in a newly segregated black school organized by the city in 1863, the year she graduated. Mann's school failed to draw sufficient enrollment and closed in 1865.[107] Unemployed, she went to Keokuk that fall and joined Caldwell and Anderson at the African School.[108]

In July 1869, less than a year after providing a new, two-story, furnished school for black students that opened in the fall of 1868, the Keokuk school board announced that it planned to replace the black staff of the African School with a white principal and white teachers. The decision touched off a "fever of excitement," and local blacks promptly organized a communitywide protest.[109] "We have competent colored teachers in our midst to instruct our children. . . . we do not desire to be taught by white teachers," they resolved. If the school board replaced their teachers, they would send their children to the all-white public schools.[110]

The threat to integrate city schools did its work: the respected and beloved black teachers continued to teach and supervise the school for African Americans. But despite the new building, capable instructors, and black pride in the school, segregation still deprived young blacks of a high school education. As one former student said, "When you reached the fourth grade, they handed you your diploma."[111] Segregation also required the youngsters to walk a considerable distance to grade school. Both circumstances led to two nearly consecutive challenges to school segregation, which continued to dominate public education in Iowa.

In the spring of 1874, Charlotta Smith, a former slave from Kentucky and the mother of sixteen-year-old Geroid, and Mrs. Mary Jane Dove, the wife of the sometimes controversial AME minister William Dove and the adoptive mother of nine-year-old Charles, each lodged a protest against segregation in Keokuk schools.[112] Smith sought Geroid's admission to the all-white high school; Dove wished to send Charles to the neighborhood grammar school, from which he could enter the high school. Both mothers escorted their sons to school; both encountered irate and obstinate white teachers, principals, and school superintendents; and both decided to engage legal counsel. In so doing, Smith and Dove participated in a regionwide pattern of mothers and children defying segregation. In response to Smith's initial efforts, the school board paid one of the male instructors at the black school to add high-school level courses. Nonetheless, a mass meeting was organized at the black Baptist church to support Smith's challenge and raise funds to pay her legal fees. "We have had a great injustice done us and our children," Reverend Dove asserted. York Anderson, a teacher, barber, Mason, and active member of the AME congregation, insisted that "we had a right to go in the . . . schools, . . . that he, for one, was ready and willing to put his shoulder to the wheel and push this thing through." It was decided at the meeting to boycott the new high school courses at the black school and urge the admittance of black students to the city high school.[113]

Both cases would be heard at court in the late fall of 1874. Meanwhile, the courage of the Dove and Smith families, and of the community that backed their challenge to segregation, must have been sorely tested when Keokuk was shaken by news of an incipient attack on the city by the Ku Klux Klan. One Sunday evening, only a month after the protest meeting, word spread that thousands of Klan members had terrorized two nearby Missouri communities and were expected to arrive at the river levee at any moment. Seven white men apparently started the rumor and persuaded an unsuspecting young black man to carry the report to the Baptist and AME churches, where services were under way. The ministers were interrupted with the news, and their congregations—as well as the larger black community—responded with "indescribable alarm and confusion." Black women gathered their children and fled the city, while their husbands seized guns from the city armory and a local gun store. "Hurrying through the streets with shotguns and pistols," they proceeded to the levee to defend their community against the invading Klan, which never materialized. According to the local paper, "some of the women who were enceinte were so badly frightened as to endanger their lives." The white men responsible for the rumor—described in local papers as the "KuKlux Jokers"—were brought to trial the next day before a courtroom packed with black spectators. The defendants insisted they had no purpose beyond a little joke; at most, they intended "to get rid of a couple colored loafers." The white jury took ten or fifteen minutes to deliberate and returned with a not guilty verdict. It was a stark reminder of how little black lives were valued and how difficult it was to obtain justice in a white courtroom.[114]

In both civil rights cases, heard in November and December 1874, the school board insisted that it did not unfairly discriminate against black students. Its defense of "white rights" was reminiscent of white opposition to black migration during the war. The board members argued that the white schools were already crowded; turning away white students to make room for black ones "would make an unjust discrimination against the white students on account of their color." They also feared that integration would "destroy the harmony . . . uniform prosperity and public usefulness" of the white schools. Furthermore, the black school had been "organized and maintained at the desire of the colored people of the city." Segregation was the preference of the majority of black families; only "a few negroes, who are some what aristocratic and feel themselves above their colored brethren, desire their children to attend with the white children."[115]

Smith and Dove won their cases in the lower courts, and the rulings were affirmed by the Iowa Supreme Court in June and December 1875. Although the 1876 school year proceeded with segregation intact, that fall about sixty black students presented themselves for admission to white neighborhood schools. By June 1876, the school board officially ended segregation, and the black school began to admit white students.

The struggle against school segregation helped create a new world of educational opportunities for some black midwesterners. Although many local school boards were slow to dismantle the practice, some black students gained unprecedented access to public education. Susan Clark graduated from one of Muscatine's desegregated schools in 1871 and delivered the commencement address; in 1878, Geroid Smith was Keokuk's first black and formerly enslaved high school graduate. Moses Mosely's daughter Susan—also a former slave— would attend local schools and be the first black graduate of Iowa Wesleyan College, where she earned a B.A. in 1885 and an M.A. in 1888.

But in the fight for equal educational opportunities, success came with real costs. While many northern black communities were clearly underserved by segregated schools that were in poor condition and understaffed, others had created valuable institutions, taught and controlled by blacks, that were lost with integration.[116] It is important to understand that the challenges to segregation in Muscatine and Keokuk were not undertaken in order to abandon or destroy the institutions black communities had worked hard to build.[117] Black schools—particularly those with black teachers—often provided significant advantages: a learning environment free of white harassment, a venue in which to hire (as teachers) and train (as students) community leaders, and the provision of a considerable and, for women, unique professional opportunity. Alexander Clark, having successfully fought school segregation on his daughter's behalf, still applauded the Republican Party's support for the creation of black schools.[118]

The loss of black schools and one of the few professional opportunities available to black women was a deprivation that young educated black women like Susan Clark and Susan Mosely would have to bear. Keokuk would not hire another black female teacher until 1965, since most white school boards refused to employ black teachers to educate white children.[119] There were exceptions: Miss Alice Anderson would teach in the public schools of the predominantly black mining community of Muchakinock in 1888, and Miss Nora Breckenridge gained certification to teach in Polk County schools by 1889. Through desegregation, black women had gained the right to a high school education, but they also saw a rare professional career path cut off with the elimination of black schools.

Frances Ellen Watkins Harper was one of the few nationally recognized African Americans to publicly address this paradox of racial progress paired with lost opportunities for black women. A well-known and highly respected writer, lecturer, and longtime activist for social equality, Harper visited Keokuk in late February 1874 to speak in the black Baptist church, the AME church, and the city courthouse. According to one resident, "her lectures are just what we are in need of; and she is well received."[120] We can only speculate about her influence on the women who would take up the challenges to segregation in the fall. But Harper explicitly addressed the collision of civil rights advances with opportunities for black women in a short story appearing in the *Christian Recorder* in 1874.[121] Here, the two protagonists—the uneducated but wise Aunt Jane and her college-educated niece, Jenny—discuss the fate of one of Aunt Jane's closest friends, who had lost her teaching job in the aftermath of civil rights legislation that closed her black school. Harper captures the individual desperation that racial progress could leave in its wake. As Aunt Jane's friend had put it, "The tidal wave of progress has reached us here and I feel that the ground has suddenly slidden from under my feet. The authorities have closed my school."[122] Responsible for supporting her widowed mother, the now-unemployed teacher did not have the luxury of taking a position in one of the South's segregated schools; nor did her pride allow her to consider domestic service. Her friend's circumstances sobered Aunt Jane. Niece Jenny responded that while she rejoiced at the passage of the civil rights bill, she felt sympathy for women who had worked hard to become teachers and now found themselves out of a profession. Through her protagonists, Harper illuminated the unique disadvantages that black women labored under even as their communities secured civil rights protections. Black women did not have the vote, they were excluded from many national civil rights meetings that black men organized; they lacked the wealth to create black-owned and operated businesses and industries that might open a gate for women as others were closed to them.¹²³ Integrated schools might allow black women to acquire an education, but the same schools refused to hire them as teachers. Harper's fictional account reveals one of the most crucial but complex civil rights struggles to emerge from slavery's destruction.

Such a loss for African American women must have weighed even more heavily considering the gains white women were making in midwestern school systems. In Iowa and Wisconsin by 1869, and in Minnesota by 1876, white women had obtained the right to participate in school elections. Voters in Mitchell County, Iowa, chose the state's first white female superintendent of county schools in 1869 (to serve in 1870 and 1871); white candidate Jennie McCowen (of Audubon County) lost her bid in 1871 to become superintendent of schools by only fifteen votes. Davenport voters had elected a white female superintendent of schools by 1874. In 1876, Minnesotans elected their first two women (both white) to school offices.¹²⁴ White women were gaining partial suffrage, the right to run for educational office, and the opportunity to lead school boards, while African American women had to sacrifice their own opportunities so their children might sooner enjoy them. Even in such circumstances, black women continued their courtroom challenges to the laws that sanctioned segregation. Of course, most experiences of illegal segregation were never heard in courtrooms; the cost of pursuing lawsuits would have been prohibitive.¹²⁵

Confronting segregation in transportation and public accommodations could be physically threatening to black women, for insisting on racial equality meant directly challenging those willing to enforce separation or exclusion. The most extreme brutality that black women encountered typically occurred in the South, but northern litigants also recounted insults, humiliations, assaults, and injury at the hands of white steamboat and railroad workers who were expected to defend the color line and the privileges enjoyed by white passengers (although some of those workers undoubtedly acted out of their own investment in white supremacy). Furthermore, most civil rights cases against common carriers were not about the exclusion of African American women from passage, but rather their exclusion from the gender-segregated cars or cabins reserved for "ladies." The alternative to ladies' cars or cabins was the forward smoker car or a mixed cabin, where men of all classes were seated, and where black women anticipated rough treatment, particularly from white men, as well as dirty, smoky, and uncomfortable conditions. When they challenged their removal to "mixed" cars or cabins, African American women were asserting their right to first-class and protected accommodations, but they were also challenging the ability of white men to protect white women from social proximity to black women, thereby undermining the race-based privileges of womanhood that white women had long claimed as their own.[126]

It is perhaps not surprising, then, that white employees on northern carriers could respond harshly when African American women asserted a claim to equal treatment. Illinois hairdresser Anna Williams, traveling from her Rockford home to Belvidere in August 1867, was denied access to the ladies' car. She testified in court that "the brakeman stopped me and told me to go in the other car. I tried to go past him, he put his hand on my shoulder and pushed me back." The brakeman used "rough and indecent language" in speaking to her. The episode played out in the presence of Williams's fourteen-year-old nephew, helpless to defend his aunt or to persuade the conductor to intervene on her behalf. She sued the railroad company for $1,000 damages, and the jury awarded her $200. The verdict withstood an 1870 appeal by the railroad company.[127] In the same year Mary Jane Chilton of St. Louis received similar treatment when she attempted to enter the ladies' car; she, too, filed suit against the railroad company.[128]

Emma Coger, a twenty-year-old schoolteacher from Quincy, Illinois, encountered a more escalated level of brutality while traveling on a steamboat from Keokuk to Quincy in early 1872. Coger had been refused a first-class ticket (one that permitted her to take her meals with "ladies," rather than below, on the guards (where freight was stacked), or in the pantry with the servants). The clerk would only sell her a second-class ticket marked "colored." Finally, Coger arranged for a gentleman onboard (who was apparently unaware that she was of African descent) to buy a first-class ticket for her. At lunchtime, Coger went to take her seat but the white clerk pulled her chair away. When she persisted, the clerk talked to her "as if speaking to a dog," then left to get the captain. Three of the five white women at the table left, refusing, they said, to eat with "a negro." The captain came and jerked her chair out from under her. When Coger held onto the table, he pulled her away—and the table setting flew to the floor. He then struck her repeatedly and literally dragged her through the ladies' and gentlemen's cabins, shoving and threatening her. Five days later Coger sued the steamboat company for damages.[129]

Coger would be vindicated, but only after a parade of white witnesses defamed her during the course of the trial. The court proceedings became a public spectacle, highlighting the current debate over who might lay claim to idealized womanhood. Coger's opponents insisted on referring to her as a "colored woman," a "negro," a "yellow girl." They said she had instigated the confrontation by attacking the captain, trying to bite him and tear his clothes, and using profane and obscene language to him and white passengers. In other words, according to these witnesses, Emma Coger was anything but a lady and therefore not entitled to the first-class accommodations reserved for white "ladies."

Adding to the complexity of Coger's case was her insistence on challenging the categories of race that segregation assumed. She testified that, as a child of a white father and a formerly enslaved mother, she had been defined as "over half white" throughout her young life and accustomed to enjoying the privileges that her light complexion afforded her. She socialized with whites and attended school with whites. In other words, Coger explicitly contested the notion that anyone with "one drop" of "colored blood" should be regarded as black, or that a "colored" woman could not claim to be a "lady." A Keokuk newspaper described her as "genteel, respectable, lady-like and well-behaved," a woman who had "a perfect right to take her seat" with other "ladies" on the ship.[130] Coger's lawyer argued that she "cannot be regarded as a colored person; that, as white blood predominates in her veins, she is, in law, to be regarded as belonging to the white race, and is not, therefore, subject to the rules or restrictions that may be imposed upon negroes."[131] Coger not only rejected popular ideas of racial categorization, but also referred to several of her character witnesses, from Quincy and from Keokuk, as biracial people who were, at most, "partially colored." This was a description they claimed for themselves as well as for Coger, noting that she had long associated "as much with white persons as those who are called colored."[132] A young woman who accompanied Coger on the steamboat was similarly defined "as white and looks as white" as any white person attending the trial, although she was referred to in court as "colored."[133]

The appeals court, ignoring Coger's challenge to contemporary definitions of race, characterized her as a "colored woman," entitled to the Fourteenth Amendment's protections—the enjoyment of "equal and inalienable rights" commensurate with those of whites. Coger herself would never describe the outcome of her case as a victory for "colored women," but rather as a victory in the ongoing national debate over the intersection of race, gender, and status in the public sphere. "The object of my suit was . . . to vindicate my right to be treated as a lady, while I acted as a lady," she asserted. The appeals court, in contrast, had concluded that "neither womanly delicacy nor unwomanly courage has any thing to do with [Coger's] legal rights and the remedies for their deprivation."[134] The court "raced" Coger; it was as an African American, rather than as a lady, that she was entitled to equal rights and the protections of the law.

Coger—along with Keokuk residents and those who read about her case in state and national newspapers—would have understood how charged was her claim to treatment as a "lady." As the legal scholar Barbara Welke has observed, northern as well as southern whites, men and women, saw physical proximity to African Americans in the public sphere as a loss of their own status in the postemancipation era. Blacks who threatened white dominion over public space risked insult, violence, arrest, and public defamation as whites sought to defend the public sphere against black incursion. Lawsuits like those pursued by Williams, Chilton, and Coger were numerous, but they only touched the surface of racialized conflicts in the public sphere. Locally, for example, arrest reports show that Keokuk police officers took it upon themselves to monitor public spaces in defense of white womanhood and racialized notions of propriety. Young African American boys were arrested and fined for using indecent language in the presence of white women; African American women indulging in boisterous behavior on city streets were arrested, fined, and defamed as lacking "a very high reputation for virtue and chastity."[135]

Courtroom victories like Coger's fueled the ongoing battles over public space, as well as public opinion.[136] A Keokuk resident wrote the *Christian Recorder* that the verdict in Coger's case indicated "the triumph of right and justice over oppression and injustice."[137] From the pages of the *New National Era*, William Vance, also of Keokuk, commended Coger's successful suit: "We as a people are still denied certain rights and privileges given to other citizens, and I think if all of us could be as bold and courageous . . . our rights would be gradually yielded to us."[138] On the other hand, a white resident wrote: "I do not want to eat with darkies, nor mix with them socially. All the liberties they possess have been generously given them by the white race. If they now attempt to push and force themselves; or, if white persons attempt to force such a mixture socially, it will only excite the prejudice now existing and make it stronger."[139]

"NOT ALTOGETHER FREE"

Given these ongoing debates, black midwesterners were among those African Americans who benefited from the Civil Rights Act of 1875. White midwesterners, too, benefited; whites who endorsed racial equality now declared an end to the struggle—"Nothing is left that can be done." The Republican Party, they thought, could finally "turn its attention to other work."[140] However, with the 1883 reversal of the 1875 legislation by the U.S. Supreme Court (under Chief Justice Samuel Freeman Miller, an Iowan), black midwesterners could no longer hope for federal protection of their civil rights, especially the right to enjoy equal accommodations.[141] Subsequently, Iowa (in 1884), Minnesota (in 1885), and Wisconsin (in 1891) were among the eighteen states to follow that reversal with civil rights legislation. Blacks in all three states had held mass meetings and organized to lobby for the measures, but, once passed, the state laws were shown to have many weaknesses.[142]

Because the Iowa Civil Rights Act of 1884 did not identify specific penalties, violations fell into a category of misdemeanors that were outside the jurisdiction of justices of the peace. Convictions therefore required, at a minimum, a fine of more than one hundred dollars or imprisonment for more than thirty days. Given what many whites felt was an overly harsh punishment, in the forty years between 1884 and 1923, when the state's NAACP finally persuaded the legislature to amend the measure, there were only three successful convictions under the Iowa law. The statute proved nearly unenforceable, depending on white juries to levy significant penalties for acts of discrimination that most whites felt should never have been criminalized to begin with.[143] Minnesota's law was equally difficult to enforce. "Something should be done," asserted the editor of the state's black newspaper, the *Appeal*, in response to the latest report (in 1890) of "prejudiced people . . . insulting and outraging respectable Colored people" in the Twin Cities.[144]

In all three states, the legislation narrowly defined the locations to which the law applied; in Wisconsin and Minnesota, African Americans regarded the penalties as insultingly small.[145] Given the limitations of state legislation, as well as the symbolic and pragmatic consequences of withdrawing federal protections for black civil rights, 1883 must be regarded as a watershed year. Black midwesterners, frustrated by the national retreat from civil rights enforcement in the context of their circumscribed political power at the state level, turned to new strategies and tactics to secure black citizenship both at home and in the South. African American women were at the forefront of this departure from the earlier civil rights era.

This new era of black activism began in 1885 and continued through the turn of the century. The most noteworthy changes in the pursuit of a black political voice and black political empowerment were found in the activism of African American women—as they began to collaborate with whites in the woman suffrage movement, as they organized with men in the nonpartisan Afro-American Council, and as they began to organize a black women's club movement. Both the successes and the failures of two decades of civil rights efforts by northern blacks had brought a change in the nature and scale of their activism.

Before 1885, there was little collaboration between African American and white women in their entirely separate struggles for broadly defined citizenship rights in the upper Midwest. In part, this was a result of the uses and abuses of antiwoman and antiblack rhetoric during the debates over the Reconstruction amendments. But it can also be attributed to the ill-considered affiliation of white feminists with the Democratic Party—viewed by African Americans as the party of slavery and race mongers—during debates over extending the franchise in the immediate postwar era. African American men felt that comparisons between their own struggle for enfranchisement and white women's demands for suffrage were rarely offered by advocates of racial equality. In legislative debates but also in the public sphere, woman suffrage was most often raised as a tactic by lawmakers to rationalize or dismiss black suffrage. The Democratic Party dismissed both black enfranchisement and woman suffrage as ridiculous and unwise, but Republican supporters responded that the women who were not allowed to vote "are supposed to be fully compensated by not being required to fight, work roads, &c." African American men, on the other hand, "have been drafted . . . put in the army, sent to the front, have fought as bravely as any other class, have contributed their full share towards putting down the rebellion and saving the government."[146] Moderate Republicans responded that the contributions of African Americans during the war were no more deserving of recognition and reward than those of other unenfranchised groups, including "the Germans, Irish, minors, and women."[147] On the successful vote to amend Iowa's constitution to enfranchise black men, one Democratic paper reported: "We can announce to the intelligent, educated, talented, moral, religious and elevated women of the State . . . that buck niggers, no matter how degraded or ignorant, are, by the laws of Iowa, esteemed above the intelligent white woman."[148]

White women were noticeably absent from the key debates and conflicts that African American women confronted in the postbellum era—the struggles for publicly funded education and equal access to public accommodations, resistance to racialized violence (which often occurred in attempted rape or rape cases involving black perpetrators and white female victims), and the full enforcement of citizenship rights. The *Woman's Journal*, published in Boston by the National American Woman Suffrage Association, frequently carried reports about white women's lectures and elections to school boards in the region; in 1878, however, it also printed excerpts from Iowa newspapers condemning two recent assaults alleged to have been committed against white women by black perpetrators. The *Journal* offered an explicit alignment with racist mob violence of which Iowa had already seen too much.[149]

Moreover, despite the enfranchisement of black men, white women more readily won elective office through school suffrage. In Iowa (by 1869), Minnesota (by 1876), and Wisconsin (by 1901), women gained the right to participate in school elections and hold elective office on school boards and as school officials, having successfully exploited popular culture's idealized views of women having a "natural" interest and indeed a moral superiority in the realm of children's education.[150] As Louise Newman has pointed out, this postbellum notion of women's moral superiority was deeply and implicitly racialized through its linkage to evolutionary ideas: "White middle-class women did not hesitate to use [the] conception of their race-, class-, and gender-specific forms of moral superiority to buttress their claims to political and social authority."[151] For their part, white men understood that school suffrage affirmed white political authority and control. Although education was a critical issue in which African American women were notably active in their own communities —in organizing, funding, staffing, and defending black schools, and in the school desegregation movement—white women were the exclusive beneficiaries of early officeholding. Until the mid-1870s, most school superintendents in Iowa rejected the idea of school desegregation and dismissed those black students who attempted to attend "white" schools.[152] African Americans might have viewed white women's new political power (however limited) as a disappointing reinforcement of the power of white supremacy, even though black men had voiced their support of woman suffrage at the 1869 Colored Labor Convention and the 1871 black convention held at Oskaloosa.[153]

White women's political toehold soon extended beyond school elections; they also appear to have gained more patronage positions in the state legislature. By 1870, the Iowa General Assembly had hired its first female clerk; by 1872, the state librarian was a woman and women were employed by both the Iowa senate and the house. Six years later, the Iowa assembly employed four women—as engrossing clerk, enrolling clerk, postmistress, and paper folder— during the 1878 legislative session.[154] To African American men seeking a political voice in the Republican parties of the Midwest, the distribution of patronage employment to white women might easily have been regarded as an affront to their expectations of masculine privilege.

Although a few Iowans had supported woman suffrage since the 1850s, and woman suffrage petitions were submitted to the state legislature as early as 1866, an organized movement would not emerge in the upper Midwest until after the ratification of the Fourteenth Amendment in 1868.[155] In Iowa, white women began to organize several local suffrage societies in 1869 and held the first statewide convention in 1870. Although participation was open to all women, it does not appear that African Americans attended (despite the fact that the convention was held in Mt. Pleasant, a town with nearly five hundred black residents in 1870). One of the officers of the convention, Democratic state legislator John Irish, was a well-known opponent of black suffrage. Both Wisconsin and Minnesota saw the formation of statewide woman suffrage associations in 1881.[156]

In the context of separate white and black suffrage movements, and thus of lost opportunities for interracial collaboration, African American women in the 1880s introduced new tactics in their pursuit of citizenship rights. For the first time, black women in Des Moines began to explore collaboration with white suffragists in a series of at least five meetings over a six-year period. In December 1885, Iowa's Polk County [white] Woman Suffrage Association met with many "of the most prominent colored" women (and apparently some men as well) of Des Moines at St. Paul's AME church.[157] It was the impression of the white suffragists that the African American women were developing an "intelligent" position on suffrage and were at "the beginning of an agitation" on the issue. In what may well have been the first attempt by upper midwestern white women to work with their African American counterparts, a white suffragist took the floor to candidly speak about three joint concerns of the white and black women assembled. First, the speaker attempted to legitimize white women's interest in black women's enfranchisement by emphasizing white women's abolitionist activities before and during the war ("throbbing in sympathy with the oppressed"). Second, she addressed what white women assumed were the sources of black men's opposition to black women's enfranchisement. Did black men truly fear that "the first breath of political freedom" would "snap . . . the chords of wifely affection?" (Such opposition was not as strong as many white women imagined it to be, according to Louise Newman.)[158] Third, the speaker issued a plea for the assistance of African American men, "with all the moral force of your race," in obtaining the ballot for "your women." She concluded her remarks with the promise of inclusiveness in the pursuit of women's right to vote. Iowa's white suffragists "would that the white women of Iowa remain forever disfranchised, if we are unwilling to share our privileges with our darker sisters."[159]

But Polk County's white suffragists did not speak for the entire state. Iowa's woman suffrage paper, the *Woman's Standard*, carried several articles over the next few years suggesting that white racism was a more significant obstacle to interracial organizing than Polk County's white suffragists imagined. For example, when turned away by election officials in November 1887, a Page County woman complained that "the vote of an exceedingly ignorant ex-slave at her side was accepted."[160] In April 1890, a white woman in Oskaloosa commented that "ignorant colored men" could be seen entering polling places to vote.[161] In January 1888, an article reprinted from a Monona County newspaper incorrectly asserted that the Emancipation Proclamation had enfranchised black men and so "made the black man, in the eye of the law, a superior to the white woman." To its credit, the paper subsequently clarified that the proclamation had not enfranchised black men, but by reprinting the original article, the *Standard* revealed a significant misunderstanding of the challenges African Americans faced in obtaining political and civil rights.[162] And in April 1893, a white suffragist of Sioux City suggested that the shortage of domestic labor and the "race problem" could both be solved by bringing southern black women to the Midwest to work as domestic servants. "The Father has placed these strong, dark children there for our use. They need our care and development; we need their strength and help," she wrote.[163]

The tentative and uneven commitment of Iowa's white suffragists to black women's citizenship, as well as the explicit racism expressed by some in the state movement, may explain why it would be more than two years before another interracial woman suffrage meeting was convened in Des Moines. On 10 January 1888, the Polk County Woman Suffrage Association convened a "parlor meeting" in the home of one of the city's leading black women, Mrs. Jane Bell, a former slave who had fled the South during the war and migrated to Iowa.[164] Although the details of Bell's journey out of slavery are unknown, it appears that she and her slave husband, Henry Bell, escaped from Alabama; made their way to Corinth, Mississippi, during the Union's siege in the spring of 1862; and arrived in Dallas County, Iowa, by 1864. By 1866 the family had moved to Polk County, where Jane Bell still resided at the time of her death in 1903. Known in the city's black community as "Mother" Bell, she would be honored at her husband's death because "her counsel and material influence brought honor and distinction to their household."[165] The woman suffrage meeting she hosted was attended by an equal number of whites and African Americans, including "colored women of culture and social standing—some who were ex-slaves—and one graduate from our city High School." A formal paper was delivered by one of the white women (described as a "brave and a loyal descendant of genuine ability and Quaker ancestry"), and "nearly every one present found a voice for her thought." They talked "earnestly and pointedly" about woman suffrage, and, according to the *Woman's Standard*, African

American women were "anxious to join forces with white women in asking for the ballot."[166]

A third meeting was held a year later, again at the home of Jane Bell.[167] Records indicate only that the meeting occurred and that a paper on "Social Vice" was read by a white woman. At their fourth interracial gathering, in January 1990, Des Moines women convened at the home of a Mrs. Robinson.[168] Like their host, the African American women who attended can be traced in the historical record only through their husbands. Among them were a Mrs. McCraven, wife of a skilled laborer (a whitewasher) and mother of an AME minister, and a Mrs. Coalson, whose husband had co-owned and operated a Des Moines barbershop for five or six years. Under the leadership of another participant, a Mrs. Poindexter (either the mother or one of her two daughters-in-law in a family that had migrated to Iowa before the war), they proposed forming a black woman's suffrage club "in the near future."[169] But based on subsequent accounts of the African American women's club movement in Iowa, it seems unlikely that this suffrage club was ever organized.

A fifth (and last recorded) interracial woman suffrage meeting was held in October 1891.[170] Once again, Mrs. Poindexter played a prominent role, representing the state's black newspapers (*Weekly Avalanche* and *Iowa Bystander*) and expressing their endorsement of woman suffrage. Support came not only from the men who published these papers, but also from a black minister in Des Moines. The Reverend H. McCraven (son of one of the women who attended the January 1890 meeting) was described in the *Woman's Standard* as "a gentlemanly colored man" who had attended the 1887 sixteenth annual meeting of the Iowa Woman Suffrage Association in Des Moines. When asked to speak, he assured the audience that "as Lucretia Mott and other noble women had helped his race to freedom, so he was ready to work with his people to help all women to political liberty."[171] Miles Bell, son of Jane Bell, was also a public supporter of the cause; he was one of the speakers at a black woman's suffrage meeting that year at the Good Templars' Hall in Des Moines.[172] Although African American women ultimately chose other kinds of organizations from which to pursue their civil and political rights, the act of reaching out to white suffragists suggests a gendered political consciousness and an effort to seek new forms of activism on the basis of that consciousness.

The second significant post-1885 change in African American women's political activism came in the 1890s, with the formation of state and national race organizations in which men and women joined together to pursue their civil and political rights. This departure in black associational life was spurred by increasing levels of violence directed against black southerners and the ongoing denial of black civil and political rights across the nation; it drew on two generations of postbellum activism within a predominantly sex-segregated environment. African American men and women now moved out of the denominational and fraternal associations that had been the core of the black public sphere and into the larger public domain. Still marginalized by the formal political process and alarmed by the withdrawal of federal oversight in the enforcement of their civil rights (with the Supreme Court's 1883 reversal of the 1875 Civil Rights Act), most African Americans agreed with Frederick Douglass's assessment at the 1883 National Convention of Colored Men in Louisville, Kentucky: Even "after twenty years of so called Emancipation. . . . in all the relations of life and death we are met by the color line."[173]

Indeed, the following year Moses Mosely published his pamphlet assessing the status of African Americans. He asked: "After all the quarreling, and fighting and shedding of blood, . . . and the expenditure of many billions of money over the question as to whether American slavery or American freedom should predominate in these United States, are the colored men all free in the true sense of the word: are they equal in the enjoyments of civil and political rights with their white fellow citizens?" No, he answered, "they are not altogether free."[174] For blacks in the upper Midwest, this state of affairs demanded new responses. These would include the formation of large state organizations, linked to their participation in the national Afro-American League and its successor, the Afro-American Council.

In early 1887, T. Thomas Fortune, a prominent black journalist of the late nineteenth century, called for the formation of a national, nonpartisan league devoted to the civil rights struggle and the protection of black voters in the South. Although Fortune envisioned the league's work as primarily southward-focused, he called on the North to help achieve its goals. Many of the northern delegates who would attend the first organizational meeting in January 1890 were already veterans of civil rights and citizenship struggles in the North as well as in the South.[175] In Minnesota, Fortune's appeal seems to have prompted action at the state level. By December 1887, John Q. Adams, a St. Paul resident and publisher of Minnesota's black newspaper, the *Western Appeal*, had called for a statewide convention in which black Minnesotans might formulate a plan for the advancement and protection of their civil rights. Energized by a recent court decision that had awarded paltry damages when a St. Paul hotel denied a black professional lodging, black Minnesotans responded eagerly to Adams's proposal. Representatives from fifteen counties attended the December meeting leading to the organization of the Minnesota Protective and Industrial League.[176]

As Fortune's call for a national organization gained support across the country, midwesterners joined in that effort. In Minnesota, ambitious black attorney Frederick McGhee called a November 1889 meeting in St. Paul to create a state chapter of the new league. With John Q. Adams presiding, the participants elected McGhee and Adams to serve as state representatives at the January 1890 organizational meeting of the league, to be held in Chicago. Local chapters were organized in Anoka, Duluth, Faribault, Minneapolis, and Stillwater as well.[177] Wisconsin and Iowa also sent delegates to the Chicago meeting. Wisconsin's African Americans had formed a state-level civil rights league immediately after Fortune's first call for a national organization, which they saw as an opportunity to expand activism within the state.[178] Iowans, too, were activated. By the following year, Iowa's new black newspaper, the *Weekly Avalanche*, published out of Des Moines, declared itself the official organ of "the Afro-American Protective Association of Iowa."[179]

The national league excited more interest within the Midwest than outside of it, which contributed to its demise in 1893. But black midwesterners had gained a new footing for their civil rights movement, with a lasting impact. Although the national league folded, black Iowans sustained the "Afro-American Protective Association," modeled on the league, with local associations in nineteen towns and cities. For women, the state association offered an unprecedented opportunity to serve as official delegates in a secular race organization. This was important for civil rights organizers not only regionally, but also nationally, since at the first, earlier meeting of the national league, no women had attended as delegates, although the league's constitution opened membership to women. The decision of black Iowans to include women was a clear indication that women expected, and were expected, to be full participants in the new organization.[180] Three sisters from Newton, Iowa (a community that received a significant influx of former slaves during the war), and a Miss Buckner of Oskaloosa joined the other fifty-one (male) delegates at their 1894 meeting, and Miss Virgie Whitsett was unanimously elected recording secretary, apparently on the strength of her contributions at the 1893 meeting.[181]

In Minnesota, state support for the national Afro-American League ended abruptly after one of the state's delegates, Samuel Hardy, en route to an 1891 meeting in Knoxville, was forced to leave the first-class railroad car when his train reached the Tennessee border. On his return, black Minnesotans prepared to sue the railroad company—but not through the league; Fortune felt that it was impossible for the league to sponsor a lawsuit. Instead, black Minnesotans organized the Minnesota Citizens Civil Rights Committee to fund the legal challenge as well as a similar case in Oklahoma. According to Frederick McGhee's biographer, Paul D. Nelson, the national league's refusal to take up the Hardy lawsuit led to hard feelings and the state's withdrawal of support. Yet the organization's impact could be measured in the formation of a statewide association to pursue the same goals as the national association and in subsequent state involvement with the revived Afro-American Council in years to follow.[182] Establishment of the national league also spurred African Americans in Wisconsin to lobby their own legislature to pass a civil rights bill and to support a civil rights case filed by a Milwaukee resident who had been denied first-class seating at an opera house.

By 1898, Fortune had resurrected the national league under a new name: the National Afro-American Council. Notably, the council included black women among its officers and speakers. Departing from the traditional male-controlled world of party politics, African Americans created an organizational framework that could draw on the talents and energy of black female activists like Ida B. Wells.[183] At the second convention, held in 1899, one of Minnesota's most experienced female activists, Mrs. Amanda Lyles, addressed the convention as a representative of an organization identified as the African American Women's National Association, but most likely the recently formed National Association of Colored Women (NACW).[184] Lyles, a "Ladies Hairdresser" and St. Paul resident since at least 1866, was viewed as an accomplished member of the black community; so, too, was her husband, Thomas H. Lyles. The couple belonged to St. Paul's elite, which included business owners, lawyers, and newspaper publishers.[185]

Iowans probably continued to maintain their state association, given their quick response to Fortune's organizing call. The following year they held a large public meeting in Des Moines to decide on the issues that Iowa's delegates should bring to the national meeting. Among those participating at the Des Moines meeting was Miss Zella Davis, who presented a paper on the "Influence of Our Women on the Race." The organization scheduled its 1910 meeting to coincide with the annual convention of the Iowa State Federation of Colored Women's Clubs, where Mrs. S. Joe Brown—a vital link between the club movement, the council, and soon the NAACP—would speak on "The Older Type of Woman, and the New." The titles of two additional council speeches—"The Dawn of Womanhood" and "The Young Man Problem"—reveal that the nineteenth-century concerns with gender relations and conventions continued to be topics of interest in the black public sphere.[186]

The third indication of a major change in black women's political work in the upper Midwest after 1885 occurred as they organized women's clubs, first at the local, then at the state and even the national levels. It appears that in the 1890s at least six clubs were formed in Iowa, including two in Davenport, two in Ottumwa, and one each in Marshalltown and Des Moines. By 1903, there were fifteen clubs; by 1910, twenty-three. United under one organization in 1902, the Iowa State Federation of Colored Women's Clubs demonstrated an unprecedented determination of African American women in the region to establish secular, black, female-led organizations that would become a gateway to community activism and leadership.[187] Perhaps the most famous clubwoman of the early twentieth-century upper Midwest, Mrs. S. Joe Brown, would become a regional leader in the NAACP and the Order of the Eastern Star. She would make a lasting impression on race organizing and the defense of black women. The regional club movement would catapult a new generation of black activists into a wide range of organizations and efforts to obtain civil rights and equal citizenship.

BY THE END of the nineteenth century, more than thirty years after the destruction of American slavery, black midwesterners still pursued full membership in the Reconstructed nation. The venues and targets of their activism ranged widely but showed the centrality of gender to northern black Reconstruction: as an organizing principle, as a source of conflict, and as a language that African American men and women employed as they pressed white allies and enemies alike to acknowledge their shared humanity. Gender conventions created different obstacles and opportunities for black men and women in their pursuit of civil rights and racial equality, even to the point of producing different costs and benefits for men and women in each hard-won victory. In lodges and temples, courtrooms and schoolhouses, sanctuaries and city streets, black men and women found that gender mattered in the black public sphere as well as in their civil rights activism. The association of rights with manhood, so vital in the context of black military service and the postwar claim for black male enfranchisement, was no less important in the struggle for racial equality within Masonry than in the contest over power and authority in black congregations. Yet even by the close of the nineteenth century, the public recognition of black manhood that so many African Americans equated with full citizenship had not been realized. To the contrary, black masculinity was increasingly vilified as a rationalization for lynching. Yet, if white midwesterners did not resort to murder in their efforts to control black womanhood, they did meet African American women's persistent claims for the privileged status of idealized womanhood with abuse, violence, and scorn.

The myth of African American consent to the exercise of white privilege politicized every confrontation with civic inequality after the Civil War, North as well as South. But for many blacks in the Midwest, the memory of slavery, war, and the struggle to become free offered visceral reminders of why they had been willing to take liberty in the rough, and why, twenty years later, they were still compelled to struggle to perfect that liberty. This memory, the persistence of white supremacy in their own communities, and their acute awareness of racism's intensifying impact in the South, all prevented any naïveté on their part about the power of the law to shape white attitudes. But these grim challenges also fueled an extraordinary range of individual decisions and organized efforts through which African Americans struggled to become fully free. Perhaps most importantly, black midwesterners—women and children, as well as men—demonstrated that they were a people determined to gain a full measure of citizenship.

7 "Agonizing Groans of Mothers" and "Slave-Scarred Veterans"

History, Commemoration, and Memoir in the Aftermath of Slavery

In the fifty years following emancipation and the close of the Civil War, African Americans sought to secure civil rights and citizenship, as well as to determine how slavery and its wartime destruction should be remembered. A culture of reunion emerged at the regional and national levels, one that encouraged sectional reconciliation by stripping the war of ideological conflict, but also by creating for white Americans a sentimental memory of slavery and emancipation.[1] Evidence of the local and lasting impact of the culture of reunion could be seen in popular, white-authored portrayals of African Americans in the Midwest that trivialized slavery. In 1927, for example, the *Des Moines Tribune* carried an interview with former slave John Hays about his life before the war. "Yes sah, the massuh was good to us. We were treated good," Hays was reported as saying.[2] The interview was accompanied by a pen-and-ink illustration of his kind master and friendly relations with the Ku Klux Klan. Similar depictions found their way into local newspapers: "Aunt" Betty Lewis was said to be an ardent sympathizer of the white South, James McDonald allegedly "Died Wishing He Was a Slave Again," and others reportedly received kind treatment at the hands of concerned masters.[3]

In the 1930s, the slave Dred Scott, who had initiated the foremost freedom suit in American history, was caricatured by a popular white columnist in the *Des Moines Register* as indifferent to his freedom and more interested in the "good-looking black girl" Harriet (his wife-to-be), presented in an accompanying illustration in a sexualized pose and revealing dress.[4] In interviews and stories, a collective, white-authored popular history portrayed slavery as an inoffensive institution and African Americans as uncivilized relics of a lost southern past who were content with white supremacy.[5]

These representations of former slaves carried over into the very popular regional literature about the Underground Railroad. Prompted, early in the 1890s, by Wilbur Siebert's solicitation of reminiscences about Underground Railroad "lines" and "conductors," an outpouring of midwestern lore offered

John Hays's life, Des Moines Tribune, *21 December 1927*.

frequently exaggerated and romanticized accounts of white sacrifice in a war against slavery, but also denigrating portrayals of the "cargo" that heroic whites were helping. This investment in a regional heritage in the fight against slavery (a "treasury of virtue," as Robert Penn Warren described it) was evident well into the 1930s, as researchers employed by the Federal Writers' Project of the Works Progress Administration prepared material for a prospective volume on Iowa black history. Several contributors wrote pieces that emphasized white heroism in the work of the Underground Railroad, and others offered character sketches about local "old time negroes."[6]

The Aftermath of Slavery

Dred Scott Sat In Iowa Shack

A black slave once lived in Iowa. His residence here convulsed the nation.

Yet nobody paid any attention at the time.

But 20 years later Dred Scott had become a fighting word. The civil war was fought over Dred Scott. History books are plastered over with the name of this lazy, squat man who caused the biggest disturbance in the supreme court from 1857 till NRA, but who hadn't the faintest idea of what it was all about. But nobody seems to remember that Dred Scott once lived in Iowa. Few Iowa histories even mention it.

Davenport Claim

Dred came with his master, Dr. John Emerson, an army surgeon, to the garrison on Rock Island in 1834.

The doctor in his spare time wandered about Davenport in what was soon to be Iowa, looking on the flower-studded prairies. His mouth watered. He entered a claim on the river bank two miles north of Davenport and built on it a little shack.

Soon Dred found himself sitting in the little shack on the claim, watching his master's property, not knowing or caring that he was in free territory.

The Private Lives of the Pioneers
BY KENT PELLETT

Bride Bought

In time the doctor sold his claim, clearing $1,000 on the deal. Dred went with him to Fort Snelling, in what is now Minnesota, and saw a good looking black girl named Harriet. She was more interesting to him than freedom. The doctor was obliging and bought her for Dred.

In 1838 Emerson was ordered back to St. Louis, taking his slaves with him. On the boat going down, Harriet had a baby. Later in St. Louis, she had another.

Dred had lived on free soil for several years. But he would not have caused any trouble about that if his master had not died. After Dr. Emerson's death, Mrs. Emerson left Dred and his family to shift for themselves while she went to Massachusetts and married an abolitionist.

When Dred got hungry and his pickaninnies began to yell, he ran to a man named Taylor Blow, whose father had once owned him. Blow did not want to take care of Dred, so he went to a lawyer to find out how to make Dred's owner support him.

Dred's X

The lawyer scratched his head, got an idea. Dred had lived in free territory, hadn't he? He was really a free man. They would have Dred sue for freedom.

More interesting to him than freedom.

Dred, who was suing, did not care about it one way or another. The man who tried to free him was a slave owner, while the woman who contested his freedom was married to an abolitionist!

Dred won, then lost, as the case went higher. The country was in a tumult over the slavery question.

At last Roger Taney, a withered old judge of the U. S. supreme court made Dred very famous when he denied him freedom, thundering out from the bench that Negroes "had no rights which the white man was bound to respect." As these words echoed and re-echoed, swords rattled all over the country.

He Didn't Care

All over a Negro who did not care. Dred was set free soon anyhow, and became a porter at Barnum's hotel in St. Louis. He was pleased and befuddled that persons should flock to see him, point him out as the famous Dred Scott, and fill his hands with nickles and dimes.

A year after the Dred Scott decision he died.

But his X mark had started something that could not be stopped. The sword rattling became the firing of guns at Fort Sumter. The civil war was on.

The Negroes of St. Louis talked of putting a monument over Dred. But they never got around to it.

With its sexualized image of Harriet Scott and its misrepresentations of the history of the freedom suit by Dred Scott, this 1930s article from the Des Moines Register *reflects popular white views on national and local African American history. MsC 295, Federal Writer's Project, Special Collections Department, University of Iowa Libraries, Iowa City.*

The Aftermath of Slavery

This "romantic memory of the Civil War era," paired with caricatures of aging African Americans expressing pleasant memories of their enslavement, served dual purposes in the white imagination of the war's causes and consequences. It allowed northern whites to rewrite the history of slavery and emancipation, and it allowed even noncombatants to claim a role in the great cause of freeing the southern slave and defending American freedom. At the same time, these collective myths allowed northern whites to ignore or overwrite their region's own history of slavery and its unresolved struggle against black citizenship, portraying African Americans as simple, naive, grateful noncitizens. Midwestern whites were more comfortable with the African Americans they imagined than with the activist men and women among them who demanded their citizenship rights and the enforcement of civil rights law.[7]

While white midwesterners caricatured the slave past and the people who had survived it, African Americans offered a very different version of the history and collective memory of slavery. When John Thompson—editor of the *Bystander*, a black newspaper in Des Moines—delivered an Emancipation Day speech in 1898, he urged a crowd of several hundred black midwesterners to

> think of being compelled to live all your life with the man who is stealing the babies from your cradle and you dare not say one word; think of being compelled to associate with the despised and hated southerner who is constantly robbing you; think of being compelled to separate from your dear brother, loving sister, only father and mother, never to see them again. The agonizing groans of mothers when separated from their crying children were heart piercing. See the slave scarred veterans who are before me today and have witness to their once cruel and inhuman treatment.[8]

This public appeal to the collective memory of slavery came only six months after Thompson had narrated a more personal, but no less vivid or less public, memorial in his mother's obituary. In that account, he documented twenty-seven years of bondage, during which time she had been bought and sold five times before fleeing to Iowa with her four children during the war. From a personal story of a mother's suffering to a collective witnessing of brutality and violence, Thompson revealed some of the ways that African Americans remembered and memorialized slavery. Particularly since he was a member of the rising class of professionals found in the black communities of the upper Midwest, Thompson's insistence on a public and collective memory of slavery contradicts many of the generalizations drawn by scholars about the desire of postemancipation black middling classes to distance themselves from the history of slavery.

In the thirty-five years since emancipation, black midwesterners had labored to define and defend black freedom and citizenship; but they had also endeavored to shape and sustain their personal and collective memories of bondage, war, and freedom. African Americans debated among themselves the uses of the collective memory of slavery. Was it an unwelcome reminder of a shameful past, used by whites to deny black progress and black individuality? Could the past be a valuable resource for contemporary black life and culture? How should the past be remembered, and how should that remembrance be represented and sustained? Thompson's Emancipation Day speech, with its devastating images of life under slavery, points to the persistent collective memories upon which he believed the official, or public, history of slavery and emancipation should be built. Although never enslaved himself, he invoked a "postmemory," as termed by literary scholar Marianne Hirsh, a second-generation memory of trauma that had deeply influenced his own family as well as most of those who gathered with him to commemorate slavery's final destruction and the role of African Americans in achieving that goal.[9]

At the time of his 1898 address, Thompson believed that if African Americans were to "make the history of our race," then they had to acknowledge that white slaveowners "stole the labor of our forefathers for 243 years, paying them in nothing but a little piece of bacon and lots of hell."[10] In contrast, white writers belonging to the "plantation school" of American literature substituted a sentimental trope of antebellum interracial kindness and mutual devotion for the harsh realities of slavery's violence and exploitation. An increasingly popular collective memory of the war, created by white authors and readers in both the North and the South, emphasized the courage of white soldiers on both sides, while disregarding black military participation as well as what the historian David Blight has described as the "emancipationist legacy" of the war.

But African Americans provided their own answers to how slavery and the war should be remembered. Some sought to recall, commemorate, and memorialize the experience and impact of slavery. Others preferred to view emancipation as the beginning of black history. And still others distanced themselves from the perceived racial legacy of slavery and the contagion of victimization and inferiority that many thought it carried, particularly as racist violence and the abrogation of African American civil rights threatened to undermine the achievements of the postemancipation generation. Yet Thompson's stirring speech reveals that black midwesterners were still deeply engaged in the questions of whether, and how, to remember and memorialize American slavery and the war that finally ended it.[11] The former slaves and their descendants struggled to shape what Saidiya Hartman and other scholars call the "afterlife of slavery."[12]

Blacks in the upper Midwest created a historical consciousness that drew on individual and collective memories of slavery and emancipation, memories that they chose to keep alive, commemorate, and circulate. Thompson's 1898 speech indicates the importance of Emancipation Day celebrations in this endeavor, but memories were sustained in other forms and venues as well. African Americans also created narrative forms of memoir that organized and preserved—in both print and oral tradition—their individual experiences of slavery and their personal role in its destruction. These memoirs include autobiographical slave narratives and expostulatory writings, recollections dictated for pension applications, and lovingly crafted obituaries (a second- or third-generation "postmemory"). Black midwesterners who produced and circulated these memoirs were influenced by diverse factors—from partisan politics to religious, financial, or filial considerations. They created an archive of African American history from their experiences, memories, observations, and testimonies about the slavery, war, and emancipation. These sites of memory and popular history through which black experiences and recollections of slavery and the Civil War were privately and publicly sustained, were passed between generations. They were asserted in opposition to a very different memory of the war created on a national scale by white Americans.

EMANCIPATION DAY CELEBRATIONS

One of the most vivid sites for the study of slavery's afterlife can be found in postbellum Emancipation Day celebrations. Drawing on the antebellum commemorative and festive calendar, African Americans incorporated the more solemn, formal rituals of commemoration (prayers, orations, recitals), the exuberant sociability of festivals (music, dancing, food, drinking), the public performance of civic and expressive culture (particularly in parades and processions), and the more private elements of indoor gatherings shielded from the white public's gaze (including "experience meetings" held in black churches). Combining performance and participation, politics and protest, the public and the private, and rural as well as urban cultures, midwestern emancipation celebrations of the nineteenth and twentieth centuries became a popular site for black expressive culture at the same time that they became the region's most important venue for articulating the dynamic relationship between history and public memories of slavery and emancipation.[13]

The record of Emancipation Day celebrations exists today in reports by the region's white press (which encompassed a wide range of political affiliations and editorial leanings) and the *Iowa Bystander*, Iowa's most successful black newspaper (operating since 1894). Published in Des Moines but covering black communities large and small across the state and region, the *Bystander* defended African Americans' civil rights and challenged racism near and far.[14] While the white press frequently offered little more than ridicule of black activities, the *Bystander*, as an advocate of black progress, emphasized the positive; it rarely dwelled on the tensions that sprang from intraracial conflicts over class and color. Neither the *Bystander* nor the white press consistently reported on what we might regard as the total matrix of Emancipation Day commemorations, such as the interactions of observers and participants and how they affected the day's events. Yet the combined record of black and white newspaper reporting provides a valuable chronicle of Emancipation Day activities and their impact on community life.

Reports of Emancipation Day celebrations portray an expressive culture developed by African Americans in a persistent effort to shape and maintain a collective memory and historical consciousness of slavery and its wartime destruction. These observances also point to the meanings and uses of the public sphere in black community life; they reveal expressive culture as both social and political practice.[15] Always multilayered (in their use of music, speech, food, visual images, costumes, and public mobilization), the celebrations were complex cultural performances, each component contributing to the total impression left on participants and observers.[16] The cheers and jeers that met the emergence of a new African American civic culture in city streets and courthouse squares exemplified how the battlegrounds of citizenship extended beyond the ballot box, spilling over into a larger public culture.

Emancipation Day celebrations also illuminate change over time. For example, John Thompson's 1898 address harkened back to an earlier nineteenth-century tradition in which African Americans acknowledged their slave past when commemorating emancipation, but it also represented a later generation's negotiation of a new era in American race relations that evoked new forms of racism and new forms of protest. By the 1890s, the struggle for black citizenship had changed, as had the meanings and uses of the history of slavery and emancipation for African Americans nationwide. But Emancipation Day celebrations already had a long history in the upper Midwest. Iowans began memorializing their freedom as early as August 1857, when the small but politically active black community in Muscatine marked the anniversary of the 1834 abolition of slavery in the British West Indies.[17] The all-day event in the modest Mississippi River town attracted local residents as well as people from elsewhere in the state and region. This earliest recorded emancipation celebration in the upper Midwest was part of a larger calendar of public commemorations that northern blacks observed before the Civil War. Many festival days—Pinkster in New York, Negro Election Day and General Training Day in New England, among others—had eighteenth-century origins. In the nineteenth century, however, new holidays and celebrations emerged to honor various state, national, and international inroads against slavery.[18] The ending of the foreign slave trade in the United States in 1808 and state legislation terminating slavery in New York in 1827 prompted commemorative holidays in several states, but West Indian liberation, initiated on 1 August 1834, superseded most of them and helped sharpen the explicit political content of emancipation celebrations. Participants contrasted Great Britain's deliverance of West Indian slaves with the continued betrayal of enslaved people by the United States, emphasized the hypocrisy of Fourth of July observances exalting American liberties, and posited an argument for a future free of slavery and racial inequality. Importantly, as the historian Genevieve Fabre has argued, emancipation celebrations reflected a "subjunctive mood," oriented toward what should or ought to be as well as toward the past.[19]

African Americans in the North memorialized these antebellum successes because slavery continued to affect their lives. Many had themselves been born into slavery, and many more had parents or other family members who had been or were still enslaved.[20] At this time, even in the Midwest, black freedom required constant vigilance against the threat of being kidnapped and sold south, against local laws that threatened involuntary servitude for African Americans who became dependent on public support, and against efforts to enforce state laws that restricted or prohibited the in-migration of free blacks.[21] Repeated attacks against black midwesterners reinforced the precariousness of their freedom in Iowa, Minnesota, and Wisconsin, even with a vocal and politically active antislavery presence in the three states.

It is not surprising, then, that African Americans used the commemoration of emancipation in the British West Indies as an opportunity to condemn slavery's persistence in the United States. At the first celebration held in Davenport, Iowa, in 1860, speakers contrasted British emancipation, "one of the greatest and most righteous deeds that ever graced the annals of history," with the unfinished work of the American Revolution. They asked "for nothing but freedom—the same freedom," they pointed out, "that the iron sons of '76 fought, bled, and died for; that which edifies a human, and places him in a position higher than a brute."[22]

When President Lincoln's Emancipation Proclamation committed the

Union to ending slavery in the Confederacy, African Americans could at long last celebrate the advent of liberty at home. The Christmas and New Year's celebrations of 1862–63 were especially jubilant. In Mt. Pleasant, Iowa, home to one of the fastest-growing communities of former slaves in the region, the holidays were infused with and apparently overtaken by the prospect of slavery's end. With "dancing every night and eating good dinners during the day," as well as several "colored balls," African Americans in that small community also marked the advent of freedom by "marching through town all night whooping, dancing, and singing 'Kingdom Coming.'" Observed a local newspaper, "They made a heavy noise."[23]

The upper Midwest's rapidly growing black population built on antebellum experiences and wartime initiatives to create a tradition that would produce hundreds of emancipation celebrations in more than thirty communities over the course of the next century.[24] That tradition was profoundly shaped by the wartime diaspora of former slaves into the region. Joined by friends, family members, returning veterans, and longer-term residents, several of the region's smaller African American communities began to celebrate their freedom. Newly emergent black communities in Burlington, Clarinda, Davenport, De Witt, Dubuque, Fort Madison, Iowa City, Muscatine, and Oskaloosa, Iowa; Twin Cities and Stillwater, Minnesota; and Racine, Wisconsin—all occasionally held celebrations by the late 1870s, some on 1 August and others on 1 January.[25] Smaller communities hosted commemorations more sporadically, although the residents may have attended festivities in a neighboring town.[26] Like county and state fairs, Emancipation Day gatherings were distinguished by all the pleasures of sociability for a scattered rural population, especially one that had only recently won freedom of movement and expression. Understandably, midwestern celebrations could attract hundreds—occasionally thousands—of participants.[27]

Such commemorations gained momentum with the contested politics of race in the public sphere.[28] The black community in Keokuk, Iowa, the region's largest in the nineteenth century, first began celebrating emancipation in 1863.[29] In 1865, black residents expressed their desire to take part in the parade that was the highlight of the city's Fourth of July activities. But the white fire company refused to march alongside the blacks, defending the traditional segregation of Keokuk's civic culture and rejecting the idea that public displays of citizenship were no longer an exclusively white privilege. Unwilling to participate except on an equal basis, local blacks boycotted the parade.[30] But if Keokuk's black residents appeared to yield to white control over civic events, they were unwilling to relinquish their claim to citizenship or their right to the ceremonial space on city streets. By 1866, local blacks supported two commemorations of emancipation—on 1 January and 1 August. Undaunted by the chill of the midwestern midwinter, they "turned out with flags and banners and transparencies" in January to parade through the city's main thoroughfares.[31]

In the upper Midwest, emancipation celebrations both invoked and evolved out of the local politics of race and civic culture. After white abolitionists in Des Moines organized and presided over the city's first emancipation commemoration in 1863, black residents presented their own Fourth of July celebrations in 1864 and 1865; beginning in 1866, they commemorated West Indian and U.S. emancipation on the first of August. The 1866 event was unprecedented in terms of its formality, the full program of events, and the number of participants: between 400 and 600 people from the city and surrounding areas attended—at a time when the black population of Des Moines numbered less than 100.[32]

The celebrations of the immediate postwar years often included what white observers described as "parades" and boisterous festivities in the city streets. But with the passage of time, more orderly processions and formal programs replaced these festivals. Black midwesterners would have been keenly aware that their every public appearance was under white surveillance and scrutiny. In this context, participants used the processions that became a core feature of Emancipation Day celebrations as a means of inserting themselves into the public sphere, while also demonstrating to hostile whites that they could do so in a respectable manner.[33] Consider the 1871 celebration in rural Clarinda:

> Early yesterday morning in every direction teams might have been seen making their way toward our city loaded with colored people who were concentrating at this place for the purpose of celebrating the anniversary of this great day to them, the Fourth of August. . . . The procession was formed in what is known as Africa, and then moved toward town, making one grand revolution around the public square, presenting an appearance seldom witnessed by our citizens, when it "struck" for the grove east of Clarinda. The procession consisted of about 50 teams, all well filled with colored folks.[34]

The orderly appearance of these processions drew the eye of white observers impressed by the "well-appearing," "very creditable," and "respectable appearance" of the black participants.[35]

From reports in white newspapers of "boisterous and disgraceful conduct" at some celebrations, however, it is evident that not all participants felt obligated to behave in an orderly or solemn manner. William Butler, a moderately successful 33-year-old plasterer, with a young wife and toddler, was one of three African American men whose "disagreement" at Keokuk's 1863 Emancipation Day picnic led to their arrest. Three years later, a "few irrepressible chaps . . . got into a row," to the annoyance of the otherwise "well-disposed" crowd, which intervened in the fracas to disarm the young men and restore the peaceful tone of the gathering. Speakers at Muscatine's 1867 commemoration were interrupted by a "crowd of young men and boys," whose noisy and boisterous behavior "made it impossible to hear anything." In 1875, Luella Lewis, a 23-year-old domestic servant, was one of four people arrested for "making a disturbance" at Keokuk's Emancipation Day activities.[36] These frustratingly incomplete reports of effusive or disruptive behavior indicate disagreement over whether Emancipation Day activities were primarily celebratory or commemorative, and whether pleasure or respectability should take center stage. In at least a few instances, vernacular culture and an emphasis on the more exuberant pleasures of a community holiday won out.

Even in light of such disagreements, several elements of the celebrations served to produce a more unified purpose. Music, for example, brought discordant voices into unison. Whether on foot or in a wagon, a band—be it a local or visiting brass band, silver cornet band, or drum corps—nearly always accompanied Emancipation Day processions. Their "martial music," "national airs," and "strains of sweet music" made the celebrations especially enjoyable. Marchers occasionally sang and offered cheers. Many nineteenth-century celebrations culminated with a dance or a more formal ball.[37]

While music enlivened and unified the day's events, flags, banners, costumes, and uniforms, as well as decorated wagons and streetcars, enhanced the visual impact created by the marchers. Flags and "expressive banners" added significant visual interest to Mt. Pleasant's parade in 1865. Muscatine's 1867 procession included a prominent lithograph of Abraham Lincoln, the "Great Emancipator." In Keokuk, the "holiday attire" of participants, and the use of transparencies along with flags and banners, helped make the parade "well appearing" in 1866, but by 1872 the event was even more elaborate, with ladies on horseback, a carriage bearing the day's key speakers, and a group of men who bore the U.S. flag. In 1876, in Clarinda, the usual caravan included a wagon that was "beautifully festooned and decorated with stars and stripes, and loaded with colored ladies, with one up front carrying a large steel engraving of Lincoln." Fancy dress would remain a major component of the town's celebrations in years to come; in 1885 and again in 1901 children in "gala costumes," as well as a costumed queen and goddess of liberty, made a dramatic impact.[38] Thus emancipation celebrations offered a feast for the eye while satisfying rural midwesterners' craving for social gatherings.

Food was another important feature of the day's events. The collective breaking of bread had deep secular and sacred connotations, and hospitality and culinary skill added appreciably to the social and festive elements of celebrations.[39] Families brought their own picnic baskets, or a "grand meal" was provided. Women's groups of local black congregations often furnished the noontime meal or an evening supper, frequently as a fund-raiser for their church, needy black families, or the local black school.[40] Like the solemn, orderly procession that reflected the mood of the community and its claim to respectability, the amount and variety of well-prepared food was not only a gesture of nurturance for the local black community, but also a symbol of female accomplishment and civilization. As the *Home Journal* noted in 1865, the repast was "worthy of any woman"; a Des Moines celebration garnered praise for "a table beauteously spread and with cookery of the best quality."[41]

In addition to these performative and material elements of expressive culture, Emancipation Day offered a diverse program of oratory that variously included recitations, prepared and extemporaneous speeches, sermons, testimonies, cheers and resolutions, and displays of the printed word. The single most common feature of postwar celebrations was the reading of the Emancipation Proclamation. (In 1876, commemorative exercises in Des Moines were suspended for two hours so organizers could locate a copy of the proclamation.)[42] Often the document was read by a prominent community member, and communities would try to capitalize on the reader's popularity as a draw to the program.[43] We also see a slight retreat from the gender politics that had excluded women from the speaker's podium; by the 1890s, women were often invited to read the proclamation.[44] This reading was regarded as a performance, and readers knew they would be judged on the quality of their execution—from high praise for a rendition "of great power and eloquence" to the criticism of another for a "tedious" delivery "which did not evidently delight any portion of the audience."[45]

The centrality of the Emancipation Proclamation to these celebrations raises several questions about the historical consciousness of the celebrants, especially how they understood the document and its relationship to the end of slavery. Although historians continue to debate its intent and impact, few Americans today have read or pondered the proclamation's significant limitations. In contrast, generations of African Americans heard the words of the proclamation every year. They would have been familiar with its pronouncement of slavery's death in the Confederate states, its exclusion of the Union's slaveholding border states as well as Union-occupied regions of the South, and its plea for nonviolence and self-sufficiency on the part of former slaves.[46]

Yet despite their familiarity with the proclamation's limitations (and their own experiences in claiming freedom well before its implementation), black midwesterners typically portrayed its author as the Great Emancipator. From the lithographs and engravings of his image carried during processions, to the cheers of those who marched, to the speakers who memorialized the "cherished" author of the Emancipation Proclamation, Lincoln was honored as "the old man" who "stretched out his long arm and smote the monster on the head with his Emancipation hammer, such a blow as none but Abe could strike."[47] In the postwar period, Lincoln became a martyred symbol of the Republican Party, even as that party assumed far more radical positions on black America than Lincoln himself had ever considered.

Although Lincoln was credited with ending American slavery, many agreed that it was God's hand that had moved the mere mortal president. "God wrought our freedom," asserted one speaker; "God willed it, and Heaven decreed it." It was a sentiment echoed on banners that read "God Says, Let the Oppressed Go Free" in an 1865 procession. Divine intent was also acknowledged by resolutions that honored Lincoln but thanked "the great Disposer of all events, that he put it into the hearts of the people, and the President of this country, to liberate the enslaved."[48] The very fact that so many emancipation celebrations began the day in church points to the belief that thanksgiving should begin in God's house.

Furthermore, celebrants generally characterized emancipation as a blessing not only for slaves, but also for the nation as a whole. In 1865, African Americans in Keokuk resolved that emancipation had been "indispensable to the cause of the Union, saving us alike from threatened foreign intervention, from disunity in executive policy, and from weakness in the prosecution of war." Three years later, speaker G. W. Guy asserted that the proclamation was "one of the greatest boons bestowed upon a Nation." Rhetorically asking "Who should celebrate this day," Guy answered: "All who love liberty."[49] Emancipation elevated the entire nation, not just the enslaved.

The complexity with which celebrants understood the wartime process of slavery's destruction is further suggested by several Emancipation Day speakers, who—to the acclaim of their audiences—directly addressed the partial victory achieved by Lincoln's actions. According to one orator in 1866, the proclamation represented only a "partial development of the principles which our Fathers sowed in Revolutionary soil"; to another, Lincoln was the slaves' "neutral friend" rather than their second Moses. After all, on his election

Lincoln "said if he thought tolerating slavery would maintain the Union, amen! and if destroying the same would do it, amen!" Only Jefferson Davis's refusal to surrender under Lincoln's terms brought down slavery. "Davis is our modern Pharaoh, and through the hardness of his heart, God wrought our freedom," argued J. Carey of Keokuk. Fairfield's James Yancey, although willing to pay "an eloquent compliment to President Lincoln," nonetheless maintained that "the Executive erred somewhat in his policy toward the slaves," perhaps referring to Lincoln's opposition to political and social equality or his early insistence on pairing emancipation with colonization.[50]

But for most black midwesterners, the clearest evidence of the proclamation's "partial" victory lay in the restrictions still placed on black citizenship by state and federal laws during the postwar era. Denied suffrage, the right to hold office, and equal access to public schools and public accommodations, and subjected to mob violence, midwestern African Americans who celebrated the end of slavery were not reluctant to express their hope that "the liberties and rights of the colored people of the Union will soon be insured."[51] Emancipation was only a partial vindication of the Declaration of Independence, but, as a "free people," black Iowans insisted that they were "destined, at no remote period, to assist in the government of this country."[52]

The politics of emancipation celebrations were shaped in part by the special honor paid both to black Civil War veterans and former slave men. A former slave was selected to serve as chief marshal of Keokuk's 1865 procession. Charles Davis, a young man still on active duty in the 65th U.S. Colored Infantry (USCI), took pride in his military service and his battle-scarred face.[53] At the Des Moines celebration in 1866 a Mr. Perkins spoke "lucidly and vigorously" about his "twenty-three years under the lash." Former slave S. J. Harris, a young man in his early twenties, was asked to address the crowd; he "spoke with some embarrassment but with considerable effect." At the same celebration, Rev. S. T. Wells—pastor of the community's African Methodist Episcopal (AME) congregation—brought a sharp yet effective tone of sarcasm to his observations about slavery: "He said he had lived in Missouri; had worked on the plantation to send his young master to college to become educated for the legal profession, so that he could learn how to catch runaway negroes with better facility; said master came back and sold his wife and children; then he (Wells) fell out with slavery, started North, and arrived there a little in advance of the Emancipation Proclamation." Thomas Gordon Jones, who organized Emancipation Day celebrations in Clarinda, spoke in 1872 about his life as a slave, giving "a general detail of the troubles, trials, and afflictions, and an interesting history of the liberation of their poor, degraded race." Jones would speak at many subsequent celebrations, elaborating on his personal experience; he did "his best to explain the difference between slavery and freedom." Former slaves were also invited to speak at Mt. Pleasant's 1868 emancipation commemoration, but that portion of the day's exercises was removed from the public eye (and no doubt that of white observers) and conducted inside the AME church as an "experience meeting," in which "old slaves related incidents connected with their slave days and their lives as free men."[54]

The testimony of former slaves kept Emancipation Day celebrations partially rooted in the memory of slavery, created ritualized events devoted to reexperiencing and reinterpreting their collective trauma, and recognized former slaves as historians of their own past. Their accounts ensured that the slave past would be incorporated in the collective memory of African Americans living in the upper Midwest.[55]

Black Civil War veterans like Charles Davis reminded participants not only of slavery's recent shadow over their lives, but also of the manliness of African Americans who had participated in the destruction of slavery and the defense of the nation.[56] It appears that celebrations offered little, if any, recognition of the role played by women in the military side of the war, such as the wives and family members who had accompanied the 60th USCI into the field, where they worked as laundresses, cooks, and nurses. Rather, the spotlight was on the veterans, who made a striking appearance as they marched "arrayed in army uniform, with swords, pistols, &c."[57] By excluding the experiences and memories of women who had also participated in the war, black midwesterners kept the focus on black manhood and men's entitlement to citizenship. On the eve of Iowa's vote on the constitutional amendment to extend the franchise to African Americans, one Emancipation Day celebration gave center stage to the community's Civil War veterans. The event began with a sunrise salute as twelve veterans formed a squad and fired their muskets, a booming reminder that African American men had willingly shouldered a citizen's responsibilities during the war.[58]

Commemorations were also gendered by the conspicuous absence of women from those who offered public testimony to their experience of slavery, although they did describe it in more sheltered settings (such as in their churches). Black communities may have been unwilling to expose their women to the judgment or contempt of white audiences. Nor were black women willing to be found lacking, either as individuals or as representatives of their race, in womanly virtue. Whether men assumed or were given the role of embodying the experience of slavery in public commemorations, they participated in a dual strategy to elevate black manhood and to protect black women. Still, these men emphasized slavery's gendered torments, including the "agonizing groans of mothers" and the subjugation of slave women to the lust of their masters.

Women did assume uniquely gendered public roles in celebrations—typically as costumed female symbols. On horseback and in decorated carriages and wagons, women and girls appeared as living images of Republicanism or as the goddesses of liberty and plenty.[59] But these were never simply decorative roles. We need only remember how white Iowans viewed the former slave women who migrated to the state during and immediately after the Civil War to understand the political statement behind these images. Black women who moved to Iowa were expected to work in circumstances and occupations that were considered demeaning to white middle-class women and denigrating to an idealized (and racialized) womanhood. When African American women sewed elaborate costumes for themselves and their daughters to wear as goddesses and queens, and when they were carried by horse and wagon rather than marching on foot, they may have been claiming for themselves and their daughters a privileged womanhood that whites actively sought to deny them. In both the roles they chose and those they avoided, black women made the commemoration of slavery about the contemporary politics of race and racialized womanhood as well as about the centrality of the past in understanding and negotiating the present.

FROM THE TURN of the century until the early 1930s, new cultural brokers took over the planning and conduct of emancipation celebrations in the upper Midwest. In Des Moines, responsibility shifted from the Old Settlers Society to the AME Church (1901, 1915), the city's black literary society (1902, 1904), and then to race and civil rights organizations: the Afro-American Council, forerunner of the Niagara movement (1907–10); the (Washingtonian) Negro Business League (1914–15); and, beginning in 1915, the NAACP.[60] Similar changes occurred in Wisconsin and Minnesota, where the Afro-American League and the NAACP assumed stewardship over celebrations.[61] Emancipation celebrations moved indoors, replacing the picnics and processions that had marked the nineteenth-century claim on the public sphere with more decorous, orderly, formal presentations. Papers were now read (a practice that had earned one nineteenth-century speaker the disdain of his audience), and vocal solos, choir performances, and recitals replaced the cheers, marching bands, and personal testimony that had been key components of earlier commemorations.

At the fiftieth anniversary of the Emancipation Proclamation celebrated by over 1,500 people in Des Moines, "there was neither boisterous declamation nor boisterous applause. Moderation prevailed in everything. It was a determined, thoughtful, ambitious body of Americans who were rejoicing over fifty years of progress and looking forward hopefully." There were speeches on the advances of the race, and the highlight of the evening's entertainment was a display in which one hundred children "representing the fifty years of our freedom" and "the future hope of the race" participated. No one spoke about the slave past.[62]

Yet black history was still deeply valued. In Des Moines, S. Joe Brown—lawyer, president of the Iowa branch of the Afro-American Council, and one of the founding members of the Des Moines branch of the NAACP—had been active at least since 1907 in the effort to make Emancipation Day a national celebration. In December 1909, he issued a call to "all local Afro-American Councils, Negro Churches, Clubs and other race organizations [to] observe the first day of January, 1910," including the reading of the Emancipation Proclamation, the singing of patriotic songs, and addresses "commemorative of that memorable occasion."[63] The Beloit, Wisconsin, branch of the NAACP not only organized Emancipation Day celebrations, but also sponsored debates on critical issues in black history (including an assessment of the Thirteenth Amendment). In St. Paul, Minnesota, the black chapter of the Woman's Relief Corps (WRC) maintained an active presence in local events, and churches arranged observances of Negro History Week.[64]

The Des Moines branch of the NAACP organized New Year's Day emancipation celebrations and added to the commemorative calendar an annual Lincoln-Douglass Anniversary celebration in February.[65] Portraying Abraham Lincoln and Frederick Douglass as the joint emancipators of the race, the Des Moines branch fostered a collective memory that centered on a national heroic narrative of black history rather than one rooted in local or regional experience or the slave past. This focus would carry over into its promotion of Negro History Week activities in 1945. One significant departure, however, occurred in 1932, when the Des Moines branch erected an award-winning booth at the Iowa State Fair, in which a variety of displays addressed local black progress and the local struggle for civil rights.[66]

The civil rights organizations that assumed responsibility for Emancipation Day celebrations throughout the upper Midwest not only relocated commemorative activities indoors and stressed a national narrative of black history rather than a regional one, but they also helped alter the gender politics of emancipation remembrances. Both the Afro-American Council and the NAACP contributed to changes in the black public sphere that made it increasingly possible for women to assume more public roles in these celebrations. Although they still prepared meals and performed musical pieces that demonstrated their refinement, women now led devotional exercises, read the proclamation, and even delivered speeches on such topics as citizenship, the history of the 60th USCI, and "the Negro problem." At the "Grand Golden Jubilee Celebration of Emancipation" held in Des Moines in 1913, Mrs. J. B. Rush addressed the audience on "Women's Progress"; the next year Mrs. Sue Brown spoke about the "Forward Movement of Colored Women."[67]

Black women were not simply beneficiaries of enlightened race organizations; at the turn of the century, they took a more public, authoritative role in Emancipation Day exercises because they had assumed that role throughout the black public sphere. From their creation of a club movement in 1890 (both Iowa and Minnesota then formed a statewide federation in 1902), to their predominance in the AME Sunday School movement in Iowa and their central role in the region's branches of the Afro-American Council and the NAACP, black women had created and expanded the opportunities by which they could organize and lead their communities.[68] Through this work, they also acquired an influence over how African American history was remembered and collectively commemorated. In 1931, the women of the Des Moines branch of the NAACP took over the planning and presentation of Emancipation Day exercises.[69]

But in Des Moines and elsewhere across the region, Emancipation Day activities became sporadic after 1935 and were eventually supplanted by Lincoln-Douglass Day celebrations. Although a few events—including Lincoln-Douglass Day and Negro History Week—seem to have been revived at the end of World War II, they died out once again until the 1950s. Yet the centennial anniversary of American emancipation in 1963 did not pass unnoticed. In fact, Iowa's NAACP branches conducted an extraordinary number of events that year, including celebrations of Emancipation Day, Lincoln-Douglass Day, and the anniversary of the Supreme Court's *Brown v. Board of Education* decision. They also participated in the March on Washington in August and Human Rights Day on 15 December.[70]

Although Emancipation Day celebrations continued in some American communities, after World War II they became infrequent.[71] Perhaps it was the promulgation of uplift ideology, the turn to a national narrative of black history that tended to exclude the local or regional, the demands of coping with the Depression and war, or the dispersal of celebration days across a larger calendar of events that allowed Emancipation Day to recede from the commemorative calendar.[72] But we should not underestimate the amnesiac influences of a white popular culture that identified slavery as a regional story anchored in the South.

"SLAVE-SCARRED VETERANS":
COMMEMORATING THE BLACK MILITARY EXPERIENCE

After the Civil War, black communities in the upper Midwest had refused to yield to whites the power to determine how the war itself would be remembered. In all-black as well as integrated posts of the Grand Army of the Republic (GAR), the Woman's Relief Corps, and the Ladies of the GAR, black midwesterners demanded public recognition of their role in the Union military victory. Nevertheless, black veterans—most of whom had been enslaved at the start of the conflict—faced an uphill battle in gaining the same respect and prestige that veteran status accorded white men. This would become most evident later in the nineteenth century with the revival of interest in the GAR, founded in 1866 but increasingly popular in the 1870s and 1880s.[73] Although the GAR had never formally adopted segregation, there were extensive debates in the 1890s about the efforts of southern departments to exclude African Americans from membership, especially in areas where blacks outnumbered whites.[74]

But segregation was not only at issue in the South. Northern GAR posts were variously integrated or segregated, and scholars have yet to ascertain the extent of or reason for this uneven pattern.[75] Keokuk's black veterans organized their own post, with at least twenty members in the 1890s, presumably because they were excluded from the white post.[76] In the same decade, the seven black veterans living in Newton, Iowa, were denied membership in the local GAR post, as were two black veterans in Iowa City who repeatedly tried to join. It took George W. Patterson three years (and three separate attempts) before white veterans would admit him in 1890.[77] By 1898, however, two posts in Des Moines accepted black members.[78]

Membership in the GAR sustained black memories of the war in several ways. First, it helped legitimate black members' claims to veteranhood. This led not only to public recognition, but also personal gain, since GAR posts helped veterans apply for a pension. Burial assistance, graveside services, and special grave markers ensured veterans an honorable burial and reinscribed black military service on the collective memory; as a practical matter, these benefits relieved heirs of burial costs. Second, the presence of black GAR members at integrated annual encampments was a visible reminder of black

Members of the Grand Army of the Republic, Biddle Circle #38, St. Paul, ca. 1945. Minnesota Historical Society.

military service. Minnesotan Henry Mack, for example, was one of only fifty-eight black veterans who attended the 1938 national encampment at Gettysburg; in 1941 he was honored by the *Minneapolis Morning Tribune* as the state's oldest living Civil War veteran, and in 1946 he was one of ten veterans to attend the Minnesota GAR encampment. His appearance at state and national gatherings and parades called attention to the fact that African Americans had played a role in the war.[79] The collective value that black midwesterners placed on their membership is rarely documented in the historical record, but the fact that one Iowa veteran willed one hundred dollars of his hard-earned estate to the GAR suggests how highly he esteemed the organization.[80]

Although it was an important site within which African Americans struggled to exercise their rightful place among veterans of the war, the GAR was also concerned with racial politics outside of the organization. By the twentieth century, the GAR frequently entered into regional and national debates about the color line and about the politics of reunion with Confederate veterans. They protested the showing of *The Birth of a Nation* and defended black veterans in the South against attack.[81] In these and other ways, African American veterans used the GAR to sustain their own memory of the war.

African American women also commemorated the black military experience through their membership in the Woman's Relief Corps and the Ladies of the GAR. According to the historian Barbara Gannon, black GAR posts were far more likely than white posts to be affiliated with women's auxiliaries.[82] Both the WRC and the Ladies of the GAR assisted GAR posts with commemorative and social activities, including Emancipation Day observances. And, like the GAR, both organizations would debate the role of black chapters and the color line. Between 1891 and 1905, the Woman's Relief Corps devoted part of every national convention to a discussion of black membership in the South and the best way to establish black chapters—especially as the corps sought to expand its membership among southern white members. Although black members did their best to challenge caricatures of African American women as illiterate, ignorant, or uninterested in the cause of national patriotism and commemoration, white members—including northern white members—frequently expressed the opinion that "there can never be in our day a Department of white and colored corps working harmoniously together."[83] African American members fought segregation in the Woman's Relief Corps as well as in the GAR. They also formed all-black corps, as they did in St. Paul, where Biddle Circle No. 38 played a significant role in commemorative events in the Twin Cities and was active at least through 1956.[84]

"ACCORDING TO MY RECKONING": AFRICAN AMERICAN MEMOIRS

In addition to public rituals and activities dedicated to the collective memories of slavery and emancipation, African Americans created narratives that preserved—in print as well as in oral tradition—their personal and familial experiences of slavery and its destruction. These narratives are best understood as memoirs. Memoir is distinguished from autobiography by its focus on particular events in history; those events, rather than the life course, form the narrative strategy of memoir. Following this usage, memoir can be seen as the act of remembering events as well as the effort to define or interpret them— that is, to illuminate and commemorate both the remembered events and the experience of those events. The production and circulation of memoirs by midwestern survivors of slavery illustrates the collective context of memory and memoir. African American memoir—especially with its broader circulation in interviews as oral testimony or in written and often published form— simultaneously served memory's individual needs as well as its compelling collective goals. These included defending black memories of the trauma of slavery and emphasizing the incomplete promise of emancipation against the forgetful tide of sectional reunion; challenging the emerging popularization and romanticization of Underground Railroad literature, which placed white heroes at center stage in the fight against slavery; and challenging the racist caricatures of black midwesterners in popular culture as well as the impact of segregation on the venues and production of emancipation-era history and memory reckoning.[85]

Segregation meant that, in the wider public sphere, African American memory and memorials entered the hierarchy of cultural authority from the bottom and were persistently relegated to the periphery of what passed for, or was projected as, "historical truth." No matter how persuasively scholars have demonstrated the subjective nature of traditional (white-authored) historical sources for the era, African American memory in all of its many forms has frequently been excluded from the central story of emancipation, war, and Reconstruction.[86] While their recollections were often untethered to the kinds of documentation on which official history typically relies, these memoirs offer firsthand observations and testimony on the trauma of slavery and the chaos of war, contributions of African Americans to the destruction of slavery and the Union military victory, and their postwar struggles for citizenship.

Among the most prolific, but also the least studied, forms of black memoir are the depositions, affidavits, and interviews contained in the pension claims of black Civil War veterans and their families, as well as the obituaries of former slaves. The varieties of recollections included in pension claims have drawn the attention of social historians, who find in these sources an unparalleled witnessing to slavery, war, and postbellum life; a unique source for the study of gender; and a window into the role of the state in defining family and familial relationships.[87] Few scholars, however, have considered this material as a form of black memoir.

The Aftermath of Slavery

The Civil War pension system was created on 14 July 1862 to provide for the veteran disabled by wounds, injuries, or disease incurred during his military service, and, in the event of his death from these causes, to furnish support for his "dependents," including his widow, dependent parents, and minor children. As described by the historian Elizabeth Regosin, "The Civil War pension system evolved through a series of subsequent acts that refined the rates for different disabilities and the qualifications for proving eligibility; increased the rates of pension for widows, children, and other relatives; and provided other specific details on such things as the order of succession of eligible relatives, the method of payment, and arrears of pension."[88]

Black Civil War veterans and family members who sought pension benefits encountered an elaborate bureaucracy, subject to changing laws and procedures, with requirements that were difficult for illiterate applicants to navigate, and agents who assumed black applicants to be likely perpetrators of fraudulent claims. Perhaps the most troublesome aspect of the pension process was the expectation that applicants could provide documentation—like family Bibles and marriage certificates—to support their claims. Since the majority of black soldiers (and their families) had been enslaved at the start of the war, they turned to the only substitute for official documentation they had access to: the sworn testimony of family members, friends, neighbors, comrades, commanding officers, and, occasionally, former masters to verify the details and veracity of their family and military histories. Thus, women, children, the elderly, and a host of others who did not officially serve in the war frequently provided their own memoir and recollections in the pension claims of black veterans.

Given the fact that claims were initiated with the goal of financial gain, historians must approach them as serving a primary need that was not necessarily an objective truth. Still, the claim process—which was more likely to reject black applicants than white, and required extensive testimonial support for the claims made by former slaves—also served as a filter that adds credence to the memories of those who testified in successful claims.[89]

The memories and recollections documented in pension claims of those who had participated in the wartime diaspora to the upper Midwest reveal common narrative features and content. Deponents frequently testified, both implicitly and explicitly, to the traumas of slavery, often in the context of explaining gaps in family histories ("They sold me away from the family when I was about 10 years").[90] Those who did not know or could not fully recall their family history relied on the veracity of collective memory in the slave quarters, as did veteran Henry Brown: "All I know is what I have been told when I was young."[91]

The Aftermath of Slavery

Since pension officials questioned the surfeit of surnames among members of the same family, former slaves often detailed the dissolution of families, slaveowners' refusal to acknowledge the surnames used by former slaves, and the postemancipation decision of former slaves to change their names to follow that of their father or mother ("I was known by the name Ellen Russell").[92] Date of birth and death, of slave marriage and separation, of sale and flight often meant tracking down family members in the South who could recollect their complex histories—in the vast majority of instances, without the aid of written sources. Through their collective memories, black midwesterners consigned their experience of slavery to an official public record.

The memoirs recorded in pension claims offer especially rich firsthand accounts of slavery's collapse and the origins of black freedom. Such testimony has several particularly notable components. One is that African Americans documented their own agency in freeing themselves. In contrast to the notion that either President Lincoln or Union troops were responsible for their freedom, claimants frequently recounted their own self-liberation.[93] A second component is the challenge that these memoirs of self-liberation posed to a growing national amnesia about slavery and slavery's significance during the war, and to the North's increasing emphasis on the role of white abolitionists (such as Underground Railroad "operators") and white soldiers in bringing freedom to enslaved people. Neither illiteracy, nor a hostile pension bureaucracy, nor declining attention to the war's emancipationist legacy prevented African Americans from using the first person in their narration of how they became free. "I ran away and went up into Iowa," asserted John Bandy.[94] A related feature of this testimony is that the recollections required for a pension application attested to the range of black military experiences and contributions to the war effort.[95]

Although African Americans—from Frederick Douglass to George Washington Williams—challenged white Americans to remember the contributions of black veterans, black soldiers and their families were largely excluded from the growing interest in Civil War stories and accounts (freighted with an intent to freeze the "true" narratives of the war in time). Nor did they profit from what David Blight has called the "reminiscence industry," as popular periodicals (among them *Century*, *Atlantic*, *Monthly Galaxy*, and *Lippincott's*), book publishers, and newspapers boosted their sales and circulation with such stories and reminiscences.[96] As the nation's dominant Civil War memories—and "official history"—moved toward sectional reconciliation, and as the war's military legacy increasingly subsumed its emancipationist consequences, pension claims became one of the largest repositories of black memoirs about slavery, the military conflict, and the destruction of American bondage.

DEATH NOTICES AND obituaries typically note the end of a life, but in such instances the black press of the upper Midwest provided another site of slave memoirs. Whether crafted by grieving family members or a newspaper's editorial staff, the obituaries that documented the passing of the region's former slaves presented a rich portrait of individual, collective, and intergenerational memories of slavery, war, and freedom. Before the emergence of clear distinctions between death notices (paid advertisements announcing the date, time, and location of funeral services) and the professionally authored obituary (a summary of the deceased's life), the region's fin de siècle black press carried elegiac accounts of the life experience of the deceased (and often excluding specific information about services and burial). The obituaries of former slaves offered an explicit counterpoint to white amnesia through their carefully crafted stories of the deceased's survival of specific traumas of slavery, the chaos of war and migration, and a life in freedom.[97]

Exemplifying the manner in which obituaries sustained both memories and histories of slavery is this notice crafted by the deceased's son, also the publisher of the *Iowa State Bystander*:

> Mrs. Thompson was born in Jackson Co. Mo., Oct. 10th, 1836, and spent 27 years in slavery[;] was bought and sold five different times; sold to a man named Martin, of Clay Co., Mo., in 1839; she was then taken to Platt Co., Mo., where she was married in 1852, to Nicholas Martin; later they were sold to Shepard, then separated from her husband and sold to Jacks. After Lincoln's proclamation of emancipation she, with four small children came to Iowa, settling in Ringgold county, working on a farm; she soon moved to Decatur county, where she was married to Mr. Andy Thompson, Nov. 16, 1866, where she spent most of her life. She was a loving and affectionate mother, sociable to her friends, kind to all, confessed religion and joined the Methodist church, of which she was a devoted member.[98]

This obituary is valuable for its specific accounting of the human costs of Thompson's experiences of slavery: sale, separation, and disrupted family, among them. It also makes clear that Thompson's emancipation was her own doing. Taking her children, she fled slavery and found work in rural Iowa as a farmhand to support her family. Even as Thomas Nelson Page and Joel Chandler Harris delighted southern and northern white readers alike with stories enacting national reconciliation and featuring faithful slaves, the families and descendants of the Midwest's former slaves—in conjunction with black newspaper publishers—memorialized a personal and collective history, one that they refused to hide or regard with shame. Indeed, the names of slaveowners who bought and sold their human property like so much chattel are given, as if to denote where the real shame of slavery ought to be laid. Through obituaries like Mrs. Thompson's, African Americans created a commemorative form in which they publicly laid claim to their family's inheritance of a memory and postmemory of enslavement, survival, self-emancipation, and, in many instances, military service. In this way, they transformed family memoir into collective memory; and through the specificity of their recollections, they deployed memoir as a form of history writing as well.[99]

A THIRD, AND widely circulated type of African American memoir in the upper Midwest, was the slave narrative. Until the Civil War and the destruction of American slavery, this was the dominant mode of African American writing. Before 1866, at least 101 such narratives appeared in book or pamphlet form.[100] Their authors participated in a collective political movement while engaging in an individual, expressive exercise that would have been liberating (engaging in a creative act), as well as traumatic (reliving the horrors of slavery). Antebellum black writers, together with members of the antislavery movement who shaped the expectations of readers and therefore the "market" for slave narratives, created a variegated structure of many voices but also a literary convention that dictated the particular topics and content that reinforced the expectations of the white reading public.

The collection of voices brought to bear in antebellum narratives typically included authenticating letters from well-known figures in the antislavery movement or from trustworthy personages in the public sphere (like members of the clergy) verifying the narrator's experience and work. They might also include excerpts from newspaper advertisements for runaway slaves; lithographs depicting moments in the former slave's life and escape; and sermons, antislavery speeches, and interjections in the narrative addressing the reader directly. All served to document the authenticity of the narrator and strengthen the antislavery appeal of the work, as well as to focus on the institution and "external reality" of slavery, rather than on the individual, subjective experience of African American people.[101]

Some scholars have argued that the slave narrative tradition left black writers "captive" to the demands and expectations of the white-dominated abolitionist movement and its strategies for securing the sympathies of the white reading public. As the literary scholar John Sekora puts it, "What remains at the center is an institutional form or experience. What is meanwhile pushed to the periphery is the unique and distinctive experience of an individual life."[102] But however limiting the slave narrative form had become by the 1840s, the political turn of events that pushed the nation closer to war also prompted black writers to push the narrative form in new directions.[103] Between the Fugitive Slave Law crisis of 1850 (which "made Canadian emigrants out of approximately 20,000 black Americans in the decade of the 1850s," according to the literary scholar William Andrews) and the *Dred Scott* Supreme Court decision of 1857, African American writers were radicalized. They demanded a new kind of textual freedom and became more willing to advocate violence as a legitimate form of resistance.[104] Their narratives were less likely to resolve the slave's flight from bondage with their arrival in a land of justice and equality. Instead, they portrayed a continuing quest for freedom and safety. On the eve of war, black writers were still searching for liberty.[105]

The most widely circulated African American memoirs in the upper Midwest after the war were *postbellum* slave narratives. Among the black midwesterners who wrote and published them were Moses Mosely and Samuel Hall.[106] At the time of the twentieth and fiftieth anniversaries of emancipation, these two Iowans presented a firsthand account of slavery and liberation. Mosely, Hall, and their families were among the thousands of African Americans who made their way to freedom in the upper Mississippi valley during the Civil War. Through their publications, they attempted to embed the African American experience of slavery and liberty in the region's public memory, history, and culture. Mosely's expostulatory and occasionally autobiographical pamphlet, *The Colored Man as Slave and Citizen of the United States* (1884), and Hall's *Forty Seven Years a Slave: A Brief Story of His Life before and after Freedom Came to Him* (1912) both offered the writers' understanding, and construction, of the past.[107] They joined with participants at Emancipation Day celebrations, veterans recalling their slavery and wartime experiences, and grieving survivors who wrote detailed obituaries of their recently deceased elders in an attempt to invoke and perpetuate a countermemory to the plantation school and Lost Cause literature that was quickly gaining credence among white northerners.

Mosely and Hall used their stories to place themselves and other black midwesterners into regional and national history, but also to return to the memory of slavery and its impact on African American views of the past, present, and future. Although working from within the slave narrative tradition, they displayed an emancipated, postbellum perspective and therefore

Samuel Hall, former slave, wartime migrant to Washington, Iowa, and author, with Orville Elder, of Samuel Hall: 47 Years a Slave: A Brief Story of His Life before and after Freedom Came to Him *(1912). Frontispiece,* Samuel Hall, *Iowa Authors Collection, Special Collections Department, University of Iowa Libraries, Iowa City.*

entered that tradition at different moments in history than did their antebellum predecessors. Scholars have concluded that emancipation marked the most significant turning point in this genre. No longer motivated or restrained by the movement against slavery, the postbellum narrative took on different purposes, and the picture of slavery that emerged from these narratives offered an important contrast to the one rendered before the war.[108]

The ninety-two or so known postbellum narratives—written by people born into slavery and published between 1866 and 1938—have yet to receive, as a body of work, the intensive study given to antebellum narratives.[109] Only three postbellum narratives have been closely examined: Booker T. Washington's *Up from Slavery* (1901), the most popular of these accounts; Elizabeth Keckley's *Behind the Scenes* (1868); and Frederick Douglass's *The Life and Times of Frederick Douglass* (1881). Scholars have argued that these three narratives reveal important distinctions between antebellum and postbellum works in that they emphasize the narrators' postbellum achievements, are less concerned with exposing the brutality of slavery (instead emphasizing the distinction between a brutal institution and the white people who presided over it), and frequently portray literal and symbolic regional reconciliation, often through what William Andrews describes as "emotionally-charged reunions between protagonists of post-bellum slave narratives and their ex-masters or mistresses."¹¹⁰ David Blight adds that market forces were at work in the changing form of postbellum narratives: that is, given the reconciliatory mood marking the post-Reconstruction nation, stories that detailed the "deprivation and humiliation of slavery, did not sell in a culture eager to purchase tales of reunion and soldiers' glory."¹¹¹ Scholars have concluded that, by the turn of the century, these narrators had moved away from a focus on the degradation of slavery and toward an emphasis on former slaves' skills and potential—tools for competing in the New South and for refuting the stereotypes of scientific racism. But the unstudied works published by Mosely and Hall depart significantly from the portrayals of slavery that scholars associate with postbellum narratives and memoirs.

Both Mosely and Hall were drawn into the wartime diaspora that took former slaves to the upper Midwest and, more specifically, to small-town Iowa. Some twenty years before he would publish his pamphlet, Mosely, his wife, and their three young children escaped from their owner in Calhoun, Missouri. They walked (Mosely carrying his youngest son in his arms) to a Union army camp about seven miles away, then were sent by rail to the contraband camp at St. Louis. From there, they made their way to Mt. Pleasant, about twenty-five miles north of Missouri and west of the Mississippi River, most likely arriving via one of the two railroad routes that served the town. They were part of the wave of migration to Mt. Pleasant that would swell the county's black population from 8 in 1856 (out of a total population close to 5,000), to 262 by the end of the war, to 401 by 1867, and to 509 by 1880.¹¹²

On the eve of the Civil War, Mt. Pleasant was a prosperous, attractive town, with brick buildings, a nearby stream and river, and several close (and valuable) stands of timber. Although it had no major industry at the time, the town's valuable natural resources, including coal along nearby riverbeds and limestone, may have steered Mosely to the craft of stonemasonry. Mt. Pleasant and the county in which it was located were also reputed to be one of Iowa's most progressive areas. Nearby Salem was the home of Quakers who had resisted the enforcement of the Fugitive Slave Law in two prominent legal cases. Henry County whites who were active in the antislavery movement petitioned the state legislature to remove the black codes and sent at least ten white town residents to abolitionist settlements in Kansas during the bloody conflict there. Mt. Pleasant's liberal environment was evident in the large number of churches, as well as in the presence of Iowa Wesleyan University, a well-attended local high school, and a female academy. Temperance and woman's rights lectures drew local support as well. However, white residents also shared some of the antiblack sentiments common among the region's white reformers. One local historian observed that even in Salem, the county's center of antislavery activism, there were no black residents; their opposition to slavery did not necessarily make local whites particularly sympathetic to African Americans living in their midst. During the war, Mt. Pleasant's Freedmen's Relief Society—which sent supplies and cash to former slaves in the South—overlooked the considerable needs of black families streaming into their community.[113]

African Americans had arrived with the earliest white pioneers in 1838, but the wartime diaspora of former slaves would dramatically alter Mt. Pleasant and Henry County. White Union officers stationed in St. Louis sent former slaves to Mt. Pleasant throughout the war, even after the military had officially ended its participation in organized relocation. For some migrants, their perilous journey to freedom ended badly, as in the case of eleven men whom a local mill owner had obtained in St. Louis in the fall of 1862 to serve as his employees. Over the winter, all eleven died from the smallpox epidemic that ran through the boardinghouse where they lived. Many others died as well; one white observer commented: "So great have been their exposures, needs or sufferings, since they came among us, that a large per cent of them have sickened and died—some eight or ten of less than fifty." Other new arrivals offered themselves to the army—some estimate that one hundred black men volunteered to serve before the War Department approved open black enlistment.[114]

Black and white neighbors found a way to coexist in Mt. Pleasant. Local whites raised funds to help construct a building that would serve the new black community as both school and church—institutions that were welcomed by the town's new black residents, even if they perpetuated segregated education. Local blacks held large, public celebrations to commemorate emancipation—a dramatic change for a white community unaccustomed to sharing the town square and its major streets with African Americans. However well or uneasily whites and blacks interacted, the war had barely ended when African Americans, including former slaves like Mosely, began demanding their rights as citizens and attempting to shape the collective memory of slavery and emancipation.[115]

ENSLAVED WITH HIS family in Tennessee, Samuel Hall made his own escape sometime in 1863 and soon brought his wife and four children (ranging from an infant to a nine-year-old) to a nearby Union camp. The Halls then were boarded on a Mississippi River steamboat and eventually arrived in Washington, Iowa. By the mid-1850s, the town of Washington—the seat of Washington County—was "a thriving place," due in part to a successful woolen factory, a flour mill, a sawmill, and a steam-boiler factory. Three public schools and a college served the town's 1,300 residents.[116] At the time of Hall's arrival, the county—directly north of Moses Mosely's home in Mt. Pleasant—had seen its black population grow from 13 people on the eve of the Civil War to at least 67 (nearly all of them in the town of Washington) at war's end. The town, initially settled in 1836 by antislavery Presbyterians, had developed a close connection with the territory's abolitionists, especially those in nearby Mt. Pleasant. Fugitive slaves had been given shelter by some of Washington's earliest white settlers, and the small handful of free blacks who migrated into the county before the war found it possible to establish safe homes and profitable trades.[117]

But come war, white opposition to the burgeoning number of black migrants in the county became pronounced. Railing against having the former slaves in their midst, Washington Democrats helped organize a petition to the legislature to block further black migration into the state and prevent black competition for jobs and school integration. Nonetheless, in 1863 an AME missionary traveling through the town saw "a number" of new black residents. "A good number having escaped from bondage have come there and settled; they are all employed, and all seem to be doing well."[118] "Quite a number [of former slaves] by this time had arrived from the South and promised the lord that they would serve him if he would give them their liberty," recalled another observer. One local African American, George Black, helped organize the purchase of a church building in 1863 with the three hundred dollars in donations raised in a canvass of town residents.[119] Samuel Hall would be described by local historians as a "pillar" of this new church, which he later served as a member of its board of trustees and an organizer of its literary society.[120]

The black community in the town of Washington was much smaller than Mt. Pleasant's and did not develop as much infrastructure as its neighbor. The church would have been all the more important in the lives of Samuel Hall, his wife Millie (born in 1832), and their six children. Although the town's black population never exceeded one hundred, it was a tightly knit society that used its church as a community center and perhaps as a place of solace from the insults and denigration encountered from local whites. Within days of his arrival, Hall found work as a farm laborer (a job he held for four years), but hostile residents were asking his white employer why he was "taking a lot of damned 'niggers' out to his place to steal everything he had." Hall's editor noted: "At the beginning of his work in the north he had some little humiliations to endure, but they were as nothing to what he had had to endure as a slave so they seemed as comparatively nothing to him. They hurt his pride a little, but in doing that they spurred him to greater honorable effort in order that he might show the white men that there were some good negroes."[121] Among his legacies would be his memoir of life under slavery, published nearly forty years after the appearance of Moses Mosely's semiautobiographical exposition of slavery and citizenship.

IN 1884, WHEN Mosely published *The Colored Man of America as a Slave and a Citizen of the United States*, black America was at a crossroads. The twentieth anniversary of emancipation had been celebrated just the year before, when black communities across the nation had spent the day in remembrance of slavery, the wartime struggle for freedom, and the postemancipation fight for citizenship.[122] Generations of black leaders assembled to honor Frederick Douglass in Washington, D.C. Lincoln Day gatherings invoked an abolitionist legacy and charged participants with the work of "wiping out the color line." African American veterans marched under the auspices of black GAR posts; Decoration Day celebrations had taken on renewed meaning. Shortly afterward, however, the Supreme Court issued its ruling in *United States v. Stanley*, limiting enforcement of the Fourteenth Amendment to the individual states and thereby undermining federal responsibility for protecting black civil rights. The decision was a bleak capstone to two decades of struggle to define and defend black freedom. Some responded in 1883 as they had to the 1850 Fugitive Slave Law and the 1857 *Dred Scott* ruling: in concluding that there was no place in America for blacks who expected equality and equal citizenship. By the 1880s the back-to-Africa movement was gaining strength, and the separatist leanings of black cultural and political institutions had intensified.

Mosely addressed both the past and the present in his pamphlet. This anniversary of emancipation sharpened a lingering issue for black Americans: How would they remember slavery and the war? Here, Mosely's narrative is instructive, as he explores such pressing issues as how to remember slavery; how to think about the recent history of secession, war, and Reconstruction; and how to prepare for the future. While more expostulatory than autobiographical, his writing shares some of the essential structural elements of the slave narrative tradition, but it also departs from that tradition in notable ways. In common with the slave narrative genre, Mosely's essay offers a polyvocal "mixed form," moving between first-, second-, and third-person perspectives; incorporating excerpts from the popular press; and, on occasion, directly confronting former masters as well as white readers.[123] There are none of the authenticating attachments common among antebellum slave narratives; Mosely relies instead on the authority of his own assessment of the slave experience and, equally boldly, emphasizes the inevitability of God's apocalyptic judgment and vengeance for the sin of slavery—in the tradition of the black jeremiad.[124] If the treatise's expostulatory style makes it somewhat difficult to delineate the autobiographical content, *The Colored Man of America* still relies on personal experience and memory to provide guiding themes for contemporary race activists.

Mosely's pamphlet opens with a complex, finely tuned assessment of racist ideology in the age of black freedom. From the overt racist who opposed emancipation "at all hazards" to the white liberal who thought immediate emancipation might make the former slave "a dangerous pest," Mosely points out a wide range of public sentiments on the issue at the close of the Civil War.[125] Laying out a schemata of twelve classes with distinct opinions, he somewhat surprisingly points to one class "who kicked a little on the freedom of the colored man," a class made up of "a very small fraction of that portion of our own race" that was free before the war (or "partially free," as he puts it). "They were looked up to by the average slaves as their superiors; they were the big A's in colored societies."[126] Free blacks before the war enjoyed the many material advantages of freedom, despite their vulnerability to racism. When it came to emancipation, this class, Mosely observes,

> was only lukewarm on the subject; there was some danger of losing their position at the head of the colored columns to be succeeded by some raw slaves from the lower grades of the human family, and this of course was not at all desirable on their part. They seemed to think that their freedom would be impeded by such an influx of contrabands. Therefore their backs were a little up: they to [*sic*], complained of the contrabands swarming into towns and other public places, taking the work from free people and often making unbecoming remarks, such as "we are none of your low, contraband niggers; we came by our freedom honorably; our old master and mistress set us all free and gave us our free papers long ago." Says another, "I was born free." Says another "I bought my time from my master."[127]

Through this commentary, Mosely alerts the reader to significant differences among African American histories and opinions. He also signals his intimate knowledge of these conflicts, turning to the first-person voice for the first time in his extended essay. Although Mt. Pleasant had a small black population on the eve of the war, by the time of emancipation more than one hundred African Americans lived in the county, and by the end of the war that rapidly growing population included recently freed as well as free-born African Americans, some penniless farm laborers, but others who owned property and were skilled artisans. Some had migrated north from Missouri; others had relocated west from free black communities in Indiana and Ohio. Mosely reveals why these differences mattered—in part because they helped shape the experiences of recently emancipated blacks in upper midwestern towns and rural communities.

Although he is willing to criticize some blacks for their attitudes toward their recently freed brothers and sisters, Mosely declares that most of the efforts to "sink the colored man still lower in the scale of degradation and shame" could be blamed on slaveowners and the institution of slavery, as well as on legislators, businessmen, and clergy who had colluded in slavery's perpetuation. In light of the post-Reconstruction effort to "redeem" the image of the Old South, Mosely rejects the notion that slaveholders were "good Christians" and that bondage served as a useful "apprenticeship" for its victims. "Although a pupil of the institution for a long term of years," he writes, "I never could like it; because it was detrimental to the best interests of the colored man in every respect." Twenty years after emancipation, Mosely believed that it would take "generations" to wipe out slavery's "poisonous influence." After all, he notes, "We began low down in life, perhaps the lowest of all others—penniless, ignorant and inexperienced in the routine of business. . . . With a few exceptions we were only farm hands and field hands and accustomed to such work as was thought in former times to require no skilled mechanics."[128] Here he offers an aside: The occupational segregation that had marked black labor under slavery persisted, shaping the northern as well as the southern workplace.

Mosely's memory of the moment of emancipation offers a rare window into the most significant transition in the nation's history. The slave, he says, "had nothing, knew nothing and desired nothing but his freedom; he regarded it as a pearl of great price. Although nothing but freedom, it was marvelous in the imagination of the slave. It filled the soul for a while; there was but little room for anything else until some of the excitement had a chance to work off." Mosely asserts that both master and slave were unprepared for "the great event." The "humble slave" and "exalted tyrant" were "far from the mark by which true manhood is gauged." Although "unprepared to occupy our places as intelligent free citizens, we were all glad enough to get our liberty in the way it came." Asking only for "a living chance and untrammeled rights," he notes, "we were willing to take it in the rough and make the best of it we can by improvement."[129]

Turning from the past to the present, Mosely considers the best strategies for "the building up of our race and repairing as rapidly as possible the breach which has been made in it by slavery." He incorporates a laissez-faire liberal political tradition as well as a harsh, apocalyptic vision of the cost of slavery and postwar racist violence.[130] He argues that efforts aimed at racial advancement should focus on former slaves, "that class of citizens who are standing far in the rear on the account of being neglected in the past."[131] For Mosely, it was best to avoid the contemporary trend toward black nationalism or race organizing, what he characterizes as "a vain attempt to re-establish the color line." After all, men, women, and children were being murdered with impunity, while black citizens across the nation waited "patiently for party reforms and party justice."[132]

Mosely urges his fellow citizens to keep foremost their memory of slavery's inhumanity, the South's rebellion, as well as God's inevitable and miraculous judgment and vengeance on the perpetrators of slavery, secession, and war. Slavery's cost to the nation should be "ever remembered." Refusing to turn away from the memory of slavery's brutality, he offers a damning litany of its cruelties; in the style of the jeremiad, he is convinced that "God was present to behold all that was going on, . . . every sorrow and groan, . . . every falling tear, . . . every ounce of blood which the lash had drawn."[133] This sentiment was not only about the past, for the wartime destruction of slavery had not yet cleansed the sin of racism from the land. Violence continued in the post-Reconstruction South, where "colored men must still be shackled a little," in "a remnant of the old pro-slavery element still at work."[134]

According to Mosely, slavery's enduring impact could be seen in white attacks on black manhood. Slavery had deprived men of the ability to provide the necessities of life for their families and raise them up respectably; slavery barred them from any employment that whites considered too honorable for black men. Slavery kept slave and slave master alike "far from the mark by which manhood is gauged"—forcing white and black men into an equally degrading brotherhood of sorts.[135] Mosely calls directly on ex-masters to "act like men" by acknowledging their responsibility for slavery and the continued oppression of black men. All men should have the same chance; black men must have "free access to all that pertains to manhood."[136]

In making black manhood his central measure for the success of emancipation, Mosely does not consider the female "colored citizen." Instead, in referring to women, his focus is on the grieving slave mother, her children taken away and sold into the slave trade—a recurring image Mosely uses to emphasize what he clearly believes to have been one of the most damning features of slavery. But he mentions freedwomen rarely and then only as victims of white mob violence. The white abolitionist Harriet Beecher Stowe is alone among women whom he acknowledges as a participant in the destruction of slavery. Mosely apparently regarded African American women as peripheral figures in the battles over slavery's repercussions, emancipation's consequences, and citizenship's ongoing struggles. It is possible that his silence on the activism of African American women was an intentional expression of a gendered ideal that was both palatable to white readers and protectionist toward black women. Perhaps he believed that the ability to protect black women from public scrutiny was an ethic of black manhood.

His aversion to discussing the black female citizen required Mosely to ignore an obvious example from his own family. In his essay, he delineates the ability to attain intellectual culture as one measure of manhood, but his oldest daughter Susan—like her father, born in slavery—would move on to a successful career in education. The year after his essay was published, Susan became the first black student to be awarded a degree from Mt. Pleasant's Iowa Wesleyan College. A beneficiary of the statewide struggle against school segregation, which had opened public high schools to black students, she would be known as one of the state's preeminent advocates of black education. Susan taught school in Iowa for two years, completed a master's degree at Iowa Wesleyan in 1888, married an AME minister, and moved south with him to do educational and missionary work among southern blacks. Returning to Mt. Pleasant in 1896, she was one of the leading speakers at the Emancipation Day celebration. She was elected to preside over the state's first black collegiate fraternity and honorary society, organized in 1899.[137] In his essay, Mosely counsels his fellow citizens that "our children are to be cared for and raised right or they will be found wanting in the many trials of life." It is worth wondering if, in his daughter's achievements, Mosely was able to see incontrovertible evidence of his own success as a man.[138]

On his death in 1916, Mosely's hometown newspaper transposed caricature onto the citizen by describing him as "a type of the old southern slave."[139] He had been "a large powerful man, honest, generous, industrious and dependable . . . respected by all who knew him," qualities that the paper forced into a "type"—one familiar to white readers—that obliterated the intellectual achievements and political claims of a person who defined himself foremost as a citizen. More than thirty years earlier, Mosely had chided white readers for perpetrating the myth that the black man could aspire to be only "an intellectual dwarf and a muscled giant."[140] Ironically, the paper also observed that Mosely had hoped to publish, before his death, "his personal recollections of his life in slavery," which was "a tale of intense personal interest." Mosely seems to have died acutely aware of the ongoing struggle over the memory and history of slavery, hoping yet to contribute to it once again.

BETWEEN THE TWENTIETH anniversary of emancipation in 1883 and the fiftieth, in 1913, the battle for the nation's memory of slavery, war, and Reconstruction was fought—and largely won—by a segregated and reconciliationist vision of national reunion. While Mosely may have been pleased that a flourishing industry of Civil War reminiscences—rather than blanketed forgetfulness—emerged in the 1880s and 1890s, he would have been dismayed indeed at the content of the popularized memory that inspired sectional reunion. Lost Cause adherents portrayed a South of pleasant plantations, built memorials to faithful servants, and applauded professional historians who concluded that Reconstruction had been a "colossal mistake," absolving southern whites of the responsibility for slavery. Northern whites, for their part, helped create a voracious market for Civil War ephemera, memoir, and literature; they nurtured a sentimentality about heroic soldiering that ignored the root causes of the conflict.

Sectional reconciliation was accomplished at great cost, as revealed by a confluence of regressive developments: the Supreme Court's imprimatur on segregation (in 1883 by reversing the 1875 Civil Rights Act, and in 1896 by its decision in *Plessy v. Ferguson*) and the marked rise in lynching and other horrific violence that finished what new voting restrictions in southern states had started. At the turn of the century, then, sectional reunion pushed black America and black American memories of slavery, war, and Reconstruction to a segregated periphery.[141]

In this context, in March 1911, ninety-three-year-old Samuel Hall set about the business of offering his own remembrance of slavery, to be published shortly before the fiftieth anniversary of emancipation.[142] Hall intended, not to write about his achievements as a free man, but rather to recount his life as a slave. As his narrative reveals, he also wished to express his opinions on slavery at a time when white Americans mistakenly believed that they could "solve the Negro problem," as he put it, without directly addressing the painful history of American bondage. Hall's was not a "reconciliationist" point of view; in fact, his autobiography and the form it took when published challenges many scholarly generalizations about the postbellum slave narrative, even as it draws so obviously on the genre.

The writing and publication of Hall's life story was accomplished in part through his association with John Orville Elder, the white publisher of the

Washington Evening Journal. According to Elder (our only source, since Hall writes nothing of their relationship), the two became "rather intimately acquainted" before 1900, when Elder, who also ran a small grocery in town, began to buy produce from Hall. At some point after the turn of the century, Hall became interested in writing his memoirs and decided to enlist the support of Elder, whose newspaper business including a publishing firm. According to Elder, the project was, in fact, Hall's idea, and it was only with Hall's constant prodding that his memoirs were published in 1912. Hall would peddle the volume in eastern Iowa in the years to come.[143]

Elder was more than a mere publisher of the project, however. Hall's story, arranged and produced by Elder, includes fourteen pages of narrative "written by himself" in the first person, surrounded by twenty-seven pages of introductory and concluding biographical material and commentary drafted by Elder. Indeed, the Library of Congress catalog lists Elder as the book's sole author. In some ways, Elder's additions to the work resemble those that white abolitionists made to antebellum slave narratives (in the form of corroborating letters, prefaces, and appendices). In this instance, Elder provided considerable biographical detail that does not appear in Hall's narrative.[144] Yet his additions do not corroborate Hall's "authenticity" in the way that such evidence was intended to serve the antebellum narrative. Neither does Elder seem to use his contribution to the work to certify his own "abolitionist pedigree," in the way that William Greenleaf Eliot manipulated—indeed, commandeered—the postbellum narrative of Archer Alexander.[145] Perhaps Elder felt it necessary to elaborate on Hall's brief narrative in order to make the work publishable; at fourteen pages, Hall's "own story" would have been too slim to bring out on its own.

Although Elder does not elaborate on the reasons for his involvement in the project, he would later confess to having "inherited the ambition to write from my mother" and having written "several things which I have never been able to get anyone to publish."[146] Besides his work on Hall's narrative and a family history, Elder wrote and published a collection of short stories, a novel, and a travel account of the Hawaiian Islands.[147] It would appear that Elder sampled a wide range of genres, and that Hall's narrative might have offered an opportunity to further extend his writing experience. Other motivations may have also influenced his involvement. Elder's father had been an abolitionist who served in the Civil War; his mother was an enthusiastic temperance crusader. From both parents, then, Elder would have learned the importance of duty and "good works."[148] It is not surprising that he chose to respond to Hall's request for assistance, whether it was with an eye to service or to his own writerly ambitions—or perhaps of both. However sympathetic Elder may have been to Hall's project, a comparison of Hall's narrative to the material contributed by Elder reveals important differences in their perspectives on slavery. Those pages reveal Hall's likely authorship of the narrative's central section, for it suggests the difference made by firsthand experience.

Samuel Hall's own narrative, clearly offset in the book by the heading "Samuel Hall's Story" and by its use of the first person singular, begins as nearly all slave narratives do: "I was born. . . ." Despite his advanced age, Hall retained a detailed memory of his family's history. He was born on 7 May 1818 in North Carolina. His father had been kidnapped from Africa at age fifteen and, along with Hall's grandmother, was sold into slavery and brought to America. In her grief at being separated from her home and her husband, Hall's grandmother refused to work, refused to learn English, and died soon afterward. After providing this brief "post-memory," Hall recounts his own earliest childhood memories, involving his uncle, his mother, and his brothers. He makes memory an important theme in the narrative by emphasizing both his father's memories and his own, establishing a patrimony of witnessing to the experience of slavery.[149]

For his part, Elder presents a brief character study of Hall before turning to his early life, repeating many of the same facts provided by Hall but adding considerably more detail. While Hall was the source of all of this information, it was Elder who wrote the words. Elder drafted more than three pages of detailed family history describing Hall's childhood and the consequences of his owner's death for his family. Based on Hall's recollections, Elder makes three important points in this section, subtitled "A Piece of Property." First, he emphasizes the devotion of Hall's mother to her children. She was inherited by a clergyman who took his slaves from North Carolina to Xenia, Ohio, where he manumitted them, but she refused to leave her family behind; Hall's mother remained in North Carolina to be near her children, who were the property of a different owner. Second, Elder reveals the complicity of slave-owning women in the institution of slavery, explaining that Hall's subsequent master was married to a woman who prevented him from freeing his slaves. Lastly, Elder describes Samuel's life under his new master as a "happy one."[150] This last point is noteworthy because Hall, in his section of the narrative, attacks the ignorance that led northern white observers to "speak about [my people] being so happy. . . . They didn't realize what the burdens of the race were."[151] While Elder seems to imply that it was the individual slaveowner that made slavery a "happy" or "sad" experience, Hall insists that it was being subjected to slavery and the will of another that damned the institution as a whole. In this fashion—by correcting the errors introduced by Elder—Hall turns the question of authenticity and corroboration in the slave narrative tradition on its head. Hall has the authority of experience, postmemory, and collective memory, and he uses them to ammend Elder's inaccurate interpretation of slavery.

The next section of Hall's narrative condemns four of the ways in which slaveowners oppressed and exploited their human chattels, using examples from his own experience: keeping slaves "in darkness" by denying them education, treating them worse than animals by assigning them unreasonably difficult tasks, separating family members through sale, and violating the slave family by interfering with the father's authority over his children and by raping slave women.[152] Noting the popular defamation of black women as sexually promiscuous, Hall asks, "How could our women live virtuous lives with such treatment as they had to endure?" Even their resistance was futile: "I have known these slave holders to take and sell husband and wife away from each other just for spite when they would attempt to stand up for themselves."[153]

Hall and Elder, in their own parts of the narrative, turn next to Hall's first marriage. Hall starts his account by describing the external constraints on slave marriage. Although he and his wife lived together for almost twelve years, their marriage was severed after his master's death. His mistress—afraid of Hall, who "had been raised to know that I was a man,"—put him on the auction block and sold him away from his wife and family.[154] While Hall's version of this turn of events is brief, almost austere, Elder's is considerably more explicit.[155] Two of his pages elaborate, in novelistic detail, Hall's sale on the auction block and dramatize what Elder imagined Hall's emotions to have been: sullen, angry, rebellious—"His temper was aroused to such a pitch that he was like a wild animal in a cage."[156] Elder portrays Hall's unrestrained emotions as animal-like. In contrast, when Hall makes use of animal images in his narrative, it is to point out that slaveowners treated slaves as if they were animals. Adults were worked like horses; children were forced to feed like pigs at a trough and sold away from their mothers like a farmer sells a calf from a cow. In Hall's version, the emphasis is on the slaveowner's inhumane treatment, rather than the animalistic quality of the slave's emotional response.

Regarding the consequences of this sale on Hall's life, the former slave emphasizes his resistance and rebellion, whereas Elder stresses Hall's victimization. Hall describes three incidents in which he refused to be beaten or broken by his new master and the angry master's failed attempt to cut Hall's throat. Hall depicts each encounter with his master as a meeting between men;

he speaks directly to his master and in an almost offhand manner informs him that he will not be taken down. He repeatedly warns his master that he will kill him; he arms himself and prepares to fight back. Ultimately, Hall's master apologizes, "saying he was wrong and begging me to go back to work. . . . I never had any more trouble with him as long as I stayed," Hall maintains, as though it were his master who had been broken. Elder, on the other hand, makes no mention of these events.[157]

Hall also describes his second marriage, which took place during this time. Although he does not give his new wife's name, he notes the date of their wedding and the fact that they lived together for more than fifty years and had nine children—six of whom survived slavery. Hall discloses as well that his wife was a full cousin of his master's wife.

Elder recounts Hall's wartime experiences, his family's flight from slavery, and his postwar life in Washington, Iowa. Although this information comes both from Hall and from Elder's observations, Elder has absolute control over the presentation of these events, since Hall chooses not to write about his wartime or postwar involvements. According to Elder, early in the war Hall and other "reluctant slaves" were forced to work for the Confederate army. As Union forces approached Tennessee, he and fellow bondsmen were sent south as refugees; but before he had traveled far, Hall turned back and headed north toward freedom. Having learned about the Emancipation Proclamation, he believed he would be "permanently safe" with the Union army. No sooner did he make his way to local Union forces than he persuaded an armed guard to return with him to his master's plantation and help him claim his wife and children. Elder then describes a powerful last encounter with the former master: Hall "delivered himself a few thoughts that were not calculated to ease Wallace's peace of mind." The Union guard apparently urged Hall to beat Wallace, but Hall took his revenge in another way. He made his ex-master "hitch up his mules, load up his wagon with hams and bacon and include in the load Sam's wife and five children and haul them all over into the union lines." Within days, Hall and his family were traveling north by boat. Hall recalled that "as the boat pulled out into the river[,] the colored people sang the most beautiful song that he has ever heard."[158] Hall's family followed a path used by hundreds, if not thousands, of former slaves—through arrangements made with midwestern Union soldiers.[159]

Hall concludes his narrative with a section on "The Cruelties of Slavery." Here he draws attention to the violence of bondage. He recounts the murder of slaves by their owners—one, an old man; another, his wife's sister. Returning to the violation of slave families, he describes an incident in which his master whipped Hall's son and threatened to kill the boy if he told Hall about it. Hall also saw mothers "fall over in a dead faint when their children were sold away from them." Like Moses Mosely, Samuel Hall centers his discussion around the traumas of enslaved mothers. "Those mothers," Hall emphasizes, "loved their little children just the same as white mothers love their little babies"; some mothers went insane, just as Hall's own mother did when her children were sold away. In relating the mistreatment of children, he says "they were raised to do just like what you would tell a dog to do."[160]

As Hall ends his narrative, he addresses the white reader directly: "Now I want to know what the reader thinks of the inhuman treatment towards my people when your people went into the wilds of Africa and brought the Negroes here . . . and placed him as a slave and kept him in bondage nigh unto three centuries; used them like a dog, yes placed him even lower than a dog, used him to his own advantage and yet," Hall charges, "they want the Negro problem solved." "Tell me," he demands of his imagined white readers, "what the Negro has done to make him a slave?" Hall was unequivocal and unrelenting in judging the sins of slaveowners and their brutal treatment of families—adults and children alike.[161]

Hall's narrative departs significantly from scholars' characterizations of the postbellum slave narrative. In his work, there is no reunion, no postwar story of uplift, and no effort to find a usable past in the slave experience. The entire narrative is a portrayal of bondage as a horrific institution. Hall denounces slavery and slaveowners; he never alludes to the postwar achievements of former slaves. He also challenges some of the misinterpretations made by his white collaborator, a criticism that extends to all northern whites who subscribed to the plantation school's depiction of happy slaves. Hall's narrative emphatically recalls a past that, by the turn of the century, much of the nation found too painful to remember.

Elder chose to bracket "Samuel Hall's story as written by himself" with more of his own writing. Because Hall was "rather meagre in his details" about his life after gaining his freedom, Elder elaborates on Hall's wartime and postwar experiences. The brief biographical information that Elder provides helps to locate Hall in the unwritten, largely forgotten history of former slaves and their diaspora to the upper Midwest.[162] But just as Elder slighted Hall's agency in contesting the power of his former masters, so he glosses over his battle with racism in his new Iowa home. What Elder blithely refers to as one of the "little humiliations" that Hall and his family were forced to endure, an "objection in the district on the part of some of the families to permitting the Negroes to go to school with their children," was in fact a personal and public confrontation with community-supported segregation. As late as 1863, a black visitor had described the town as "the right kind of place for our people," at least in part because African Americans had access to public schools "without any restriction."[163] But by 1865, in response to wartime black migration, Washington's white residents decided to segregate their schools. As a result, the school board rented a room for black students in Washington's new AME church.[164]

Dissatisfied with this inequitable arrangement, Hall, in the late 1860s or early 1870s, tried to enroll his children in one of the county's rural white schools. He was not the only black parent to do so. In December 1870, Wesley Moore, another "pillar" of the AME church, attempted to enroll his son in the (white) public school. A controversy ensued over which white child would be made to sit next to a black one. The school board soon became involved, dictating new seating arrangements in the classroom. The dispute apparently continued for some time, and its resolution is unclear in local records.[165] However, it is from these local records, not from Elder's account, that we learn the extent of white opposition to integration. Elder implies that there was official white support for Hall's efforts and that everyone was happily reconciled before a month had passed. What Elder so easily passes off as "some little humiliations" was part of a recurring pattern of discrimination that shaped postwar life and opportunities in Iowa, as it did throughout the upper Midwest. To understand the meaning of this struggle for Hall, we might take our cue from his narrative. Hall valued education very highly and viewed the South's denial of schooling for slaves as a way of keeping them "in the darkness." "From the day they shut off the learning from the Negro they began to bind them tighter" in slavery, he asserts.[166] Elder points out that Hall "always felt that education was the one thing that was needed to bring his people up," yet he excludes from his account Hall's challenge to school segregation.[167]

This brings us to the question of facts and authenticity in this postbellum slave narrative. Samuel Hall and Orville Elder chose to stress different kinds of information in their accounts of Hall's life as a slave, and their choices are telling. Elder clearly took it upon himself to fill in names, dates, and locations—all, of course, gathered from Hall himself in conversations or interviews that neither writer makes note of. It appears that Elder viewed the purpose of the postbellum slave narrative to be primarily biographical, whereas Hall intended it to document slavery's many wrongs and the cruelty of slaveowners.

Written at a moment in history when white Americans had willingly suspended their knowledge of and connection to slavery, Hall's narrative can be seen as a deliberative act of resistance against the tide of national forgetting. Although Elder seems unaware of it, Hall's account mirrors the commemorative work of other black midwesterners who also insisted, in private and in public arenas, that the nation remember slavery, the sins of white southerners, the bravery of black soldiers on Civil War battlefields, the national failures of Reconstruction. The more acceptable reconciliation had become to white Americans, the more demonstrative black midwesterners were in remembering and honoring their past. Throughout the fifty years following the end of the war, black midwesterners participated in the struggle over public memory. In Iowa, they insisted on including the remaining veterans of the state's black regiment in the 1894 Flag Day celebrations, they fought to integrate the state's GAR posts, they turned out en masse to hear Judge Albion Tourgée speak about a past that must be remembered, they continued to organize Emancipation Day celebrations. Into the 1890s, the *Iowa Bystander*, the state's black newspaper, carried stories about families who finally had tracked missing and separated members and were reunited for the first time since slavery. And, in a final testament to Iowa's men and women who had lived under slavery, well into the twentieth century the *Iowa Bystander* printed respectful obituaries giving precise accounts of the violence and brutality that these former slaves had once endured.[168]

THE MEANINGS OF American slavery and emancipation among the black residents of the upper Midwest would not fade easily, thanks to postbellum memoirs; the recollections circulated among veterans, their friends, and families; the obituaries that persistently documented the trauma of slavery; and the Emancipation Day celebrations that were a regular feature of the region's commemorative calendar. But it is striking that, as prevalent and dogged as were these efforts to sustain slavery in collective memory, there seems to have been no corresponding memory of the wide-ranging Reconstruction-era activism for citizenship and civil rights. These are downplayed in Samuel Hall's narrative, and they are rarely referred to in post–Reconstruction Emancipation Day speeches or obituaries recounting the achievements of former slaves and their descendants. The postwar challenges to white racism—to expand the meaning of black freedom, to claim and defend black citizenship—apparently had no Clio in the region's black communities. For their part, white midwesterners preferred to remember that theirs had been among the first northern states to enfranchise northern black men, substituting that complicated political compromise for the long history of white resistance to black citizenship in the region. But African Americans themselves seem to have paid remarkably little commemorative attention to the activism of their forebears in carving out a fuller citizenship.

For the historian, silence is a tricky thing to interpret. In this instance, however, silence about the postemancipation struggles of African Americans in the upper Midwest must shape our understanding of the history and memory of slavery. For the region's more recent arrivals as well as its longer-term black residents, the trauma, memory, and continued effects of slavery (especially the racism that had sustained it) seem to have been more crucial to their collective identity than the memory of postwar activism. Perhaps this was because African Americans, even in the ostensibly unlikely location of the upper Midwest, saw slavery as "ground zero"—not only for their past, but also for their present and future. They may have viewed their activism in courtrooms, voting booths, public streets, and congregations at its most fundamental: as an effort to heal and redress the personal experience and national sin and shame of slavery. Indeed, by linking their second-class citizenship in the North and their enslavement (whether in the South, the East, or the upper Midwest), African Americans in the upper Midwest were defining slavery and emancipation as national events with inseparable national consequences. Modern historians would do well to follow their lead.

Epilogue

Emancipation and Reconstruction brought short-term and long-term consequences to the upper Midwest. Black freedom, migration, and relocation to Iowa, Minnesota, and Wisconsin had unprecedented social and cultural repercussions. For antebellum African American residents of the region, local slavery and the attenuated nature of black freedom were both superseded by the immediacy of southern slavery's wartime collapse and destruction, the call to military service, and the wider citizenship claims that black men's military service seemed to imply. In the South, thousands of men, women, and their families used war's confusion and chaos to their advantage as they fled their masters and either made their own way north into the upper Mississippi valley or found temporary safety in Union army camps. From the camps, many were relocated to the upper Midwest.

This geographic dislocation of former slaves, which accelerated when women and children overwhelmed the ability and willingness of Union military officials to cope with them, contributed to the social dislocation that emancipation induced—even in the Midwest. Across the North, white Americans contemplated—and feared—how black freedom would alter the prerogatives that they had so long enjoyed. Although many northern whites developed sympathy for southern slaves over the course of the war and supported humanitarian efforts on their behalf, when those same former slaves migrated to the upper Midwest, emancipation suddenly became a vigorously debated issue of public policy at the local, regional, and national levels.

To northern whites, the *physical* mobility of African Americans also suggested their potential *social* mobility; whites feared black encroachment on what had been a freely exercised custom of white privileges and domination. Wartime black migration forced into the open the extent to which white midwesterners claimed white supremacy and were willing to defend it. As a consequence, racial hostility directed at black newcomers intensified during and immediately after the war. Whites, too, were targeted. Volunteers who aided in relocation efforts, women and men who hired black workers, and even white soldiers who returned from the South with former slaves to employ as servants and farmhands were derided in the press, visited by threatening mobs, and in some instances became the victims of mob violence.

The regional and local racial prerogatives and hierarchies that emancipation seemed to threaten were indeed dislocated and renegotiated as longtime black residents, black veterans, and black newcomers set out to make their freedom real. Their struggles—which initiated a long-term process of redefining and extending citizenship—were reinforced by federal Reconstruction policy in the South. Northern Republicans could not afford the political risk of imposing black enfranchisement on the South while failing to endorse it in the North. Neither could they rationalize the denial of citizenship's prerogatives to black men who had so willingly accepted citizenship's obligations and risks in military service to their country. By the close of the Civil War, the national debates over the extent and form of the Reconstruction amendments, federal initiatives, and legislation were assessed, by upper midwesterners, not just in terms of their likely impact on the South, but on the North as well.

"Northern Reconstruction" may seem like an oxymoron: Northern states had not seceded, so there was no debate over how they might be brought back into the Union. But what does Reconstruction mean? For most scholars, the evolution of Reconstruction legislation in the South and federal policy over the return of seceded states to the Union no longer defines the parameters of the era. An entire generation of scholarship has recentered historians' attention to include the experiences of all those who lived through this era, especially the freed women and men who ensured the destruction of slavery in the South. *Emancipation's Diaspora*, with its story of emancipation's very real consequences in the North and the ensuing conflicts between African Americans and whites, as well as between black men and women over the meaning of citizenship, reveals that the history of slavery, emancipation, and Reconstruction was national in scope. Just as American slavery defined the meaning of freedom for all Americans, so the destruction of American slavery reverberated across the nation and shaped the historical experience of what race was understood to mean for all Americans. Emancipation did not depend on an African American diaspora into the upper Midwest to have deep consequences there, but black migration exacerbated and exaggerated what white midwesterners had anticipated and feared.

Notes

ABBREVIATIONS

BAP	C. Peter Ripley, ed., *The Black Abolitionist Papers*
BPL	Burlington Public Library, Burlington, Iowa
CWPF	Civil War Pension Files, RG 15
DOM	Department of the Missouri
FWP	Federal Writers' Project
IML	Iowa Masonic Library, Cedar Rapids, Iowa
ISA	Illinois State Archives, Springfield
IWA	Iowa Women's Archives, University of Iowa, Iowa City
KPL	Keokuk Public Library, Keokuk, Iowa
LC	Library of Congress, Washington, D.C.
LCHS	Lee County Historical Society, Keokuk, Iowa
MHS	Minnesota Historical Society, St. Paul
MO/SA	Missouri State Archives, St. Louis
MO/SHS	Missouri State Historical Society, St. Louis
Musser	Musser Public Library, Muscatine, Iowa
NA	National Archives, Washington, D.C.
NACW	National Association of Colored Women's Clubs
NPS	National Park Service, U.S. Department of the Interior
NVHM	Nodaway Valley Historical Museum, Clarinda, Iowa
OR	U.S. War Department, *The War of the Rebellion: A Compilation of the Official Records of the Union and Confederate Armies*, 128 vols., Washington, D.C., Government Printing Office, 1880–1901. *OR* citations take the following form: volume number (part number, where applicable): page number. Unless otherwise indicated, all volumes cited are from series 1.
RG 15	Record Group 15: Records of the Veterans Administration, NA RG 94 Record Group 94: Records of the Adjutant General's Office, 1780s–1917, NA
RG 108	Record Group 108: Records of the Headquarters of the Army, NA
RG 393	Record Group 393: Records of U.S. Army Continental Commands, 1821–1920, NA
SC/UI	Special Collections, University of Iowa, Iowa City
SHS/DM	State Historical Society of Iowa, Des Moines
SHS/IC	State Historical Society of Iowa, Iowa City
URR	Underground Railroad Binder, NVHM
UWDC	University of Wisconsin Digital Collections
WHMC/C	Western Historical Manuscript Collection, Columbia, Mo.
WHMC/SL	Western Historical Manuscript Collection, St. Louis
WHS	Wisconsin Historical Society, Madison

INTRODUCTION

1. See, e.g., Berlin et al., *Slaves No More*; Hahn, *Nation under Our Feet*; Hunter, *To 'Joy My Freedom*; Bercaw, *Gendered Freedoms*; Frankel, *Freedom's Women*; Schwalm, *"A Hard Fight for We"*; Thomas J. Brown, *Reconstructions*.

2. *Harper's Weekly*, 28 June 1862; Voegeli, *Free but Not Equal*; Lofton, "Northern Labor and the Negro"; Bernstein, *New York City Draft Riots*.

3. This process has been most clearly revealed by the fine work of Joanne Pope Melish in *Disowning Slavery*. See also Leslie M. Harris, *In the Shadow of Slavery*; Berlin, *Many Thousands Gone*; Hodges, *Root and Branch*; Nash and Soderlund, *Freedom by Degrees*; Zilversmit, *First Emancipation*; Litwack, *North of Slavery*; Shane White, *Somewhat More Independent*.

4. See, e.g., Cohen, *At Freedom's Edge*.

5. Frey, *Water from the Rock*; Schama, *Rough Crossings*.

6. Tadman, *Speculators and Slaves*; Deyle, *Carry Me Back*; Walter Johnson, *Soul by Soul*.

7. Voegeli, "A Rejected Alternative"; Faulkner, *Women's Radical Reconstruction*; Michael P. Johnson, "Out of Egypt."

8. U.S. Census Bureau, State and County QuickFacts. In 1870, those percentages were .0048 (Iowa), .0017 (Minnesota), and .002 (Wisconsin).

9. Finkelman, "Evading the Ordinance" and "Slavery, the 'More Perfect Union' "; Ekberg, "Black Slavery in Illinois"; Grivno, " 'Black Frenchmen' " and "African-Americans at Fort Snelling"; VanderVelde and Subramanian, "Mrs. Dred Scott"; Spangler, *Negro in Minnesota*, 19–21; Dykstra, *Bright Radical Star*, 3–5; Williams-Searle, "Intimate Empires."

10. See, e.g., the otherwise excellent studies by Wang, *Trial of Democracy*, and McPherson, *Struggle for Equality*.

11. See, e.g., Davison M. Douglas, *Jim Crow Moves North*, and Fishel, "North and the Negro."

12. Schwalm, "Emancipation Day Celebrations"; Kachun, *Festivals of Freedom*; Fabre and O'Meally, *History and Memory*; Blight, *Race and Reunion*.

CHAPTER 1

1. *Iowa State Bystander*, 18 Feb. 1898; Rev. J. B. Rogers, *War Pictures*, 126–29, and photograph, RG 98S-CWP 145.54, U.S. Army Military History Institute (Carlisle, Pa.); affidavit by Jane Morgan, 11 Mar. 1874, pension file of Alfred Morgan, Mother C 167990, CWPF; notes by Board of Review, 14 Aug. 1918, 4 May 1920, pension file of Walter Bucklin, WC 892542, CWPF. The people named in this chapter were all migrants to the upper Midwest.

2. *Dubuque Daily Express and Herald*, 17 June 1857; *Delavan Enterprise*, 13 Feb. 1986 (second quotation, by Oscar McClellan).

3. Orville Elder, *Samuel Hall*.

4. *Delavan Enterprise*, 13 Feb. 1986; *Christian Recorder*, 25 Aug. 1866 (Titus and Ellen Shropshire); William Brown, *Life Story*; affidavit by Nathaniel Adams, 9 Feb. 1889, pension file of Adams, IC 472578, CWPF; deposition by Fannie Robinson (née Jackson),

12 Oct. 1904, pension file of John R. Robison, WC 586639, CWPF; Clarissa Cox obituary, *Newton Record*, 24 Feb. 1898; Charles Thompson, *Biography of a Slave*; Rawick, *American Slave*, 115. William Wells Brown (*Narrative*) writes eloquently of his observations of the Mississippi valley slave trade.

5. As Walter Johnson has noted, "The history of the slave trade is as much the story of those left behind as it is the story of those carried away" (*Soul by Soul*, 41). Jonathan D. Martin makes the same point about the experience of slave hiring; see *Divided Mastery*, esp. chap. 2.

6. Orville Elder, *Samuel Hall*, 29–30.

7. This includes both civilians and former slaves who enlisted in the Union army once arriving in Iowa.

8. On the sale of slaves out of Virginia, see Tadman, *Speculators and Slaves*; Deyle, *Carry Me Back*; and Gumestad, *Troublesome Commerce*.

9. In 1850, white migrants born in Virginia were most likely to choose Kentucky, followed by Tennessee and Missouri, as their destinations in the slave South. Virginians were especially drawn to Missouri's most slave-intense regions—the bottomlands of the Missouri and Mississippi rivers. This migratory flow contributed to the growth of Missouri's white population (which nearly doubled between 1820 and 1860), as well as its slave population (which increased more than tenfold during the same period). On migration out of Virginia, see Fischer and Kelley, *Bound Away*, 231, 135–80. Missouri's slave population was concentrated in the Missouri River region known as "Little Dixie," where the slave population on the eve of the Civil War ranged from 22 to 37 percent. St. Louis (both the city and the county) also held a significant slave population. (On Missouri slavery, see Hurt, *Agriculture and Slavery*, esp. chap. 9; on St. Louis, 217, 220–23).

10. Tadman, *Speculators and Slaves*, 138, 147.

11. Ibid., 175.

12. Tadman (*Speculators and Slaves*, 31) places his estimate at 30 to 40 percent, but more recently Walter Johnson (*Soul by Soul*, 6–7) estimates that in addition to the two-thirds of a million people "moved through the interstate trade, there were twice as many who were sold locally. Sales from neighbor to neighbor, state-supervised probate and debt sales, or brokered sales within a single state do not yet show up in the statistics that have been used to measure the extent and magnitude of the slave trade."

13. Affidavit by Henry Vance, 25 Jan. 1893, pension claim of Frederick Douglass, Father C 367268, CWPF; Mrs. Kate Thompson obituary, *Iowa State Bystander*, 18 Feb. 1898.

14. Martin, *Divided Mastery*, 36–38.

15. William Brown, *Life Story*, 3–12.

16. Martin, *Divided Mastery*, 8. An excellent overview can also be found in King, *Stolen Childhood*, 102–8.

17. Undated clipping, *Page County Democrat*, URR; Rosa Dandridge Pryor, "The Dandridge Family History" (typewritten MS, 1971), pp. 11–12, box 1, Harper Papers, IWA.

18. Robinson, *From Log Cabin to the Pulpit*, 29, 40.

19. Orville Elder, *Samuel Hall*, 22.

20. See, e.g., Michael McManus's claim that slavery "had vanished from Wisconsin" by 1844 in *Political Abolitionism*, 3.

21. For example, while Illinois territorial law permitted African Americans to hold other blacks in bondage, they were not permitted to hold whites in servitude (N. Dwight Harris, *History of Negro Servitude*, 9).

22. The territory included in the "Illinois Country" changed over time; initially referring to the small section of southwestern Illinois first explored by the French in 1673, the lands it referred to expanded, sometimes extending to the Rocky Mountains; at other times it was regarded as the southern border of "New France," or the northern border of Louisiana. After the British acquired the region in 1763, it was regarded as the territory bordered on the west by the Mississippi River, on the east by the Wabash, on the north by the Illinois, and to the south by the Ohio (Ekberg, *French Roots*; Alvord, *Illinois Country*).

23. Ekberg, *French Roots*, 150–53.

24. Murphy, *Gathering of Rivers*; Magnaghi, "Red Slavery."

25. Finkelman, "Evading the Ordinance" and "Slavery, the 'More Perfect Union'"; Ekberg, "Black Slavery in Illinois."

26. N. Dwight Harris, *History of Negro Servitude*, 6–67. See also Williams-Searle, "Intimate Empires."

27. N. Dwight Harris, *History of Negro Servitude*, 7–14, 99–107; Database of Servitude and Emancipation Records, ISA. Illinois laws governing black servitude are well cataloged in Middleton, *Black Laws*, 269–342.

28. I use "white supremacy" to refer to a dynamic ideology that asserted the social, cultural, and biological superiority of whites relative to other "racial" groups. On white supremacy and the Midwest, see Litwack, *North of Slavery*; Berwanger, *Frontier against Slavery*; Voegeli, *Free but Not Equal*; Rosenberg, *Iowa on the Eve of the Civil War*; Arnie Cooper, "Stony Road"; and Dykstra, *Bright Radical Star*. Useful state histories include Noyes, "Negro in Wisconsin's Civil War Effort," 71–72, and Bergmann, *Negro in Iowa*.

29. On the development and prevalence of slavery in upper Mississippi valley forts, see Grivno, "'Black Frenchmen'" and "African-Americans at Fort Snelling"; VanderVelde and Subramanian, "Mrs. Dred Scott"; Spangler, *Negro in Minnesota*, 19–21; and Dykstra, *Bright Radical Star*, 3–5. Fragmentary evidence makes it difficult to ascertain the exact number of enslaved people at these forts, but snapshots are provided by census data. For example, the Wisconsin Territorial Census for 1836 shows 17 slaves among the 313 residents at Fort Crawford (WHS, *First Wisconsin Territorial Census*, 254). The federal census for 1850 shows, in the village of Fort Winnebago, Wis., 17 black residents, of whom 8 had been born in slave states—such as Jim and Jack Reed, teenagers boarding with the white Reed family—and gave New Orleans as their place of birth (Ancestry.com, *1850 United States Federal Census*). Also on Fort Winnebago, see Rev. E. Mathews, *Autobiography*, 124–25.

30. Harriet and Dred Scott were among Taliaferro's slaves at Fort Snelling (VanderVelde and Subramanian, "Mrs. Dred Scott," 1048–49).

31. *Daily State Register*, 31 Mar. 1869.

32. According to the federal census of 1810 for Hendersonville, Ky., Posey owned eleven slaves. Patsey's name appears as both "Patsey" and "Patsy" in the historical record.

33. Indiana territorial law stated that male indentured servants could serve until age 35, females until age 32; children born in slavery could be made to serve thirty years. See

N. Dwight Harris, *History of Negro Servitude*. Paragraph 2, Article IV, of the 1818 Illinois Constitution provided the exception for Shawneetown slaveowners.

34. In two cases (*Cornelius v. Walsh*, Breese 92 [1825], and *Boon v. Juliet, a woman of color*, I Scammon 258 [1836]), Illinois courts rejected a master's claim to the labor of his servant's children, but these rulings were based on procedural error and an instance where the children had been born prior to the passage of the indentured servitude law. See Middleton, *Black Laws*, 333–40.

35. WHS, *First Wisconsin Territorial Census*, 254.

36. *Daily State Register*, 3 Feb. 1867; Porter, *Annals of Polk County*, 904.

37. Dykstra, *Bright Radical Star*, 45; Welty, *Fair Field*, 103–4; *History of Jefferson County*, 420–21.

38. George Wilson, "First Territorial Adjutant"; Rayman, "Joseph Montfort Street"; Howard, "Des Moines Negro"; Ancestry.com, *1810 United States Federal Census*, Henderson, Ky., *1820 United States Federal Census*, Gallatin County, Ill., *1830 United States Federal Census*, Crawford County, Mich., WHS, *First Wisconsin Territorial Census*, *1850 United States Federal Census*, Wapello County, Iowa, and *1860 United States Federal Census*, Keokuk, Lee County, Iowa; Servitude and Emancipation Records, Slave Register, Gallatin County, 1:44, 50, ISA.

39. Berwanger, *Frontier against Slavery*; Davidson, *Negro Slavery in Wisconsin*, 218; Workers of the Writers' Program, WPA, *Negroes of Nebraska*.

40. Essie M. Britton, "The Negro in Iowa: History of the Colored Race of People Residing in Keokuk and Vicinity" and "Freedom for the Negroes," WPA notes, and clipping, *Daily Gate City*, 13 Apr. 1939, all in "Ethnography-Negroes," KPL; entry for June 1835, Mrs. Caroline Phelps Diary, transcribed by Bridgett Williams Searle, in author's possession; *History of Jefferson County*, 166–70.

41. Porter, *Annals of Polk County*, 904 (Samuel Cochran); *History of Johnson County, Iowa*, 463 ("Uncle" Cassius); Britton, "The Negro in Iowa" (the Jackson family); Davidson, *Negro Slavery in Wisconsin*, 211–14 ("Bart" Hannah, the Jones siblings, the Godar family), 218 (America and family), 214 (Proctor); photograph of Jerry Seers, R. James and Abby Mendenhall Papers, MHS (Jerry Seers); Edna L. Jones, *Nathan Littler's History*, 82 (Henry Hannah); Mrs. Caroline Phelps Diary, transcribed by Bridgett Williams-Searle ("Black" Charlotte); *1850 United States Federal Census*, Wayne County, Iowa; Howell and Smith, *History of Decatur County*, 1:184 (Moses Franklin).

42. Essie M. Britton, "Freedom for the Negroes," WPA notes, and clipping, *Daily Gate City*, 13 Apr. 1939, both in "Ethnography-Negroes," KPL; "A Slave Owner in Iowa," *Palimpsest*; Davidson, *Negro Slavery in Wisconsin*, 211–14; Rev. Edward Mathews, *American Slavery and the War*, 4–5; *Lyons Mirror*, 26 Nov. 1857; *Iowa Weekly Citizen*, 2 Dec. 1857. Many slaves were also taken to Minnesota by vacationing southern slaveowners; see Spangler, *Negro in Minnesota*, 24–29. The Wisconsin State Historical Society's online "Dictionary of Wisconsin History," <http://www.wisconsinhistory.org/dictionary> (15 June 2008) notes, under its heading "Slavery in Wisconsin," that "between 90 and 100 slaves" were taken to Wisconsin during its territorial era.

43. From as early as 1807 until the Civil War, Missouri law allowed enslaved people to challenge their status in courts if they could provide evidence that they were wrongfully

held as slaves. Until 1845, the law also permitted enslaved plaintiffs to apply, as paupers, for court-appointed attorneys. Many of these suits were initiated in the St. Louis circuit courts, where almost three hundred suits were pressed by enslaved people. See St. Louis Circuit Court Historical Records Project, MO/SA.

44. However, Finkelman notes that between 1837 and 1852, no significant freedom suits were brought before the Missouri Supreme Court (*Imperfect Union*, 218–28). The other southern states ruling favorably on freedom suits until the 1840s were Kentucky, Louisiana, and Mississippi.

45. *Rachel, a woman of color, v. Walker, William* (November 1834), *Henry, James, a boy of color, v. Walker, William* (November 1834), *Peter, a man of color v. Richardson, John* (November 1841), and *Milly, a woman of color v. Duncan, James* (November 1835), all in St. Louis Circuit Court Historical Records Project, MO/SA; Catrerall and Hayden, *Judicial Cases*, 116–17. All of the plaintiffs experienced retaliation by their owners for having filed suit. Milly testified to having begun her effort to gain her freedom in Dubuque and to being removed to St. Louis as a result; Peter said he had been imprisoned for a year.

46. Acton and Acton, "A Legal History of African-Americans," 62–65 (Rachel Bundy, Ralph, Jim White); Dykstra, *Bright Radical Star*, 7–18; Davidson, *Negro Slavery in Wisconsin*, 214; Parish, *George Wallace Jones*, 66 (Paul Jones).

47. Dykstra, *Bright Radical Star*, 27, refers to Iowa's 1839 "sojourners provision." Rhode Island, Pennsylvania, New York, Indiana, and Iowa were among the northern states explicitly providing for the right of slaveowners to retain their slave property while temporarily visiting or traveling through a free state. Other states, including Minnesota, Wisconsin, Ohio, and Illinois, had no explicit law but permitted the practice. Most northern courts protected sojourners' rights until the 1830s, when Massachusetts (1836), Connecticut (1837), Pennsylvania and New York (1840s), Ohio (1857), and Vermont (1858) revoked either the law or the practice allowing southern slaveowners to retain claim to their slave property, even during periods of transit or temporary residence. Don Fehrenbacher and William Wiecek see this change as a sign of increasing sectional conflict. Iowa legislators chose to pass such a law in light of the trend away from protections for sojourning slaveowners. See Fehrenbacher, *Dred Scott Case*, 54–57, 60–61, 611 n.17; Wiecek, *Sources of Antislavery Constitutionalism*, 53, 142–43, 195; Finkelman, *Imperfect Union*; Christy M. Clark, "Business of Slavery."

48. *In re the matter of Ralph* (1839); *Rachel [Bundy] v. William Walker* (1836). Sojourner protections were claimed as late as 1860 (although unsuccessfully) by a Colonel Christmas in his effort to retain claim over Eliza Winston, a slave he took to Lake Harriet, Minn., to join other summering southern slaveowners. For comments on slaveowners who vacationed in Minnesota, see Potter, *101 Best Stories*, 124–27; Hiram Stevens, *History of the Bench*, 1:30–36; Spangler, *Negro in Minnesota*, 28–32; Hennessy, *Past & Present*, 24–29; *Stillwater Democrat*, 19 May 1860; *Daily Hawk-Eye and Telegraph*, 13 June 1857; *St. Paul Pioneer Press*, 5 May 1895. For examples of midwestern slaveowners illegally evading the distinction between sojourning and permanent residence, see Walker, *Free Frank*, 76.

49. Ancestry.com, *1850 United States Census, 1860 United States Census, 1870 United States Census*, Muscatine County; Anderson obituary, A. Clark file; Musser, *History of Muscatine County*, 528; *Portrait and Biographical Album of Muscatine County, Iowa*, 220; Dykstra, *Bright Radical Star*, 14.

50. Olive Cole Smith, *Mt. Pleasant*, 15–16; *Portrait and Biographical Album of Henry County*, 474; Genealogy.com, <http://www.slaveryinamerica.org/geography/slave_laws_VA.htm>.

51. For Kentucky law pertaining to free blacks, see Walker, *Free Frank*, 64, and Berwanger, *Frontier against Slavery*, 36 n.17. On the Gillihans and their slaves, see memoir and clippings, URR.

52. Harry Herndon Polk, "Old Fort Des Moines," SHS/IC; Porter, *Annals of Polk County*, 904.

53. Undated clipping, Richter Papers, SHS/IC.

54. Ancestry.com, *1840 United States Federal Census*, Windsor County, Morgan County, *Iowa State Census*, Cedar Rapids, Linn County, 1856, and *1860 United States Federal Census*, Muscatine, Muscatine County; *Phylaxis* 2, no. 2 (March 1975): 62–65; Old Settlers Register, p. 83, Musser; "Bio. Notes—A. Clark," A. Clark File, Musser; *History of Muscatine County*, 598; Census for 1846, Auditor's Office, Johnson County; Nosek, "Historical Detective Work." Patrick Cheadle's given and surname are spelled variously in census records (Paddock, Paddick, Cheidle, etc.).

55. Clipping, *Burlington Hawk-Eye*, 12 Aug. 1971, in "Race Relations" clippings file, Musser; *Daily Hawk-Eye*, 12 Sept. 1863.

56. Steinfield, *Invention of Free Labor*; Thornbrough, *Negro in Indiana*; N. Dwight Harris, *History of Negro Servitude*; Melish, *Disowning Slavery*; Finkelman, "Evading the Ordinance."

57. Aurner, *Leading Events in Johnson County*, 463–64; Ancestry.com, *1860 United States Federal Census*, Johnson County, Iowa; *Daily Iowa State Register*, 14, 21, 28 Feb. 1860; *Linn County Register*, 11 Feb. 1860; *Franklin Record*, 5 Mar. 1860.

58. Herbert M. Hoke, "Negroes in Iowa: Evidence of Negroes Here in the Early Days," typescript MS, 7 May 1940, WPA Federal Writers' Project, Iowa, SC/UI.

59. Clippings File, Afro-Americans, SHS/IC.

60. Davidson, *Negro Slavery in Wisconsin*, 211–14 ("Bart" and the Jones siblings); Edna L. Jones, *Nathan Littler's History*, 82 (Henry Hannah); Ancestry.com, *1850 United States Federal Census*, Keokuk, Lee County (Augustus Tindle), and Wayne County; Howell and Smith, *History of Decatur County*, 1:184 (Moses Franklin). Among the unnamed children was a ten-year-old boy purchased at Iowa City by O. H. W. Stull, the secretary of Iowa Territory, in 1841; Stull subsequently sold the young boy to his brother-in-law in Maryland (Stiles, *Recollections*, 10, 14).

61. Melish, *Disowning Slavery*.

62. As Leslie Harris (*In the Shadow of Slavery*, 12) notes, "The system of racial slavery became the foundation of New Yorkers' definitions of race, class, and freedom far into the nineteenth century."

63. Over 3,500 African Americans remained in bondage in northern states as of 1830; New Jersey and New York, the largest slaveowning states of the North, did not abolish slavery until 1827 and 1846, respectively. See McManus, *Black Bondage in the North*.

64. *Daily Express and Herald*, 17 June 1857.

65. Green, "Race and Segregation"; Spangler, *Negro in Minnesota*, 27–40.

66. *National Era*, 29 Oct. 1857; Libman, "Minnesota and the Struggle," 11, 14–15, 38; McManus, *Political Abolitionism*; Dykstra, *Bright Radical Star*.

67. Erbe, "Militia under the Constitution of Iowa"; Dykstra, *Bright Radical Star*, 26, 108–12.

68. "A Citizen" to editor, *Burlington Hawk-Eye*, 4 Dec. 1851.

69. Donnel, *Pioneers of Marion County*, 70–76. Neither of the McGregors can be traced through the Illinois census.

70. Territory of Iowa, *Statute Laws*, 65–67. This law required newly arriving free black residents to post a $500 bond, an amount well beyond the resources of most African Americans.

71. *Burlington Hawk-Eye*, 4 Dec. 1851.

72. Wisconsin law prevented black suffrage (and exempted blacks from the poll tax). It also excluded black men from service in the state militia, while permitting them to own property, serve on juries, testify against whites, and attend public schools; there were no legal prohibitions on interracial marriage (McManus, *Political Abolitionism*, 34–5). In Minnesota in 1849, African Americans were barred from voting in congressional, territorial, county, and precinct elections; by 1851, they were also banned from village elections, and by 1853, from voting at town meetings (David Vassar Taylor, "The Blacks," 74). They were also barred from serving in public office and on juries, and their children had to attend segregated schools at least until 1869 (Libman, "Minnesota and the Struggle," 11–14; Spangler, *Negro in Minnesota*, 34–35). On black exclusion laws, see Dykstra, *Bright Radical Star*, 108–13; Spangler, *Negro in Minnesota*, 27, 44; State of Wisconsin, *Journal of the Senate, 1863*, 633–37, and *Journal of the Assembly . . . 1863*, 287, 529–31; and *St. Paul Daily Press*, 10 Feb. 1863 (this and all subsequent references to the *St. Paul Daily Press* come from transcriptions collected in FWP, Annals of Minnesota, MHS).

73. Dykstra, *Bright Radical Star*, 45.

74. An Alderman Stumbaugh, of Lyon, Clinton County, Iowa, introduced a black exclusion measure to the Lyon City Council in December 1859 (*Iowa Weekly Citizen*, 14 Dec. 1850).

75. The regulation of free blacks in Iowa was enforced by "all township and county officers" (*Burlington Hawk-Eye*, 4 Dec. 1851). See Martha and Francis Reno Bond, BL 160, folder 29, SHS/IC; Minutes, City Council meeting, 17 Dec. 1855, City Clerk's Office, Iowa City; Aurner, *Leading Events in Johnson County*, 252. The Garner family of Fremont County posted bonds in 1850 (Todd, *Early Settlement*, 90–91). Elizabeth Thompson filed her bond in Keokuk (clipping, *Gate City and Constitution*, 7 May 1847, in Bickel Collection, KPL). According to an 1839 statute, black migrants who failed to follow the letter of the law could be arrested and hired out to the highest bidder for six months; whites who employed or "harbored" illegal migrants were subject to a $100 fine (Dykstra, *Bright Radical Star*, 27).

76. In 2003, the $500 bond required in 1839 was equivalent to $9,824.29, based on the Consumer Price Index, or $92,171.85 if compared with the unskilled wage of the period. See *What Is the Relative Value*, at the Economic History Services website, <http://eh.net>.

77. Kerr, "Whittenberg Manual Labor College"; Jordan, "William Salter and the Slavery Controversy"; Rev. E. Mathews, *Autobiography*, 186–93; Schwalm, "Antislavery and Reform Activities"; McManus, *Political Abolitionism*; Dykstra, *Bright Radical Star*; Connor, "Antislavery Movement in Iowa"; Berrier, "The Underground Railroad in Iowa," in *Outside In*, ed. Silag, 44–59; *Frederick Douglass' Paper*, 14 April 1854.

78. Dykstra, *Bright Radical Star*, 33 (quotation). The most well-known defenses of

fugitive slaves were those associated with trials, including the defense of nine fugitive men, women, and children by Salem, Iowa, whites (see entries for June 1848, Nathan Isabell Diary, SHS/DM, and Sherman Booth's prominent role in the rescue of Joshua Glover in Milwaukee in McManus, *Political Abolitionism*, 87–88).

79. Dykstra, *Bright Radical Star*, 37. Chambers, a Kentucky Whig and newly appointed governor of the territory, set up "a country place near Burlington which he called Grouseland, where he spent much of his time in bucolic pursuits," according to an Iowa historian, presumably including exercising his dominion over enslaved people (Cole, *History of the People of Iowa*, 164–65). According to the 1840 U.S. census for Mason, Ky., he owned nineteen slaves (Ancestry.com, *1840 United States Federal Census*).

80. "A Slave Owner in Iowa," *Palimpsest*. Allen shows up in the 1850 U.S. census for Buncombe County, N.C., as the owner of a thirteen-year-old slave boy (Ancestry.com, *1850 United States Federal Census*). Both he and his wife Mary were born in 1826, and in 1850 they had a one-year-old child of their own. Allen listed his occupation as laborer, <http://content.ancestry.com/iexec/?htx=View&r=an&dbid=8054&iid=NCM432_622-0257&desc=L+Allen&pid=12599109> (10 Aug. 2005).

81. Spangler, *Negro in Minnesota*, 28; *New York Tribune*, 30 Oct. 1858.

82. In the 1848 presidential elections (the first in which a Free Soil candidate appeared on the ballot), Wisconsin's Free Soil Party won 28 percent of the votes cast—compared to 10 percent nationally; Robert Dykstra argues that Free Soil voters cost the Whig candidate Taylor the state's presidential election. See McManus, *Political Abolitionism*, 55, and Dykstra, *Bright Radical Star*, 84–85.

83. Plumbe, *Sketches of Iowa and Wisconsin*, 12. See also *Description and History of Marshall County*, 8: "There is but one negro in the entire county."

84. This issue is insightfully investigated in Colleen K. Kelley, "'Beautiful Land of the White Man.'"

85. Remarks of Hon. J. C. Hall, in Iowa Colonization Society, *Annual Report . . . 1857*, 9–11. The 1855 Iowa Democratic Convention endorsed the colonization of people of African descent (*National Era*, 22 Feb. 1855).

86. *Provincial Freeman*, 21 Mar. 1857. On Dudley, see Vollmar, "Negro in a Midwest Frontier City," 2, and Miller, *Search for a Black Nationality*, 175; on Douglas's tour, see *Davenport Daily Gazette*, 13 Dec. 1859; *Oskaloosa Weekly Times*, 15, 22 Dec. 1859. A biographical essay on Douglas can be found in Ripley, *United States, 1847–1858*, vol. 4 of *BAP*, 78–79. Miller's study provides an excellent overview of the emigrationist movement; an essay that places the movement in the larger context of black activism is Ripley, *United States, 1830–1846*, vol. 3 of *BAP*, 3–69.

87. *Oskaloosa Weekly Times*, 24 Mar. 1859. According to the 1860 U.S. census for Oskaloosa (Mahaska County), there were only six black residents of Oskaloosa (Ancestry.com, *1860 United States Federal Census*).

88. *Oskaloosa Weekly Times*, 24 Mar. 1859.

89. Ibid.; *Cedar Democrat*, 4 June 1859; *Anamosa Gazette*, 15 July 1859, citing an article in the *Mason City Press*. See U.S. census for 1860, Spring Creek Township, Tama County, Iowa (Ancestry.com, *1860 United States Federal Census*).

90. Vincent, *Southern Seed, Northern Soil*, 30–31.

91. Edward L. Sheppard to brother, 29 Aug. 1858, Charles Sheppard Papers, UWDC.

92. In 1860, the U.S. census counted 112 black city residents (Ancestry.com, *1850 United States Federal Census*).

93. The church's charter members included 19 women and 15 men, and reflected the core families of the black community: the Clarks, Mathews, Andersons, Motts, Mannings, Pritchards, Jacksons, and others.

94. *Weekly Journal*, 27 Jan. 1888, transcribed clipping, in Clark File, Musser. Clark and Jacob Pritchard (who was similarly active in Muscatine's petitioning and convention activities) were Iowa's earliest Masonic members, joining at least by 1851, when they both belonged to Prince Hall Lodge No. 10 (Ohio Register) in St. Louis (A. G. Clark, *Prince Hall Freemasonry*, 25). Bishops Richard Harvey Cain and William Paul Quinn were involved in establishing churches in the upper Midwest, as well as deacons Edward Carroll Joiner and Abram T. Hall, men who, accompanied by their wives who were also very active in the denomination, traveled the region, attended midwestern conferences and represented the region at the denomination's annual general conference.

95. This process is astutely discussed in Jacqueline Jones, *American Work*, chap. 8.

96. Hope D. Williams, *Oral History*, interview by Lillian Justice with Dorothy Katherine Mitchell Childress; affidavit by Milton Howard, 17 Dec. 1916, pension file of Harvey Brooks, WC 825854, CWPF.

97. Petition #11, 17 Jan. 1855, "Petitions, Blacks and Mulattos, Rights of," General Assembly, Secretary of State Records, SHS/DM. Richard Harvey Cain (1826–87), the fourteenth bishop of the AME Church, was born in Greensboro County, W.Va., and as a child moved with his parents to Ohio, where he converted in 1841; he subsequently went to Hannibal, Mo., and was licensed in 1844. Cain joined the AME Church and was admitted to the Indiana Conference in 1854. Muscatine was his first charge. In 1859 he was ordained deacon and the next year entered Wilberforce. In 1861 he moved to New York and in 1865 to South Carolina, where he served as a state senator and was sent to Congress. Cain was elected bishop in 1880. Wright, *Centennial Encyclopedia*, 269.

98. *Provincial Freeman*, 21 Mar. 1857.

99. Richman, "Congregational Life in Muscatine."

100. Hallie Q. Brown, *Homespun Heroines*, 34–45; T. H. Batcheler to David W. Kilburne, 31 Mar. 1854, Kilburne Papers, SHS/DM; *Frederick Douglass' Paper*, 9 Feb. 1855; *New York Times*, 2 Aug. 1855; Essie M. Britton, "Early Negro Families in Iowa," WPA Project, "Ethnography-Negroes," KPL.

101. Faye Emma Harris, "Frontier Community," 112–14.

102. *History of Lee County*, 640; *Christian Recorder*, 17 May, 7 June 1862, 29 Dec. 1866, 4 Feb. 1865. On the school, see Keokuk Public School Superintendents Records, SHS/IC.

103. Keokuk Public School Superintendents Records, SHS/IC.

104. See Ross, *Justice of Shattered Dreams*, 41–45, 49, for an excellent overview of the panic's economic impact on Keokuk.

105. Ibid., 45.

106. *Daily Gate City*, 2–6 June 1857; *Daily Hawk-Eye and Telegraph*, 3 June 1857; *Davenport Daily Gazette*, 13 June 1857; *Dubuque Daily Express and Herald*, 5 June 1857. The captain's name is given in reports as both Straw and Stran. An H. B. Straw appears as a

slaveowner on the 1860 census for Natchez, Miss. (Ancestry.com, *1860 United States Federal Census*).

107. *Keokuk Weekly Times*, 4 June 1857; *Daily Gate City*, 5, 6 June 1857; *National Era*, 27 Aug. 1857; Dykstra, *Bright Radical Star*, 171–77.

108. Horton and Horton, *In Hope of Liberty*.

CHAPTER 2

1. On the Busey family, see *Davenport Democrat and Leader*, 8 Mar. 1908, 4 Dec. 1913, and undated clipping, Richter Papers, SHS/IC. On wartime Kentucky, see Berlin et al., *Wartime Genesis . . . Upper South*, ser. 1, vol. 2, of *Freedom*, 625–38.

2. [Blakeley, David], *Annual Report of the Secretary of State*; Hull, *1836–1880: Census of Iowa*. At least 700 African men served in the armed forces credited to Wisconsin, Minnesota, and Iowa; see Berlin et al., *The Black Military Experience*, ser. 2 of *Freedom*, 12. This number does not include the men and women officially and unofficially attached to white units as military laborers, who also would have been overlooked by the summer 1865 census.

3. [Blakeley, David], *Annual Report of the Secretary of State*; Hull, *1836–1880: Census of Iowa*.

4. The highest net increase in the nation occurred in Nevada (693 percent), from 45 to 357. In contrast, New York saw an increase of 6 percent; Pennsylvania, 15 percent; Massachusetts, 45 percent; and Ohio, 72 percent. There were other examples: by 1870, the proportion of African Americans in Iowa's southernmost county increased from 12 percent to 27 percent; in Wisconsin's rural Fond du Lac County, the proportion grew from 6 percent to 22 percent; and the black population of St. Paul more than doubled (from 1860 and 1870 census, U.S. Historical Census Data Browser, <http://fisher.lib.virginia.edu/collections/stats/histcensus/index.html>). St. Paul's census returns are reported in David Vassar Taylor, "Pilgrim's Progress," 22–23. The census is subject to a considerable rate of error, including the undercounting of African Americans; Ransom and Sutch estimate an undercount of 6.6 percent in the 1870 census (*One Kind of Freedom*, 54, 329n.). For a fuller discussion of the range of error in census-based migration statistics, see Cohen, *At Freedom's Edge*, 299–300.

5. *Manitowoc Pilot*, 17 Apr. 1863; *Fond du Lac Commonwealth Reporter*, 25 Oct. 1862; *History of Dodge County*, 711–12; Meyer, "Germans in Wisconsin," 36.

6. *Minneapolis Spokesman*, 14 Mar. 1958, and "History, Pilgrim Baptist Church: The First Negro Church in St. Paul," MHS (the *War Eagle*); *St. Paul Pioneer*, 6 May 1863 (the *Northerner*); *St. Paul Pioneer*, 15 May 1863, and *St. Paul Daily Press*, 16 June 1863 (the *Davenport*). See also Harpole, "Black Community."

7. These figures are drawn from my database containing biographical information on 2,247 black residents of Iowa (887 women and 1,344 men, 16 of unidentified gender). These black Iowans, who resided in the state between 1865 and 1880, were identified through census records, city directories, military service and pension records, county histories, newspaper articles, denominational reference works, biographical dictionaries, and a host of additional primary source materials.

8. Faulkner, *Women's Radical Reconstruction*; Michael P. Johnson, "Out of Egypt." Johnson's study, which covers Ohio, Michigan, Indiana, Illinois, Iowa, and Kansas, describes the wartime departure of former slaves from the South as the largest migration of free African Americans in the nation's first century. See also Thornbrough, *Negro in Indiana*, 183–205; Salvatore, *We All Got History*, 114; Castel, "Civil War Kansas and the Negro,"128.

9. William Brown, *Life Story*, 12.

10. Maj. John Clopper to Maj. George Merrill, 21 Mar. 1863, Letters Received, DOM, ser. 2593, RG 393, pt. 1; deposition by Martilla Newbern, 9 July 1895, pension file of William Newbern, WC 453072, CWPF.

11. Michael P. Johnson, *Abraham Lincoln, Slavery*, 116–18, provides a brief but excellent overview. He argues that this phase dominated Lincoln's strategy until the Emancipation Proclamation of January 1863, but Johnson's vantage point is dominated by developments (political and military) in the eastern theater of the war.

12. On the conduct of the war and its relationship to slavery in the Mississippi valley, see Berlin et al., *Destruction of Slavery*, ser. 1, vol. 1, of *Freedom*, 249–69, and Gerteis, *From Contraband to Freedman* (Kentucky), 493–518. See also McPherson, *Battle Cry of Freedom*, chap. 9.

13. Quoted in Louis S. Gerteis, *Civil War St. Louis*, 267.

14. As McPherson (*Battle Cry of Freedom*, 422) notes, during this short period "Union forces conquered 50,000 square miles of territory, gained control of 1,000 miles of navigable rivers, captured two state capitals and the South's largest city, and put 30,000 enemy soldiers out of action." One might more accurately describe it as a "river and rail" war, given the significance of such railway centers as Corinth, Memphis, and Nashville to the progress of war in the western theater during this second phase. Among the Union victories during this period were the capture of Fort Henry (6 Feb. 1862), Fort Donelson (16 Feb. 1862), Nashville (25 Feb. 1862), Shiloh (7 Apr. 1862), Island No. 10 (8 Apr. 1862), New Orleans (25 Apr. 1862), and Corinth (25 May 1862). On Celia Curran and William Brickley, see affidavit by William Brickley, 1 Feb. 1908, pension file of William Brickley (aka Brickler), IC 565196, CWPF.

15. These numbers, from my database of African Americans in the upper Midwest, are based on 245 of the total wartime migrants to Iowa. The sample comprises those migrants to Iowa whose wartime place of departure could be identified. Some of these were veterans and their families; others were civilians unaffiliated with military service.

16. Gerteis, *Civil War St. Louis*, 267; *Liberator*, 14 Feb., 2 May 1862 (detailing the efforts of soldiers and an officer in the Iowa 3rd to protect a fugitive slave from recapture by his Unionist owner in Missouri).

17. On 30 Nov. 1861, the *Burlington Daily Hawk-Eye* reprinted a commentary from the *Cincinnati Gazette* on Halleck's appointment and his exclusionary order. The paper stated that Halleck "had not the courage to face the popular consequences of reversing Fremont's policy towards the slaves of rebels . . . so he slanders the slaves, calls them spies, and orders them rigidly excluded from our camps." The arrest of Union officers for violating Halleck's order drew the attention and protests of midwestern politicians. See the *Liberator*, 2 May 1862, in which Sen. James W. Grimes criticizes the arrest of an officer of an Iowa unit for failing to abide by the order, and the *Liberator*, 15 Aug. 1862, in which Iowa's governor complains to the president about Halleck's action.

18. Maj. Geo. E. Waring to Acting Maj. Gen. Asboth, 19 Dec. 1861, *OR* 8:451–52.

19. Berlin et al., *Destruction of Slavery*, ser. 1, vol. 1, of *Freedom*, 400.

20. Ibid., 396–400, 423. On the use of city jails to threaten and intimidate fugitive slaves (and free blacks), see the extensive correspondence between John Latty and Mr. Kennett in 1862 and 1863, Kennett Family Papers, MO/SHS.

21. *OR* 8:444–45; Berlin et al., *Destruction of Slavery*, ser. 1, vol. 1, of *Freedom*, 419–20. The *Daily Missouri Democrat* of 22 Feb. 1862 reported the flight of thirty or forty slaves from Missouri's "Little Dixie" to the city, with the chief of police on active lookout for their recapture. Many examples of conflict with the state militia over the disposition of fugitive slaves can be found in the papers of Gov. Hamilton R. Gamble, including James Campbell to Gamble, 9 Sept. 1862, and Burton Bates to Gamble, 12 Sept. 1862, Gamble Collection, MO/SHS. See also Col. Wm. Pope to Maj. Gen. S. R. Curtis, 16 Jan. 1863, and Capt. D. P. Whitman to Curtis, 2 Feb. 1863, both in Letters Received, DOM, ser. 2593, RG 393, pt. 1; Greer W. Davis to Maj. Gen. S. R. Curtis, 24 Feb. 1863, Letters Received, DOM, p. 111, #83, ser. 2592, vol. 26/140 DMo, RG 393, pt. 1.

22. The *Daily Missouri Democrat*, the city's Republican newspaper, took a close interest in the use of the jail by slaveowners to retain custody of their slaves. On 9 Mar. 1863, a St. Louis grand jury investigated and condemned the practice. See *Daily Missouri Democrat*, 9, 10, 11, 16 Mar. 1863.

23. Ibid.

24. John Latty to Mr. Kennett, 20 Sept. 1862, Kennett Family Papers, MO/SHS.

25. Benton Barracks is described by Emily Parsons in her *Memoirs*, 72–73. Constructed at the beginning of the war, Benton Barracks was a large facility that could accommodate about 30,000 troops. In addition to the hospital, it contained a troop cantonment, parole encampment, contraband camp, and camp for white refugees. For further information and photographs, see Missouri Civil War Museum, <http://www.missouricivilwarmuseum.org/>.

26. *Daily Missouri Democrat*, 9 Jan. 1862.

27. William D. Wood to H. R. Gamble, 10 Nov. 1862, Gamble Collection, MO/SHS.

28. *Daily Missouri Democrat*, 9 Jan. 1862. See also Wm. D. Wood to H. R. Gamble, 10 Nov. 1862, Gamble Collection, MO/SHS.

29. See, e.g., *Daily Missouri Democrat*, 2, 15 Aug. 1862, and Wm. D. Wood to H. R. Gamble, 10 Nov. 1862, Gamble Collection, MO/SHS. For an excellent overview of the claims made by enslaved women in particular, see Romeo, "Freedwomen in Pursuit of Liberty."

30. Gerteis, *Civil War St. Louis*, 270–71; Berlin et al., *Destruction of Slavery*, ser. 1, vol. 1, of *Freedom*, 403, 435. Curtis, a resident of Keokuk, Iowa, was a three-term congressman, serving from 1847 until his death in 1866 *(In Memoriam . . . Curtis)*.

31. Berlin et al., *Destruction of Slavery*, ser. 1, vol. 1, of *Freedom*, 403; Gerteis, *Civil War St. Louis*, 271.

32. A. Lincoln to Maj. Gen. S. R. Curtis, 10 Jan. 1863, *OR* 22(2):30; William Eliot to (brother), 14, 18 Jan. 1863, Eliot Family Papers, MO/SHS. Lincoln hoped that the Missouri legislature then in session would pass a gradual emancipation bill (it did not).

33. Eliot, *Archer Alexander*, 60–61.

34. Louisa Alexander to Archer, 16 Nov. 1863, Eliot Family Papers, MO/SHS.

35. Ibid.

36. Asst. Provost Marshal O. A. A. Gardner to Maj. Gen. S. R. Curtis, 16 Feb. 1863, and

Green W. Dare to Curtis, 24 Feb. 1863, Letters Received, DOM, ser. 2593, RG 393, pt. 1; John Latty to Mr. Kennett, 20 Sept., 4 Oct. 1862, 15 Apr. 1863, Kennett Family Papers, MO/SHS; affidavit by James Montgomery, 24 July 1889, pension file of Gerrit Brown aka Gerrit Montgomery, Minor C 471639, CWPF.

37. The bill would initiate gradual emancipation in 1870 but would leave African Americans under the control of their former owners until 1876; see Gerteis, *Civil War St. Louis*, 279.

38. E. P. Cayce to M. P. Cayce, 19 June 1863, and Col. C. W. Parker to Col. John B. Gray, 21 July 1863, Letters Received, DOM, ser. 2593, RG 393, pt. 1; M. P. Cayce to Hamilton B. Gamble, 22 June 1863, Gamble Collection, MO/SHS.

39. "The guerillas have shown a singular and inhumane ferocity towards them," reported one commanding officer, who described the murder of two men, a woman, and two children by bushwackers who were helping slaveowners prevent the widespread escape of slaves to Union forces (Brig. Gen. Thomas Ewing to Lt. Col. C. W. Marsh, 3 Aug. 1863, Letters Received, DOM, ser. 2593, RG 393, pt. 1). See also Berlin et al., *Destruction of Slavery*, ser. 1, vol. 1, of *Freedom*, 406.

40. Gerteis, *Civil War St. Louis*, 288.

41. T. R. Mitchell to J. T. Sweringen, December 1863, 15 Jan. 1864, Sweringen Papers, MO/SHS. See also Latty to Mr. Kennett, 3 Mar. 1864, Kennett Family Papers, MO/SHS.

42. See Berlin et al., *Wartime Genesis . . . Upper South*, ser. 1, vol. 2, of *Freedom*, 625–38.

43. *Appleton Motor*, 10 July 1862. A soldier from Davenport, Iowa, noted from Corinth that "slaves . . . are not permitted to enter our picket line. To employ them would be shocking. My mess has not had a cook for three weeks. We might not be permitted to serve our country much longer if we hired one of the slaves about here as a cook, and it were discovered" (*Davenport Daily Gazette*, 29 July 1862).

44. Moore Diary, 26 June 1862, UWDC.

45. That September, some 400 contraband men were employed on Helena fortifications and another 500 women and children in the camp (Berlin et al., *Wartime Genesis . . . Lower South*, ser. 1, vol. 3, of *Freedom*, 665). By 2 Jan. 1863, there were about 4,000 freedpeople at Helena: 1,800 men, 1,200 women, and 1,000 children under age 15 (Emancipation League, *Facts Concerning the Freedmen*, 7). A Confederate raid in July 1863 devastated the camp, but even so, by the end of the year the camp population had returned to 2,228 (Yeatman, *Condition of the Freedmen*, 5; Berlin et al., *Wartime Genesis . . . Lower South*, ser. 1, vol. 3, of *Freedom*, 637).

46. Deposition by Mary A. Robison (née Crutchfield), 7 Dec. 1904, pension file of John A. Robison, WC 586639; affidavit by A. J. Hardin, 16 Feb. 1904, pension file of Perry Weeden, WC 568627; deposition by Martilla Newbern, 9 July 1895, pension file of William Newbern, WC 453072; affidavit by Enos Luckadoo, 2 July 1888, pension file of Enos Luckadoo, IA 593448; affidavit by Nathaniel Adams, 9 Feb. 1889, pension file of Adams, IC 472578—all in CWPF. See also affidavit by Ephraim P. Ford, 25 Jan. 1910, pension file of Ford, IC 935141, CWPF. All of these men and women would make their way from Helena to Iowa during the war.

47. Berlin et al., *Destruction of Slavery*, ser. 1, vol. 1, of *Freedom*, 30.

48. *Janesville Daily Gazette*, 1 Dec. 1862.

49. David James Palmer to ——— [illegible], 29 Aug. 1863, Palmer Papers; Robert

Moyle to ——— [illegible], 26 Dec. 1862, Robert Moyle Collection (quotation); and Oliver Boardman to ——— [illegible], 12 Feb. 1862, Oliver Boardman Collection—all in SC/UI. See also Henry Eggleston to Elizabeth, 4 July 1862, box 2, folder 2, Eggleston Letters, UWDC.

50. WPA Iowa Federal Writers' Project, "The Negro in Iowa," 387–88, SHS/IC; annotation on undated photographic portrait of Elizabeth Fairfax, Clinton County Historical Society Archives, Clinton, Iowa; Thomas Montgomery to Dear Parents and Brothers, 23 Mar., 19 May 1864, Montgomery Papers, MHS; Urwin and Urwin, *History of the 33d Iowa*, 68; Miss Rhonda Amanda Shelton Diary, 23 Apr. 1864, Shelton Family Papers, SC/UI.

51. Judson Wade to My Dear Sister, 26 Feb. 1863, Wade Papers, MHS. See also *Daily Hawk-Eye*, 18 Sept. 1862, and *Muscatine Journal*, 5 Aug. 1863.

52. Berlin et al., *Destruction of Slavery*, ser. 1, vol. 1, of *Freedom*, 403.

53. Ibid., 265–66, 249–51.

54. Eberhart, *History of the Eberharts*, 242–45.

55. See W. G. Eliot to Maj. Gen. J. M. Schofield, 19 Nov. 1863, Family Eliot Papers, MO/SHS; Berlin et al., *Destruction of Slavery*, ser. 1, vol. 1, of *Freedom*, 411, 587–89; and Berlin et al., *Black Military Experience*, ser. 2 of *Freedom*, 245–26.

56. At age fifteen, Alfred Morgan was taken into service by his owner Col. Ed. A. Kutzner, of the Enrolled Missouri Militia, until he fled and enlisted in the Union army (affidavit by Jane Morgan, 17 Apr. 72, pension file of Alfred Morgan, Mother C 167990, CWPF). Henry Webb was also taken by his owner's nephew into the Confederate service (undated clipping, Black History Binder I, BH 0040–41, NVHM).

57. To avoid the terms of the confiscation acts, Missouri slaveholders sold their slaves to traders, who transported the slaves to Kentucky and sold them there; Gerteis describes one such incident in *Civil War St. Louis*, 272–73.

58. Deposition by Ellen Hays, 19 Dec. 1891, pension file of Anderson Hays, WC 344064; affidavit by Rosanna Woods, 5 Dec. 1895, pension file of Phillip Woods, WC 451267; affidavit by Saphronia Carter, 23 June 1896, and by Charlotte Harding, 1 Feb., 24 June 1918, pension file of John Carter, WC 427881—all in CWPF; *Douglass' Monthly*, April 1863. For other examples of forced removal during the war, see affidavit by Delila Ray, 22 Oct. 1910, pension file of Antoine Crawford, WC 711140, CWPF; and Minnesota interview with George Johnson, in George Johnson Ex-Slave Narrative, LC.

59. Urwin and Urwin, *History of the 33d Iowa*, 293 n.2.

60. This rough calculation is drawn from the best available information. The Freedmen and Southern Society Project at the University of Maryland estimates that, by the spring of 1865, some 474,000 former slaves and free blacks took part in Federally sponsored free labor arrangements in the Union-occupied South. Of the total, 93,542 were soldiers. Deducting that number, as well as 61,364 (the 6.2 percent of the black population estimated to consist of free blacks), leaves approximately 319,094 southern slaves who, in choosing to abandon their masters, joined the population of displaced people at some point during the war. (This is clearly a low estimate, as the number of southern blacks counted by Union officials were not likely to have included all free blacks in the South.) See Berlin et al., *Wartime Genesis . . . Lower South*, ser. 1, vol. 3, of *Freedom*, 77–80; Berlin et al., *Black Military Experience*, ser. 2 of *Freedom*, 12; Boles, *Black Southerners*, 135.

61. Schwalm, *"A Hard Fight for We,"* 75–144; Robinson, "Day of Jubilo," 226–44.

62. One authority has estimated that 250,000 white southerners were displaced during the war—the vast majority of whom were women. See Massey, *Women in the Civil War*, 291–316.

63. Cashin, "Into the Trackless Wilderness"; Faust, *Mothers of Invention*, 40–45; Rable, *Civil Wars*, 181–92.

64. This was not always the case; some slave women were forced to accompany their owners who became displaced during the war; others became reluctant refugees in light of guerrilla attacks, and still others were forcibly displaced by Union policy. See Schwalm, *"A Hard Fight for We,"* 108–14; Faust, *Mothers of Invention*, 53–79; Cashin, "Into the Trackless Wilderness," 42–43; Glymph, "'This Species of Property.'"

65. Urwin and Urwin, *History of the 33d Iowa*, 309–10 n.7. See also Thomas Montgomery to parents, 18 Mar. 1864, Montgomery Papers, MHS.

66. Asst. Provost Marshal O. A. A. Gardner to Maj. Gen. S. R. Curtis, 16 Feb. 1863, Letters Received, DOM, ser. 2593, RG 393, pt. 1.

67. Drew Faust (*Mothers of Invention*, 40–45) has argued for a further distinction: that the term "refugee" was reserved in fact for elite southern whites and carried a pejorative meaning, implying a lack of patriotism in the decision to flee. Southern whites with fewer resources, she suggests, might more accurately be termed "displaced persons." On social constructions of the role of noncombatants in war, see Elshtain, *Women and War*, 180–93. For another critique of the passivity implied in the term, see Glymph, "'This Species of Property.'"

68. William Ault Civil War Papers, UWDC.

69. See, e.g., the comments of Henry S. Eggleston, a commissioned officer of a Wisconsin regiment, who observed that of the contrabands "flocking" into his company's camp, "quite a proportion were women & children, who could be of no use to us whatever," prompting him to issue an order excluding them from the camp (see box 2, folder 7, Eggleston Letters, UWDC).

70. Schultz, *Women at the Front*, 21–22. Schultz is careful to point out that the 21,208 female hospital attendants documented in the records of the U.S. Record and Pension Division offer only a baseline, not the total number of women who worked for pay or otherwise on behalf of the Union army.

71. Elizabeth Stuart, a former slave who had lived in Iowa for five years, for example, left Iowa for Helena to visit her husband during the war. She stayed for a year, cooking for the regiment's sutler (affidavits by William Stuart and Elizabeth Stuart, 28 Aug. 1886, pension file of London Triplett, WA 266564; affidavit by G. W. Pittman, 25 July 1884, pension file of William Stuart, WC 607408—all in CWPF).

72. Lucius Hubbard to Aunt Mary, 8 Sept. 1862, Hubbard Family Papers, MHS. Hubbard, a resident of Red Wing, Minn., enlisted as a private in the 5th Minnesota but obtained the rank of general before the end of his war service. He would go on to serve as a member of the Minnesota state senate, 16th District (1872–75), and later as governor of the state (1882–87), <http://politicalgraveyard.com/bio/hubbard.html> (4 Mar. 2006).

73. These developments are summarized in Gerteis, *From Contraband to Freedman*, 119–81; Berlin et al., *Destruction of Slavery*, ser. 1, vol. 1, of *Freedom*, 1–56, 249–69, 395–412;

Berlin et al., *Wartime Genesis . . . Lower South*, ser. 1, vol. 3, of *Freedom*, 1–83, 621–50; and Berlin et al., *Wartime Genesis . . . Upper South*, ser. 1, vol. 2, of *Freedom*, 551–64.

74. George Johnson Ex-Slave Narrative, LC.

75. History, Pilgrim Baptist Church, "The First Negro Church in St. Paul," Hampton Smith's folder on black history, MHS.

76. Undated clipping, Black History Binder I, BH 0092, NVHM; *Iowa State Bystander*, 9 Feb. 1912.

77. Affidavit by Milton Howard, 17 Dec. 1916, pension file of Harvey Brooks, WC 825854, CWPF.

78. *Newton Record*, 29 Oct. 1897.

79. Sarah J. Novell to Commissioner of Pensions, 13 June 1895, pension file of John Anderson aka Norvell, WA 271609, CWPF.

80. "Mrs Richard Lewis," *Dial of Progress*, 26 Feb. 1959.

81. Louis S. Gerteis provides a finely detailed discussion of Missouri emancipation in *Civil War St. Louis*, chap. 9. Missouri would ratify the Thirteenth Amendment in January 1865; see Parrish, *Turbulent Partnership*, 130–48, 201.

82. *Canton Press*, 16 June 1864, quoted in Lee, *Slavery North of St. Louis*, 165.

83. On slave flight to Kansas, see Quintard Taylor, *In Search of the Racial Frontier*, 95–99; to Illinois, see testimony of Dr. George Park, 21 May 1881, of Eveline Pace, 4 March 1879, and of Mathilda Henderson, 5 Mar. 1879—all in pension claim of George C. Young, XC 133472, CWPF, and Berlin et al., *Wartime Genesis . . . Upper South*, ser. 1, vol. 2, of *Freedom*, 555–56. On Catherine Thompson's flight from Missouri to Ringgold County, Iowa, with her four young children, see *Iowa State Bystander*, 18 Feb. 1898. A south-central Iowa newspaper published "accounts of negro stampedes from all parts of Missouri" (*Iowa City Republican*, 2 Sept. 1863). On contrabands in St. Louis, see Forman, *Western Sanitary Commission*, 133–34; Freedmen's Relief Society, *Annual Report*; Samuel Sawyer to Brig. B. M. Gen. Prentiss, 16 Mar. 1863, and Lucien Eaton to Maj. Gen. J. M. Schofield, 30 May 1863, Letters Received, DOM, 1861–67, ser. 2593, RG 393, pt. 1.

84. Railroad officials and steamboat operators feared their liability for inadvertently transporting fugitive slaves; their careful policing of black passengers limited escape options for fleeing slaves and constrained the efforts of the Union army to relocate fugitives northward. See T. C. Hanford to S. W. McKissock, 2, 3 May 1863, G. R. Taylor (President, Central Pacific Railroad) to Maj. Gen. J. M. Schofield, 10 June, 5 Aug. 1863, Isaac Sturgeon (President, Northern Missouri Railroad) to Schofield, 23 May, 9 Sept. 1863—all in Letters Received, DOM, 1861–67, ser. 2593, RG 393, pt. 1; Berlin et al., *Wartime Genesis . . . Upper South*, ser. I, vol. 2, of *Freedom*, 557; Berlin et al., *Destruction of Slavery*, ser. 1, vol. 1, of *Freedom*, 407–8; and Berlin et al., *Black Military Experience*, ser. 2 of *Freedom*, 228–30. On the pursuit of fugitive slaves into Iowa, see Rev. J. Cross to Rev. S. S. Jocelyn, 9 Sept. 1863, American Home Missionary Association Papers, SHS/IC. See the *Missouri Democrat*, 8 Nov. 1863, on the recapture of a group of slave women and children heading for southern Iowa.

85. Lt. Col. and Provost Marshal Gen. F. A. Dick to Maj. Gen. S. R. Curtis, 6 May 1863, encl. Lt. Henry, Asst. Provost Marshal, to Col. [Gen.] Dick, Letters Received, DoM, ser. 2593, RG 393, pt. 1.

86. For retrospective accounts, see *Milwaukee Journal*, 19 Apr. 1981; *Mukwonago Chief*, 14 Nov. 1984; *Stevens Point Journal*, 22 May 1975; Newson, *Pen Pictures*, 396; Abram L. Harris, *Negro Population*, 6; *St. Peter Tribune*, 30 Aug. 1865; *Minneapolis Spokesman*, 27 May 1949; and *New Ulm Review*, 21 Apr. 1915. For the most comprehensive overview of the widely varying policies of commanders in the Mississippi valley, see Berlin et al., *Destruction of Slavery*, ser. 1, vol. 1, of *Freedom*, 249–69. Midwestern regiments served largely, although not exclusively, in the western theater of war; most of the fugitive slaves with whom they made arrangements were from the Mississippi valley, but those white soldiers who served in the East also sent former slaves to their midwestern homes (Cohen, *At Freedom's Edge*, 92).

87. Berlin et al., *Destruction of Slavery*, ser. 1, vol. 1, of *Freedom*, 398–401, 404–10, and *Daily Hawk-Eye*, 18 Sept. 1862.

88. For an example of a Minnesota soldier refusing to return slaves, see Berlin et al., *Destruction of Slavery*, ser. 1, vol. 1, of *Freedom*, 467–68. See also Maj. Geo. E. Waring Jr. to Acting Maj. Gen. Asboth, 19 Dec. 1861, *OR* 3:451–52. A March 1862 act of Congress prohibited the use of Union soldiers in returning slaves to their former masters (Berlin et al., *Destruction of Slavery*, ser. 1, vol. 1, of *Freedom*, 22). On soldiers' appreciation for the labor of fugitive slaves in their camps, see *Daily Hawk-Eye*, 18 Dec. 1862, and Judson Wade to My Dear Mother, 26 Feb. 1863, Wade Papers, MHS, and Thomas Montgomery to parents and brother, 23 Mar. 1864, Montgomery Papers, MHS. On the employment of contraband women in army camps, see Jonathan Ricketts to Peter Mowrer, 1 Sept. 1862, Ellen Mowrer Miller Collection, IWA.

89. Hubbard to My Dear Aunt Mary, 13 Oct. 1862, Lucius F. Hubbard Family Papers, MHS; Rev. J. B. Rogers, *War Pictures*, 127–30.

90. Edward Redington to Mary Redington, 24 Jan. 1863, Redington Papers, UWDC.

91. *Racine Journal*, 22 Feb. 1922.

92. Danbom, "'Dear Companion,'" 537–43 (quotation, 538). For other instances, see *Christian Recorder*, 7 Sept. 1872; John L. Mathews to sister, 14 Aug. 1863, Mathews Letters, SHS/IC; Spangler, *Negro in Minnesota*, 48–49; *Daily Hawk-Eye*, 17 Mar. 1864; Berlin et al., *Destruction of Slavery*, ser. 1, vol. 1, of *Freedom*, 476; Mae L. Christenson, "Reminiscences of the Ex-Slave," 20 Jan. 1937, WPA Iowa Federal Writers' Project, SC/UI.

93. These included, e.g., Lew Johnson (*Stevens Point Journal*, 22 May 1875), Gus Cowan (*Mukwonago Chief*, 14 Nov. 1984), George Hall (deposition by Diana Hall, 30 May 1913, pension file of George Hall, IC 554990, CWPF), James Robinson (*Fairfield Ledger*, 26 June 1862), William H. Black (undated clipping, Black History Binder I, BH 016, NVHM), Julius Todd (*Minneapolis Spokesman*, 27 May 1849), Matt Bernard (Herdegen, *Men Stood Like Iron*, 60, Mrs. Turner (*Iowa State Bystander*, 12 Oct. 1894), "Aunt" Millie (Newson, *Pen Pictures*, 396), and a number of families (*St. Paul Daily Press*, 6 June 1863, and *Wisconsin Patriot*, 27 July 1863).

94. M. A. Rogers, "Iowa Woman in Wartime," 614.

95. Edward Redington to Mary, 28 Mar. 1863, transcribed letter, quoted in ibid.

96. On Elizabeth Estell, see Thomas Montgomery to mother, 27 May, 14 June, 22, 31 Aug., 12, 27 Oct., 27 Nov. 1864, 1, 14 Jan. 1864 [1865], 16 Jan., 29 May, 11 June, 5 Dec.

1866; Montgomery to parents and brothers, 22 Oct. 1864, 5, 23 Sept. 1866; Montgomery to Charles, 26 Oct., 17 Dec. 1864, 21 Feb. 1865, 29 Mar. 1866; Montgomery to father, 22 Mar. 1865, 23 Feb. 1866—all in Montgomery Papers, MHS.

97. *Constitution*, 13 Feb. 1863. Shortly before Craig attempted to leave Kirkwood's employment, Craig's father, a recently arrived former slave from Arkansas who had befriended a wealthy white man in Lyons, Iowa, tracked his son down and initiated correspondence with Kirkwood about his son (Benjamin Lake to Kirkwood, 5 Feb. 1863, box 2, folder 4, Kirkwood Papers, SHS/DM. On a similar case (of the employment of children), see *Burlington Hawk-Eye*, 6 Feb. 1863. In a related incident, an Indianola, Iowa, hotelkeeper attacked a recruiting agent for the state's black regiment when he tried to talk with a former slave whom the hotelkeeper had brought from St. Louis to work in his hotel (*Muscatine Journal*, 14 Nov. 1863). On such episodes reported in eastern Iowa, see *Daily Democrat and News*, 2 Feb., 25 Apr., 26 May 1863.

98. On the Fairfield incident, see the *Fairfield Ledger*, 26 June 1862. A similar case at Fort Snelling, Minn., is reported in the *St. Paul Daily Pioneer*, 12 Feb. 1868. On relocated blacks who were left at the Lee County poorhouse, see the *Constitution*, 20, 21 Oct. 1862. For an example of the threat of return to the South, see Thomas Montgomery to Dear Mother, 23 Sept. 1866, Montgomery Papers, MHS.

99. Iowa's law was only sporadically implemented; the last attempt to enforce it occurred in the winter of 1863 in an effort to return a recent arrival from slavery in Arkansas, a case that ultimately overthrew the law as unconstitutional. Several hundred petitioners requested a similar law in Wisconsin in 1863, and an unknown number petitioned Minnesota in 1863. See Dykstra, *Bright Radical Star*, 198–200; Spangler, *Negro in Minnesota*, 44; State of Wisconsin, *Journal of the Senate*, 633–37, and *Journal of the Assembly*, 286–87, 529.

100. Thomas Montgomery to father, 22 Mar. 1865, Montgomery Papers, MHS.

101. There were occasional organized relocations prior to 1862, but they were quite secretive. See W. H. Hicks to Dear Bro. Salter, 18 July 1861, and P. B. Bell to William Salter, 28 Oct. 1861, Race Relations, BPL.

102. *Douglass' Monthly*, November 1862.

103. On the army's response to the large numbers of fugitive slaves gathering behind Union lines, see Maj. Gen. B. M. Prentiss to Maj. Gen. J. M. Schofield, Helena, Ark., 16 June 1863, Letters Received, DOM, ser. 2593, RG 393, pt. 1. Although some historians date the origin of the camps to the onset of winter in 1862, the three camps discussed here were established several months earlier.

104. Moneyhon, "From Slave to Free Labor," 138.

105. Berlin et al., *Wartime Genesis . . . Lower South*, ser. 1, vol. 3, of *Freedom*, 659–60. On the arrival of women and children, see also p. 665.

106. In September 1862, the post commander at Helena was directed by one superior officer to feed contrabands with army rations but warned by another that in so doing he was violating official policy; see ibid., 665.

107. On the estimated population at Helena, see ibid., 665, and Emancipation League, *Facts Concerning the Freedmen*, 7. On the impact of the Emancipation Proclamation, see Col. Cyrus Bussey to Maj. Gen. S. R. Curtis, from Helena, 13 Jan. 1863, *OR* 22(2):39.

108. Maria R. Mann to Rev. Ropes, 13 Apr. 1863, Mary Peabody Tyler Mann Papers, LC.

109. Samuel Sawyer to Maj. Gen. S. R. Curtis, from St. Louis, 18 Apr. 1863, Letters Received, DOM, ser. 2593, pt. 1, boxes 8–11 (for 1863), RG 393, pt. 1.

110. Berlin et al., *Wartime Genesis... Lower South*, ser. 1, vol. 3, of *Freedom*, 674–76.

111. *Weekly Gazette and Free Press*, 16 Jan. 1863.

112. Berlin et al., *Wartime Genesis... Lower South*, ser. 1, vol. 3, of *Freedom*, 674–75.

113. Henry Eggleston to wife, 21 July 1862, box 2, folder 2, Eggleston Letters, UWDC.

114. See T. C. Hanford to S. W. McKissock, 2, 3 May 1863, G. R. Taylor (President, Central Pacific Railroad) to Maj. Gen. J. M. Schofield, 10 June, 5 Aug. 1863, and Isaac Sturgeon (President, Northern Missouri Railroad) to Schofield, 23 May, 9 Sept. 1863—all in Letters Received, DOM, ser. 2593, RG 393, pt. 1; and Berlin et al., *Wartime Genesis... Upper South*, ser. 1, vol. 2, of *Freedom*, 557; Berlin et al., *Destruction of Slavery*, ser. 1, vol. 1, of *Freedom*, 407–8; Berlin et al., *Black Military Experience*, ser. 2 of *Freedom*, 228–30. On unhappy white crew members, see Samuel Sawyer to Brig. Gen. B. M. Prentiss, 16 Mar. 1863, Letters Received, DOM, ser. 2593, 4 boxes, 8–11 (for 1863), RG 393, pt. 1.

115. Both Cairo (later replaced by a camp on Island No. 10) and St. Louis were recipients of contraband slaves forwarded by military authorities from places further south; for instance, several thousand contrabands were sent to St. Louis from Arkansas and to Cairo from Union forces occupying northern Alabama and Vicksburg (see, e.g., testimony of Ellen Reed, 10 Dec. 1896, pension file of Cassius Reed, WC 411436, CWPF). For an early outline of the relocation program, see S. A. Duke to Maj. Gen. S. R. Curtis, 9 Mar. 1863, Letters Received, DOM, ser. 2593, RG 393, pt. 1.

116. Rev. J. B. Rogers, *War Pictures*, 211–13.

117. Brig. Gen. J. M. Tuttle to Hon. Edwin M. Stanton (Secretary of War), 18 Sept. 1862, *OR*, ser. 3, 2:569.

118. *Douglass' Monthly*, November 1862.

119. *New York Times*, 27 Oct. 1862.

120. *New York Times*, 4 Nov. 1862.

121. Berlin et al., *Wartime Genesis... Upper South*, ser. 1, vol. 2, of *Freedom*, 677–80, 686; Maj. R. E. Lawder, 2nd Ohio Cavalry and Superintendent and Provost Marshal, R & F (St. Louis), to Brig. Gen. J. Sprague, Asst. Cmdr. (Freedmen's Bureau), 4 Sept. 1865, Letters Received, DOM, ser. 2593, RG 393, pt. 1; *First Annual Report of the Educational Commission for Freedmen*, 9.

122. Rev. J. B. Rogers, *War Pictures*, 211–13.

123. Ibid., 211–23; Job Haldey to James Wright, 22 Feb. 1863, Wright Letterbook, SHS/DM; Berlin et al., *Wartime Genesis... Lower South*, ser. 1, vol. 3, of *Freedom*, 691–92.

124. Maj. R. E. Lawder to Brig. Gen. J. Sprague, 4 Sept. 1865, Letters Received, DOM, ser. 2593, RG 393, pt. 1.

125. *Douglass' Monthly*, November 1862.

126. The number is reported in the *Daily Hawk-Eye*, 1 Sept. 1862. On Stanton's authority, see *OR*, ser. 2, 2:569. See also the *Pioneer and Democrat*, 23 Sept. 1862. Large numbers of contrabands similarly gathered in September 1862 at Helena, Ark.; Jackson, Tenn.; and Corinth, Miss., added cumulatively to the pressure on Grant and Secretary of War Stanton to authorize their relocation to northern employers; see Berlin et al., *Wartime Genesis... Upper South*, ser. 1, vol. 2, of *Freedom*, 27–29, 665–70.

127. *OR*, ser. 3, 2:569; *New York Times*, 2 Nov. 1862.

128. *Weekly Journal*, 1 Oct. 1862.

129. Letter to W. R. Arthur, Superintendent, Ill., Central Railroad Co., 10 June 1863, Letters Sent (No. 241/586 DKy), DOM, ser. 1085, no. 28, RG 393, pt. 2.

130. Lucius Hubbard to My Dear Aunt Mary, 8 Sept., 13 Oct. 1862, Hubbard Family Papers, MHS.

131. Voegeli, *Free but Not Equal*, 13–20, 34–35, 60–63; Berlin et al., *Wartime Genesis... Upper South*, ser. 1, vol. 2, of *Freedom*, 28–29.

132. "Contrabands Arriving from the South: Extraordinary Demand for their Service," reported one St. Louis observer (*New York Evangelist*, 2 Apr. 1863).

133. Rev. J. B. Rogers, *War Pictures*, 125–27, 132. Rogers served as superintendent of the camp at Cairo from Fall 1862 until April 1863. *Fond du Lac Commonwealth Reporter*, 13 Oct. 1933, 25 Oct. 1862; H. G. Shane to Annie Wittenmyer, 20 Mar. 1863, folder 5, box 2, Wittenmyer Papers, SHS/DM. Samuel Sawyer, superintendent of contrabands in St. Louis, faced tremendous obstacles in his effort to send the fugitives north by rail, in violation of the state code to prevent the transport of slaves by common carrier without the permission of the master. See T. C. Hanford to S. W. McKissock, 3 May 1863, and Hanford to McKissock (telegram), 2 May 1863, Letters Received, DOM, ser. 2593, RG 393, pt. 1. For further accounts of organized relocation, see the *Missouri Democrat*, 20 Mar. 63; *Constitution*, 5, 9, 10, 20, 21, 23, 25 Oct. 1862; *Daily Gate City*, 20 Aug., 29 Oct. 1862, 1 Apr. 1863; *Iowa City Republican*, 1 Apr. 1863; Voegeli, *Free but Not Equal*, 89–90; Samuel Sawyer to Brig. Gen. B. M. Prentiss, 16 Mar. 1863, Sawyer to Maj. Gen. S. R. Curtis, 20 Apr. 1863, and Chaplain H. D. Fischer (5th Kansas Volunteers) to Maj. Gen. J. M. Schofield, 22 June 1863, Letters Received, DOM, ser. 2593, RG 393, pt. 1; Forman, *Western Sanitary Commission*, 133–34; Berlin et al., *Wartime Genesis... Upper South*, ser. 1, vol. 2, of *Freedom*, 566, 598, 615.

134. Samuel Sawyer to Maj. Gen. S. R. Curtis, 16 Mar. 1863, Letters Received, DOM, ser. 2593, RG 393, pt. 1.

135. *OR* 22(2):147.

136. Samuel Sawyer to Brig. Gen. B. M. Prentiss, 16 Mar. 1863, Letters Received, DOM, ser. 2593, RG 393, pt. 1.

137. Maj. Gen. B. M. Prentiss to Maj. Gen. J. M. Schofield, 16 June 1863, Letters Received, DOM, ser. 2593, RG 393, pt. 1.

138. Affidavit by A. J. Hardin, 9 Sept. 1902, and by L. A. Cox, 3 Sept. 1902, pension file of Perry Weeden, WC 568627; affidavit by Nathaniel Adams, 9 Feb. 1989, pension file of Adams, IC 472578—all in CWPF.

139. Samuel Sawyer to Brig. Gen. B. M. Prentiss, 16 Mar. 1863, Letters Received, DOM, ser. 2593, RG 393, pt. 1; *Daily Missouri Democrat*, 20 Mar. 1863.

140. T. C. Hanford to S. W. McKissock, 3 May 1863, Letters Received, DOM, ser. 2593, RG 393, pt. 1. Sawyer's efforts drew complaints by the officers of the railroad company he wished to use, both because it was illegal to transfer the slaves of loyal owners without those owners' permission and because Sawyer included wives and children as well as unmarried women among those he targeted for relocation to St. Louis.

141. Samuel Sawyer to Maj. Gen. S. R. Curtis, 18 Apr. 1863, Letters Received, DOM, ser. 2593, RG 393, pt. 1; *Daily Missouri Democrat*, 22 Apr. 1863; Lucien Eaton to Maj. Gen. J. M. Schofield, 30 May 1863, Letters Received, DOM, ser. 2593, RG 393, pt. 1.

142. Brown's comments were made on 28 June 1864 (see Ivers, *Congressional Globe*, 3836).

143. *Daily Missouri Democrat*, 23 Jan. 1863.

144. Freedmen's Relief Society, *Annual Report*; *Daily Missouri Democrat*, 9 Mar., 15 June 1863; Lucien Eaton to Maj. Gen. J. M. Schofield, 30 May 1863, Letters Received, DOM, ser. 2593, RG 393, pt. 1. Later reports indicate the higher number (Berlin et al., *Wartime Genesis . . . Upper South*, ser. 1, vol. 2, of *Freedom*, 581–84).

145. *New York Evangelist*, 2 Apr. 1863.

146. *Iowa City Republican*, 1 Apr. 1863; Harriet Stevens, *Graybeards*, 1, 12.

147. *Douglass' Monthly*, August 1863; *Daily Missouri Democrat*, 30 Sept. 1865.

148. *Daily Missouri Democrat*, 27 Aug. 1863.

149. *Daily Missouri Democrat*, 26 Feb., 30 Sept. 1863.

150. *Daily Missouri Democrat*, 9–11, 16 Mar., 17 Apr. 1863; Anonymous communication #104, 28 Apr. 1863, p. 146, Letters Received, ser. 2592, and Samuel Sawyer to Maj. Gen. S. R. Curtis, 18 Apr. 1863, Letters Received, DOM, ser. 2593, RG 393, pt. 1.

151. Undated and unsigned endorsement by Maj. Gen. S. R. Curtis, 21 Apr. 1863, enclosing Col. Henry Almstedt to Curtis, 22 Apr. 1863, and Col. B. S. Bonneville to Capt. H. C. Fillebrown, 28 May 1863, all in Letters Received, DOM, ser. 2593, RG 393, pt. 1.

152. Jackson, *Story of Mattie J. Jackson*, 14–15.

153. Before his transfer, Curtis arranged for contrabands who had been gathered at various posts across Missouri to be brought into the city and forwarded to free states; see Lucien Eaton to Maj. Gen. J. M. Schofield, 30 May 1863, Letters Received, DOM, ser. 2593, RG 393, pt. 1. His efforts led to several lawsuits brought by slaveowners against railroad companies—more than thirty against one company—for transporting slaves without their owners' permission; see G. Taylor (President, Pacific Railroad Co.) to Maj. Gen. J. M. Schofield, 5 Aug. 1863, Letters Received, DOM, ser. 2593, RG 393, pt. 1.

154. Gerteis, *Civil War St. Louis*, 279–80. See also Berlin et al., *Destruction of Slavery*, ser. 1, vol. 1, of *Freedom*, 408–9.

155. Berlin et al., *Wartime Genesis . . . Upper South*, ser. 1, vol. 2, of *Freedom*, 581–84.

156. Deposition by Mary A. Robison, 7 Dec. 1904, pension file of John R. Robison, WC 586639, CWPF.

157. Berlin et al., *Wartime Genesis . . . Upper South*, ser. 1, vol. 2, of *Freedom*, 597–98.

158. Col. Wm. A. Pile to Lt. Col. O. N. Greene, 28 Dec. 1863, Letters Received, DOM, ser. 2593, RG 393, pt. 1. A report in the *Missouri Daily Democrat* on 7 Jan. 1864 put the number at 2,200.

CHAPTER 3

1. *Iowa City Republican*, 1, 8 Apr. 1863. Fears of being inundated by African Americans were much exaggerated. Although Johnson County's black population doubled between 1860 and 1865, the numbers were low: from 38 to 79.

2. *Muscatine Daily Courier*, 2 Oct. 1862.

3. Consider, for example, the race riots that erupted in Cincinnati in 1829 and 1841, five that occurred in Philadelphia between 1832 and 1849, and, in the 1830s and 1840s, those that occurred in Pittsburgh, Columbia, and Burlington, Pa., Canaan, N.H., Washington,

D.C., Boston, and New York City (Litwack, *North of Slavery*; Horton and Horton, *In Hope of Liberty*; James Oliver Horton, *Free People of Color*; Grimsted, *American Mobbing*). On emigration and colonization, see Miller, *Search for a Black Nationality*; Blight, *Douglass' Civil War*, chap. 6.

4. *New York Independent*, 21 Aug. 1862.

5. Silber and Sievens, *Yankee Correspondence*, 74; *Constitution*, 5 Sept. 1862. A surprisingly scant scholarship has explored emancipation's meaning and impact in the North. An important exception is *Free but Not Equal*, V. Jacque Voegeli's 1967 landmark study of wartime black migration to the Midwest. Herbert Wubben, *Civil War Iowa*, and Robert Dykstra, *Bright Radical Star*, assess the impact of white Iowans' racial attitudes on Civil War–era electoral politics. On white abolitionists and wartime race relations in the North, see McPherson, *Struggle for Equality*, and Frederickson, *Inner Civil War*, chap. 8. On the varied racial attitudes of northern white soldiers, see Glatthaar, *Forged in Battle*, and McPherson, *For Cause and Comrades*.

6. *Harper's Weekly*, 5, 19 Apr., 6 June, 28 Oct. 1862; *Liberator*, 14 Feb. 1862.

7. This statement, by Robert Hamilton, appeared in his paper, the *Weekly Anglo-African*, on 26 Sept. 1863. On Hamilton, see Ripley, *United States, 1859–1865*, vol. 5 of *BAP*, 27–29. See also Paludan, *"People's Contest,"* 220–21; McPherson, *Struggle for Equality*, 235–37. See Blight, *Douglass' Civil War*, for an excellent overview of wartime black activism, as well as Ripley, *Witness for Freedom*, chap. 5.

8. See Melish, *Disowning Slavery*.

9. On the Lincoln administration's advocacy for colonization, see Blight, *Douglass' Civil War*, 134–47.

10. *Muscatine Daily Courier*, 2, 13 Oct. 1862.

11. This conceptualization of wartime politics follows Jean H. Baker's study of the nineteenth-century Democratic Party (*Affairs of Party*). Helpful, too, is Mary Ryan's *Civic Wars*, as is a review essay by Joanne Pope Melish, "Of Politics and Publics." The best recent study of the expression of the wartime politics of race in popular literature (including songs, stories, cartoons, illustrations, and pictorial envelopes) is found in Fahs, *Imagined Civil War*. My thinking about the broader public politics of northern racism draws on feminist critiques of and revisions to the work of Jürgen Habermas on the public sphere; see Fraser, "Rethinking the Public Sphere," and Ryan, "Gender and Public Access," both in Calhoun, *Habermas and the Public Sphere*, 109–42, 259–88; Ryan, *Women in Public*; and Brown, "Negotiating and Transforming the Public Sphere," in Dailey et al., *Jumpin' Jim Crow*, 28–66.

12. W. H. Hicks to William Salter, from Denmark, 18 July 1861, History: "Slavery/Underground Railway," BPL; P. B. Bell to Rev. Wm. Salter, Burlington, Iowa, 28 Oct. 1861 (photocopy of original), Race Relations, BPL; J. Cross to Rev. S. V. Jocelyn, 6 Apr. 1862, American Missionary Association Papers, SHS/IC. The sources for information on wartime migration to the upper Midwest—military correspondence, personal correspondence, and contemporary accounts in newspapers—offer no evidence of organized relocation prior to the winter of 1862.

13. See, e.g., the *Liberator*, 14 Apr. 1862, on Lt. Leffingwell of Company C, 3rd Iowa, in northern Missouri, who took in a fugitive slave and helped his unit spend three hours sawing off the iron collar riveted to his neck in punishment for helping his wife escape to

Illinois. See also the *Liberator*, 2 May 1862, in which Grimes criticized the arrest of an officer of an Iowa unit for failing to abide by Halleck's exclusionary order; and 15 Aug. 1862, in which Kirkwood complained to the president about the same issue.

14. Consider the actions of Capt. James Reeve, of the 32nd Iowa, who liberated slaves despite at the risk of his commission and sent one of the freed slaves (whom he called "Joe darkey") to his family in Franklin County, Iowa (*Liberator*, 7 Aug. 1863).

15. Of some 1,600 newspapers published in the North during the war, 80 percent were political in character (Neely, *Union Divided*, 193 [quotation]; see also 63, 70). And see Neely, *Boundaries of American Political Culture*.

16. On the politics of wartime relief work, see Faulkner, *Women's Radical Reconstruction*; Leonard, *Yankee Women*; and Frederickson, *Inner Civil War*.

17. For example, it would be November 1863 before the Western Sanitary Commission, organized in late 1861, began to provide aid to freedpeople in the Mississippi valley. See Western Sanitary Commission to Abraham Lincoln, 6 Nov. 1863 (broadside), Gilder Lehrman Collection, New-York Historical Society, <http://www.gilderlehrman.org/collection/1545.11.pdf> (20 Mar. 2006).

18. Salem Meeting, vol. 2: Minutes, Iowa Yearly Meeting of Friends (Oskaloosa, 1866), 17–88, 21–22, microfilm 84, Local Quaker Meetings, SHS/IC; [Wisconsin Methodist Church], "State of the Country" statement, October 1862, *Minutes of the Sixteenth Annual Session of the Wisconsin Conference*, 16–17, and *Minutes of the Seventeenth Annual Session of the Wisconsin Conference*, 22–24.

19. *Mankato Semi-Weekly Record*, 24 May 1862.

20. *Burlington Daily Hawk-Eye*, 10 Oct. 1862. James Stewart, in a letter to David Palmer of 14 Feb. 1863, noted that Washington County abolitionists "don't want the negroes to go North, no more than the Democrats do, and don't care what becomes of them, if we can only close the war" (typed transcripts of correspondence, Palmer Papers, SC/UI).

21. Benjamin, *History of Envelopes*, 25–26; Fahs, *Imagined Civil War*, 150–54.

22. See Jean H. Baker, *Affairs of Party*, esp. chaps. 6, 7; Klement, *Copperheads*; and Adam I. P. Smith, "Partisan Politics."

23. On the print culture of the Civil War, see Fahs, *Imagined Civil War*; Diffley, *To Live and Die*; and Richards, "U.S. Civil War Print Culture."

24. An intraparty split, argues Frank Klement, prevented Iowans from enjoying the "full benefits of the political trend" (*Copperheads*, 37–38). See also Current, *Civil War Era*, 404–5, and Voegeli, *Free but Not Equal*, 62. Democrats captured a majority of congressional seats in the states of the old Northwest and made notable gains in Minnesota and Wisconsin.

25. On the association of the Republican Party with an increasingly large, centralized, and powerful state, see Bensel, *Yankee Leviathan*, 236, 423, and Montgomery, *Beyond Equality*, 102. See also Bernstein, *New York City Draft Riots*, 8–10, 190–91.

26. *Mankato Semi-Weekly Record* (first quotation), 23 Apr. 1862; *Manitowoc Pilot*, 5 Dec. 1862; *Milwaukee Sentinel*, 9 Apr. 1863. See also Frank Malcolm's 1864 letters from his Tennessee post to his wife (in James J. Robertson Jr., "Such is War: The Letters of an Orderly in the 7th Iowa Infantry," unidentified clipping, Civil War Files No. 1, Musser), and *St. Paul Pioneer*, 31 Jan. 1863. Similar rhetoric was offered by *Vanity Fair* on 22 Mar. 1862 (p. 139): "The Gorilla of the cotton-field is doubtless an interesting creature, ethno-

logically considered, but his comfort and recreation are not with the disbursement of over a Million *per diem*, and the slaying of the very flower of our generation."

27. See, e.g., petitions to the Iowa state legislature for a law that would block migration of former slaves into the state, from residents of Polk, Warren, Linn, and other counties (State of Iowa, *Journal of the Senate*, 19, 38, 47). Douglas is quoted in Litwack, *North of Slavery*, 268–69.

28. *Manitowoc Pilot*, 12 Dec. 1862. The same editor later complained that "while our volunteers are yet unpaid and their families suffering actual want, the public money is to be further wasted on the liberation of a class whom we shall have to feed afterwards" (30 Jan. 1863).

29. Florence Chapman of Indianola, Iowa, wrote that many people in her town felt the entire purpose of the war was to elevate the Negro and degrade the white man (Florence Chapman to Philo Chapman, 25 Apr. 1863, Chapman Family Papers, SHS/IC). On white privilege, see Roediger, *Wages of Whiteness*, and Jacobson, *Whiteness of a Different Color*, esp. 13–31, 204–5.

30. For the centrality of their relations with Native Americans in the creation of a midwestern white consciousness, see Gray, "Stories Written in the Blood"; Bruce M. White, "Power of Whiteness"; and Green, *Peculiar Balance*. The contrast between the upper Midwest, where Indian populations persisted at midcentury, and their displacement from the lower Midwest is noted by Cayton and Gray, "Story of the Midwest." For a substantive treatment of the events leading up to and following the August 1862 Dakota uprising, see Josephy, *Civil War in the American West*, 95–154; Prucha, *Great Father*; 437–47; Current, *Civil War Era*, 319–24; and Holmquist, *They Chose Minnesota*, 17–23. In addition to some 40,000 Minnesotans who fled into Wisconsin, panic also struck such towns as Manitowoc, Menomonie, Superior City, Sheboygan, Milwaukee, and Wauwatosa. See Trask, *Fire Within*, 132–340; *Manitowoc Herald*, 4 Apr. 1862; Gov. Edward Salomon's message to the Wisconsin Senate and Assembly, reprinted in *Manitowoc Herald*, 18 Sept. 1862; Quaife, "Panic of 1862"; and Klement, *Wisconsin and the Civil War*, 38–42.

31. Secretary of War Stanton refused to take seriously the request by Gov. Salomon of Wisconsin for assistance against the rumored Indian invasion of the state. The alarm and outrage this inspired among residents was not allayed by later developments, including the War Department's organization of the Dept. of the Northwest and the army's pursuit of the Minnesota Sioux across the plains.

32. *St. Paul Pioneer*, 10 Feb. 1863.

33. *St. Paul Daily Press*, 6 June 1863; *St. Paul Pioneer*, 6 May, 6 June 1863.

34. For an excellent account of the impact of the panic of 1857 on one midwestern town, see Ross, *Justice of Shattered Dreams*, chap. 3. See also Klement, *Wisconsin and the Civil War*, 25–27, 38–42.

35. On race and military service, see the *Iowa City Republican*, 1 July 1863; *Fairfield Ledger*, 19 Mar. 1863; comments by a midwestern soldier and Wisconsin officer quoted in Herdegen, *Men Stood Like Iron*, 58; Berlin et al., *Black Military Experience*, ser. 2 of *Freedom*, 85; *Oskaloosa Times*, 5 Mar. 1863; *Mankato Semi-Weekly Record*, 23 Apr. 1862; *St. Paul Pioneer*, 21 Dec. 1862, 10 Feb. 1863. On pensions, see *Washington Democrat*, 23 Aug. 1864. On Sumner, see *Pioneer and Democrat*, 1 Oct. 1862. On mortgages, see *Mankato*

Semi-Weekly Record, 21 June 1862. St. Louis shoemakers are quoted in the *Missouri Democrat*, 14 Apr. 1864.

36. *Liberator*, 14 Feb. 1862; Florence Chapman to Phil Chapman, 1 Feb. 1863, Chapman Family Papers, SHS/IC. The wide debates about race extended even to the design of new letterhead for the state of Wisconsin. There was some concern about the dark complexion of the two Wisconsin men represented on a draft version of the letterhead, requiring reassurances from the governor that the men would appear much lighter-complected in the final version of the design (H. Seiferd to W. H. Watson, Esq., 7 Mar. 1863, Edward Salomon Papers, WHS).

37. Quoted in Bodnia, "Racial and Political Attitudes," 77–78.

38. *Mankato Semi-Weekly Record*, 21 June 1862.

39. *St. Paul Pioneer*, 21 Dec. 1862.

40. *Manitowoc Pilot*, 13 Feb. 1863; *St. Paul Pioneer*, 21 Dec. 1862 (soldiers' rations); *Oskaloosa Weekly Times*, 5 Mar. 1863, and *Constitution*, 8 Oct. 1863 (relations between white soldiers and blacks); *Constitution*, 12 Feb. 1863 (exclusion of white soldiers from public events). Quotations are from Florence Chapman to Philo Chapman, 1 Feb. 1863, Chapman Papers (on soldiers kept off trains), and the *Washington Democrat*, 23 Aug. 1864.

41. *Daily Democrat and News*, 30 Jan. 1863 (first quotation); *Fairfield Ledger*, 7 Aug. 1862 (2nd quotation). According to white observers, while in the South, blacks acted like they knew "their place" in white society, but "a few weeks or months in the North entirely ruins" them, making them worse than useless. A correspondent from St. Louis reported that in St. Louis, "a nigger *is* a nigger, *and he knows it*. There is no such thing as niggers crowding white people off the sidewalk here, like in Keokuk" (*Constitution*, 5 Sept. 1862).

42. Maria Mann to Miss Peabody, 19 Apr. 1863, Mann Papers, LC.

43. *St. Paul Pioneer*, 7, 28 June 1863.

44. Bernstein, *New York City Draft Riots*, 122–23.

45. Paludan, *"People's Contest,"* 182–83.

46. Jacqueline Jones, *American Work*, 13.

47. For examples of employers hiring black labor (either in the Midwest or recruited from St. Louis), see Jaynes, *Highlights of Henry County*, 41–42.

48. *Constitution*, 5 Sept. 1862; see also *St. Paul Pioneer*, 26 Mar. 1863.

49. *Constitution*, 15 July 1864. The *Muscatine Daily Courier* of 6 Oct. 1862 printed a letter from "J. P. C." at Camp Strong noting that the soldiers understood "a certain gentleman of your city discharged his faithful white girl, who had been in his family for years, to make room for one of the late importations from the land of Dixie."

50. *Constitution*, 5 Sept. 1862.

51. *Fairfield Ledger*, 4 Dec. 1862.

52. Lincoln's message to both Houses of Congress, 1 Dec. 1862, reprinted in the *Manitowoc Pilot*, 12 Dec. 1862.

53. *Fairfield Ledger*, 28 Apr. 1863 (1st quotation); *Iowa City Republican*, 8 Apr., 6 May 1863; J. Cross to Rev. S. S. Jocelyn, 4 June 1863, American Missionary Association Papers, SHS/IC (2nd quotation); *Daily Hawk-Eye*, 28 Sept. 1863, 6 Apr. 1864; *Muscatine Journal*, 1 Aug. 1863 (3rd quotation); *St. Paul Daily Press*, 6, 15, 16 May, 16 June 1863. See also *St. Paul Pioneer*, 4 Jan., 7 May 1863, and *Fond du Lac Commonwealth Reporter*, 13 Oct. 1933.

54. Mrs. Francis Harris Shirley, who was among those relocated to Fond du Lac by Chaplain James Rogers, recalled the attack in a 1933 interview; see *Fond du Lac Commonwealth Reporter*, 13 Oct. 1933. On Rogers himself, see Berlin et al., *Wartime Genesis . . . Lower South*, ser. 1, vol. 3, of *Freedom*, 667–70, and Rogers's memoir, *War Pictures*.

55. *Fond Du Lac Commonwealth Reporter*, 29 Mar. 1879.

56. On the wartime agricultural economy, see Paludan, *"People's Contest,"* chap. 7, and Wubben, *Civil War Iowa*, 134–36. On midwestern urban economies, see Russell Lee Johnson, "Army for Industrialization."

57. Paludan, *"People's Contest,"* 168.

58. *Daily Gate City*, 29 Oct. 1862, 25 Mar. 1863; *St. Paul Pioneer*, 26 Mar. 1863.

59. On the involvement of midwestern soldiers in the relocation of former slaves, see John L. Mathews to sister, 14 Aug. 1863, Mathews Letters, SHS/IC; Spangler, *Negro in Minnesota*, 48–49; Lucius F. Hubbard to Aunt Mary, 8 Sept., 13 Oct. 1862, Hubbard Family Papers, MHS; Orrin Densmore to Daniel Densmore, 24 Mar. 1864, Densmore Family Papers, MHS; Current, *Civil War Era*, 390–91; *Daily Hawk-Eye*, 10 Feb., 17 Mar. 1864; *Constitution*, 20 Oct. 1862; *Iowa City Republican*, 1 Apr. 1863; *Fairfield Ledger*, 26 June 1862; *Daily State Register*, 13 June 1863; *Weekly Commonwealth*, 22 Oct. 1862; Glaze, *Incidents and Anecdotes*; *Delevan Enterprise*, 13 Feb. 1986; *Milwaukee Journal*, 19 Apr. 1981; *Racine Journal-News*, 22 Feb. 1922. See also Berlin et al., *Destruction of Slavery*, ser. 1, vol. 1, of *Freedom*, 476. For other instances, see Mae L. Christenson, "Reminiscences of the Ex-Slave."

60. Wubben, *Civil War Iowa*, 62.

61. The rioters were arrested and, under a suspension of the writ of habeas corpus, were imprisoned indefinitely until the Wisconsin Supreme Court ruled for their release; see Klement, *Wisconsin and the Civil War*, 50–51, and Rippley, *Immigrant Experience*, 38–42.

62. On wartime labor unrest in midwestern towns and cities, see Wubben, *Civil War Iowa*, 137–38, 151–52; on ethnicity and race, see Jacobson, *Whiteness of a Different Color*, 15–55, Ignatiev, *How the Irish Became White*; Roediger, *Wages of Whiteness*, 144–56, 167–76; Holmquist, *They Chose Minnesota*, 130–52; and Jacqueline Jones, *American Work*, 270–72, 281–92. Consider Dubuque's alchemy of ethnicity and class: immigrants represented a large proportion of the city's working class—two-thirds of all persons with occupations in the 1860 census—but three-fourths of the working class and less than half of the business class. The city's largest concentration of immigrants were Germans, but the Irish provided the bulk of unskilled workers. Native-born whites accounted for over half of the business class. See Russell Lee Johnson, "Army for Industrialization," 128–29.

63. *Christian Recorder*, 6 Dec. 1862. One of the ways in which native-born ambivalence about the racial identity of Irish immigrants was expressed was in the manuscript census, where Iowa census takers recorded Irish as "mulatto"; see, e.g., 1856 manuscript census for Davenport, Scott County, p. 27, and 1869 manuscript census for 1st Ward, Keokuk, Lee County, p. 22, SHS/IC.

64. *St. Paul Daily Press*, 15, 16 May 1863 (quotations). For attacks by Irish workers on black workers, see the *Mankato Semi-Weekly Record*, 14 June 1862; *Daily Hawk-Eye*, 6 Apr. 1864; Russell Lee Johnson, "Army for Industrialization," 343; and Wubben, *Civil War Iowa*, 158. For attacks on contrabands arriving at St. Paul, see *St. Paul Daily Press*, 6, 16 June 1863.

65. *Northwestern Bulletin*, 5 May 1923.

66. Mosely, *Colored Man of America*, 3.

67. Midwestern newspapers commented frequently on the composition of the groups of former slaves being sent north, often noting a majority of women and children. See, e.g., *Daily State Register*, 24 Sept. 1862; *Fairfield Ledger*, 30 Oct. 1862; *Constitution*, 13 Feb. 1863; *St. Paul Daily Press*, 17 May 1863; and *Daily Hawk-Eye*, 18 Dec. 1863. In a similar vein, see also Wubben, *Civil War Iowa*, 81, 132.

68. M. W. Sandford of Bentonsport, Iowa, to Annie Wittenmyer, n.d. [filed in folder 14], and Mrs. John Shane to Wittenmyer, 27 Oct., 8 Dec. 1862, 20 Mar. 1863, both in Wittenmyer Papers, SHS/DM; Father [Orrin Densmore] to son [Benjamin Densmore], Red Wing, 20 Aug. 1864, and Orrin Densmore Jr. to Daniel Densmore, 27 Oct. 1864 ("wench fever"), Densmore Family Papers, MHS. On Vinton, see [?] to Annie Wittenmyer, 27 Oct. 1862 (unsigned) [filed in folder 14], Wittenmyer Papers. For similar developments in wartime Iowa, see H. G. Shane to Annie Wittenmyer, 20 Mar. 1863, Wittenmyer Papers. The demand for black servants would continue in some settings well after the war; in 1880, the operator of a hotel at Lake Minnetonka, Minn., transported fifty African Americans from the South to work as servants in the facility (see *Minneapolis Tribune*, 19 May 1880, in Annals of Minnesota, MHS).

69. *New York Times*, 2 Nov. 1862.

70. *New York Times*, 4 Nov. 1862.

71. On midwestern white women's farm labor during the war, see Hurn, *Wisconsin Women*, 78–82; *Dubuque Herald*, 16 July 1862; *Daily Gate City*, 1 June 1864; *McGregor News*, 24 May 1864; *Dubuque Daily Times*, 30 July, 15 Aug., 5 Nov. 1862; and Wubben, *Civil War Iowa*, 81. Black women were described as "rough" and "able-bodied" in Job Headley to James Wright, 22 Feb. 1863, Wright Letterbook, SHS/DM. The phrase "athletic" women comes from Senator Waitman T. Willey of West Virginia in his 14 June 1864 discussion of finding employment for former slaves (Ivers, *Congressional Globe*, 2934).

72. Job Headley to James Wright, 22 Feb. 1863, Wright Letterbook, SHS/DM; W. H. Corkhill to O. D. Greene, 27 Apr. 1864, endorsement by Brig. Gen. Wm. A. Pile, 27 Apr. 1864, Letters Received, DOM, ser. 2593, box 12, 1864 [C-153], RG 393, pt. 1.

73. *Daily Missouri Democrat*, 22 Apr. 1863. In 1863, the Union commander headquartered at Helena suggested relocating hundreds of former slaves north, but "I only propose to send off the women and children who could earn a support if distributed with farmers families." Brig. Gen. N. B. Buford (commanding District of Eastern Arkansas, headquarters at Helena) to Lt. Col. H. Binmore, A.A.A.G., 10 Oct. 1863, Letters Sent, ser. 4664, Dept. of Arkansas, District of Eastern Arkansas, vol. 37/96, 97, 98, Dark, RG 393, pt. 2.

74. *St Paul Pioneer*, 24 Feb. 1863.

75. *St. Paul Daily Press*, 17 May 1863.

76. Orrin Densmore to Daniel Densmore, 28 Apr. 1864, Densmore Family Papers, MHS.

77. For example, a farmer in Elm Grove, Wis., "has talked of sending for a 'contraband' to fill the place of the transitory Swedes" (Orrin Densmore to Benjamin Densmore, 11 June 1863, Densmore Family Papers). Another man from the same town complained that "the prices for labor are so high and the day labor is more independent than the employer"

(Norman Densmore to Daniel Densmore, 15 Jan. 1864, ibid.). In Red Wing, Minn., Orrin Densmore complained when immigrant day workers gave notice of their intention to "go into the country through harvest for higher wages" (Orrin Densmore to Daniel Densmore, 10 July 1864, ibid.). See also Orrin Densmore to Daniel Densmore, 1 Aug. 1864, ibid. Residents of McGregor, Iowa, angry that local white women welcomed the arrival of former slave women, "advised the Norwegian, German and Irish girls to emigrate to the region of the Rocky Mountains and thus make room for the new order of things" (Wubben, *Civil War Iowa*, 132–33).

78. White men were not immune to the attractions of status that the employment of black workers seemed to offer; as one such employer was caustically portrayed, "Look at me, I am able to keep a colored gentleman as my hired hand, and prefer him for his fidelity and suitableness, to any white man in the land" (*Davenport Daily Gazette*, 1 Sept. 1865).

79. *Iowa City Republican*, 8 Apr. 1863; *Daily State Register*, 31 Jan. 1863. R. E. Robinson, on discovering two black children playing in a farmyard in Monroe County, Iowa—where the wartime black population increased from 2 to 26—pulled up his wagon and offered passing farmers taking produce to market an agitated, impromptu address on "the evil consequences resulting from the emancipation of the black race," including "the debasement and ultimate coalescence of the two races" (Hickenlooper, *History of Monroe County*, 183).

80. Urwin and Urwin, *History of the 33d Iowa*, xxv–xxvi.

81. On northern white women's wartime activism, see Leonard, *Yankee Women*, esp. chap. 2; Massey, *Women in the Civil War*, esp. chap. 4; and Clinton and Silber, *Divided Houses*.

82. Jean H. Baker, *Affairs of Party*, 256. On popular political participation, see also Adam I. P. Smith, "Partisan Politics," 83.

83. *Davenport Daily Gazette*, 23 July 1862.

84. Voegeli, *Free but Not Equal*, 13–20, 34–35, 60–63; Berlin et al., *Wartime Genesis . . . Upper South*, ser. 1, vol. 2, of *Freedom*, 28–29.

85. In 1864, Senate debates over the Freedmen's Bureau bill revealed the continuing influence of northern opposition to organized relocation. Disagreement erupted over whether the bureau would be given authority to operate in border states, as well as an amendment directing the bureau commissioner to correspond with northern governors about the possibility of relocating freedpeople to their states (a hostile amendment intended to sink the bill entirely). Supporters of the latter amendment insisted that Republican resistance to relocation revealed the hypocrisy of the party's emancipationist rhetoric: "Sit not quietly in your homes and shed crocodile tears over the barbarism of slavery and the inhumanity of southern slave holders when you have the opportunity to go and take this oppressed race not only to live in your midst, but to take them to your heart and cherish them as philanthropic men should cherish the object of their pity" (Ivers, *Congressional Globe*, June 28, 1864, 2933–34, 3328–36).

86. *Daily Democrat and News*, 1 May 1862; Wubben, *Civil War Iowa*, 79.

87. Lincoln's advocacy for colonization took several forms during the war. It included investigating potential colonies at Chiriqui (present-day Panama), Honduras, Costa Rica, and Vache Island and obtaining significant appropriations for the support of colonization schemes by Congress. It was paired with efforts to persuade the nonseceding border states

to initiate compensated, gradual emancipation, and it was included in the First and Second Confiscation Acts. See Vorenberg, "Abraham Lincoln."

88. *Home Journal*, 14 Dec. 1861; Vorenberg, "Abraham Lincoln"; Gue, *History of Iowa*, 15–34; Mason, *Election in Iowa*. See also McManus, *Political Abolitionism*, 161–63, and Voegeli, *Free but Not Equal*, 22–25.

89. *Davenport Daily Gazette*, 30 Aug. 1862; *Iowa State Journal*, 3 Sept. 1862. See petitions submitted from Marion, Polk, Warren, and Lee counties, State of Iowa, *Journal of the Senate*, 19, 47; *St. Paul Daily Press*, 10 Feb. 1863; and *St. Paul Pioneer*, 23 Feb. 1863.

90. *Daily State Register*, 6 Jan. 1863.

91. *Davenport Daily Gazette*, 12 Sept. 1862.

92. *Daily State Register*, 31 Jan. 1863.

93. *Daily Hawk-Eye*, 5 Feb. 1863.

94. On the enforcement and repeal of the exclusion law, see Dykstra, *Bright Radical Star*, 199–202; "Polk County, Delaware Township Justice of the Peace Documents," SHS/IC; *Daily State Register*, 18, 20–22, 25, 27, 31 Jan., 3 Feb. 1863; *Daily Hawk-Eye*, 24 Jan., 5, 6 Feb. 1863; Coffin, "Case of Archie P. Webb." On the employment of other contrabands in Delaware Township, see *Daily State Register*, 25 Jan. 1863. Webb disappears from the historical record after 1867 (*Daily State Register*, 27 Aug. 1867).

95. On Minnesota's petitioning, see *St. Paul Daily Press*, 10 Feb. 1863; on Wisconsin's efforts, see *St. Paul Pioneer*, 23 Feb. 1863. See also memorial of Nelson Bowers and 170 others regarding the interests of white men, 14 Mar. 1863, State of Wisconsin, *Journal of the Senate*, 404; Memorial of Chas. Walter and 338 others opposing compensated emancipation and prohibiting black settlement in Wisconsin, 19 Feb. 1863, State of Wisconsin, *Journal of the Assembly*, 286–87.

96. Quotations are from *Muscatine Daily Courier*, 13 Oct. 1862, and *Fairfield Ledger*, 28 Apr. 1863.

97. In April 1862, the Washington, D.C., City Council urged Congress to reject the emancipation bill for the district, fearing that it would make the capital "an asylum for free negroes, a population undesirable in every American community" (Berlin et al., "'To Canvass the Nation,'"). On Canada West, see Rhodes, *Mary Ann Shadd Cary*, 151. On wartime violence against northern blacks, see Bernstein, *New York City Draft Riots*; Jacqueline Jones, *American Work*, 290–92; Thornbrough, *Negro in Indiana*, 185–92; Voegeli, *Free but Not Equal*, 34–35; and Lofton, "Northern Labor and the Negro."

98. Shootings and other attacks by white assailants are reported in the *Daily Democrat and News*, 26 Dec. 1863, *Davenport Daily Gazette*, 23 Aug. 1864; *Daily State Register*, 1, 9 July, 20 Aug. 1864; and Porter, *Annals of Polk County*, 524.

99. In 1860, of 4,441,830 African Americans, 226,152 (5 percent) resided in the North; 3,953,760 slaves (89 percent) lived in the South, as did 261,918 free blacks. See Trotter, *African American Experience*, 1–23.

100. Mosely, *Colored Man of America*, 7.

CHAPTER 4

1. Affidavit by Henry Tolliver, 22 July 1890, pension file of Tolliver, IC 555868, CWPF.

2. White masculinity in the context of Union military service is discussed insightfully by Reid Mitchell in "Soldiering, Manhood, and Coming of Age."

3. African Americans who enlisted from the upper Midwest served in a number of units. In addition to the 49 men recruited for the 60th USCI from Minnesota, another 38 black soldiers, assigned to the 68th, 69th, 30th, and 18th USCI, were credited to the state. These units were organized in Missouri, Arkansas and Tennessee, Maryland, and Missouri, respectively. Excluding the men recruited for the 60th, many were signed up in the South and credited to Minnesota. Credited to Wisconsin were 272 African Americans; another 81 men from other states stood in as substitutes for white draftees. Most of these men were in Company F of the 29th USCI (organized in Quincy, Illinois), although Wisconsin men also served in the 5th, 12th, 14th, 21st, and 40th USCI (organized in Ohio [5th], Tennessee [12th, 14th, 40th], South Carolina [21st], and Louisiana [49th]). See Rusk and Chapman, *Roster of Wisconsin Volunteers*, 954–60; Noyes, "The Negro," 75; and Civil War Soldiers and Sailors System, NPS.

4. The possible range falls between 267 and 431. The number cannot be determined with precision. Although 384 soldiers were credited to Iowa, not all of these were actually recruited in the state. A much smaller number, 220, gave Iowa as their residence when they mustered out. See Logan, *Official Roster*, 1585–1687.

5. *Oskaloosa Times*, 14 Aug. 1862.

6. Billings D. Sibley to Dear Sister Anna, Winchester, Tenn., 12 Aug. 1862, Sibley Papers, MHS.

7. *Daily State Register*, 23 Dec. 1862; Nell, *Colored Patriots*.

8. Newman, *White Women's Rights*, 10–11.

9. *Daily State Register*, 5 Nov. 1863.

10. See, e.g., *Daily Democrat and News*, 4 Oct. 1862.

11. *Iowa Daily Statesman*, 27 Aug. 1863.

12. Miss Charlotte Thomas, 10 May 1863, vol. 1, p. 848, entry 13, ser. 361: Letters Received, 60th USCI, Records of Colored Troops, RG 94.

13. Quoted in Herdegen, *Men Stood Like Iron*, 59.

14. The first quotation is from James M. Stewart, "Old Putrid's Washington County Democrat on Abolitionists," 14 Feb. 1863, typed transcript, Palmer Papers, Special Collections, University of Iowa. The second quotation is that of the Iowa governor's secretary in his August 1862 response to an offer to raise black companies in the state (Wubben, "Uncertain Trumpet," 413–14).

15. In Davis Letters, 16 Apr. 1863, 17 Jan. 1865, SC/UI.

16. Hiram Russell to Maria Russell, 10 July 1863, transcribed by Thomas J. Russell, c/o Bruce Hanson, personal correspondence in possession of author.

17. *Davenport Daily Gazette*, 15 Aug. 1862.

18. *Home Journal*, 28 Feb. 1863.

19. *Iowa City Republican*, 19 Aug. 1863.

20. Noyes, "The Negro," 73.

21. E-mail from Chandra Miller to author, 13 Nov. 2001; Throne, *Diary of Cyrus F. Boyd*; manuscript census return for Marion County, Iowa (Ancestry.com, *1850 United States Federal Census*).

22. Noted in Zachary Cooper, *Black Settlers*, 23; however, this could not be confirmed on the Civil War Soldiers and Sailors System website, NPS, as of 20 June 2006.

23. There were no bars against Native American service in white regiments during the Civil War, although Wisconsin's governor and other state officials rejected offers by native men to organize Native American regiments early in the war, and the 1862 Enrollment Act exempted native men who were not citizens. Despite these obstacles, a number of Native Americans enlisted in midwestern regiments early in the war; in fact, 500 to 600 of Wisconsin's Native American population of 9,000 served during the war (Russell Horton, "Unwanted in a White Man's War," 18–27). John and William Revels are listed as "dark"-complected in their service files. However, although Revels family members and genealogists have documented their Cherokee origins, during their lifetime and after, whites identified them as people of African descent; see Herdegen, *Men Stood Like Iron*, 60–61, and James K. Phillips to Mrs. Clinton Nuzum, 1 Nov. 1956, in Wisconsin—Negroes, Explanatory Materials, WHS (this letter notes that the Revels clan could be traced to the 1830 North Carolina census as a family of free blacks). Co-residence and social intimacy among the area's African and Native American–descended families undoubtedly played a role in whites' identification of the settlement's inhabitants. Members of the Revels family were neighbors of, and intimately familiar with, local African Americans (e.g., a sister of John and William was a midwife to Lydia Allen when her husband served in the 29th USCI; see J. L. Davenport, Commissioner, to Commissioner, General Land Office, 26 Aug. 1912, in pension file of Charles Allen, WC 354849, CWPF). The extended Revels family also had previously lived in a community that included former slaves in Hamilton County, Ind. (Ancestry.com, *1860 United States Federal Census* for Hamilton County). The best accounts of the Revel family are offered by genealogists; see <http://genforum.genealogy.com/revels/messages/152.html> (13 Jan. 2008).

24. See pension file of Leonard Barton, IA 360582, CWPF. His father's and grandfather's emancipation papers are recorded in the Database of Illinois Servitude and Emancipation Records, ISA. A number of black men served in northern white regiments; among those identified were H. Ford Douglas (95th Illinois Infantry), George E. Stephens (26th Pennsylvania Infantry), and William H. Johnson (8th Connecticut Infantry)—see Redkey, *Grand Army*, 9–250; Charles R. Pratt (11th Ohio Volunteers) and four additional men from the 1st Ohio Cavalry, noted but not named in Berlin et al., *Black Military Experience*, ser. 2 of *Freedom*, 18n. 29; and Beverly Jefferson, grandson of Thomas Jefferson and Sally Hemings, whose family moved to Wisconsin in 1852 and passed as white, changing their names from Hemings to Jefferson. Jefferson served in the 1st Regiment, Wisconsin Infantry (Thomas Jefferson Memorial Foundation, *Report of the Research Committee*, App. H, Sally Hemings and Her Children). See also Ancestry.com., *1870 United States Federal Census*, and Civil War Soldiers and Sailors System, NPS). Felix Barton is found in Rusk and Chapman, *Roster of Wisconsin Volunteers*, 958.

25. *Davenport Daily Gazette*, 13 Aug. 1862; *Cedar Falls Gazette*, 8, 15 Jan. and 5 Feb. 1864.

26. Brig. Gen. N. B. Buford to Brig. Gen. Asboth, 11 June 1863, Letters Received, DOM, ser. 1085, vol. 241/586 DKy, RG 393, pt. 2.

27. Meier, "Lorenzo Thomas." On black enlistment in the broader Midwest, see Michael O. Smith, "Raising a Black Regiment," and Washington, *Eagles on Their Buttons.*

28. *Home Journal*, 9 May 1863.

29. Meier, "Lorenzo Thomas," 261.

30. Gooding, *On the Altar of Freedom*, 3–4, 17.

31. Mathew Griffin to Garrett Douglas, 28 Mar. 1865, in pension file of Griffin, WC 552781, CWPF.

32. *Iowa City Republican*, 1 July 1863.

33. *Iowa City Republican*, 19 Aug. 1863.

34. Gov. Samuel Kirkwood to Gen. [Henry Halleck], 5 Aug. 1862, Letters Received, ser. 22, RG 108. See also *St. Paul Pioneer*, 22 July 1864, in which Frances Collins, commanding a company of the 49th USCI, urges the residents of his hometown to allow him to recruit among runaway slaves at the rear of Sherman's army, to be credited to St. Paul and Minnesota.

35. *Burlington Weekly Hawk-Eye*, 15 Oct. 1864.

36. Noyes, "The Negro," 73; Dykstra, *Bright Radical Star*, 196.

37. *Home Journal*, 10 Mar. 1863; Charlotte Thomas to [?], 10 May 1863, p. 848, entry 13, ser. 361, [Minn. Asst. Secretary of State to ?], 15 June 1863, p. 505, entry 19, and Gov. Salomon to [?], 24 July 1863, p. 940, entry 63, all in Letters Received, Records of Colored Troops, RG 94; G. Van Steenwyk to Gov. Edw. Salomon, 29 Oct. 1863, Executive Dept., Administration of the Army, ser. 1 / 1 / 5–11 (new ser. 58), box 16, WHS.

38. *Home Journal*, 22 Aug. 1863.

39. See "The Call for Colored Soldiers: Will They Fight? Should They Fight?," *Christian Recorder*, 14 Feb. 1863; Blight, *Douglass' Civil War*, 149–50; and Kantrowitz, "Fighting like Men."

40. Robert Dykstra reports that Alexander Clark appealed to Kirkwood in 1862 for permission to raise black military companies in the state, only to be rebuffed by the governor's secretary; see *Bright Radical Star*, 196. I have been unable to locate Clark's letter.

41. Pile had already organized his first regiment and designated it an Arkansas unit. His recruiting efforts were undoubtedly boosted by the 1 July 1863 passage of a gradual emancipation law in Missouri, which, though starting in 1870, would keep some African Americans in bondage as late as 1897. The law confirmed for many enslaved people that flight or enlistment were their only avenues to freedom. Missouri's gradual emancipation law dictated that slaves over age 40 would live out their lives as apprentices; slaves under age 12 in 1870 would remain apprentices until they reached age 23, and all others would be free on 4 July 1870 (Trexler, *Slavery in Missouri*, 236–37).

42. John Cleghorn to Gov. Kirkwood, n.d., Adjutant General Records, SHS/DM.

43. Camp Lincoln was established in 11 Aug. 1862; see Donald C. Elder, *Damned Iowa Greyhound*, 183 n.1. See also *Constitution*, 12 Sept. 1863.

44. Seven of the recruits who joined the 60th USCI gave Iowa as their birthplace; of these, only three can be found in the census to confirm their Iowa residence. Seven additional men demonstrated through their pension applications that they had resided in

Iowa prior to the war; three of these were brothers, born in Wisconsin to Patsey Street, whose history of midwestern enslavement was discussed in Chapter 1. None of the signatories to two antebellum petitions from Muscatine's antebellum black residents enlisted in the regiment (Petitions #11, 1855, and #11b, n.d., Petitions, Blacks and Mulattos, Rights of, Secretary of State Records, SHS/DM). No recruits gave Minnesota as their birthplace; similar patterns shaped Wisconsin enlistments in Company F of the 29th USCI (Vollmar, "Negro in a Midwest Frontier City," 73–77).

45. Affidavit by Henry Tolliver, 22 July 1890, pension file of Tolliver, IC 555868, CWPF.

46. George Hall to Mr. Davenport (Commissioner of Pensions), 14 Dec. 1903, pension file of Hall, IC 554990; affidavit by Ephraim Piles Ford, 25 Jan. 1910, pension file of Ford, IC 935141—both in CWPF.

47. Affidavit by James Bradford, 18 May 1904, pension file of Bradford, WC 933600, CWPF. See also Capt. Bates, endorsement, 8 May 1903 (pension file of George W. Coleman, IA 1374395, CWPF), describing the work of John Wesley.

48. *Racine Journal-News*, 22 Feb. 1922. William H. Harrison left his master in Brunswick, Mo., in October 1862 and "fell in with" Col. Merrill's cavalry regiment to serve as Merrill's bodyguard until he left for Keokuk and enlisted in August 1863 (affidavit by Harrison, 12 May 1883, pension file of Harrison, IC 884167, CWPF). Before enlisting, Raymond Lewis also worked as a servant in a Union regiment, and Alfred Morgan was a servant in the Missouri militia (affidavit by Raymond Lewis, 10 Jan. 1883, pension file of Lewis, WC 299926, and affidavit by Jane Morgan, 17 Apr. 1872, pension file of Alfred Morgan, Mother C 167990, CWPF). Escaping from his owner's large farm ten miles from Helena, Nathaniel Adams made his way to Helena "and cooked for about 5 months for soldiers there"; in the spring of 1863, he headed for Keokuk, where he lived and worked until he could enlist (affidavit by Adams, 9 Feb. 1889, pension file of Adams, IC 472578, CWPF). Former slave Alfred Mason also cooked for a Union regiment before enlisting (affidavit by Mason, 4 July 1898, pension file of Mason, IC 698900, CWPF).

49. *St. Paul Pioneer*, 6, 15 May 1863; *St. Paul Daily Press*, 6, 16 June 1863; *Daily Missouri Democrat*, 15 June 1863.

50. Affidavit by Antoine Crawford, 2 Dec. 1895, pension file of George Johnson, WC 419018, CWPF. See also affidavit by Crawford, 9 Apr. 1886, pension file of Alexander Lambert, WC 236371; affidavit by Perry Malvan, 17 Apr. 1876, pension file of Robert Draper, Minor C 177212, and declaration by Charles H. Crockett, 21 Sept. 1863, pension file of Crockett, WC 368575—all in CWPF.

51. See, e.g., affidavit by John Reed, 17 Apr. 1886, pension file of Alexander Lambert, WC 236371, CWPF.

52. Robert Huhn Jones, *Civil War in the Northwest*, 63–67; *St. Paul Daily Press*, 27, 30 Sept. 1863; *Washington Press*, 2 Dec. 1863, cited in Rawick's version of the Iowa Negroes WPA Project, 385.

53. John Wesley earned $35 per month working as a teamster for the Union army at Little Rock. When he became a soldier, his pay dropped to $7 per month until soldiers' pay was equalized in June 1864 (Capt. Bates, endorsement, 8 May 1903, pension file of George W. Coleman, IA 1374395, CWPF).

54. Affidavit by William Logan, 11 May 1889, pension file of George Young, MC

133472, CWPF. Although the proclamation did not apply to Missouri or the other loyal border states, both Union soldiers and enslaved people acted on the assumption that it did.

55. Affidavit by Henry C. Cooper, 9 Aug. 1888, pension file of William C. Early, IC 419454; affidavit by Jason Green, 4 Aug. 1881, pension file of Green, WC 481796—both in CWPF.

56. Affidavit by Milton Howard, 17 Dec. 1916, pension file of Harvey Brooks, WC 825854, CWPF.

57. Affidavit by William Logan, 11 May 1889, pension file of George C. Young, MC 133472, CWPF.

58. Deposition by Arge Washington, 17 Mar. 1886, pension file of Robert Wilson, IC 327417, CWPF.

59. Affidavit by Leroy Stevens, 8 June 1920, pension file of Walter Bucklin, WC 892542, CWPF.

60. No member of the 60th indicated Wisconsin as his residence at the time he mustered out; fifty-nine mustered out to Illinois.

61. Compiled from service and pension records.

62. Capt. William A. Stuart to Capt. Brownell, 31 July 1864, box 40, 60th USCI, RG 94.

63. On the encounter at Big Creek, see *OR* 41(1):18–20. The 60th lost one commissioned officer and three men killed and ten wounded. The entire U.S. force consisted of 150 cavalry, 360 colored infantry, and a section of colored light artillery (*OR* 41(2):401).

64. Early in the war, the secretary of the U.S. Sanitary Commission, Frederick Law Olmsted, reported to the secretary of war that more than half of the time, physical exams on entry into the service were not conducted at all. Army regulations prescribed thorough examinations: recruits were to be undressed and subjected to inspection of the head, eyes, ears, nose, jaw, neck, chest, and genital and urinary organs. See George Worthington Adams, *Doctors in Blue*, 11–13, and Patten, *Patten's Army Manual*. After the passage of the Enrollment Act of 3 Mar. 1863 establishing the draft, enrollment boards were required to administer still very thorough exams, but the boards also faced considerable pressure to work briskly. John David Smith ("Kentucky Civil War Recruits") found four Kentucky examiners seeing an average of 75 to 100 men daily. See also Doyle and Smith, " 'Best Soldiers in the World.' "

65. Deposition by Abram Myers, 8 Feb. 1887, pension file of Manual Achan, WC 496793, CWPF.

66. Deposition by Arge Washington, 21 Mar. 1887, pension file of Washington, IC 312408, CWPF.

67. Deposition by George Kebo, 22 Mar. 1887, pension file of Arge Washington, IC 312408, CWPF.

68. Deposition by William Early, 27 July 1883, pension file of Alexander Fine, WC 895031, CWPF. Donald Shaffer, in examining pension records for men from several black units, found testimony on exams that ranged from superficial to thorough. Calvin Gales, of the 27th USCI, reported that "I was examined by being stripped and required to hop across the room, and so pronounced sound" (Shaffer, "Sable Arm Speaks").

69. William Henry Harrison Clayton, a white recruit, described being required to undress for his exam at Keokuk; see Donald C. Elder, *Damned Iowa Greyhound*, 6. Indeed, the

regulations of the Provost Marshal Bureau dictated that recruits be stripped for their exams (noted by Bartholow in *Manual of Instructions*, 168–69, although Bartholow and others recalled wartime exams performed with clothed subjects). Alfred Johnson recalled: "I was made to strip and submit to inspection in the presence of Dr. Patton and an asst. surgeon" (affidavit by Alfred Johnson, n.d., pension file of Johnson, WC 876983, CWPF). On the commodification of enslaved people's bodies, see Walter Johnson, *Soul by Soul*, 25–26, 138–39, 150–51.

70. Not all recruits received such thorough examinations; John Scott passed his, despite the fact that his feet were significantly malformed, causing a serious lameness (Certificate of Disability for Discharge for Private John Scott, 13 June 1865, pension file of Scott, IA 102128, CWPF). An additional eleven men were rejected by mustering officers by 11 Jan. 1864 (Iowa, Adjutant General's Office, *Report of the Adjutant General*, 199–227, SHS/IC. Alexander Clark is referred to as "Sergeant" in the *Muscatine Journal* of 27 Sept. 1863; his disability is noted in the *Washington Press*, 2 Dec. 1863, quoted in Rawick's version of the Iowa Negroes WPA Project MS, 385, and *Muscatine Journal*, 16, 20 Nov. 1863.

71. Deposition by George Kebo, 22 Mar. 1887, pension file of Arge Washington, IC 312408, CWPF. Kebo's examiner may have been guided by Bartholow's 1863 *Manual of Instructions*, which notes that a black soldier with white ancestry was "prey to scrofula, loses the power of reproduction, and becomes extinct in a few years." According to Bartholow (pp. 206–7), blacks were well suited for fatigue duty but lacked the intellect to lead. Yet he also asserted that besides a black's distinct color, "shape of cranium, length of forearm, thinness of calves, and flatness of feet," there were no other "physical peculiarities making him different from white men" (p. 207). In addition, though his manual proposes careful inspection for hemorrhoids, there is no specific suggestion for a close check of the penis ("The testes and cords should be examined for chronic enlargements, varicocele, circocele, hydrocele, or sarcocele. The next step is to require the recruit to lean forward upon his hands and place his feet widely apart; whilst in this position, the surgeon should separate the nates for hemorrhoids, fissures of the anus, fistula in ano, or urinary fistula" [pp. 173–74]).

72. On discipline and manhood, see Lapsansky, "'Discipline to the Mind'"; Cullen, "'I's a Man Now'"; and Rotundo, "Learning about Manhood."

73. *Chicago Times*, 25 Aug. 1863.

74. *Constitution*, 8 Oct. 1863.

75. On name changes, see affidavit by Benjamin Henry, 12 Feb. 1896, pension file of John Anderson aka Norvell, WA 271609; affidavit by Henry D. Brown, 28 Feb. 1891, pension file of Brown, IC 660715; affidavit by Isaac Cox, 5 July 1899, pension file of Cox, IC 353446; affidavit by Emeline Ross, 27 July 1921, pension file of Joseph Ross (aka Porter), IC 482911; and deposition by Nelson Shelby, 2 Jan. 1888, pension file of Shelby, IC 391883—all in CWPF

76. See, e.g., the comments of Cyrus Boyd (a white Iowan) as noted in Mitchell, *Vacant Chair*, 6.

77. Entries for 5, 31 Nov. 1863, Private Notebook of Lt. Col. Collins, LCHS.

78. Thomas Montgomery to Dear Parents, 16 Dec. 1863, Montgomery Papers, MHS; Private Notebook of Lt. Col. Collins, 5 Nov. 1863, LCHS; *Keokuk Weekly Gate City*, 25 Nov. 1863.

79. *Christian Recorder*, 31 Dec. 1864.

80. *Missouri Democrat*, 21 Nov. 1863; *Muscatine Journal*, 26 Nov. 1863; entries for 20 and 21 Nov. 1863, Private Notebook of Lt. Col. Collins, LCHS.

81. Entry for 28 Nov. 1863, Private Notebook of Lt. Col. Collins, LCHS. The best overview of the pay issue can be found in Berlin et al., *Black Military Experience*, ser. 2 of *Freedom*, 362–68.

82. Berlin et al., *Black Military Experience*, ser. 2 of *Freedom*, 484–85.

83. Quoted in Shea, "Semi-Savage State," 95.

84. Moneyhon, "From Slave to Free Labor," 178.

85. By August 1864, the total force at Helena was about 3,100 men; see *OR* 41(2):711–16.

86. Taylor Robinson suffered a hernia while trying to carry a cartridge box and a heavy knapsack (affidavit by Taylor Robinson, 10 Sept. 1891, pension file of Robinson, IC 699571); Nelson Shelby was crushed beneath a heavy box of provisions he tried to unload from a boat (affidavit by Shelby, 16 Sept. 1887, pension file of Shelby, IC 391883); John H. Bandy broke his collarbone while trying to move an officer's mess chest (affidavit by Bandy, 10 Aug. 1892, pension file of Bandy, IC 840217); George Patterson was hurt while building a bridge (declaration by Patterson, 23 Mar. 1898, pension file of Patterson, IC 64409); Clement Graves suffered an injury by heavy timbers while repairing fortifications (affidavit by Anderson Hays, n.d., pension file of Clement, WC 772597); both Samuel Webster and William Anderson were run over by wagons and mule teams (affidavit by Richard Elliott, 12 Mar. 1900, pension file of Webster IC 1027540, and declaration by William Alexander, 5 Mar. 1891, pension file of Alexander, WC 485836)—all in CWPF. For complaints by commanders of black regiments and black soldiers in the Mississippi valley about the assignment of heavy fatigue and guard duty to black troops, see Berlin et al., *Black Military Experience*, ser. 2 of *Freedom*, 504–16.

87. Affidavit by Charles Richardson, 4 Apr. 1883, and by Sally Deberry, 7 Jan. 1891, pension file of Richardson, IC 287414, CWPF.

88. Urwin and Urwin, *History of the 33d Iowa*, 14–15; Urwin, "'A Very Disastrous Defeat.'"

89. Entry, 20 Dec. 1863, Private Notebook of Lt. Col. Collins, LCHS. The second and third quotations are from Shea, "Semi-Savage State," 96.

90. A white observer described the shantytown as "a regular town of niggers who have run away from slavery, they keep every thing clean around them but the streets are not laid out very regular." He also noted that "there is a large Fort about two miles below town, called . . . Fort of Freedmen, where all the niggers who are unable to work or cannot get any are sent and supported by the U.S. until they can find work" (George Adams to Abby, 5 Aug. 1864, folder 2, Adams Papers, MHS). The hospital for blacks, according to one inspection in December 1862, was "dirty, uncomfortable and cheerless." Moreover, "cruelties and barbarities" were perpetrated on black patients to the extent that the inspector recommended, and authorities concurred, that a radical change was necessary (*Weekly Gazette and Free Press*, 16 Jan. 1863).

91. Entry, 12 Jan. 1864, Private Notebook of Lt. Col. Collins, LCHS.

92. Entries for 15, 25, 26 Jan. 1864 and undated concluding entry, Private Notebook of Lt. Col. Collins, LCHS. In January, one inspector at Helena pronounced the 60th "the best African Regiment in the field." By late February, an inspection pronounced the men to be

"well-disciplined, well drilled," with a "good soldierly appearance" (entry, 16 Jan., 1864, ibid.; Capt. T. S. Ellsworth, ADC, to Brig. Gen. L. Thomas, 26 Feb. 1864, Letters Received, box 40, 60th USCI, RG 94).

93. Musser, *Soldier Boy*, 20.

94. *Constitution*, 5 Oct. 1863; deposition by Abram Myers, 2 Jan. 1888, pension file of Nelson Shelby, IC 391883, CWPF). Mason Lewis lost several toes from the cold on the trip to Helena (affidavit by Lewis, 13 Aug. 1867, pension file of Lewis, IC 161945, CWPF), as did Manual Achan (affidavit by Arge Washington, 8 Feb. 1887, pension file of Achan, WC 496793, CWPF); see also entries for 1 Jan., 21–23 Dec. 1864, Private Notebook of Lt. Col. Collins, LCHS. George Thomas lost toes from both feet while on picket duty at Helena (affidavit by Mat Cheatham and Jackson Henry, 23 Dec. 1869, pension file of Thomas, WC 816806, CWPF); affidavit by George Kebo, 16 Apr. 1884, pension file of Daniel Tate, WC 361052, CWPF.

95. Gooding, *On The Altar of Freedom*, 55.

96. Logan, *Official Roster*, 1585–1687.

97. Linderman, *Embattled Courage*, 115.

98. *Weekly Gate City*, 7 Oct. 1863; affidavit by David Robinson, 11 Feb. 1889, pension file of Nathaniel Adams, IC 472578, and affidavit by John H. Bandy, 10 Aug. 1892, pension file of Bandy, IC 840217, CWPF.

99. *Daily State Register*, 28 Nov. 1863.

100. On the "second wave" of disease, see Linderman, *Embattled Courage*, 115. As John David Smith ("Let Us All Be Grateful," 42) has pointed out, black troops throughout the Mississippi valley suffered horrific mortality rates from disease.

101. Entry, 26 Dec. 1863, Private Notebook of Lt. Col. Collins, LCHS; Logan, *Official Roster*.

102. Affidavit by Ralph Teller, 15 Apr. 1884, pension file of Daniel Tate, WC 361052, CWPF. Interestingly, there were significant variations in the death rate for soldiers depending on where they enlisted (keeping in mind that this is sometimes an indication of where they were credited to, rather than their actual residence at the time of enlistment). The highest death rate was among men enlisted in Illinois (94 percent, 34 enlisted men); in Helena, the rate was 86 percent (6 enlisted men); in Missouri, 85 percent (187); in Iowa, 66 percent (120); and in Minnesota, 48 percent (John David Smith, "Let Us All Be Grateful," 10).

103. Affidavit by Ned Dunn, 22 Oct. 1884, pension file of Peter Jackson, WC 314291, CWPF.

104. Deposition by Peter Jackson, 22 Nov. 1881, pension file of Jackson, WC 314291, CWPF.

105. Endorsement, Eli Ramsey, John C. Black to Ramsey, 4 Oct. 1886, pension file of Henry White, IC 92134, CWPF.

106. Deposition by Henry Cooper, 13 Jan. 1898, pension file of John Williams WC 463670, CWPF.

107. Reimer, "Smallpox and Vaccination in the Civil War." On inequities in the health care provided to black soldiers, see Berlin et al., *Black Military Experience*, ser. 2 of *Freedom*, 633–37.

108. According to James Henry Gooding (*On the Altar of Freedom*, 12) of the Massachusetts 54th, the regimental surgeon vaccinated his entire regiment before it left Massachusetts.

109. Joseph Jones, *Researches upon "Spurious Vaccination."*

110. Affidavit by Ralph Teller, 10 Sept. 1883, and affidavit by Emanuel Aikens, 28 Aug. 1886, pension file of London Triplett, WA 266564, CWPF.

111. Affidavit by Freeman Knowles, M.D., n.d., and George Kebo to Mr. Dudley, 14 July 1884, pension file of Kebo, WC 919204, CWPF.

112. Affidavit by George Jenkins, 1 Apr. 1886, pension file of London Triplett, WA 266564, CWPF.

113. Affidavit by Emanuel Aikens, 28 Aug. 1886, pension file of London Triplett, WA 266564, CWPF.

114. One widow's application for a pension on the basis of her husband's death from syphilis, contracted by vaccination while in the army, was denied on the assumption by white examiners that he had come by the disease "in the usual way," contrary to extensive testimony on the administration of impure vaccine to Triplett and other members of the regiment. See Capt. H. Sweeney to Commissioner of Pensions, 20 Mar. 1884, pension file of Henry Allen, WC 834236, CWPF; Special Examiner C. P. Eppert to Commissioner John C. Black, 29 Aug. 1886, and Special Examiner A. W. Clegg to Black, 5 Apr. 1886, pension file of London Triplett, WA 266564, CWPF.

115. Racist characterizations of African Americans as likely carriers of venereal disease ignored the fact that its incidence was lower among black troops (77 cases per 1,000 men) than white troops (82 cases per 1,000 men) (Lowry, *Story the Soldiers Wouldn't Tell*, 104). A study of three white California physicians who examined recruits during the war found that none of these doctors associated venereal diseases with blacks, though all three maintained explicitly racist views (Doyle and Smith, "'Very best Soldiers in the World'").

116. Donald C. Elder, *Love amid the Turmoil*, 278. William Vermillion had warned his wife Mary to avoid the vaccine at all costs (p. 281).

117. Kohl, "'This Godforsaken Town.'"

118. Urwin and Urwin, *History of the 33d Iowa*, 16.

119. Berlin et al., *Black Military Experience*, ser. 2 of *Freedom*, 633–37; see also Shaffer, *After the Glory*, 16–17.

120. Linderman, *Embattled Courage*, 116; Blight, "No Desperate Hero," 64–67.

121. Berlin et al., *Black Military Experience*, ser. 2 of *Freedom*, 654.

122. Ibid., 637–55.

123. *Weekly Gate City*, 30 Sept., 7 Oct. 1863; *Constitution*, 12 Sept. 1863.

124. General Orders No. 67, DOM, General Court-Martial of McCoy, MO/SHS.

125. *Daily State Register*, 28 Nov. 1863; General Orders No. 6, 6 Dec. 1863, Col. John G. Hudson, Benton Barracks, Mo., box 41, unbound Regimental Records, 60th USCI, RG 94; entry for 15 Dec. 1863, Private Notebook of Lt. Col. Collins, LCHS.

126. Lt. R. A. Phelan to Col. A. D. Greene, 6 Nov. 1863, and endorsement by Capt. Sweeney, 10 Nov. 1863, Headquarters DOM, St. Louis, ser. 2593, RG 393, pt. 1.

127. See, e.g., General Orders No. 7, 30 Jan. 1864, by order of Brig. Gen. N. B. Buford, District of East Arkansas Helena, 60th USCI, box 41, RG 94.

128. Affidavit by Milton Howard, 17 Dec. 1916, pension file of Harvey Brooks, WC 825854, CWPF; deposition by Martilla Newbern, 9 July 1895, pension file of William Newbern, WC 453072, CWPF.

129. Deposition by Martilla Newbern, 9 July 1895, pension file of William Newbern, WC 453072, CWPF.

130. Brockett and Vaughn, *Women's Work*, 697–703; Notice, Col. John G. Hudson, 22 June 1865, Little Rock, box 40, unbound Regimental Records, 60th USCI, RG 94. According to one black observer at Helena, many men in the 60th USCT had learned enough to read and sign their names on the payroll (*Christian Recorder*, 31 Dec. 1864).

131. Quotations from *OR, Supplement, Part II—Record of Events*, vol. 78, serial no. 90, 358; AWOL charges against Thomas Allison, 18 Mar. 1865, folder 9, John G. Hudson Papers, WHMC/C; General Orders No. 40, Col. John G. Hudson, 22 Dec. 1864, Helena, Ark., Headquarters, 60th USCI, unbound records, box 40, Letters Received; General Orders No. 26, 25 July 1865, Col. J. G. Hudson, Headquarters, 2nd Brigade, Little Rock, Ark., unbound records, box 41, both in Regimental Records, 60th USCI, RG 94; Brig. Gen. N. B. Buford to Maj. W. D. Green, 23 Mar. 1864, District of Eastern Arkansas, Dept. of Arkansas, ser. 4664, vol., 37/96–98, RG 393, pt. 2.

132. Affidavits by Lafayette Franklin, 31 July 1891, and Eli Ramsey, 23 Feb. 1891, pension file of Henry D. Brown, IC 660715, CWPF.

133. Affidavits by Mary White Brown, 20 Dec. 1882, 22 June 1887, pension file of Henry White, IC 92134, CWPF. Brown's nursing prevented White from having to go to the hospital. Subtitle from affidavit by Virginia Linebaugh, 15 June 1885, ibid.

134. *Chicago Defender*, 6 Mar. 1915.

135. Jane Schultz estimates that 10 percent of the female workers officially employed by the Union army as nurses, cooks, laundresses, and in other positions were African Americans; like black soldiers, black Union nurses received lower wages than did whites (Schultz, *Women at the Front*, 21–22, 39).

136. Affidavit by Violet Moulton, 26, 29 Oct. 1878, pension file of Robert Hutchinson, WC 142814, CWPF.

137. Affidavit by Nancy Richards, 8 June 1877, pension file of James Richards, WC 162287, CWPF.

138. Affidavit by Violet Moulton, 26 Oct. 1878, pension file of Robert Hutchinson, WC 142814, CWPF.

139. Affidavit by William Stuart and Elizabeth Stuart, 28 Aug. 1886, pension file of London Triplett, WA 266564, and affidavit by G. W. Pittman, 25 July 1884, pension file of W. Stuart, WC 607408—both in CWPF.

140. For Patsey and London Triplett, who were owned by the Street family prior to the war, see Chapter 1.

141. Federal census for Lee County, Iowa, 1860 and 1870; statement by J. B. McNamara, Deputy Clerk of Courts, 3 Apr. 1883, pension file of London Triplett, WA 266564, CWPF.

142. Affidavit by Mary Hardin, 21 Jan. 1887, pension file of London Triplett, WA 266564, CWPF.

143. Affidavit by Mary Hardin, 1 Apr. 1886, ibid.

144. Ibid.

145. Affidavits by Elizabeth Stuart, George Thomas, William Stuart, 28 Aug. 1886, and

Arge Washington, 27 Aug. 1886, pension file of London Triplett, WA 266564, CWPF. William Stuart also noted that "some called it the clap, some called it the pock."

146. Affidavit by Elizabeth Stuart, 28 Aug. 1886, pension file of London Triplett, WA 266564, CWPF.

147. See "Congenital Syphilis," Medline Plus, <http://www.nlm.nih.gov/medline plus/ency/article/001344.htm> (28 May 2006).

148. Affidavit by Emmanuel Aikens, 28 Aug. 1886, pension file of London Triplett, WA 266564, CWPF.

149. Jane Schultz kindly shared, from her own research, the names of the African American relief workers that could be located in the Carded Service Records and on pension applications—both at the National Archives and Records Administration. Her research is described in her book, *Women at the Front*.

150. Berlin et al., *Black Military Experience*, ser. 2 of *Freedom*, 709. The order was issued on 3 Feb. 1865.

151. General Orders No. 8, 2 Apr. 1865, Col. John G. Hudson, Helena, Ark., Headquarters 60th USCI, box 40, unbound Regimental Records, RG 94.

152. See, e.g., Fleche, "'Shoulder to Shoulder,'" 175–77.

CHAPTER 5

1. Mosely, *Colored Man of America*, 7.
2. Melish, *Disowning Slavery*, offers an excellent overview of New England's trajectory from slavery to a mythically free region.
3. *Christian Recorder*, 25 Dec. 1873.
4. Of the northern states, only Illinois (1891), New York (1876), and Ohio (1883) passed laws after the war to recognize the legality of slave marriages; see Stephenson, *Race Distinctions*, 74.
5. For example, when members of the Colored Debating Society of Fond du Lac, Wis., decided to "imitate" their "white brethren" with an "ambitious" move to relocate their debates from the local black church to the public Opera Hall, they were portrayed as offering whites "laughable and side-splitting entertainments" (*Milwaukee Sentinel*, 9 May 1878).
6. Some scholars use the term "cultural citizenship" to capture the aspects of belonging and identity that lay outside the arena of formal rights. See Shafir, *Citizenship Debates*; Flores and Benmayor, *Latino Cultural Citizenship*; and Flint, "Toni Morrison's *Paradise*." My appreciation to Andrea Friedman for pointing me to this literature.
7. Quoted in *Christian Recorder*, 10 Feb. 1866. "Enterprise" was not the only advocate for westward emigration. Before the war, St. Paul resident Thomas Albert Jackson promoted the region's "free and pay for labor system, our free and general circulation of knowledge, and our general and public improvements" (*Douglass's Paper*, 23 Feb. 1855). AME Bishop Wayman urged black residents of the large eastern cities to move to Davenport, Iowa, if they wanted "to become owners of property, and get good wages . . . for there is a great demand for them there" (*Christian Recorder*, 16 Nov. 1872). Rev. J. W. Malone advocated western emigration over African colonization: "We must become owners of the land and cultivators of the soil. We need more farmers among us; we must be producers as well as

consumers; there are too many among us in towns and cities; we need more of our people on farms and on the broad prairies. Therefore, instead of colonizing Africa, why not colonize the territories and broad prairies of the West?" (*Christian Recorder*, 22 Mar. 1883).

8. *Daily Hawk-Eye*, 5 May 1869. The ad was placed by a hotel seeking dining room servants and porters.

9. *St. Louis Globe-Democrat*, 13 Aug. 1876 (reprinting a story from the *Constitution*).

10. The following summaries are based on my database containing 2,247 records of 887 women, 1,344 men, and 16 whose gender is unknown. These black Iowans, who resided in the state between the end of the war and 1880, were identified through census records, city directories, military service and pension records, and a host of primary source material. There is no single source that reliably reports occupations or work experiences among African Americans in the postbellum Midwest. The 1870 census is useful but typically vague for adult men; it is even less useful or accurate in documenting the income-generating activities of women and children. For that reason, I draw on narrative, testimony, and other sources to ascertain occupations in the postwar era. The data are admittedly spotty and imperfect, as well as inappropriate for more sophisticated studies of persistence or occupational mobility, but they are nonetheless useful for gaining a sense of broader patterns of employment and work experience.

11. Rosa Dandridge Pryor, "The Dandridge Family History," 1971 MS, bound vol., Harper Papers, IWA.

12. Russell Johnson, in his community study of wartime Dubuque, offers useful analyses of white occupations and households against which to contrast findings from my database of black Iowans. On white women taking in boarders, see Johnson, *Warriors into Workers*, 54.

13. Alfred L. Triplett to Veteran's Bureau, 19 Nov. 1941, pension file of London Triplett, WA 266564, CWPF.

14. Affidavit by Elmer Wilson, 9 Nov. 1891, pension file of Isaac Hutchinson, WC 390736, CWPF.

15. Affidavit by Nancy Richards, 8 June 1877, pension file of James Richards, WC 162287, CWPF.

16. Russell Johnson, *Warriors into Workers*, 38.

17. Hunter, *To 'Joy My Freedom*, 50–51.

18. Tera Hunter estimates those wages in the postwar urban South as $4–$8 per month (*To 'Joy My Freedom*, 52).

19. Deposition by Rebecca Rakes, 11 Feb. 1893, and affidavit by Henry Vance, 25 Jan. 1893, both in pension claim of Frederick Douglass, Father C 367268, CWPF.

20. According to my database, of 154 black Iowans residing in white households, 32 were age 16 and younger. Three were under 10 years old, 8 were ages 10 to 13, and 21 were between 14 and 16. The oldest group represented 14 percent of all African Americans living in white households according to the 1870 census.

21. On white children in Dubuque, see Russell Johnson, *Warriors into Workers*, 52–54.

22. Of these, 18 percent identified themselves as farm laborers or farmers.

23. Sixty percent of black men (see n. 10 above), contrasted to 36 percent in 1870 Dubuque (Russell Johnson, *Warriors into Workers*, 332).

24. Statement by Isaac Cox, 23 Oct. 1899, in pension file of Cox, IC 353446; deposition by Edward Swanson, 1 Nov. 1888, in pension file of Swanson, IC 695396—both in CWPF.

25. Affidavit by Ann Johnson, 31 Dec. 1895, pension file of George Johnson, WC 419018, CWPF.

26. For example, two years after the war, more than two dozen black men left St. Paul for Cottage Grove, Minn., to work the harvest; *St. Paul Daily Press*, 14 June 1867.

27. Deposition by Kansas Wilson, 13 Jan. 1898, pension file of John Williams, WC 463670, CWPF.

28. Affidavit by Henry Vance, 25 Jan. 1893, pension file of Frederick Douglass, Father C 367268, CWPF.

29. Affidavit by Mary Brown née White, 22 June 1887, pension file of Jerry (aka Henry) White, WA 269343, CWPF.

30. Pension file of Frederick Douglass, Father C 367268, CWPF. Able-bodied men made $20 a month and board, according to the affidavit by Alexander E. Fine, 21 July 1883, pension file of Fine, WC 895031, CWPF.

31. Affidavit by Alexander E. Fine, 21 July 1883, pension file of Fine, WC 895031, CWPF.

32. Affidavit by Walker Waldron, 25 July 1883, pension file of Alexander E. Fine, WC 895031, CWPF. For a description of farm tenant households, see Rugh, *Our Common Country*, 135.

33. Pryor, "The Dandridge Family History," IWA. On tenancy, see Winters, *Farmers without Farms*, 106–8. Stephen A. Vincent, in his study of rural black communities in Indiana, found that after 1870 the increasingly volatile economy, the expense of agricultural innovations in machinery, and the trend toward commercial farming decreased both the persistence of black farming households and the demand for farm laborers (Vincent, *Southern Seed, Northern Soil*, 112–17).

34. Davis Scrapbook, 295–99, microfilm, KPL.

35. Anderson, *From Slavery to Affluence*, 48–51.

36. Alfred L. Triplett to Veteran's Bureau, 19 Nov. 1941, pension file of London Triplett, WA 266564, CWPF.

37. Jacqueline Jones, *American Work*, 258–65.

38. *Home Journal*, 27 Apr. 1866.

39. Hickenlooper, *History of Monroe County*, 187; Schweider, Hraba, and Schweider, *Buxton*, 13–39; see also *New York Times*, 24 July 1881. The *Christian Recorder* of 29 Apr. 1880 reported that 300 black miners were wanted for employment at Albia and 600 at Ottumwa.

40. *Davenport Daily Gazette*, 25 Mar. 1881.

41. On midwestern whites, see Russell Johnson, *Warriors into Workers*, 332; on northern free blacks, see Horton and Horton, *In Hope of Liberty*, 115; on blacks in Washington, D.C., see James Oliver Horton, "Race, Occupation, and Literacy in Reconstruction Washington, D.C.," *Free People of Color*, 192.

42. *Christian Recorder*, 10 June 1886.

43. Russell Johnson, *Warriors into Workers*, 332; Horton and Horton, *In Hope of Liberty*, 119–20.

44. Affidavit by William Stuart, 4 Mar. 1891, pension file of Henry D. Brown, IC 660715, CWPF.

45. Hotel runners typically gathered on wharfs and levees to meet disembarking passengers and solicit business for their respective employers. This often included carrying the passenger's luggage to the hotel.

46. Deposition by Rachel Jackson, 17 May 1918, pension file of Charles M. Jackson, WC 859558, and affidavit by John H. Warwick, n.d. [1887], pension file of Charles Gifford, IA 592932—both in CWPF.

47. *Fairfield Ledger*, 17 Nov. 1897, 14 Jan. 1903.

48. Keo-Mah Genealogical Society, *History of Mahaska County*, 44. The 1870 census lists a Robert (55, born in North Carolina) and Eliza (48, born in Tennessee) Warren in Oskaloosa's first ward (Ancestry.com. *1870 United States Federal Census*).

49. *Christian Recorder*, 14 July 1887.

50. *Christian Recorder*, 20 Dec. 1865. Religious scholar Jualynne E. Dodson (*Engendering Church*, 13) has noted the important grassroots work of African American women in the formative years of the AME Church: "Their work, and the women themselves, created African Methodism and became revered legends of Church and community."

51. *Christian Recorder*, 21 Apr. 1887.

52. Bailey, in *Around the Family Altar*, documents the dramatic increase in membership during the postwar years.

53. *Christian Recorder*, 3 Dec. 1870.

54. Ibid. Consider the comments of abolitionist and Presbyterian minister John Cross, of College Springs, Iowa, about former slaves who arrived in his community and worshipped in his congregation during the war: "I find the evils of slavery . . . deeply rooted in this portion of our community . . . the most prominent traits of which, are falsehood, and licentiousness. Can these strong propensities be corrected? and How? . . . One great difficulty exists, in making parties, who have 'taken up' with each other, & have children, some of them adults, or nearly so, feel the necessity of being legally married. Some have in this matter yielded to our advice; others, as yet, have not done so." Rev. J. Cross to Rev. S. S. Jocelyn, 4 July 1864, AMA Letters, SHS/DM.

55. Higginbotham, *Righteous Discontent*, 53–55.

56. Iowa Baptist State Convention, *Journal of the Sixth Annual Meeting of the Iowa Baptist Association, 1884* (Muchakinock), 4–5.

57. Iowa Baptist State Convention, *Proceedings of the Iowa Baptist Association, 1886*, 25–26.

58. Iowa Baptist State Convention, *Minutes of the 57th Annual . . . Convention*, and *Minutes of the 55th Annual . . . Convention*, 55.

59. Higginbotham, *Righteous Discontent*, 25.

60. *Christian Recorder*, 9 Feb. 1888; Bailey, *Around the Family Altar*, 39–41.

61. *Christian Recorder*, 12 Mar. 1874.

62. *Christian Recorder*, 17 May, 2 Aug., 25 Oct. 1862.

63. *Christian Recorder*, 18 Apr. 1863.

64. *Christian Recorder*, 7 July 1862.

65. *Oskaloosa Herald*, 30 Nov. 1865; *Davenport Daily Gazette*, 13 Dec. 1865.

66. *Christian Recorder*, 10 Mar. 1866; *Daily Davenport Democrat*, 29 Dec. 1871; *Daily Gazette*, 14 Aug. 1873; *Davenport Gazette*, 22 Apr., 3 June 1875.

67. *Daily State Register*, 1 Jan. 1867, 24 Apr. 1873.

68. WPA Church Records Form, "WPA—Churches," vertical file, KPL; *Christian Recorder*, 17 May, 2 Aug., 25 Oct. 1862; 18 Apr. 1863, 29 Dec. 1866 (on the church at Keokuk); *History of Muscatine County*, 527–28 (Muscatine). *Minneapolis Spokesman*, 25 Apr. 1958 (St. Paul); Butler, "Communities and Congregations," 124–25. In an envelope addressed to Mrs. Betty Schaile, with St. John A.M.E. Church letterhead, is the "History of St. John African Methodist Episcopal Church, Burlington, Iowa, 1867–1976," compiled by Geraldine Brown (2 pp. typescript), BPL. Jualynne E. Dodson (*Engendering Church*, 26–33) finds women dominating the early AME church.

69. Martha S. Jones elaborates on this point in her work, *All Bound Up Together*.

70. *Christian Recorder*, 3 Jan. 1863.

71. See Schwalm, "Emancipation Day Celebrations."

72. Bailey, *Around the Family Altar*, 38; *Christian Recorder*, 28 May 1864.

73. *Christian Recorder*, 29 Oct. 1891. Duffin was eighty when she died.

74. Campbell, *Songs of Zion*, 51.

75. *Christian Recorder*, 18, 5 June 1884, 11 Aug. 1887; Campbell, *Songs of Zion*, 52.

76. *Christian Recorder*, 15 July 1865.

77. Campbell, *Songs of Zion*, 52; *Christian Recorder*, 15 May 1873, 5 Apr. 1888; Dodson, *Engendering Church*, 58–59. Martha S. Jones (*All Bound Up Together*, 151) has noted that, in contrast, women of the African Methodist Episcopal Zion (AMEZ) Church gained the right to vote and hold office in 1876.

78. See, e.g., Iowa Baptist State Convention, *Minutes . . . , 1878* (Bedford), 35, and *Journal of the Sixth Annual Meeting of the Iowa Baptist Association* (Muchakinock), 6. The black Iowa Baptist Association boasted far more female clerks than did the state's white Baptist Convention.

79. Bailey, *Around the Family Altar*, 44–45. For example, the Educational Report of the *Proceedings of the Iowa Baptist Association, 1885*, asserts: "Bodily contortions, animal magnetism or volumes of vehement sounds may make people 'feel happy' as it is termed, but the intellect will not be reached, the conscience will not be stirred, the will not be influenced" (pp. 26–27).

80. See, e.g., *Christian Recorder*, 6 Nov. 1869, 2 Oct. 1873, 15 Nov. 1888, 1 Jan., 13 Aug. 1891, 3 Aug. 1893.

81. *Muscatine Journal*, 28 May 1864, and *Davenport Daily Democrat*, 25 June 1864 (Muscatine); *Davenport Daily Gazette*, 27, 29 July 1875 (Davenport); *Burlington Weekly Hawk-Eye*, 30 Dec. 1875 (Ottumwa); *Daily Gate City*, 3 Jan. 1893 (Fort Dodge); *Daily InterOcean*, 3 June 1895 (St. Paul); Nelson, *Fredrick L. McGhee*, 54 (Minnesota).

82. Martha S. Jones, *All Bound Up Together*, 156.

83. *Christian Recorder*, 25 May 1872. On matrimonial vows as viewed by the denomination, see Allen and Tapisco, *Doctrines and Discipline*, 139, for the African-Methodist connection in the United States.

84. *Christian Recorder*, 12 Aug. 1880.

85. *Christian Recorder*, 18 Jan. 1883.

86. For attempted lynchings, see *Muscatine Journal*, 28 May 1864; *Daily Davenport Democrat*, 25 June 1864; *Des Moines Register*, 18 Apr. 1868; *Davenport Daily Gazette*, 23 July 1875; *Daily Gate City*, 3 Jan. 1893; and *Daily InterOcean*, 3 June 1895. For lynch mobs, see *Burlington Weekly Hawk-Eye*, 20 Dec. 1875, and *Davenport Daily Gazette*, 3–5 June 1879. For murders, see *Chicago Daily Tribune*, 27 June 1883, and *New York Times*, 18 Aug. 1883. See also *Daily Gate City*, 3 Apr. 1874.

87. *Woman's Journal*, 28 Sept. 1878.

88. *Daily Iowa State Register*, 10 Jan. 1865, 25 Oct. 1867, 29 Apr., 10 Oct. 1868, 15 Apr. 1875; *Davenport Daily Gazette*, 9 Aug. 1865, 29 Sept. 1869; 1881 unidentified clipping, Black History Binder I, BH 006, NVHM; *Davenport Weekly Gazette*, 3 Aug. 1881.

89. Patricia A. Schechter (*Ida B. Wells-Barnett and American Reform*) makes an important argument about the significance of reputation to former slave women.

90. *Chicago Tribune*, 17 Jan. 1863.

91. Ibid.

92. Ibid.

93. Ibid.

94. Ibid.

95. *Christian Recorder*, 21 Feb. 1863; *Chicago Tribune*, 17 Jan. 1863.

96. *Chicago Tribune*, 17 Jan. 1863.

97. *Christian Recorder*, 21 Feb. 1863.

98. *Christian Recorder*, 14 Feb. 1863.

99. *Christian Recorder*, 5 Sept. 1863.

100. *Chicago Times*, 23 Aug. 1863; *Chicago Daily Tribune*, 25 Aug. 1863.

101. *Christian Recorder*, 7 Feb. 1889.

102. *Chicago Daily Tribune*, 26 Dec. 1874. This was Wisconsin's third AME church when it was organized in 1869. On AME history in Wisconsin, see *Christian Recorder*, 31 July 1869, and "History: St. Mark's African Methodist Episcopal Church," in *Souvenir Program, 78th Session Chicago Annual Conference of the African Methodist Episcopal Church September 6th thru 11th, 1960* (n.p., n.d.), 1, in Fisher Papers, WHS.

103. *Christian Recorder*, 18 Nov., 9 Dec. 1875.

104. *Fond Du Lac Commonwealth Reporter*, 27 Mar. 1880; Worthing, *History of Fond du Lac County*, 109–10.

105. "The speaker next introduced was S. J. Harris, a colored boy of perhaps 23 years of age, who spoke with some embarrassment but with considerable effect. He said he was uneducated. But we judge he has made excellent use of his time since he has been free. He had evidently prepared himself somewhat. His sentences were singularly correct; and altogether he made a considerable sensation" (*Daily Iowa State Register*, 2 Aug. 1866). The Burns AME Chapel was named for Francis Burns, the first black bishop of Episcopal Methodism.

106. *Daily State Register*, 3 Jan. 1867.

107. Ibid.

108. Martha S. Jones, *All Bound Up Together*, 171–84; Schechter, *Wells-Barnett*; Higginbotham, *Righteous Discontent*; Gilmore, *Gender and Jim Crow*.

109. Skocpol and Osler, "Organization Despite Adversity," 370.

110. On "female degrees," see Prince Hall Grand Lodge of Missouri, *Proceedings of the . . . York Masons . . . July [1869]*, 18, IML.

111. *Christian Recorder*, 20 May 1865.

112. On the history of the HOJ, see <http://phaglmo.org/HOJ/history.htm> (15 Mar. 2005). St. Mary's Court No. 1 was organized in Missouri in 1863 (HOJ, WHMC/SL). Noted in the United Grand Lodge of Iowa, *Proceedings* (1895), 13, IML, is a silver anniversary meeting of a Mahaska County lodge, thus dating its origin to 1870.

113. Amanda Smith, *Autobiography*, 61–62.

114. Before the war, Delany used the St. Louis Court system to sue for her freedom and was active in the war work of black women. See Delany, *From the Darkness Cometh the Light*, 62–63.

115. Essie M. Britton, "The Negro in Iowa: History of the Colored Race of People Residing in Keokuk and Vicinity," WPA notes, "Ethnography-Negroes," KPL.

116. Skocpol, Leazos, and Ganz, *What a Mighty Power*, 70–71.

117. Fahey, *Temperance and Racism*, 60–61; Pilgrim Baptist Church, *We've Come This Far*, 17–18 (Marceline, Mo.).

118. Fahey, *Temperance and Racism*, 60–61; *Daily State Register*, 29 Nov. 1866; *State Press*, 5 Dec. 1866; *Minneapolis Spokesman*, 27 May 1949; *St. Paul Daily Press*, 19 Oct. 1872.

119. Fahey, *Temperance and Racism*, 65–66.

120. Information on Dickson is imprecise and sometimes conflicting. I rely on Rev. J. J. Pipkin, *Story of a Rising Race*, 481–84. Pipkin was born in Cincinnati in 1824; both of his parents had died by the time he reached age fourteen. Nonetheless, he acquired an education and the skills of barbering, which he used to secure employment on Mississippi River steamboats, traveling throughout the river valley, north and south. In 1844, he organized a secret abolition society, the Knights of Liberty, out of St. Louis, which assisted slaves in their flight to freedom. He apparently served during the Civil War and afterward took up the causes of education, relief for exodusters, and Republican Party activism. He was licensed by the AME Church in 1866, and, in addition to his work with the Knights and Daughters of Tabor, he was a prominent Mason.

121. Dickson, *Manual of the Knights of Tabor*; *Daily InterOcean*, 13, 14, 16 Aug. 1879, 10 Apr. 1893; *St. Louis Globe-Democrat*, 10 Aug. 1880, 14 Aug. 1886.

122. In "Organization Despite Adversity," Theda Skocpol and Jennifer Lynn Osler describe black fraternal associations as "generators and sustainers of vast and intricate network linkages," 374.

123. See Grand Lodge of Iowa, *Constitutions of the Freemasons*, 147–49, IML.

124. Skocpol and Osler, "Organization Despite Adversity," 385; see also *Christian Recorder*, 7 Oct. 1865, and A. G. Clark, *Prince Hall Freemasonry*, IML. A. G. Clark was the son of Alexander Clark.

125. Contrary to the conclusion of Skocpol and Osler that charitable and social welfare work was a minor component of black fraternal organizational life, midwestern Masons made support for widows and orphans an integral part of their associational mission; see, e.g., Prince Hall Grand Lodge of Missouri, *Proceedings of the . . . York Masons . . . July [1869]*, 16, IML. See also the *Daily InterOcean*, 22 Aug. 1892, for the organized efforts of Chicago Masons to build a home for Masonic widows and orphans in 1892.

126. See *Provincial Freeman*, 21 Mar. 1857; *Christian Recorder*, 13 Sept. 1862, 15 Apr. 1875; A. G. Clark, *Prince Hall Freemasonry*, 34, IML; <http://www.clpgh.org/exhibit/neighborhoods/downtown/down_n105.html> (15 June 2008); *History of Muscatine County, Iowa*, 527–28; Census: Union, Fayette County, Pa., 1830, 1840; Muscatine, Iowa, 1850, 1852, 1860; Kansas City, Mo., 1870. During the 1860s, Pritchard worked as a steward on a steamboat.

127. Records suggest that Iowa and Minnesota Masons did not extend their reach to Wisconsin until 1894, when they organized a lodge at West Superior (see A. G. Clark, *Prince Hall Freemasonry*, 132, IML). White Masons had a longer history and a larger following in the Midwest. They had established lodges in Wisconsin in 1843, in Iowa in 1844, and in Minnesota in 1853. By 1865, there were 6,166 white Masons in Iowa alone (here I rely on the authority of Iowa's Masonic librarian and historian, Bill Krueger).

128. Grand Lodge of Iowa, *Constitutions of the Freemasons*, 147–48, IML.

129. Ibid.

130. Grand Lodge of Minnesota, *Proceedings . . .* , [1876], 48, and *Proceedings . . .* , [1877], 33, IML.

131. Grand Lodge of Iowa, *Proceedings . . . at Its Twenty-fourth Grand Annual Communication*, 486–97, 540–41, 555, IML.

132. Prince Hall Grand Lodge of Missouri, *Proceedings of the Special Communication . . . 1866*, 21–22, IML.

133. Summers, *Manliness*, 25–65.

134. The significance of correspondence with other lodges was reflected both in an elected committee charged with this task and in the priority assigned to this item in lodge budgets. One of the core disputes over whether Prince Hall Freemasonry was "clandestine" or legally constituted focused on the question of whether two separate Grand Lodges could exist within one state. If integrated masonry was impossible, then (from the perspective of white lodges) this "ancient landmark" meant that all black lodges organized in states with preexisting white Grand Lodges were clandestine, or illegitimate. For a fuller description of this issue, see <http://mastermason.com/jjcrowder/dictionary/dictionary.htm> (15 June 2008) and the research of Paul M. Bessel, published at <http://bessel.org/masrec/>.

135. Any man who was not a bondsman at the time of his petition for membership and who was age twenty-one or older, honest, temperate, and industrious, of sound mind, and with no physical disabilities was eligible for membership. Prince Hall Grand Lodge of Missouri, *Proceedings of the . . . York Masons . . . July [1869]*, 16–17, IML. The core and unchangeable beliefs of Masonry constitute what is referred to as its "Ancient landmarks."

136. Prince Hall Grand Lodge of Missouri, *Proceedings of the . . . York Masons . . . July 3rd 1871*, 52–53, IML.

137. Prince Hall Grand Lodge of Missouri, *Proceedings of the York Masons . . . July 1st 1872*, 7, IML. Clark's optimism overlooks the vicious attack on his own Masonic virtue and that of Prince Hall Masonry generally by Mark M. Pomery, in the pages of his New York paper, the *Democrat*, described in Prince Hall Grand Lodge of Missouri, *Proceedings of the York Masons . . . July 1st 1872*, 17–26, IML.

138. Prince Hall Grand Lodge of Missouri, *Proceedings of the Special Communication . . . 1866*, 21–22, IML.

139. Prince Hall Grand Lodge of Missouri, *Proceedings of the . . . York Masons . . . July [1869]*, 16–17, and *Proceedings of the . . . York Masons, July 3rd 1871*, 19, IML.

140. Summers, *Manliness*, 54.

141. See, e.g., the description of "a very grand affair" in Nashville, Tenn., in the *Christian Recorder*, 10 Aug. 1867. Bill R. Kreuger, Iowa Grand Lodge librarian, notes that the ceremony is highly symbolic. "The stone must be perfectly square on its surface and a cube in shape. The square is a symbol of mortality, the cube a symbol of truth. The cornerstone is usually laid on the northeast corner of a building, the north is the place of darkness and the east is the place of light, symbolizing the Masonic progress from darkness to light. The stone is carefully examined after it is deposited in its location. It is examined using tools of the operative Masons, the square, level, and plumb and is then declared to be 'well formed, true and trusty.' The symbolism here has to do with virtues that are tested by the 'Master Builder' as being worthy for eternal life. Finally there are deposited on the stone corn, wine and oil, symbolic of nourishment, refreshment, and joy which are to be rewards of a faithful and true life" (Kreuger, Librarian, IML, to Leslie Schwalm, e-mail correspondence, 29 June 2004).

142. *Daily Gazette*, 23 Nov. 1869; Prince Hall Grand Lodge of Missouri, *Proceedings of the . . . York Masons . . . July 1st 1872*, 17, IML; *Christian Recorder*, 8 Dec. 1881; *Daily Iowa State Register*, 26 June 1866. Masons could not invite candidates to apply for initiation; men interested in the order had to approach Masonry on their own. Public ceremonies would have been important recruiting occasions.

143. Grand Lodge of Iowa, *Proceedings . . . at Its Twenty-seventh Grand Annual Communication*, 127–29, IML.

144. Ibid., 178–79; African Grand Lodge . . . of Iowa, *Ancient Constitutions* (1880), 66, IML.

145. Wesley, *History of Prince Hall Grand Lodge*.

146. Ibid.

147. Grand Lodge of Minnesota, *Proceedings . . .*, [1876], 21–29, IML.

148. Grand Lodge of Minnesota, *Proceedings . . .*, [1877], 40–54, IML.

149. Ibid., 32–36.

150. Ibid., 134.

151. Prince Hall Grand Lodge of Missouri, *Proceedings of the First Annual Communication . . . 1867*, 33–34, IML.

152. A. G. Clark, *Prince Hall Freemasonry*, 30–33, IML

153. Prince Hall Grand Lodge of Missouri, *Proceedings . . . Keokuk . . . 1872*, 7, IML; *St. Louis Globe-Democrat*, 26 Aug. 1879; African Grand Lodge, *Organization and Proceedings . . . 1881*, undated newspaper clipping, app., IML.

154. A. G. Clark, *Prince Hall Freemasonry*, 92, IML.

155. Significantly, while Alexander Clark would condemn the "riotous acts" of "unlawful strikes" that "disturbed the peace and commercial prosperity" of the nation in 1886 and 1887, when over 1,500 strikes were organized by American workers, both Grand Lodges would organize Masons among Iowa's relatively prosperous black coal workers who were recruited to replace striking white miners beginning in 1880 and 1881 (A. G. Clark, *Prince Hall Freemasonry*, 113, IML; Schweider et al., *Buxton*, 16–39).

156. Clark was scheduled to attend the Ecumenical Conference of the Methodist

Episcopal Church in London in September 1881 as a delegate of the AME Church. Some of his critics charged that he delayed the formation of the independent lodge so he might attend that conference as a representative from the very large and powerful Missouri Grand Lodge rather than as a member of the much smaller Iowa Grand Lodge. Later, members of the African lodge would continue to level charges of un-Masonic conduct against him: "Bro. Clark has had the respect and esteem of the Iowa Masons, but the disposition he has shown to make trouble and dissatisfaction and contention, has caused a reaction, and some of the best men . . . are getting tired, and think it time to call a halt" (African Grand Lodge, *Proceedings of the . . . Fourth Annual Session . . . 1885*, 61–62, IML). The key difficulty in assessing motives lay in the subjective nature of contemporary accounts and the fact that the most authoritative history of Iowa Prince Hall Masonry was written by Clark's son.

157. A. G. Clark, *Prince Hall Freemasonry*, 42–43, IML.

158. Ibid., 44–47.

159. Ibid., 53. Referring to President Andrew Johnson's disastrous reelection campaign tour (known as his "swing around the circle") in 1866, Iowa Grand Lodge members would recall that "our Moses swung around the circle himself . . . to try and organize a Grand Lodge in Iowa, but as he failed to rule, he now seeks to ruin" (African Grand Lodge, *Proceedings . . . 1883*, IML). The communities were Burlington, Council Bluffs, Ottumwa, Des Moines, and Keokuk.

160. In addition to St. Paul, the additional communities included Albia, Newton, Mt. Pleasant, Chariton, and Marshalltown.

161. The eight cities and towns were Des Moines, Oskaloosa, Keokuk, Red Oak, Cedar Rapids, Davenport, Centerville, and Muchakinock.

162. African Grand Lodge, *Proceedings . . . 1884*, 6, and *Proceedings . . . in Its Fourth Annual Session . . . 1885*, 7, IML.

163. African Grand Lodge, *Proceedings . . . in Its Fourth Annual Session . . . 1885*, 16, IML.

164. In October 1885, e.g., both Grand Lodges sent representatives to a meeting with the Illinois Grand Lodge, competing for that state's recognition. Each representative had an opportunity to present his version of the recent developments leading up to the existence of two Grand Lodges in Iowa, and Illinois advised that the two lodges settle their differences. John G. Jones, the "father" of Illinois black Masonry and the state's most prominent political activist and advocate for black civil rights, was a strong opponent of the African lodge (*St. Louis Globe-Democrat*, 16 Oct. 1885).

165. A. G. Clark, *Prince Hall Freemasonry*, 100.

166. Ibid., 125.

167. Ibid., 92, 134.

CHAPTER 6

1. Mosely, *Colored Man of America* (chapter title). Delaware refused to ratify the Thirteenth Amendment in 1865 (Vorenberg, *Final Freedom*, 216–17).

2. Because northern states have been excluded from most Reconstruction histories, we do not have a record of black voting and officeholding in the North between the end of the war and the end of Reconstruction, nor an accounting of black involvement in and

impact on party politics. The most comprehensive survey of African Americans in the Reconstruction-era North is still Fishel, "The North and the Negro, 1865–1900."

3. Hahn, *Nation under Our Feet*, 7.

4. Vorenberg, *Final Freedom*, 222.

5. Wang, *Trial of Democracy*, 41–42. Importantly, the Fourteenth Amendment did not provide a remedy to school segregation, as pointed out by Davison M. Douglas in *Jim Crow Moves North*, 69–71.

6. William Gillette describes Democratic opposition in *Right to Vote*, 113–58.

7. On Ohio and Delaware, see Stephenson, *Race Distinctions*, 292–93; on New York, see Quigley, *Second Founding*, 80–83.

8. Eric Foner, *Reconstruction*, 315; Wang, *Trial of Democracy*, 5, 17–22; Valelly, *Two Reconstructions*, 2; Gillette, "Right to Vote"; Fishel, "Northern Prejudice." New York rejected a proposal to end property limitations on black voters. Earl Maltz (*Civil Rights*, 11–12) points out that while Republicans often supported postbellum suffrage referenda by significant majorities, those majorities were not sufficient to carry the vote.

9. Valelly, *Two Reconstructions*, 3, 39–41; Hahn, *Nation under Our Feet*, 177, 190–98. Union Leagues functioned as political education and activist organizations; they were closely allied with the Republican Party.

10. Wang, *Trial of Democracy*, 41.

11. Maltz, "Reconstruction without Revolution," 222–26.

12. On segregated cemeteries in Iowa, see *Davenport Daily Gazette*, 21 Feb. 1885.

13. On black manhood and citizenship rights, see Shaffer, *After the Glory*; Hahn, *Nation under Our Feet*; and Elsa Barkley Brown, "Negotiating and Transforming," 107–46.

14. Quoted by McPherson in *Ordeal by Fire*, 512.

15. *Appleton Motor*, 19 Apr. 1866.

16. *Davenport Daily Gazette*, 4 Nov. 1865, and *Christian Recorder*, 18 Nov. 1865 (conference proceedings). On the return of the regiment to Iowa, see *Davenport Daily Gazette*, 25–26 Oct. 1865; *Daily Davenport Democrat*, 25, 30 Oct. 1865.

17. On the struggle for the franchise in the upper Midwest, see Spangler, *Negro in Minnesota*, 38–39; Wubben, "Uncertain Trumpet," 409–10; Fishel, "Wisconsin and Negro Suffrage," 184, 189–90, and "Northern Prejudice," 8–26; and Gillette, *Retreat from Reconstruction*, 6–11.

18. This, of course, was true for the Republican Party throughout the North; see Gambill, *Conservative Ordeal*, 36–37, and Wang, *Trial of Democracy*, 39–41.

19. Dykstra, *Bright Radical Star*, 209–10. See also the speech by Maj. Gen. C. C. Andrews (a Democratic state senator from St. Cloud, Minn., before the war), in St. Paul, advocating black suffrage in the context of white political recalcitrance in the South (*Milwaukee Daily Sentinel*, 2 Nov. 1865).

20. Warrington Howe, "Impartial Suffrage and Equal Rights," 17 Nov. 1865, *Home Journal*.

21. Dykstra, *Bright Radical Star*, 207.

22. *Appleton Motor*, 5 Oct. 1865.

23. See, e.g., *Janesville Weekly Gazette*, 1, 7 Sept., 12 Oct. 1865.

24. *Appleton Motor*, 19 Oct. 1865.

25. McManus, *Political Abolitionism*, 19–35; *North American and United States Gazette*,

25 Dec. 1849, 28 Dec. 1857; *Appleton Motor*, 9 Mar., 16 Nov. 1865; *Daily Milwaukee News*, 12 Nov. 1865; *Chicago Tribune*, 30 Mar., 18 Nov. 1866; *Gillespie v. Palmer and Others*; Ancestry.com, *1860 United States Federal Census*.

26. McManus, *Political Abolitionism*, 35. There seems to have been some confusion about jury service; on 25 Apr. 1875, the *Burlington Weekly Hawk-Eye* reported that a James Green had served not only as Wisconsin's first black jury member, but also as jury foreman.

27. *St. Paul Daily Press*, 20 Jan. 1865; Green, "Race and Segregation," 147–48.

28. *St. Paul Daily Press*, 1 Mar., 16 Aug. 1865. Griswold would play a major role in challenging white Masons to abandon their racially exclusive policies.

29. Libman, "Minnesota and the Struggle"; Spangler, *Negro in Minnesota*, 38–39; Green, "Race and Segregation," 146.

30. *Milwaukee Daily Sentinel*, 23 June 1865.

31. Warrington Howe, "Impartial Suffrage and Equal Rights," *Home Journal*, 17 Nov. 1865.

32. *Daily Iowa State Register*, 8 Oct. 1865.

33. *Home Journal*, 18 Aug. 1865.

34. *Christian Recorder*, 3 Feb. 1866.

35. Rev. Malone's address was reprinted in the *Daily Gate City* of 20 Feb. 1868. It did not appear in the pamphlet version of the proceedings, although Clark's address did (Iowa State Colored Convention, *Proceedings . . . 1868*, 10–12).

36. *Bangor Daily Whig & Courier*, 26 Nov. 1868; Green, "Race and Segregation," 147 n.18. This was not the first black convention in the state. In early August 1865, some of Minnesota's black veterans assembled to endorse the recent decision by the St. Paul School Board to provide black schools with black teachers for the growing African American population, rather than integrate the existing schools. The veterans declared that, if the black schools were not established, they would stop paying school taxes and seek strict enforcement of a recently passed state law forbidding the exclusion of children from public schools on account of color. *St. Paul Pioneer*, 9 Aug. 1865; *St. Paul Daily Press*, 15 Aug. 1865; Green, "Race and Segregation," 145.

37. *Northwestern Bulletin*, 5 May 1923.

38. *Proceedings of the Convention*, 18, 13, 29–31. Among the white speakers were Gov. Marshall, St. Paul Mayor J. H. Stewart, Gen. L. Nutting, and former lieutenant governor and congressman Ignatius Donnelly.

39. *Daily Gate City*, 7 Nov. 1868.

40. *Washington County Press*, 11 Nov. 1868 (reprinted from *Davenport Daily Gazette*).

41. *Daily State Register*, 8 Jan. 1868.

42. Libman, "Minnesota and the Struggle," 195.

43. *Iowa City Republican*, 17 Feb. 1869.

44. *Weekly Journal*, 5 Mar. 1869.

45. Valeria Weaver ("Failure of Civil Rights," 369) noted that after 1883, several northern states included in their civil rights acts (passed after the U.S. Supreme Court's reversal of the 1875 Civil Rights Act) guarantees of the right to serve on juries.

46. One of the earliest reports of conflict over the jury service of an African American man in the region came in January 1869, when Albert Sappington, a fifty-eight-year-old Tennessee-born resident of Ottumwa, Iowa, received notice to serve on a district court jury.

But on appearing, he was promptly dismissed by the presiding judge (*Davenport Daily Gazette*, 23 Jan. 1869).

47. *Weekly Journal*, 13 June 1869; *Chicago Tribune*, 14 June 1869.

48. *Davenport Daily Gazette*, 29 Sept. 1869. The jury was assembled in Linn County, Iowa.

49. *Chicago Tribune*, 16 Apr. 1870; see also *Daily Gazette*, 29 Aug. 1873.

50. *Davenport Daily Gazette*, 29 Mar. 1869. To the contrary, most of the jurors had been free before the Civil War and were members of the local black population's elite. See also *St. Paul Daily Pioneer*, 25 Mar. 1869 (in FWP, Annals of Minn., MHS).

51. *Davenport Daily Gazette*, 15 June 1869; *Iowa City Republican*, 16, 23 June 1869. Scott County elected two black delegates, while Polk, Muscatine, Lee and Dubuque each named one.

52. *Davenport Daily Gazette*, 30 Sept. 1869.

53. *Daily Gate City*, 6 Oct. 1869.

54. Hahn, *Nation under Our Feet*, 219.

55. *Davenport Daily Gazette*, 23 Nov. 1869; U.S. census for Perry Township, Tama County, Ancestry.com, *1870 United States Federal Census*; http://www.15thwisconsin.net/p-thomas.htm (15 June 2008). By 1890, Thomas owned thirteen acres in Racine County (*1890–91 Farmers and Land Owners Directory*). On Blagburn's election, see Lufkin, "Founding and Early Years," 441; on his activism in the Afro-American League, see *Iowa State Bystander*, 20 Jan., 10 Feb. 1899.

56. *Appeal*, 25 Apr. 1891.

57. John Frank Wheaton (1866–1938) was nominated at age twenty-one as a Republican candidate to the Maryland legislature. Active in the state's Republican Party, he was an alternate delegate to the national party convention in 1888 and his state convention's temporary chairman in 1889. Although nominated by Maryland's black Republicans to represent them at the 1892 national convention in Minneapolis, the convention rejected his credentials. The following year he moved to Minneapolis, graduated from the law school at the University of Minnesota, and became a highly respected attorney and politician. As well as his service as a state legislator, Wheaton was a clerk in the U.S. Congress, clerk of the Minnesota legislature, and clerk of the Minneapolis municipal court. See Shutter, *Progressive Men*, 350–51; Nelson, *McGhee*, 66–68; "Pioneering Black Politicians," 31; Brady, "Minnesota Then," 23. Lucien Palmer, born in 1855 in Huntsville, Ala., was a successful Wisconsin businessman in the resort and catering industry in the 1880s and 1890s. In addition to serving in the state legislature, he held a number of appointive positions, including "U.S. Weigher of Mails," "Commissioner for Negro Exhibits at the New Orleans Exposition," "Checking Clerk at U.S. Marshall's Office," and "Messenger of the U.S. District Court." See Beck, *Blue Book of the State of Wisconsin*, 1161.

58. Dykstra, *Bright Radical Star*, 249.

59. Black voters in Muchakinock also tried to nominate Rev. L. H. Reynolds as a candidate for the state assembly in 1885, but after five ballots at the Republican state convention, he withdrew his name, pointing to the significant opposition to a black candidate (WPA, "The Negro in Iowa," MS, p. 15, folder 69, box 9, ser. 2, Rawick Papers, University of Missouri Archives). Rev. Thomas Cheek, of Des Moines, served as doorkeeper to the state legislature from 1883 until his death in April 1884 (*Burlington Weekly*

Hawk-Eye, 13 Dec. 1883; *Chicago Daily Tribune*, 7 Apr. 1884; *New York Times*, 6 Apr. 1884). Cheek had been a Republican Party activist in Illinois beginning with Grant's presidential campaign in 1872. He moved to Iowa around 1875, serving AME congregations in Dubuque (1876), Mt. Pleasant (1879), and Des Moines (1880–?).

60. Newspaper clipping, Black History Binder BH007 (1877); *New York Times*, 8 and 28 Mar. 1872; *Davenport Daily Gazette*, 15 June 1869; *Iowa City Republican*, 23 June 1869; *Weekly Journal*, 24 Sept. 1869, 9 Aug. 1872.

61. *Davenport Daily Gazette*, 19 and 22 Sept. 1869; *Daily Gate City*, 19 Sept. 1874.

62. *New York Times*, 26 Sept. 1871; *Milwaukee Sentinel*, 26 Sept. 1871.

63. Quoted in Klingman and Geithman, "Negro Dissidence and the Republican Party," 178.

64. On Downing, see Ripley, *United States, 1847–1858*, vol. 4 of *BAP*, 317–18. J. Sella Martin also endorsed the Liberal ticket; Lewis, "Political Mind of the Negro," 196–97. The meeting was announced in the *New National Era*, 3 Oct. 1872. The Iowa delegates, William Tann and John Tucker, had no previous record of public activism in the region. At the time of the 1870 federal census, Tann was a forty-one-year-old New York–born barber living in McGregor, Iowa. Tucker does not appear in any nineteenth-century census records for Iowa.

65. Gillette, *Retreat from Reconstruction*, 58; see also Wang, *Trial of Democracy*, 102–10. The *Christian Recorder* of 5 Nov. 1874 referred to a "Colored Liberal Republican Club" in New York City. Clark's remark is found in the *Weekly Journal*, 22 Jan. 1876.

66. *New York Times*, 27 Aug. 1872; *St. Paul Daily Press*, 23 Aug. 1872.

67. Valelly, *Two Reconstructions*, 47; *Burlington Weekly Hawk-Eye*, 9 Apr. 1874.

68. Valelly, *Two Reconstructions*, 47, 60; Biles, "Black Mayors," 110.

69. See, e.g., *Christian Recorder*, 24 Feb. 1887 (on black voters "bolting" from the party when it refused to endorse black candidates for local office in Pennsylvania), and Lewis, "Political Mind," 196–202.

70. *St. Louis Globe-Democrat*, 20 Aug. 1883.

71. Coston, *Freeman and Yet a Slave*, 31–33. Coston attended Yale Preparatory School (1875–80), Wilberforce University (with the support of the AME Church), and Yale Seminary (1884–87). As an ordained pastor, he subsequently served a number of conferences of the AME Church, including Mt. Pleasant. During the Spanish-American War he was chaplain to two black regiments and afterward was editor of *Ringwood's Home Magazine* for African American women; Talbert, *Sons of Allen*, 232–33.

72. *New York Times*, 27 Apr. 1884; *Davenport Daily Gazette*, 10 May 1884.

73. *Chicago Daily Tribune*, 4 June 1884.

74. Schweider, Hraba, and Schweider, *Buxton*. In the fall of 1883, an estimated 150 black emigrants, largely from Virginia, had made their way to southeastern Iowa to join another 600 already working in the coal mines as "a safeguard against suspension from strikes" (*St. Louis Globe-Democrat*, 2 Sept. 1883).

75. *New National Era*, 9 July 1885; *New York Times*, 1 July 1885. Priestly, born in Tennessee, had lived in Iowa least since 1866—Oskaloosa in 1870 (where he worked as a day laborer) and Burlington in 1880 (where he, his wife Fanny, and their two sons were employed as hotel servants). See Ancestry.com, *1870 United States Federal Census* and *1880 United States Federal Census*. By 1902, prominent black lawyer George H. Woodson would

be selected to preside over the Mahaska County Republican Convention; see *Des Moines Leader*, 20 May 1902.

76. *Freeborn County Standard*, 7 Oct. 1885. Howard N. Rabinowitz ("Three Reconstruction Leaders," 195) has characterized Bruce as an "accommodationist, who favored gradual change and sought to avoid taking strong stands on controversial issues."

77. *Chicago Daily Tribune*, 23 Sept. 1890. The speaker, Rev. John Laws, at a gathering of black delegates to the Republican National Convention in 1884, had similarly urged the party to adopt a platform that addressed race issues (*Chicago Daily Tribune*, 4 June 1884).

78. Nelson, *McGhee*, 35–36.

79. *Mt. Pleasant Journal*, 12 June 1884.

80. Ibid.; Welke, *Recasting American Liberty*, 301 n.72. Welke's original and penetrating analysis focuses largely on the experience of southern litigants. Stephen J. Riegel, in his survey of reported cases appearing in the lower federal courts, found more than forty cases between 1865 and 1896, 70 percent originating in ex-Confederate states ("Persistent Career of Jim Crow," 21). J. Morgan Kousser, *Dead End*, identifies forty-seven civil rights cases concerning school segregation between 1865 and 1903. There has been no systematic study of female litigants in northern civil rights cases.

81. *Clark v. Board of Directors* (1868); *State ex rel. Garners v. McCann* (1871); *Cory v. Carter* (1874); *Ward v. Flood* (1874); *Dove v. The Independent School District of Keokuk* (1875); *Smith v. The Directors of the Independent School District of Keokuk* (1875); *Allen v. Davis* (1881); *People ex rel. King v. Gallagher* (1883); *Knox v. Board of Education of the City of Independence* (1891).

82. These include cases reported in the *New York Times* (1 Aug. 1874, Marion, Ind.; 15 Mar. 1868, Hartford, Conn.; 28 Sept. 1867, 16 May 1868, Buffalo, N.Y.), in the *Cleveland Gazette* (17 Dec. 1887, Xenia, Ohio; 19 Dec. 1896, Carlisle, Pa.; 24 Oct. 1896, Davis County, Ind.; 2 June 1888, Columbus, Ohio; 6 Apr. 1889, Richmond, Ohio), and in the *Christian Recorder* (10 Mar. 1881, Monmouth, N.J.; 7 Oct. 1875, N.Y.).

83. Douglas, *Jim Crow Moves North*, 68.

84. Lurie, "Fourteenth Amendment." On federal courts, see Riegel, "Persistent Career of Jim Crow."

85. The quoted phrase comes from a discussion of the distinctions between social and civil rights by an anonymous black writer in the *Oshkosh Northwestern*, 21 Nov. 1883.

86. Minutes, City Council meeting, City Clerk's Office, Iowa City.

87. SHS, BL 160 f29.

88. Arnie Cooper, "Stony Road," 120; *History of Johnson County, Iowa*, 647.

89. Arnie Cooper, "Stony Road," 130–33.

90. Todd, *Early Settlement*, 90–91; Sarah Parker to mother, 10 Mar. 60, Parker Collection, sec. 2, Letters #4, 1860s folder, Grinnell College Archives, Grinnell, Iowa; Lucas, "Men Were Too Fiery."

91. *Christian Recorder*, 3 Dec. 1870.

92. *Weekly Journal*, 1 Oct. 1862.

93. *Daily State Register*, 18 Jan. 1866.

94. *Daily State Register*, 8 Oct. 1867, 1216 Feb. 1868; *Daily Iowa State Register*, 1 June 1865; *Dubuque Weekly Herald*, 30 Jan. 1867; *Washington County Press*, 19 Jan. 1870.

95. Neither the Civil Rights Act of 1866 or 1875 nor the Fourteenth Amendment encompassed school segregation, and only two court cases in the nineteenth century found that school segregation violated the Fourteenth Amendment; Douglas, *Jim Crow Moves North*, 70.

96. *New National Era*, 27 Feb. 1873.

97. McPherson (*Struggle for Equality*, 221–37, and "Abolitionists") points to the persistence of segregation and the activism of white abolitionists to challenge discriminatory laws and practices in the North. But most white activism occurred at a safe distance from the day-to-day operation of white supremacy, where African Americans were forced to confront the practices and the people who denied them equal citizenship.

98. Legal challenges involving black female students included Mary Ward of San Francisco (*Ward v. Flood*, Cal. LEXIS 94, January 1874), Theresa B. King of Brooklyn, N.Y. (*People ex rel. King v. Gallagher*, N.Y. LEXIS 302, 18 June 1883), Eva McCullom of Xenia, Ohio (*Cleveland Gazette*, 17 Dec. 1887), the daughter of the Rev. J. W. Gazaway of Springfield, Ohio (*Cleveland Gazette*, 12 Jan. 1884), as well as the many children involved in lawsuits brought by parents in Monmouth Co., N.J. (*Christian Recorder*, 28 Sept. 1882), Hartford and Buffalo, N.Y. (*New York Times*, 28 Sept. 1867, 16 May 1868), and Marion, Ind. (*New York Times*, 1 Aug. 1874).

99. Barbara Welke (*Recasting American Liberty*, 88–89) surveys the common law requirement that prevented married women from bringing suit on their own behalf: a married woman's legal identity was subsumed within that of her husband's until property laws of the postwar period enabled married women in some states to file suit independently. As Welke notes, these laws were unevenly structured and unevenly enforced; some states retained the common law requirement until the twentieth century. Iowa state law was inconsistent on this matter; according to Ruth Gallaher (*Legal and Political Status*, 29–33), by 1870 state law permitted married women to sue on their own, but at least as late as 1894, judges were still denying married women damages, making awards to husbands instead.

100. Wisconsin was the only midwestern state without de jure segregation of its public school system (Douglas, *Jim Crow Moves North*, 38). Douglas reports that in 1868, the Wisconsin superintendent of public instruction asserted that he knew of no separate schools for black children, nor of any schools in the state that excluded black children from attending (p. 100). But it is also true that after the Civil War, Milwaukee saw a significant drop in the rates of school attendance among black children (Vollmar, "Negro in a Midwest Frontier City," 86).

101. Green, "Race and Segregation," 138–49; *St. Paul Daily Press*, 27 Feb. 1864, *St. Paul Pioneer*, 9 Aug. 1865, *St. Paul Daily Pioneer*, 14 Mar., 15 Apr. 1869, *Minneapolis Spokesman*, 28 Feb. 1958, and *St. Paul Daily Minnesotan*, 9 Mar. 1959 (all in FWP, Annals of Minnesota, MHS); Cummings, "Segregated Education," 26–28.

102. *Muscatine Daily Courier*, 8 Sept. 1865.

103. *Cedar Falls Gazette*, 18 Dec. 1868.

104. *Clark v. Board of Directors* (1868).

105. *Christian Recorder*, 17 May, 7 June 1862, 29 Dec. 1866, 4 Feb. 1865; *History of Lee County*, 640; Keokuk Public School Superintendents Records, SHS/IC.

106. Anderson evidently gained quick acceptance in the Keokuk community; in the fall of 1865, as the only official agent of the Colored People's National Lincoln Monument

Association west of Ohio, she was able to raise nearly $100 for the memorial; *Christian Recorder*, 9, 23 Sept. 1865. See also Savage, *Standing Soldiers*, chap. 3.

107. *"Cookhouse Talk,"* 3–4, LCHS; McCaul, *Black Struggle*, 55–72. A Democratic city government amended Chicago's charter in 1863 to require school segregation; see Daniel, "Segregation-Discrimination Dilemma," 126.

108. *Christian Recorder*, 16 Nov. 1867.

109. *Daily Gate City*, 23, 25 July 1869.

110. *Daily Gate City*, 23, 25 July, 9 Nov. 1869.

111. Rosa Dandridge Pryor, "The Dandridge Family History," 1971 MS, bound vol., Harper Papers, IWA.

112. These women were able to file suit under changes to the 1870 state code, which allowed married women to sue on their own behalf (Gallaher, *Legal and Political Status*, 30). Another incident of racial discrimination made the news that spring, when Keokuk's hotels refused accommodations to the "Tennesseans," a black singing troupe (*Cedar Falls Gazette*, 1 May 1874).

113. *New National Era*, 1 Oct. 1874.

114. *Iowa State Register*, 4, 5 Nov. 1874; *Daily Gate City*, 7 Nov. 1872; C. R. Rasmussen, "Keokuk's Ku Klux Scare of Long Ago," 29 Jan. 1927; "Ethnography-Negroes," KPL.

115. *Smith v. The Directors of the Independent School District of Keokuk* (1875).

116. See, e.g., Nikki M. Taylor, *Frontiers of Freedom*, 161–74.

117. Patrick Rael makes a similar point in *Black Identity and Black Protest*, 51.

118. *Daily Gate City*, 7 Oct. 1869.

119. *Daily Gate City*, 18 Aug. 1965.

120. *Daily Gate City*, 26 Feb. 1874; *Christian Recorder*, 12 Mar. 1874.

121. "Fancy Etchings," *Christian Recorder*, 15 Jan. 1874. In the 1870s, Harper published several short stories that focused on social issues then facing black communities; Peterson, *Doers of the Word*, 214–15.

122. "Fancy Etchings," *Christian Recorder*, 15 Jan. 1874.

123. Here Harper might be referring to a national convention held in December 1873 that advocated equal access (*New York Times*, 11 Dec. 1873). An 1869 national convention had seen significant debate on the floor about admitting women, including those who had been duly elected as delegates, but the convention voted to refuse their credentials. Iowa's Alexander Clark joined Sella Martin and four others in supporting the admittance of women; Foner and Walker, *Proceedings of the Black National and State Conventions*, 354, 367.

124. Bystrom, "From Voting to Running for Political Office"; Catt and Shuler, *Woman Suffrage*, 214; Noun, *Strong-Minded Women*, 231; Wood, *Freedom of the Streets*, 60; *Woman's Journal*, 11 July 1874, 13 May 1876.

125. Marshall, "Mount Pleasant," 51; *Daily Hawk-Eye*, 21 May 1867.

126. See Barbara Welke's important, southern-focused article, "When All the Women Were White,"

127. *The Chicago & Northwestern Railway Company v. Anna Williams* (1870), LEXIS 338; see also *Weekly Journal*, 26 Nov. 1869. Mrs. Green of Parsons, Pa., encountered similar treatment in Wilkes-Barre during 1875 as she and her husband prepared to board a train. As Green approached the ladies' car, escorted by her husband, the white brakeman permitted two white women to enter but then "pushed [Green] back [off the step] and pointed

to the front car." When Green, with her husband's assistance, persisted in trying to gain entrance, the brakeman chained and then locked the door. In its finding, the court rejected claims by the brakeman that Mrs. Green had been smoking, an implicit charge of unladylike behavior, instead asserting that she "was behaving in a very proper manner so far as testimony shows"; she was awarded $500 in damages. *Central R. of New Jersey v. Green* (1878).

128. Chilton's case was not resolved until 1893; see Barbara Welke's incisive treatment of this and similar cases in *Recasting American Liberty*.

129. *Daily Gate City*, 13 Feb. 1872. Coger sued for $5,000 damages and was awarded $250. Ironically, one of her lawyers, George W. McCrary, a future congressman and secretary of war, had favored the exclusion of black children from public schools before the Civil War (Dykstra, *Bright Radical Star*, 203). Coger was not the first African American to sue a packet line for denial of first-class service while traveling on the upper Mississippi River; in 1870, Chicago resident J. H. Washington sued the St. Louis and Keokuk Packet Co. for denying him first-class service and violently ejecting him from the ship when he attempted to travel from St. Louis to Quincy (*Chicago Tribune*, 15 Apr. 1870).

130. *Daily Gate City*, 12 Sept. 1872.

131. *Coger v. North West Union Packet Co.* (1873), State Law Library of Iowa, Des Moines, 153.

132. One of these character witnesses was George Caldwell, an active member of Keokuk's Prince Hall Masons.

133. Neither Coger nor her friends were unusual in the challenges they posed to the ideological constructions of race. In 1890, Naomi Anderson of Wichita, Kans., in a letter to the *Woman's Tribune*, asserted: "There are very few negroes in this country, if any. . . . We have adopted the name, Afro-American because we are color-stained, but we belong to no race at all. We are bone and flesh of every nationality of white men on this continent, and will continue to be so as long as our women remain unprotected and the power of the Anglo-Saxon . . . predominates. We are not a separate people, deny it who will. We are a manufactured people. . . . My father was Indian and German, and my mother African And Irish (What am I?)" (*Woman's Tribune*, 22 Mar. 1890).

134. *Daily Gate City*, 13 Feb. 1872.

135. *Weekly Gazette*, 7 June 1872; *Daily Gate City*, 27 May 1874.

136. *Oshkosh Northwestern*, 21 Nov. 1883.

137. *Christian Recorder*, 27 Feb. 1873.

138. *New National Era*, 27 Feb. 1873.

139. *Daily Gate City*, 15, 17 Feb. 1873.

140. *Burlington Weekly Hawk-Eye*, 4 Mar. 1875.

141. Wang, *Trial of Democracy*, 212–15 (reversal of the Civil Rights Act); Ross, *Justice of Shattered Dreams* (Justice Miller).

142. *Milwaukee Sentinel*, 2 Nov. 1883; David Vassar Taylor, "The Blacks," in *They Chose Minnesota*, 80; *Capital Times*, 18 May 1979.

143. Iowa's bill shared the weaknesses of the federal Civil Rights Act in that it excluded schools, churches, and cemeteries. See Goostree, "Civil Rights in Iowa," 18–29, and Weaver, "Civil Rights Act of 1875."

144. *Appeal*, 15 Mar. 1890. St. Paul's Harris Theater had refused to give Mrs. R. C. Howard, an African American, the first-class seats she requested.

145. Weaver, "Civil Rights Act of 1875," 65–66, 69.

146. *Home Journal*, 4 Aug. 1865.

147. *Home Journal*, 18 Aug. 1865.

148. *Iowa City Republican*, 18 Nov. 1868, quoting *Des Moines Statesman*.

149. *Woman's Journal*, 28 Sept. 1878.

150. Although the Wisconsin legislature approved school suffrage for women in 1886, subsequent court cases forced a review of the law and Wisconsin women were unable to vote in school elections until 1901. But they were apparently able to run for seats on school boards as early as 1869. See *Woman's Journal*, 25 Dec. 1886, and Bystrom, "From Voting to Running for Political Office."

151. Newman, *White Women's Rights*, 60.

152. *Daily State Register*, 12 Feb. 1868.

153. *Weekly Journal*, 10 Dec. 1869; *Washington County Press*, 11 Jan. 1871.

154. Noun, *Strong-Minded Women*, 125–26; *Woman's Journal*, 2 Mar. 1872, 2 Feb. 1878.

155. In January 1866, Sen. James Crookham of Oskaloosa (who supported extending the franchise to all soldiers, black and white) proposed limited female suffrage in Iowa. That year, the state legislature received a petition from 27 Clinton County women; Noun, *Strong-Minded Women*, 44, 56–57. Several more petitions were submitted over the next three years, and at least three nationally recognized woman suffrage speakers lectured at various locations in Iowa (ibid., 85–95).

156. Wisconsin's suffragists launched a statewide campaign in 1882 and (somewhat unexpectedly) won women's right to participate in school elections in 1886. The poorly worded law was immediately challenged in court, suspending school elections for Wisconsin women until 1901 and leading to a downturn in the woman suffrage movement until the 1890s. Genevieve McBride (*On Wisconsin Women*, 118) describes the passage of the school suffrage bill as "an afterthought," an assembly-sponsored compromise measure.

157. "Colored Women Want to Vote," 10 Dec. 1885, folder 1, box 4, Woman's Suffrage Corr. 1869–1910, Iowa Woman's Suffrage Records, SHS/DM. My thanks to Jennifer Imsande for bringing this to my attention.

158. Newman, *White Women's Rights*, 63–64.

159. "Colored Women Want to Vote," Iowa Woman's Suffrage Records, SHS/DM.

160. *Woman's Standard*, February 1887. The *Woman's Standard* was the monthly newspaper of the Iowa Woman Suffrage Association.

161. *Woman's Standard*, April 1890.

162. *Woman's Standard*, January, February 1888.

163. *Woman's Standard*, April 1893.

164. *Woman's Standard*, February 1888.

165. *Iowa State Bystander*, 5 Oct. 1894.

166. *Woman's Standard*, February 1888.

167. Untitled, 4 Jan. 1889, folder 2, box 2, Iowa Woman's Suffrage Records, SHS/DM.

168. *Woman's Standard*, January 1890.

169. Ibid.

170. Untitled, October 1891, folder 2, box 2, Iowa Woman's Suffrage Records, SHS/DM.

171. *Woman's Standard*, February 1887.

172. *Woman's Standard*, May 1891.

173. Frederick Douglass, "Address of the Colored National Convention: To the People of the United States," p. 14, MS, 1883, Speech, Article, and Book File, Douglass Papers, LC. Minnesota blacks met in August 1883 to prepare for the late September convention, electing a delegate to attend and passing several resolutions to be raised in Louisville; *St. Louis Globe-Democrat*, 22 Aug. 1883. No record of similar meetings in Iowa or Wisconsin has been uncovered.

174. Mosely, *Colored Man of America*, 7, 12.

175. Among the northern delegates would be Rev. J. W. Malone, representing Iowa at the 1890 convention. Malone was well known in the AME Church for his advocacy of black-led churches; he had been a fiery speaker at the 1868 black convention called to support the cause of black suffrage.

176. David Vassar Taylor, "The Blacks," 80.

177. Ibid.; *Appeal*, 9 Nov. 1889. Although membership was open to women, all of the appointed officers were men.

178. Fishel, "The Genesis of the First Wisconsin Civil Rights Act," 327.

179. The only surviving issue of the paper is from 20 Jan. 1893. "Protective League" and "Protective Association" were synonymous with the organization; see Fortune's proposal for the "creation of a Protective League," quoted in Alexander, "'We Know Our Rights,'" 12.

180. According to Shawn Alexander, Fortune believed women's participation would be central to the success of the national league, but no states had elected female delegates to attend the 1890 organizational meeting. See Alexander, "We Know Our Rights," 36–37, 43 (on the constitutional plank admitting women).

181. *Iowa State Bystander*, 6 July 1894. The paper reported that the meeting was under-attended due to strikes by railroad workers at the time. On lagging interest in Minnesota, see *Appeal*, 15 Mar. 1890.

182. David Vassar Taylor, "The Blacks," 80; Nelson, *McGhee*, 31–33; *Appeal*, 21 Nov. 1891.

183. Schechter, *Wells-Barnett*, 117, 119, 123, 128–29, 137, 182–83.

184. The NACW was established in 1896 when the National Federation of Afro-American Women, organized in Boston in 1895, and the Colored Women's League, organized in Washington, D.C., in 1893, united. NACW, "History of the National Association."

185. *St. Paul City Directory*; *Minneapolis Spokesman*, 27 May 1949; *St. Paul Daily Dispatch*, 7 July 1876; Nelson, *McGhee*, 147–55. Born in Ohio in 1855, Amanda Lyles's father was of German ancestry; her mother was a native of Missouri. Thomas Lyles and his parents were Maryland-born. As early as March 1889, the *Appeal* announced that her "Hair Bazaar" had opened, and it carried regular advertisements for her business (see 22 June 1889). Nelson makes the important point about the impermanence and vulnerability of class status among the black elite; not all, for example, enjoyed the benefits of formal education, and some were vulnerable to severe cash-flow problems. See also Summers, *Manliness*, 6–7.

186. Iowa State Federation of Colored Women's Clubs, *Programme of the Eighth Annual Session*.

187. Retrospective accounts of the dates of club formation sometimes varied; see Iowa State Federation of Colored Women's Clubs, *Minutes of the Fifth Annual Meeting*, 18, *Minutes of the Sixth Annual Meeting, Programme of the Eighth Annual Session, Proceeding of the Tenth Annual Session*, and *Proceeding of the Eleventh Annual Session*, all in Iowa Association of Colored Women, Records, box 1, SHS/IC. See also Allen, "Sowing Seeds of Kindness."

CHAPTER 7

1. Blight, *Race and Reunion*, 251.
2. *Evening Tribune*, 21 Dec. 1927.
3. *Davenport Democrat and Leader*, 11 Feb. 1912; *Des Moines Register*, 10 Nov. 1929; George Wilson, "First Territorial Adjutant," 574; *Chariton Leader*, 4 Nov. 1947.
4. Kent Pellett, "Dred Scott Sat in Iowa Shack: The Private Lives of the Pioneers," undated newspaper clipping, SC/UI. Scott's lawsuit was based on his residence in free territory in the upper Midwest.
5. Blight, *Race and Reunion*, 231–54, 284–91; Silber, *Romance of Reunion*, chap. 5.
6. Siebert's work was published as *The Underground Railroad from Slavery to Freedom*. Warren's phrase "the treasury of virtue" comes from his *Legacy of the Civil War*, 59. There are two versions of the WPA Federal Writers' Project manuscript, "The Negro in Iowa." One is located at the State Historical Society of Iowa, Iowa City. The second is a revised version found in the George P. Rawick Papers at the University of Missouri Archives, St. Louis. The manuscript was never published.
7. Blight (*Race and Reunion*, 232, 236) first offered the notion of an "alternate veteranhood." Contemporary black activism included opposition to D. W. Griffith's 1915 film, *The Birth of a Nation*, in Davenport (*Iowa State Bystander*, 29 Oct. 1915), in Des Moines ("14 Reasons Why You Should Join the N.A.A.C.P.," reel 10, frame 687, and S. Joe Brown, *History of the Des Moines Branch, National Association for the Advancement of Colored People* (n.d., n. p.), 3–4, reel 10, frame 800, both in NAACP Papers, Collections on Microfilm); in Sioux City, Iowa (*Chicago Defender*, 11 Sept. 1915), in Milwaukee (*Chicago Defender*, 15 July 1915), in Oshkosh, Wis. (*Chicago Defender*, 25 Sept. 1915), and in Minneapolis (*Chicago Defender* 21 Aug., 23, 30 Oct. 1915).
8. Newspaper clipping, 4 Aug. 1898, "Ethnography-Negroes," KPL. Thompson's mother, Mrs. Catherine (Kate) Thompson, was born into slavery in Missouri. She took her children to Ringgold County, Iowa, during the war, then moved to Decatur City and subsequently Des Moines by 1866. See her obituary in the *Iowa State Bystander*, 20 Nov. 1903. Thompson edited the *Bystander* from 1896 until 1919. On earning his law degree in 1898, he was the only African American to pass the state bar exam that year and the second black Iowan admitted to practice in federal courts; Allen W. Jones, "Equal Rights to All," 77.
9. According to Hirsh (*Family Frames*, 22), "Postmemory is distinguished from memory by generational distance and from history by deep personal connection." She also asserts that "postmemory characterizes the experience of those who grow up dominated by narratives that preceded their birth, whose own belated memories are evacuated by the stories of the previous generation shaped by traumatic events that can be neither understood nor recreated." Although intended to illuminate the memories constructed by and for the

children of Holocaust survivors, Hirsch's conceptualization is also valuable for understanding the memories of slavery passed down by survivors to their children and descendants. A note on terminology: I use "history" to refer to the events of the past and rigorous reconstruction of those events by academic historians. I use "memory" to refer to direct, personal recollections of lived experience. I use "collective memory" to refer to shared experiences and those passed down through generations (much as Hirsh uses postmemory). As David Blight (*Beyond the Battlefield*, 2) has observed, "History asserts the authority of academic training and recognized canons of experience; memory carries the often more powerful authority of community membership and identity."

10. Newspaper clipping, 4 Aug. 1898, "Ethnography-Negroes," KPL.

11. Charles Chesnutt's short story, "The Wife of His Youth" (*Atlantic Monthly*, July 1898, 55–61), poignantly explores these conflicting forces of memory and amnesia among former slaves. Literary scholar Henry Louis Gates Jr., writing in the *New York Times* (9 Feb. 2003), has argued that at the turn of the century "slavery had become something of an embarrassment to an aspiring black elite desperate to integrate into a gilded American age." See Blight, *Race and Reunion*, 216–31, 284–91, and *Beyond the Battlefield*, 120–52; Savage, *Standing Soldiers*, 89–128; and Kammen, *Mystic Chords of Memory*, 121–23.

12. Hartman, *Lose Your Mother*, 6, 45, 73, 107, 133.

13. This analysis draws on a rich literature, including Kachun, *Festivals of Freedom*; Fabre and O'Meally, *History and Memory*; Gravely, "The Dialectic of Double-Consciousness"; Kathleen Clark, "Celebrating Freedom" (107–32), and Brundage, "No Deed but Memory" (1–28), in Brundage, *Where These Memories Grow*; Shane White, " 'It Was a Proud Day' "; Wiggins, *O Freedom!*; Rael, *Black Identity*, 54–81; and Higman, "Remembering Slavery."

14. The *Bystander*'s editors—and editorial positions—changed over time, becoming more politically conservative in the 1920s and 1930s, although the paper would remain community-oriented. With a circulation of 1,750 by 1899, the *Bystander* claimed subscribers in three-fourths of Iowa's counties, in more than half the states of the Union, and in two foreign countries. Whereas white newspapers survived primarily on advertising revenue, black newspapers typically relied on subscriptions, so the paper's success in covering community events across the state was critical to its survival; Allen W. Jones, "Equal Rights to All."

15. See Houston A. Baker, "Critical Memory"; Shane White, "Question of Style"; Elsa Barkley Brown, "Negotiating and Transforming," 107–46; Saville, "Rites and Power"; Hunter, *To 'Joy My Freedom*; and Robin D. G. Kelley, *Race Rebels*.

16. Although some scholars emphasize speeches and oration as the most important element of the exercises, the complex assemblage of parades, picnics, banners, and dancing all contributed to the meaning of the celebrations. My approach to this complex performance draws on Susan Davis's exploration of parades as "street theater" in her *Parades and Power*, 13–20, and Ryan, *Civic Wars*.

17. Dykstra, *Bright Radical Star*, 16–17. By 1857, Muscatine's black population (counted at 69 in the 1850 U.S. Census) had already helped protect a fugitive slave, sent a delegate to the National Colored Convention held at Rochester, N.Y. (1853), petitioned Iowa legislature to repeal the 1851 law limiting black migration into the state, and organized Iowa's first black convention, which met at Muscatine within days of the August 1857 commemoration. See J. P. Walton, "Unwritten History of Bloomington (now Muscatine) in Early Days";

Muscatine Journal, 27 Jan. 1888 (typewritten transcription), Alexander Clark File, Musser; Petition #11, 17 Jan. 1855, "Petitions, Blacks and Mulattos, Rights of," General Assembly, Secretary of State Papers, SHS/DM; and Dykstra, *Bright Radical Star*, 151, 154, 173.

18. See Shane White, " 'It Was a Proud Day,' " and Rael, *Black Identity*.

19. Fabre, "African American Commemorative Celebrations," 72–73.

20. For example, Charlotta Pyles, a former slave from Kentucky who went to Keokuk after she and most of her family were manumitted, struggled to buy her remaining family members out of slavery. This prompted a trip east in 1855 for a fund-raising tour. One of her stops included an Emancipation Day celebration in New York City, where she encountered a sympathetic audience. *New York Times*, 2 Aug. 1855; Essie M. Britton, "Early Negro Families in Iowa," "Ethnography-Negroes," KPL; Hallie Q. Brown, *Homespun Women*, 34–45.

21. The 1853 kidnapping of Milton Howard and his family from their Muscatine home is described in his testimony in a comrade's pension application (affidavit by Howard, 17 Dec. 1916, pension file of Harvey Brooks, WC 825854, CWPF) and in a 1978 interview by Lillian Justice with Howard's niece, Dorothy Katherine Mitchell Childress, in Williams, "An Oral History of the Black Population of Davenport, Iowa," at the Davenport Public Library. Several Iowa newspapers reported Archie Webb's prosecution in 1863 for violating Iowa law against black migration. See *Daily State Register*, 18 Jan.–3 Feb. 1863; *Daily Hawk-Eye*, 24 Jan., 5, 6 Feb. 1863. See also "Polk County, Delaware Township Justice of the Peace Documents Related to Removal of Free Negro, Jan. 1863," SHS/IC, and Dykstra, *Bright Radical Star*, 199–200.

22. *Davenport Daily Gazette*, 3 Aug. 1860.

23. *Home Journal*, 3 Jan. 1863. A celebration was also held in Des Moines on 5 or 6 January (contemporary accounts disagree), organized and attended by white abolitionists; from existing records, it is impossible to determine whether or how many of the city's African Americans attended. See *Daily State Register*, 7 Jan. 1863, and *Daily Hawk-Eye*, 9 Jan. 1863.

24. Based on numerous state newspapers, as well as the *New York Times* and the *Christian Recorder* from the 1850s through 1963. Although by no means a complete survey of the region's celebrations, my research has identified over two hundred commemorations in Iowa alone. More fragmentary evidence for Wisconsin and Minnesota suggests that celebrations became more popular in those states later in the nineteenth and early twentieth centuries.

25. Given the difficulty of holding an outdoor celebration in the cold of midwestern winters, the 1 August celebration date might simply have been the most convenient choice. However, contemporary reports suggest a clear consciousness of the significance of the August date. In 1867, Keokuk blacks announced that by celebrating in August, both West Indian emancipation and the issuance of Lincoln's preliminary Emancipation Proclamation could be honored (*Daily Gate City*, 1 Aug. 1867). Other communities explicitly described their celebrations as commemorating West Indian, or Jamaican, emancipation. See *Dubuque Times*, 2 Aug. 1882, 2 Aug. 1894.

26. In 1867, delegations from Davenport and Washington, Iowa, attended Muscatine's celebration; *Muscatine Courier*, 3 Jan. 1867. In 1868 Des Moines invited residents of Oskaloosa, Newton, Washington, Grinnell, and Chariton to participate in their commem-

oration (*Daily State Register*, 21 July 1868), and Davenport invited residents of Rock Island and Moline, Ill., as well as those of West Liberty, to theirs (*Daily Davenport Democrat*, 31 July 1868). In 1872, the "colored fellow citizens of Davenport, Clinton, Lyons, Fulton, Moline, Rock Island, Muscatine, De Witt, Cedar Rapids, and Chicago" celebrated together at De Witt (*Davenport Daily Democrat*, 31 July 1872). In 1874, Mt. Pleasant invited residents of Des Moines, Ottumwa, Burlington, and Keokuk (Marshall, "Mount Pleasant," 51). In 1894, Oskaloosa organizers touted their celebration as a "statewide" event and invited more than twelve communities, including Des Moines and Keokuk, to their festivities (*Iowa State Bystander*, 3 Aug. 1894).

27. The *Oshkosh Daily Northwestern* of 2 Aug. 1894 reported a gathering of over two hundred at a Racine (Wis.) celebration; the *Stevens Point Gazette*, 10 Aug. 1910, reported a gathering in Oshkosh of over three hundred.

28. *Constitution*, 12 Aug. 1863.

29. Ibid.; Wubben, *Civil War Iowa*, 153–54. In 1900, Keokuk was surpassed by Des Moines in the size of its black population; Goudy, "Selected Demographics, 41."

30. Faye Emma Harris, "Frontier Community," 389. Fourth of July celebrations were sites of class as well as racial conflict; see the insightful assessments of Susan Davis in *Parades and Power*, 40–48.

31. *Daily Gate City*, 3 Jan., 2 Aug. 1866.

32. *Daily Iowa State Register*, 2 Aug. 1866.

33. For white hostility toward Keokuk's growing black population, see, e.g., *Constitution*, 5 Sept. 1862.

34. Unidentified clipping, [1871], Black History Binder II, NVHM. For a full discussion of the move away from boisterous street festivities to "respectable" processions among African Americans by the 1830s, see Kachun, *Festivals of Freedom*, 54–75; Rael, *Black Identity*, 54–81; and White, "It Was a Proud Day," esp. 28–31, 34–41. The evolution of urban parades into a more elaborate ceremonial form by the eve of the Civil War is also noted by Mary Ryan in *Women in Public*, 20–23. Kachun (*Festivals of Freedom*, 236–48) discusses the increasing concerns of black leaders with the projection of respectability in public commemorations in the 1880s.

35. *Daily Gate City*, 3 Jan. 1866; *Home Journal*, 28 Aug. 1865; *Daily State Register*, 2 Aug. 1867.

36. *Constitution*, 12 Aug. 1863 (Butler appears in the 1860 census—see Ancestry.com, *1860 United States Federal Census*); *Daily Gate City*, 2 Aug. 1866, 3 Jan. 1875; *Muscatine Courier*, 3 Jan. 1867.

37. *Christian Recorder*, 4 Feb. 1865; *Iowa State Bystander*, 3 Aug. 1894, 9 Aug. 1895; *Home Journal*, 3 Jan. 1863; *Minneapolis Tribune*, 31 July, 1 Aug. 1879 [WPA Annals of Minn., MHS]; *Oshkosh Daily Northwestern*, 2 Aug. 1890; unidentified clipping, [1871], Black History Binder II, and 1877 clipping, Underground Railroad Binder, both in NVHM; *Dubuque Times*, 2 Aug. 1882; *Burlington Hawk-Eye*, 2 Aug. 1894; *Constitution*, 6 Jan. 1864; *Daily State Register*, 7 July 1864; *Iowa State Register*, 26 July 1876. The *Tipton Advertiser* of 3 Dec. 1896 announced a "cake walk."

38. *Home Journal*, 28 Aug. 1865; *Muscatine Courier*, 3 Jan. 1867; *Daily Gate City*, 1 Jan. 1866, 31 Dec. 1871; unidentified newspaper clipping, Black History Binder I, BH007

(1876), transcribed clipping, Black History Binder I, BH 0056 (1885), and 1901 program, Black History Binder, BH 110—all in NVHM.

39. *Christian Recorder*, 15 Aug. 1863, 13 Nov. 1873, 3 Apr. 1890; *Oshkosh Daily Northwestern*, 1 Aug. 1877, 2 Aug. 1890; *Madison Democrat*, 2 Oct. 1912.

40. *Home Journal*, 28 Aug. 1865; *Weekly Courier*, 3 Jan. 1867; *Daily Gate City*, 1 Jan. 1866, 31 Dec. 1871; unidentified newspaper clipping, Black History Binder, BH007 (1876), transcribed clipping, Black History Binder, BH 0056 (1885), and 1901 program, Black History Binder I, BH 110—all in NVHM); *Keokuk Daily Constitution*, 2 Aug. 1882; *Daily Gate City*, 31 Dec. 1871; *Daily Iowa State Register*, 2 Aug. 1866; *Daily State Register*, 1 Jan. 1867; *Davenport Daily Gazette*, 29 Dec. 1865; *Dubuque Times*, 2 Aug. 1882.

41. *Home Journal*, 28 Aug. 1865; *Iowa State Register*, 2 Aug. 1876. On the cultural politics of foodways and the commodification of black women's work in the kitchen, see Super, "Food and History"; Witt, *Black Hunger*; and Manring, *Slave in a Box*.

42. *Iowa State Register*, 2 Aug. 1876.

43. See the announcement of Alexander Clark's role in Muscatine's exercises in the *Muscatine Courier*, 3 Jan. 1867; Susan Mosely's part in Mt. Pleasant's 1896 celebration in the *Iowa Wesleyan*, 15 Oct. 1896; and local speakers for various programs in the *Daily State Register*, 31 July 1867, *Daily Gate City*, 23 July 1874, and *Twin City Star*, 16 Sept. 1910.

44. See, e.g., the list of female readers in the *Muscatine Courier*, 7 Jan. 1869; *Tipton Advertiser*, 2 Jan. 1896; and the *Iowa State Bystander*, 4 Jan. 1901, 8 Jan. 1909 (for Newton and Des Moines).

45. *Daily Iowa State Register*, 2 Aug. 1866. See also *Burlington Hawk-Eye*, 2 Aug. 1894, and *Iowa State Bystander*, 4 Jan., 16 Aug. 1901.

46. Berlin, "Who Freed the Slaves?"

47. *Christian Recorder*, 4 Feb. 1865; unidentified clipping, Black History Binder I, BH 007, NVHM; *Daily Gate City*, 4 Jan. 1868.

48. *Christian Recorder*, 4 Feb. 1865. See also 1890 clipping, Black History Binder II, NVHM.

49. *Christian Recorder*, 4 Feb. 1865; *Daily Gate City*, 4 Jan. 1868. In 1868, Guy was a teacher in Keokuk's black public school, where between 1869 and 1873 he served as the principal ("Schools," Bickel Collection, KPL). Politically active in the state's black convention movement, Guy occasionally served as a delegate to AME regional conferences; see Jenifer, *Centennial Retrospect History*, 114–15.

50. *Daily Iowa State Register*, 2 Aug. 1866. Carey, a Baptist minister, was active in the state's black convention movement, and in 1869 he defended the employment of black teachers in Keokuk's black public school; *Daily Gate City*, 25 July 1869. Yancey, a Keokuk barber, moved to Iowa with his wife Nancy and infant daughter in 1857. Known locally as a skilled orator, he spoke at Emancipation Day celebrations in Keokuk, Mt. Pleasant, and Des Moines before his death in 1878. See Prill and Prill, *Jefferson County Records*, 5:356–57; 1870 Federal Manuscript Census (Ancestry.com, *1870 United States Federal Census*), Population, Ward 2, Fairfield, Jefferson County; *Home Journal*, 28 Aug. 1865; *Daily Iowa State Register*, 2 Aug. 1866; *Daily State Register*, 31 July 1867.

51. *Daily Iowa State Register*, 2 Aug. 1866; *Davenport Daily Democrat*, 2 Aug. 1872.

52. *Daily Gate City*, 4 Jan. 1868.

53. Davis enlisted in January 1864 from Sangamon County, Ill., and was mustered into Company G, 65th USCI; he was mustered out on 8 Jan. 1867; Bickel's Civil War Binder, Bickel Collection, KPL. According to the 1870 census, at the time of Keokuk's 1865 celebration, Davis—born into slavery in Missouri—was in his twenties, was illiterate, and worked as a servant while residing in the household of a Georgia-born black family who had moved to Iowa during or immediately after the war. Davis was a "familiar figure" in Keokuk. "He was very proud of his war service and displayed a rifle bullet wound scar on his face. . . . Charlie was a quiet, cheerful old fellow and friendly to everyone"; *Daily Gate City*, newspaper clipping and notes (1951), Negro History File, LCHS.

54. *Iowa State Register*, 2 Aug. 1866; clipping, 5 Aug. 1871, Black History Binder II, NVHM; clipping, 6 Aug. 1901, Black History Binder II, BH110, NVHM; *Home Journal*, 25 Sept. 1868; *Henry County Free Press*, 16 Sept. 1868. See also the invitation extended to Civil War veterans for Davenport's 1915 celebration in the *Davenport Democrat and Leader*, 27 Dec. 1914, and the announcement that "former slaves and civil war veterans will be guests of honor" at the 1915 Des Moines celebration in the *Register and Leader*, 27 Dec. 1914.

55. My understanding of the process of collectivizing slavery's trauma draws on Eyerman, *Cultural Trauma*.

56. See, e.g., the role of veterans in the St. Paul celebration of 1913 (*Twin City Star*, 3 Oct. 1913).

57. *Muscatine Weekly Courier*, 3 Jan. 1867.

58. Lowenthal, *Past Is a Foreign Country*, 213.

59. In her assessment of the role of women in postbellum civic parades and ceremonies, Mary P. Ryan has noted the prevalence of similar performances across a range of ethnic, racial, and religious communities. She finds that the prevalence of Goddesses of Liberty and other living icons reinforced distinct gender roles but emphasized civic unity (*Civic Wars*, 244–58).

60. Formed in 1898, the Afro-American Council was a rebirth of the Afro-American League, which organized out of a national meeting convened in Chicago in 1890 by T. Thomas Fortune, editor of the *New York Age*. Without adequate support, the league failed, but the council was organized on the same basis—i.e., to challenge the disenfranchisement of southern black men and to protest lynching, the chain-gang system, discrimination in public schooling and accommodations, and wage and occupational discrimination. Iowa delegates, including *Bystander* editor John Thompson, attended the league's 1890 meeting in Chicago as well as the council's conventions in Indianapolis in 1900 and St. Paul in 1902. See Afro-American League, *Official Compilation of Proceedings*, and Cyrus Field Adams, *National Afro-American Council*. Booker T. Washington organized the National Negro Business League in 1900 to advance the economic interests of elite businessmen. See Harlan, *Booker T. Washington*, 266–71; Lorini, *Rituals of Race*, 194–207; *Iowa State Bystander*, 8 Jan. 1915. The NAACP was organized nationally in 1909, and a Des Moines branch was formed in 1915. See Lufkin, "Founding and Early Years."

61. See, e.g., *Appeal*, 27 Dec. 1890; *Chicago Defender*, 13 Jan. 1923 (on Beloit, Wis.).

62. *Iowa State Bystander*, 3 Jan. 1913, 6 Dec. 1912. See also programs published in the *Bystander*, 8 Jan. 1904, 25 Dec. 1908, 31 Dec. 1909, 26 Dec. 1913.

63. *Iowa State Bystander*, 4 Jan. 1907, 3 Dec. 1909. In its first year, the Des Moines branch of the NAACP initiated an important (although ultimately unsuccessful) legal challenge to the showing of *The Birth of a Nation* in city theaters. The film, based on Thomas Dixon's novel, *The Clansman*, offered a distorted, Lost Cause portrait of Reconstruction, caricaturing black men as rapists and attempting to justify lynching. See Lufkin, "Founding and Early Years," 450–52. In 1923, Sue Brown, Joe's wife, who was also active in the NAACP, chaired the advisory board of the Frederick Douglass Memorial and Historical Association, organized to maintain and preserve the Douglass home as well as the Douglass Papers. See Mrs. S. Joe Brown to Hon. J. W. Johnson, 31 July 1923, frame 634, reel 10, NAACP Papers, Collections on Microfilm. The Des Moines Interracial Commission, formed in 1924, called for "the introduction of a course in Negro History into the Des Moines Public Schools" as one of its fourteen "Desiderata" (S. Joe Brown et al., *Twenty Years*).

64. *Chicago Defender*, 13 Jan. 1923 and 29 Mar. 1924 (Beloit), 5 June 1926 and 9 Feb. 1935 (St. Paul).

65. Existing newspaper accounts and NAACP records—which may be incomplete—document NAACP commemorative activities in Iowa from 1915 to 1928 and in 1930, 1932, 1935, 1945, 1955, and 1963. For the NAACP's involvement with the memorialization of black history, as well as with changing the form in which that history was presented, see Lorini, *Rituals of Race*, 208–56, and Blight, *Race and Union*, 361–97.

66. The branch also distributed a pamphlet it had prepared for the fair, entitled *A Few Facts about Iowa Negroes*. The eight-page paper was primarily given over to brief biographies of leading black men and women, rather than providing a historical narrative about African Americans in the state. Ten thousand copies were distributed, and the NAACP won two prizes at the 1932 fair; frame 1018–26, reel 10, NAACP Papers.

67. *Iowa State Bystander*, 3 Jan., 26 Dec. 1913. See also the programs described in the *Bystander*, 4 Jan. 1901, 1 Jan. 1904, 4 Jan. 1907, 1 Jan. 1909, 1 Jan. 1910, 3 Jan. 1913.

68. On the African American women's club movement in Iowa, see Allen, "Sowing Seeds of Kindness." On Milwaukee's black club women, see *Chicago Defender*, 11 Sept. 1915. Minnesota's state federation of African American Women's Clubs was organized in 1902 (*Appeal*, 24 May 1902). On the AME Sunday School convention, see *Iowa State Bystander*, 12 May, 9 June 1899, 22 June 1900. On women and the Afro-American Council, see *Iowa State Bystander*, 25 Aug. 1899, 3 Dec. 1909. On black women and the Des Moines NAACP branch, see S. Joe Brown, *History of the Des Moines Branch*. Two excellent sources on twentieth-century African American women's activism in secular and denominational organizations are Deborah Gray White, *Too Heavy a Load*, and Higginbotham, *Righteous Discontent*.

69. *Bystander*, 26 Dec. 1930.

70. *Bystander*, 3 Jan. 1963.

71. Wiggins, *O Freedom!*, pays particular attention to the celebrations of the mid-twentieth century.

72. For the past thirteen years, Juneteenth has emerged as Iowa's most popular emancipation celebration date. It commemorates 19 June 1865, the day Union general George Granger belatedly informed Texas slaves of their freedom. Celebrations are found in a

handful of Iowa cities, and the state is one of seven to have declared Juneteenth a state holiday—in accordance with a national movement to secure a federally recognized day of remembrance. See *www.juneteenth.com/3iowa_us.htm* (15 June 2008).

73. Kammen, *Mystic Chords of Memory*, 105–6.

74. See *Chicago Daily Tribune*, 25 Jan. 1890, 30 Aug. 1891, and Davies, "Problem of Race Segregation."

75. Shaffer, *After the Glory*, 152–59; Gannon, "The Won Cause." Gannon identifies 200 black posts in 23 states and the District of Columbia (59).

76. *Iowa State Bystander*, 3, 17 Aug. 1894.

77. *Iowa State Bystander*, 17 Aug. 1894; Membership files, GAR, Samuel J. Kirkwood Post No. 8, SHS/IC.

78. Membership files, GAR, Samuel J. Kirkwood Post No. 8, SHS/IC. At Des Moines, these included 6 of 461 members in good standing in Crocker Post No. 12 and 3 black members in Kinsman Post No. 7

79. *American Legacy*, Spring 2004.

80. *Iowa State Bystander*, 13 Jan. 1911.

81. *Chicago Defender*, 14 Apr. 1911, 29 Jan. 1916, 10 Feb. 1917, 8 June, 13 July 1918, 4 May 1929.

82. Gannon, "The Won Cause," 70.

83. Woman's Relief Corps, *Journal of the Tenth Annual Convention*, 35–36; *Journal of the Eleventh Annual Convention*, 252–54; *Journal of the Twelfth Annual Convention*, 256–57; *Journal of the Fourteenth National Convention*, 215, 248–49, 262–63; *Journal of the Fifteenth National Convention*, 224–25, 241–42, 320–30; and *Journal of the Twenty-third National Convention*, 81, 245, 299–300, 425–26.

84. See *Chicago Defender*, 14 Sept., 16 Nov. 1935, 8 Jan. 1938; inventory for the MS collection, "Ladies of the Grand Army of the Republic," and photograph of members (ca. 1945), negative no. 24630, MHS.

85. Blight, *Race and Reunion*, 231–37. The quotation in the subheading comes from an interview with Ansel Clark, published in the *Chicago Defender*, 1 Jan. 1949.

86. The objectivity of traditional sources of "official history" has been thoughtfully reconsidered by a number of scholars, including Caron, " 'How Changeable Are the Events of War' "; Irvine, "Genesis of the Official Records"; Fahs, *Imagined Civil War*, esp. 287–310; McConnell, "Epilogue: The Geography of Memory"; and Blight, *Race and Reunion*.

87. See, e.g., Regosin, *Freedom's Promise*; Shaffer, *After the Glory*; Schwalm, *"A Hard Fight for We"*; Frankel, *Freedom's Women*; and Bercaw, *Gendered Freedoms*.

88. Regosin, *Freedom's Promise*, 31.

89. On the rejection rate of claims, see ibid., 19.

90. Affidavit by Emmeline Porter, 16 Jan. 1922, pension file of Joseph Porter, IC 482911, CWPF.

91. Affidavit by Henry Brown, 11 Apr. 1913, pension file of Henry Brown, IC 782140.

92. Ellen Hayes to Commissioner of Pensions, 1890, pension file of Anderson Hayes, WC 344064. On family reconstitution, see deposition by Martha Jackson, 14 Oct. 1913, pension file of Preston Jackson, WC 774574; affidavit by Phillis Taylor, 22 July 1889, pension file of Gerrett Brown, aka Gerrett Montgomery, Minor C 471639; affidavit by Lucy Bassett, 23 Sept. 1911, pension file of Edward Boyd, IC 694102.

93. Affidavit by Benjamin Henry, 12 Feb. 1896, pension file of John Anderson aka Norvell, WA 271609.

94. Affidavit by John H. Bandy, 10 Aug. 1892, pension file of John H. Bandy, IC 840217.

95. See, e.g., affidavit by William Camp, 4 Mar. 1892, pension file of William Camp, IC 754265; affidavits by Virginia Linebaugh and Amerlia Spence, 15 June 1885, pension file of Jerry aka Henry White, IC 921134; affidavit by George Kebo, 16 Apr. 1884, pension file of Daniel Tate, WC 361052.

96. Blight, *Race and Reunion*, 179, and *Douglass' Civil War*, chap. 10; Fahs, *Imagined Civil War*, 287–310; Diffley, *To Live and Die*, 1–24.

97. See, e.g., the following obituaries in the *Iowa Bystander*: Margaret Rose (23 Mar. 1896), Susan White (31 May 1901), Mrs. Jennie Bell (13 Feb. 1903), Mary Anne Shepard (20 Nov. 1903), Nathan E. Morton (10 Feb. 1905), Henry Bell (14 May 1909). In the *Chicago Defender*, see Robert T. Motts (22 July 1911), Ansel Clark (30 Apr., 7 May 1932), Curry Reed (16 July 1938), Henry Mack (14 Apr. 1945). In the *Burlington Hawk-Eye*, see Irene McPike (11 May 1900).

98. *Iowa State Bystander*, 18 Feb. 1898.

99. On the cultural history of death and obituary for African Americans, see Lois Brown, "Memorial Narratives," and Holloway, *Passed On*.

100. My source here is the bibliography prepared by William L. Andrews, series editor of the DocSouth collection, "North American Slave Narratives," <http://docsouth.unc.edu/neh/chron.html> (15 June 2008). Five of the 102 (20 percent) were written by women.

101. As William Andrews ("First Century of Afro-American Autobiography," 5) has noted, the reception of a black narrative as truthful "depended on the degree to which his artfulness could hide his art." The success of a slave narrative not only benefited a political movement; it also ensured the writer a career as a lecturer. The narratives of former slaves were frequently oriented to speaking tours to promote the antislavery cause as well as to provide their bread and butter. See also Sekora, "Black Message/White Envelope"; Foster, *Witnessing Slavery*; Gates, "The Language of Slavery," and James Olney, "'I Was Born,'" both in Davis and Gates, *Slave's Narrative*, xi–xxxiv, 148–75; and Andrews, *To Tell a Free Story*.

102. Sekora, "Black Message/White Envelope," 503.

103. This periodization of American slave narratives draws on Andrews, *To Tell a Free Story*, and Heglar, *Rethinking the Slave Narrative*.

104. Andrews, *To Tell a Free Story*, 170.

105. Harriet Wilson's *Our Nig*, with its emphasis on racism and restricted opportunities for blacks in the North, is an example.

106. Two additional postbellum narratives that touch far more lightly on experiences in the upper Midwest are Robinson, *From Log Cabin to the Pulpit*, and Anderson, *From Slavery to Affluence*.

107. Mosely, *Colored Man of America*; Orville Elder, *Samuel Hall*.

108. Among the scholars who have considered the meaning of emancipation for the slave narrative tradition, Henry Louis Gates ("Language of Slavery," xii–xiii, xxii) has argued that "once slavery was formally abolished, no need existed for the slave to write himself into the human community through the action of first-person narrative." Gates has concluded

that emancipation offers an absolute cutoff date for the slave narrative tradition, but other scholars—including William Andrews, Frances Smith Foster, and Kimberly Rae O'Connor—have argued convincingly that the slave narrative tradition, in O'Connor's ("To Disembark," 35) words, "is ongoing in its formation." See also Andrews, "The Representation of Slavery."

109. Andrews, "North American Slave Narratives," <http://docsouth.unc.edu/neh/chron.html> (15 June 2008). Recently, David Blight (*A Slave No More*) has brought to light two previously unpublished postbellum narratives: "Memories of the Past," by John M. Washington, and "The Journal of Wallace Turnage."

110. Andrews, "Reunion in the Post-bellum Slave Narrative," 5. Other studies of the postwar slave narrative include Andrews, "Representation of Slavery" and "Towards a Poetics of Afro-American Autobiography"; Foster, *Written by Herself*; Fleischner, *Mastering Slavery*; and Sorisio, "Unmasking the Genteel Performer."

111. Blight, *Race and Reunion*, 313.

112. Obituary of James Mitchell Mosely, undated newspaper clipping, vertical file, Mt. Pleasant Public Library, Iowa; U.S. Historical Census Data Browser, University of Virginia.

113. On the history of Mt. Pleasant, see Parker, *Iowa as It Is*, 139–41; *Daily Hawk-Eye*, 8 July 1857; Hair, *Iowa State Gazetteer*; Olive Cole Smith, *Mt. Pleasant Recalls*; Isabell Diary, SHS/DM; P. C. Tiffany, "Reminiscences," *Dial of Progress*, 22 July 1899, Clippings File, Henry County—Reminiscences, SHS/IC.

114. W. H. Corkhill, Hospital Chaplain and Superintendent of Contrabands, to O. D. Greene, Asst. Adj. Gen., 27 Apr. 1864, Letters Received, DOM, ser. 2593, box 12, RG 393, pt. 1; Jaynes, *Highlights of Henry County*, 41–42; *Burlington Hawk-Eye*, 27 Oct. 1919; *Home Journal*, 10 Jan. 1863, 6 Jan. 1864 (quotation).

115. *Home Journal*, 3 Jan., 13 June 1863; Elihu Gunn to Rev. G. S. Backer, 14 July 1863, Gunn Papers (unprocessed collection), SHS/IC; *History of Henry County, Iowa*, 526, 532.

116. Parker, *Iowa Handbook for 1856*, 76.

117. U.S. Historical Census Data Browser, University of Virginia; Dykstra, *Bright Radical Star*, 31; *Bystander*, 25 Sept. 1914; Edna L. Jones, *Nathan Littler's History*, 82.

118. Wubben, *Civil War Iowa*, 79; *Christian Recorder*, 11 July 1863.

119. *Washington Evening Journal*, 26 Apr. 1913. The piety of the former slaves became well known. At one revival meeting in rural Washington County, "the interest was not a little increased by the presence of a contraband preacher, whose frequent songs of Zion and warm exhortations and soul felt prayers, were ever ready to aid in the good work" (Rev. W. H. Westerwelt to Brother Jocelyn, 22 Jan. 1863, AMA Letters from Iowa, microfilm, SHS/DM).

120. Although church membership, along with the town's black population, peaked in the last decades of the nineteenth century, the congregation was still active in the 1920s, when the literary society and Sunday school were still important components of the church's work. In 1925, the church hosted a statewide Sunday School convention as well as a local branch of the NAACP. Burrell, *History of Washington County*, 252, 55; entry for 1893, AME Church, bound volumes (unpaginated), Washington Public Library, Iowa; *Washington Evening Journal*, 3 Apr. 1926.

121. Orville Elder, *Samuel Hall*, 42.

122. My summary of the year's events relies heavily on the account provided by David

Blight in his well-researched and thoughtfully analyzed chapter, "Black Memory and Progress of the Race," in his *Race and Reunion*.

123. On the "mixed form" in the genre, see James Olney, "I Was Born," 151–53.

124. On the black jeremiad, see Andrews, *To Tell a Free Story*, 14–19 (which discusses the use of the jeremiad in the black autobiographical tradition prior to the Civil War); Jeremiah Moses Wilson, *Black Messiahs* (which emphasizes the antebellum use of the jeremiad to protest slavery); Howard-Pitney, "Enduring Black Jeremiad" (which extends Wilson's argument by exploring the uses of the jeremiad to protest racial injustice after the war); and Blight, *Douglass' Civil War*, 114–21 (which explores Douglass's use of the jeremiad).

125. Mosely, *Colored Man of America*, 2.

126. Ibid., 2–3.

127. Ibid., 3.

128. Ibid., 6.

129. Ibid., 6–7.

130. Ibid., 7. Mosely's simultaneous deployment of secular political idealism and a national millennialism was not unique in African American letters. David Blight has insightfully traced the influence of these same traditions in Frederick Douglass's efforts to shape American memory of the war. See Blight, "Frederick Douglass and the American Apocalypse," *Douglass' Civil War*, 101–21.

131. Mosely, *Colored Man of America*, 8.

132. Ibid., 16–18.

133. Ibid., 9.

134. Ibid., 12.

135. Ibid., 6.

136. Ibid., 17.

137. On Susan Mosely, see *Historical Sketch and Alumni Record*, 232, Iowa Wesleyan College, Mt. Pleasant; *Mt. Pleasant Daily News*, 27 Feb. 1897; *Iowa Wesleyan*, 15 Oct. 1896; and *Iowa Bystander*, 14 July 1899.

138. Mosely, *Colored Man of America*, 17.

139. The report of Mosely's death appeared in the *Mt. Pleasant Daily News*, 13 May 1916.

140. Mosely, *Colored Man of America*, 18.

141. *Mt. Pleasant Daily News*, 13 May 1916; Blight, *Race and Reunion*, 284. This overview draws heavily on Blight's account, but see also Silber, *Romance of Reunion*; Savage, *Standing Soldiers*; and the essays in Brundage, *Where These Memories Grow*.

142. Orville Elder, *Samuel Hall*.

143. Ibid., 6–7; *Davenport Democrat and Leader*, 30 June 1912.

144. Stepto, *From Behind the Veil*, 3; and "I Rose and Found My Voice: Narration, Authentication, and Authorial Control," in Davis and Gates, *Slave's Narrative*, 225–41.

145. See Thomas, "Post-Abolitionist's Narrative."

146. Orville Elder, *David and Isabella Elder*, 79.

147. Orville Elder, *The Frank Stories, Mickey Peck*, and *A Trip to the Hawaiian Islands*.

148. Orville Elder, *David and Isabella Elder*.

149. Orville Elder, *Samuel Hall*, 26.

150. Ibid., 11.
151. Ibid., 28.
152. Ibid., 27–28.
153. Ibid., 29.
154. Ibid.
155. Ibid., 15.
156. Ibid., 16.
157. Ibid., 34. This scenario bears a clear resemblance to the encounter with slave breaker Edward Covey that Frederick Douglass describes in his own *Narrative* (71–73).
158. Orville Elder, *Samuel Hall*, 22–25.
159. Ibid., 40–44.
160. Ibid., 36–38.
161. Ibid., 38.
162. Ibid., 40–44.
163. Ibid., 43–44; *Christian Recorder*, 11 July 1863.
164. *Washington Evening Journal*, 26 Apr. 1913.
165. *Washington County Press*, 19 Jan. 1870.
166. Orville Elder, *Samuel Hall*, 28.
167. Ibid., 43.
168. *Iowa Bystander*, 10 Aug. 1894 (Flag Day celebrations); *Iowa Bystander*, 20 Sept. 1894 (Tourgée's visit); *Iowa Bystander*, 12 Oct. and 14 Dec. 1894 (families of former slaves reunite). For an example of the many obituaries published in the *Bystander*, see the report on Henry Bell's life and death, 13 Dec. 1903.

Bibliography

PRIMARY SOURCES
Manuscript Collections

Illinois
 Springfield
  Illinois State Archives
   Database of Servitude and Emancipation Records (1722–1863), <http://www
    .cyberdriveillinois.com/departments/archives/servant.html>. 2 Aug. 2005.
   Servitude and Emancipation Records, Slave Register, Gallatin County, 1815–39
Iowa
 Burlington
  Burlington Public Library
   History: "Slavery/Underground Railway," vertical file
   "History of St. John African Methodist Episcopal Church, Burlington, Iowa,
    1867–1976," compiled by Geraldine Brown, vertical file
   Race Relations, vertical file
 Cedar Rapids
  Iowa Masonic Library
   Clark, A. G., Jr. *Clark's History of Prince Hall Freemasonry, 1775–1945*. Des
    Moines: United Grand Lodge of Iowa, A.F & A.M., 1947.
   Grand Lodge of Iowa. *The Constitutions of the Freemasons with the Constitution
    and By-Laws of the Grand Lodge of Iowa*. 7th ed. Des Moines: Mills and Co.,
    Steam Printing House, 1866.
   ———. *Proceedings of the Grand Lodge of Iowa of Ancient, Free and Accepted
    Masons at Its Twenty-fourth Grand Annual Communication, Held at
    Davenport, Tuesday, June 4, . . . 1867*. Davenport: Publishing House of Luse
    and Griggs, 1867.
   ———. *Proceedings of the Grand Lodge of Iowa of Ancient, Free, and Accepted
    Masons, at Its Twenty-seventh Grand Annual Communication Held at
    Davenport, Tuesday June 7 . . . 1870*. Davenport: Griggs, Watson, and Day,
    Printers, 1870.
   ———. *The Ancient Constitutions, with the Constitution and By-Laws and Masonic
    Code with a Digest of Decisions of the Grand Lodge of Iowa, A.F. & A.M.*
    Burlington: Acres, Blackmar and Co., Printers, 1880.
   ———. *Organization and Proceedings of the Most Worshipful African Grand Lodge of
    Free and Accepted Masons, for the State of Iowa and Its Masonic Jurisdiction,
    Held in the City of Keokuk, Iowa, Commencing August 9th, 1881*. N.p., n.d.
   ———. *Proceedings of the Most Worshipful African Grand Lodge of Free and
    Accepted Masons, for the State of Iowa and Its Masonic Jurisdiction, Held at*

Burlington, *July 10, 11 and 12, 1883*. Des Moines: P. C. Kenyon, Publisher Law Briefs, 1883.

———. *Proceedings of the Most Worshipful African Grand Lodge of Free and Accepted Masons, for the State of Iowa and Its Masonic Jurisdiction, Held at Ottumwa, July 8, 9, and 10, 1884*. Des Moines: P. C. Kenyon, Publisher Law Briefs, 1884.

———. *Proceedings of the Most Worshipful African Grand Lodge of Free and Accepted Masons, in Its Fourth Annual Session for the State of Iowa and Its Masonic Jurisdiction, Held at St. Paul, July 14, 15 and 16, 1885*. Des Moines: Hunnel and Simpson, Printers, 1885.

Grand Lodge of Minnesota. *Proceedings of the Grand Lodge of A.F. & A.M. of Minnesota, at Its Twenty-fourth Grand Annual Communication Held at St. Paul*. [St. Paul: St. Paul Pioneer Press, 1876].

———. *Proceedings of the Grand Lodge of A.F. & A.M. of Minnesota, at Its Twenty-fifth Grand Annual Communication Held at St. Paul*. [St. Paul: St. Paul Pioneer Press, 1877]

Prince Hall Grand Lodge of Missouri. *Proceedings of the Special Communication of the Most Worshipful Grand Lodge of the Most Ancient and Honorable Fraternity of Free and Accepted Masons for the State of Missouri and Its Jurisdiction, Convened in the City of St. Louis, Dec. 20, A.D. 1866*... N.p., n.d.

———. *Proceedings of the First Annual Communication of the Most Worshipful Grand Lodge of the Most Ancient and Honorable Fraternity of Free and Accepted Masons for the State of Missouri and Its Jurisdiction, Convened in the City of St. Louis, June 1, A.D. 1867*. N.p., n.d.

———. *Proceedings of the Most Worshipful Grand Lodge of Free and Accepted Ancient York Masons for the State of Missouri and Its Jurisdiction; Convened in the City of St. Louis, July [1869]*. St. Louis: Missouri Democrat Book and Printing House, 1869.

———. *Proceedings of the Most Worshipful Grand Lodge, Free and Accepted Ancient York Masons for the State of Missouri and Its Jurisdiction; Convened in the City of Memphis, Tenn., July 3rd 1871*. Keokuk: Gate City Steam Printing House, 1871.

———. *Proceedings of the Most Worshipful Grand Lodge, Free and Accepted Ancient York Masons for the State of Missouri and Its Jurisdiction; Convened in the City of Keokuk, Iowa, July 1st 1872*. Keokuk: Gate City Steam Printing House, 1872.

United Grand Lodge of Iowa, A.F. & A.M. *Proceedings of the United Grand Lodge of Iowa and Its Jurisdiction*. 1895.

Clarinda
  Nodaway Valley Historical Museum
    Black History Binder, I and II
    Underground Railroad Binder
Clinton
  Clinton County Historical Society Archives

Des Moines
   State Historical Society of Iowa
      Adjutant General Records, Record Group 101
      American Missionary Association Letters
      Des Moines Pioneer Club Annual Banquet, *HS2513.D4 D4
      Iowa Woman's Suffrage Records, 1866–1951, MS 71
      Nathan Isabell Diary, 1830–56, D8, folder 1
      David W. Kilburne Papers, Business Correspondence, 1854, vol. 3, file 9
      Samuel J. Kirkwood Papers, 1841–94, MS 37
      Secretary of State Records, Record Group 081
      Annie Wittenmyer Papers, 1861–1901, MS 25
      Dr. James Wright Letterbook, vol. 3, 1862–63, #3467
   State Law Library of Iowa
      Coger v. North West Union Packet Co. (1873), Supreme Court Records

Grinnell
   Grinnell College Archives
      L. F. Parker Collection

Iowa City
   Iowa City Clerk's Office
      Minutes, City Council Meetings (microfilm)
   State Historical Society of Iowa
      American Home Missionary Association Papers, ser. 1, Incoming Correspondence, Iowa Files, 1838–93, MF 32
      Chapman Family Papers, 1855–66, MS 233
      Clippings File, Afro-Americans
      Clippings File, Henry County—Reminiscences
      Grand Army of the Republic, Samuel J. Kirkwood Post No. 8, Records, R70
      Elihu Gunn Papers, 1852–65, BL 375
      Iowa, Adjutant General's Office. *Report of the Adjutant General and Acting Quartermaster General of the State of Iowa, January 1, 1863 to January 11, 1864.* Des Moines: F. W. Palmer, State Printer, 1864.
      Iowa Association of Colored Women's Clubs, Records, 1903–70, MS 193
      Iowa City Schools, Minutes of School Boards, 2 June 1858, Book I, p. 4, School Records, box 8, and Keokuk Public School Superintendents Records, 1859–66, box 2, Iowa School Records, 1849–1958, R28
      Iowa Yearly Meeting of Friends, Salem Meeting of Friends Minutes, 1859–70, *BX7607.IF9P
      John L. Mathews Letters, 1861–89, BL331
      Harry Herndon Polk, "Old Fort Des Moines," Des Moines Pioneer Club Banquet, 20 Jan. 1940 [MRC4]
      "Polk County, Delaware Township Justice of the Peace Documents Related to Removal of Free Negro, Jan. 1863," BL 316 f7
      Francis Reno, Freedman's Bond, BL 160 f29

August P. Richter Papers, ca. 1884–1925, Negroes in Iowa News Clippings, MS 103

WPA Iowa Federal Writers' Project, "The Negro in Iowa" Collection, 1935–42, MS 232

University of Iowa
 Iowa Women's Archives
  Virginia Harper Papers
  Ellen Mowrer Miller Papers
 Special Collections
  Correspondence and Journals, 1861–63: Oliver Boardman Collection, MsL B6621
  Letters, 1862–1905: Edward E. Davis Letters, MsL D2615c
  Federal Writers' Project, Iowa, MsC 295
  Letters to [Mr. and Mrs. Moyle]: Robert Moyle Collection, Hillsboro, Iowa, 1862–64, MsL M938c
  David James Palmer Papers, 1862–87, MsC 438
  Shelton Family Papers, 1864–66, 1908, MsC 7

Johnson County
 Auditor's Office
  Census of Johnson County for 1846, MS

Keokuk
 Keokuk Public Library
  Bickel Collection, Underground Railroad Binder
  Caleb Forbes Davis Scrapbook (microfilm)
  "Ethnography-Negroes," vertical file
  "WPA—Churches," vertical file
 Lee County Historical Society
  Negro History File
  Private Notebook of Lieutenant Colonel Milton Collins

Mt. Pleasant
 Iowa Wesleyan College
  Chadwick College
   Historical Sketch and Alumni Record of Iowa Wesleyan College. Mt. Pleasant, 1917.
   Iowa Wesleyan
 Mt. Pleasant Public Library
  Churches of Mt. Pleasant, clippings file

Muscatine
 Musser Public Library
  Alexander Clark File
  Civil War Files No. 1
  Old Settlers Register
  "Race Relations" clippings file

Washington
   Washington Public Library
      African Methodist Episcopal Church, bound volumes
Minnesota
  St. Paul
     Minnesota Historical Society
        George R. Adams Papers, 1862–64, P1663
        Benjamin Densmore and Family Papers, 1797–1955, A/.D413
        Federal Writers' Project, Annals of Minnesota: Subject files, Nationality Groups—Negroes, 1852–87, 1892, 1895, reel 104 [microform], M529
        Lucius F. Hubbard and Family Papers, 1842–72, 1956, A/.H875
        Ladies of the Grand Army of the Republic, Department of Minnesota, ALPHA
        R. James and Abby Mendenhall Papers, P1578
        Thomas Montgomery Papers, 1862–67, M235
        Pilgrim Baptist Church (St. Paul). *125th Anniversary Book, 1863–1988*. (Marceline, Mo.: Walsworth Publishing Co., 1988), BX6480.S2 P664 1988.
        ———. *Centennial: 1863–1963*. St. Paul: F. D. Fredell, 1963. BX6480.S2 P6.
        Billings D. Sibley Papers, A.S564b
        Judson Wade Papers, box 1, P1922
Missouri
  Columbia
     Western Historical Manuscripts Collection
        John G. Hudson Papers, Collection 3553
  St. Louis
     Missouri Civil War Museum, <http://www.missouricivilwarmuseum.org/>. 14 June 2004.
     Missouri State Archives
        General Orders No. 67, Department of the Missouri, St. Louis, 7 May 1864, General Court-Martial of Chauncey D. McCoy, bound volume
        St. Louis Circuit Court Historical Records Project, <http://stlcourtrecords.wustl.edu>. 15 June 2008
        Henry, James, a boy of color, v. Walker, William, November 1834, Case No. 83, Circuit Court Case Files, Office of the Circuit Clerk, City of St. Louis, [15 July 2005]
        Milly, a woman of color, v. Duncan, James, November 1835, Case No. 63, Circuit Court Case Files, Office of the Circuit Clerk, City of St. Louis, [15 July 2005]
        Peter, a man of color, v. Richardson, John, November 1841, Case No. 84, Circuit Court Case Files, Office of the Circuit Clerk, City of St. Louis, [15 July 2005]
        Rachel, a woman of color, v. Walker, William, November 1834, Case No. 82, Circuit Court Case Files, Office of the Circuit Clerk, City of St. Louis, [14 July 2005]

Missouri State Historical Society
William Greenleaf Eliot Family Papers, 1832–1961, A 0446
Hamilton Rowan Gamble Collection, 1787–1964, A0549
Kennett Family Papers, 1840–1932, A0812
James Tower Sweringen Papers, A 11595
University of Missouri Archives
George P. Rawick Papers
Western Historical Manuscripts Collection
Heroines of Jericho, St. Louis, History and Proceedings, Msl 105

New York
New-York Historical Society
Gilder Lehrman Collection

North Carolina
Wilson Library, University of North Carolina at Chapel Hill
North American Slave Narratives, Documenting the American South, <http://docsouth.unc.edu/neh>. 15 June 2008.

Washington, D.C.
Library of Congress
Frederick Douglass Papers, <http://memory.loc.gov/mss/mfd/24/24003/0001d.jpg>. 4 Feb. 2007.
Mary Peabody Tyler Mann Papers
National Archives
Record Group 15: Records of the Veterans Administration
Record Group 94: Records of the Adjutant General's Office, 1780–1917
Record Group 108: Records of the Headquarters of the Army
Record Group 393: Records of U.S. Army Continental Commands, 1821–1920
U.S. Department of the Interior
National Park Service
Civil War Soldiers and Sailors System, <http://www.itd.nps.gov/cwss/index.html>. 20 June 2006.

Wisconsin
University of Wisconsin
Digital Collections
William Ault Civil War Papers, 1864–65, box 3, p. 3, <http://digital.library.wisc.edu/1711.dl/WI.WillAult>.
Henry S. Eggleston Letters, 1861–62, box 2, folder 2, <http://digital.library.wisc.edu/1711.dl/WI.HenryEdo1>.
William Moore Diary: History of Company G, 10th Regiment Wisconsin Volunteers, 7 Sept. 1861–26 June 1862, <http://digital.library.wisc.edu/1711.dl/WI.WillMoore>.
Edward S. Redington Papers, 1862–67, <http://digital.library.wisc.edu/1711.dl/WI.EdRedo1>.
Charles Sheppard Papers, 1850–58; Platteville Micro 2, <http://digital.library.wisc.edu/1711.dl/WI.Shepard3a>.

Madison
  Wisconsin Historical Society Archives
    Edward Salomon Papers, ser. 33, box 2
    Wisconsin Governor Papers, Military Correspondence, 1837–1910, ser. 49, box 16
    Wisconsin—Negroes, Explanatory Materials, SC 457
Milwaukee
  Wisconsin Historical Society, Milwaukee Area Research Center (UWM Libraries, University of Wisconsin—Milwaukee)
    Cecil A. Fisher Papers, 1921–66, Milwaukee Small Collection 51

Collections on Microfilm

National Association for the Advancement of Colored People. NAACP Papers, Part 12, Selected Branch Files, 1913–39. Ser. C: The Midwest.

Published Letters, Diaries, Memoirs

Anderson, Daisy. *From Slavery to Affluence: Memoirs of Robert Anderson, Ex-Slave.* Steamboat Springs, Colo.: Printed by the Steamboat Pilot, 1927.
Brown, William. *The Life Story of (Rev.) Wm. Brown.* N.p., 1930.
Brown, William Wells. *Narrative of William Wells Brown, a Fugitive Slave, Written by Himself.* Boston: Anti-Slavery Office, 1847.
Cookhouse Talk: A Dialogue between William Talbot, President, Lee County Historical Society, and Leon Bland, Old Time Steamboat Hand and Chef... Keokuk: Lee County Historical Society, 1965.
Coston, W. H. *A Freeman and Yet a Slave.* Burlington, Iowa: Wohlwend Bros., 1888.
Delany, Lucy A. *From the Darkness Cometh the Light; or, Struggles for Freedom.* St. Louis: Publishing House of J. T. Smith, n.d.
Douglass, Frederick. *Narrative of the Life of Frederick Douglass, an American Slave.* Boston: Anti-Slavery Office, 1849.
Eberhart, Rev. Uriah. *History of the Eberharts in Germany and the United States.* N.p.: Donohue and Henneberry, 1891.
Elder, Donald C., III, ed. *A Damned Iowa Greyhound: The Civil War Letters of William Henry Harrison Clayton.* Iowa City: University of Iowa Press, 1998.
———, ed. *Love amid the Turmoil: The Civil War Letters of William and Mary Vermillion.* Iowa City: University of Iowa Press, 2003.
Elder, Orville, with Samuel Hall. *Samuel Hall: 47 Years a Slave: A Brief Story of His Life before and after Freedom Came to Him.* Washington, Iowa: Journal Print Co., 1912.
Eliot, William Greenleaf. *The Story of Archer Alexander: From Slavery to Freedom.* 1885. Reprint, New York: Negro Universities Press, 1970.
Gooding, Corporal James Henry. *On the Altar of Freedom: A Black Soldier's Civil War Letters from the Front.* Edited by Virginia Matzke Adams. Amherst: University of Massachusetts Press, 1991.
Harpole, Patricia C., ed. "The Black Community in Territorial St. Anthony: A Memoir." *Minnesota History* 49, no. 2 (Summer 1984): 42–53.

Jackson, Mattie J. *The Story of Mattie J. Jackson . . . Written and Arranged by Dr. L. S. Thompson.* Lawrence, Kans.: Sentinel Office, 1866.

Mathews, Rev. E. *The Autobiography of Rev. E. Mathews.* New York: American Baptist Free Mission Society, 1866.

Mosely, Moses. *The Colored Man of America as a Slave and a Citizen of the United States.* Mt. Pleasant, Iowa: Journal Co. Printers, 1884.

Musser, Charles O. *Soldier Boy: The Civil War Letters of Charles O. Musser, 29th Iowa.* Edited by Barry Popchock. Iowa City: University of Iowa Press, 1995.

Newson, T. W. *Pen Pictures of St. Paul, Minnesota and Biographical Sketches of Old Settlers.* St. Paul: Brown, Treacy and Co., Printers, 1886.

Parsons, Emily. *Memoirs of Emily Elizabeth Parsons.* Boston: Little, Brown, 1880.

Rawick, George P., ed. *The American Slave: Arkansas, Colorado, Minnesota, Missouri, & Oregon & Washington Narratives.* Supp. ser. I, vol. 2. Westport, Conn.: Greenwood Press, 1978.

Ripley, C. Peter, ed. *Witness for Freedom: African American Voices on Race, Slavery, and Emancipation.* Chapel Hill: University of North Carolina Press, 1993.

Robinson, William H. *From Log Cabin to the Pulpit; or, Fifteen Years in Slavery.* 3rd ed. Eau Claire, Wis.: James H. Tifft Publishing Printer, 1913.

Rogers, Rev. J. B. (Chaplain, 14th Wisconsin Volunteers). *War Pictures: Experiences and Observations of a Chaplain in the U.S. Army, in the War of the Southern Rebellion.* Chicago: Church and Goodman, 1863.

Rogers, M. A. "An Iowa Woman in Wartime, Part II." *Annals of Iowa* 35, no. 8 (Spring 1961): 594–615.

Silber, Nina, and Mary Beth Sievens, eds. *Yankee Correspondence: Civil War Letters between New England Soldiers and the Home Front.* Charlottesville: University Press of Virginia, 1996.

Smith, Amanda. *An Autobiography: The Story of the Lord's Dealings with Mrs. Amanda Smith[,] the Colored Evangelist.* Chicago: Meyer and Brother, Publishers, 1893.

Thompson, Charles. *Biography of a Slave; Being the Experiences of Rev. Charles Thompson, a Preacher of the United Brethren Church, while a Slave in the South: Together with Startling Occurrences Incidental to Slave Life.* Dayton, Ohio: United Brethren Publishing House, 1875 (at Documenting the American South, University of North Carolina-Chapel Hill <http://docsouth.unc.edu/neh/thompsch/thompsch.html>, 10 June 2004.)

Throne, Mildred, ed. *The Civil War Diary of Cyrus F. Boyd, Fifteenth Iowa Infantry, 1861–1863.* Millwood, N.Y.: Kraus Reprint Co., 1977.

Todd, Rev. John. *Early Settlement and Growth of Western Iowa; or, Reminiscences.* Des Moines: Historical Department of Iowa, 1906.

Urwin, Gregory J. W., and Cathy Kunzinger Urwin, eds. *History of the 33d Iowa Infantry Volunteer Regiment, 1863–66, by A. F. Sperry.* Fayetteville: University of Arkansas Press, 1999.

Wilson, Harriet E. *Our Nig; or, Sketches from the Life of a Free Black . . .* Boston: C. Rand and Avery, 1859.

Newspapers and Periodicals

Anamosa Gazette (Iowa)
Appeal (St. Paul, Minn.)
Appleton Motor (Wisconsin)
Bangor Daily Whig & Courier (Maine)
Burlington Hawk-Eye (Iowa)
Burlington Weekly Hawk-Eye (Iowa)
Bystander (Des Moines, Iowa)
Capital Times (Madison, Wis.)
Cedar Democrat (Tipton, Iowa)
Cedar Falls Gazette (Iowa)
Chariton Leader (Iowa)
Chicago Daily Tribune
Chicago Defender
Chicago Times
Christian Recorder
Cleveland Gazette
Constitution (Keokuk, Iowa)
Daily Davenport Democrat (Iowa)
Daily Democrat and News (Davenport, Iowa)
Daily Express and Herald (Dubuque, Iowa)
Daily Gate City (Keokuk, Iowa)
Daily Gazette (Davenport, Iowa)
Daily Hawk-Eye (Burlington, Iowa)
Daily Hawk-Eye and Telegraph (Burlington, Iowa)
Daily InterOcean (St. Paul, Minn.)
Daily Iowa State Register (Des Moines)
Daily Milwaukee News (Wisconsin)
Daily Missouri Democrat (St. Louis)
Daily State Register (Des Moines, Iowa)
Davenport Daily Gazette (Iowa)
Davenport Democrat and Leader (Iowa)
Delavan Enterprise (Wisconsin)
Des Moines Leader (Iowa)
Des Moines Register (Iowa)
Dial of Progress (Mt. Pleasant, Iowa)
Douglass' Monthly
Dubuque Daily Express and Herald (Iowa)
Dubuque Times (Iowa)
Dubuque Herald (Iowa)
Evening Tribune (Des Moines, Iowa)
Fairfield Ledger (Iowa)
Fond du Lac Commonwealth Reporter (Wisconsin)

Franklin Record (Hampton, Iowa)
Freeborn County Standard (Albert Lea, Minn.)
Gazette (Cedar Falls, Iowa)
Harper's Weekly
Henry County Free Press (Iowa)
Home Journal (Mt. Pleasant, Iowa)
Iowa City Citizen (Iowa)
Iowa City Republican (Iowa)
Iowa Daily Statesman (Des Moines)
Iowa State Bystander (Des Moines)
Iowa State Journal (Des Moines)
Iowa State Register (Des Moines)
Iowa Weekly Citizen (Des Moines)
Janesville Daily Gazette (Wisconsin)
Janesville Weekly Gazette (Wisconsin)
Keokuk Daily Constitution (Iowa)
Keokuk Weekly Constitution (Iowa)
Keokuk Weekly Gate City (Iowa)
Keokuk Weekly Times (Iowa)
Liberator
Linn County Register (Iowa)
Lyons Mirror (Iowa)
Madison Democrat (Wisconsin)
Manitowoc Herald (Wisconsin)
Manitowoc Pilot (Wisconsin)
Mankato Semi-Weekly Record (Minnesota)
Mason City Press (Iowa)
McGregor News (Iowa)
Milwaukee Journal (Wisconsin)
Milwaukee Sentinel (Wisconsin)
Minneapolis Morning Tribune (Minnesota)
Minneapolis Spokesman (Minnesota)
Mt. Pleasant Daily News (Iowa)
Mt. Pleasant Journal (Iowa)
Mukwonago Chief (Wisconsin)
Muscatine Courier (Iowa)
Muscatine Daily Courier (Iowa)
Muscatine Journal (Iowa)
Muscatine Weekly Journal (Iowa)
National Era
New National Era (Humeston, Iowa)
Newton Record (Iowa)
New Ulm Review (Minnesota)
New York Evangelist

New York Independent
New York Times
New York Tribune
North American and United States Gazette
Northwestern Bulletin (Minnesota)
Oshkosh Daily Northwestern (Wisconsin)
Oshkosh Northwestern (Wisconsin)
Oskaloosa Herald (Iowa)
Oskaloosa Times (Iowa)
Oskaloosa Weekly Times (Iowa)
Phylaxis
Pioneer and Democrat (Minnesota)
Provincial Freeman (Chatham, Canada West)
Racine Journal (Wisconsin)
Racine Journal-News (Wisconsin)
Register and Leader (Des Moines, Iowa)
Reporter (Fond du Lac, Wis.)
St. Louis Globe-Democrat (Missouri)
St. Paul Daily Dispatch (Minnesota)
St. Paul Daily Pioneer (Minnesota)
St. Paul Pioneer (Minnesota)
St. Paul Pioneer Press (Minnesota)
St. Peter Tribune (Minnesota)
State Press (Iowa City, Iowa)
Stevens Point Gazette (Wisconsin)
Stevens Point Journal (Wisconsin)
Stillwater Democrat (Minnesota)
Tipton Advertiser (Iowa)
Twin City Star (Minnesota)
Washington Democrat (Iowa)
Washington Evening Journal (Iowa)
Washington Press (Iowa)
Weekly Anglo-African (New York)
Weekly Commonwealth (Fond du Lac, Wis.)
Weekly Courier (Muscatine, Iowa)
Weekly Gate City (Keokuk, Iowa)
Weekly Gazette (Davenport, Iowa)
Weekly Gazette and Free Press (Janesville, Wis.)
Weekly Journal (Muscatine, Iowa)
Wisconsin Patriot (Madison)
Woman's Journal
Woman's Standard (Des Moines, Iowa)
Woman's Tribune

Legal Cases

Allen v. Davis, 10 WNC 156 (Pa., 1881)
Boon v. Juliet, a woman of color, I Sammon 258 (1836)
Central R. of New Jersey v. Green, 86 Pa. 421 (1878)
The Chicago & Northwestern Railway Company v. Anna Williams, 55 Ill. 185 (1870)
Clark v. Board of Directors, 40 Iowa 518 (1867)
Clark v. Board of Directors, 24 Iowa 266 (1868)
Coger v. North West Union Packet Co., 37 Iowa 145 (1873)
Cornelius v. Walsh, Breese 92 [1825]
Cory v. Carter, 48 Ind. 327 (1874)
Dove v. The Independent School District of the City of Keokuk, 41 Iowa 689 (1875)
Gillespie v. Palmer and Others, 28 Wis. 544 (1866)
In re the matter of Ralph, 1 Morris 1 (Iowa 1839)
Knox v. Board of Education of the City of Independence, 45 Kans. 152 (1891)
People ex rel. King v. Gallagher, 93 N.Y. 438 (1883)
Rachel [Bundy] v. William Walker (1836)
Smith v. The Directors of the Independent School District of the City of Keokuk, 40 Iowa 518 (1875)
State ex rel. Garners v. McCann, 21 Ohio 198 (1871)
Ward v. Flood, 48 Cal. 36 (1874)

Genealogical and Census Resources Published Online

Ancestry.com. *1810 United States Federal Census* [database online]. Provo, Utah: Generations Network, Inc., 2004. Original data: U.S. Bureau of the Census. *Third Census of the United States, 1810*. Washington, D.C.: National Archives and Records Administration, 1810. RG 29, M252, 71 rolls.

Ancestry.com. *1820 United States Federal Census* [database online]. Provo, Utah: Generations Network, Inc., 2004. Original data: U.S. Bureau of the Census. *Fourth Census of the United States, 1820*. Washington, D.C.: National Archives and Records Administration, 1820. RG 29, M33, 142 rolls.

Ancestry.com. *1830 United States Federal Census* [database online]. Provo, Utah: Generations Network, Inc., 2004. Original data: U.S. Bureau of the Census. *Fifth Census of the United States, 1830*. Washington, D.C.: National Archives and Records Administration, 1830. RG 29, M19, 201 rolls.

Ancestry.com. *1840 United States Federal Census* [database online]. Provo, Utah: Generations Network, Inc., 2004. Original data: U.S. Bureau of the Census. *Sixth Census of the United States, 1840*. Washington, D.C.: National Archives and Records Administration, 1840. RG 29, M704, 580 rolls.

Ancestry.com. *1850 United States Federal Census* [database online]. Provo, Utah: Generations Network, Inc., 2005. Original data: U.S. Bureau of the Census. *Seventh Census of the United States, 1850*. Washington, D.C.: National Archives and Records Administration, 1850. RG 29, M432, 1,009 rolls.

Ancestry.com. *1860 United States Federal Census* [database online]. Provo, Utah: Generations Network, Inc., 2004. Original data: U.S. Bureau of the Census. *Eighth*

Census of the United States, 1860. Washington, D.C.: National Archives and Records Administration, 1860. RG 29, M653, 1,438 rolls.

Ancestry.com. *1870 United States Federal Census* [database online]. Provo, Utah: Generations Network, Inc., 2003. Original data: U.S. Bureau of the Census. *Ninth Census of the United States, 1870*. Washington, D.C.: National Archives and Records Administration, 1870. RG 29, M593, 1,761 rolls.

Ancestry.com. *Minnesota Census Schedules for 1870* [database online]. Provo, Utah: Generations Network, Inc., 2003. Original data: U.S. Bureau of the Census. *Ninth Census of the United States, 1870*. Washington, D.C.: National Archives and Records Administration, 1870. RG 29, T132, 13 rolls.

Ancestry.com and The Church of Jesus Christ of Latter-day Saints. *1880 United States Federal Census* [database online]. Provo, Utah: Generations Network, Inc., 2005. 1880 U.S. Census Index provided by The Church of Jesus Christ of Latter-day Saints © 1999 Intellectual Reserve, Inc. All rights reserved. All use is subject to the limited use license and other terms and conditions applicable to this site. Original data: U.S. Bureau of the Census. *Tenth Census of the United States, 1880*. Washington, D.C.: National Archives and Records Administration, 1880. RG 29, T9, 1,454 rolls.

Ancestry.com. *1890 Veterans Schedules* [database online]. Provo, Utah: Generations Network, Inc., 2005. Original data: U.S. Bureau of the Census. *Special Schedules of the Eleventh Census (1890) Enumerating Union Veterans and Widows of Union Veterans of the Civil War*. Washington, D.C.: National Archives and Records Administration, 1890. RG 29, M123, 118 rolls.

Ancestry.com. *1900 United States Federal Census* [database online]. Provo, Utah: Generations Network, Inc., 2004. Original data: U.S. Bureau of the Census. *Twelfth Census of the United States, 1900*. Washington, D.C.: National Archives and Records Administration, 1900. RG 29, T623, 1854 rolls.

Ancestry.com. *1910 United States Federal Census* [database online]. Provo, Utah: Generations Network, Inc., 2006. Original data: U.S. Bureau of the Census. *Thirteenth Census of the United States, 1910*. Washington, D.C.: National Archives and Records Administration, 1910. RG 29, T624, 1,178 rolls.

Ancestry.com. *Iowa State Census Collection, 1836–1925* [database online]. Provo, Utah: Generations Network, Inc., 2007. Original data: Microfilm of Iowa State Censuses, 1856, 1885, 1895, 1905, 1915, 1925, as well various special censuses from 1836 to 1897 obtained from the State Historical Society of Iowa via Heritage Quest.

Genealogy.com. Revels Family Genealogical Forum, <http://genforum.genealogy.com/revels/messages/152.html>. 13 Jan. 2008

<http://www.slaveryinamerica.org/geography/slave—laws—VA.html>. 9 Aug. 2005.

University of Virginia, Geospatial and Statistical Data Center. U.S. Historical Census Data Browser, <http://fisher.lib.virginia.edu/collections/stats/histcensus/index.html>. 15 June 2008.

U.S. Census Bureau, State and County QuickFacts, <http://quickfacts.census.gov/qfd/states/55000.html>, <http://quickfacts.census.gov/qfd/states/27000.html>, and <http://quickfacts.census.gov/ qfd/states/19000.html>. 15 June 2008.

Wisconsin Historical Society. *First Wisconsin Territorial Census*, Crawford County, 1836, <http://content.wisconsinhistory.org/v?/whc,5850>. Source: Collections of the State

Historical Society of Wisconsin, edited and annotated by Reuben Gold Thwaites, Corresponding Secretary of the Society, vol. 13, Madison, Democrat Printing Co., State Printer, 1895, p. 254.

Other Published Primary Sources

Adams, Cyrus Field, comp. *The National Afro-American Council, Organized 1898: A History of Its Organization* . . . N.p., n.p., 1902.

Afro-American League. *Official Compilation of Proceedings of the Afro-American League National Convention, Held at Chicago, January 15, 16, 17, 1890* . . . Chicago: J. C. Battles and R. B. Cabell, 1890.

Allen, Richard, and John Tapisco. *The Doctrines and Discipline of the African Methodist Episcopal Church.* Philadelphia: John H. Cunningham, Printer, 1817.

Bartholow, Roberts. *Manual of Instructions for Enlisting and Discharging Soldiers.* . . Philadelphia: J. B. Lippincott and Co., 1863.

Beck, J. D., ed. *The Blue Book of the State of Wisconsin.* Madison: Democrat Printing Co., State Printer, 1907.

Berlin, Ira, Barbara J. Fields, Thavolia Glymph, Joseph P. Reidy, and Leslie S. Rowland, eds. *The Destruction of Slavery.* Ser. 1, vol. 1, of *Freedom: A Documentary History of Emancipation, 1861–1867.* Cambridge: Cambridge University Press, 1985.

Berlin, Ira, Thavolia Glymph, Steven F. Miller, Joseph P. Reidy, Leslie S. Rowland, and Julie Saville, eds. *The Wartime Genesis of Free Labor: The Lower South.* Ser. 1, vol. 3, of *Freedom: A Documentary History of Emancipation, 1861–1867.* Cambridge: Cambridge University Press, 1990.

Berlin, Ira, Steven F. Miller, Joseph P. Reidy, and Leslie S. Rowland, eds. *The Wartime Genesis of Free Labor: The Upper South.* Ser. 1, vol. 2, of *Freedom: A Documentary History of Emancipation, 1861–1867.* Cambridge: Cambridge University Press, 1993.

Berlin, Ira, Leslie S. Rowland, and Joseph P. Reidy, eds. *The Black Military Experience.* Ser. 2 of *Freedom: A Documentary History of Emancipation, 1861–1867.* Cambridge: Cambridge University Press, 1982.

[Blakeley, David]. *Annual Report of the Secretary of State to the Legislature of Minnesota.* St. Paul: N.p., 1866.

Brockett, L. P., M.D., and Mrs. Mary C. Vaughn. *Women's Work in the Civil War: A Record of Heroism, Patriotism and Patience.* Philadelphia: Zeigler, McCurdy and Co., 1867.

Brown, S. Joe. *History of the Des Moines Branch, National Association for the Advancement of Colored People.* N.p., n.p., 1927.

Brown, S. Joe, et al., comps. *Twenty Years of Interracial Work in Des Moines, Iowa; Brief History of the Des Moines Interracial Commission.* N.p., n.p., 1944.

Catrerall, Helen Tunnicliff, and James J. Hayden, eds. *Judicial Cases Concerning American Slavery and the Negro.* Vol. 4. Washington, D.C.: Carnegie Institution of Washington, 1937.

Catt, Carrie Chapman, and Nettie Rogers Shuler. *Woman Suffrage and Politics: The Inner Story of the Suffrage Movement.* New York: Scribner's, 1923.

Convention of Colored Citizens of the State of Minnesota. *Proceedings of the Convention of Colored Citizens of the State of Minnesota, in Celebration of the Anniversary of*

Emancipation, and the Reception of the Electoral Franchise on the First of January, 1869. St. Paul: Press Printing Co., 1869.

Description and History of Marshall County, Iowa. Marshalltown: Taylor and Barnhart, 1862.

Dickson, Moses, P. G. M. *A Manual of the Knights of Tabor, and Daughters of the Tabernacle . . .* St. Louis: G. I. Jones, Publisher, 1879.

1890–91 Farmers and Land Owners Directory of Racine Co., Wisconsin. St. Louis: Benson Brothers, 1891.

Emancipation League. *Facts Concerning the Freedmen: Their Capacity and Destiny.* Boston: Press of Commercial Printing House, 1863.

First Annual Report of the Educational Commission for Freedmen, May 1863. Boston: Prentiss and Deland, Book and Job Printers, 1863.

Foner, Philip S., and George E. Walker, eds. *Proceedings of the Black National and State Conventions, 1865–1900.* Vol. 1. Philadelphia: Temple University Press, 1986.

Forman, Jacob G. *The Western Sanitary Commission: A Sketch.* St. Louis: R. P. Studley and Co., 1864.

Freedmen's Relief Society. *The Annual Report of the Freedmen's Relief Society, of Saint Louis, Missouri, for 1863.* St. Louis: Published at the Office of the Missouri Democrat, 1864.

Hair, James T., ed. *Iowa State Gazetteer, Shippers' Guide and Business Directory.* Chicago: Bailey and Hair, 1865.

Hull, John T. *1836–1880: Census of Iowa for 1880.* Des Moines: F. M. Mills, 1883.

In Memoriam: Maj. Gen. Samuel Ryan Curtis: Died, December 26th, 1866. Keokuk, Iowa; Rees' Job Office, 1867.

Iowa Baptist State Convention. *Minutes of the Iowa Baptist State Convention, 1878.* Oskaloosa, Iowa: Herald Steam Book and Job Print, 1898.

———. *Journal of the Sixth Annual Meeting of the Iowa Baptist Association, 1884.* Keokuk: R. B. Ogden and Son, 1884.

———. *Proceedings of the Iowa Baptist Association, 1885.* Keokuk: R. B. Ogden and Son, 1885.

———. *Proceedings of the Iowa Baptist Association, 1886.* Ottumwa: Keokuk: R. B. Ogden and Son, 1886.

———. *Minutes of the 55th Annual Iowa Baptist State Convention.* Washington, Iowa: S. W. A. Athearn, Printer, 1896.

———. *Minutes of the 57th Annual Iowa Baptist State Convention.* Iowa City: Iowa Citizen Publishing Co., 1898.

Iowa Colonization Society. *The Annual Report of the Colonization Society of the State of Iowa, with the Proceedings of the Second Anniversary, in the Capitol, January 22, 1857.* Iowa City: Sylvester, Harrison and Brother, Printers, 1857.

Iowa State Colored Convention. *Proceedings of the Iowa State Colored Convention Held in the City of Des Moines, Wednesday and Thursday, February 12th and 13th, 1868.* Muscatine: Daily Journal Book and Job Printing House, 1868.

Iowa State Federation of Colored Women's Clubs. *Minutes of the Fifth Annual Meeting of the Iowa State Federation of Colored Women's Clubs.* N.p., 1906.

———. *Minutes of the Sixth Annual Meeting of the Iowa State Federation of Colored Women's Clubs.* N.p., 1907.

———. *Programme of the Eighth Annual Session of the Iowa State Federation of Colored Women's Clubs and Ninth Annual Session of the Iowa State Afro-American Council.* Muscatine, Iowa: Press of Conaway-Porter, 1910.

———. *Proceedings of the Tenth Annual Session of the Iowa State Federation of Colored Women's Clubs.* Muscatine, Iowa: Press of Conaway-Porter, 1911.

———. *Proceedings of the Eleventh Annual Session of the Iowa State Federation of Colored Women's Clubs.* [Muscatine, Iowa: Press of Conaway-Porter], 1912.

Ivers, John C. *The Congressional Globe: Containing the Debates and Proceedings of the First Session of the Thirty-eighth Congress.* Washington, D.C.: Congressional Globe Office, 1864.

Jenifer, John T., D.D. *Centennial Retrospect History of the African Methodist Episcopal Church.* Nashville: Sunday School Union Print, n.d. [ca. 1916].

Jones, Joseph, M.D. *Researches upon "Spurious Vaccination," or the Abnormal Phenomena Accompanying and Following Vaccination in the Confederate Army during the Recent American Civil War, 1861–1865.* Nashville: University Medical Press, 1867.

Logan, Guy E., Iowa Adjutant General. *Official Roster and Record of Iowa Soldiers in the War of the Rebellion.* Washington, D.C., Des Moines: E. H. English State Printer, 1911.

Mason, Charles. *The Election in Iowa.* New York: Society for the Diffusion of Political Knowledge, 1863.

Mathews, Rev. Edward. *American Slavery and the War.* Wirksworth: J. Buckley, Printer, [1864].

Middleton, Stephen. *The Black Laws in the Old Northwest: A Documentary History.* Westport, Conn.: Greenwood Press, 1993.

Parker, Nathan H. *Iowa as It Is in 1856: A Gazetteer for Citizens, and a Hand-book for Emigrants.* Chicago: Keen and Less, 1856.

———. *Iowa Handbook for 1856.* Boston: J. P. Jewett and Co., 1856.

Patten, George. *Patten's Army Manual: Containing Instructions for Officers in the Preparation of Rolls, Returns and Accounts Required of Regimental and Company Commanders, and Pertaining to the Subsistence and Quartermasters' Departments. . . .* New York: J. W. Fortune Co., 1862.

Pilgrim Baptist Church. *We've Come This Far by Faith: 125th Anniversary Book, 1863–1988.* Marceline, Mo.: Walsworth Publishing Co., 1988.

Plumbe, John, Jr. *Sketches of Iowa and Wisconsin . . .* St. Louis: Chambers, Harris and Knapp, 1839.

Porter, Will. *Annals of Polk County, Iowa and City of Des Moines.* Des Moines: George A. Miller Printing Co., 1898.

Prill, Orville Louis, and Mary Barnes Prill, comps. *Jefferson County Records.* 13 vols. Fairfield, Iowa: N.p., 1966.

Ripley, C. Peter, ed. *The United States, 1830–1846.* Vol. 3 of *The Black Abolitionist Papers.* Chapel Hill: University of North Carolina Press, 1991.

———, ed. *The United States, 1847–1858.* Vol. 4 of *The Black Abolitionist Papers.* Chapel Hill: University of North Carolina Press, 1991.

———, ed. *The United States, 1859–1865.* Vol. 5 of *The Black Abolitionist Papers.* Chapel Hill: University of North Carolina Press, 1991.

———, ed. *Witness for Freedom: African American Voices on Race, Slavery, and Emancipation.* Chapel Hill: University of North Carolina Press, 1993.

Rusk, Jeremiah M., and Chandler P. Chapman, comps. *Roster of Wisconsin Volunteers, War of the Rebellion, 1861–65.* Vol. 2. Madison: Democrat Printing Co., 1886.

State of Iowa. *Journal of the Senate at the Extra Session of the 9th General Assembly.* Des Moines: F. W. Palmer, State Printer, 1862.

State of Iowa. Iowa Adjutant General. *Report of the Adjutant General and Acting Quartermaster General of the State of Iowa, January 1, 1863 to January 11, 1864.* Des Moines: F. W. Palmer, State Printer, 1864.

State of Wisconsin. *Journal of the Assembly of the State of Wisconsin, 1863 Annual Session.* Madison: State Printer, 1863.

———. *Journal of the Senate, 1863 Annual Session.* Madison: State Printer, 1863.

———. *Roster of Wisconsin Volunteers, War of the Rebellion, 1861–65.* Vol. 2. Madison: Democrat Printing Co., State Printers, 1886.

St. Paul City Directory, 1889–1990. St. Paul: R. L. Polk and Co., 1890.

Territory of Iowa. *The Statute Laws of the Territory of Iowa, Enacted at the First Session of the Legislative Assembly of Said Territory, Held at Burlington, A.D. 1838–39.* Dubuque: Russell and Reeves, Printers, 1839.

U.S. War Department. *The War of the Rebellion: A Compilation of the Official Records of the Union and Confederate Armies.* Washington, D.C.: GPO, 1880–1901.

Williams, Hope D. *An Oral History of the Black Population of Davenport, Iowa.* Davenport: Palmer Junior College, [1979].

[Wisconsin Methodist Church]. *Minutes of the Sixteenth Annual Session of the Wisconsin Conference.* Milwaukee: N.p., 1862.

———. *Minutes of the Seventeenth Annual Session of the Wisconsin Conference.* Milwaukee: N.p., 1863.

Woman's Relief Corps. *Journal of the Tenth Annual Convention of the Woman's Relief Corps, Auxiliary to the Grand Army of the Republic, Washington, D.C., Sept. 21st, 22d, 23d and 24th, 1892.* Boston: E. B. Stillings, 1892.

———. *Journal of the Eleventh Annual Convention of the Woman's Relief Corps, Auxiliary to the Grand Army of the Republic, Indianapolis, Ind., September 6th, 7th and 8th, 1893.* Boston: E. B. Stillings, 1893.

———. *Journal of the Twelfth Annual Convention of the Woman's Relief Corps, Auxiliary to the Grand Army of the Republic, Pittsburgh, Pa., September 12th, 13th and 14th, 1894.* Boston: E. B. Stillings, 1894.

———. *Journal of the Fourteenth National Convention of the Woman's Relief Corps, Auxiliary to the Grand Army of the Republic, St. Paul, Minn., September 3d and 4th, 1896.* Boston: E. B. Stillings, 1896.

———. *Journal of the Fifteenth National Convention of the Woman's Relief Corps, Auxiliary to the Grand Army of the Republic, Buffalo, N.Y., August 26th and 27th, 1897.* Boston: E. B. Stillings, 1897.

———. *Journal of the Twenty-third National Convention of the Woman's Relief Corps, Auxiliary to the Grand Army of the Republic, Denver, Colorado, September 7th and 8th, 1905.* Boston: E. B. Stillings, 1905.

Wright, Richard R. *Centennial Encyclopedia of the African Methodist Episcopal Church.* Philadelphia: Book Concern of the A.M.E. Church, 1916.

Yeatman, James E. *Report upon the Condition of the Freedmen of the Mississippi, Presented to the Western Sanitary Commission, Dec. 17, 1863.* St. Louis: N.p., 1864.

SECONDARY SOURCES

Books and Articles

Acton, Lord Richard, and Patricia Nassif Acton. "A Legal History of African-Americans from the Iowa Territory to the State Sesquicentennial, 1838–1996." In *Outside In: African-American History in Iowa, 1838–2000,* edited by Bill Salag, 60–89. Des Moines: State Historical Society of Iowa, 2001.

Adams, George Worthington. *Doctors in Blue: The Medical History of the Union Army in the Civil War.* New York: H. Schuman, 1952.

Allen, Annie Beiser. "Sowing Seeds of Kindness—and Change: A History of the Iowa Association of Colored Women's Clubs." *Iowa Heritage* 83 (Spring 2002): 2–13.

Alvord, Clarence W. *The Illinois Country, 1673–1818.* Springfield: Illinois Centennial Commission, 1920.

Andrews, William L. "The First Century of Afro-American Autobiography: Theory and Explication." In *Studies in Black American Literature, Vol. 1: Black American Prose Theory,* edited by Joe Weixlmann and Chester Fontenot, 4–42. Greenwood, Fla.: Penkevill Publishing Co., 1984,

——. "The Representation of Slavery and the Rise of Afro-American Literary Realism, 1865–1920." In *Slavery and the Literary Imagination,* edited by Deborah E. McDowell and Arnold Rampersad, 62–80. Baltimore: Johns Hopkins University Press, 1989.

——. "Reunion in the Post-bellum Slave Narrative: Frederick Douglass and Elizabeth Keckley." *Black American Literature Forum* 23 (Spring 1989): 5–15.

——. *To Tell a Free Story: The First Century of Afro-American Autobiography, 1760–1865.* Urbana: University of Illinois Press, 1986.

——. "Towards a Poetics of Afro-American Autobiography." In *Afro-American Literary Study in the 1990s,* edited by Houston A. Baker Jr. and Patricia Redmond, 78–90. Chicago: University of Chicago Press, 1989.

Aurner, Charles Ray. *Leading Events in Johnson County[,] Iowa History.* Cedar Rapids: Western Historical Press, 1912.

Bailey, Julius H. *Around the Family Altar: Domesticity in the African Methodist Episcopal Church, 1865–1900.* Gainesville: University Press of Florida, 2005.

Baker, Houston A., Jr. "Critical Memory and the Black Public Sphere." In *The Black Public Sphere: A Public Culture Book,* edited by The Black Public Sphere Collective, 7–37. Chicago: University of Chicago Press, 1995.

Baker, Jean H. *Affairs of Party: The Political Culture of Northern Democrats in the Mid-Nineteenth Century.* Ithaca: Cornell University Press, 1983.

Benjamin, Maynard H. *The History of Envelopes, 1840–1900.* [Alexandria, Va.?]: Envelope Manufacturers Association, 1997.

Bensel, Richard Franklin. *Yankee Leviathan: The Origins of Central State Authority in America, 1859–1877.* New York: Cambridge University Press, 1990.

Bercaw, Nancy D. *Gendered Freedoms: Race, Rights, and Politics of Households in the Delta, 1861–1875*. Gainesville: University Press of Florida, 2003.
Bergmann, Leola Nelson. *The Negro in Iowa*. Iowa City: State Historical Society of Iowa, 1948.
Berlin, Ira. *Many Thousands Gone: The First Two Centuries of Slavery in North America*. Cambridge, Mass.: Belknap Press of Harvard University Press, 1998.
———. "Who Freed the Slaves?" In *Union and Emancipation: Essays on Politics and Race in the Civil War Era*, edited by David W. Blight and Brooks D. Simpson, 105–21. Kent, Ohio: Kent State University Press, 1997.
Berlin, Ira, Wayne Durrill, Steven F. Miller, Leslie S. Rowland, and Leslie Schwalm. " 'To Canvass the Nation': The War for Union Becomes a War for Freedom." *Prologue* 20 (1988): 235–36.
Berlin, Ira, Barbara J. Fields, Steven F. Miller, Joseph P. Reidy, and Leslie S. Rowland. *Slaves No More: Three Essays on Emancipation and the Civil War*. Cambridge, England: Cambridge University Press, 1992.
Bernstein, Iver. *The New York City Draft Riots: Their Significance for American Society and Politics in the Age of the Civil War*. New York: Oxford University Press, 1990.
Berrier, G. Galin. "The Underground Railroad in Iowa." In *Outside In: African-American History in Iowa, 1838–2000*, edited by Bill Salag, 44–59. Des Moines: State Historical Society of Iowa, 2001.
Berwanger, Eugene H. *The Frontier against Slavery: Western Anti-Negro Prejudice and the Slavery Extension Controversy*. Urbana: University of Illinois Press, 1967.
Biles, Roger. "Black Mayors: A Historical Assessment." *Journal of Negro History* 77 (Summer 1992): 109–25.
Blight, David W. *Beyond the Battlefield: Race, Memory and the American Civil War*. Amherst: University of Massachusetts Press, 2002.
———. *Frederick Douglass' Civil War: Keeping Faith in Jubilee*. Baton Rouge: Louisiana State University Press, 1989.
———. "No Desperate Hero: Manhood and Freedom in a Union Soldier's Experience." In *Divided Houses: Gender and the Civil War*, edited by Catherine Clinton and Nina Silber, 55–75. New York: Oxford University Press, 1992.
———. *Race and Reunion: The Civil War in American Memory*. Cambridge: Harvard University Press, 2001.
———. *A Slave No More: Two Men Who Escaped to Freedom, Including Their Own Narratives of Emancipation*. Orlando, Fla.: Harcourt, 2007.
Blight, David W., and Brooks D. Simpson, eds. *Union and Emancipation: Essays on Politics and Race in the Civil War Era*. Kent, Ohio: Kent State University Press, 1997.
Boles, John B. *Black Southerners, 1619–1869*. Lexington: University Press of Kentucky, 1983.
Brady, Tim. "Minnesota Then: Barely There." *Minnesota Monthly* 38 (August 2004): 23–26.
Brown, Elsa Barkley. "Negotiating and Transforming the Public Sphere: African American Political Life in the Transition from Slavery to Freedom." *Public Culture* 7 (1994): 107–46.

Brown, Hallie Q. *Homespun Women and Other Women of Distinction.* Xenia, Ohio: Aldine Publishing Co., 1926.

Brown, Lois. "Memorial Narratives of African Women in Antebellum New England." *Legacy* 20 (2003): 38–61.

Brown, Thomas J., ed. *Reconstructions: New Perspectives on the Postbellum United States.* New York: Oxford University Press, 2006.

Brundage, W. Fitzhugh, ed. *Where These Memories Grow: History, Memory, and Southern Identity.* Chapel Hill: University of North Carolina Press, 2000.

Burrell, Howard A. *History of Washington County Iowa from the First White Settlement to 1908.* Chicago: S. J. Clarke Publishing Co., 1909.

Butler, Jon. "Communities and Congregations: The Black Church in St. Paul, 1860–1900." *Journal of Negro History* 56, no. 2 (April 1971): 118–34.

Bystrom, Dianne. "From Voting to Running for Political Office: The Role of Women in Midwestern Politics." Carrie Chapman Catt Center for Women and Politics, Iowa State University, <http://www.iastate.edu/cccatt/midwestwomen.htm>. 23 Feb. 2007.

Calhoun, Craig, ed. *Habermas and the Public Sphere.* Cambridge: MIT Press, 1992.

Campbell, James T. *Songs of Zion: The African Methodist Episcopal Church in the United States and South Africa.* Chapel Hill: University of North Carolina Press, 1998.

Caron, Timothy P. " 'How Changeable Are the Events of War': National Reconciliation in *The Century Magazine's* 'Battles and Leaders of the Civil War.' " *American Periodicals* 16 (2006): 151–71.

Cashin, Joan E. "Into the Trackless Wilderness: The Refugee Experience in the Civil War." In *A Woman's War: Southern Women, Civil War, and the Confederate Legacy,* edited by Edward D. C. Campbell Jr., 29–53. Charlottesville: University Press of Virginia, 1996.

Castel, Albert. "Civil War Kansas and the Negro." *Journal of Negro History* 51 (1966): 125–38.

Cayton, Andrew R. L., and Susan E. Gray. "The Story of the Midwest: An Introduction." In *The American Midwest,* edited by Cayton and Gray, 14–15. Bloomington: Indiana University Press, 2001.

Clark, Kathleen. "Celebrating Freedom: Emancipation Day Celebrations and African American Memory in the Early Reconstruction South." In *Where These Memories Grow: History, Memory, and Southern Identity,* edited by W. Fitzhugh Brundage, 107–32. Chapel Hill: University of North Carolina Press, 2000.

Clinton, Catherine, and Nina Silber, eds. *Divided Houses: Gender and the Civil War.* New York: Oxford University Press, 1992.

Coffin, Nathan E. "The Case of Archie P. Webb: A Free Negro." *Annals of Iowa* 11 (1913): 200–214.

Cohen, William. *At Freedom's Edge: Black Mobility and the Southern White Quest for Racial Control, 1861–1915.* Baton Rouge: Louisiana State University Press, 1991.

Cole, Cyrenus. *A History of the People of Iowa.* Cedar Rapids: Torch Press, 1921.

Connor, James. "The Antislavery Movement in Iowa." *Annals of Iowa* 40 (1970): 450–70.

Cooper, Arnie. "A Stony Road: Black Education in Iowa, 1838–1860." *Annals of Iowa* 48 (Winter/Spring 1986): 113–34.

Cooper, Zachary. *Black Settlers in Rural Wisconsin*. Madison: State Historical Society of Wisconsin, 1977.
Cullen, Jim. " 'I's a Man Now': Gender and African American Men." In *A Question of Manhood: A Reader in U.S. Black Men's History and Masculinity*, edited by Darlene Clark Hine and Earnestine Jenkins, 1:489–501. Bloomington: Indiana University Press, 1999.
Current, Richard N. *The Civil War Era, 1849–1873*, Vol. 2 of *The History of Wisconsin*. Madison: State Historical Society of Wisconsin, 1976.
Danbom, David B. " 'Dear Companion': Civil War Letters of a Story County Farmer." *Annals of Iowa* 47 (Fall 1984): 537–43.
Daniel, Philip T. K. "A History of the Segregation-Discrimination Dilemma: The Chicago Experience." *Phylon* 41 (1980): 126–36.
Davidson, J. N. *Negro Slavery in Wisconsin*. Milwaukee: Parkman Club, 1896.
Davies, Wallace E. "The Problem of Race Segregation in the Grand Army of the Republic." *Journal of Southern History* 13 (1947): 354–72.
Davis, Charles T., and Henry Louis Gates, eds. *The Slave's Narrative*. New York: Oxford University Press, 1985.
Davis, Susan G. *Parades and Power: Street Theatre in Nineteenth-Century Philadelphia*. Philadelphia: Temple University Press, 1986.
Deyle, Steven. *Carry Me Back: The Domestic Slave Trade in American Life*. New York: Oxford University Press, 2005.
Diffley, Kathleen, ed. *To Live and Die: Collected Stories of the Civil War, 1861–1876*. Durham: Duke University Press, 2002.
Dodson, Jualynne E. *Engendering Church: Women, Power, and the AME Church*. Lanham, Md.: Rowan and Littlefield, 2002.
Donnel, William M. *Pioneers of Marion County: Consisting of a General History of the County*. Des Moines: Republican Steam Printing House, 1872.
Douglas, Davison M. *Jim Crow Moves North: The Battle over Northern School Segregation, 1865–1954*. Cambridge, England: Cambridge University Press, 2005.
Doyle, Julie A., and John David Smith. " 'The Very Best Soldiers in the World': Two Surgeons Examine California's Civil War Recruits." *Military History of the West* 27 (Spring 1997): 59–82.
Dykstra, Robert R. *Bright Radical Star: Black Freedom and White Supremacy on the Hawkeye Frontier*. Cambridge: Harvard University Press, 1993.
Ekberg, Carl J. "Black Slavery in Illinois, 1720–1765." *Western Illinois Regional Studies* 12 (1989): 5–19.
———. *French Roots in the Illinois Country: The Mississippi Frontier in Colonial Times*. Urbana: University of Illinois Press, 1992.
Elder, Orville. *David and Isabella Elder and Those Who Came After Them*. Washington, Iowa: N.p., 1928.
———. *The Frank Stories*. Chicago: Rogers and Smith, 1905.
———. *Mickey Peck: A Novel*. Boston: Roxburgh Publishing Co., 1918.
———. *A Trip to the Hawaiian Islands with the Press Congress of the World*. Washington, Iowa: Evening Journal, 1922.

Elshtain, Jean Bethke. *Women and War*. New York: Basic Books, 1987.

Erbe, Carl Herman. "The Militia under the Constitution of Iowa." *Iowa Journal of History and Politics* 24 (April 1926): 270–89.

Eyerman, Ron. *Cultural Trauma: Slavery and the Formation of African American Identity*. Cambridge, England: Cambridge University Press, 2001.

Fabre, Genevieve. "African American Commemorative Celebrations in the Nineteenth Century." In *History and Memory in African American Culture*, edited by Genevieve Fabre and Robert O'Meally, 72–77. New York: Oxford University Press, 1994.

Fabre, Genevieve, and Robert O'Meally, eds. *History and Memory in African American Culture*. New York: Oxford University Press, 1994.

Fahey, David M. *Temperance and Racism: John Bull, Johnny Reb, and the Good Templars*. Lexington: University Press of Kentucky, 1996.

Fahs, Alice. *The Imagined Civil War: Popular Literature of the North and South, 1861–1865*. Chapel Hill: University of North Carolina Press, 2001.

Faulkner, Carol. *Women's Radical Reconstruction: The Freedmen's Aid Movement*. Philadelphia: University of Pennsylvania Press, 2004.

Faust, Drew Gilpin. *Mothers of Invention: Women of the Slaveholding South in the American Civil War*. Chapel Hill: University of North Carolina Press, 1996.

Fehrenbacher, Don E. *The Dred Scott Case: Its Significance in American Law and Politics*. New York: Oxford University Press, 1978.

Finkelman, Paul. "Evading the Ordinance: The Persistence of Bondage in Indiana and Illinois." *Journal of the Early Republic* 9 (Spring 1989): 21–51.

———. *An Imperfect Union: Slavery, Federalism, and Comity*. Chapel Hill: University of North Carolina Press, 1981.

———. "Slavery, the 'More Perfect Union,' and the Prairie State." *Illinois Historical Journal* 80 (1987): 248–69.

Fischer, David Hackett, and James C. Kelley. *Bound Away: Virginia and the Westward Movement*. Charlottesville: University Press of Virginia, 2000.

Fishel, Leslie H., Jr. "The Genesis of the First Wisconsin Civil Rights Act." *Wisconsin Magazine of History* 49 (1966): 324–33.

———. "Northern Prejudice and Negro Suffrage, 1865–1870." *Journal of Negro History* 39 (1954): 8–26.

———. "Wisconsin and Negro Suffrage." *Wisconsin Magazine of History* 46 (Spring 1963): 180–96.

Fleche, André. "'Shoulder to Shoulder as Comrades Tried': Black and White Union Veterans and Civil War Memory." *Civil War History* 51 (2005): 175–201.

Fleischner, Jennifer. *Mastering Slavery: Memory, Family, and Identity in Women's Slave Narratives*. New York: Oxford University Press, 1996.

Flint, Holly. "Toni Morrison's *Paradise*: Black Cultural Citizenship in the American Empire." *American Literature* 78, no. 3 (September 2006): 585–612.

Flores, William V., and Rina Benmayor, eds. *Latino Cultural Citizenship: Claiming Identity, Space, and Rights*. Boston: Beacon Press, 1997.

Foner, Eric. *Reconstruction: America's Unfinished Revolution, 1863–1877*. New York: Harper and Row, 1988.

Foster, Frances Smith. *Witnessing Slavery: The Development of Ante-Bellum Slave Narratives*. Westport, Conn.: Greenwood Press, 1979.

———. *Written by Herself: Literary Production by African American Women*. Bloomington: Indiana University Press, 1993.

Frankel, Noralee. *Freedom's Women: Black Women and Families in Civil War Era Mississippi*. Bloomington: Indiana University Press, 1999.

Frederickson, George M. *The Inner Civil War: Northern Intellectuals and the Crisis of the Union*. New York: Harper and Row, 1965.

Frey, Sylvia R. *Water from the Rock: Black Resistance in a Revolutionary Age*. Princeton: Princeton University Press, 1991.

Gallaher, Ruth A. *Legal and Political Status of Women in Iowa*. Iowa City: State Historical Society of Iowa, 1918.

Gambill, Edward L. *Conservative Ordeal: Northern Democrats and Reconstruction, 1865–1868*. Ames: Iowa State University Press, 1981.

Gerteis, Louis S. *Civil War St. Louis*. Lawrence: University Press of Kansas, 2001.

———. *From Contraband to Freedman: Federal Policy Towards Southern Blacks, 1861–1865*. Westport, Conn.: Greenwood Press, 1973.

Gillette, William. *Retreat from Reconstruction, 1869–1879*. Baton Rouge: Louisiana State University Press, 1979.

———. *The Right to Vote: Politics and the Passage of the Fifteenth Amendment*. Baltimore: Johns Hopkins University Press, 1965.

Gilmore, Glenda Elizabeth. *Gender and Jim Crow: Women and the Politics of White Supremacy in North Carolina, 1896–1920*. Chapel Hill: University of North Carolina Press, 1996.

Glatthaar, Joseph T. *Forged in Battle: The Civil War Alliance of Black Soldiers and White Officers*. New York: Free Press, 1990.

Glaze, A. T. *Incidents and Anecdotes of Early Days and History of Business in the City and County of Fond Du Lac*. Fond Du Lac, Wis.: P. B. Haber, 1905.

Glymph, Thavolia. " 'This Species of Property': Female Slave Contrabands in the Civil War." In *A Woman's War: Southern Women, Civil War, and the Confederate Legacy*, edited by Campbell, Edward D. C., Jr., and Kym S. Rice, 55–71. Charlottesville: University Press of Virginia, 1996.

Goudy, Willis. "Selected Demographics: Iowa's African American Residents, 1840–2000." In *Outside In: African-American History in Iowa, 1838–2000*, edited by Bill Salag, 22–43. Des Moines: State Historical Society of Iowa, 2001.

Gravely, William B. "The Dialectic of Double-Consciousness in Black American Freedom Celebrations, 1808–1865." *Journal of Negro History* 67 (1982): 302–17.

Gray, Susan E. "Stories Written in the Blood: Race and Midwestern History." In *The American Midwest*, edited by Andrew R. L. Cayton and Gray, 123–39. Bloomington: Indiana University Press, 2001.

Green, William D. *A Peculiar Balance: The Fall and Rise of Racial Equality in Early Minnesota*. St. Paul: Minnesota Historical Society, 2007.

———. "Race and Segregation in St. Paul's Public Schools, 1846–1869." *Minnesota History* 55 (Winter 1996–97): 138–49.

Grimsted, David. *American Mobbing, 1828–1861: Toward Civil War*. New York: Oxford University Press, 1998.

Grivno, Max L. "African-Americans at Fort Snelling, 1820–1840: An Interpretive Guide." 1997. Typed MS in possession of author.

———. " 'Black Frenchmen' and 'White Settlers': Race, Slavery, and the Creation of African-American Identities along the Northwest Frontier, 1790–1840." *Slavery and Abolition* 21 (December 2000): 75–93.

Gue, Benjamin F. *History of Iowa*. Vol. 2. New York: Century History Co., 1903.

Gumestad, Robert H. *A Troublesome Commerce: The Transformation of the Interstate Slave Trade*. Baton Rouge: Louisiana State University Press, 2003.

Hahn, Steven. *A Nation under Our Feet: Black Political Struggles in the Rural South from Slavery to Emancipation*. Cambridge: Harvard University Press, 2003.

Harlan, Louis R. *Booker T. Washington: The Making of a Black Leader, 1856–1901*. New York: Oxford University Press, 1972.

Harris, Abram L. *The Negro Population in Minneapolis: A Study of Race Relations*. Minneapolis: Urban League and Phyllis Wheatley Settlement House, [1926].

Harris, Leslie M. *In the Shadow of Slavery: African Americans in New York City, 1616–1863*. Chicago: University of Chicago Press, 2003.

Harris, N. Dwight. *The History of Negro Servitude in Illinois*. Chicago: A. C. McLurg and Co., 1904.

Hartman, Saidiya. *Lose Your Mother: A Journey along the Atlantic Slave Route*. New York: Farrar, Straus and Giroux, 2007.

Heglar, Charles J. *Rethinking the Slave Narrative: Slave Marriage and the Narratives of Henry Bibb and Ellen Craft*. Westport, Conn.: Greenwood Press, 2001.

Hennessy, William Bradley. *Past & Present of St. Paul, Minnesota*. Chicago: S. J. Clarke Publishing Co., 1906.

Herdegen, Lance J. *The Men Stood Like Iron: How the Iron Brigade Won Its Name*. Bloomington: Indiana University Press, 1997.

Hickenlooper, Frank. *An Illustrated History of Monroe County, Iowa*. Albia, Iowa: N.p., 1896.

Higginbotham, Evelyn Brooks. *Righteous Discontent: The Women's Movement in the Black Baptist Church, 1880–1920*. Cambridge: Harvard University Press, 1993.

Higman, B. W. "Remembering Slavery: The Rise, Decline and Revival of Emancipation Day in the English-Speaking Caribbean." *Slavery and Abolition* 19 (1998): 90–105.

Hirsh, Marianne. *Family Frames: Photography, Narrative, and Postmemory*. Cambridge: Harvard University Press, 1997.

The History of Dodge County, Wisconsin. Chicago: Western Historical Co., 1880.

The History of Henry County, Iowa. Chicago: Western Historical Co., 1879.

The History of Jefferson County. Chicago: Western Historical Co., 1879.

The History of Johnson County, Iowa. Iowa City: N.p., 1883.

The History of Lee County. Chicago: Western Historical Co., 1879.

The History of Muscatine County, Iowa. Chicago: Western Historical Co., 1879.

Hodges, Graham Russell. *Root and Branch: African Americans in New York and New Jersey, 1613–1863*. Chapel Hill: University of North Carolina Press, 1999.

Holloway, Karla F. C. *Passed On: African American Mourning Stories*. Durham: Duke University Press, 2003.
Horton, James Oliver. *Free People of Color: Inside the African American Community*. Washington: Smithsonian Institution Press, 1993.
Horton, James Oliver, and Lois E. Horton. *In Hope of Liberty: Culture, Community and Protest among Northern Free Blacks, 1700–1860*. New York: Oxford University Press, 1997.
Horton, Russell. "Unwanted in a White Man's War: The Civil War Service of the Green Bay Tribes." *Wisconsin Magazine of History* 88 (Winter 2004–5): 18–27.
Howard, Lawrence C. "The Des Moines Negro and His Contribution to American Life." *Annals of Iowa* 30 (January 1950): 211.
Howard-Pitney, David. "The Enduring Black Jeremiad: The American Jeremiad and Black Protest Rhetoric, from Frederick Douglass to W. E. B. Du Bois, 1841–1919." *American Quarterly* 38 (1986): 481–92.
Howell, J. M., and Herman C. Smith, eds. *History of Decatur County Iowa and Its People*. 2 vols. in 1. Chicago: S. J. Clarke, 1915.
Hunter, Tera. *To 'Joy My Freedom: Southern Black Women's Lives and Labors after the Civil War*. Cambridge: Harvard University Press, 1997.
Hurn, Ethel Alice. *Wisconsin Women in the War between the States*. Original Papers No. 6. Wisconsin History Commission, 1911.
Hurt, R. Douglas. *Agriculture and Slavery in Missouri's Little Dixie*. Columbia: University of Missouri Press, 1992.
Irvine, Dallas D. "The Genesis of the Official Records." *Mississippi Valley Historical Review* 24 (September 1937): 221–29.
Jacobson, Matthew Frye. *Whiteness of a Different Color: European Immigrants and the Alchemy of Race*. Cambridge: Harvard University Press, 1998.
Jaynes, Peter H., ed. *Highlights of Henry County: Iowa History, 1833–1976*. Burlington, Iowa: Doran and Ward Publishing Co., 1976.
Thomas Jefferson Memorial Foundation. *Report of the Research Committee on Thomas Jefferson and Sally Hemings*. 2000, <www.monticello.org/plantation/hemingscontro>. 20 June 2006.
Johnson, Michael P. "Out of Egypt: The Migration of Former Slaves to the Midwest during the 1860s in Comparative Perspective." In *Crossing Boundaries: Comparative History of Black People in Diaspora*, edited by Darlene Clark Hine and Jacqueline McLeod, 223–45. Bloomington: Indiana University Press, 1999.
———, ed. *Abraham Lincoln, Slavery, and the Civil War: Selected Writings and Speeches*. Boston: Bedford/St. Martin's, 2001.
Johnson, Russell L. *Warriors into Workers: The Civil War and the Formation of Urban-Industrial Society in a Northern City*. New York: Fordham University Press, 2003.
Johnson, Walter. *Soul by Soul: Life Inside the Antebellum Slave Market*. Cambridge: Harvard University Press, 1999.
Jones, Allen W. "Equal Rights to All, Special Privileges to None: The Black Press in Iowa, 1882–1985." In *The Black Press in the Middle West, 1865–1985*, edited by Henry Lewis Suggs, 71–106. Westport, Conn.: Greenwood Press, 1996.

Jones, Edna L., ed. *Nathan Littler's History of Washington County, 1835–1875.* Washington, Iowa: Gestetner Press, 1977.

Jones, Jacqueline. *American Work: Four Centuries of Black and White Labor.* New York: Norton, 1998.

Jones, Martha S. *All Bound Up Together: The Woman Question in African American Public Culture, 1830–1900.* Chapel Hill: University of North Carolina Press, 2007.

Jones, Robert Huhn. *The Civil War in the Northwest.* Norman: University of Oklahoma Press, 1960.

Jordan, Philip D. "William Salter and the Slavery Controversy, 1837–1864." *Iowa Journal of History and Politics* 33 (1935): 101.

Josephy, Alvin M. *The Civil War in the American West.* New York: Vintage Books, 1991.

Kachun, Mitch. *Festivals of Freedom: Memory and Meaning in African American Freedom Celebrations, 1808–1915.* Amherst: University of Massachusetts Press, 2003.

Kammen, Michael. *Mystic Chords of Memory: The Transformation of Tradition in American Culture.* New York: Vintage Books, 1991.

Kantrowitz, Stephen. "Fighting Like Men: Civil War Dilemmas of Abolitionist Manhood." In *Battle Scars: Gender and Sexuality in the American Civil War*, edited by Catherine Clinton and Nina Silber, 19–40. New York: Oxford University Press, 2006.

Kelley, Robin D. G. *Race Rebels: Culture, Politics, and the Black Working Class.* New York: Free Press, 1994.

Keo-Mah Genealogical Society and Mahaska County Historical Society. *The History of Mahaska County, Iowa, 1984.* Dallas, Tex.: Curtis Media Corp., 1984.

Kerr, Robert Y. "The Whittenberg Manual Labor College." *Iowa Journal of History and Politics* 24 (April 1926): 129–35.

King, Wilma. *Stolen Childhood: Slave Youth in Nineteenth-Century America.* Bloomington: Indiana University Press, 1995.

Klement, Frank L. *The Copperheads in the Middle West.* Chicago: University of Chicago Press, 1960.

———. *Wisconsin and the Civil War.* Madison: State Historical Society of Wisconsin, 1963.

Klingman, Peter D., and David Geithman. "Negro Dissidence and the Republican Party, 1864–1872." *Phylon: The Review of Race and Culture* 40, no. 2 (June 1979): 172–82.

Kohl, Rhonda M. "'This Godforsaken Town': Death and Disease at Helena, Arkansas, 1862–63." *Civil War History* 50 (June 2004): 109–44.

Kousser, J. Morgan. *Dead End: The Development of Nineteenth-Century Litigation on Racial Discrimination in Schools.* Oxford: Clarendon Press, 1986.

Lapsansky, Emma Jones. "'Discipline to the Mind': Philadelphia's Banneker Institute, 1854–1872." In *A Question of Manhood: A Reader in U.S. Black Men's History and Masculinity*, edited by Darlene Clark Hine and Earnestine Jenkins, 1:399–414. Bloomington: Indiana University Press, 1999.

Lee, George R. *Slavery North of St. Louis.* Canton, Mo.: Lewis County Historical Society, 1999.

Leonard, Elizabeth D. *Yankee Women: Gender Battles in the Civil War.* New York: Norton, 1994.

Lewis, Eliza. "The Political Mind of the Negro, 1865–1900." *Journal of Southern History* 21 (May 1955): 189–202.

Linderman, Gerald F. *Embattled Courage: The Experience of Combat in the American Civil War.* New York: Free Press, 1987.
Litwack, Leon F. *North of Slavery: The Negro in the Free States, 1790–1860.* Chicago: University of Chicago Press, 1961.
Lofton, Williston H. "Northern Labor and the Negro during the Civil War." *Journal of Negro History* 34 (July 1949): 251–73.
Lorini, Alessandra. *Rituals of Race: American Public Culture and the Search for Racial Democracy.* Charlottesville: University Press of Virginia, 1999.
Lowenthal, David, *The Past Is a Foreign Country.* Cambridge, England: Cambridge University Press, 1985.
Lowry, Thomas P. M. D. *The Story the Soldiers Wouldn't Tell: Sex in the Civil War.* Mechanicsburg, Pa.: Stackpole Books, 1994.
Lucas, Thomas A. "Men Were Too Fiery for Much Talk: The Grinnell Anti-Abolitionist Riot of 1860." *Palimpsest* (Spring 1987): 12–21.
Lufkin, Jack. "The Founding and Early Years of the National Association for the Advancement of Colored People in Des Moines, 1915–1930." *Annals of Iowa* 45 (Fall 1980): 439–61.
Lurie, Jonathan. "The Fourteenth Amendment: Use and Application in Selected State Court Civil Liberties Cases, 1870–1890—A Preliminary Assessment." *American Journal of Legal History* 28 (1984): 295–313.
Magnaghi, Russell M. "Red Slavery in the Great Lakes County during the French and British Regimes." *Old Northwest* 12 (1986): 201–17.
Maltz, Earl. *Civil Rights, the Constitution, and Congress, 1863–1869.* Lawrence: University Press of Kansas, 1990.
———. "Reconstruction without Revolution: Republican Civil Rights Theory in the Era of the Fourteenth Amendment." *Houston Law Review* 24 (March 1987): 221–80.
Manring, M. M. *Slave in a Box: The Strange Career of Aunt Jemima.* Charlottesville: University Press of Virginia, 1998.
Martin, Jonathan D. *Divided Mastery: Slavery Hiring in the American South.* Cambridge: Harvard University Press, 2004.
Massey, Mary Elizabeth. *Women in the Civil War.* Lincoln: University of Nebraska Press, 1966, 1994.
McBride, Genevieve G. *On Wisconsin Women: Working for Their Rights from Settlement to Suffrage.* Madison: University of Wisconsin Press, 1993.
McCaul, Robert L. *The Black Struggle for Public Schooling in Nineteenth-Century Illinois.* Carbondale: Southern Illinois Press, 1987.
McConnell, Stuart. "Epilogue: The Geography of Memory." In *The Memory of the Civil War in American Culture,* edited by Alice Fahs and Joan Waugh, 258–66. Chapel Hill: University of North Carolina Press, 2004.
McManus, Edgar J. *Black Bondage in the North.* Syracuse, N.Y.: Syracuse University Press, 1973.
———. *Political Abolitionism in Wisconsin, 1840–1861.* Kent, Ohio: Kent State University Press, 1998.
McPherson, James M. "Abolitionists and the Civil Rights Act of 1875." *Journal of American History* 52 (December 1865): 493–510.

———. *Battle Cry of Freedom: The Civil War Era*. New York: Oxford University Press, 1988.
———. *For Cause and Comrades: Why Men Fought in the Civil War*. New York: Oxford University Press, 1997.
———. *The Struggle for Equality: Abolitionists and the Negro in the Civil War and Reconstruction*. Princeton: Princeton University Press, 1964.
Meier, Michael T. "Lorenzo Thomas and the Recruitment of Blacks in the Mississippi Valley, 1863–1865." In *Black Soldiers in Blue: African American Troops in the Civil War Era*, edited by John David Smith, 249–75. Chapel Hill: University of North Carolina Press, 2002.
Melish, Joanne Pope. *Disowning Slavery: Gradual Emancipation and "Race" in New England, 1780–1860*. Ithaca: Cornell University Press, 1998.
———. "Of Politics and Publics." *Radical History Review* 709 (Winter 2001): 157–67.
Miller, Floyd J. *The Search for a Black Nationality: Black Emigration and Colonization, 1787–1863*. Urbana: University of Illinois Press, 1975.
Mitchell, Reid. "Soldiering, Manhood, and Coming of Age." In *Divided Houses: Gender and the Civil War*, edited by Catherine Clinton and Nina Silber, 43–54. New York: Oxford University Press, 1992.
———. *The Vacant Chair: The Northern Soldier Leaves Home*. New York: Oxford University Press, 1993.
Moneyhon, Carl H. "From Slave to Free Labor: The Federal Plantation Experiment in Arkansas." *Arkansas Historical Quarterly* 53 (Summer 1994): 137–60.
Montgomery, David. *Beyond Equality: Labor and the Radical Republicans, 1862–1872*. Urbana: University of Illinois Press, 1981.
Murphy, Lucy. *A Gathering of Rivers: Indians, Metis, and Mining in the Western Great Lakes, 1737–1832*. Lincoln: University of Nebraska Press, 2000.
Nash, Gary B., and Jean Soderlund. *Freedom by Degrees: Emancipation in Pennsylvania and Its Aftermath*. New York: Oxford University Press, 1991.
National Association of Colored Women's Clubs. "History of the National Association of Colored Women's Clubs, Inc.," <http://www.nacw.org/about/history.php>. 2 Feb. 2007.
Neely, Mark E., Jr. *The Boundaries of American Political Culture in the Civil War Era*. Chapel Hill: University of North Carolina Press, 2006.
———. *The Union Divided: Party Conflict in the Civil War North*. Cambridge: Harvard University Press, 2002.
Nell, William Cooper. *The Colored Patriots of the American Revolution, with Sketches of Several Distinguished Colored Persons . . .* Boston: Robert F. Wallcut, 1855.
Nelson, Paul D. *Fredrick L. McGhee: A Life on the Color Line, 1861–1912*. St. Paul: Minnesota History Society Press, 2002.
Newman, Louise Michele. *White Women's Rights: The Racial Origins of Feminism in the United States*. New York: Oxford University Press, 1999.
Nosek, Pamela. "Historical Detective Work: The Story of Alexander and Catherine Clark." *Iowa Griot* 4 (Winter 2004): 4–5.
Noun, Louise R. *Strong-Minded Women: The Emergence of the Woman-Suffrage Movement in Iowa*. Ames: Iowa State University Press, 1969.

Noyes, Edward. "The Negro in Wisconsin's Civil War Effort." *Lincoln Herald* 69 (Summer 1967): 70–82.
O'Connor, Kimberly Rae. "To Disembark: The Slave Narrative Tradition." *African American Review* 30 (Spring 1996): 35–57.
Paludan, Phillip Shaw. *"A People's Contest": The Union and the Civil War, 1861–1865*. New York: Harper and Row, 1988.
Parish, John Carl. *George Wallace Jones*. Iowa City: State Historical Society of Iowa, 1912.
Parrish, William E. *Turbulent Partnership: Missouri and the Union, 1861–1865*. Columbia: University of Missouri Press, 1963.
Peterson, Carla. *Doers of the Word: African-American Speakers and Writers in the North, 1830–1880*. New Brunswick: Rutgers University Press, 1995.
"Pioneering Black Politicians and Public Officials in Hennepin County." *Hennepin History* 63 (Summer 2004): 31.
Pipkin, Rev. J. J. *The Story of a Rising Race: The Negro in Revelation, in History and in Citizenship*. St. Louis: N. D. Thompson Publishing Co., 1902.
Portrait and Biographical Album of Henry County, Iowa. Chicago: Acme Publishing Co., 1888.
Portrait and Biographical Album of Muscatine County, Iowa. Vol. 2. Chicago: S. J. Clarke Publishing Company, 1911.
Potter, Merle. *101 Best Stories of Minnesota*. Minneapolis: Harrison and Smith Co., 1931.
Prucha, Francis Paul. *The Great Father: The United States Government and the American Indians*. Lincoln: University of Nebraska Press, 1984.
Quaife, Milo M. "The Panic of 1862 in Wisconsin." *Wisconsin Magazine of History* 4 (December 1920): 166–95.
Quigley, David. *Second Founding: New York City, Reconstruction, and the Making of American Democracy*. New York: Hill and Wang, 2004.
Rabinowitz, Howard N. "Three Reconstruction Leaders: Blanche K. Bruce, Robert Brown Elliott, and Holland Thompson." In *Black Leaders of the Nineteenth Century*, edited by Leon Litwack and August Meier, 191–218. Urbana: University of Illinois Press, 1988.
Rable, George C. *Civil Wars: Women and the Crisis of Southern Nationalism*. Urbana: University of Illinois Press, 1989.
Rael, Patrick. *Black Identity and Black Protest in the Antebellum North*. Chapel Hill: University of North Carolina Press, 2002.
Ransom, Roger L., and Richard Sutch. *One Kind of Freedom: The Economic Consequences of Emancipation*. New York: Cambridge University Press, 1977.
Rayman, Ronald A. "Joseph Montfort Street: Establishing the Sac and Fox Indian Agency in Iowa Territory, 1838–1840." *Annals of Iowa* 43 (Spring 1976): 261–74.
Redkey, Edwin S. *A Grand Army of Black Men*. New York: Cambridge University Press, 1992.
Regosin, Elizabeth. *Freedom's Promise: Ex-Slave Families and Citizenship in the Age of Emancipation*. Charlottesville: University Press of Virginia, 2002.
Reimer, Terry. "Smallpox and Vaccination in the Civil War." National Museum of Civil War Medicine, <http://www.civilwarmed.org/articles.cfm>. 26 May 2006.

Rhodes, Jane. *Mary Ann Shadd Cary: The Black Press and Protest in the Nineteenth Century*. Bloomington: Indiana University Press, 1998.

Richards, Eliza. "U.S. Civil War Print Culture and Popular Imagination." *American Literary History* 17 (2005): 349–59.

Richman, Irving B. "Congregational Life in Muscatine, 1843–1893." *Iowa Journal of History and Politics* 21 (1923): 356–58.

Riegel, Stephen J. "The Persistent Career of Jim Crow: Lower Federal Courts and the 'Separate but Equal' Doctrine, 1865–1896." *American Journal of Legal History* 28 (1984): 17–40.

Rippley, La Vern J. *The Immigrant Experience in Wisconsin*. Boston: Twayne Publishers, 1985.

Roediger, David R. *The Wages of Whiteness*. 1991. Revised ed., New York: Verso, 1999.

Rosenberg, Morton M. *Iowa on the Eve of the Civil War: A Decade of Frontier Politics*. Norman: Oklahoma University Press, 1972.

Ross, Michael A. *Justice of Shattered Dreams: Samuel Freeman Miller and the Supreme Court during the Civil War Era*. Baton Rouge: Louisiana State University Press, 2003.

Rotundo, Anthony. "Learning about Manhood: Gender Ideals and the Middle Class Family in Nineteenth-Century America." In *Manliness and Morality: Middle Class Masculinity in Britain and America, 1800–1940*, edited by J. A. Mangan and James Walvin, 35–51. New York: St. Martin's Press, 1987.

Rugh, Susan Sessions. *Our Common Country: Family Farming, Culture, and Community in the Nineteenth-Century Midwest*. Bloomington: Indiana University Press, 2001.

Ryan, Mary P. *Civic Wars: Democracy and Public Life in the American City during the Nineteenth Century*. Berkeley: University of California Press, 1997.

——. *Women in Public: Between Banners and Ballots, 1825–1880*. Baltimore: Johns Hopkins University Press, 1990.

Salvatore, Nick. *We All Got History: The Memory Books of Amos Webber*. New York: Random House, 1996.

Savage, Kirk. *Standing Soldiers, Kneeling Slaves: Race, War, and Monument in Nineteenth-Century America*. Princeton: Princeton University Press, 1997.

Saville, Julie. "Rites and Power: Reflections on Slavery, Freedom and Political Ritual." *Slavery and Abolition* 20 (1999): 81–102.

Schama, Simon. *Rough Crossings: Britain, the Slaves and the American Revolution*. New York: HarperCollins, 2006.

Schechter, Patricia A. *Ida B. Wells-Barnett and American Reform, 1880–1930*. Chapel Hill: University of North Carolina Press, 2001.

Schultz, Jane E. *Women at the Front: Hospital Workers in Civil War America*. Chapel Hill: University of North Carolina Press, 2004.

Schwalm, Leslie A. "Emancipation Day Celebrations: The Commemoration of Slavery and Freedom in Iowa." *Annals of Iowa* 62 (Summer 2003): 291–332.

——. *"A Hard Fight for We": Women's Transition from Slavery to Freedom in South Carolina*. Urbana: University of Illinois Press, 1997.

——. "'Overrun with Free Negroes': Emancipation and Wartime Migration in the Upper Midwest." *Civil War History* 50 (June 2004): 145–74.

Schweider, Dorothy, Joseph Hraba, and Elmer Schweider. *Buxton: Work and Racial Equality in a Coal Mining Community*. Ames: Iowa State University Press, 1987.

Sekora, John. "Black Message/White Envelope: Genre, Authenticity, and Authority in the Antebellum Slave Narrative." *Callaloo* 10 (1987): 482–515.

Shaffer, Donald R. *After the Glory: The Struggles of Black Civil War Veterans*. Lawrence: University Press of Kansas, 2004.

Shafir, Gershon, ed. *The Citizenship Debates: A Reader*. Minneapolis: University of Minnesota Press, 1998.

Shea, William L. "A Semi-Savage State: The Image of Arkansas in the Civil War." In *Civil War Arkansas: Beyond Battles and Leaders*, edited by Anne J. Bailey and Daniel E. Sutherland, 85–100. Fayetteville: University of Arkansas Press, 2000.

Shutter, Marion D. *Progressive Men of Minnesota*. Minneapolis: Minneapolis Journal, 1897.

Siebert, Wilbur H. *The Underground Railroad from Slavery to Freedom*. New York: Macmillan, 1898.

Silag, Bill, ed. *Outside In: African-American History in Iowa, 1838–2000*. Des Moines: State Historical Society of Iowa, 2001.

Silber, Nina. *The Romance of Reunion: Northerners and the South, 1865–1900*. Chapel Hill: University of North Carolina Press, 1993.

Skocpol, Theda, Ariane Leazos, and Marshall Ganz. *What a Mighty Power We Can Be: African American Fraternal Groups and the Struggle for Racial Equality*. Princeton: Princeton University Press, 2006.

Skocpol, Theda, and Jennifer Lynn Osler. "Organization Despite Adversity: The Organization and Development of African American Fraternal Associations." *Social Science History* 28, no. 3 (Fall 2004): 367–437.

"A Slave Owner in Iowa." *Palimpsest* 22, no. 11 (November 1941): 344–45.

Smith, Adam I. P. "Partisan Politics and the Public Sphere: The Civil War North." *American Nineteenth-Century History* 2 (Summer 2001): 82–103.

Smith, John David. "Kentucky Civil War Recruits: A Medical Profile." *Medical History* 24 (1980):187–88.

Smith, Michael O. "Raising a Black Regiment in Michigan: Adversity and Triumph." In *A Question of Manhood: A Reader in U.S. Black Men's History and Masculinity*, edited by Darlene Clark Hine and Earnestine Jenkins, 1:502–16. Bloomington: Indiana University Press, 1999.

Smith, Olive Cole. *Mt. Pleasant Recalls Some of the Happenings of Her First Hundred Years*. Mt. Pleasant, Iowa: Henry County Historical Society, 1942.

Sorisio, Carolyn. "Unmasking the Genteel Performer: Elizabeth Keckley's *Behind the Scenes* and the Politics of Public Wrath." *African American Review* 34 (2000): 19–28.

Spangler, Earl. *The Negro in Minnesota*. Minneapolis: T. S. Denison and Co., 1961.

Steinfield, Robert J. *The Invention of Free Labor: The Employment Relation in English and American Law and Culture, 1350–1870*. Chapel Hill: University of North Carolina Press, 1991.

Stephenson, Gilbert Thomas. *Race Distinctions in American Law*. 1910. Reprint, New York: Negro Universities Press, 1969.

Stevens, Harriet, ed. *Graybeards: The Family of Major Lyman Allen during the American Civil War*. Iowa City: Press of the Camp Pope Bookshop, 1998.
Stevens, Hiram F. *History of the Bench and Bar of Minnesota*. Vol. 1. Minneapolis: Legal Publishing and Engraving Co., 1904.
Stepto, Robert B. *From Behind the Veil: A Study of Afro-American Narrative*. 2nd ed. Urbana: University of Illinois Press, 1991.
Stiles, Edward. *Recollections and Sketches of Notable Lawyers and Public Men of Early Iowa*. Des Moines: Homestead Publishing Co., 1916.
Summers, Martin. *Manliness and Its Discontents: The Black Middle Class and the Transformation of Masculinity, 1900–1930*. Chapel Hill: University of North Carolina Press, 2004.
Super, John C. "Food and History." *Journal of Social History* 36 (2002): 165–78.
Tadman, Michael. *Speculators and Slaves: Masters, Traders, and Slaves in the Old South*. Madison: University of Wisconsin Press, 1989.
Talbert, Rev. Horace. *The Sons of Allen: Together with a Sketch of the Rise and Progress of Wilberforce University*. Xenia, Ohio: Aldine Press, 1906.
Taylor, David Vassar. "The Blacks." In *They Chose Minnesota: A Survey of the State's Ethnic Groups*, edited by June Drenning Holmquist, 73–91. St. Paul: Minnesota Historical Society Press, 1981.
Taylor, Nikki M. *Frontiers of Freedom: Cincinnati's Black Community, 1802–1868*. Athens: Ohio University Press, 2005.
Taylor, Quintard. *In Search of the Racial Frontier: African Americans in the American West, 1528–1990*. New York: Norton, 1998.
Thomas, Joseph M. "The Post-Abolitionist's Narrative: William Greenleaf Eliot's *The Story of Archer Alexander*." *New England Quarterly* 73 (2000): 463–81.
Thornbrough, Emma Lou. *The Negro in Indiana before 1900: A Study of a Minority*. 1985. Revised ed., Bloomington: Indiana University Press, 1993.
Trask, Kerry A. *Fire Within: A Civil War Narrative from Wisconsin*. Kent, Ohio: Kent State University Press, 1995.
Trexler, Harrison Anthony. *Slavery in Missouri, 1804–1865*. Baltimore: Johns Hopkins University Press, 1914.
Trotter, Joe William, Jr. *The African American Experience*. Boston: Wadsworth Publishing, 2006.
Urwin, Gregory J. W. " 'A Very Disastrous Defeat': Arkansas in the Civil War." *North and South: The Official Magazine of the Civil War Society* 6 (2002): 26–39.
Valelly, Richard M. *The Two Reconstructions: The Struggle for Black Enfranchisement*. Chicago: University of Chicago Press, 2004.
VanderVelde Lea, and Sandhya Subramanian. "Mrs. Dred Scott." *Yale Law Journal* 106 (December 1996–January 1997): 1033–1122.
Vincent, Stephen A. *Southern Seed, Northern Soil: African-American Farming Communities in the Midwest, 1765–1900*. Bloomington: Indiana University Press, 1999.
Voegeli, V. Jacque. *Free but Not Equal: The Midwest and the Negro during the Civil War*. Chicago: University of Chicago Press, 1967.
———. "A Rejected Alternative: Union Policy and the Relocation of Southern 'Contrabands' at the Dawn of Emancipation." *Journal of Southern History* 69 (November 2003): 765–90.

Vorenberg, Michael. "Abraham Lincoln and the Politics of Black Colonization." *Journal of the Abraham Lincoln Association* 14 (1993): 1–45.
———. *Final Freedom: The Civil War, the Abolition of Slavery, and the Thirteenth Amendment*. Cambridge, England: Cambridge University Press, 2001.
Walker, Juliet E. K. *Free Frank: A Black Pioneer on the Antebellum Frontier*. Lexington: University Press of Kentucky, 1983.
Walton, J. P. "Unwritten History of Bloomington (now Muscatine) in Early Days." *Annals of Iowa* 1 (1882): 47–49.
Wang, Xi. *The Trial of Democracy: Black Suffrage and Northern Republicans, 1960–1910*. Athens: University of Georgia Press, 1997.
Warren, Robert Penn. *The Legacy of the Civil War*. New York: Random House, 1961
Washington, Versalle F. *Eagles on Their Buttons: A Black Infantry Regiment in the Civil War*. Columbia: University of Missouri Press, 1999.
Weaver, Valerie W. "The Failure of Civil Rights: 1875–1883 and Its Repercussions." *Journal of Negro History* 54 (October 1969): 368–82.
Welke, Barbara Young. *Recasting American Liberty: Gender, Race, Law, and the Railroad Revolution, 1865–1920*. Cambridge, England: Cambridge University Press, 2001.
———. "When All the Women Were White, and All the Blacks Were Men: Gender, Class, Race, and the Road to *Plessy*, 1855–1914." *Law and History Review* 13 (1995): 261–316.
Welty, Susan Fulton. *A Fair Field*. Detroit: Harlo Press, 1968.
Wesley, Charles H. *The History of Prince Hall Grand Lodge of Free and Accepted Masons of the State of Ohio, 1849–1960*. Wilberforce, Ohio: Central State College Press, n.d. <http://users.1stnet/fischer/prince01.htm>. 30 Oct. 2006.
White, Bruce M. "The Power of Whiteness; or, The Life and Times of Joseph Rolette Jr." In *Making Minnesota Territory, 1849–1858, Special Issue of Minnesota History*, edited by Anne R. Kaplan and Marilyn Ziebarth (1999): 26–45.
White, Deborah Gray. *Too Heavy a Load: Black Women in Defense of Themselves, 1894–1994*. New York: Norton, 1999.
White, Shane. " 'It Was a Proud Day': African Americans, Festivals, and Parades in the North, 1741–1834." *Journal of American History* 81 (1994): 13–50.
———. "A Question of Style: Blacks in and around New York City in the Late 18th Century." *Journal of American Folklore* 102 (1989): 23–44.
———. *Somewhat More Independent: The End of Slavery in New York City, 1770–1810*. Athens, Ga.: University of Georgia Press, 1991.
Wiecek, William M. *The Sources of Antislavery Constitutionalism in America, 1760–1840*. Ithaca: Cornell University Press, 1977.
Wiggins, William H., Jr. *O Freedom! Afro-American Emancipation Celebrations*. Knoxville: University of Tennessee Press, 1987.
Wilson, George. "George Wilson: First Territorial Adjutant of the Militia of Iowa." *Annals of Iowa* 4 (January 1901): 763–76.
Wilson, Jeremiah Moses. *Black Messiahs and Uncle Toms: Social and Literary Manipulations of a Religious Myth*. University Park: Pennsylvania State University Press, 1982.

Winters, Donald L. *Farmers without Farms: Agricultural Tenancy in Nineteenth-Century Iowa*. Greenwood, Conn.: Greenwood Press, 1978.
Witt, Doris. *Black Hunger: Food and the Politics of U.S. Identity*. New York: Oxford University Press, 1999.
Wood, Sharon E. *The Freedom of the Streets: Work, Citizenship, and Sexuality in a Gilded Age City*. Chapel Hill: University of North Carolina Press, 2005.
Workers of the Writers' Program, Works Progress Administration in the State of Nebraska. *The Negroes of Nebraska*. Lincoln: Woodruff Printing Co., 1940.
Worthing, Ruth Shaw. *The History of Fond du Lac County, as Told by Its Place Names*. Oshkosh, Wis.: Globe Printing Co., 1976.
Wubben, Hubert H. *Civil War Iowa and the Copperhead Movement*. Ames: Iowa State University Press, 1980.
———. "The Uncertain Trumpet: Iowa Republicans and Black Suffrage, 1860–1868." *Annals of Iowa History* 47 (Summer 1984): 409–29.
Zilversmit, Arthur. *The First Emancipation: The Abolition of Slavery in the North*. Chicago: University of Chicago Press, 1967.

Unpublished Secondary Sources

Alexander, Shawn Leigh. "'We Know Our Rights and Have the Courage to Defend Them': The Spirit of Agitation in the Age of Accommodation, 1883–1909." Ph.D. diss., University of Massachusetts, 2004.
Bodnia, George. "The Racial and Political Attitudes of Minnesota Soldiers during the Civil War." Master's thesis, University of Minnesota, 1974.
Clark, Christy M. "The Business of Slavery and the Struggles of Emancipation: African Americans in Rhode Island, 1650–1850." Ph.D. diss., University of Iowa, in progress.
Cummings, Frank W. "Segregated Education in St. Paul, Minnesota." Fifth-year paper for the M.Ed. degree (Department of Education), Macalester College, 1961.
Fishel, Leslie H., Jr. "The North and the Negro, 1865–1900: A Study in Race Discrimination." Ph.D. diss., Harvard University, 1953.
Gannon, Barbara A. "The Won Cause: Black and White Comradeship in the Grand Army of the Republic." Ph.D. diss., Pennsylvania State University, 2005.
Goostree, Robert Edward. "Civil Rights in Iowa: The Statute and Its Enforcement." Ph.D. diss., University of Iowa, 1950.
Harbour, Jennifer Rebecca. "'Bury Me in a Free Land': African-American Political Culture and the Settlement Movement in the Antebellum and Wartime Midwest." Ph.D. diss., University of Iowa, 2008.
Harris, Faye Emma. "A Frontier Community: The Economic, Social, and Political Development of Keokuk, Iowa, from 1820 to 1866." Ph.D. diss., University of Iowa, 1965.
Johnson, Russell Lee. "An Army for Industrialization: The Civil War and the Formation of Urban-Industrial Society in a Northern City." Ph.D. diss., University of Iowa, 1996.
Kelley, Colleen K. "'Beautiful Land of the White Man': Promotional Literature in Iowa, 1836–1865." Master's essay, University of Iowa, 2005.
Libman, Gary. "Minnesota and the Struggle for Black Suffrage, 1849–1870: A Study in Party Motivation." Ph.D. diss., University of Minnesota, 1972.

Marshall, Robert D. "Mount Pleasant: 'The Athens of Iowa,' 1865–1875." Master's thesis, University of Iowa, 1963.
McKerley, John. "Citizens and Strangers: The Politics of Race in Missouri from Slavery to the Era of Jim Crow." Ph.D. diss., University of Iowa, 2008.
Meyer, Sister Mary Demetria. "The Germans in Wisconsin and the Civil War." Master's thesis, Catholic University, 1937.
Robinson, Armstead Louis."Day of Jubilo: Civil War and the Demise of Slavery in the Mississippi Valley, 1861–1865." Ph.D. diss., University of Rochester, 1977.
Romeo, Sharon E. "Freedwomen in Pursuit of Liberty: St. Louis and Missouri in the Age of Emancipation." Ph.D. diss., University of Iowa. In progress.
Schwalm, Leslie A. "The Antislavery and Reform Activities of Women in Wisconsin." Master's thesis, University of Wisconsin, 1984.
Shaffer, Donald R. "The Sable Arm Speaks: Union Pension Files Giving Voice to Black Union Soldiers." Paper presented at Annual Meeting of the Society for Military History, University of Mississippi, Oxford, 20 May 2006. In possession of author.
Taylor, David Vassar. "Pilgrim's Progress: Black St. Paul and the Making of an Urban Ghetto, 1870–1930." Ph.D. diss., University of Minnesota, 1977.
Vollmar, William J. "The Negro in a Midwest Frontier City: Milwaukee, 1835–1870." Master's thesis, Marquette University, 1968.
Weaver, Valerie Whittemore. "The Civil Rights Act of 1875: Reactions and Enforcement." Master's thesis, University of California, Berkeley, 1966.
Williams-Searle, Bridgett. "Intimate Empires: Domestic Order, Property Relations, and the Law in the Western Country, 1760–1830." Ph.D. diss., University of Iowa, 2005.

Index

Abolitionists, 29–31, 228, 247, 250
Achan, Manuel (aka Emmanuel Aikens), 301 (n. 65), 304 (n. 94), 305 (nn. 110, 113), 307 (n. 148)
Adams, John Q., 213–14
Adams, Nathaniel, 11, 59, 77, 268 (n. 4), 280 (n. 46)
African Americans: divisions among, 96–97; enfranchisement, 176–79, 181–89; migration, feared by whites, 28–29, 31–34, 41, 81, 83–90, 101, 105, 182; "place," 1, 5, 82–83, 85, 105–6, 109; place of birth, 12, 35, 38, 45, 135; population, in upper Midwest, 3, 35, 38, 277 (n. 4)
African American women: and auxiliary organizations, 158–59; and black churches, 144–50, 155–57; caricatured, 93–94, 156, 219–22; and civil rights activism, 154, 176, 179, 194, 197–200, 204–6; club movement, 179–80, 215–16; employment of, 71, 97–99, 149, 177; and family life, 151, 179; political activism of, 179–80; and respectability, 136, 151; violence against, 66, 150–51; and wartime dislocation, 64–65. *See also* Contrabands; Occupations; Slavery; Slaves; Whites
African Methodist Episcopal, 35, 37, 39, 131–32, 135, 143–45, 147–55, 159–61, 165, 195, 197, 200, 202, 234, 236, 249, 255, 261
African Methodist Episcopal Zion (AMEZ), 155
Afro-American Council, 180, 213, 215, 234–36. *See also* National Afro-American Council
Afro-American League, 213–14, 234
Afro-American Protective Association of Iowa, 214; female members and officers, 214, 326 (n. 180)
Aikens, Emanuel. *See* Achan, Manuel
Alexander, Archer, 56, 256
Alexander, H. McGee, 170
Alexander, Louisa, 56
Alexander, William, 303 (n. 86)
Allen, Henry, 305 (n. 114)
Allen, Maj. Lyman, 78, 81
Anderson, Alice, 202
Anderson, Benjamin, 24
Anderson, Daniel, 24
Anderson, Ellen, 24
Anderson, John, 67
Anderson, Martha, 198
Anderson, York, 200
Andrews, William, 246–47
Ankrom, Jacob, 25
Applewhite, Lydia, 27
Arkansas locales: Big Creek, 118, 123; Ft. Curtis, 124; Helena, 50, 59, 69, 73–75, 78–80, 103, 116, 118, 124–27, 129–33; Little Rock, 59–60, 123; Marks Mills, 63
Army, U.S.: black enlistment, 56–57, 61, 68, 102, 110–14; contraband policy, 50, 61–62, 68, 107–8, 112; employment of African Americans, 44, 50, 53, 58, 66, 73, 102; exclusion of African Americans, 92–111; freedom certificates, 55, 59, 79–80; Quartermaster, 62, 73
Ault, William, 66

Bailey, Julius H., 146, 148–49
Baker, Jean, 101, 289 (n. 11)
Ball, Thomas A., 69
Bandy, John, 242
Baptists (African American), 34, 144–46, 159, 165, 200, 202
Barton, Felix, 112, 298 (n. 24)

Barton, Leonard, 111–12, 298 (n. 24)
Bassett, Lucy, 334 (n. 92)
Bell, Henry, 211, 335 (n. 97)
Bell, Jane (aka Jennie), 211–12, 335 (n. 97)
Bell, Miles, 212
Benton Barracks (St. Louis), 54, 80, 121–22, 125, 128–29, 279 (n. 28)
Bernstein, Iver, 94
Birney, John W., 114
Birth of a Nation, 239
Black, George, 249
Black, John C., 304 (n. 105)
Black, William H., 284 (n. 93)
Black conventions, 36; Colored Labor Convention (1869), 209; Davenport, Iowa (1865), 180–81; Des Moines, Iowa (1868), 185; Milwaukee, Wisc. (1865), 182–83; Minnesota (1883), 191; Muscatine, Iowa (1857), 36; National Convention of Colored Men 1883 (Louisville), 213; Oskaloosa, Iowa (1871), 209; Rochester, N.Y. (1853), 36; St. Paul, Minn. (1869), 185–86
Black newspapers, 114, 161, 194, 206; *The Bystander* (Iowa), 212, 222, 225, 243, 262; *The Weekly Avalanche* (Iowa), 212, 214; *Western Appeal* (Minnesota), 213. See also *Christian Recorder*
Blagburn, Frank, 189
Bland, Austin, 173
Blight, David, 223, 242, 247
Bowser, B., 37
Boyd, Edward, 334 (n. 92)
Bradford, James, 116, 300 (n. 47)
Breckenridge, Nora, 202
Brickley (aka Brickler), Celia, 50, 130
Brickley (aka Brickler), William, 50, 130
Brooks, Harvey, 301 (n. 56)
Brooks, Stephen, 103
Brown, Sen. Benjamin Gratz, 78
Brown, Edwin, 110
Brown, Gerrett (aka Gerret Montgomery), 334 (n. 92)
Brown, Henry D., 120, 241, 310 (n. 44)
Brown, Lucy, 14

Brown, Mary, 306 (n. 133)
Brown, Sue M., 215–16, 235–36
Brown, William, 10, 13–14, 268 (n. 3)
Brownell, Capt., 118
Brown v. Board of Education, 236
Bruce, Blanche K., 192
Bucklin, Walter, 9, 268 (n. 1)
Buckner, Miss, 214
Busey, James, 43–44, 47
Busey, Matilda, 43–44, 47
Busey, Tom, 43–44
Butler, Gen. Benjamin, 58–59
Butler, Cornelius, 114
Butler, George, 112
Butler, William, 229

Cain, Rev. Richard Harvey, 36–37, 144
Caldwell, George, 142
Caldwell, Susan, 198–99
Camp, William, 335 (n. 95)
Campbell, James, 148
Carey, J., 232
Carter, John, 281 (n. 58)
Carter, Sophronia, 63, 281 (n. 58)
Cassius, "Uncle," 21
Charlotte, "Black," 21, 271 (n. 41)
Cheatham, Matt, 304 (n. 94)
Cheek, Rev. Thomas, 319–20 (n. 59)
Chestnutt, Charles, 328 (n. 11)
Chilton, Mary Jane, 204, 206
Christian Recorder, 36, 114, 135, 137, 144–45, 148–50, 152, 155, 194, 202, 206
Citizenship: cultural, 307 (n. 6); as defined by black midwesterners, 136–37, 175–76, 179, 216–17; and gender ideologies, 5, 216; and military service, 108, 113, 118, 133, 180–81, 208; as viewed differently by men and women, 5–6, 179
Civil rights, 136–37; enforcement, 207; female litigants, 199–202, 204–6; and Fourteenth Amendment, 194, 196, 205, 210; organized pursuit of, 207, 213–15
Clark, Alexander, 36–37, 114, 116–17, 119–22, 142, 161, 164–65, 170–73, 180, 185, 188–91, 201

Clark, Ansel, 335 (n. 97)
Clark, Catherine, 25–26, 36
Clark, Susan, 197–98, 201–2
Coalson, Mrs., 212
Cochran, Samuel, 21
Coger, Emma, 204–6
Coleman, George W., 300 (n. 47)
Collins, Milton, 115, 122, 124–25
Colonization, 36; American Colonization Society, 32; Colonization Society of the State of Iowa, 32–33
Combs, George, 118
Confiscations Acts, 50, 53, 55, 59–60, 80, 123
Congregationalists, 31, 37
Conklin, O. S., 141
Contraband Relief Society (St. Louis), 78, 80
Contrabands: abuse of, by soldiers and locals, 75–76, 79; camp conditions, 73–76, 79–80; caricatured by whites, 84–85, 87–89; children, 65, 74, 76–77; criticism of policy on, 90; female, 60, 65–66, 74, 76, 77; kidnapped, 62, 79; murdered by Confederates, 63; organized relocation of, 62, 72–78, 85, 99; and other African Americans, 96–97; Union policy on, 50, 65–66, 68; vulnerability to capture or return, 61–62, 79–80; wartime employment of men, 68–69, 76, 78; wartime employment of women, 61, 112. *See also* Enlistment
Conway, Joseph, 79
Cooper, Henry, 117, 126
Copperheads, 67, 114
Coston, Rev. William Hilary, 191
Cowan, Gus, 284 (n. 93)
Cox, Isaac, 140
Cox, Mary, 13
Cox, Clarissa, 11, 269 (n. 4)
Craig, Emmanuel, 71
Crawford, Antoine, 116–17, 281 (n. 58)
Crockett, Charles H., 300 (n. 50)
Crutchfield, Mary. *See* Robison, Mary
Curran, Celia. *See* Brickley, Celia

Curtis, John L., 26
Curtis, Gen. Samuel R., 55, 58–59, 73, 77–80

Dais, Henry, 131
Dakota Uprising of 1862, 90–92, 116–17, 121, 163
Dandridge family, 14, 269 (n. 17)
Dandridge, Matilda, 138–39
Dandridge, Rufus, 141
Davis, Charles, 232–33
Davis, Edward, 110
Davis, Lucy Ann, 79
Davis, Zella, 215
Delaney, Martin, 161
Delany, Lucy, 159
Democratic Party, 109–10, 176, 182; and black relocation, 89–90; and female suffrage, 208; in Iowa, 41; and newspapers, 85–86, 120
Densmore, Orrin, 98
Deuster, Peter, 96
Diaspora, 1–3, 44–46
Dick, "Uncle," 25
Dickson, Moses, 160–61, 165, 170–72
Diffley, Kathleen, 89
Domestic service, 97–99; and race, 99–100, 139
Domestic sphere, 97
Doolittle, Sen. James R., 102, 182
Douglas, Davison, 194
Douglas, H. Ford, 34
Douglass, Frederick, 114, 190, 213, 242, 246; as memory, 235–36, 246, 250
Douglass, Frederick (veteran), 140, 269 (n. 13)
Dove, Charles, 199, 201
Dove, Mary Jane, 153–54, 199
Dove, Rev. William, 148–49, 151–54, 199–200
Draper, Robert, 300 (n. 50)
Dudley, Ambrose, 33–34
Duffin, Elizabeth, 148
Dunn, Ned, 304 (n. 103)

Early, William C., 117, 119
Eaton, Chaplain John, Jr., 60
Eberhart, Chaplain Uriah, 61–2
Education. *See* Schools
Elder, Orville, 255–62
Elective office, and black midwesterners, 189–90, 191–93
Eliot, William Greenleaf, 256
Elliott, Richard, 303 (n. 86)
Emancipation: in Missouri, 51–52, 56–57, 67–68; northern white reactions to, 83–89, 92, 163, 175
Emancipation Day celebrations, 6, 37–38, 147, 155, 224–37
Emancipation Proclamation, 50, 61, 73, 85, 90, 102–3, 117, 230
Emigration, 33–34, 36, 82
Employment: of African Americans during wartime, 70–71, 91, 94–96, 105–6; of children, 139–40; comparison of black and white workers, 137–41
Enlistment of African Americans: advocated, 108, 110; opposed, 108, 110, 114
Estell, Elizabeth, 71
Exclusion Laws: challenged by black midwesterners, 36, 102–4, 274 (n. 75); enforced, 30–31, 102; passed, 30; sought by midwestern whites, 29, 82, 102–3, 105, 274 (n. 74)

Fabre, Genevieve, 226
Fahey, David, 159
Fahs, Alice, 88–89
Fairfax, Liz, 60
Faulkner, Carol, 46
Federal Writers' Project, 220
Felkerson, Monroe, 62
Fine, Alexander, 301 (n. 68)
Finkelman, Paul, 16, 21
Ford, Ephraim Piles, 116, 280 (n. 46)
Forrester, Charles, 19, 31
Fortune, T. Thomas, 213–15
Franklin, Moses, 21, 27
Fraternal and sororal organizations, 157–74, 216

Freedom, 135; antebellum black, 23–25, 97, 142
Freedom papers, 24–26
Freedom suits, 21–24, 39–40, 271–72 (n. 43); Rachel Bundy, 22–23, 272 (n. 48); Milly, 22, 272 (n. 45); Peter, 22, 272 (n. 45); Rachel, 22, 272 (n. 45); Ralph, 22–23; Dred and Harriet Scott, 21–22, 33, 39, 168; Jim White, 22
Free labor ideology, 99
Free Soil, 32, 275 (n. 82)
Frémont, Gen. John C., 51–53
Fugitives: antebellum, 30–31, 36, 41; wartime, 44–45, 53–54, 58–59. *See also* Slaves: flight during wartime
Fugitive Slave Law, 33, 85, 245, 250

Gamble, Gov. Hamilton R., 52, 115
Gannon, Barbara, 239
Gerteis, Louis, 55–56
Gifford, Charles, 310 (n. 46)
Gillespie, Ezekial, 183
Gillette, William, 176, 191
Gillihan, Catherine, 25
Gillihan, Jack, 25
Godar, Alexis, 21
Godar, Jule, 21
Godar, Rachel, 21
Gordon, Ellen, 38
Gore, Ben, 26
Gore, Kitty, 26
Grand Army of the Republic (GAR), 237–39, 250; Ladies of the GAR, 237, 238
Grant, Gen. Ulysses S., 43, 53, 57, 60, 62, 74, 76; presidential campaigns, 190
Graves, Clement, 303 (n. 86)
Gray, E. W., 112–13
Gray, John Henry, 104
Green, James, 318 (n. 27)
Green, Jason, 117
Green, Jerry, 114
Green, John, 192
Green, Thomas, 67, 111
Griffin, Mathew, 113
Grimes, Sen. James W., 85

Griswold, Charles, 168–69, 183, 186
Guy, G. W., 231

Hahn, Steven, 176
Hall, Abram T., 146
Hall, George, 116, 284 (n. 93)
Hall, Johanna, 146
Hall, Samuel, 10–12, 14, 60, 245, 247–50, 255–62
Halleck, Gen. Henry W., 52–53, 55, 58, 85, 113
Hannah, Bart, 21, 27
Hannah, Henry, 21, 27
Hardin, Mary, 306 (n. 142)
Harding, Charlotte, 281 (n. 58)
Hardy, Samuel, 214–15
Harlan, Sen. James, 102, 183–84
Harper, Frances Ellen Watkins, 202–3; on school integration, 202
Harris, Joel Chandler, 243
Harris, Samuel J., 155, 232
Harris, Hannah, 155–56
Harrison, William, 120
Hartman, Saidiya, 224
Hayden, Lewis, 168
Hays, Anderson, 67, 281 (n. 58)
Hays, Ellen, 281 (n. 58)
Hays, Henderson, 67
Hays, John, 219
Henderson, Betsey, 25
Henderson, Charles, 25
Henderson, Mathilda, 283 (n. 83)
Henry, Benjamin, 302 (n. 75)
Henry, Jackson, 131
Henry, Malinda, 131
Henry, Sherrod, 131
Henry, Violet (née Moulton), 131, 306 (n. 138)
Hilyard, James Kidd, 189
Hiner, John, 38, 142, 189
Hirsh, Marianne, 223
Hoge, Jeff, 110
Holloway, Jefferson, 10
Horton, James, 41
Horton, Lois, 41

Howard, Milton, 36, 67, 117
Howe, Warrington, 182, 317 (n. 20), 318 (n. 31)
Hubbard, Lucius, 67–68, 76
Hudson, John G., 133
Hutchinson, Harriet, 130
Hutchinson, Isaac, 308 (n. 14)
Hutchinson, Nellie, 139
Hutchinson, Robert, 130

Illinois locales: Belvidere, 204; Cairo, 44, 51, 53, 74–76, 78–79, 95, 112, 114, 116; Chicago, 39, 76, 151–54, 160, 214; Ft. Armstrong, 18; Galena, 148; Moline, 34; Quincy, 204–5; Rockford, 34, 204; Rock Island, 34; Shawneetown, 16, 18
Illinois Country, 270 (n. 22); indentured servitude in, 16–17, 26; and slavery, 15–18; as source of midwestern slave trade, 15–20, 22
Immigrants: German, 96, 208; Irish, 39, 96, 208, 293 (n. 63); Norwegian, 294–95 (n. 77); Swedish, 99
Indiana, 30, 104
Iowa: civil rights law, 207; constitutional conventions (1857), 29; Democratic convention (1862), 101; slavery, 25, 37–38; voting rights, 180–88
—locales: Albia, 117, 141; Amity, 31; Anamosa, 34; Appanoose Co., 127; Audubon Co., 203; Bentonsport, 98; Bonaparte, 196; Burlington, 22, 26–27, 29, 32, 39–40, 107, 144–45, 147, 188, 227; Camp Lincoln, 120, 128; Cedar Rapids, 144; Clarinda, 227–29, 232; Davenport, 25, 34, 44–45, 96, 107, 147, 180–81, 187, 203, 216, 226–27; Denmark, 31; Des Moines, 25, 67, 71, 103–4, 107, 118, 120, 139, 147, 155, 159, 162, 173, 185–86, 189, 191, 196, 210–12, 216, 225, 228, 232, 234–37; DeWitt, 227; Dubuque, 19, 21–22, 37, 103, 142, 227; Fairfield, 19, 71, 143; Ft. Des Moines, 18, 21; Ft. Madison, 40, 140, 227; Grinnell, 195; Henry Co., 114, 247–48; Iowa

City, 26, 36, 50, 78, 81, 110, 159, 188, 194–95, 227, 237; Jefferson Co., 31; Johnson Co., 81, 95, 100; Keokuk, 20–21, 27, 35, 37–41, 67, 71, 77, 80, 107, 114–15, 117–18, 120–22, 125, 129–32, 137–38, 141–42, 144–47, 152–54, 159, 173, 186, 189, 191–92, 198–202, 204–6, 227, 229, 231, 237; Lee Co., 37, 71, 141, 162, 185; Lucas Co., 141; Marshalltown, 216; Mason City, 34; Mitchell Co., 196, 203; Mt. Pleasant, 37, 67, 97, 107, 114, 118, 135, 141, 144, 191–92, 210, 227, 233, 247–48, 251, 254; Muchakinock, 141–42, 192, 202; Muscatine, 24, 26, 33, 35–39, 41, 76, 116, 144, 147, 161, 184, 188, 197–98, 201, 227, 229; Newton, 67, 107, 118, 237; Oskaloosa, 30, 34, 92, 143, 147, 192, 211, 227; Ottumwa, 34, 195, 216; Page Co., 25, 95, 189, 211; Perry, 189, 195; Polk Co., 202, 210–11; Poweshiek Co., 100; Ringgold Co., 21, 32; Salem, 31–32, 247; Tabor, 31, 196; Tama, 69; Tama Co., 34, 189; Taylor Co., 196; Tipton, 34; Vinton, 77, 98; Wapello Co., 18–19, 95; Warren Co., 21; Washington, 10, 31, 144, 196, 248–49, 259; Waterloo, 112; Whittenberg, 31
Iowa State Federation of Colored Women's Clubs, 215–16
Irish, John, 210

Jackson, Andrew, 21
Jackson, Charles M., 310 (n. 46)
Jackson, John, 21
Jackson, Martha, 334 (n. 92);
Jackson, Mary Jane, 21
Jackson, Preston, 334 (n. 92)
Jackson, Mattie J., 288 (n. 152)
Jackson, Peter, 304 (n. 103)
Jackson, Rachel, 14, 310 (n. 46)
Jackson, Rev. Thomas H., 150
James, Manson, 189
Jeffries, Thomas, 111
Jenkins, George, 305 (n. 112)
Johnson, Alfred, 302 (n. 69)

Johnson, Ann, 309 (n. 25)
Johnson, George, 11, 67
Johnson, Lew, 284 (n. 93)
Johnson, Louisa, 99
Johnson, Michael, 46
Joiner, Edward Carroll, 276 (n. 94)
Jones, Alice, 79
Jones, Charlotte, 21, 27
Jones, Jacqueline, 94
Jones, Martha S., 150
Jones, Nicholas, 187
Jones, Paul, 21–22, 27
Jones, Thomas Gordon, 67, 232–33
Jones, William, 67, 189
Judy, "Aunt," 25
Jury service, 29, 188

Kansas-Nebraska Act, 33
Kay, William, 128
Kebo, George, 119–20, 125, 127
Keckley, Elizabeth, 246
Kennet, F. B., 54
Kentucky, 25, 43–44, 47, 57–58; Columbus (contraband camp), 44, 57; Ft. Heiman, 43, 47
Kirkwood, Gov. Samuel, 71, 85, 102, 113–15
Knowles, Freeman (M.D.), 305 (n. 111)
Ku Klux Klan, 219; rumored attack (1874), 200

Labor, 94, 99
Ladies Union Aid Society (St. Louis), 78
Lambert, Alexander, 300 (n. 51)
Law: black codes, 15–16, 27–31; Civil Rights Act (1866), 163–64., 176, 178, 196; Civil Rights Act (1875), 191, 206–7, 213, 255; Dred Scott decision, 176, 245, 250; First Reconstruction Act (1867), 176; and Fourteenth Amendment, 164, 176, 194, 196, 205, 10, 250; and Fifteenth Amendment, 176, 178, 181; *Plessy v. Ferguson*, 255; Supreme Court reversal (1883), 191, 207, 213, 255; and Thirteenth Amendment, 175–76, 182; *United States v. Stanley*, 250

Lewis, "Aunt" Betty, 219
Lewis, Luella, 229
Lewis, Mason, 304 (n. 94)
Lewis, Raymond, 300 (n. 48)
Liberal Republican Party: Colored National Liberal Republican Convention (1872), 190; and Frederick Douglass, 190; and George Downing, 190; Great Plains meeting (1871), 190
Liberty Party, 31, 33
Libman, Gary, 188
Lincoln, Abraham, 55, 90–91, 95; and slavery, 43, 52–53, 57, 67, 102; as memory, 229, 231–32, 235–36
Linderman, Gerald F., 125
Linebaugh, Virginia, 335 (n. 95)
Logan, William, 117, 300–301 (n. 54)
Louisiana, 110
Louisiana Purchase, 3
Luckadoo, Enos, 59, 280 (n. 46)
Lyles, Amanda, 215
Lynch, John R., 192

Mack, Henry, 238
Malone, Rev. John W., 143–46, 185
Mann, Mary, 198–99
Marriage, 133, 150; interracial, 30. *See also* 60th U.S. Colored Infantry; Slaves
Martin, Jonathan D., 13
Mary, 25
Mary (slave of John L. Curtis), 26
Maryland, 11–13
Masculinity: and denominational authority, 148–51, 155–56; and franchise, 177, 179; and fraternal associations, 157, 160–61, 164–65; and gender role performance, 5–6, 204; and military service, 108–9, 120–21, 123, 128, 131; and race, 100–101, 109, 142, 149
Mason, Alfred, 300 (n. 48)
Mason, Charles, 23, 102
Matthews, Edward, 24
McClellan, Oscar, 10
McCowen, Jennie, 203
McCraven, Rev. and Mrs. H., 212

McDonald, James, 219
McGhee, Frederick, 214–15
McGregor, Rose Ann, 30
McIntosh, A., 153
McNeely, Mark, 85
McPherson, James, 47, 57
McPike, Irene, 335 (n. 97)
Meier, Michael T., 112
Melish, Joanne Pope, 27
Memoir, 224, 240; and obituaries, 224, 243–44; and pensions, 224, 241–43; and slave narratives, 224, 244–47
Methodist, African American, 145; Wesleyan, 38
Migration, 34; African American, 12, 43–47, 51, 64–68, 71–72, 137; "paths to freedom," 66–75; wartime, 34–35, 45–47, 51, 62–75, 80–81; white, 13, 24–25, 64
Military experience: of African American men, 107, 113, 122, 277 (n. 2); of African American women, 61, 66, 68, 130, 132–33, 277 (n. 2), 306 (n. 135); black enlistment, 50, 56–57, 61, 68, 102, 107–8, 110–15; and black masculinity, 113, 118, 128; and citizenship, 108, 113; and married couples, 129–33; and off-duty activities, 128–29; and soldiers' families, 56–57, 117, 129–33; of white men, 109; white opinions on black soldiers, 92–93, 109, 117. *See also* 60th U.S. Colored Infantry
Miller, John, 67
Miller, Samuel Freeman, 207
Millie, "Aunt," 284 (n. 93)
Minnesota: civil rights, 197, 207, 213–15; female suffrage, 209; migration to, 45; voting rights, 177–78, 181, 183–84, 186, 188, 191, 192–93
—locales: Anoka, 214; Cleveland, 71; Duluth, 214; Faribault, 214; Ft. Snelling, 18, 21–22, 116–17; Minneapolis, 29, 45, 214, 227, 239; Red Wing, 98; St. Anthony, 29, 45; St. Paul, 45, 67, 96, 104, 107, 117, 159, 183–84, 186, 188–

381

Index

89, 191, 197, 227, 235, 239; Stillwater, 214, 227; Wabashaw Co., 188
Minnesota Citizens Civil Rights Committee, 214–15
Minnesota Industrial and Protective League, 213
Mississippi locales: Corinth, 95; Vicksburg, 56, 59, 61, 116
Mississippi valley: lower, 51, 58–64; middle, 51–58; upper, 16–17, 20, 34, 42, 85
Missouri locales: Boone Co., 67; Canton Co., 68; Chariton Co., 67; Chillicothe, 55; Grundy Co., 117; "Little Dixie," 54; Platte City, 54; Rolla, 52; St. Louis, 21, 44, 51, 53–54, 56, 67–68, 77–79, 81, 121–22, 125, 128–31, 247; Shelby Co., 117; Warrenton, 67; Washington Co., 54
Missouri Hotel, 77–80
Montgomery, James, 56
Montgomery, Thomas, 60, 65, 72
Moore, Wesley, 261
Moore, Capt. William, 58
Morgan, Alfred, 268 (n. 1), 281 (n. 56), 300 (n. 48)
Morgan, Jane, 9, 268 (n. 1), 281 (n. 56)
Morton, Nathan E., 335 (n. 97)
Morton, Rachel, 77
Mosely, James Mitchell, 336 (n. 112)
Mosely, Moses, 97, 106, 201, 213, 245, 247, 249–55, 260
Mosely, Susan, 201–2, 254
Motts, Robert T., 335 (n. 97)
Motts, Thomas, 36
Moulton, Violet. *See* Henry, Violet
Moyles, Robert, 60
Music, 224, 225, 227, 229, 234, 235
Myers, Abram, 119, 301 (n. 65)

National Afro-American Council, 215
National Association of Colored Women's Clubs, 180, 215
National Association for the Advancement of Colored People, 180, 207, 215, 234–36
Nativism, 96

"Negrophobia," 84
Nelson, Capt. Charles, 69
Nelson, Paul D., 215
Newburn, Martilla, 46, 59, 280 (n. 46)
Newburn, William, 278 (n. 10), 280 (n. 46)
Newman, Louise Michelle, 109, 209–10
New York, 23, 104, 176–77; Morris Grove, 38
Nichols, Aleck, 67
Northwest Ordinance, 3, 15–16, 26
Nuckols, Albert, 187
Nurses, African American female, 66

Occupations, 35–37, 138–43, 201–3
Ohio, 25, 101, 168–70, 176–77; Cincinnati, 34, 36, 101
Organized relocation. *See* Contrabands
Osler, Jennifer Lynn, 157, 161

Pace, Eveline, 283 (n. 83)
Page, Thomas Nelson, 243
Paine, Col. Halbert E., 58
Palmer, David James, 59
Palmer, Lucien, 189
Patterson, George, 237
Payne, Rev. J. H. D., 154–56
Payne family, 24–25
Pearson, Lt. Benjamin F., 63
Peck, Campbell, 162–63, 165
Pennsylvania, 23, 177
Perkins, Mr., 232
Petitioning, 86, 104, 178, 182, 183, 185
Phelps, Caroline, 271 (n. 41)
Pile, Col. William, 115
Pillow, Gideon J., 76
Pittman, George, 115, 131, 282 (n. 71)
Poindexter, Mrs., 212
Porter, Emmeline, 334 (n. 90)
Porter, Joseph, 334 (n. 90)
Posey, Thomas, 18
Prentiss, Brig. Gen. B. M., 77
Prescott, Dr. J., 34
Price, Hiram, 110
Priestly, Fanny, 320 (n. 75)
Priestly, John, 189, 192, 320 (n. 75)

Index

Prince Hall Masons, 36, 158–74
Pritchard, Jacob, 158, 161
Public sphere, 136–37, 166, 179, 289 (n. 11); celebrations, 147; churches, 147, 157; parades, 224, 225, 227, 228, 229, 231; speeches, 222, 223, 225, 226–29, 231–33, 235, 236
Pyles, Charlotta, 38, 41
Pyles, Harry, 38, 41
Pyles, Julian, 38

Quinn, Rev. William Paul, 144, 153, 276 (n. 94)

Race: categories of, challenged by African Americans, 121, 122, 136, 165, 168, 203–6, 253, 324 (n. 133); and male authority, 81, 101, 121, 187; and mob actions, 75–76, 95, 101, 104–5, 288–89 (n. 3), 293 (n. 64); and political behavior, 29, 40–41, 100–101, 176–78, 181–82, 185, 189–90; and political rhetoric, 40–41, 84; and respectability, 205, 228–29, 234, 323–24 (n. 127), 330 (n. 34)
Racial egalitarianism, 63–65
Racial hierarchies, linked to location, 82, 83–85, 87, 92, 93, 290 (n. 20), 292 (n. 41), 295 (n. 85), 296 (n. 97)
Racial ideologies, 9, 27, 29, 83–84, 98–100, 105–6, 157, 160, 162–63, 166–69, 179–80, 219–20, 251–52, 270 (n. 28), 292 (n. 36), 293 (n. 63), 295 (n. 79), 305 (n. 115), 310 (n. 54); and partisan politics, 101–2, 316–17 (n. 2); and public culture, 82, 83–84, 93, 105, 227, 289 (n. 11), 307 (n. 5); and science, 87, 127–28, 302 (n. 71)
Rakes, Rebecca, 139
Ramsey, Eli, 304 (n. 105)
Rankin, Col. John W., 71
Rape, 151, 208
Ray, Delia, 281 (n. 58)
Reconstruction: northern, 5, 175-217; southern, 175
Red, Samuel, 141

Redington, Edward, 69, 71
Redington, Mary, 71
Reed, Cassius, 286 (n. 115)
Reed, Ellen, 286 (n. 115)
Reeve, Capt. James, 290 (n. 14)
Regosin, Elizabeth, 241
Reno, Martha, 194
Republican Party: and Aspiring Club (Des Moines), 191–92; and black convention delegates, 188–90, 193; and black suffrage, 41, 176–77, 186–89, 208; and black voter criticism, 190–92; and Cobblers and Tanners Clubs, 190; and contraband (relocation), 76, 101; and female suffrage, 208; and newspapers, 86–87; and party discipline, 190; patronage and race, 209. *See also* Liberal Republican Party
Revels, John, 111, 298 (n. 23)
Revels, Micajah, 111
Revels, Mourning, 111
Revels, William, 111, 298 (n. 23)
Richards, James, 130–31
Richards, Nancy, 130–31, 139
Richardson, John, 188
Riots: anti-draft, 96; race, 101, 104
Robinson, Fanny, 11, 268–69 (n. 4)
Robinson, James, 71
Robinson, Rosy, 14
Robinson, Taylor, 303 (n. 86)
Robinson, William H., 14
Robison, John, 269 (n. 4)
Robison, Mary (née Crutchfield), 280 (n. 46), 288 (n. 156)
Rogers, Rev. J. B., 74, 77, 95
Rogers, Mary Ann Graham, 69
Rohrer, David, 22
Rose, Margaret, 335 (n. 97)
Ross, Emeline, 302 (n. 75)
Ross, Joseph, 302 (n. 75)
Rowland, Thompson, 54
Rush, Mrs. J. B., 236

St. Louis Ladies Union Aid Society, 78
Salomon, Gov. Edward (Wisconsin), 111, 114

Sappington, Albert, 318–19 (n. 46)
Sawyer, Samuel, 77–78
Schofield, Gen. John M., 80
School elections: and white female candidates, 325 (n. 50); and white female voters, 325 (n. 56)
Schools, 136, 142; African American ("African"), 39, 47; and black educators, 197–99, 201–3; and integration, 195–201, 209, 296 (n. 100), 321 (n. 81), 322 (n. 98); and taxes, 36, 194–95
Schultz, Jane, 66
Scott, Dred, 21, 219
Scott, Harriet, 21, 219
Scott, John, 166–67
Seers, Jerry, 21
Segregation: customary, 5, 83; legal, 83; public accommodations, 20; public schools, 194–99; transportation, 82–83, 203–6. *See also* Iowa; Minnesota; Wisconsin
Sekora, John, 245
Servitude, indentured, 17, 26, 271 (n. 34)
Sexuality: and black churches, 136, 150–53; and regimental culture among black soldiers, 127–28, 132; regulated by military, 305 (n. 115); and standards to which men were held, 150–51; and standards to which women were held, 132, 151
Shear, Mrs., 154–55
Shelby, Nelson, 303 (n. 86)
Shelton, Rhonda Amanda, 60
Shepard, Mary Anne, 327 (n. 8)
Shepherd, John, 65
Sheppard, Edward, 35
Shirley, Mrs. Francis Harris, 293 (n. 54)
Shropshire, Ellen, 10
Shropshire, Titus, 10
Sibley, Henry H., 116–17, 121
Siebert, Wilbur, 219
60th U.S. Colored Infantry: camp conditions, 124–25; disease, 124–26, 130–31; enlistment, 107–8, 114–18; examinations (medical), 118–20; family members, 122, 129–32; flag, sewn and presented, 122; impure smallpox vaccinations, 126–28, 130–31; injuries to soldiers, 123–24, 128; names/identity, 120; off-duty activities, 128–29; organized, 114–15; public image, 120–21; strategic role, 123–25; unequal pay, 122; women's labor in camp, 130, 132–33
Skocpol, Theda, 157, 161
Slaveowners, midwestern: L. P. Allen, 21, 32; Judge Frank Ballinger, 21; John Chambers, 32; Patrick Cheadle, 25–26; John L. Curtis, 26; Augustus L. Gregoire, 21; Gen. George W. Jones, 22; Stephen Kearney, 21; Rev. James Mitchell, 21; Joseph Smart, 18; and sojourning, 23, 272 (n. 47); T. B. W. Stockton, 22; Gen. O. H. W. Stull, 27; Ned Thomas, 14; George Williams, 25; George Wilson, 19
Slavery: impact on ideas about citizenship, 168; Indian, 15–16, 18; in military, 17–21, 70–71; memorialized, by African Americans, 222–24, 232–34, 239–42, 243–44, 244–47, 253, 255–62, 327–28 (n. 9), 335 (n. 101); midwestern, 15–23, 31–32, 270 (nn. 21, 29), 271 (n. 42), 272 (nn. 47, 48); New England, 27–29; by whites, 219–22, 254–62; and Union policies, 47–58, 60–63, 79–80; wartime collapse, 46, 47–50, 52–53, 56–57, 80, 83, 105; westward expansion, 12
Slaves: childhood, 10, 11, 14, 19, 21, 22, 25, 26, 27, 54–55; families, 9–12, 38, 43, 56, 80, 232, 310 (n. 54); fathers, 10, 232, 285 (n. 97); flight during wartime, 9, 37–38, 43–46, 52–56, 59, 61, 66–69, 282 (n. 69), 303 (n. 90); fugitive, wartime, 54–55; hiring, 13–14; husbands, 14; involuntary migration, 20–21, 25; manumission, 25–26; mothers, 9, 11, 19–20, 22, 24, 60, 62, 64–66, 68, 329 (n. 20); "refugeeing", 62; refugees, wartime, 62–65; relocation, wartime, 64, 66–78, 286 (n. 115), 287 (n. 133); sales of, wartime,

54, 61, 79–80; trade, 11, 12–13, 269 (nn. 5, 9, 12); treated as animals, 10; violence against, 14, 58, 62–63, 74; wartime employment, 52–53, 58–61, 69, 76–78, 116; wives, 14; women, 11, 14, 17, 18–20, 22, 25–26, 32, 38, 59–60, 64–66, 129–33, 272 (n. 48), 282 (nn. 64, 69, 71)
Smith, Amanda, 158–59
Smith, Geroid, 199, 201
Smith, Charlotta (née Pyles), 199–200
Soldiers: African American in white regiments, 111–12; white, 58, 59, 60, 65, 66, 68–72, 73–74, 92, 93, 98, 109, 110, 111, 113–14, 128–29, 182
"Sons of Freedom," 186
South Carolina, 110; Beaufort, 82, 86
Spence, Amerlia, 335 (n.95)
Spence, Van, 95
Sperry, A. F., 60
Stevens, Leroy, 301 (n. 59)
Stone, William, 95, 185
Story, Flora, 38
Stowe, Harriet Beecher, 82, 254
Street, Gen. Joseph M., 18–20, 31
Stuart, Elizabeth, 131–32, 282 (n. 71)
Stuart, William, 118, 131, 142
Suffrage
—black: celebrated, 186–87; exercised, 187–88; in Iowa, 41, 178, 181–89; in Minnesota, 178, 181–85, 187–89; and northern Reconstruction, 176–77; in northern states, 177–78, 187; and Republican party, 177, 182, 184, 186–89, 319 (n. 57); and southern Reconstruction, 177; white opposition to, 176–77, 182–83; in Wisconsin, 178, 181–83, 188–89, 274 (n. 72)
—female: and African American women, 208–12; endorsed by African Americans, 190, 208–12; endorsed by black men, 209; and interracial meetings, 210–12; partial, 208–9; and race, 209; and white women, 184, 203, 208–12
Summers, Martin, 164, 166
Sumner, Charles, 92

Swanson, Edwin, 140
Swisshelm, Jane, 32

Tadman, Michael, 12
Taliaferro, Maj. Lawrence, 18
Tate, Daniel, 304 (n. 94)
Taylor, Phillis, 334 (n. 92)
Teller, Ralph, 304 (n. 102)
Tennessee locales: Ft. Henry, 43, 59; Ft. Pillow, 116; Jackson, 76; Memphis, 61, 78; Tiptonville, 74
Thomas, George, 304 (n. 94)
Thomas, Gen. Lorenzo, 61, 112–14, 128
Thomas, Peter, 69, 116, 189
Thompson, Rev. Charles, 11
Thompson, Catherine (Kate), 9, 13, 269 (n. 13)
Thompson, Elizabeth, 274 (n. 75)
Thompson, John, 222–25
Tindle, Augustus, 27
Todd, Julius, 284 (n. 93)
Tolliver, Henry, 297 (n. 1)
Tourgée, Judge Albion, 262
Triplett, Alfred, 139
Triplett, Henry, 19–20
Triplett, Lewis, 19
Triplett, London (father), 18–19, 131
Triplett, London (son), 19, 127, 131–32
Triplett, Mary, 131–32, 139
Triplett, Newton, 19
Triplett, Patsey, 18–20, 22, 131
Turner, Mary A., 149

Underground Railroad, as memory, 219–20, 240
Union League, 177, 188
U.S. Colored Troops. *See* 60th U.S. Colored Infantry

Valelly, Richard, 177
Vance, Henry, 13, 140, 269 (n. 13)
Vance, William, 206
Vessy, 26
Veterans, African American, 175, 178, 180–81, 183, 232, 233, 237–39

Vincent, Stephen, 34
Violence, white on black, 104–5, 151, 203, 208–9. *See also* Race: and mob actions; Whites: threats against white employers of African Americans
Virginia, 24–25; Ft. Monroe, 58, 90

Waldron, Walker, 309 (n. 32)
Wang, Xi, 177
Warfield, David, 24;
Warfield, Major O.A., 24
Waring, Gen. George, 52–53
Warren, Eliza, 143
Warren, Robert Penn, 220
Wartime economic hardship, 70–71, 90, 92, 94, 100–101; impact on gender relations, 100
Warwick, John H., 310 (n. 46)
Washington, Arge, 117, 119
Washington, Booker T., 246
Washington, Mr. (orator), 186
Washington, Reuben, 67
Wayman, Alexander Walker, 144, 154
Webb, Archie, 102–4
Webb, Henry, 190, 281 (n. 56)
Webster, Samuel, 303 (n. 86)
Weeden, Rachel, 59
Weeden, Perry, 280 (n. 46)
Wells, Rev. S. T., 155–56, 232
Wesley, John, 300 (n. 47)
Western Sanitary Commission, 129
Wheaton, John Frank, 189, 319 (n. 57)
White, Henry, 306 (n. 133)
White, Jerry (aka Henry), 129–30, 140
White, Mary (née Brown), 129–31
White, Susan, 335 (n. 97)
Whites: attitudes toward African Americans, 10,15–23, 27–34, 40–41, 82–83, 84, 85–89, 109–10, 153–54, 162–63, 166, 168–69, 186, 219–22, 254, 291 (n. 35); expectations of race-based privilege, 29–30, 38–39, 83, 90, 92, 93, 108–9, 124, 162–63, 169, 176–78, 190, 95–96, 200–201, 209, 211, 237, 239, 261, 91 (nn. 28, 29); fear of black migration, 28–29, 1, 34, 41, 81, 83–90, 101, 105; fear of employment competition, 84, 94–95, 99, 103, 137; employment of African Americans, 24–25, 52, 70–71, 88, 94, 95–96, 97, 101, 137, 285 (n. 97); negative characterization of white employers, 81, 86, 94–96, 113, 295 (n. 77); perceived erosion of privilege, 41, 83–84, 90, 93, 109–10; threats against African Americans, 82, 84–85, 95, 104–5; threats against white employers of African Americans, 86, 95, 100, 105; "wages of whiteness," 90, 94–95, 137–43, 291 (n. 29)
White supremacy, 82, 138, 162–64, 175, 270 (n. 28). *See also* Racial ideologies
Whitsett, Virgie, 214
Williams, Anna, 204, 206
Williams, George Washington, 242
Williams, John, 304 (n. 106)
Williams, Liz, 155
Wilson, Elmer, 308 (n. 14)
Wilson, Kansas, 140
Wilson, Robert, 117
Wisconsin: civil rights, 188, 197, 207; migration to, 45; voting rights, 177,178, 181, 182–83; female suffrage (limited), 209
—locales: Beaver Dam, 45; Beloit, 69, 235; Burlington, 31; Cheyenne Valley, 111; Delevan, 31; Fond du Lac, 45, 77, 95, 155; Ft. Crawford, 18–19, 22, 131; Ft. Winnebago, 18; Janesville, 159; Kenosha, 114; Lacrosse, 69, 114, 182; Lancaster, 21–22; Madison, 159, 188; Manitowoc, 90, 291 (n. 30); Menomonie, 291 (n. 30); Milwaukee, 31, 154–55, 182; Potosi, 21; Prairie du Chien, 19, 67; Racine, 31, 45, 227; Racine Co., 189; Sheboygan, 291 (n. 30); Superior, 291 (n. 30); Trenton, 45; Wauwatosa, 291 (n. 30); Whitewater, 69
Wittenmyer, Annie, 97
Woman's Relief Corps (WRC), 235, 237, 240
Woman's Standard (Iowa), 210–12

Women
—African American: caricatured, 93–94, 219, 221; dress, 93–94, 229, 234
—white: employment, 69, 71, 139; employment of African Americans, 69–70, 97–99; relief work with contrabands, 78, 85–86; unwaged, 98–99; and wartime relocation, 64–65; and "wench fever," 98
Woods, Phillip, 281 (n. 58)
Woods, Rosanna, 281 (n. 58)
Woodson, George, 189
Wright, James, 103–4
Wright, Melville, 103

Yancey, James, 232
Yancey, Nancy, 142–43
Young, George C., 117, 300 (n. 54)

www.ingramcontent.com/pod-product-compliance
Lightning Source LLC
LaVergne TN
LVHW040409260326
834688LV00032B/441